THE MIDDLE EAST PEACE PROCESS

VISION VERSUS REALITY

THE MIDDLE EAST PEACE PROCESS
VISION VERSUS REALITY

Edited by

JOSEPH GINAT, EDWARD J. PERKINS,
AND EDWIN G. CORR

Foreword by
HRH Prince El Hassan bin Talal of Jordan

Preface by
David L. Boren, President of the University of Oklahoma

University of Oklahoma Press : Norman

U.S. edition © 2002
University of Oklahoma Press, Norman, Publishing Division of the University,
by special arrangement with
SUSSEX ACADEMIC PRESS
PO Box 2950
Brighton BN2 5SP, UK.

Library of Congress Cataloging-in-Publication Data

The Middle East peace process : vision versus reality / [edited by] Joseph Ginat,
Edward J. Perkins, Edwin G. Corr
p. cm
Includes bibliographical references and index
ISBN 0-8061-3522-0 (hc)
1. Arab-Israeli conflict—1993- —peace—Congresses. I. Ginat, J.   II. Perkins, Edward J.
(Edward Joseph), 1928-.   III. Corr, Edwin G.

DS119.76 .M475   2003
956.05'3—dc21

2002026633

Typeset and designed by G&G Editorial, Brighton, UK.
Printed by Bookcraft, Midsomer Norton, Bath, UK.
This book is printed on acid-free paper.

Contents

PART II
Countries with Peace Agreements with Israel: Egypt and Jordan

PART III
Countries without Peace Agreements with Israel

Foreword

HRH Prince El Hassan bin Talal
President of the Club of Rome
Moderator of the World Conference on Religion and Peace
Chairman of the Arab Thought Forum

───────

Anticipating the future security requirements of a Palestinian–Israeli peace is a process shaped, in large part, by the complex nature of the Middle East, the multiplicity of its actors, and the sources of conflict within it. There exists a high degree of political permeability and strategic vulnerability between the states in the region – for reasons of geography, history, society, and culture – which give rise to constant instability.

This, in turn, emphasizes the role to be played by external powers, especially given the proximity of southern Europe, the former Soviet Republics and South Asia; not to mention the global role and Cold War heritage that have introduced the United States as a key player in regional Middle Eastern affairs.

In the short term, however, the most important issue that we face today is the successful conclusion of Middle East peace negotiations. A united voice for our region should envisage the conclusion of a just, comprehensive and peaceful solution to the Palestinian–Israeli conflict and broader Arab–Israeli hostility. The achievements of the past have proved fragile; the death toll for both Palestinians and Israelis continues to mount, and escalation of violence seems to worsen every day. Improvements in the quality of life and opportunity in the Middle Eastern region are yearned after but remain hindered by the struggle between Palestinians and Israelis – a powerful preventive force curtailing our capacity to contribute positively and effectively towards international promotion of humanitarian aspirations.

Clearly, resolving the Palestinian–Israeli conflict is essential for the immediate future of the Middle East. Furthermore, peace between Israel and Syria would unlock peace between Israel and Lebanon. This, in turn, would open up trade and diplomatic relations between Israel and the rest of the Arab World, and stimulate investment in the region. Extremists, whether religious or nationalistic, would lose much of the fuel that feeds their cause; and those who support and direct radical movements would increasingly be marginalized by the unfolding of a new geopolitical order. The interest shown in the recent "land for peace" proposal by Saudi Arabia's Crown Prince Abdullah indicates that credible solutions can be sought from within the region as well as without.

For the present, our Middle-Eastern or Western-Asian region does not possess any institutional mechanism for the avoidance, prevention, or resolution of conflicts. It is a complex geopolitical area in which most people cannot realize their aspirations in terms of security and a decent human environment.

What is needed is a historic reconciliation, not a temporary political settlement. Pertinent UN Security Council Resolutions listed the requirements for such a reconciliation to be achieved. Essentially, in our view, Israel must give up its dream of a greater Israel and recognize a Palestinian State on the Palestinian territories occupied in 1967, and the Arabs must give up the dream of a historical Palestine and recognize the right of Israel to exist within recognized and secure borders.

Since September 11, 2001, a quantum leap has occurred in our shared vulnerability and therefore in the need for our shared shouldering of responsibility. A desirable international relationship is often described as "interdependent"; but I believe we need to move further – towards a state I have often described as *intra-independent*, in which independent identities are fostered by a supportive network of multilateral relationships within a region. In such a relationship one might, perhaps, speak of "multiple modernities" sharing core values, rather than thinking in terms of one cultural model to which all should subscribe.

I am more convinced than ever that the greatest challenges facing not only the Middle East but the whole of the international community in this millennium include a much firmer management of conflicts, better cross-cultural links, promotion of religious tolerance, maintaining the growth of the global economy, eradicating poverty and maximizing the benefits of the information revolution so as to manage effectively food supply, water shortages, and other environmental challenges.

Yet many nations in Africa and Asia continue to suffer from huge debt burdens, famine, epidemics, and natural disasters. One-sixth of the world's population still lives on less than one dollar a day. When the human race holds all human life to be precious, regardless of religion, nationality or ethnic origins; when justice prevails for all, and the pursuit of freedom, happiness, and dignity is the right of all peoples and not just a few; when all human beings are equal before God, and when all life is sacred; this is when we will overcome most of the challenges that face us – in our region and beyond.

The 1991 Madrid Conference marked the beginning of a complex and difficult peace process. After long decades of strife, the parties involved came to realize that negotiations and endeavors to find peaceful solutions to the area's problems constitute the best means for confronting many of the challenges facing the Middle Eastern communities. We in Jordan pride ourselves on having made the hard decisions to attain the cherished objective of peace. After eleven years of the Madrid Peace Conference, however, the ultimate objective of total and comprehensive peace continues to be evasive. Thorny issues, such as the status of Jerusalem, remain unsolved.

The ideological, historical, and political paradigm of Jerusalem is seen as an obstacle to the ultimate goal of sustainable and durable peace between the Palestinians and Israelis. The challenge here is how to change the concept of "obstacle" to the concept of "bridge" in building peaceful coexistence around the city of Jerusalem. The Israeli ideological approach, which strives towards a scenario in which Israel is the single player on the Jerusalem stage, prohibits negotiation to build a sustainable peace between the Israelis and Palestinians on the basis of mutual concessions. The Palestinian demands are more realistic and pragmatic, based on removing the occupation dating from 1967. East Jerusalem would become the capital of the envisaged Palestinian State and West Jerusalem the capital of the Israeli State.

The problems we now face should be addressed by formulating a humanitarian code of conduct which emphasizes obligation and adherence to international norms with no exception. Further, such a code should distinguish between politics and policies, between slogans and substance. The fight against terror should be conducted through comprehensive joint efforts to address effectively the root causes of terror.

Throughout the history of civilization, we encounter examples of harmony between the "sons of Abraham" in the Torah, the Qur'an and the Gospel. Before enmity erupted, we find worship of the unique God, faith in love, mutual help, respect for the family, ethics, tolerance, and above all "love thy neighbour." However, this convergence among Semitic faiths has erupted into conflict – not on religious grounds but rather for political and demographic reasons.

Under the auspices of the University of Oklahoma, a conference entitled "Negotiating Jerusalem: Guiding Principles" was held in January 2000 in Amman, Jordan and attended by a number of respected scholars from Israel, the Arab region, the United States, Europe, and the international community. There, a comprehensive proposal was reached concerning the status of Jerusalem which was then forwarded to concerned parties – including the chairman of the Palestinian Authority, the King of Jordan, the President of Egypt, and the Prime Minister of Israel. The proposal emphasizes the principles of equity, fairness and reciprocity among the parties in searching for a lasting settlement, and puts forward guiding principles for the final settlement of the Jerusalem issue:

"JERUSALEM IS TO BE THE CAPITAL of both Israel and Palestine in Jewish West and Arab East of the city, respectively and on equal footing" and "Palestinians and Israelis shall be sovereign over their respective capitals."

"THE UNIQUE RELIGIOUS, cultural, and historical importance of the walled part of Jerusalem to both sides requires special arrangement to be negotiated by the parties."

"THE WHOLENESS OF JERUSALEM should be upheld with open access to Israelis and Palestinians alike."

"GOVERNANCE OF THE CITY must be respectful of Jerusalem's important pluralist and multicultural character. The protection and preservation of the unique religious interests of Christians, Jews, and Muslims must be guaranteed; and freedom of worship and access to holy places must be granted."

"THE STATUS QUO in the administration of holy places should be maintained, and a coordination mechanism among the various religious authorities should be introduced."

"PRINCIPLES OF SELF-GOVERNANCE of all communities and at all levels must be equitable and democratic."

"IT IS NECESSARY TO RESOLVE the issue of Jewish neighbourhoods/ settlements in and around Jerusalem beyond the 1967 'green line', and to reconcile existing realities with the existing agreements between the parties and with relevant international resolutions."

"RESIDENTS OF JERUSALEM, including non-citizens, shall be subject to equitable rules and regulations to be agreed upon by Israel and the Palestine Liberation Organisation."

"MUNICIPAL ARRANGEMENTS in Jerusalem must be consistent with the above principles. Among the possible arrangements consistent with these principles is the establishment of two municipal councils in the two respective capitals and a coordination commission for the entire city with equal representation."

"NO UNILATERAL STEP that would affect the final status and boundaries of Jerusalem beyond the 1967 green line should be taken prior to final agreement."

We should learn from our history to date that it is high time to make Jerusalem a haven for dialogue among cultures, religions, and traditions. Jerusalem may become the future melting pot, mosaic, or crossroads of civilizations. Jerusalem is qualified to become a regional seat of conflict resolution and of dialogue among the three Abrahamic religions for mutual respect, tolerance, and appreciating cultural diversity. It may yet unite the worshippers of God under one roof.

Xenophobia (as a morbid fear of the stranger, the foreigner, and what is different) and racism (as antagonism between different races of men) are forms of intolerance: refusal, blind rejection, and a destructive and nega-tive attitude. Tolerance is recognition that no individual culture, nation, or religion possesses a monopoly on knowledge or truth. Tolerance is a form of freedom – freedom from prejudice and freedom from dogma.

The global environment and culture in which we live and work is not simply a heritage, but also a dynamic and evolving process. Cultural iden-tity is not only linked to the past; it is constantly evolving and renewing into the future – through interaction with other cultures. These different cultures need each other; they are regenerated through encounters and exchanges, enriched by coming face to face with each other, recognizing their differences and, by recognizing those differences, learning to know themselves. This interaction is as inevitable as it is enlightening.

The sense of understanding others, experiencing cultural diversity, rejecting violence and seeking peaceful solutions must become inherent in the way of life of future generations. It is by joining our efforts through solidarity and sharing that we shall build our own identity and, simultane-ously, combat xenophobia and pledge tolerance – not only to each other, but also to our children's children.

What is needed, I may add, is a new, not self-centred view of humanism – a view in which humans are constantly moving towards broader horizons, towards a *metanoia* or change of heart. Conversation should be predicated on self-giving instead of an attempt to assimilate "the other." In Asian-Buddhist idiom, I refer to that self-transgression which "opens the flood-gates of *metta* (loving-kindness) and *karuna* (compassion)."

Unfortunately, the criminal attacks of September 11 and the war in Afghanistan have cast their shadow on dialogue between civilizations. But I find it appropriate to refer today to another voice that spoke out eight centuries ago from Balkh, in a happier Afghanistan. Jalal ud-Din ar-Rumi, one of the greatest poets of the Islamic world, wrote:

> Come now whoever you are!
> Come without any fear of being disliked.
> Come whether you are a Muslim, a Christian or a Jew.
> Come whoever you are!
> Whether you believe or do not believe in God.
> Come also if you believe in the sun as God.
> This door is not a door of fear.
> This is a door of good wishes.

Preface

DAVID BOREN, PRESIDENT OF THE UNIVERSITY OF
OKLAHOMA

———

This book provides historical information and analyses about the negotiating states and parties involved in the Middle East peace process. It
examines the political issues and positions of the contending parties, looks
at control and management of the holy sites, and proposes solutions and
compromises to overcome obstacles to achieving a peace agreement
between Israel and Palestine and a comprehensive agreement among
the Middle East states. In *The Middle East Peace Process, Vision
Versus Reality*, co-editors Professor Joseph Ginat, Ambassador Edward J.
Perkins, and Ambassador Edwin G. Corr assembled the thoughts and
knowledge of some of the most respected scholars, former practitioners,
and long-time observers and analysts of the Middle East. Collectively this
group of contributors – composed of Israelis, Palestinians, Jordanians,
Lebanese, Europeans, and Americans; and of Jews, Muslims, Christians,
Druze, and secularists – reprocess previously made proposals and offer new
creative ideas that if seized and acted upon with political will can put to an
end the many decades of violence, bloodshed and struggle.

This volume is the second book in the Studies in Peace Politics in the
Middle East series. The first was *Palestinian Refugees: Old Problems – New
Solutions* published jointly by the University of Oklahoma Press and
Sussex Academic Press in 2001. That book grew out of a conference held
at the University of Oklahoma in December 1999 by the Center for Peace
Studies, whose secretariat is based at the International Programs Center at
the University of Oklahoma. The four institutions that constitute the
Center are Bethlehem University in the Palestinian Authority, the Horizon
Institute in Jordan, Haifa University in Israel, and the University of
Oklahoma in the United States.

This book is the result of a Center for Peace Studies conference that took
place at the University of Haifa in March 2000. The conference dealt with
different aspects of the peace process and the countries involved. It was

unique in that it examined not only the Israeli–Palestinian conflict but also the results of Egypt's and Jordan's peace agreements with Israel; the history, attitudes and critical factors for the negotiation of peace agreements of Syria, Lebanon and Iraq with Israel; and also the role of the Palestinian Arabs who are Israeli citizens. Knowledge of all these subjects is essential to successful negotiation of a comprehensive peace in the Middle East, despite the fact that some of the countries considered do not currently appear as players in peace talks.

In January 2000, prior to the Haifa conference, the Center for Peace Studies held a special conference on the status of Jerusalem that took place in Amman, Jordan, and concluded in Jerusalem. The Arab and Israeli participants in that conference instead of merely presenting scholarly papers, discussed and deliberated issues that must be resolved to achieve an agreement on Jerusalem. The Declaration of Principles for Jerusalem that was agreed upon and signed by the participants is included in full in chapter 27 and partially by HRH Prince El Hassan bin Talal in the Foreword.

During the past half-century events have consistently over-taken recently published descriptions of the current situations of the Middle East and of peacemakers' efforts to resolve the long-standing problems and strife there. This book is no different in that respect. As is pointed out in the following *Introduction*, the papers that constitute the chapters of this book were written in a period of relative optimism prior to the outbreak of the second Intifada in 2001 after the collapse of peace talks. However, the lapse in peace negotiations, because of violence and counter-violence, does not diminish the worth of this book. The current breakdown in the peace process, in a sense, enhances the value of the information and innovative, sound proposals contained herein; because, though I cannot predict precisely when, I am confident that the contending parties inevitably will and must return to the negotiating tables. There really is no other lasting alternative. And when the official negotiators of the contending states and Palestinian Authority do return, I hope they will have read and digested the contents of this book.

The editors and contributors offer a variety of views and experiences, not only from the Middle East but also from editors who have been involved in other seemingly unsolvable conundrums of intra-state, regional and complex conflicts. The Middle East contributors' remarkable foresight in proposing viable solutions to specific issues in the Middle East peace process benefits from their personal experiences and from thought over many years of meditation on and analyses of the region.

The contributors and editors do not, in fact, provide absolute answers for a comprehensive, final peace agreement for the Middle East, but within this volume are the blue prints and necessary ingredients for creative negotiator's of good will to fashion an acceptable, compromise agreement that all contenders can accept, though it will not satisfy perfectly all of any of the contenders' aspirations. Thus are the final solutions to long-standing, seemingly intractable, complex disputes – especially those across differing cultures and religions.

Though the prospects of peace in the Middle East at the time of this writing seem more dismal than they have for some years, the pragmatism and vision I find in this book, plus the sage advice and negotiating philosophy of my good friend and former colleague in the US Senate, George J. Mitchell, give me hope for the future. Senator Mitchell, as President Clinton's envoy to Northern Ireland, was a critical actor in helping to move the adversaries of that centuries-long dispute toward peace. His personal involvement in the Middle East in 2001 as the leader of the Mitchell Commission to aid in the search for peace in the region again produced the elements for a giant leap forward toward peace, if only the weary and hardened leaderships of Israel and the Palestinian Authority will take heed.

Senator Mitchell made a superb presentation at the University of Oklahoma on February 25, 1999 at our annual foreign policy conference in which he spoke on the negotiation of settlements to seemingly interminable conflicts, and in which he set forth certain universal principles for peace making in such cases. These are included in the book Ed Perkins and I co-edited on the basis of that conference that was centered around the personage and advice of Lady Margaret Thatcher, and featured other prominent seekers of peace, such as Archbishop Desmond Tutu, as well as Senator Mitchell. That book is entitled *Democracy, Morality, and the Search for Peace in America's Foreign Policy* (University of Oklahoma Press, 2002). Here are Senator Mitchell's four principles, and they ring loud and clear when applied to the Middle East conflict.

"*First,* . . . there is no such thing as a conflict that cannot be solved. Conflict is created and sustained by human beings, and it can be ended by human beings. There must be a determination on the part of all concerned to bring it to an end, and that requires an extraordinary amount of patience and perseverance . . . Patience is as important as perseverance.

"*Second,* . . . it is important to establish early, and to repeat consistently, a determination not to yield to men of violence. In every circumstance . . . men of violence on both sides will be determined to wreck the peace process . . . to bomb, murder, assassinate, and destroy to get their way, in the hope that the other side would eventually capitulate.

"*Third,* . . . there must be a willingness among the negotiators to genuinely listen to the other point of view and to enter into principled compromise. That is easy to say but very hard to do because it

requires political leadership willing to take risks for peace . . . but
it must be done . . . [or] there will be no hope for peace.

   "There is a *fourth* and final principle . . . outside the area of
conflict . . . which . . . universally affects such conflicts. This is the
importance of employment and well-being."

The adoption of these principles by Middle East leaders and their
supporters, combined with the pragmatic yet visionary ideas and proposals
to specific issues that are set forth in this book, can, and eventually will,
produce a comprehensive peace in the Middle East. The tragedy is the delay
and postponement by Middle East leaders to accept these principles and to
seek to apply the knowledge and proposals of this and other books and
experts. The leaders of the Middle East, of America and of Europe should
determine to begin without surcease to negotiate a viable solution; they
must prevent the men of violence of both sides of the Israeli–Palestinian
conflict from having sway and wrecking the peace process; and they must
be willing to listen to their adversaries points of view and to enter into principled compromise to end the violence and secure a lasting peace.

   It is, of course, ultimately the responsibility of the leaders in the area to
resolve the problems of unemployment and well-being of their peoples,
but the United States' and European Union's leaders can make a vital
contribution to the peace process by making available the resources
required to address the challenges of reconstruction and economic development. That aid of course should be strongly conditioned, but it should
be committed and announced as early as possible so that it can serve both
as an enticement to move to peace and then for implementation of the
peace.

   If the Israeli and Arab leaders were to commit themselves to the principles of negotiation set forth by Senator Mitchell, I think the Middle East
and the world could take a giant step forward to fulfill in the Holy Land
and Jerusalem the vision of an ancient prophet, a vision which in my interpretation would be satisfactory to peoples of the three great religions of the
monotheistic tradition:

"Behold I will create new heavens and a new earth.
The former things will not be remembered
   nor will they come to mind.
Be glad and rejoice forever in what I will create,
   for I will create Jerusalem to be a delight
   and its people a joy.
I will rejoice over Jerusalem and take delight in my people;
   the sound of weeping and of crying will be heard no more.
"Never again will there be in it an infant who lives but a few days
   or an old man who does not live out his years . . .
"They will not toil in vain or bear children doomed to misfortune . . .

"The wolf and the lamb will feed together
 and the lion will eat straw like the ox, . . .
"They will neither harm nor destroy on all my holy mountain."
                                    From Isaiah 65, *The NIV Study Bible*
                                    (Grand Rapids, MI: Zondervan, 1995)

The Center for Peace Studies focuses upon urgent issues of international relationships by drawing on analytic tools from the social sciences, humanities, sciences and technology, and business administration. It fosters a multidisciplinary discussion of contemporary conflicts among societies, cultures, and political entities. Studies and conferences sponsored by the Center have initially concentrated on the pressing issues of the Arab–Israeli peace process. The Center is creating an international community of scholars and advisors. Symposia held under the leadership of the Center attempt to identify solutions to the critical disputes that stand in the way of a lasting peace in the Middle East. As governments around the world struggle to find the bases for building peace, their citizens must develop mechanisms that support those efforts. The Center serves this process by contributing to and influencing new policies as they are conceived and implemented.

Our hope is that the leadership and the peoples of the Middle East can cease to be prisoners of the violence and history of the region, determine to secure peace and well-being for their peoples, and use the information and ideas of this book to end bloodshed and provide opportunity, prosperity and freedom to their long-suffering peoples.

Acknowledgments

We, the editors, recognize that this book shares the experiences, knowledge, thought, and wisdom on the Middle East peace process of two dozen distinguished professionals from several countries and academic disciplines. We thank these scholars and practitioners for attending a conference at Haifa University sponsored by the Center for Peace Studies (constituted by the University of Oklahoma, Haifa University, Bethlehem University, and the Horizon Institute) where as participants they presented ideas and papers, and, with our help afterward, for writing informative and innovative chapters that make up this book.

In addition, we wish to express our appreciation to the following individuals without whom publication of this book would have been much more difficult, if not impossible.

The President of the Board of the Center for Peace Studies, His Royal Highness Prince El Hassan bin Talal, for writing the foreword. The support of the President of the University of Oklahoma, David L. Boren, for writing the preface and his support for the Center for Peace Studies.

Mr. Anthony Grahame, the Editorial Director at Sussex Academic Press for his patience and professional guidance; and, at the University of Oklahoma Press, Director John Drayton and Acquisitions Editor Jean Hurtado and her assistant Susan Garrett for their advice and assistance. We also want to thank Mr. Danny Kolker of University Seminars International and Mr. Jared Willis of Brandeis University for their help in compiling and editing the papers of the contributors.

At the International Programs Center of the University of Oklahoma, where the co-editors work and where the Center for Peace Studies' headquarters is, we gratefully acknowledge the assistance of Julie Horn, Kathy Shahan, Gary Miller, and Donna Cline. Donna is worthy of special mention because of her months of dedication, meticulous work, research, and vital help in the editing of this book.

The conference in which these works were presented was made possible by the financial support of The University of Oklahoma, The University of Haifa, the Jewish Federation of Greater Oklahoma City, Oklahoma Israeli

Exchange, Inc., the Jewish Federation Foundation of Tulsa, Mr. Jack Golsen, and Mr. Paul Stewart.

Finally, we thank Mr. Edward R. and Sumya Adwon whose generous donation to the University of Oklahoma for the Center for Peace Studies made possible the book's publication. They made the gift in the hope that this volume will assist in bringing peace to the Middle East. So do we.

This book is dedicated to

TAHSEEN BASHEER (1924–2002)

a distinguished Egyptian, intellectual, diplomat, statesman
and influential man of peace
who participated in two Center for Peace Studies conferences
and wrote a chapter of the Center's
The Palestinian Refugees: Old Problems – New Solutions.

Ambassador Basheer had a vision of peace and was an advocate of
peaceful co-existence in the Middle East, and
normal relations among Arab nations and Israel.

His clear and strong voice for peace is missed!

CHAPTER 1

Introduction: Vision versus Reality

JOSEPH GINAT, EDWARD J. PERKINS, AND EDWIN G. CORR

In the first book of this series *The Palestinian Refugees: Old Problems – New Solutions,* the co-editors stated that the two main problems of the peace process between Israel and the Palestinians are the refugees question and the status of Jerusalem. While most of the chapters of the second volume deal with the history and politics of the peace process, there are also chapters that focus on specific unresolved issues, including the political status of Jerusalem and its holy sites. The latter part of this introduction will include brief summaries of the chapters.

The Breakdown in the Peace Process

This introduction is being written about a year after the start of the second *Intifada* following the collapse of the Camp David talks. The chapters herein were written in a period of relative optimism with respect to the achievement of a final peace accord between Israel and the Palestinian Authority. Aside from the deterioration in Israeli-Palestinian relations that has taken place, the *Intifada* has fundamentally altered the relationship between Israel and the Arab countries of Egypt and Jordan with whom Israel already had reached peace. Egypt regards itself as the leader of the Arab world, and as such feels that is should protect Palestinians from what they regard as Israeli aggression and failure to comply with UN resolutions. A few months into the *Intifada*, Egypt recalled its ambassador. Jordan did not reappoint a new ambassador to fill a vacancy. Even prior to the *Intifada* the intellectuals and trade unions in each country had initiated a boycott of Israel.

Aggressive attitudes of the citizens of Arab countries and of Israel have only become more acute since the *Intifada*'s outbreak. In Syria, after the death of President Assad and the inauguration of his son Bashar, there was a brief period of hope that the young, western-educated leader would reform the country and lead it toward democracy. Similarly, it was hoped Bashar would be more open to resuming talks with Israel to reach a peace agreement. But this was not the case, and the *Intifada* seemingly has only hardened the Syrian position. Because of Syrian influence in Lebanon, it is unlikely that Lebanon would conduct any peace negotiations with Israel without prior Syrian agreement.

David L. Boren, the President of the University of Oklahoma and former US Senator and Governor of Oklahoma, succinctly and competently laid out in the Preface the value of the content of this book. When the madness of violence and counter-violence ends, hatreds are quelled, and committed negotiators of good will can again conscientiously seek the arrangements and principled compromises necessary for peace, security and the well-being of their peoples in that region of great historic and religious value for all mankind, the information and innovative proposed solutions set out in this volume will come into play.

Men and women on both sides of the conflict who are committed to an enduring peace and a mutually beneficial co-existence – founded on mutual respect, if not deep friendship – are advised to study and contemplate this book (and others similar to it) so they will be ready to move rapidly and effectively when the opportunity again presents itself. As editors, we are convinced that this will occur, sooner or later, and that in the meantime peoples on both sides must prepare themselves for the negotiation of a just and final peace agreement.

The *Intifada* and the Disintegration of the Oslo Peace Process

The failure of the Camp David Summit in the late 2000, hosted by President William J. Clinton and attended by Palestinian Chairman Yassir Arafat and Prime Minister Ehued Barak, led to the creation of a semi-consensus in both the Israeli and Palestinian societies that the Oslo Agreement, signed September 13, 1993, was no longer productive. Menachem Klein claims that the Oslo model was dead even before the *Intifada* started. The Palestinians lost faith in the goodwill of the Israelis when the stipulations of the agreement – such as the release of prisoners and a settlement freeze – remained unimplemented. The Palestinians were further discouraged by what they saw as Israel's constant delaying of final status talks. Israel, on the other hand, felt the Palestinians were not fulfilling their obligations to stop the terrorism,[1] and indeed were consciously using violence as a negotiating tactic.

The underlying assumption of the Oslo Accords was that the very process would in itself lead toward coexistence between Israelis and Palestinians and lessen the chance of another war. Ron Pundak, one of the participants in the secret talks that led to the Oslo agreement, argues that the final agreement must deal with all the relevant issues: refugees, settlements, Jerusalem, security arrangements, borders, water, and the economy. He rejects suggestions to leave some of the more complicated issues open for later negotiation; because, he says, if issues are left unresolved, the implementation of any semi-agreement is likely to remain hostage to extremists on both sides. To show that reaching a final agreement is possible, Pundak and Dr. Yair Hirschfeld engaged in an intensive dialogue that resulted in the "Beilin–Abu Mazen Agreement," dated October 31, 1995. The agreement, of course, was not an official document, but it constituted a jointly attained proposal and demonstrated that well intentioned Palestinians and Israelis can reach acceptable solutions on the basis of coexistence, mutual respect, and good neighborliness. The agreement covered all the specific and relevant issues.[2] The co-editors use the Beilin-Abu Mazen draft provisions illustratively in this Introduction to show a number of possible solutions.

Gilad Sher, who was the Israeli negotiator at the Camp David Summit, claims that the Israeli goal during those talks was to exchange territory for a final end to the conflict. Instead, Arafat, he says, chose to attempt to achieve his goals by the use of violence.[3] The consensus of the editors of the present volume is that the Americans and Israelis were doomed to failure (though not necessarily mistaken) in trying to achieve a final agreement within the very short period allowed for negotiations at the Camp David Summit. Neither Yasser Arafat nor any other Palestinian leader could have signed a comprehensive agreement without solving the Palestinian refugee issue and without the tacit consent of some Arab states to the solution. The Beilin–Abu Mazen Agreement stipulates a right of return to the Palestinian state, and recognition of Palestinian suffering as a result of the 1947-49 war. It further acknowledges the refugees' right to compensation and rehabilitation to be implemented under the supervision of an international committee. This committee would be responsible for raising the necessary resources.[4] Such a solution might have gained acceptance at Camp David had there been more time. Although some politicians suggested that the failure of Camp David was because of the Temple Mount issue, President Clinton himself stated that the refugee issue was the true obstacle.[5]

The Settlements

It has been asserted that the *Intifada* broke out due to the settlements issue. While the *Intifada* is directed partially against the settlements, that issue in and of itself was not the cause. According to the Beilin–Abu

Mazen document, a few blocks of settlements would be annexed to Israel. Settlers living in scattered communities would remain under the Palestinian Authority, or residents would be compensated to relocate. Barak also referred to a similar solution for the settlements in his proposal at Camp David.

Since the *Intifada*, there has been huge international pressure on Israel related to the growth of the settlements. The European Community claims that the settlements are one of the major obstacles for peace.[6] Klein claims that there is a parallel between the colonial situation in Algeria under the French and the Palestinian territories. In some cases the State of Israel sent settlers to the Palestinian territories, while in other instances they encouraged large groups of citizens to build communities there. The Palestinian inhabitants of the area settled by the Jews have a historical, cultural, religious, ethnic, and political identity completely different from the new settlers. The settlers did not move to Palestine to be integrated into the local society, but instead to enlarge the boundaries of their mother country. Starting with relatively small numbers and initially occupying temporary shelters, the settler movement has become an institutionalized method to alter the population make-up of the territories.[7]

The editors of this book do not necessarily agree with the comparison of Israeli settlers with the French settlers in Algeria, but do agree with Klein's basic analysis. Dr. Yossi Beilin, interviewed by the Israeli newspaper *Ha'aretz*, said the final agreement will include the annexation from the West Bank territory of Ariel and Gush Etzion, and the Jewish settlements within the Jerusalem area in return for sovereign Israeli territory in Halutza (in the Negev), plus the territory of a safe passage route (between the Gaza Strip and the West Bank). He also believes it will be necessary to uproot all the settlements in the Gaza Strip and about 100 small settlements in the West Bank, totaling roughly 40,000 settlers. Concludes Beilin, "I think our silence in the face of the expanding settlements was a mistake."[8]

There have been several attempts to find a diplomatic agreement that would halt the *Intifada*. However, there are Palestinians who claim that the *Intifada* is a liberation struggle for independence, and that the motivation for the *Intifada* will remain as long as there is an Israeli occupation. Abd el-Khalim Kindil writes, "Has the Palestinian Authority become more important than the Palestinian cause?" He contends that the Palestinian Authority did not listen to warnings and surrendered to outside pressure.[9] Hani el-Masri claims that the *Intifada* can and must continue until all its goals are fulfilled and that it can only succeed as a popular uprising under one leadership.[10]

The Mitchell Report

Unlike the first *Intifada* (1987–1993), the second one is not merely a popular rebellion of demonstrations and stone throwing. The second *Intifada* is being fought with guns, mortars, and suicide attacks. In the interest of preventing even further escalation, the United States again offered to mediate between the sides. The Palestinians want international involvement and intervention whereas Israel insists on mediation only. There are three possibilities in the current "game:" the sides will succeed in reaching a compromise that can lead to a final solution; the situation will continue as is; or, an escalation will lead to regional war. A limited confrontation can remain self-confined to skirmishes between Israelis and Palestinians, or escalation in the violence might lead to a war involving the surrounding Arab countries. The Americans are acutely aware of this possibility.

Stemming from agreements signed after the start of the *Intifada*, former US Senator George Mitchell and a committee of experts were sent to the Middle East to investigate the causes of the violence. Their report, however, focused little on the original causes of the violence and instead offered guidelines for returning to the political track. Following are the Mitchell report recommendations:

END THE VIOLENCE
The GOI [Government of Israel] and the PA [Palestinian Authority] should reaffirm their commitment to existing agreements and undertakings and should immediately implement an unconditional cessation of violence.

The GOI and PA should immediately resume security cooperation.

REBUILD CONFIDENCE
The PA and GOI should work together to establish a meaningful "cooling off period" and implement additional confidence building measures, some of which were detailed in the October 2000 Sharm el-Sheikh Statement and some of which were offered by the United States on January 7, 2001 in Cairo (see Recommendations section for further description).

The PA and GOI should resume their efforts to identify, condemn and discourage incitement in all its forms.

The PA should make clear through concrete action to Palestinians and Israelis alike that terrorism is reprehensible and unacceptable, and that the PA will make a 100 percent effort to prevent terrorist operations and to punish perpetrators. This effort should include immediate steps to apprehend and incarcerate terrorists operating within the PA's jurisdiction.

The GOI should freeze all settlement activity, including the "natural growth" of existing settlements.

The GOI should ensure that the IDF [Israeli Defense Forces] adopt and enforce policies and procedures encouraging non-lethal responses to unarmed demonstrators, with a view to minimizing casualties and friction between the two communities.

The PA should prevent gunmen from using Palestinian populated areas to fire upon Israeli populated areas and IDF positions. This tactic places civilians on both sides at unnecessary risk.

The GOI should lift closures, transfer to the PA all tax revenues owed, and permit Palestinians who had been employed in Israel to return to their jobs; and should ensure that security forces and settlers refrain from the destruction of homes and roads, as well as trees and other agricultural property in Palestinian areas. We acknowledge the GOI's position that actions of this nature have been taken for security reasons. Nevertheless, the economic effects will persist for years.

The PA should renew cooperation with Israeli security agencies to ensure, to the maximum extent possible, that Palestinian workers employed within Israel are fully vetted and free of connections to organizations and individuals engaged in terrorism.

The PA and GOI should consider a joint undertaking to preserve and protect holy places sacred to the traditions of Jews, Muslims, and Christians.

The GOI and PA should jointly endorse and support the work of Palestinian and Israeli non-governmental organizations involved in cross-community initiatives linking the two peoples.

RESUME NEGOTIATIONS
In the spirit of the Sharm el-Sheikh agreements and understandings of 1999 and 2000, we recommend that the party's meet to reaffirm their commitment to signed agreements and mutual understandings, and take corresponding action. This should be the basis for resuming full and meaningful negotiations.[11]

The Tenet and Zinni Mediations for a Cease-Fire

The second stage of American involvement was when President George Bush sent CIA Director George Tenet to the Middle East. The setting for this visit was a unilaterally declared cease-fire, first declared by Prime Minister Sharon and then by Yasser Arafat. The Tenet cease-fire text attempted to formalize the de facto cessation in violence while providing a timetable to move toward implementing the Mitchell recommendations. The document specified that the Israelis and Palestinians would immediately resume security cooperation, including meetings between security officials as well as joint patrols. Furthermore, both sides would strictly enforce the cease-fire, and would not initiate attacks on the other side or otherwise permit violence. A subsequent stipulation was that the Palestinian Authority re-arrest all terrorists while the Israelis would avow not to "liquidate" suspected perpetrators. Another condition dealt with methods to alleviate the pressure at certain "flashpoints" between the sides; to this end Israel agreed to a redeployment of forces to positions held before September 28, 2000. The final clause stipulated that within a certain time frame Israel would be responsible for lifting the closure on the Palestinian population (from entering Israel), and restrictions on Palestinians movement through border crossings and the Gaza airport would be eased as well.

Although both sides accepted the Tenet cease-fire, there was skepticism as to whether it could be implemented. Professor Shlomo Avinery, a well-known Israeli political scientist, said that while it was still possible to reach a final solution, it was simply not possible at that point in time.[12] He is one of many who believe in reaching a comprehensive final solution, and advocates unilateral separation from and recognition of the Palestinians. Professor Ya'akov Bar-Siman-Tov asserts that the fast transition from negotiation attempts to renewed wide-scale violence once again raises the question of whether the two sides are ready for peace. While the Israelis had always claimed that the Palestinians were not "ripe" for a resolution to the conflict, it looks like the Israelis were not either.[13] Avinery asserts that now it is not possible to reach a comprehensive solution, reminding that questions concerning the region's "ripeness" for peace were not raised before the current *Intifada*. Avinery seems to imply that the time when it will be possible to make peace is still far in the future.

President Bush in November 2001, following a major speech by Secretary of State Colin Powell on the peace process, sent Assistant Secretary of State for Near Eastern Affairs William J. Burns and Special Envoy Marine Corps General, Retired, Anthony C. Zinni to push again for talks on the basis of the Mitchell and Tenet reports. Zinni has returned to the region several times.

The editors of this volume believe that for the implementation of the Tenet document both sides have to work in stages, tackling one problem at a time. In negotiations perhaps a new strategy should be tried, where the sides tackle the most difficult issues first, such as Jerusalem and the refugees. The big uncertainty is the future of Yasser Arafat and whether the Hamas and the Islamic Jihad will obey the Palestinian Authority and halt their suicide bombings and any other terrorist activity, and whether Ariel Sharon is truly committed to the concept of a viable Palestinian state, or simply wants to scuttle the concept and make Palestine a weak dependency. In the event that there is not an adequate cessation of violence, it does not appear there will be the opportunity for the parties to advance toward the trust-building stages or negotiations.

Hudna

If the current American approach fails, among alternative approaches might be introducing a culturally based cease-fire (*hudna* in Arabic). While the blood feud has been a part of Arab custom and Islam for many centuries, Arab culture has also developed an important and traditional mechanism for solving such conflicts. Approaching the Palestinians with a proposal rooted in their own culture might actually enhance its chances for success.

In traditional Arab society once a *hudna* is declared, all violence and revenge attacks halt, and after a period of time the families involved enter into negotiations to resolve the roots of the conflict. Even Sheikh Ahmde Yassin of Hamas has spoke several times in favor of a *hudna* with the Jews and Israel, even if his terms were clearly unacceptable to Israel. But the mere fact that he mentioned a *hudna* with Israel means even the fundamental Islamic groups would under certain circumstances cease their attacks against Israel.

The concept of *hudna* received much attention in the Middle East and the United States in December of 2001 when Israeli President Moshe Katsav agreed to speak to the Palestinian Legislative Council about *hudna*. Joseph Ginat, Eyal Ehrlich, a former journalist and now businessman, and former Member of the Knessett Abdubwahol Darawshe had approached the president. But Prime Minister Ariel Sharon stopped the planned Katsav trip to Ramallah. However, *hudna* has now been widely discussed at the highest levels of government of both Israel and the Palestinian Authority, and also in other Arab capitals, and it has gained a modicum of acceptance. It is unlikely the concept will disappear, especially if a cease-fire is not obtained through other devices or channels. The use of *hudna* would show the Arab world respect for its mentality and customs, and thus increase the chances for success.[14] Under the cultural/religious umbrella there is a great chance that all factions, including the extremist Islamic one, would find the *hudna* cease-fire acceptable. During the time frame allowed by the *hudna* political discussions between the sides could begin.

Culture and Negotiations in the Middle East

An understanding of cross-cultural conflicts among Israelis, Arabs, and the West aids comprehension of political events in the region and facilitates negotiations. Professor Gabi Sheffer, in his paper "Political Cultural and Possibilities for Solving the Israeli–Palestinian Conflict," refers to cultural gaps between the two societies.[15] Sheffer claims there is asymmetry between the two cultures that influences political discourse, resulting in a barrier to finding a solution between the two nations. He asserts that both the Israeli and Arab ethno-religious societies are dealing with the building of their distinct national identities, in which the dominant factors are not necessarily rational. Emotion and collective memory of historical trauma both have a great influence. Both cultures are inundated with calls to resist the "stranger" and the "other." This phenomenon has poisoned the current and future generations with mistrust and hatred.

In negotiations the parties come to know the basic cultural norms and customs of the other side. This familiarity helps to break down barriers to sincere discussion, compromise, and accord. For example, when people from Western cultures negotiate with those of East Asia they have to be aware that body contact is inappropriate. In Arab culture the situation is the opposite; not only do Arabs shake hands when they meet, they compete so as not to be the last person to kiss the other on both sides of the cheek. As in Southeast Asia, sitting postures must be taken into account. Showing ones feet in both the Middle East and parts of Southeast Asia is considered a sign of disrespect. In cease-fire negotiations a senior US official sat crossed-legged, pointing the sole of his foot toward Arafat, which caught the attention of Arab negotiators and disturbed them. The same situation occurred during a secret visit to Oman by a minister in the Israeli cabinet. He did not understand the uneasiness in the room, until he dropped his foot to the ground and saw the entire atmosphere change.

In Arab cultures there is the concept of "opening a new page," meaning to forget the past and start afresh. This notion has a much deeper significance in Arab cultures than in the West. Arabs do not actually forget the past but pretend to do so for the purpose of building a new relationship. The late King Hussein and Yasser Arafat were archenemies during the 1970s, and yet they reconciled during the 1980s. This is an example of "opening a new page."[16]

In the course of the first Camp David Summit between Israel and Egypt, the late President Sadat and late Prime Minister Begin shook hands after reaching agreement on all details. That night Begin discussed the details with his cabinet minister Ariel Sharon. Sharon suggested asking Sadat if some Israeli settlements could remain in northern Sinai. The following day, before the official signing of the agreement, Begin raised Sharon's proposal with Sadat. The Egyptian president was very disturbed and asked his aids to pack his suitcases, announcing that they were flying back home. The Israeli Foreign Minister Moshe Dayan then addressed Sadat with an old Arab proverb, "haste suits the devil." As a result the atmosphere improved and Sadat remained. The mistake was not in asking for changes in the agreement but that Begin raised the point after they had already shaken hands.

Another example of a lost political opportunity stemming from cultural insensitivity and misunderstanding occurred following the failed Paris talks between Barak and Arafat. Egyptian President Mubarak had invited the parties to a further round of talks the next day in Sharm el-Sheikh, and Barak declined. Such an invitation coming from an Arab leader indicates that Barak would not have left those talks without some sort of gain. Furthermore, by refusing to attend, Barak also insulted Mubarak.

During the talks between Israeli and Syrian diplomats in Washington the Israeli delegation once again failed to take advantage of cultural norms. The Syrian delegation had been instructed by then President Assad not to shake hands with the Israelis. However, had the Israelis, for example, asked the Syrian negotiators to sit down with them during coffee breaks, the Syrians culturally would have been unable to refuse. Informal conversation might have made possible some progress.

In addition to cultural differences, political discourse between Israelis and Palestinians is also plagued by asymmetry and its resulting mis-understandings. On a purely behavioral level, Israelis are considered to be far more informal, frank, and direct – behavior that borders on arrogance and tactlessness. The Palestinians are more ceremonial, formal, polite, and less open. Professor Gobi Golan claims that the disparity is not only in behavior but also influences the self-perceptions of the sides and the "roles" they assign themselves.[17] Palestinians have been conscious of the fact that they are not equal in military and economic power to the Israelis, and that the situations of occupier and occupied cannot be ignored or fudged into a false atmosphere of normality. The asymmetry of power is apparent in the Israeli tendency to view themselves as "giving" the Palestinians something, as conceding "more," and that for this a reward or some return from Palestinians is expected. At the same time, the Palestinians regard Israeli "concessions" as no more than what is due to them, was theirs to begin with, and their "right." The Palestinians view a peace agreement as being of mutual interest and not an Israel concession.

If the negotiators and political leaders were to pay more attention to cultural behavior, not only could crucial misunderstandings be avoided by such sensitivity on their part, it could actually lead to gains in negotiations.

Prince Hassan's Four Stages to Sustainable Peace

His Royal Highness Prince Hassan bin Talal of Jordan asserted that the Arab world is fearful of an Israeli and Western cultural invasion and has proposed a process to overcome barriers to cultivate a "culture of peace."

"I suggest that there are four stages to be passed through before a real and sustainable peace can be achieved. In the first stage there needs to be a clear definition of how each side sees itself in terms of its history, its present condition, and its vision of the future. In the second stage there needs to be knowledge of one another, now, alas, largely lacking on both sides. In the third stage knowledge must lead to understanding, which is not the same thing. And in the fourth, and hopefully final stage, there needs to be an imaginative "leap" from the present state of mutual distrust and distaste to a new mutual respect, a shared perception of common interests, and a real and sincere desire to live together in peace. There is the need therefore on both sides of the Arab-Israeli conflict for a "culture of peace." Where can this culture of peace best be nurtured and propagated other than in the mosque, the synagogue and the church; in the school and the university; and most importantly in the family, where all life and society begin, and where we are all created "free and equal."[18]

We, the co-editors, believe that all concerned with this conflict – the Israelis, Palestinians, other Arabs, Europeans and Americans – should immediately adopt the Arab concept of "opening a new page." We should start afresh to negotiate a final peace. In this process, however, we cannot forget the past but must build on it with creativity and daring to reach an acceptable and enduring peace arrangement. This book presents the information and new thinking that can be used in this compelling and opportunity-establishing endeavor for the peoples of the Middle East and the world.

This book has twenty-seven chapters written by Israeli, Arab, European and North American experts. The chapters after this introduction are organized into four parts. The following are brief summaries of the chapters.

Part I, *The Oslo Agreement, the Palestinian Track, and New Options in the Middle East* comprises chapters 2–11.

Robert Rothstein, in "Oslo and the Ambiguities of Peace," endeavors to provide criteria by which the peace process can be judged. He states that breakdowns of the peace process have had more to do with the way in which Oslo and other similar peace agreements have been regarded and because of the multiple goals/audiences of the negotiators rather than because of the presumed inadequacies of the draft agreements' terms. Adapting to the status quo, demonizing, and perceiving that one's constituencies' total existence is at stake, constrain the peace process. Weak leaders are risk averse and are unwilling to take chances. Rothstein points out these problems and makes suggestions for improvement.

Gabriel Ben-Dor, in "The Oslo Peace Process: Patterns, Paradoxes, and Prospects," analyzes the reasons leading to the breakthrough to the Oslo Peace Process in 1993. He also concludes that there were several major paradoxes involved. He shows that the same reasons that made the initial phase of the Oslo process successful doomed the later phase to failure. Among those were the role of the mediators, the level and character of the negotiators, the secret nature of the talks, the approach to confidence building, and the decision to postpone the more fundamental issues of the conflict to the remote future. Ben-Dor urges an all-out effort for a permanent agreement, and suggests concrete solutions for tough issues related to refugees, settlements, and Jerusalem. His discussion of Palestinian–Israeli relationships within the context of Israeli Arab-Palestinian relationships is insightful. If and when negotiations resume with Syria, his discussion on this subject will be of value.

Fredrik Barth, in "The Changing Structure of Public Opinion in the Middle East," analyzes the rise in Internet technology in the Arab world and what influence it could have on the peace process. Users engage in debates that are free from any pre-established and enduring social relations or differentials of authority. The Internet, he says, will reshape significant membership and participation in "imagined communities" and establish a new cadre of self-confident opinion leaders. It could contribute to the spread of irrational and irresponsible opinions, or its permeable technology could be co-opted and deployed to bring beneficial effects to the level of the debates, the range of expressed ideas and opinions, and the possibilities for more moderate and peaceful societies.

Shlomo Gazit, in "Are Real Coexistence and Normalization Possible?," reviews the Israeli and Arab goals for peace. The contrast of these goals is the key to understanding what is happening today as well for the future. He discusses the differences in ethnicity, language, religion, economy, technology, and attitudes toward each other. He sees complications in the peace process even after an agreement. Nevertheless, he is optimistic that by taking into account these differences and difficulties, and because a hot war is the only alternative, a cold peace can be achieved.

Menachem Klein, in "The Official Israeli–Palestinian Track: An Assessment," assesses the official Israeli-Palestinian negotiating track. He states that final status talks have remained relatively static, actually having started three times. Interim agreements on issues have neither been completely concluded nor implemented, and all agreed-upon timetables have consistently been violated. Moreover, the Labor and Likud governments have held fundamentally different positions in terms of Israeli relations with the Palestinians. Whereas Labor was disposed to work with the Palestinian Authority within the Oslo process toward a peace agreement, the Likud still regards the PLO as a terrorist organization and resists recognizing it as an eventual juridically equal state.

Khalil Elian's objective in "The Peace Process and Scenarios for a Permanent Solution of the Palestinian Question," is to explore several scenarios for a peaceful and permanent solution for the Palestinian question in all of its aspects: identity, statehood, land, borders, Jerusalem, the refugees, and the settlements. He explains the difference between a state, a federation, and a confederation. He then describes models of each form that could apply to the area, including a Swiss-style federation.

Onn Winckler's economic analysis in "The Long-Term Economic Benefits of Peace Stability in the Middle East," starts by describing the enormous direct and indirect economic damage that the Middle East conflict has caused. In addition, high population growth rate has harmed many countries. He shows that the peace agreements have significantly improved the economies of Egypt and Jordan. In comparison with other economic activities, tourism has the greatest potential to spur the economic development of the countries of the Middle East, and tourism is directly affected by the peace and stability of the region. Peace has become an economic imperative.

Ephraim Yuchtman-Ya'ar in "The Oslo Process and Jewish Public Opinion in Israel: A Story of Disappointment," describes the disparity and change of feelings in Israeli public opinion about the Oslo peace process. His surveys cover one year of the Barak government and the first three months of the Sharon government. The steep decline in support for the Oslo process, which occurred over almost the entire period of Barak's tenure, explains to a great extent his debacle in the elections. The profile of most of those who held positive attitudes for Oslo clearly consists of secular left-wing voters who belonged to the high socioeconomic stratum.

Shaul Mishal, in "How Hamas Thinks," examines Hamas' ideology, leadership, pragmatism and strategy, and its tactics in dealing with the Palestinian Authority, Israel, and others. Hamas remains committed in the long-term to a Palestinian state "from the river to the sea," and to the elimination of Israel. However, the "inside" leadership (those within the Palestinian Authority) has been disposed to accept a short-term establishment of a Palestinian state without abandoning Hamas' long-term Islamic vision and objective. Mishal states that Hamas has been remarkably successful in balancing Palestinian national interests with its allegiance to its vision of Islam. Hamas' political flexibility within the Authority has been far different from its world image of fanaticism, fundamentalistism, and intransigence. This flexibility has been productive and kept Hamas from becoming completely isolated in the local Palestinian, inter-Arab, and international arenas.

Reuben Aharoni and **Joseph Ginat**, in "The Palestinian Citizens of Israel and the Peace Process," address the situation of the Palestinian citizens of Israel. Fifty years of disappointment have clarified to them the need for a separate, collective definition. Despite claims that the Arabs in Israel are increasing their interest in national Palestinian issues, this chapter shows that Israeli Arabs have expended most of their energy on internal Israeli state issues related to equality and their status in Israel.

Part II, *Countries with Peace Agreements with Israel: Egypt and Jordan*, comprises chapters 12–16.

David Kushner, in "Lessons from Greek/Turkish Relations for the Arab–Israeli Conflict," analyzes the history of the peace process between Greece and Turkey over Cyprus. He compares and contrasts its success and failure with the Arab–Israeli peace process. He emphasizes three crucial lessons learned from the case of Cyprus: (1) the vision and farsightedness of the Greek and Turkish leaders who stood against historical myths and unrealizable aspirations contributed to the peace process; (2) Turkish and Greek relations functioned best under conditions of maximum separation of populations; and (3) it is unreasonable to think that the affinities between Arabs of other countries and Palestinian Arabs do not elicit support, and, therefore, solving the Palestinian problem is crucial to full reconciliation between the Israel and Arab world.

Yoram Meital, in "Peace with Israel in Egypt's Policy," reviews Egypt's policy of peace with Israel. He traces the historical roots of the agreement and shows it to be part of a broader transformation encompassing Egypt's domestic, economic, and security policies. Egypt regards itself as the leader of the Arab world in achieving stability for the region and in negotiating against Israeli policies that it sees as harmful. The Egyptian public believes it was Egypt that broke the log-jam and set the Middle East on the road toward a negotiated peace, that failure to finally achieve a comprehensive agreement will hurt Egypt, and that Israel is responsible for the lack of progress. Egyptians are increasingly critical of the United States, and they oppose Shimon Peres' idea of "the New Middle East."

Mohanna Haddad, in "Jordan's Perspectives of Peace," gives historical reasons why Jordan has been able to establish a distinct identity and set its own path within the Arab world. Economic progress would bring Jordan even greater recognition. However, even though Jordan is intrinsically connected with the Palestinians and Israel, Jordan is often ignored by the two parties in decisions that have a direct effect on Jordan.

Joseph Nevo, in "The Jordanian–Israeli Peace: The View from Amman," focuses on how the Jordanian public has perceived and evaluated the Jordan–Israel peace. He looks at the advantages and the shortcomings of the peace for the people and the nation. He juxtaposes King Hussein's and King Abdallah's perceptions of peace and normalization with Israel, and examines the various constraints with which each of the two kings has had to cope. Of importance is his description of the Jordanian forces opposing normalization of relations with Israel.

Rateb Amro, in "The Peace Process: A Jordanian Perspective," discusses the Jordanian point of view and Jordan's absolute commitment to the peace process. He stresses the great difficulty that conflict imposes on the region, the positive worldwide implications of regional peace, and the opportunities the Jordanian–Israeli peace accord opens to the peoples of both countries. He creates a vision for the region's political and economic future. In painting this picture he examines issues of nuclear weapons, water, energy and security.

Part III, *Countries Without Peace Agreements with Israel,* comprises chapters 17–21.

Kais Firro, in "Lebanon's Position in the Peace Process," states that Israeli attempts to separate the Palestinian, Lebanese, and Syrian negotiating tracks might lead to success in the shortrun but not in the longrun. He explores the historical Israeli–Lebanese relationship, the Syrian presence in Lebanon, its implications for Lebanese internal politics, and the future of Palestinian refugees now in Lebanon.

Marius Deeb, in "Lebanon and the Arab–Israeli Conflict," describes how Lebanon is an unwilling participant in the Arab-Israeli conflict, having been dragged into the dispute by Syria. Through Syrian military occupation and Hizballah, supported by Iran and Syria, the Lebanese are kept from practicing pluralism, democracy and a non-confrontational relationship with Israel. The solution to the violence is to end Syria's military occupation of Lebanon. Were Syria to depart, Hizballah would not survive because, contrary to appearances, Hizballah is not accepted by the vast majority of the Lebanese people.

Moshe Ma'oz, in "Syrian–Israeli Relations on the Eve of the Peace Process," identifies Israel and Syria as the two major protagonists in the Middle East conflict during the past two decades. Although Israel's policy toward Syria has not changed much since 1967, Syria's policy has gone through serious changes in diplomatic maneuvers and military build-up. From 1988, and with the Gulf War, Syria changed policy again and appealed to the United States for help with Israel. Between 1992 and 1996 significant progress was made, but despite negotiation in 1999–2000, the differences were not overcome. Syria continued to exert pressure via Hizballah and to demand full withdrawal by Israel from the Golan. This account of Syrian diplomacy is valuable to any future negotiations.

Eyal Zisser, in "Israeli–Syrian Peace Negotiations (December 99–March 2000) – Missed Opportunity?," writes of the problems of establishing a peace process between Israel and Syria. He explores the attempts by both sides to move toward peace talks and what precluded them each time. Zisser analyzes Israeli and Syrian feelings toward the actual and perceived issues involved. He focuses on the near-miss situation when hopes were high that Asad would try to reach a settlement before he died. As in the Ma'oz chapter, Zisser's contribution provides background knowledge essential to negotiators for making progress on this front of the peace process.

Amatzia Baram, in "Iraq and the Middle East Process," traces Iraq and the Middle East peace process from 1968. He outlines the origins of radical pan-Arabism in Iraq, the role that the question of Palestine has played in internal Iraqi politics, and the policy phases through which the Ba'ath party and Saddam Hussein have evolved. Baram predicts that Iraq will eventually enter into the peace process, and provides compelling evidence for this view.

Part IV, *Jerusalem and the Peace Process* comprises chapters 22–27.

Enrico Molinaro, in "Creative Approaches to Coexistence of National and Religious Identities in Jerusalem," proposes creative approaches for the coexistence of national and religious identities in Jerusalem. He explains the meaning of temporary "status quo," arrangements in Jerusalem for the Holy Places. He outlines important aspects of the holy sites in the controversy over Jerusalem and suggests practical solutions for each.

Manuel Hassassian, in "Jerusalem in the Peace Process," starts with the premise that lasting peace in the Middle East can be attained only with the establishment of an Independent Palestine with East Jerusalem as its Capital. His perception is that Israel does not have a good record of implementing past agreements, and its policies to build settlements and to control East Jerusalem have been flawed – they have not changed the de facto demographic situation. Both sides must learn lessons from previous talks. Israeli peace forces and the Palestinian mainstream must find common ground. Hassassian believes any solution must promote the ideals of justice and inclusion, and promote civil society and democracy. He provides in his conclusions facts from the Palestinian perspective for negotiations, and he asserts the need for an international force to guarantee implementation of the final peace agreement.

Moshe Amirav, in "The Palestinians: From the Sidelines to Major Player in Jerusalem," reviews the modern history of the struggle for the control of Jerusalem. The Palestinians accomplished moving from being a player on the sidelines of the political arena to major player. He discusses how events, circumstances, and policy tools led to a shift in the "Jerusalem problem" paradigm. Neither the Palestinians' "success" nor the Israelis' "failure" alone constitutes an explanation of the policy paradigm change. It was the result of circumstances and events in which many players took part.

Menachem Klein, in "Demarcating Jerusalem's Borders" argues that the peace process should be led first and foremost by elite groups, mainly political leaders. He argues that the question of Jerusalem can be resolved. Israel's attempts to change the de facto demographics have failed. There is international consensus that Jerusalem must be the capital of both Israel and Palestine, and that the city must not be divided by barriers. The city is currently divided by at least five "soft" lines, and these give flexibility in negotiating the boundary between Israeli and Palestinian parts of Jerusalem. Klein shows that Jerusalem is not an exclusively religious matter, and argues it should be possible politically to manage the religious conflicts over holy sites in the city, such as the Temple Mount. He ends with a list of "foundations" for a Palestinian-Israeli agreement.

Ephraim Yuchtman-Ya'ar's poll results, detailed in "The Future Status of Jerusalem: Views of the Israeli and Palestinian Publics," show clearly that the future status of Jerusalem is by far the most prominent issue both for the Israelis and Palestinians. Both the Israelis and the Palestinians are unwilling to compromise on the future status of Jerusalem, even if this would ensure the signing of a peace agreement. Yuchtman-Ya'ar believes that both the Israeli and Palestinian publics can be persuaded to accept the idea of keeping Jerusalem functionally undivided while dividing it politically into two capitals.

In "Temple Mount – al Haram al-Sharif," **Joseph Ginat** sets forth his and Ephraim Yuchtman-Ya'ar's proposal for a solution for the Temple Mount. As background, they provide a consensus document agreed to by Arabs and Israelis, "Negotiating Jerusalem: Guiding Principles." Ginat outlines his and Yuchtman-Ya'ar's discussion of the Temple Mount proposal with Israeli and Arab political and religious leaders. Ginat and Yuchtman-Ya'ar argue that whereas in the near past it was believed that political issues should be negotiated prior to tackling the resolution of control and management of religious sites, now because of the prolonged period of violence, addressing and quickly resolving the Temple Mount issue could enhance negotiations on political issues for a comprehensive peace agreement. The authors believe that their Temple Mount proposal offers an opportunity to solve this issue, which is so important to both Jews and Muslims.

Notes

1　Menachem Klein, "Is the Israeli-Palestinian Conflict Solvable." Paper in a conference conducted by the Tammy Steinmetz Center for Peace Studies, Tel Aviv University, June 22–23, 2001.

2　Ron Pundak, "Peace, Security, and Fairness: Towards a Final Israeli–Palestinian Agreement." Tammy Steinmetz Center for Peace Studies, September 2000.

3　Gilad Sher, "Peace Process – Vision versus Reality." Tammy Steinmetz Center for Peace Studies, June 2001.

4　Pundak, "Peace, Security and Fairness," pp. 6–7.

5　*Newsweek*, June 29, 2001.

6　Aluf Benn, *Ha'aretz*. April 10, 2001.

7　Klein, "Is the Israeli–Palestinian Conflict Solvable."

8　Yossi Beilin, *Ha'aretz*, June 15, 2001.

9　Abd el-Khalim Kindil, *El Istiklal*, June 21, 2001.

10　Hani el-Masri, *Al-Ayyam*, June 23, 2001.

11　Sharm el-Sheik Fact-Finding Committee, George J. Mitchell, chairman. Other members of the committee included Suleyman Demirel, Thobjoern Jagland,

Warren B. Rudman, and Javier Solana. U.S. Department of State, Internal Information Programs, April 30, 2001, http://usinfo.state.gov/regional/nea/mitchell.htm

12   Shlomo Avinery, *Introductory Remarks* in conference conducted by the Tammy Steinmetz Center for Peace Studies, Tel Aviv University, June 22–23, 2001.

13   Ya'akov Bar-Siman-Tov, "Dialectics between Conflict Management and Conflict Resolution." Paper in conference conducted by the Tammy Steinmetz Center for Peace Studies, Tel Aviv University, June 22–23, 2001.

14   In the battles between Saladin and the Crusaders there were eight cease-fires, some requested by Saladin and others by the Crusaders. Kreutz A., Ehren. *Saladin*. New York. 1972

15   Gabi Sheffer, *"Culture, Political Culture and the Possibility of Solving the Israeli–Palestinian Conflict."* Paper in conference conducted by the Tammy Steinmetz Center for Peace Studies, Tel Aviv University, June 22–23, 2001.

16   See Joseph Ginat, *Blood Revenge* (Brighton and Portland: Sussex Academic Press, 1997).

17   Galia Golan, "Cultural Aspects of Peace." Paper in conference conducted by the Tammy Steinmetz Center for Peace Studies, Tel Aviv University, June 22–23, 2001.

18   HRH Prince El Hassan bin Talal, *Foreword*. In Shaul Mishal, Ranan Kuperman, David Boas. *Investment in Peace* (Brighton and Portland: Sussex Academic Press, 2001), p. vii.

Part I

The Oslo Agreement, the Palestinian Track, and New Options in the Middle East

CHAPTER 2

Oslo and the Ambiguities of Peace

ROBERT L. ROTHSTEIN

Can there be a bad peace, and how would we know?

The Oslo peace process has generated an increasing amount of opposition. Some of that opposition erupted with the very signing of the agreement in September 1993. Thus the Israeli right wing (both secular and religious) insisted that too much had been given away, and the Palestinian left (as well, of course, as the Islamic fundamentalists) insisted that not enough had been gained or guaranteed for the future to justify entering an uncertain peace process. In the years since the signing of Oslo, the opposition, especially in the Palestinian camp, has grown even stronger. This is partly because the peace process lost momentum, staggering from one crisis to another; partly because standards of living for the Palestinian community have continued to deteriorate; and partly because the performance of Mr. Arafat's Palestinian Authority (PA) has been dismal and disappointing to all sides. A group of twenty Palestinian intellectuals and legislators not only denounced the record of the PA, but the Oslo peace process as well, for having sold out the national aspirations of the Palestinian people.[1]

Does this suggest or imply that Oslo and other similar agreements (such as the Dayton and the Good Friday agreements) that have also engendered dissent are necessarily "bad" agreements? Since these agreements are more like exploratory truces than genuine peace settlements, any attempt to render a final judgment is decidedly premature – although not wholly irrelevant because enough time has passed to render some tentative judgments. It should be noted that this effort to establish criteria for a good or bad peace, however provisional or uncertain it may be, is only an academic exercise. Without such criteria or an attempt to think through how exploratory truces should be assessed, we have no convincing response to critics who assert that Oslo is a failure – or to enthusiasts who insist that

Oslo has or will eventually generate a mutually beneficial peace settlement. Thus, unanswered criticisms can lead to a downward spiral or a negative self-fulfilling prophecy as assumptions of failure produce the kind of actions or policies that virtually guarantee that the critics will be proved correct, even at great cost to the peace process itself.[2] Again, however, the criteria that emerge are likely to be inherently ambiguous, because what is (or is not) good or bad is largely subjective, since each side's judgment is likely to shift with changing circumstances. Therefore, any exploratory truce is only part of a potentially prolonged series of negotiations. These criteria, however unsatisfying, may still be useful, however, if they increase awareness of the importance of considering such issues, and alert both analysts and practitioners to the fact that we should not compare Oslo to some abstract notion of a good or bad peace, but rather to what was good or bad contextually.

Can one discover the criteria for a bad peace by looking at those neces- sary for a good one? Unfortunately, the answer is no, because the latter criteria are also subjective and ambiguous. For example, we might argue that a good peace is a stable peace that neither side wants to alter signifi- cantly because each has achieved enough of its essential aims to compensate for the costs of concessions, and is willing to implement its terms effectively. This will not suffice here, however, because the potential costs and bene- fits of these trade-offs are very difficult to calculate and changes will be imperative as the negotiating process continues. Nor can we argue that a good peace is one that extracts the most that is available at the time. These are complex, multilevel bargaining games that are not yet established; which is to say that we cannot know what is available except in a nominal sense – what emerges from the negotiating process is pretty much what is available. Finally, one might argue that a good peace is a peace that both sides perceive as fair and just. But justice is a very subjective concept in this case, as each side begins with different premises about what is "just." Thus, debates about a just settlement may generate more conflict and not a deeper peace.[3]

There are a variety of suggestions about the criteria for a bad peace.[4] Any peace agreement can have bad effects if it is not implemented, or if it demands a degree of compliance that asks too much too soon from one or both parties, as with the decommissioning issue in Northern Ireland. It can also have negative results if it threatens a leader who may be a necessary component of the negotiating process, or if one or both parties signed only to get breather to re-arm or to increase external support. It can also have negative results if it is an agreement forced upon the parties by an external patron with his own political agenda, or if it is oversold and increases expec- tations that cannot be met, and thus likely to fail in a hailstorm of recriminations and bitterness. In short, a bad peace increases the probability of a return to violence and makes it likely that the next attempt to jumpstart a peace process will be even more unsuccessful in implementing than the first one.

The key point here, however, is not that there are a variety of factors that can generate a bad peace, but rather that most of the reasons for breakdown of the process have more to do with the way in which Oslo and other similar peace agreements have been implemented than with any presumed inadequacies of their terms. This is *not* meant to deny that there are differences in quality among different agreements – that some agreements are relatively more equitable than others, or that some more closely approximate the minimally acceptable terms of agreement for both sides. Nevertheless, all peace agreements that attempt to begin the process of resolving protracted (and sometimes existential) conflicts are inevitably flawed, incomplete, and fragile (for reasons that I shall discuss in the next section). Thus, while it may be unfortunate that the Oslo, Dayton, or Good Friday agreements are only partially satisfactory to either side, they should not be criticized for failing to do the impossible or to more fully approximate someone's ideal of what ought to be done, and done quickly. No peace agreement in the present context is going to meet all the needs or demands of both parties. None is going to clarify and resolve the central symbolic and substantive issues that drive the conflict. No peace agreement should be called "bad" for such failings.

In short, such agreements – or exploratory truces – are largely blank canvases that remain to be filled in, that await the skill and imagination of the painters/peacemakers. At least there is a canvas on the easel and a willingness to begin discussing what can and should be drawn on it. To expect more, given the inherited and continuing patterns of conflict and the cognitive limitations and political weaknesses of most political leaders, is to make the best the enemy of the good – or perhaps the good the enemy of the possible. Only a victor's peace could promise more; and, apart from the fact that neither side has conceded defeat, such a peace may only create more problems in the long run than it resolves. Moreover, the alternatives offered by the naysayers: a return to violence and the "politics of the last atrocity"[5] are hardly superior.

This argument necessarily implies that the standards we should use in evaluating Oslo and other such agreements must be as tentative, provisional, and open-ended as are the agreements themselves. We can only know whether Oslo is good or bad after some time has passed and some of the painters/peacemakers have had a chance to show some of their skills – and even more crucially, their intentions.[6] Even a peace that leaves a very large gap between aspirations and achievements, as Oslo does, may turn out reasonably well if both sides implement it in good faith and seek to build on it rather than manipulate it as merely another stage in the conflict.

No peace (or exploratory truce) can be quite as bad as its severest critics suggest if one can append to its list of failures:

- that it has stopped the majority of the violence most of the time;
- that it has recognized the other side as a necessary negotiating partner; and
- that it has opened up the opportunity to establish new procedural rules (as to how to go about resolving issues of contention) and perhaps to explore whether there is room for compromise on substantive issues.

What is "bad" in these circumstances is not a flawed agreement that may represent the most that can be achieved either politically and psychologically at a particular time, but rather the failure to grasp the opportunities and to see *both* the limits and possibilities of a fragile and incomplete agreement that must be strengthened, but that can also make a conflict that has been drawn out even more insoluble.

The central question, in effect, is not whether Oslo is a good or a bad peace – for we do not yet know – but whether leaders and their key external supporters are willing, able, or wise enough to make something more out of it. The limiting case argument here is rather like a paraphrase of Churchill's famous comment on democracy. Oslo is no one's idea of a good peace, except when we look at the alternatives. Oslo was a product of a period when both sides (for different reasons) were willing to explore the possibility of a new relationship, but were also distrustful and suspicious of each other. They were not in full control of their domestic constituencies, and were thus unwilling to risk much or to attempt a high risk/high gain strategy (as Camp David). Each was always too ready to interpret the failings of the other as justification for a return to conflict.

Before we explore the Oslo process itself, we need to understand why such cautionary and ambivalent responses to the peace process are "normal" and even rational in the context of protracted, and at least in part, existential conflict. Therefore, we may still conclude that the leaders on both sides failed miserably in their task of transforming an exploratory truce into a genuine peace process that resolved critical issues; but we will also have a deeper understanding of why they failed – and perhaps what needs to be done to give them a better chance at succeeding in the future.

Existential Conflict:
Fear, Distrust and the Absence of Empathy

The costs of extended conflicts are devastating: brutal and unending violence; the tensions of living in fear in a neighborhood of hatred; the perversion of civic values as unsavory tactics generate more unsavory tactics, thus destroying lawful rule; the economic losses from high levels of military expenditures and low levels of foreign investment and regional cooperation; the shame of pariah status or the sorrows of a life in exile; and the inability to be accepted as an "ordinary" state. Why, then, with elites and publics increasingly desperate to find a way out, and affected by battle fatigue as well as a sense of futility, has it been so difficult to negotiate compromise settlements more bearable than an ugly status quo?[7]

One part of the answer is familiar. Both sides, leaders and followers alike, have learned to adapt to what only seems an unbearable status quo. However, even this status quo may seem preferable to relinquishing deeply held and sometimes theologically ordained maximalist goals of victory in the future, however difficult the present is. It is impossible to disprove the belief that victory by a long war strategy of attrition is possible.[8] Moreover, the limited offers that weak leaders can submit to each other and the uncertainty that such offers will be implemented or produce enough benefits quickly mean that what can be offered and what can be obtained are insufficient. Thus it seems more prudent to complain bitterly about the status quo but to risk very little to change it. The flawed and fragile agreements that do emerge rarely produce a basic shift in the calculus of conflict. Each continues to fear that compromise offers will lead only to new demands or to an appearance of weakness, and the peace process – sadly – becomes the continuation of conflict by other means.

Once conflicts begin, perhaps because of governmental failure and conflicts of interests, they may escalate and deepen as psychological biases and cognitive limitations fuel animosities and generate a process of demonization. These factors make conflicts of interest more difficult to resolve, especially because most peace negotiations focus on compromising interests, thus leaving the subjective factors for treatment at a later time. Unfortunately, the latter may undermine the peace process because they create patterns of hostility and distrust and may take much longer to diminish or contain. There is an obvious need to deal with both levels of conflict, as many books on conflict resolution attest to, but the difficulty of doing so, given the different time scales, may delay, impede, or even undermine any peace process.

These difficulties are exacerbated if a conflict is largely or in an important part existential. Conventionally, in these existential conflicts, one or both sides feel that their literal existence is at stake, or that they could lose their cultural or ethnic identity.[9] In addition, in such conflicts, one usually finds that each side has a lack of empathy for the other – that there is instead a rejoicing in whatever pain can be inflicted on the other.[10] There may also be an indifference to learning about each other. Because the only acceptable outcome for either party is total victory, the argument goes like this: Why learn about the other party whose fate is about to be destroyed? Hence, most political energies thus focus on sustaining commitment among one's own supporters as opposed to "reaching across the great divide to the other."[11]

This backward focus on sustaining the faith of the committed also keeps alive the dreams of triumph. (Parenthetically, these comments may be truer for the exiles who have little contact with the enemy than with the local community left behind and in regular contact with it. The locals may be less likely to hold extreme views, more knowledgeable about who the enemy is, what terms he is likely to accept, and more willing to push for compromise.)

One needs to be very careful, however, not to carry the idea of existential conflict too far, for few if any conflicts are completely existential. There are always some issues that can be negotiated, even with sworn enemies, if such issues are initially largely procedural or peripheral, as opposed to symbolic or fundamental. These compromises may help to sustain a negotiating process that gradually diminishes purely existential elements, although this is obviously vastly more difficult if memories of atrocities are recent (as in Bosnia and Kosovo). Too simplistic a view of existential conflict may also generate the view that there is no solution to the conflict, or, as Richard Rose said of the Northern Ireland situation in 1971, "no solution is immediately practical."[12] But some movement is always possible. Not everyone is always a "true believer" in apocalyptic visions of the conflict; and by taking the "no solution" view too literally, one may miss chances for compromise by ignoring changes that may be occurring in one or both communities.[13]

Nevertheless, while it is important not to overstate the consequences of existential (or even partially existential) conflict, it is equally true that such conflicts are especially difficult to resolve. Hatreds and grievances have deep roots; issues are frequently emotional and symbolic, and traditional interest-based bargaining strategies do not work well; and levels of distrust (as well as skepticism about the possibility of peace or the likelihood of implementation of commitments) are so high that each side may demand immediate confirmation of an acceptable final outcome before making any concessions itself. Compromise in such circumstances is likely to seem treasonable certainly to the extremists, and opposition to compromise may be the only position that can maintain unity. Because the stakes of the conflict are so high and because it is believed that the other can never be trusted and is always seeking to do the worst, the conflict and any peace process proceeds in the context of a permanent sense of fear and insecurity. Nothing the other side says is ever taken at face value and constant demands for strong evidence of the other side's sincerity are prevalent – although such demands ignore the other side's difficulties in bringing a constituency for peace into being, thus threatening the peace process itself.[14]

These attitudes and beliefs fuel the conflict but, even more critically, they set constraints on the kind of peace process that is likely to emerge and develop.[15] The key point is that neither side is likely to make a full commitment to the process because initial offers will be minimal, doubts about the other's willingness or ability to offer more or to implement promises beyond the procedural will be great, there will be widespread fears on both sides about either's ability to get a substantive agreement through domestic political processes, and both will be unhappy about the terms of any agreement, thus constantly seeking to push its limits or renegotiate its terms. Since these fears and doubts are rational, given the laden history and the persistence of the conditions that have sustained the conflict, reluctant and tentative commitment to a low risk/low gain strategy is intrinsic to the end game of protracted, existential conflict.[16] Generosity will be limited, demands to dot every "i" and cross every "t" will be pervasive, and haggling over every inch of territory or every symbolic concession will be nasty. The temporary truce is likely to revert quickly to renewed conflict as each seeks to manipulate the peace process to gain more or to be stronger at the next stage. Risk aversion will be high because fear of failure will be high, and leaders will seek to protect themselves from these risks to themselves and to the peace process rather than to increase the chances of success by altering attitudes and patterns of behavior.[17]

How does one get beyond this rather grim picture of the peacemaking process, one that stands in sharp contrast to the (premature) euphoria generated by ceremonies on the White House lawn? "Big Bang" negotiations like Camp David or Dayton are not likely to work, and the normal process of incremental adjustment and gradual convergence is also at great risk in an existential bargaining game that probably requires entirely different bargaining rules. The latter is especially true because there is an ineradicable risk to both sides that any apparent shift toward peace is merely tactical – a new slower, presumably less violent way to achieve old goals by stages. The fear of being duped is especially strong in the early stages of the peace process because distrust is pervasive. The need for reassurance is great, and the consequences of being wrong about the intentions of the other could be catastrophic for both leaders and followers. This probably explains why demands for strong, tangible, and early indications of a serious commitment to peace are inevitable, but dangerous when weak leaders have serious rivals and an insecure domestic base. Thus there may be a conflict between what each leader needs to bolster domestic support and increase his own willingness to run risks, and what is necessary to convince the other side that the peace process is genuine, that momentum needs to be maintained, and that the risks are worth taking.

Are there means available to avert a "race to the bottom," that is, a peace process that rapidly degenerates into an exchange of recriminations and renewed threats? There are some more or less conventional answers, none of which we can discuss here: reliance on pressures and assistance from third parties; the hope that leadership changes will bring more flexible negotiating postures; the hope that battle fatigue on the part of mass supporters (and a sense that time is turning against one's own side on the part of the leadership) will energize what must initially be a top-down nego-tiational process; and perhaps greater efforts to cultivate a domestic constituency for peace much earlier and much more thoroughly.[18] I would submit here, however, that while these and other measures may be helpful or even necessary, they will not suffice unless we also recognize the intrinsic limitations, constraints, and inconsistencies of these kind of peace processes and the kind of policy adjustments and adaptations that must ensue.

In short, the stop/go, off/on, crisis driven negotiating process that developed after Oslo is not simply the result of flawed leaders and un-predictable political events. Rather, it is intrinsic to any peace process that seeks to take the first uncertain steps toward the long and painful road to peace. Too much is at stake, the risks are too high, and the mental reservations and implicit doubts about the sincerity and commitment of the other are too profound to expect much more than a willingness to explore and an escape hatch to the comforts of the familiar. It is unrealistic to expect a leap of faith into a new world that might never eventuate and might be worse than the past (especially for leaders who have risked exploration of a new path).[19]

These comments put the failures of the Oslo process in a somewhat different light. Everyone has their favorite scapegoat for what has tran-spired – usually Arafat for the Israelis and Netanyahu for the Palestinians – not to mention the Clinton administration for both. And no one could possibly deny that plenty of mistakes have been made (thus tilting a poten-tially good peace toward a potentially bad one). But weak leaders threatened by internal rivals and an insecure domestic base, and fearful for their own survival, can only hedge their bets, move slowly, be ambiguous about how much has been conceded, and unwisely optimistic about what benefits can be expected and how soon.[20] When Arafat proclaims a "peace of the brave" to the Israelis and the Americans but simultaneously tells his own people that "the struggle continues" and what has been gained is only a stage in gaining more, he violates the norms of conventional bargaining theory. And Netanyahu does the same sort of thing when he demands from Arafat and the PA a degree of compliance with the commitment to control terrorism that would threaten Arafat's increasingly shaky and unpopular rule.[21] But rather than merely denouncing the waffling, the speaking with two voices, and the endless haggling over small details, one needs to under-stand that ambiguity, ambivalence, and anxiety are intrinsic to the early stages of a tentative peace process. Indeed, they are the very warp and woof of the process, which should be expected and anticipated and dealt with as the "normal" cost of a dangerous venture into unknown territory.[22]

Moreover, while such behavior may clearly have negative long-run consequences, for leaders intent above all on short-run survival, such tactics are not irrational. After all, protecting one's back, keeping options open, and evading reciprocity for as long as possible are well-known tactics in much less risky political environments. In any case, it is surely wrong as an exercise in prudential bargaining to tell such leaders to risk more, or to take actions that threaten their basic power, positions, or (as Irish scholars have said of the demand for immediate decommissioning of arms) to "set them up for an exam that they cannot pass."[23]

A final point about the end game of existential conflicts is worth emphasis. In conventional, interest-based conflicts the most important level of interaction is usually between the parties themselves as they engage in a process of concession and convergence. However, in the conflicts that concern us here, it is usually two other levels that dominate. Because there is so much doubt as to the commitment of the other side and so much fear of being duped, leaders (especially those leaders weakened by past failures or unstable domestic coalitions) are likely to focus first on not getting too far ahead of a domestic constituency that may still believe in promises of ultimate victory or still believe in a demonic view of the other. In addition, such leaders may view the third level of interaction with actual or potential patrons as the most critical, not only because of the hope of access to external financial resources, but also because of the added bargaining leverage from a newly gained diplomatic access. These calculations may have been dominant for Sadat at Camp David, for Arafat at Oslo, and perhaps also for Assad of Syria in his on again/off again negotiations with Israel. What is critical here is that the most essential level – face-to-face negotiations with the old enemy – becomes a residual of the other levels and may come to seem almost epiphenomenal to other bargaining games that are very important but also of less importance if the face-to-face talks fall apart.

When a tentative peace process does begin, the initial stage frequently involves a crucial trade-off: a temporary end to most violence in exchange for recognition of each other as a legitimate and necessary bargaining power. This changes the terms of the conflict and opens up new opportunities for movement, but it is obviously a long way from a genuine peace settlement. The road ahead is perilous largely because the initial agreement and subsequent agreements are not self-executing. Terms are constantly exposed to divergent interpretations and the process of implementation bounces from crisis to crisis, and from misunderstanding to misunderstanding.

The Oslo peace process has begun to deal with a whole range of familiar substantive issues: borders, Jerusalem, the right of return for refugees, etc. It is far from clear at the time of this writing (March 2000) that a "contract zone" exists on any of these issues, especially if the bargaining game remains focused solely on limited and symmetrical concessions for concessions. This is because, in the final analysis, these conflicts are not merely about resolving difficult substantive issues, as important as that may be; but they are also conflicts dealing with learning to live together and how to establish new rules of engagement or coexistence. There is, of course, no possibility that a new bargaining relationship can be established from the start just because exploratory talks have begun. Perhaps it will never be possible to do more than muddle through to a bearable but always risky compromise. Even that, however, may be difficult without strong leadership and continued external financial and political support.

Oslo and Its Aftermath

Oslo was not a victor's peace process; it was an unequal process. Israel was strong and prosperous, but internal changes (battle fatigue, a desire to live a "normal" life, etc.), external pressures (from the US as well as from the desire to participate in the global economy), and uncertainty about how to deal with the *Intifada* generated a willingness to risk an uncertain peace process.[24] The factors pushing Arafat and the PLO to join the Oslo process were obvious but the associated dangers were much greater. Arafat's disastrous decision to support Iraq during the Gulf War led to a massive loss of financial support; the continued building of settlements by the Israelis raised fears about how much of the West Bank and Gaza would be left for the Palestinians; and the growing support for the Islamic fundamentalists and the emergence of an alternative local leadership during the *Intifada* suggested that challenges to Arafat's leadership (and his loyalists in Tunis) were likely to grow. In light of these factors and in light of the asymmetries in power between Israel and the Palestinians (which implied that Arafat would be negotiating from weakness), Arafat's "peace of the brave" appeared to be a "peace of the desperate."[25]

Arafat did not come away from Oslo empty-handed. He and the PLO, threatened by failure, were recognized by Israel as legitimate negotiating partners, if only because there was no obvious alternative. In addition, he acquired access to the White House and Washington, which at least generated hopes that Arafat could induce the Clinton administration to persuade Israel to do what it would not otherwise be willing to do. In addition, there was also the implicit hope that a new bargaining game had been established with the Israelis and that this game might produce mutually bearable terms of separation.[26]

Arafat also had to make some painful concessions, however. The most important of these was that Arafat agreed to join an interim negotiating process – an exploratory truce – without any guarantees about the central issues in the conflict: statehood, borders, Jerusalem, refugees, etc. Over the years, he had insisted that he would not do this, which may only indicate how desperate he was.[27] He also had to agree to cooperate in repressing terrorism, although this threatened his domestic base and would make it difficult to integrate the fundamentalists into the political process. The Israeli and US demand to act strongly against terrorism, while obviously understandable, also violated a basic precept of bargaining theory: it asked Arafat to do something that threatened his domestic power base and to do so without much in return for the Palestinians in the West Bank and Gaza.[28] In any case, it was not surprising that the Oslo Agreement was controversial from the start, generating significant dissent among Palestinian elites and only fluctuating and lukewarm support from the masses.[29] And what support there was gradually weakened on both sides as endless delays destroyed momentum, disagreement about terms grew increasingly bitter, and brutal acts of terrorism undermined support for the process and helped to elect a harsh critic of the peace to office in Israel.

I have argued that a peace process like Oslo is inextricably fragile, unstable, and erratic. Weak leaders reluctantly make tentative commitments to an uncertain process, leave loopholes for a quick exit back to "the good old days" of intense but frozen conflict, and speak with different accents to different audiences. The context of choice is dominated by risk, and even a strong and wise leader would have trouble adopting and implementing a high risk, high gain strategy. This context, which is the result of an accumulation of grievances, suspicions, and hatred in a protracted, existential conflict, sets the framework within which the peace process – before and after Oslo – must unfold. But how deep and pervasive the damage to the peace is depends on the interacting decisions of opposing leaders. The situation is difficult and dangerous but there is still room to make it better or worse. Unfortunately, Arafat and Netanyahu, among the Israeli leaders, have failed the test disastrously. The Oslo process has steadily deteriorated and, while it may or may not have been saved by a new agreement between Barak and Arafat, it is clear that time was lost, bitterness intensified, and the likelihood of continued conflict *after* a new agreement is still very high.[30]

The pessimism of the last point reflects more than the usual difficulties, already noted, of ending a protracted conflict. It also reflects more than the worsening of the situation after the initial agreement. The central point is that a Barak–Arafat agreement did not emerge because Arafat was too weak internally to take what Barak offered, and because he believed it was unlikely to fulfill all of the demands of the Palestinians and Arab backers. Thus, in response to the Israeli demand for a definitive settlement, the Palestinians were bound to see the agreement as merely another stage of the conflict – which as yet remains unresolved. This obviously portended continued instability. Moreover, continued economic deterioration and very high population growth rates raise troubling questions about whether the West Bank and Gaza will ever be able to provide enough jobs and an improved standard of living for the Palestinian populace.[31] Regional instability will not help matters during a slow and potentially bloody transition to democratization and while the market gets underway.

The period after a peace agreement has been signed is an unusual hybrid since many of the factors that deepened and sustained the conflict in the past are still present but the new opportunities opened by the agreement require new patterns of thought and behavior. Because the masses may still firmly believe in the rhetoric of the past and may not be aware of some of the external pressures pushing toward peace, the initial agreement *and* the new patterns necessary during the transition period are largely the responsibility of the leadership.[32] I lack the space here to deal with this crucial post-peace period but I want to make a few summary comments about two areas that are bound to be crucial in any post-peace period: political cooperation and the achievement of some level of economic development (especially development that provides immediate benefits to the Palestinians in the West Bank and Gaza).

There were three political areas in which progress toward a new relationship might have been generated: growing ties between the leaders themselves as they began to realize that they would hang together or hang separately; an emerging consensus within each elite group and between elite groups across the old lines; and the beginning of a genuine movement toward democracy in the PA. The record in all three areas has been almost completely negative.

In several conflicts (for example, in South Africa between Mandela and de Klerk and in Northern Ireland between Trimble and Adams) ancient enemies have gradually come to realize that they need each other and that they can each benefit from helping the other.[33] This tacit alliance may be transient but it may also be crucial for surviving the transition period and sustaining the momentum of the peace process. This never happened after Oslo, for Arafat and Netanyahu were weak leaders who were more concerned about strengthening their own domestic base than helping the other. Each sought to manipulate the peace for partisan purposes, and neither ever asked what the other needed to stay in power. The value of the elite consensus both within and between each side is also apparent since it protects the leader's back and may thus increase willingness to take some risks, and because it may help to allay or diminish mass resistance to concessions for peace. It suffices here to note that it never occurred after Oslo, either within each community or across the lines. The peace polarized each community and there did not seem to be any major consensual groups emerging across the lines. Perhaps this was because even groups who opposed or supported the peace did so for different reasons.

The achievement of democracy can be a mixed blessing because democracy can have both good and bad effects in different circumstances.[34] But the debate was never joined in regard to the PA because Arafat rapidly created a rather typical Middle Eastern autocracy: power centralized in his hands; eight different security organizations repressing dissent; loyalty dominating competence in appointments; rampant corruption; and indifference to the legal and political institutions of the PA.[35] Perhaps it was too much to hope that Arafat, a man of limited vision with no experience of democracy but plenty of experience with the conspiracies and paranoia of exiled rebel groups, would understand the benefits of democracy. He was able to enact these disastrous policies largely because Israel and the United States preferred a strong leader who would implement Oslo and control terrorism to a weaker leader who might have to worry about public opinion and securing a victory in the next election. He answered his critics by asserting that democracy was a luxury that the Palestinians could not afford; that priority had to be given to state-building and economic development, although his policies undermined these goals also. As in the Cold War, however, external support for corrupt authoritarianism probably sacrificed long-run stability for uncertain short-run gains.

The international financial institutions, the United Nations, and the US Agency for International Development recognized from the beginning that support for peace needed to be bolstered by rapid improvements in standards of living. People needed to feel as if they had something to lose if the peace failed. Unfortunately, the exact opposite happened: standards of living deteriorated, per capita income declined, and joblessness increased.[36] The World Bank, the lead agency, had worked out an intelligent two-track strategy for development: a short-run track to provide immediate benefits and a long-run track to begin the process of sustained development.[37] The Bank also insisted on its usual standards of accountability and transparency before dispensing funds.

All of this was for naught, however, as Arafat refused to abide by these standards, insisting that all funds be controlled by his office, hiring large numbers of Tunis loyalists for the PA bureaucracy and his security services, and awarding import monopolies to his cronies – thus creating an incompetent and corrupt administration that expended money designated for development of current expenditures. Arafat justified his actions by saying that jobs had to be found for the many unemployed and that inflating the bureaucracy was the only available option. The Bank and the other agencies went along with this because they felt they had no choice: the "tyranny of weakness" worked again because a future without Arafat seemed more perilous than a future with him – "the devil you know" idea, etc. But this distorted short-term development, delayed long-term development, and rapidly decreased support for Arafat, the PA, and the peace process. Whether a sensible compromise was available between Arafat's efforts to control everything and reward all his friends and the economically sophisticated but politically naïve strategies of the donors is an issue that I cannot explore here.[38]

Some people seem to think that peace will come easily – that since all the issues are well known and have been discussed for years, a "final settlement" can be achieved in weeks or months.[39] There is absolutely no doubt that eventually another agreement between Israel and Palestine is not merely likely but highly probable. That agreement is also likely, whatever its deficiencies, to be an important step beyond Oslo – a step, one hopes, that will bring both sides somewhat closer to a settlement of substantive issues that both believe are definitive. Nevertheless, for reasons that I have already articulated, that agreement, even if it is wise and generous, is not likely to be final – unless we are extraordinarily fortunate in the way in which socioeconomic events unfold, how the transitions to a new political order occur, and in the obtaining of good leaders in the next generation. Short of that, progress will still be possible, but only if we are realistic about what we can expect and how quickly we can expect it in a conflict that has been built and grown, brick by brick, over decades, if not longer.

There is no choice but to continue negotiations despite the constraints and limitations, because the potential benefits of success are so much greater than the risks of an unstable peace process (except to the leaders who have to make crucial concessions) and because the risks of not negotiating are even greater than those of negotiating. The risks of peace can be hedged but the risks of stonewalling only increase the likelihood of more conflict with even more deadly weapons than before. Moreover, even if the official negotiating process continues to stagger from crisis to crisis, there may be changes beneath the surface (especially in unofficial and informal contacts between academics, professionals, businessmen, and students) that will gradually stiffen the spines of leaders reluctant to take risks. Resistance to peace can be powerful but brittle (as many authoritarian regimes have turned out to be) and the accumulation of pressures and a change in the psychological environment (bargaining over the terms of coexistence, not the terms of confrontation) may gradually turn the Oslo process into something more than an exploratory truce.[40] Whether we shall obtain the leaders who can see the need for an "imagined partnership" to work out new rules of engagement remains an open question.

Notes

1   For the statement by the twenty Palestinian notables, see *The New York Times*, November 29, 1999, p. A7. The response of the PA and Arafat was to jail seven of the signers, threaten others, and violently attack another – ironically, or sadly, providing evidence to sustain some of the charges in the statement.

2   The obverse is not necessarily true: the idea that the peace is "good" may not generate a benign self-fulfilling prophecy because it may not help much in resolving substantive and symbolic issues and because it could create a moral

hazard (if peace is inevitable, one does not need to do much more to insure its arrival.)

3   This complex issue deserves more discussion than I can give it here. For an interesting analysis, see David A. Welch, *Justice and the Genesis of War* (Cambridge: Cambridge University Press, 1993).

4   They are not always a mirror image of the criteria for a good peace but they certainly may be in some cases.

5   Edward Said has suggested the creation of a bi-national state in which Israelis and Palestinians share power and live together peacefully. In the abstract, this makes a good deal of sense, especially economically. However, it must also be said that the idea has attracted almost no support from *either* side and it is unclear how peaceful coexistence would be. For a recent statement, see Edward W. Said, *The End of the Peace Process – Oslo and After* (New York: Pantheon Books, 2000). I might also add that advocating an essentially utopian proposal and dismissing the Oslo process out of hand loses the opportunity to make small gains that can be built on and generates more support for extremist options that could destroy the possibility of any progress.

6   The answer to the question about how much time needs to pass is unclear; as the economists always say, "it all depends." Perhaps we can say that the jury is still out as long as the negotiating process continues and there has not been a return to full-scale violence and demands for all-or-nothing solutions from one or both sides.

7   For more extended comment on these issues, see Robert L. Rothstein, "Fragile peace and Its Aftermath," in Robert L. Rothstein, ed., *After the Peace: Resistance and Reconciliation* (Boulder: Lynne Rienner, 1999), pp. 241–4.

8   A number of rebel groups, after discovering victory is not imminent, have adopted a "long war" strategy to minimize short-run losses and keep the "dream" alive. See, for example, Brendan O'Brien, *The Long War: The IRA and Sinn Fein, 1985 to Today* (Syracuse: Syracuse University Press, 1995).

9   See Meron Benvenisti, *Intimate Enemies – Jews and Arabs in a Shared land* (Berkeley: University of California Press, 1995), pp. 77–88 and 199–200.

10 On the lack of empathy, see Paul Arthur, *"The Anglo-Irish Peace Process: Obstacles to Reconciliation,"* in Rothstein, *After the Peace*, pp. 95–7.

11 For example, Yossi Beilin notes that Abu Ma'azen, a very high-ranking Palestinian official, told him (Beilin) that the Palestinian leadership before Oslo took pride in knowing nothing about Israel and the Israelis: Israel was demonized and no distinction was made between different views or perspectives(Israel would simply have to disappear. When (or if) this commitment to ignorance among the exiled leadership changed is unclear. See Yossi Beilin, *Touching Peace – From the Oslo Accord to a Final Agreement* (London: Weidenfeld and Nicolson, 1999), p. 168.

12 Quoted in John McGarry and Brendan O'Leary, *Explaining Northern Ireland – Broken Images* (Oxford: Blackwell Publishers, 1995), p. 354. Note that Rose seemed largely correct for about two decades but that gradual changes were occurring politically, psychologically, economically – that finally led, as with Oslo, to a tentative breakthrough in the mid-1990s.

13 One might add that another effect of the "no solution" perspective may be a turning away from the quest for substantive agreement to focus instead on first

"irrigating the desert" (as someone suggested for Northern Ireland) – an understandable, perhaps even necessary, approach but one that also might be too passive and limited.

14   Again, it may be prudent to emphasize that these comments are not meant to suggest that these effects of existential conflict apply everywhere and at any time. There are instances when the effects can be diminished or overcome by other factors and at different times, thus the discussion illustrates a general trend line only.

15   There have been many attempts to specify exactly what combination of factors must come together to break an existing stalemate and induce the leaders on both sides to take the risk of entering peace talks. Since my focus is on the talks and their aftermath I shall not discuss this issue here. It is worth noting, however, that various attempts to specify when a conflict is "ripe" for resolution (or at least negotiations) have not yielded much that is analytically useful. And note that the de Klerk–Mandela breakthrough in South Africa fit none of the models of ripeness.

16   On the structural and procedural conditions that deepen conflicts of interest and generate protracted, existential conflict, see my essay "In Fear of Peace: Getting Past Maybe," in Rothstein, *After the Peace*, pp. 1–25.

17   Camp David was a "big bang" negotiation that worked precisely because the conflict was not existential, there was a relatively easy trade-off of different interests, and each saw clear and important short-term gains. But these were special circumstances that do not often appear (as Dayton may illustrate) – and have not in any event led to a "warm peace" between Egypt and Israel. I shall return to this issue.

18   The top/down peace process obviously needs mass support, especially in the difficult transition period just after the initial agreement has been signed. As we shall see below, the effort to give the masses a greater stake in peace by demonstrating that the "peace dividend" would quickly improve standards of living failed miserably, thus helping to undermine support for Oslo.

19   Lustick has argued for a high-risk, high-gain strategy in the Oslo process but my argument attempts to explain why it is very likely that a low-risk, low-gain strategy will be chosen and, indeed, why the high-risk strategy, were it to be chosen by *both* sides, might end very badly. See Ian S. Lustick, "Necessary Risks: Lessons for the Israeli–Palestinian peace Process from Ireland and Algeria," *Middle East Policy*, Vol. 3, No. 3 (1994), p. 42ff.

20   A weak leader can be deliberately ambiguous about the latter point because the war has not yet been clearly lost or won. So he can act as if time is still on his group's side and that the dream is still alive.

21   Lustick sharply and justifiably criticizes the tactics of Netanyahu and the right (Israeli and American) in this sense. See Ian S. Lustick, "Ending Protracted Conflicts: The Oslo Peace Process Between Political Partnership and Legality," *Cornell International Law Journal*, Vol. 30, No. 3 (1997), pp. 741–57.

22   And note that the tactic of speaking with different voices is hardly confined to Arafat. For a similar instance in regard to South Africa see Tom Lodge, "Guerrilla Warfare and Exile Diplomacy: The African National Congress and the Pan Africanist Congress," in Lodge et al., *All, Here, and Now: Black Politics in South Africa in the 1980s* (New York: Ford Foundation, 1991),

p. 185; on Northern Ireland, see the report of a speech in New York by a Sinn Fein official that contradicted Sinn Fein statements in Belfast in Warren Hoge, "New Obstacle Seen as Ulster is Given Date of Home Rule," *The New York Times*, November 21, 1999, p. 4.

23 Eamonn Mallie and David McKittrick, *The Fight for Peace – The Secret Story Behind the Irish Peace Process* (London: Heinemann, 1996), p. 349.

24 A similar set of linked factors seems to have created the breakthrough to peace in South Africa. See Patti Waldneir, *Anatomy of a Miracle – The End of Apartheid and the Birth of the New South Africa* (New York: W.W. Norton and Company, 1997), p. 82.

25 See Benvenisti, *Intimate Enemies*, p. 225, for a similar characterization.

26 One should also note that Arafat and the PLO got substantial promises of aid, which might have been used to improve standards of living and thus support for peace – if Arafat wanted to use the money for those purposes.

27 See Beilin, *Touching Peace*, pp. 133–4.

28 As distinct from Arafat and his loyalists in Tunis who did get access to aid, jobs, and status.

29 See Itamar Rabinovitch, *Waging Peace – Israel and the Arabs at the End of the Century* (New York: Farrar, Straus and Giroux, 1999), p. 71–3, for a discussion of this issue.

30 Rumors of the outline of a deal (as of May 2000), suggest Barak's willingness to cede 90 percent of the West Bank, give Arafat the Jerusalem suburb of Abu Dis, and a minimal right of return for refugees with close family ties to Israeli Arabs. If this is true, it is more generous in a territorial sense than anticipated, although unsatisfactory on a variety of other issues to the Palestinians. Whether Barak could get this deal through the Knesset and a popular referendum is unclear.

31 As one illustration of looming problems, see Deborah Sontag, "Cramped Gaza Multiplies at Unrivaled Pace," *The New York Times*, February 24, 2000, pp. A1 and A10.

32 The situation has some similarities to the transition, to democracy stage in a number of countries. Note also that it is obviously true that a top/down peace process needs popular support, which was thwarted in this case by the political and economic policies Arafat chose to pursue (see below).

33 As one illustration, the growing ties between Mandela and de Klerk are discussed in Waldneir, *Anatomy of a Miracle*, pp. 162–6.

34 For more extended comment, see my two essays in Edy Kaufman, Shukri Abed and Robert L. Rothstein, eds., *Democracy, Peace, and the Israeli–Palestinian Conflict* (Boulder: Lynne Rienner, 1993).

35 One of the best sources on this is Glen E. Robinson, *Building a Palestinian State: The Incomplete Revolution* (Bloomington: Indiana University Press, 1997). See also the statement by twenty leading Palestinian notables, roundly denouncing Arafat and his policies, in *The New York Times*, November 29, 1999, p. A7.

36 For the depressing record, see Sara Roy, "De-Development Revisited: Palestinian Economy and Society Since Oslo," *Journal of Palestine Studies*, Vol. XXVII, No. 3 (Spring 1999), pp. 64–82.

37 The best discussion of the relationship between the international aid agencies

and Arafat and the PA is Rick Hooper, "The International Politics of Donor Assistance to the Palestinians in the West Bank and Gaza Strip, 1993–1997," in Sara Roy, ed., *The Economics of Middle East Peace: A Reassessment* (Stamford, CT: JAI Press, 1999), pp. 59–95.

38 Providing jobs was crucial, just as Arafat said. But they did not have to be provided via a bloated bureaucracy and so many security services. The aid agencies might have tried a compromise strategy with more jobs created through agencies like the New Deal's Work Progress Administration and Conservation Corps.

39 Barak has implied this in various statements and a number of Palestinian and Israeli commentators have done the same.

40 This may be another version of the currently popular argument that the accumulation of small events (what economists call a "cascade of information") can generate large effects in certain circumstances.

CHAPTER 3

The Oslo Peace Process: Patterns, Paradoxes, and Prospects

GABRIEL BEN-DOR

The Oslo Peace Process is one of the marvels of modern diplomacy, as it represents a uniquely dramatic and drastic attempt at conflict resolution in a bitter and protracted international conflict. Yet, more than half a decade after the initial breakthrough not only has the original sense of euphoria disappeared, but the process has come to a stalemate and there is a real concern over the prospect of an ultimate failure.

This chapter analyzes the reasons for the success leading to the original breakthrough in 1993, and concludes that there are several major paradoxes involved. Above all, analysis shows that the very same reasons that made the initial phase successful doomed the later phases to failure. Among these are the role of the mediators, the level and character of the negotiators, the secret nature of the talks, the approach to confidence building, and the decision to postpone the more fundamental issues of the conflict into the more remote future, after the conditions in the region improve.

The Israeli–Palestinian peace process does not fit into any predetermined pattern. Almost everything about it has been unconventional and full of exceptions to all generalizations. It goes without saying that in such situations the degree of creative diplomacy necessary is even higher than in other cases of protracted conflict.

What is so exceptional about this particular conflict?

- Two national movements still demand more or less the same piece of land, and in the extreme cases in its entirety. This is not seen very much around the world anymore.
- One protagonist is a more or less established state, whereas the other is not.

- The protagonist that is not a state nevertheless enjoys quite a few of the attributes and assets of autonomy, without really being a state.
- The non-state is recognized by as many forces around the world as the state, and in fact historically has been often supported by more of them.
- The non-state is part of a large area of political culture and identity, a fact that historically turned the old intercommunal civil war into a major international issue.
- All this takes place on land considered holy by hundreds of millions, thereby bringing into the political picture religious and spiritual factors that make the conflict even more complicated.
- The parties have perceived this as an existential conflict, raising threats to their very ability to survive as political entities, hence the fears and sentiments of the most extreme kind that on both sides.
- The stronger actor even now considers itself not only historically weak, but a "victim people," and indeed that party has been subject to the most horrible persecutions imaginable, including the worst crimes of genocide in history.
- As a result of everything above, many outside forces have been involved in the conflict.

In this complex situation, it is hard to point exactly to the moment in history when things started changing dramatically. Just a few years ago it seemed that we would be doomed to live with the conflict in a very extreme and violent form for many decades, if not centuries.

In fact, in the recent past this conflict has even contributed to the outbreak of other wars in the region. Among them the 1967 war between Israel on the one hand, and Egypt, Syria and Jordan on the other; the war in Lebanon in 1982; and the first Arab–Israeli war in 1947–9. So there had been little expectation of any kind of peace in the foreseeable future.

Even the diplomatic wrangling about Palestinian representation at the Madrid conference in 1991 seemed to indicate that more conflict was in the offing, and that no solution could be expected at that time. Yet two years later there was the dramatic breakthrough in Oslo, leading to the Declaration of Principles.

The Declaration changed everything as far as the basic formalities were concerned. It included the mutual recognition of the Government of Israel and the Palestine Liberation Organization as the legitimate representative of the Palestinian people. It led to the establishment of self-government for the Palestinians in Israeli-held territory, first in the Gaza Strip and the Jericho area. It established a framework for a series of interim settlements, as well as for the negotiation of a permanent settlement within five years of the start of the agreement's operative phase. This agreement took place in May 1994 with the Israeli withdrawal from Gaza and Jericho and the establishment of Palestinian self-government in these years.

In order to allow for an agreement to be reached and implemented, the parties tried to concentrate on issues where they could find mutual interests and consent. The other thornier issues were postponed to the more remote future.

The logic behind this method is best expressed in a series of statements, more or less as follows:

- The conflict has created an inhospitable climate for resolving difficult issues.
- Therefore, it is imperative to start changing that climate by reaching partial agreement on the easier issues.
- These partial agreements will create a new reality on the ground.
- The new reality will generate more trust and will improve the climate for the foreseeable future.
- In the new climate it will be possible, or at any rate easier, to tackle the issues now left in abeyance.

The above makes logical sense, but things have not worked out as anticipated, for several reasons:

- The difficulty of implementing the complex agreement on the ground;
- The failure to make clear to the relevant political communities that the peace process pays quick and high dividends in terms of the everyday lives of the people;
- The lack of support for the agreements, exactly because they are partial and do not seem to resolve the basic problems;
- The opposition of extremists and others on both sides;
- Dramatic acts of Islamic terrorism against the agreement, in the heartland of Israel;
- The Israeli reactions to these acts, creating a vicious cycle;
- The assassination of Israeli Prime Minister Rabin, and subsequent change of governments in Israel; and
- The passing of time, which instead of steadily improving the relationship has led many people to feel that nothing is changing in the basic contours of the situation.

As a result, not only have things not worked out in the psychological aspect of future expectations, but also:

- There has been difficulty in implementing the interim agreements, and, when they were implemented, this was done with great acrimony and invariably behind schedule.
- There has been no progress in the critical area of the permanent settlement.

- There has been no consistent mechanism for handling permanent settlement issues.

None of these facts should be taken to mean that the Oslo process was wrong, or that it was not necessary. Nor is it possible now to point to a much better alternative to it. But it behooves us to remember that creativity in diplomacy means not only engineering historical break-throughs, but also ensuring that a process of peacemaking and conflict resolution continues in a consistent and ongoing manner. In order to accomplish that, it may be necessary to expand upon the original concept in several ways:

- No more secret negotiations or secret deals, because they take away much of the ability to mobilize crucial public support.
- A general effort is needed to build stronger constituencies for the agreements, beyond any temporary or narrow coalitions.
- There should be a greater effort to bring home the impact of the process on daily lives, in order to show somehow that peace pays.
- It is no longer possible to postpone problems to the future.
- To the contrary, the permanent settlement issues should be tackled soon and with vigor. These issues include:
  1. Jerusalem
  2. Settlements
  3. Refugees
  4. The nature of the emerging Palestinian entity
  5. Security
  6. Water
  7. The future relationship between the two peoples once the settlement is implemented.

Some people will argue it is still early to talk about the difficult issues. But this argument will always be true and false simultaneously. There will never be an ideal climate for discussing thorny issues dividing two peoples that have been at conflict literally for decades. Indeed the climate is not yet ripe for the kind of resolution that both parties may hope for; yet that climate will not come about on its own. It has to be created, and it cannot be created without tackling the big issues, showing the public what the agreement will look like, and then building around the new future.

In order for an agreement to be successful certain requirements will have to be met, many of which will be quite difficult to achieve:

- A continued high degree of creativity;
- A sensitivity to the needs and concerns of the other side;
- A feeling of historical mission that should not be allowed to falter, and

a historical opportunity that must not be missed under any circumstances;
- A strong standing in each community of the leaders in question, to
  ensure that they can make the necessary concessions and compromises
  and then still sell it to their respective constituencies; and
- A policy of linkage, making concessions where it hurts less while
  standing firm on the most painful issues.

The last point is worth stressing. Reaching a permanent settlement
between parties to a protracted conflict is possible if the agreement is seen
by both as a package in the full sense of the term. Discussing the issues one
by one is not likely to lead to a resolution, because neither party will be
satisfied with the outcome, which is bound to fall short of expectations.

On the other hand, there is a better chance for an acceptable solution if
the agreement is understood as a way to resolve the violent and open form
of the conflict. If this is the case, the agreement must paint a reasonably
promising picture for the future so that both parties will have a sense of
optimism and satisfaction in their achievements. This, and only this perception, can help alleviate the feelings of disappointment and sorrow over
the inevitable losses that are entailed in the process.

In the wake of the 1948–9 war the state of affairs from the Zionist
perspective in Israel was very bleak. In that war, not only did the small
Jewish community lose thousands of casualties, but it also failed to defend
the Old City of Jerusalem. The Jewish Quarter was captured, and some of
the holiest places to Judaism were lost. The road to Jerusalem was narrow
and threatened from each direction, the airport at Lod was within range of
cannons from across the borders, and the seashore in Israel was some
eleven miles from the border at the narrow waist of Netanya.

On the other hand, there was a Jewish state with the attributes of independence and sovereignty, the possibility to continue the Zionist
revolution, the challenge to absorb millions of immigrants, the possibility
of living a full Jewish life in Israeli society, and the cause of further developing Jewish culture, science and all forms of social life. These circumstances
were sufficient for the leadership at the time not to pursue the option of
continuing the war in 1949 when the situation was very much in Israel's
favor on most battlefields.

Solutions can be forced that will lead to an acceptable modus vivendi, if
not to the nationalist elation of triumphing over one's enemies totally. For
example, the following components of a package should be considered:

- Israeli concessions on the refugee question, which should not be considered a zero-sum game. It is possible to make practical progress on
  this issue, which is most important to the Palestinian sense of minimal
  justice:

1. International financing can be obtained for assisting many of the refugees in need.
2. Quite a few of them may want to come back to the new Palestinian entity, and Israel should agree to that.
3. Israel should continue an existing project of family unification and expand it to allow for a sense of its participation in the solution.
4. Some way needs to be found to express the Israeli concern with the unfortunate fate of the refugees, without compromising the basic Israeli positions and without accepting guilt or blame in any way.

- At the same time, it will be necessary for the Palestinian side to make heavy concessions on the issue of Israeli settlements in the territory, no matter how unpalatable that may seem. This is a question involving many tens of thousands of Israelis directly, and hundreds of thousands by family or social affiliation. Alienating all these elements might make too many enemies to the peace process, and in addition there are numerous human difficulties involved. Even in purely ideological terms, many Israelis who support the peace process reject the necessity to uproot tens of thousands of their fellow citizens to make the point of total control over territory.

This means that the old models of total and pure sovereignty will have to accommodate several new elements, which might assist in finding acceptable solutions to a settlement of the conflict. Some of the following possibilities seem self-apparent:
1. Some Israeli settlements will remain under Israeli rule, in return for Israeli land ceded to the Palestinians, under some form of exchange.
2. Some other settlements will have to be allowed to remain where they are, even if the land is under Palestinian sovereignty, by some formula that will allow the settlers to remain Israeli citizens and to commute freely to Israel for work and other purposes.
3. Theoretically, Palestinian citizenship should be offered to those settlers who want it, but this is not practical, for reasons obvious to those familiar with the history of the problem and the conflict.
4. When there is no better solution, it may be necessary to allow Israel to lease some Palestinian territory containing settlements for a transition period lasting some decades, which will allow the process necessary for solving the question. This will be painful, but insisting on dismantling the settlements on all territory out of Israeli control before 1967 will bring about the collapse of the talks and the entire process.

So just as Israel will have to make concessions on the refugee issue, the Palestinians will have to make concessions on the settlement issue.

On Jerusalem, too, the positions are seemingly irreconcilable. Israel insists on full sovereignty in the entire city, undivided, which will be the eternal capital of the State. And the Palestinians insist on their state, with East Jerusalem as its capital. From this seemingly total impasse there emerged the truly creative idea of the Abu Dis solution, which according to press reports, was considered in talks between Abu Ma'azen and Yossi Beilin.

Jerusalem has become by now more a symbolic concept than a historical or geographic reality. Most parts of the city, and certainly those new neighborhoods that have sprung up since 1967, are so far from the center or the holy places that they are considered to be "Jerusalem" only because they have been defined as such in political and psychological terms. Political and psychological perceptions are key in crafting a solution. It is possible to take the Arab township of Abu Dis, which is geographically a suburb of Jerusalem, and define it as part of East Jerusalem. As such it is possible to establish the seat of the future Palestinian government and parliament there. Thereby the Palestinians will be able to claim that this is East Jerusalem, the capital of their state, whereas the Israeli government will be able to continue to claim that it has not given up control or sovereignty over "all of Jerusalem," as it has been defined until now.

Of course these solutions require not only creativity but also tolerance on the part of the two sides. Yet the point is that clearly there are possible solutions to the most intractable problems, if the conditions are ripe.

None of these possible solutions are ideal, and none of them may be tolerable enough for the parties to consider as the basis for resolving that particular problem. But that is not the point. Rather, the point is that if the parties wish to undertake a departure from the old pattern of their relationship and look for a fresh beginning, then the solutions to their mutual problems should be linked together. Thus the new relationship will be more satisfying, and it will allow for a better quality of life for both parties in the long run.

Indeed, this is one of the theoretical foundations of the theory of confidence building: the parties undertake steps that are not to be assessed only in their own right, but also – in fact mostly – as contributing to the relationship with the other party. A better relationship with the neighbor and protagonist has value that should be cherished, which has not been the case between Israelis and Palestinians.

It is not clear whether or not any actions of the sort described above will take place in the near future. After all, the conflict has gone on for many decades, and the feelings of bitterness, hatred, frustration and disappointment on both sides are virtually endless. Nonetheless there is still hope, in part due to many new changes and trends:

- The international system has changed, and it is not so easy to find support for continued, endless and violent conflict.
- The people on both sides are increasingly tired of the costs of protracted conflict, and they wish to improve their lives, even if this involves political costs.
- The leadership on both sides is now more pragmatic than perhaps ever in the past.
- There is the important precedent of peace treaties between Israel and major Arab countries, like Egypt and Jordan.
- There is renewed hope for negotiations between Israel and Syria about possible peace between them.

Up to mid-December 1999, the Palestinians had stood at the absolute center of the regional and global stage. Whenever the fashionable peace process in the Middle East was mentioned, it was the Palestinians who were assumed to hold the key to its success. A common assumption around the world is that the Palestinian problem is at the heart of the Arab–Israeli conflict. Therefore, its solution is considered the true key to real Middle East peace. This assumption has given the Palestinians a lot of moral strength and also a lot of favorable publicity around the world.

However, with the announced breakthrough in Israeli–Syrian relations in December 1999 and the resumption of the talks between these two heavy-weights, it seemed suddenly that the term "peace process" referred primarily to the Syrians. Until those talks aborted, the future of the region seemed to depend on the success of that particular process, not on the one that had began in Oslo six years before.

In other ways, too, the Palestinians have suffered a diminution in their standing. They took a beating even in terms of their image in public relations, which had been one of their strongest points in world affairs. They have not been able to handle some bothersome problems:

- There are allegations of corruption in the Palestinian National Authority, and a lot of evidence to prove it. Various commissions of inquiry have failed to solve the problem or even to inspire confidence in the Palestinian public or others.
- There is a lot of inefficiency, much of it associated with the corruption. Hence a lot of outside investment and assistance does not reach its intended target, and is instead mismanaged or wasted. Hence a lot of foreign donors and investors shy away from putting more money into the Palestinian-controlled territory.
- There is oppression and repression. Human rights organizations complain about massive violations, and every so often we witness opponents and critics of the ruling regime who are arrested and beaten,

or disappear. This creates a very bad impression at a time when the Palestinians are trying hard to utilize the potential of democracy to make their point in the region and around the world.

In the light of all this, the entire Palestinian issue is not as popular around the world as it once was. Nonetheless the Palestinians have some advantages that will allow them to enjoy considerable sympathy in the future as well, despite the problems that will inevitably surface in their political system. In a sense, the Palestinians are now enjoying their status as the "twin" of Israel:

- Visiting dignitaries who come to Israel make it a point to visit the Palestinian territories as well.
- International bodies and forums who have Israeli participation now also allow Palestinian membership.
- Various international donors who give money to Israel now also give some of it to the Palestinians.
- Various international moves are tied to the peace process between Israel and the Palestinians.
- It has become a ritual in European political forums to preach about the need to make progress in the Palestinian–Israeli peace process, and to stage appropriate occasions for making this point at a high political level.

The Palestinians are still trying to establish their own state, and they are able to make the point that they are fighting for minimal rights after decades of destruction and persecution. Countries feel varying degrees of guilt in the Israeli–Palestinian connection, and the Palestinians are able to utilize this, at times quite skillfully:

- Countries like Germany still feel guilt for the wrongs done to the Jews in the past. Hence they will not condemn Israel for anything, but are happy to help the Palestinians within the context of peace with Israel, which leaves them in good conscience.
- Other countries in Europe feel a vague sense of guilt as a result of the Holocaust. They are happy that they can rectify this now within the context of the peace process.
- Various circles on the left and among liberals like to identify Israel with the West and imperialism, whereas the Palestinians are identified with the "good guys" in the so-called Third World, with all its extensions and manifestations.

Thus, the Palestinians still have considerable political and moral capital in the West, and their blunders and deficiencies have not yet wasted this resource. But how about the Arab world, their natural audience? Here the situation is more complicated. On the one hand, the Arab countries continue to argue that they are committed to the cause of the Palestinians, and they quote the injustice done to them as the core of the conflict with Israel. They also support the Palestinian cause in general terms, and certainly so on the verbal level. On the other hand, the Arab countries – like any other political community – are basically self-centered, and they pursue their own interests above all. When convenient, they use the Palestinian card, but when they find this burdensome they go about their business granting minimal attention to the issue. This game has been going on for decades, and it has been extensively documented by the Palestinians themselves as well as by others.

The feeling of being exploited by the whims of others was one major reason that the Palestinians entered into the Oslo process. While this process has given them far less than their historical ambitions, it has allowed them to build up independent capabilities on territory that they themselves control. They call this the "independence of decision," and the fact that this independence is limited by Israel strangely plays as an advantage for the Palestinians. Israeli interference lacks legitimacy and is bound to cease, sooner or later, while Arab interference will not go away as easily. Moreover Arab involvement enjoys a much higher degree of legitimacy than any that Israel could ever hope for. From this more or less independent territory the Palestinians have been building the infrastructure of the future state they hope for, and are apparently certain to achieve in the foreseeable future:

- As mentioned before, independently ruled territory that keeps expanding with every new agreement;
- The structures of a government;
- The techniques of ruling, among them collecting taxes and enforcing the law;
- Widespread international recognition in some form (indeed more states have recognized the Palestinian Authority than have recognized the State of Israel);
- Diplomatic relations with numerous countries around the world, again with more states than Israel itself;
- The nucleus of a future army, in the form of the large Palestinian police force;
- A harbor and an airport, which are critical for future independent transportation;
- A broadcasting network, critical for future independent communications;
- The ability to control the educational network and thereby to cultivate national identity.

While much has been accomplished, there is still a lot to be done:

• Most territory in the West Bank is still in Israeli hands.
• There are numerous restrictions imposed by Israel on independent actions by the Palestinian National Authority.
• It is difficult to move between parts of the territory, despite the progress made by the opening of the safe passage between the Gaza Strip and the West Bank.
• There are huge economic problems, both internal as well as those that have to do with the dependence on Israel.
• There is widespread unemployment.
• There is a general feeling of frustration over the fact that little progress has been made on the big issues that matter so much to the future of the Palestinians:
  1. The nature of the state
  2. The status of Jerusalem
  3. The presence of the Jewish settlements and settlers
  4. The location of the future borders
  5. The future relationship with the State of Israel
  6. The sharing of water resources

For a brief period after December 1999, it appeared that Israel and Syrian secret talks would turn into serious negotiations and perhaps an agreement. This process was regarded with concern by some Palestinians, who felt a general sense of inferiority toward Syria in this context, and for several good reasons:

• Syria is a state and the Palestinians were not that yet.
• Syria is one of the leading military powers in the region, and hence peace with it makes a huge difference to strategic security in the area, which is decidedly not the case with the Palestinian entity at this time.
• Syria is perhaps the best-known advocate of Arab nationalism and Arab unity, and is known to have made huge sacrifices in the name of the cause; hence it cannot be accused of treason with any degree of credibility. This is not the case with the new Palestinian National Authority.
• Syria is an important center of inter-Arab and regional activity, with allies such as Libya and Iran, which of course cannot be said of the small Palestinian entity in its present form.

Should the Syrian–Israeli negotiating track re-open, the Palestinians have very limited options, considering that if they choose not to support the peace process they would be considered outside the family of civilized nations. They can only give their blessing to the process, and express the hope that their process, which is still the heart of the conflict, will also be given its due attention. The Palestinians have several options:

- They can approach the Syrians directly, and lobby them to be included in their agenda more forcefully, but of course that course of action would not be particularly promising given the realities of power politics in the region.
- They can approach the other Arab states and ask them to apply pressure on the various parties, but of course those Arab states also have their own interests and preferences.
- They can approach the Americans, and to some extent the Europeans, and try to persuade them to keep the pressure on Israel for the continuation of the negotiations.
- Most intriguing of all, they might approach Israel directly, and make sure that the talks go ahead speedily, despite the Syrian diversion. This would work perhaps if they were to offer Israel something tangible by way of reasonable – from the Israeli point of view – concessions.

This last point raises a host of interesting ideas and possibilities. After all, the Palestinians might feel that this is precisely what is expected of them: to play along in a game in which they are virtually blackmailed into making concessions for fear that otherwise Israel might pursue another track for peace. For that reason alone they might not want to cooperate in the game in which they can only lose.

On the other hand, the Israeli–Palestinian relationship is nothing like the Syrian–Israeli one. The Israelis and the Palestinians have been sitting at the table for over six years now, and of course, due to geographic reasons they also know each other intimately well. Whatever the form of the permanent peace settlement, they are doomed to live together and experiment with various forms of cooperation; otherwise the country will not be big enough for both of them. And having lived together for so long, the Israelis and the Palestinians also resemble each other to a surprising extent, something that certainly cannot be said about the Israelis and the Syrians.

It would not be so surprising to find in the relationship room for the Palestinians to approach the Israelis directly, perhaps even on a personal basis. The Palestinians could try to talk to many of their friends in Israel and make the point that being left out in the cold because of the preference for the Syrian track is likely to damage the relationship and to cause long-term harm, something that Israelis would certainly wish to avoid. In general, the Palestinians have acquired a surprising ability to penetrate the Israeli political system, and to use their allies in it for their advantage.

CHAPTER 4

The Changing Structure of Public Opinion in the Middle East

FREDRIK BARTH

Public opinion does not determine war and peace between states – governments do. Yet, public opinion is not without effects on what governments do, whether in democracies or dictatorships, whether in Israel or in Arab countries. To assess and promote the prospects of the peace process in the Middle East we therefore need to give close attention also to public opinion, and to the factors that influence it. This essay invites you to consider the ways that some of the very ground underlying public opinion in the Middle East may be shifting due to the development of electronic communication and information technology.

These technologies increase peoples' access to information and knowledge, they enhance the uses to which this information can be put, and they extend the forms and reach of communications between people. What is more, as these technologies become increasingly available and affordable to people, they have effects not only on public knowledge and attitudes but also on the very structure of the public; they redirect the flows of communication and interaction between people, and thus affect the very communities into which parts of the public are organized. One need not subscribe to the more imaginative scenarios of the cyber visionaries to recognize that current developments in these technologies may be highly significant factors in shaping public political attitudes.

What role has the electronic media played so far in the Middle East? Besides easier and more rapid travel, the increasing availability and use of long-distance telephone have promoted more active and intimate participation in the lives of kin and friends regardless of physical distance. Incrementally, satellite TV has given audiences global access to entertainment and news, exposing them to a somewhat bizarre but greatly expanded range of information and images of life outside their own community. More recently, they have also introduced various formats of talk shows and discussion programs, where diverse and opposed opinions are presented. These changes are increasingly reintegrating the diaspora of overseas migrants in an active role in local social life of the areas from which they came, while simultaneously expanding the awareness and participation of locals in a larger world.

Last, and perhaps potentially most groundbreaking, are the processes entailed in the development of the Internet. This development adds two new powers to the users of electronic technology: interactive facility and the means to form new interactive communities. With the Internet, users can access information at will, as well as introduce and distribute messages of their own – leveling the power relations that govern traditional mass communication. By establishing web sites, e-mail lists, chat clubs, and the like, net users can express and disseminate personal opinions and enter into dialogue, discussion, and debate on an equal footing with others on the net. They obtain a voice, reach out across geographical space, dissolve social authority, and challenge established opinions. Moreover, by such operations the user also seizes the power to create new social organizations and communities, transcending and bisecting the existing boundaries and institutions of natural communities and established states.

These last points deserve to be spelled out. Eickelman and Anderson,[1] who have been in the forefront of exploring these changes in the Arab world, rightly point out that the fact of public dialogue is nothing new in the Middle East. The spirited conversations and arguments that variously unfold in mosque, majlis, and café are certainly ubiquitous features of Arab public life. Even within the family circle, e.g., as audiences before the family TV, women and men exercise a striking freedom in expressing individual and idiosyncratic opinion and judgment despite the marked inequalities of positioning that obtain within the family.

What *is* radically new in many of the fora that emerge on the Internet are two other aspects. One is that the users engage in debates within circles that are free from the constraints of *any* pre-established and enduring social relations or differentials of authority. In the traditional fora, whether family, groups of friends and peers, or public gatherings, no one speaks without an acute awareness of who is present. The face-to-face community in which they are embedded monitors all expression. The social controls, memories, and conventions of such groups certainly curtail both what will be said, and what meanings will be read into each statement. The anonymity and equality that is obtained on the Internet, on the other hand, lends a freedom of expression to the user that vastly expands the scope and reach of individual thought and opinion. According to generally accepted theory, it simultaneously trains users in new skills of criticism. They must learn to critique and judge the validity of messages by internal criteria of content and logic, no longer by the credentials of the sender, i.e., by standards of traditional authority. The need for such critical exercise used to be characteristic mainly of communications in the market place. On the Internet, it permeates all fields and topics.

The second aspect arises from the fact that Internet groups form without regard to locality and region. This means that they are based, at least initially, simply on the community of interests that has drawn the participants together. As a consequence, these cyber groups form communities of a new kind: focused in their topical attention and unconstrained by the myriad circumstances of existence that govern the natural communities of families, neighborhoods, cities, and nations. That means that they may be more free to surge ahead in debate and opinion-forming, and give rise to attitudes and views according to an internal dynamics of their own – influenced, but not determined by ideas drawn from a new and larger world than the one any particular member has previously occupied. We do not know yet what consequences this will have on the dynamics of public opinion. But I would expect such arenas to stimulate the emergence of a range of far more volatile and innovative opinions and attitudes than those that form in natural communities.

How far may such factors have affected the structure of public opinion, and popular political attitudes in Middle Eastern countries as of today? To judge this, we need to know how far the electronically carried information and its virtual communities have diffused; how the technologies are indeed being used at this stage by local residents and diasporas; and how their results mingle with other currents of communication and opinion. A monitoring of this may arguably provide the most important background information by which to assess current trends in public opinion in the Middle East. Public opinion in any large population is always obscure, especially in authoritarian states where neither independent investigators, the local regime, nor the public itself can know what larger segments of the population are thinking. To gauge public opinion even in the most accessible and widely polled populations is, as we can see in the United States for example, at best a difficult and inexact art. To do so in the complex and unpolled field of Middle Eastern publics, the best method may be to identify and monitor the main *sources* of influence within them, and base an informed judgment of current public opinion on how those influences are changing at the present time.

Looking strictly at the physical bases for current Internet influence, Anderson[2] reports that by January 1998, the total number of households with Internet access ranged from 3 percent in Qatar and the United Arab Emirates to 0.1 percent in Egypt. This may seem negligible, but that was more than several years ago and the technology is spreading quickly. Moreover, its effects may be considerably augmented by the institution of "Internet cafés" as found in Amman. Beirut, Cairo, Kuwait, and the Gulf, abetted by the open radio and TV programs, featuring a range from the famous debate in 1997 between the liberal Sadeq al-Azm and the conservative Shaykh Yusuf al-Qaradawi on Qatar's al-Jazira TV to more modest other open fora and occasions.

Another important question concerns the predominant uses to which the technologies so far have been put by the population. In the Gulf, where Internet is most diffused, the main interest has been in its commercial uses.[3] Diaspora overseas Arab users have employed it to bring the homeland internationally on-line and to present information on Islam to the encompassing global society, as well as to circulate information about the homeland and about travel and overseas facilities to each other, and to discuss the problems of maintaining a Muslim identity in minority situations overseas.[4] In addition, there are probably e-mail circles connecting overseas university students from each of the Middle Eastern states, as there are among most other national student groups and some use of these technologies in building political resistance *within* Middle Eastern states. Modest as most of this may seem, such are the overt concerns at present; but deeper effects may already be making themselves felt. Thus, Eickelman and Anderson feel justified in opening their volume of essays on the effects of the new media with the strong statement that, "A new sense of public is emerging throughout Muslim-majority states and Muslim communities elsewhere."[5]

These changes impinge directly on public opinion information in several ways, of which I would emphasize three. First are the effects on people's own conceptual geography, what may be called their *imagined communities* of significant membership and participation. The meanings of terms like nation, Arab, and Muslim will inevitably be reshaped by new information and new forms of participation. Commitments and views will be built from the inflows and outflows of information through the new electronic media, as well as the traditional sources. A more active vicarious participation in the lifeworld of diaspora members with whom local people identify may be particularly effective in expanding the awareness among those of the larger world. The growing diversity and scale of potential and actual participation of such communities will lead to the embracement of new dreams, new memberships, and new commitments, and thus, to new issues and influences on public opinion.

Secondly, changes may be expected to affect specifically the *self-images* of net users. The use of the new media requires particular initiatives and skills. Although easy to learn and not very taxing in their simpler forms, they are nonetheless quite distinctive and strongly associated with a sense of individuality and modernity. Coping with changes therefore gives the net user a personal experience of skill, modernity, and sophistication. More dramatically, it lends a sense of autonomy and power to the advancing user, epitomized by the teen-age computer hackers in the West who take on civil institutions and global corporations in their cyber-space tournaments. Thus, a new cadre of self-confident opinion leaders, with new ideas and new competencies, may be emerging. The insertion of such persons with their new sources of empowerment and self-esteem in an otherwise traditional world will give significant impetus to intellectual and political restlessness and dissent, and will in due course erode the hegemony of traditional authorities and powers.

Thirdly, we should be alert to a characteristic feature of cyber-based communities. While natural communities are usually well demarcated and conceptually self-evident, the nature and very existence of a cyber-based community is more difficult to conceptualize and grasp, also for its own members. Such communities come into being in the virtual world of the Internet, and are emergent and self-creating through the coding and clicking operations of unknown members of physically isolated actors. What may be the internal sociological and political processes that are set into motion *within* such a cyber-network community? Among its members, a need will surely arise for the symbolic work that constitutes their community as a more palpable and subjectively imaginable entity by making its boundaries more definable and its identities more embraceable. Such work must take the form of a theatre of constructing images for the new entity: defining shared treasures and identities, and developing collective ways to identify valued and disvalued members.

Conflict is a particularly powerful way to mark social boundaries and identities in public space. In the political realm, these means have normally been monopolized by local regimes, who have often manipulated external conflicts to create solidarity and bolster authority within. Now, with the expanded information flows and multiple communicative processes we have reviewed, these means move increasingly out of the state's control; but similar processes may be set in motion within cyber-communities for their own boundary defining purposes. These are not necessarily benign changes. There has been a simplistic assumption among social scientists and information technologists that more information and freedom of information are by definition good for globalizing democratic processes and for promoting international peace. But it is not only a matter of becoming more cosmopolitan and better informed.

As the need arises for embraced identities within the cyber-based communities of information and opinion exchange, there is no assurance that they may not engage in a similar manipulation of enmity, exclusion, and symbolic villainizing to create their boundaries and define their unities as do state regimes. And while regimes, whatever their morality, are forced to be rather long-term, rational, and careful in their policies, popular opinion can at times be impulsive, irrational, and irresponsible. Now virtual communities, as temporary and single-purpose creations without the constraints of the multiple concerns of a natural community, and without the self perpetuating imperative of a regime, may be extreme in their freedom to develop irrational, impulsive, and irresponsible opinions when these serve their symbolic purposes. Such a danger will only be exacerbated by the increasing participation of the diaspora in the formation of public opinion in the homeland.

Diaspora persons are, after all, often under special kinds of emotional and identity stresses, but physically safe from violence and war in the homeland. Consequently, they can feel less need to play safe, and more free to urge for emotional, impulsive, and dramatic symbolic action – symbolic, that is, for them, but very real in their consequences for the locally resident population. Thus arises a greater freedom for these cyberspace-based communities to thrive by imagining themselves in aggressive enmity with someone outside their group, and cultivate extremist opinions through a symbolic politics that creates stronger identities, internal solidarity, and symbolic leadership. These tendencies, in extreme form, can be seen in the many "hate groups" that have emerged on the Internet. Perhaps the global proliferation of terrorist organizations today may be a direct reflection of the general de-territorialization of the contemporary world. If so, one can indeed expect the new media to exacerbate this trend.

What are the outcomes of these new media for political relations between peoples in the Middle East? It is for others, with direct access to the living communities in the area, to assess their direct and indirect effects on public opinion in Middle Eastern nations. But an awareness of the character, and modes of operation, of electronic communication and information technology will in itself be an aid in monitoring these changes, by sensitizing us to the indicators we should watch. We urgently need to know *what to look for*, now that the scene is changing through the addition of new processes of communication, new sources of popular knowledge, and new modes of community formation.

But these changes in technology also provide entirely new opportunities for people-to-people peace efforts. They offer the opportunity for an active engagement in new forms of opinion formation. Internet arenas are accessible, as means to communicate the message of peace. But even more importantly, those that are currently providing arenas for opinion formation that may work against peace are by the nature of their technology *permeable*. Thus, they can be co-opted with messages that work against negative opinion trends, thus influencing the emerging consensus's toward which the communicative communities are moving. What these virtual communities may gain by transcending borders and distances, they may lose by losing control of their own boundaries as communities: they can be infiltrated.

Whereas the intelligence services of concerned countries may no doubt be doing just that, there is no obvious reason why broadly based democratic organizations or scholarly communities should not do the same. Such a strategy could bring beneficial effects to the level of debates, the range of expressed ideas and opinions, and the mixture of voices even in the otherwise narrowly conceived cyber communities. If cyberspace is changing the dynamics of public opinion formation in Middle Eastern countries, there is every reason why constructive imagination and action should engage and be deployed in it.

Notes

1   Dale F. Eickelman and Jon W. Anderson, eds., *New Media in the Muslim World* (Bloomington, IN: Indiana University Press, 1999), p. 1.
2   Jon W. Anderson, *Arabizing the Internet,* The Emirates Center for Strategic Studies and Research, Occasional Papers No. 30 (1998), p. 29.
3   Ibid., p. 20.
4   Ibid., pp. 13–18.
5   Eickelman and Anderson, eds., *New Media in the Muslim World,*.p. 1.

CHAPTER 5

Are Real Coexistence and Normalization Possible?

SHLOMO GAZIT

Allow me to begin from the end. I am a strong supporter of the urgent need, for both sides, to negotiate and to reach political agreements that will bring an end to the long and bitter bilateral conflict between the Jewish people in Israel and the Arab countries.

I believe that we are facing a unique opportunity and that such agreements are possible. The overall conditions – in the international arena, in the Middle East, and in every one of the individual countries involved, including Israel, of course – are responsible for creating this unique window of opportunity. I have no way to tell how long will this window will remain open.

Nevertheless, I have to be realistic. When all agreements have been reached and signed and even implemented by both sides in the most scrupulous and perfect way, we will not necessarily see the development of true friendship, normalization, and coexistence between the two parties. I cannot provide prophecies,; and yet I strongly believe that these agreements and their implementation are still a vital *pre-condition* to coexistence. But these agreements will not be enough in and of themselves to guarantee coexistence. We shall need a long period of adaptation; we shall need decades, and very possibly even generations, before we may see real peace. We shall first have to see changes in the political, cultural, and social systems of both Arab and Israeli culture to assure a lasting coexistence. In the mean time, we shall have to satisfy ourselves with what we might call a "Cold Peace."

Below, I concentrate on a description of the present as well as on an attempt to provide a list of the needed changes that will make true coexistence possible.

The Goals and the Aspirations of Both Sides

There is neither love nor any mutual respect. Both sides, if they only could achieve it, would rather see the other side disappear. In the past there was an Israeli minister, Yisrael Galili, who used to define the Arab–Israeli conflict as an agrarian problem. "Which party will succeed in burying the other one in the ground?" The problem originates from the asymmetry and conflict in goals of both parties, even as they actively strive to agree on peace treaties.

Israel's goal is a genuine attempt to see peace. Israel does not do so out of respect and love for its Arab neighbors but out of its basic desire to remove the threat of war, the threat to both its national existence as well as the threat to its individual citizens. Israel hopes that peace would permit a revolutionary change of its national priorities and thus it would be able to dedicate its efforts to its true and traditional goals:

- To serve as a shelter and home to all Jews wherever they may be;
- To deal with the very difficult challenge of the Israeli melting pot and the balanced development of Israeli nation and the society.
- To develop its economy.
- To achieve scientific, technological, and moral excellence.

The Arab goals, and there is a difference between the goals of Arabs in general and Palestinian goals, are first and foremost to rid the Arab Middle East from the alien Israeli element, the unwanted and annoying entity from every point of view. Arabs (and I assume, almost without exception) share the hope and the strong belief that ultimately this goal will be reached – be it by force, be it by an overwhelming demographic superiority, or be it through political pressures in the international arena. This is not because of its rejection of foreigners. Again, Arabs claim, and rightly so, that Jews used to live peacefully in the Arab countries as an ethnic-religious minority among the Arab-Moslem majority.

- TheyArabs reject, however, a Zionist Israel that has imposed itself on the Arabs;
- An Israel that projects its superiority, in every sphere of Arab life and culture;
- An Israel that they consider, right or wrong, as the arm serving Western imperialism;
- And, for the key countries in the region, there is a genuine fear that Israel does threaten their hegemony in the Arab world.

As for the Palestinians, in addition to the above goals, which they share with all other Arabs, they define their conflict with Israel as a zero-sum problem. Both Israel and the Palestinians are two political entities that claim the same territory, Eretz Yisrael or Palestine. Furthermore, not only do both sides claim 100 percent of the territory, but they also see the process as an incessant race to establish new facts that would ultimately favor their side (as well as prevent the other side from establishing its own new facts).

This asymmetry of goals is the key to understanding what is happenings today as well as what the prospects are for the future. We are in the process of negotiating peace agreements, and an agreement will ultimately be signed. But the mere signing of the treaty will not eliminate the strategic goals of either side. Thus the true chance of establishing peace and reaching coexistence will depend mainly on the chance of changing these goals.

In this essay I shall try to portray a realistic picture of the present, and in spite of my belonging to one of the parties I hope to do so in an objective way. I see three major areas of difference and conflict: The ethnic–cultural difference, the religious difference, and the economic–technological difference.

The Ethnic–Cultural Difference

Israel is a Western country from almost every point of view, irrespective of the original sources of the various components of its society. The original settlers of the Zionist immigration have introduced the western way of life: true democracy, liberal attitudes, freedom of speech, western curriculum, art, music, literature, etc. On the other side stands an Arab-Moslem society that wants to preserve its traditional way of life.

On top of it, the parties do not share a common language that would allow human communication. We in Israel pay lip service to the need to learn Arabic, but we do very little about it. It is even worse when it comes to studying and understanding the history, the culture, and, of course, the Koran and the New Testament. Neither Israeli nor Arab Muslim school children study these subjects; thus, they know literally nothing about the other side.

The Religious Gap

Both religions, Islam and Orthodox Judaism, are extreme faiths,. Each is dominated by an extreme, radical, and fundamentalist leadership that does not accept any compromise or flexibility. We have on both sides radical groups that are motivated by extreme religious ideology and can easily be incited to violent acts.

These are two religions that dominate all aspects of civilian life on both sides. And thus they forbid any intimate relationship between individuals on either side (intermarriage, etc.). We have, on either side, ethnic–racist societies that give clear priority and advantage to its own ethnic group.

The Economic–Technological Gap

Israel clearly belongs to the bloc of developed countries. It has a modern economy and it enjoys an educated and highly professional work force. Israel's standard of living is high, and the ratio between the Israeli income per-capita to Arab income per-capita is at least 10:1. Israel's economy is in the process of eliminating all its economic activities that depend on cheap manual labor. Like most western economies Israel is importing cheap manual labor from all over the world, including Palestinian and other Arab workers from across the border.

This reality develops a rather complicated relationship between the Israeli employer and his Arab employee, and this is a permanent source of friction. Part of it is the natural humiliating treatment of these low-cost manual workers. But there is also a direct connection between political violence and Palestinian and Arab workers in Israel. Fear of terrorist acts, Palestinian boycotts of work in Israel, and the instability of this labor have forced Israeli employers to import "safe" workers from abroad as an alternative to the "dangerous" Arab. And this creates a problem, as this trend of importing non-Arab workers will be very difficult to reverse in the future.

One has to understand and remember that Israel is probably the only developed "frontier" country that shares borders with a mass of underdeveloped countries. This naturally invites difficulties: friction and confrontation, even without the political problems between the two sides.

Public Opinion and Positions

If we try to project future relations between the parties it is interesting to analyze Israeli and Arab public opinion following the signature of the peace treaties with Egypt and Jordan, as well as the Oslo Declaration of Principles. Israelis do not believe or trust the Arab. Public opinion polls that have been conducted since 1962 show that about half of the Israelis believe that the Arabs want to conquer and to destroy Israel. Fifty-four percent believe that another Arab–Israeli war is unavoidable. When asked about the kind of relations they would like to have with the Arabs, 91 percent insist on having formal peace treaties and full diplomatic relations. Thirty-six percent of Israelis are convinced that the Arabs do not want to have peace with Israel.

The main reason Israelis give for their insistence on keeping the occupied territories is Israel's national and historical right to the land (again, some 50 percent). The average Israeli does not want to be integrated into the region nor does he want to develop close relations with the Arabs surrounding Israel. This is the answer to the question why do so few Israelis learn and speak Arabic, and know so little about Arab culture, history, tradition, and religion.

The political agreements that had been reached with Arab countries had very little effect in changing the Israeli attitude toward their Arab neighbor. Average Israelis look at whoever belongs to the Middle East as inferior, frightening and threatening, irrational and dangerous. The peace agreements that have been signed with the Arabs establish a peace that has been signed with someone different. It did not make the Arab any closer and, even more disturbing, it did not generate interest in his life and culture. If we want to reach any conclusions in regard to the longer run, one should examine the answers to desired cultural and regional orientation. Sixty-five percent would like to see life in Israel similar to that of Western Europe. New immigrants are even more adamant about this direction; 87 percent among them want to live like persons in Western Europe.[1]

There is a mirror image to these very same attitudes among the Arabs, possibly even in a more extreme manner. A public opinion poll was conducted in Lebanon, Syria and Jordan following the Oslo Declaration of Principles of September 1993. Asked if the peace agreement between Arabs and Israelis would hold, 88 percent answered in the negative. Answering another question, "Would you support the present peace treaties with Israel if, some time in the future, geo-strategic conditions would change against Israel?", 92 percent answered in the negative. And to the question, "What do you think is the alternative to the peace talks?, 75 percent answered "A new military confrontation with Israel!"[2]

The Input of Future Implementation Process

These factors cast a very dark shadow on the chances of developing a genuine and deep peace between Israel and its neighbors for the foreseeable future, even if peace agreements are eventually reached with all the Arab countries surrounding Israel. And yet, the present positions and attitudes of both sides, and the chances of seeing a positive change in the future, will not be the sole factors that determine future developments.

Let us not forget that between the signing of the treaties between Israel and Syria, Lebanon, and the Palestinians and the completion of the implementation of these agreements, we shall see the passing of many years, possibly a generation if not more. This will be a period during which both parties will have to diffuse many mines spread all throughout the area. The removal of these mines will be dangerous and there is a possibility that some of them will blow up in our faces. Furthermore, there will be many on both sides who will do their utmost in order to derail the quiet and conscientious implementation.

The most critical problems in the implementation process will be coping with the Palestinians. There will be a need to deal with Palestinian problems both within the borders of the future Palestinian state as well with the Palestinian Diaspora that comprises the majority of the refugees. We do not have to enumerate these problems, but we should not underestimate their importance and the magnitude of their capability to spoil the entire process. Furthermore, each of these problems will directly influence the process and the timetable as well as, indirectly, strengthen the negative attitudes on both sides, the very attitudes that make deep and true peace so distant.

In Conclusion

I am not pessimistic. On the contrary, I believe we have better chances to reach an agreement if we understand the many obstacles that have to be overcome. I am not pessimistic because I am very much aware that all parties simply have no alternative but to negotiate an agreement. Furthermore, I know that a true and deep peace will need a very long time to realize. But the phases we have to go through are first the negotiations, then the implementation, and then a long and very cold peace that will only gradually warm up.

Notes

1   Asher Arian, *Security Threatened: Surveying Israeli Opinion on Peace and War* (Cambridge: Cambridge University Press, 1955). These figures are from the Hebrew language version by Diyunon Press, 1997, pp. 32–56.

2   Hilal Khashan, "Partner or Pariah," The Washington Institute for Near East Policy, Policy Paper 41, 1996.

CHAPTER 6

The Official Israeli–Palestinian Track: An Assessment

MENACHEM KLEIN

In an analysis of the official Israeli–Palestinian peace negotiating track, one may discover the following four characteristics:

First, since the Oslo Declaration of Principles (DoP) was signed in September 1993, this track has remained relatively static, especially the talks on final status issues. Interestingly, the final status talks between Israel and the Palestine Liberation Organization (PLO) began officially three times. The first was in May 1996 at a ceremony in Taba (Egypt), when Peres tried to secure the election and gain legitimization as Rabin's successor. The Netanyahu administration, which replaced Peres' government in May 1996, succeeded in delaying and postponing any discussion on final status issues. Therefore, the second opening ceremony occurred only in October 1999, when Barak became prime minister and David Levy replaced Uri Savir as the Israeli colleague of Abu Ma'azen.

The third ceremony took place in December of 1999 when the negotiating teams headed by Oded Eran from Israel and Yasser Abed Rabo from the Palestinian Authority (PA) began to operate. The negotiation meetings actually occurred five months after the target date by which the final status agreement should have been achieved. Currently there is no intensive negotiation on final status issues.

On this note I will lead into my second conclusion, which is that final status talks have officially been opened, though interim agreement issues are not yet completely concluded nor implemented. The Oslo II Agreement of September 1995 did not put an end to the discussion over the Israeli military redeployment in the West Bank, but rather resulted in the signing of the Hebron Agreement almost a year later. This in turn brought about the signing of the Sharm el-Sheikh memorandum in the summer of 1999. Yet the debate over the implementation of these signed agreements continues. Israel was forced to recognize the PLO and withdraw from certain areas in the 1967 Occupied Territories; therefore, it has had a problem adjusting itself to this new reality. In parallel, the PLO has had to change from being the sole legitimate political organization representing the Palestinian people to an elected ruling power providing not only representation but also different kinds of services and security to its people at a reasonable cost and efficiency.[1] In other words, the agreements with Israel caused a historical change in the PLO's status. Since 1994 the Palestinian Authority has ruled over its people and territories, and enjoyed international recognition as well as domestic legitimization, achieved in January 1996 by general elections.

Arafat and his colleagues, by founding in 1959 the Fatah movement (the Arabic acronym for the Palestinian National Liberation Movement, the dominant organization in the PLO), have traveled a long distance from the margin of the Palestinian arena to hold key positions in international and regional politics, and actually did hold the key to ending the Arab–Israeli and the Muslim–Israeli conflicts.[2] However, the Jewish state-in-being was able to arrive at better cooperation with the British mandatory authorities than the Arab Palestinians were, and the Israelis even integrated part of the Authority's manpower into the British mandates bureaucracy in order to learn from the British Empire experience in state management and military methods. This was highly important for a people that remained outside of political history for almost 2,000 years. At the same time, the Palestinians suffered from their social and political weaknesses, especially after 1939. Since the Nakba of 1948,[3] the Palestinians have had to rebuild their national movement with their leadership located outside of Palestine most of the time, not only excluded from the Palestinian land and people but also without access to state power and substantial ruling positions. At the most, the PLO leadership ruled its organization and some refugee camps in Jordan between 1967–70 and in Lebanon between the years 1971 and 1982.[4]

Since 1967, members of the Palestinian political movement have not been allowed to participate in the Israeli military or civil administration. Thus since 1994, the Palestinian national movement's leadership has had to develop its own methods of ruling and state building, and base them on its former experience at the PLO establishment – while simultaneously negotiating with Israel over power, authority, and territory.

The third conclusion relates to the very fact that all agreed-upon timetables within the Israeli–Palestinian agreements have consistently been violated. This began with the DoP of 1993 when the Israeli withdrawal from Gaza Strip and Jericho was not implemented after the agreed-upon two months, but instead after nine. In January 2000, both sides failed to hold a marathon of discussions in mini-teams in order to meet a very ambitious timetable of concluding a core agreement in February 2000 and a detailed one in September. In March 2000, a new Israeli–Palestinian timetable was agreed upon accordingly; a core agreement on final status issues was to be concluded by May 2000; and Israel was to have completed its withdrawals from the West Bank (except army bases and Jewish settlements) by July. Thereafter, both sides were obliged to conclude a comprehensive peace agreement by September 2000. As all know, this did not happen.

My fourth conclusion relates to the differences between Labor and Likud governments' attitudes with respect to their Palestinian partner. Although developing the Israeli–Palestinian track was not Rabin's first choice but rather one of default, Israel's Labor government and the Palestinians had an unwritten understanding that breathed life into the Oslo Accords. The PLO and the Palestinian Authority were to pass a series of tests as a condition for transforming themselves from a terrorist organization to a state. This began with the signing of the first Oslo Agreement in September 1993, in which Israel accepted the PLO as a legitimate negotiating partner.

The Labor government maintained that fundamentally and over time Arafat had passed the tests. In this view, the tests imposed by the Oslo Accords were bilateral – Israel also had to pass them. The question of whether the two parties could live side by side, which was the basis of reaching an interim agreement before a permanent settlement, was a question that applied to both sides. Quite naturally, Israel took Palestinian violations of the Oslo Accords very seriously while minimizing the importance of its own unilateral actions, (such as the imposition of a harsh and thorough closure on Palestinian areas) and of its own violations, (such as the failure to open the safe passage routes between the West Bank and Gaza Strip on time and its failure to free Palestinian prisoners). Nevertheless, throughout the service of their governments, Rabin and Peres were cognizant of Israel's violations.

The Palestinians accepted Israel's violations and unilateral actions because they had received the status of an equal partner, and understood that Israel had difficulty in accepting restrictions on its power and in moving instantly from being an occupier to a situation in which the occupied people had equal status to it. The Oslo process gave both sides hope and enlarged the capacity of each side to accept the other's violations.[5]

The Likud government brought an entirely different outlook to the agreements, acting as if the learning process that the Oslo Accords laid out had been a one-sided one. The Palestinians were to pass all their tests in full, and only after that would they be moved from the status of members of a terrorist organization, or of organizations that encourage terror, to the status of an interlocutor- – and even then, one of inferior status. The Likud government did not want the permanent settlement to create a Palestinian state with a status equal to that of the State of Israel, but merely to exercise Palestinian autonomy over several disconnected territorial enclaves covering just half of the West Bank, with broad powers left to Israel. To achieve this objective, Netanyahu's Likud government launched three parallel paths.

- The first was to allot half a year to permanent status negotiations, which were to begin immediately, on the assumption that it would succeed in forcing the Palestinians to accept these terms. The Palestinians rejected this outright because they wanted to enter the permanent status negotiations while proceeding along the Oslo path and implementing it to its fullest.
- Netanyahu's second path was to enter into violent confrontation with the Palestinians. The Palestinian Authority acted cautiously and initially did not fall into this trap. The violent reactions to the Har Homa project were discrete, controlled, and supervised.
- Third, the Likud government acted to expand the Israeli settlements in general, and Jewish housing in Jerusalem in particular, with the aim of taking control of land that, in its view, had to be under Israeli sovereignty.

Unilateral action thus replaced agreements with the Palestinians, and the Likud government stood behind the Oslo Agreements only in word. To achieve broad public support for its actions, the Likud government chose to concentrate its efforts on Jerusalem. The capital, it believed, was an area that in the national consensus was valued as sacred and that was worth sacrifice and even fighting for. However, to achieve even broader support, it kept silent about this last argument, and instead formulated its goal negatively. The Labor government, it claimed, had begun the process of handing the city over to the Palestinians.[6] The Likud's policy turned Jerusalem into the essence of the dispute, rather than a separate issue. During the Labor government, which had followed the Oslo path, Israel and the Palestinians reached an understanding of Jerusalem as a problem of its own – not a local and marginal problem, but also not a problem that epitomized the Israel-Palestinian dispute and not the principal dispute between the two sides. The Likud's policy was diametrically opposed, because for the Likud Jerusalem was at the very heart of the confrontation. The way of getting off the Oslo track, or at least of stopping the process in its tracks, was to go through Jerusalem by engaging in intensive unilateral activity there.

The Palestinians viewed Jerusalem as a place in which they could force the Likud government to continue along the Oslo road.[7] In order to re-isolate the Jerusalem problem from the rest of the pending problems between the Palestinian Authority and Israel, they had to create a controlled diplomatic and violent confrontation with Israel over the opening of the Western Wall tunnel and Har Homa. From the point of view of the Palestinians, the confrontation over Jerusalem was not meant to blow up or halt the Oslo process, but rather to advance it. When Israel put Jerusalem at the focus of the dispute, the Palestinians also began hardening their position. Jerusalem turned from a different and special issue to the essence of the dispute between Israel and the Palestinians. Arafat stopped talking publicly about a creative solution to the problem and maintained that Jerusalem was the Palestinians' red line.

> "The struggle for Jerusalem is for us a question of life or death . . . we will mobilize all efforts and abilities to save Jerusalem and against Israel's policy . . . Israel is a red line."[8]

Notes

1   Menachem Klein, "Quo Vadis? Palestinian Authority Building Dilemmas Since 1993," *Middle Eastern Studies* 33 (1997): 383–404.
2   On the history of Fatah and the PLO, see Yezid Sayigh, *Armed Struggle and the Search for State* (Oxford: Clarendon, 1997); Helena Cobban, *The Palestinian Liberation Organization – People, Power and Politics* (Cambridge: Cambridge Unversity Press, 1984).
3   Disaster, the Palestinian name to their collapse in the 1948 war. See Baruch Kimmerling and Joel S. Migdal, *Palestinians – The Making of People* (Boston: Harvard University Press, 1994) pp. 96–156.
4   Rashid Khalidi, "The Palestinians in Lebanon: Social Repercussions of Israel's Invasion," *The Middle East Journal,* Spring 1984, 38 (2): 225–66; Sayigh, ibid., pp. 447–63.
5   For further discussion see Menachem Klein, *Jerusalem – The Future of a Contested City* (New York: Hurst & Co., March 2001).
6   *Ha'aretz*, March 19, 1997, March 20, 1997.
7   *Ha'aretz*, April 24, 1997.
8   *al-Quds*, March 8, 1998, July 2, 1998.

CHAPTER 7

The Peace Process and Scenarios for a Permanent Solution of the Palestinian Question

KHALIL ELIAN

The Palestinian question has continued without a proper solution for several generations and has led to three major wars of 1948, 1967, and 1973, in addition to the invasion of Lebanon in 1982. Nonetheless there have been several attempts to have a permanent solution since the 1920s: the White Paper Solution by the British in the early 1940s; the Partition of Palestine into two states by the UN in 1947; Resolutions 242 and 338 of the Security Council; Camp David in 1979; the Madrid Conference in 1991; the Oslo Agreement in 1993; and the Wadi Araba Agreement in 1994.

The 1948 Arab–Israeli war was a catastrophe (Nakba) for the Palestinian people and a deep shock to the Arab People.

The 1967 war dealt an even heavier blow to the Palestinians, Jordanians, and the rest of the Arabs when Israel occupied the West Bank and Gaza, including East Jerusalem.

The 1973 war did not restore to the Palestinians their rights but it did lead to the Camp David Agreement in 1979, which was the first Arab–Israeli treaty. The Agreement marks a turning point in the course of the Arab–Israeli conflict in that it neutralized Egypt, the most populous Arab state. This treaty upset the regional balance of power in the Middle East.

Then came the Israeli invasion of Lebanon in 1982 to destroy the PLO. But this did not bring a permanent solution to the Palestinian problem or achieve peace for Israel.

In the mid-1980s, the *Intifada* started and continued for several years, which gave a message to Israel that the Palestinians reject the occupation and want to restore their rights.

In 1991, the Peace Conference in Madrid led to the Israel–PLO Oslo

Agreement in 1993, which subsequently paved the way for the Wadi Araba Treaty in 1994 between Jordan and Israel.

The *objective* of this chapter is to explore several scenarios or options for a peaceful and permanent solution for the Palestinian question in all of its aspects of identity, statehood, land, borders, Jerusalem, the refugees, and the settlements.

The *significance* of the objective stems from the fact that neither the wars, nor the agreements, nor the status quo until now will bring a comprehensive peace to the region as long as the central issue – the Palestinian question – lacks a permanent and convincing solution. Thus, the discussion that follows of the possible scenarios of a comprehensive and permanent solution to the Palestine issue gives the decision-makers on both sides "food for thought" as to the available alternatives that could help achieve a solution.

The *methodology* is based on the descriptive and analytical approaches of the mainly qualitative data available to the researcher. Such an approach was selected due to the nature of these types of studies, which rely on vision and a future-based outlook with less dependence on historical data from other sources.

The organizational structure of this study includes the following sections: (I) Conceptual Framework; (II) Establishing a Palestinian state beside Israel and Jordan; (III) A Confederation of Jordanian and Palestine States; (IV) A Swiss Model Federation of Israel and Palestine with a Unified Jerusalem as its Capital and Refugees being absorbed in the Federation; (V) A Confederation between Palestinian and Israeli States; (VI) A Confederation between Palestine, Jordan, and Israel; (VII) Continued Conflict under the Status Quo; (VIII) Conclusions and Policy Implications.

I Conceptual Framework of the Study

A *state* is a sovereign entity made up of a social group(s) that occupies a defined territory, is organized under common political institutions, has an effective government, and is formally recognized by other states.[1] An independent state has its own head of state, army, ministries, borders, flag, passport, and citizens. Recognition of the state by other countries in the community of nations adds strength to the state. A state could enter into a confederation or into a full union without losing its own sovereignty, but if the state enters into a federation it loses some aspects of its sovereignty and independence in the matters of defense and foreign affairs in favor of the federation or the federal government. This is true also in terms of membership in the United Nations.

A *federation* is a union of states in which the member states recognize the sovereignty of a central authority or government while retaining certain residual powers and rights to be exercised and administered by the states. Concrete examples of such federations are the United States of America (USA) and the Federal Union of Switzerland. The federal government is responsible for the foreign affairs, defense, federal tax, and federal budget while each state is responsible for the remaining administrative issues, such as municipalities, education, health, etc.[2]

A *confederation* is an association of states that seek to achieve national objectives through common political and economic institutions. A confederation differs from a federation in that member states retain full sovereignty. The states coordinate policies of external defense, foreign policy, and external trade with the other states. There are several examples of a confederation, such as the Confederation of the Southern States that seceded from the United States in 1860 and 1861 and the Confederation of Independent States constituted by Russia and twelve former republics of the Union of Soviet Socialist Republics.[3]

The Palestinian question includes the aspects of statehood; citizenship, sovereignty over land, borders, water, and population; East Jerusalem; the refugees; and the settlements.

II Establishing a Palestinian State beside Israel and Jordan

Among the Palestinians there is substantial consensus supporting the establishment of an independent state in the pre-1967 territories of the West Bank and Gaza. (This would constitute 22% of the pre-1948 Palestine Mandate which is less than the 49% allotted to the Palestinian state in the United Nations Partition Plan of 1947.) The Palestinian state would have recognized borders with East Jerusalem as its capital. Achievement of the state would require a just solution for the Palestinian refugees (of 1948 and 1967) and for the Jewish settlements established after 1967.

Adnan Abu Audeh – a well-known politician in Jordan who has been a political advisor to his Majesty King Abdulla, the Minister of Information, and who held senior posts at the Ministry of Foreign Affairs – made the following analogy in his book *Jordanians, Palestinians and The Hashemite Kingdom*. Before the year 1948, the status quo of the Palestinians, Jordanians, and Jews was as three persons in one room, with two seats for the Palestinians and Jordanians and no seat for the Jews. After 1948, there were two seats for the Israelis and Jordanians with no seat for the Palestinian. The Arabs failed to destroy the Jewish dream for an Israeli state and the Israelis failed to destroy the Palestinian dream for a state of their own. The Jordanians and Israelis survive with their own states. Hence, there is a necessity to create a new seat for the Palestinian in the form of a Palestinian state.[4]

Such a new state would give the Palestinians a recognized entity, a government, a parliament, a flag, passports, borders, a capital, and lands of their own. If established, it might be recognized by more than a three-fourths majority of the member states of the United Nations.

Most of the Arab states, including Jordan, would recognize the new state. His majesty King Abdullah II and his majesty the Late King Hussein have declared more than once that if the Palestinians decided to have a state of their own, Jordan would support and recognize it.[5]

Many neutral observers believe that a Palestinian state would satisfy Palestinian demands and be a stabilizing factor in the region. As a state with only a small lightly armed army, it would not be a threat to its neighbors. A majority of Palestinians truly believe that they have had enough war and suffering, and that it is their destiny to co-exist with Israel as a neighbor state.

III A Confederation between Jordan and a Palestine State

The idea of a confederation between Jordan and Palestine has reappeared on several occasions in the media, during the years following the Oslo and Wadi Araba Agreements. Several officials from both the Palestinian and Jordanian sides have supported the idea.

Due to the special relationship between Jordan and the Palestinians in the West Bank and Gaza because of the social, economic, and historical bonds, the scenario of a federation between the two parties might be feasible.

From the Palestinian side, the Head of the Palestinian Authority has expressed his support for a confederation between Jordan and Palestine in order to keep up the strong bonds and ties with Jordan. Jordan is crucial to the survival of a Palestinian state economically and politically. For Palestinians, Jordan is one of a few doors, besides Egypt and Israel, to the rest of the world, and in particular to the Arab countries. Moreover, the Palestinian side thinks that a confederation with Jordan might lessen the objections of Israel and the western world to the Palestinian state, since Jordan has good relations with all parties.

From the Jordanian side, different views are expressed by a number of high officials about the desirability of such a confederation. His Majesty King Abdullah II, following the same strategy as his father, his majesty the late King Hussein, has not committed Jordan to such a confederation. Some observers assert that it is too early to discuss the feasibility of such a confederation before the establishment of a Palestinian state in the West Bank and Gaza. Creation of a Palestinian state depends on solving the issues of Jerusalem, the refugees, and the settlements. For example, Mr. Ahmad Obeidat – a former prime minister, a former head of the intelligence department, and a current senator in the Jordanian Parliament –

stated that in the absence of a just solution for the thorny issues such as the refugees, Jerusalem, the Jewish settlements, the borders, and the creation of a Palestinian state, a Jordanian–Palestinian Confederation is unacceptable.[6]

Many Jordanians fear the increase in the number of Palestinians that the proposed confederation would bring into the Jordanian Kingdom – no less than 75 percent, compared to the current majority of 60 percent or more.[7] However, to my knowledge, a substantial majority of the Jordanians of Palestinian origin prefer some kind of confederation or even a federation between both banks of Jordan.

Mr. Adnan Abu Audeh mentioned in his book *Jordanians, Palestinians, and the Hashemite Kingdom* that the presidency of the suggested confederation could be rotated between His Majesty the King and the President of the future Palestinian state, or that there might be a symbolic presidency of the federation held by his Majesty the King with much of the authority in the federation in the hands of a Federation Council of Ministers.

IV A Swiss Model Federation of Israel and Palestine with a Unified Jerusalem as its Capital and Refugees being Absorbed in the Federation

This scenario seems to be the best long-term option to solve the Palestinian question in all of its aspects – mainly the refugees, the borders, Jerusalem, the settlements, statehood, and the security issues for both Israelis and Palestinians. Such a solution would be a permanent one. The general features of the proposed federation may be imagined as follows:

1. The federal state would be called "The Holy Land/ Al-Aradi Al-Mokadaseh," replacing the names of Israel and Palestine. This name should be acceptable to the Jews, Moslems, and Christians.
2. The new entity would be divided into several cantons for the Israelis and others cantons for the Palestinians. Each canton would have its own administration, budget, and municipality.
3. The capital of the Federal State would be a united Jerusalem.
4. The borders of the Federal State would be pre-1948 Palestine, as under the British Mandate.
5. There would be a new passport for the citizens of the federation in the name of the Holy Land in English, Hebrew, and Arabic, with the symbol of a Crescent and the Star of David (inside the Crescent) on the passport cover.
6. The Federal State would have dual official languages of Hebrew and Arabic.

7. The President of the Federal State would be selected annually and rotated among the cantons. The president might be Jewish, Moslem, or Christian.
8. The members of the Parliament of the Federal State would be elected from all the cantons.
9. There would be no official religion in the Federal State.
10. The issue of the settlements would disappear, since every citizen of the Federal State would have the right to settle anywhere he or she could afford.
11. The issue of the refugees would be solved by their settlement in the Federal State or by providing them dual nationality in the new federated state and in the country of current residence, if a refugee so chooses.
12. The flag of the Federal State would consist of the Red Crescent and the Blue Star of David inside it.
13. The currency of the Federal State would bear the word Palestine on one face and the word Israel on the other face.

V   A Confederation between a Palestinian State and Israel

Should the Israelis and the Palestinians find it hard to accept the federation option as an ideal and permanent solution for the long run, they might start with a confederation between them as a first phase. A Palestinian state must first be established in the West Bank and Gaza, with East Jerusalem as capital. The Palestinian state would then have to enter into a confederation with Israel. The advantages of such a solution to the Israelis and the Palestinians are as follows:

1. The problem of security for Israel would disappear because the two entities would have to coordinate their foreign and defense policies.
2. The issue of the borders would be no longer be a problem since the security policies of both states would be coordinated within the confederation.
3. Movement of the Israelis and the Palestinian in and out of united Jerusalem would be guaranteed, since the two parts of the city would be open for all citizens of the new confederation.
4. Free movement of persons and goods between the two states would be guaranteed within the confederation.
5. Normalization between the Israelis and the Arabs would be much easier within the confederation. The confederation would serve as a bridge between the Jews and Arabs, and present barriers would disappear between the confederation and the rest of the Arab countries.
6. The refugees would be given dual nationality of the confederation and

the country of residence, should they decide not to return to the proposed confederation.[8]

7.   The president of the proposed confederation would have symbolic protocol type authorities, and the office would be filled, in rotation, by Israelis and Palestinians.

VI A Confederation between Palestine, Jordan, and Israel

Ninety percent of the Palestinian people are dispersed among the West Bank and Gaza, Jordan, and Israel. A confederation among the three entities would serve to re-establish bonds among the Palestinians by making them into one undivided people. The Israelis would no longer need to fear the Palestinians in the Diaspora. Jordan would benefit from the new investments, trade, technology, and economies of scale, besides gaining new outlets to the Mediterranean. The problems of Jerusalem, borders, and settlements would all be solved by the confederation. However, the nearly 10 percent or more Palestinians in the Diaspora remaining outside the countries of the confederation would need to resettle within the confederation, or to be given a dual citizenship if they decide not to return.

VII Continued Conflict under the Status Quo

Everyone in the Middle East – including the Palestinians, the Israelis, the rest of Arabs, and the rest of the world – has suffered dearly from the continued conflict, which has lasted for almost seven decades. By all standards, the Arab–Israeli conflict – with the Palestinian question at the core of it – is considered one of the most dreadful conflicts that humanity has seen.

The urgency of solving the Palestinian question stems from the reality that future conflicts in the Middle East will be even more destructive than before. Weapons of mass destruction such as the long-range rockets, forbidden chemicals, and nuclear bombs could be used. Hence, a permanent solution for the Palestinian question is crucial for every Palestinian, Israeli, and Arab, and for the rest of the human race.

VIII Conclusions and Policy Implications

In spite of repeated attempts to solve the Palestinian question during the last five decades, there has been no permanent solution. This study has attempted to shed light on the various scenarios or options that are still open to the decision makers in this region of the Middle East to find a permanent solution. This bloody conflict seems endless to many people, but the conflict is potentially solvable, like most of the conflicts worldwide. What all of us need, is wise, brave, and determined leaders armed with the political will and the vision of peace – such as that of the late President Charles De Gaulle of France who gave Algiers its full independence – so that the Palestinians, the Israelis, the rest of Arabs, and the rest of the world can live in peace and dignity without the threat of war and destruction. Then the spirit of cooperation, not confrontation, will prevail in the Holy Land.

Notes

1   Jack C. Plano and Roy Olton, *The International Relations Dictionary, 4th Edition* (Oxford: Cleo Press Ltd, 1988), p. 277.
2   *Al-Mawred Arabic English Dictionary* (Beirut: Munir Baal Baki, 1999).
3   *The American Heritage Dictionary of the English Language* (New York: Dell Publishing Co., 1982).
4   Such views were expressed by H.E Mr. Adnan Abu Audeh, the Political Advisor of His Majesty the King and a former minister for several governments and a former Representative of Jordan in the UN in New York in his book *Jordanians, Palestinans and the Hashemite Kingdom* (Washington, D.C.: United States Institute of Peace, 1999.)
5   His Majesty King Abdulla II and H.E the Prime Minister Mr. Abdul-Raof Al-Rawabdeh have lately declared that the Palestinians have the right to establish their own state and that the Palestinian Refugees have the right of return (*al-Arab Alyawm*, February 14, 2000).
6   H.E Mr. Ahmad Obeidat expressed these views during a lecture held at the Showman Forum on Jordan and the Future Challenges, on February 14, 2000. Amman.
7   It is informally estimated that the Jordanians of Palestinian origin constitute around 60 percent or more of Jordan's populations, or around 3 million out of 5 million. The population of the West Bank and Gaza is estimated to be around 2.7 million. Thus, a confederation between Palestine and Jordan might have around 6 million people at the end of the year 2000. Thus, the Jordanians of Palestinian origin might constitute around 75 percent of the Federation's population.
8   During a recent symposium on Palestinian–Jordanian relations, which was held in Gaza, Dr. Said Al-Tel, a former deputy of the Prime Minister, expressed his views against such a double nationality of the Jordanians of Palestinian origin (*al Arab al-Yawm*, February 22, 2000). Moreover, H.E Saleh al-Kalab, Minister of Information and Culture in Jordan expressed similar views versus the idea of a dual nationality for the Palestinian refugees in Jordan (*al-Rai Newpaper*, February 23, 2000).

CHAPTER 8

The Long-Term Economic Benefits of Peace Stability in the Middle East

ONN WINCKLER

The Economic Damage of the Conflict

In addition to its huge human costs, the long-standing Arab–Israeli conflict has caused significant economic damage to the countries involved, particularly the Palestinians, Jordan, Egypt, Lebanon and Syria. This damage can be divided into two main categories.

First is *the direct damage*. In the case of Egypt, such damage included the loss of the oil fields in Sinai, the inability to explore the oil fields in the west bank of the Suez Canal as a result of the instability in this area, the closure of the Suez Canal between 1967–1975, and the destruction of the cities along the Canal. Syria lost the Golan Heights with its natural resources to Israel in the June 1967 war. In addition, Syria was forced to absorb approximately 150,000 refugees from the Golan Heights. The country that has suffered the greatest economic damage from the conflict is Jordan. As a result of the June 1967 war, Jordan lost the West Bank, including East Jerusalem, with almost 40 percent of the Kingdom's population and a large part of its agricultural land and water resources, as well as some major tourism sites.

The second category is *the indirect damage*. This includes first and foremost the loss of tourism income and a low scale of foreign investments – well below the original potential of the region.

Moreover, the conflict forced the Middle Eastern countries to allocate immense resources to military purposes rather than to economic and social development. During the past three decades, the military and security expenditures in the Middle East were higher than in any other developing region worldwide, amounting to more than 10 percent of the GDP. In Syria during the 1980s, military expenditures constituted more than half of the total governmental budget.

Rapid Population Growth and its Economic Consequences

In parallel to the economic damage caused by the Arab–Israeli conflict, another factor constituting a major barrier to rapid economic development in the Middle East during the second half of the twentieth century was that of rapid population growth as a result of high fertility levels combined with decreasing death rates. The economic consequences of the rapid population growth in the Middle East were many and varied, including increased water shortages, food imports, public expenditures on subsidies of basic foodstuffs, a rapid urbanization process, the creation of housing shortages in the major cities absorbing most of the rural migrants, traffic problems, and air pollution and other environmental problems caused by high population density in the major cities.

The prolonged high natural increase rates in population have led to the creation of a wide-based age pyramid. By 1997, the total population of the Middle East and North Africa amounted to 325.8 million, of whom 46.9 million were under the age of 5 and 153.1 million were under the age of 18. The meaning of this wide-based age pyramid is that despite the fertility reduction during the past two decades, Middle Eastern populations will continue to grow rapidly in the coming generation as well. One major consequence of this trend is the need to provide sufficient work opportunities for the rapidly growing workforce, which will continue to grow until the number of those entering the workforce, namely, those in the age group of 20–24, will be equal to those leaving the workforce at the age of 60–65. This will happen, according to the various demographic projections, only in the middle of the twenty-first century.

Thus, the current poor economic situation in many Middle Eastern countries, particularly in the case of Egypt, Syria, and Jordan, which have been directly involved in the Arab–Israeli conflict, is the result of high military expenditures and economic damage from the conflict, combined with rapid population growth.

The Current Economic Benefits of the Middle East Peace Process

Indeed, the Middle East peace process has substantial economic benefits for the countries involved in it. As a result of the peace treaty with Israel from March 1979, Egypt has been enjoying an annual grant of $2.3 billion and substantial foreign investments creating a large number of work opportunities, has regained the oil fields in Sinai, has had the Suez Canal reopened in 1975; and most importantly, has taken in revenues of more than $2 billion annually from tourism. All in all, it seems that Egypt's direct economic benefits from the peace with Israel amount to at least $10 billion annually. The Jordanian economic benefits from the October 1994 peace treaty with Israel have also been considerable. These include the removal of a large part of the Jordanian foreign debt; an increase in water sources; a rise in foreign investments; substantial expansion of foreign aid, particularly from the United States; and most importantly, growth in tourism revenues. For the Palestinians, a peace treaty with Israel means an independent state for the first time in their history. However, these benefits, albeit substantial, have not led to a macro-level change in the economies of the countries involved in the Middle East peace process.

Tourism: The Major Lever for Future Middle Eastern Economic Growth

During the 1970s and 1980s, the major lever for Middle Eastern economic development consisted of the huge oil revenues that were largely distributed among many Middle Eastern countries, both through direct grants from the oil states to the poorer countries and via workers' remittances, which represented the most lucrative source for hard currency among the larger labor-exporting countries, i.e., Egypt, Jordan, Syria, Yemen, Tunisia, and Sudan. In addition, large-scale labor emigration led to a substantial decline in the employment pressures in these countries. Thus, during the 1970s and 1980s, *rent sources* constituted the major part of the Middle Eastern economy, not only in Gulf oil economies.

However, during the 1990s, both the workers' remittances and the grants of the Gulf oil-rich countries substantially declined. The subsequent economic development of the non-oil Middle Eastern countries has been very slow. In the case of Jordan and Syria during the past two years, the GDP growth rates in per capita terms were negative. By 1998, according to United Nations Economic and Social Commission for Western Asia estimates, the per capita GDP (in current prices) was $1,381 in Egypt, $1,538 in Jordan, and $1,593 in Syria.

Thus, the most important question is: Except for oil, which is concentrated primarily in a small number of countries, what are the other options for the Middle Eastern countries to achieve a substantial and stable economic growth in order to improve the current low standard of living and reduce the high unemployment rates?

The achievement of this goal through *the agriculture sector*, which was the major lever for rapid economic development in the region during the nineteenth century, is no longer a viable option. This is the result of increasing water shortages for agricultural purposes due to rapid population growth as well as the fact that most of the available agricultural lands in the region are already in use, particularly in Egypt and Jordan.

A second option, *rapid industrial development*, which was the major lever for rapid economic development in the emerging economies in East Asia, such as in Taiwan and Korea, is not a realistic option, at least not in the foreseeable future. This is because it would be a long and difficult process, if possible at all, to compete with the Western industrialized countries in the area of high-tech products, on the one hand, or the cheap products of the Far East, mainly from China, on the other. In Syria, for example, the industrial sector increased by less than one percent in 1997. Moreover, rapid industrial development would be require many changes in the political as well as in the tariff and the exchage rate systems currently prevailing in the Middle East, which by itself is a long process.

My thesis is that currently the only option for both rapid economic growth and a substantial increase in available employment opportunities is through development of *the tourism industry*. During the past three decades, tourism has emerged as one of the world's major industries, exceeding many other industries in number of employees and foreign currency earnings. For a growing number of countries, tourism has become the largest economic sector, both in terms of percentage of the GDP and number of employees.

What does the Middle East have to offer to the World Tourism Industry?

The Middle East offers some very important advantages over other tourism destinations in the world. The most prominent among them are as follows:

1. First and foremost is *religious tourism*. The Middle East is rich in holy sites – such as Jerusalem, the Sea of Galilee, and Bethlehem, for example – for all the three monotheist religions.
2. Second, the region is rich in cultural and historical sites, such as Petra in Jordan and the Pyramids in Egypt.
3. Third, the Middle East is very close to Europe, being only a few hours by air. Thus, the travel expenses are relatively low.
4. Fourth, the Middle East region offers at the same time winter in the north and summer in the south within a distance of no more than a few hundred kilometers.
5. Fifth, the Middle East has great potential in the area of beach resort holidays throughout almost all the seasons of the year.

However, it must be emphasized that the fundamental requirement for using these advantages is the ability to cross borders freely; otherwise, the costs would be too high.

What does Tourism have to Offer the Middle East?

For the Middle Eastern economies, in particular, the tourism industry has many advantages, the five most prominent being as follows:

1. *Increasing governmental revenues through taxation.* Today, due to the low per capita income in most of the Middle Eastern countries, the governmental revenues from taxation are very low. In the Gulf Coast countries, with the highest per capita income in the Middle East, taxes are not imposed on the personal income of nationals for political reasons. However, in the tourism industry, taxation is applied to the tourists themselves. These taxes can be used to expand the infrastructure facilities, which will also be used for other purposes.
2. *Tourism as a lever for the development of other related industries.* The tourism industry serves as a major catalyst for the development of other economic sectors, such as construction, transportation, agriculture, fisheries, etc., insofar as they supply the goods and services used in the tourism industry.
3. *Tourism as a heavily labor-intensive industry.* In contrast to other industries, particularly high-tech, the number of potential work opportunities in the tourism industry is enormous. Moreover, work opportunities in the tourism industry, as compared with other industries and advanced services, are relatively quick and cheap to create. In addition, the tourism industry provides work opportunities in a wide variety of skills and professions, from the top managerial positions to unskilled occupations in hotels, restaurants, tourist sites, etc.
4. *Foreign currency earnings.* The vast majority of the revenues from the tourism industry are in foreign currencies. Thus, these revenues could compensate for the balance of trade deficits, which currently characterize all of the non-oil Middle Eastern economies.
5. *Promotion of foreign investments.* The tourism industry, in particular, promotes foreign investments, especially in the construction of new hotels and tourism sites.

Summary and Conclusions

The peace process has raised awareness of the tremendous tourism potential of the Middle East. Geoffrey Lippman, the head of the World Travel and Tourism Council, has stated: "We have enormous faith in this region." However, it must be emphasized that the tourism industry, more than any other industry, is very sensitive to both internal and external security situations. Thus, a stable peace in the Middle East is a basic and fundamental requirement for further development of the tourism industry. A report of the World Tourism Organization noted in this regard that: "The Middle East region has lost ground as a destination region over the past two decades for the major tourist generating markets of Western Europe because of its political problems." During the past few years, the share of the Middle Eastern and North African countries in the world tourism industry was only 2.5 percent. The potential, according to the various studies conducted in this field, is much higher, amounting to at least 10 to 13 percent. This gap translates into hundreds of billions of dollars every year, as well as millions of new work opportunities. Thus, given the current economic situation in the Middle East, the inescapable conclusion is that a stable peace in this region is no longer a matter of option, but simply a matter of economic survival.

CHAPTER 9

The Oslo Process and Jewish Public Opinion in Israel: A Story of Disappointment?

EPHRAIM YUCHTMAN-YA'AR

This chapter examines the developments that have occurred in the Israeli Jewish public's attitudes toward the Oslo process during the Barak government and the Sharon government, as well as the social basis of these attitudes. As a point of departure for this analysis, it should be recalled that since the beginning of the Israeli–Palestinian negotiating process following the two sides' signing of the Oslo Agreement in September 1993, the Israeli Jewish public has been divided into distinct camps of supporters and opponents of the agreement. At the base of the rift between the two camps lie differences in both ideological outlooks and pragmatic considerations.

Ideologically speaking, on one side are various groups that uphold the idea of the Greater Land of Israel, some of them motivated by a religious worldview ("and to thy seed I will give this land") and others by the Zionist ideology that regarded and regards Jewish settlement in all parts of the Land of Israel as a main aspect of fulfilling the vision of establishing a Jewish state in the historical homeland. Most of those on the other side certainly identify with the Zionist ideology and the Jewish nation's historical right to the Land of Israel, but at the same time recognize the fact that there is also a Palestinian people in this land that is also entitled to realize its national aspirations in it by establishing a state of its own. Furthermore, the Oslo supporters emphasize the moral problem of dominating another people, and the contradiction between this reality and Israel's commitment to democratic values. From this standpoint, then, the solution of "two states for two peoples" will strengthen Israel's ability to exist as a Jewish and democratic state.

In pragmatic terms, the gaps between the two camps mainly concern the question of whether it is possible to set up on such a small and resource-poor territory (the entire Land of Israel west of the Jordan comes to about 28,000 square kilometers) two states that could effectively function economically while maintaining their political independence. Moreover, the Oslo opponents argue that the establishment of a Palestinian state, particularly if it would require an Israeli withdrawal to the 1967 borders, would constitute a strategic threat to Israel's existence, since such a state could ally itself with other Arab states, including those belonging to the "rejectionist front" that regard Israel's existence as illegitimate.

Underlying this claim is the notion that Israel cannot allow itself to trust the Palestinians, and that even if a peace agreement was signed with them, Israel's existence would be under perpetual threat. Indeed, such apprehensions also exist among many of the Oslo supporters, leading them to raise various proposals of maintaining Israel's security control in certain areas of the West Bank, such as the Jordan Valley, as well as the demand that the Palestinian state would be limited in the size of its army and the types of weapons it could possess. On the other hand, this camp essentially believes that Israel's security would in fact be strengthened by arriving at a peace treaty with the Palestinians and the other Arab states, since it could then direct its human and material resources to pursuing social and economic objectives in cooperation with the peoples of the region (i.e., the "New Middle East" vision of Shimon Peres).

Ultimately, the gap between the two camps manifests itself in the degree of readiness for a territorial compromise between the two peoples on the one hand, and in the belief that this would lead to the end of the two people's historical conflict on the other. At the same time, it is important to keep in mind that beyond the disagreements between them, the two camps are united in desiring to preserve the Jewish character of the state, and that is why there is a broad consensus among the Israeli Jewish public against the Palestinian claim for realizing the Arab refugees' right of return insofar as this refers to their return to territories within the State of Israel. In other words, even the camp that favors a solution based on territorial compromise is not prepared to compromise on what it regards as an existential threat, as is clear from the reaction to the demand for the refugees' right of return to Israel itself.

What, then, are the relative proportions of the two camps among the Israeli Jewish public and what is the social basis of their composition? To answer these questions we will make use of data obtained by the Tami Steinmetz Center for Peace Research of Tel Aviv University, which since June 1994 has conducted monthly surveys that have consistently examined the Israeli public's attitudes toward different aspects of the peace process. On the basis of several questions that are regularly included in these surveys, it is possible to track widespread trends in Israeli public opinion by means of the "peace indexes," one of which focuses on the Oslo Agreement.

The Oslo index consists of two questions, one of which measures the degree of support or opposition to the "Oslo formula," and the second the degree of belief that it will lead to a permanent peace agreement between Israel and the Palestinians. This chapter deals with the developments in public opinion regarding the two questions over two years only, i.e., from May 1999 to April 2001. This period begins with the Barak government's taking office and ends in the third month of the Sharon government's tenure. To facilitate presenting the findings, we divided the overall period into three subperiods: the first three months of the Barak government (May–July 1999), the last three months of this government (November 2000–January 2001), and the first three months of the Sharon government (February–April 2001). The findings for each month are based on representative samples of the entire, adult Israeli Jewish population, including residents of the occupied territories.

Trends over Time

In the first period of the Barak government the level of support for the Oslo Agreement came to 63 percent of the entire Jewish public, and the level of belief that it would lead to a permanent peace agreement came to 58 percent. These are among the highest rates that were obtained for the Oslo index since we began measuring it in June 1994. Note that the level of belief in the Oslo process was slightly lower than the level of support for it, though the gap was only 5 percent. The findings show, however, that during the Barak government the rate of support fell from 63 percent to 46 percent, and of belief from 58 percent to 33 percent. That is, toward the end of the Barak government's tenure less than half of the Jewish public supported Oslo and only about a third of it still believed in the chances of reaching a peace agreement with the Palestinians according to the "Oslo formula."

Interestingly, though the decline was in both components of the index, it was much greater in the dimension of belief than of support, so that the gap between the two grew to 13 percent. This indicates that part of the public continued to support the Oslo Agreements while no longer believing in them. The data obtained for the first period of the Sharon government show that the trend of decline in both components continued, though at lower rates. Thus, the level of support in this period stood at 43 percent and the level of belief at 28 percent. In other words, a substantial majority of the public (57%) did not support the Oslo formula and a much larger majority (72%) did not believe in it. It should also be noted that in this period belief continued to decline slightly more than support, so that the gap between them reached 15 percent.

In general, the trend of a steep decline in the Oslo index, which occurred over almost the entire period of Barak's tenure, explains to a great extent his débâcle in the February 2001 elections. Other Peace Index data indicate what caused the erosion in the Oslo formula's status among the public. The Israeli Jewish public seems to have been disappointed, first and foremost, by the Palestinians' reactions to Barak's peace proposals even before the Palestinian *Intifada* again broke out late in September 2000.

Thus, the findings of the survey for July 2000, the month in which the second Camp David conference was held, show that most of the public (67%) believed it was the Palestinians who were responsible for the failure of the conference, with only 12 percent putting the blame on the Israeli side. Furthermore, only 9 percent thought Barak's positions at the conference were too tough, whereas 35 percent thought they were balanced and 45 percent saw them as too accommodating. Indeed, some 60 percent opposed Barak's offer at the conference that Israel transfer to the Palestinians "slightly more" than 90 percent of the territories of the West Bank and the Gaza Strip, compared to 37 percent who supported it. Similarly, only 29 percent agreed to a division of Jerusalem with East Jerusalem becoming the capital of the Palestinian state, if this meant "removing the last obstacle on the path to a peace agreement," compared to 65 percent who opposed this solution. As for the offer, which was reported in the media, that Israel would allow 100,000 refugees to return to Israel proper, the level of those opposing it came to 76 percent compared to 17 percent who supported it. Thus, on these issues there was a large degree of consensus among the Jewish public that included at least half of the supporters of the Oslo Agreement.

However, the criticism of Barak involved not only the sort of concessions he was prepared to make but also his handling of the negotiations with the Palestinians. To the question: "Which side handled the negotiations more wisely in terms of its interests?," twice as many Israelis responded that the Palestinians had done better than those who believed the Israelis had shown more acumen. Not surprisingly, in the wake of the Palestinian *Intifada* that broke out, as noted, in late September 2000, the opposition to Barak's policy intensified along with a further decline in support and belief in the Oslo process, as we saw earlier. It is interesting that in contrast to the dissatisfaction with Barak's policy, which was manifested in the results of the elections held early in February 2001, a large majority of the public supports Sharon's policy even though the *Intifada* continues to claim many victims and the Oslo index continues to sink. The support for the Sharon government seems to stem, on the one hand, from the fact that it is a national unity government as the public already desired in the days of the Barak government, and on the other, from the belief that Sharon would handle negotiations with the Palestinians more firmly and more carefully than Barak.

The Social Basis of the Oslo Supporters and Opponents

Thus far we have discussed trends in the development of Jewish public opinion toward the Oslo process, based on a distinction between rates of supporters and believers in the Oslo formula and rates of opponents and nonbelievers in it. We will now consider the demographic composition of the two camps, that is, whether there are systematic and consistent differences between their social attributes. Because Israeli citizens show extremely high political involvement in foreign and security issues, with their electoral behavior being primarily affected by the positions of the political parties' leaders on these issues, one may reasonably hypothesize that there is a large degree of concordance between the public's positions toward Oslo and the positions of the parties that it supports.

To test this, we classified the respondents to the Peace Index surveys into voters for the left-wing parties, voters for the right-wing parties, and the nonidentified, and examined the three groups' positions toward Oslo. Because of space considerations we will discuss only the levels of support for the agreement, comparing the beginning of the Barak period and the beginning of the Sharon period. It should be recalled, however, that the corresponding percentages for belief in the agreement are much lower than the percentages for support, as we saw earlier.

The findings show that in the first period of the Barak government the level of support for the Oslo process came to 87 percent of the voters for the left-wing parties compared to 38 percent of those for the right-wing parties, while among the nonidentified it stood at 63 percent. These numbers indicate a large (and expected) gap between the left- and right-wing voters in this period in their attitudes toward Oslo, as well as the fact that during this span the Left exhausted almost the full potential of its voters' support for its policy, while at the same time a significant minority of right-wing voters adopted the left-wing parties' positions. Thus, whereas almost 9 out of 10 left-wing voters supported the Oslo process, only 6 of 10 right-wing voters *opposed* it. In other words, in the first period of its tenure the Barak government's policy enjoyed the full support of the left-wing voters, as well as relatively large (close to 40%) support from the right-wing voters and even more (63%) from the nonidentified ones.

A look at the findings from the surveys in the first period of the Sharon government shows that the pattern of differences in the levels of support for Oslo is similar to that for the corresponding period of the Barak government, though the levels of support declined to various degrees among all three groups of voters, with a sharper rate of decline among the left-wing ones than among the right-wing ones. Thus, for the left-wing voters the level of support stood at 65 percent, i.e., a decline of 22 percent compared to the first period of the Barak government, whereas among the right-wing voters support came to 25 percent, a decline of 13 percent. Interestingly, among the nonidentified the level of support stood at 41 percent (a similar rate of decline to the Left's. Overall, the gap between the left- and right-wing voters narrowed in the direction of the Right, though it remained large indeed (40%).

Sociological research on Israeli society has often shown that one of the most important parameters that distinguish between the attitudes and behavior of its Jewish citizens in different areas of life is their degree of commitment to religious observance and beliefs. Hence, the Jewish population is customarily classified into four groups according to degree of religiosity: ultra-Orthodox (about 8% of the Jewish population), religious (about 10%), traditional (about 30%), and secular (about 52%). When we examined the relation between the religiosity of the respondents, according to their self-labeling, and their degree of support for Oslo, we found a particularly strong link, only slightly less pronounced than the link in regard to party voting. This pertained both to the Barak and Sharon periods, as we see below:

	Barak period	Sharon period (in percentages)
Ultra-Orthodox	33	15
Religious	32	24
Traditional	58	34
Secular	76	54

These data show that in both periods the rates of support for Oslo were in inverse proportion to the degree of religiosity – the higher the religiosity, the lower the support. It should be stressed that in the recent period the greatest opposition to the Oslo Agreement is in fact seen among the ultra-Orthodox community, most of which is known to be anti-Zionist. This is in contrast to the religious sector, almost all of which belongs to the Zionist camp. It appears that the ultra-Orthodox represent the hard core of nationalism with a religious-fundamentalist character.

When we compare the two periods, we find that the rates of decline for the traditional and secular sector were larger than for the ultra-Orthodox and the religious, similar to what we saw for the rates of decline in the support of the Left and the Right. In both cases one must take into account that the numerical potential for decline was higher among the two groups whose support for Oslo was higher in the first place, namely, left-wing voters and the secular and traditional sector. Note also that despite the existence of a certain overlap between the two parameters (voting and religiosity), we found in statistical analyses that each of the two parameters has an independent effect on attitudes toward Oslo.

Beyond these effects, it appears that the camps of Oslo supporters and opponents also differ from each other in socioeconomic and demographic terms, though to a smaller extent compared to the attributes of voting and religiosity. Thus, the rates of support for Oslo are consistently higher among those with high levels of education and income. For example, at the beginning of the Barak period these rates stood at 56 percent among those with low education (partial high school or less), 62 percent of the medium-education group (full high school), and 70 percent of those with high education (partial or full academic). Although these gaps indeed narrowed at the end of the period because the rates of support declined in the high-education group, essentially the gap between the three groups remained.

A similar tendency was found for the effects of income level: the higher it is, the higher the support for Oslo. As for the demographic variables, we found, first, that the rates of support for Oslo rise with age, though to a limited extent. In the first period of the Barak government, the levels of support corresponded to the age of the respondents as follows: young (18–34) – 60%, middle age (35–54) – 65%, old and elderly (55 and over) – 68%. In the third period the gaps between the two higher age groups disappeared, while the young group continued to show the lowest levels of support. Although these are relatively small disparities, the finding that young people tend to support the Oslo process less than older people is most interesting since studies in various democratic countries have found that young people tend to identify more with the "peace camp."

An additional and consistent gap in the levels of support for Oslo was found between men and women, with the levels being slightly higher among women both at the beginning and end of the period surveyed. Furthermore, whereas the gaps between the segments of the different groups narrowed during the period, as we saw above, the gap between men and women remained as it was and even grew somewhat. Thus, in the first period of the Barak government the levels of support were 65 percent for women and 61 percent for men, whereas for the Sharon-government period the respective figures were 46 percent and 39 percent. However, in both gender groups a substantial decline in support occurred, as we found for all the other groups. Finally, The findings show that support for Oslo also seems to be influenced by the ethnic factor, being lower among Sephardim than Ashkenazim. It emerges from multivariate statistical analyses, however, that the gaps between these two communities disappear when one takes into account the effects of the other attributes, particularly religiosity and education.

In summary, there are sharp and consistent differences between the social attributes of the sector that supports and believes in the Oslo Agreement and those of the sector that opposes and does not believe in it. The profile of those with positive attitudes clearly consists, first and foremost, of secular left-wing voters who belong to the high socioeconomic stratum. It also shows a relatively high representation of older and elderly people and of women. The profile of those taking negative positions consists of ultra-Orthodox or religious right-wing voters, those of low socioeconomic status, as well as a disproportion of young people and of men. As we have seen, the gaps between the two camps have narrowed over the past two years, as part of the process of erosion in the status of the Oslo Agreement – an erosion that has encompassed the entire Jewish public and especially the social stratum from which most of the Oslo supporters and believers came. Nevertheless, even today that stratum expresses a more positive attitude toward Oslo than the other sectors of this public, and under certain conditions it may return to the dimensions that characterized it in the not very distant past.

CHAPTER 10

How Hamas Thinks

SHAUL MISHAL

Much of Hamas's politics can be explained in terms of its dogmas and practical needs. This interaction is manifested in the tensions among fulfillment of the Islamic duty of holy war (*jihad*) against Israel as the most effective means of political mobilization, reviving the spirit of Palestinian national activism in an Islamic context, and the movement's realistic considerations of political survival and access to resources.

Hamas's effort to secure a dominant public position by committing itself to promote Palestinian national interests while at the same time maintaining its allegiance to an Islamic vision generates an acute predicament. The problem, inherent since the movement's establishment during the early months of 1988, was sharply aggravated by the signing of the September 1993 Israel–Palestine Liberation Organization (PLO) Oslo Accord and the creation of the Palestinian Authority (PA) in Gaza and Jericho in June 1994. Hamas's awareness of the need to secure its presence and influence within the Palestinian population, often at the expense of competition with the popular PA, necessitated flexibility in its uncompromising attitude toward a settlement with Israel.

Yet, by adopting such a strategy, Hamas runs the risk of losing its standing as the normative opposition to the PLO, thus heightening the danger of friction within the movement and opening itself to manipulation by the PA. Adherence to the dogmatic vision also produces confusion and uncertainty, whereas Hamas's conformity to its stated religious doctrine strengthens its credibility among followers and adversaries alike. However, by taking actions that bring Israeli retaliation it runs the risk of undermining the support of large segments of the Palestinian public, which seek an early end to social and economic hardships in the Israeli-held territories – as well as in now PA-administered areas.

A close examination of the decision-making processes shows that Hamas has been markedly balanced, combining realistic considerations with traditional beliefs and arguments, emphasizing visionary goals but also immediate needs. They have demonstrated conformity with the formal Hamas doctrine while showing signs of political flexibility. While a final peace settlement with Israel was forbidden, Hamas left open the option of an agreement provided it assumed a temporary form.[1] And while Hamas rejected the PLO's right to represent the Palestinian people, it did not exclude the possibility of a political coalition "on an agreed program focused on *jihad*."[2]

Hamas demonstrated its flexibility by differentiating between the short-term objective of a Palestinian state in the West Bank and Gaza and the long-term goal of establishing a Palestinian Islamic state on the whole territory of Palestine that would supplant Israel. Adopting this order of objectives, Hamas effectively subordinated the former to the latter by emphasizing the transitional nature and provisional status of any political settlement with Israel.

By interpreting any political agreement involving the West Bank and Gaza Strip as merely a pause on the historic road of *jihad*, Hamas achieved political flexibility without forsaking its ideological credibility. Having adopted the strategy of a temporary settlement, Hamas was ready to acquiesce in the 1993 Oslo process without recognizing Israel; to support the establishment of a Palestinian state in the West Bank and Gaza Strip without ending the state of war or renouncing its ultimate goals; and to consider restraint, but not to give up the armed struggle. Political activity here and now was thus justified in terms of the hereafter. Acceptance of a political settlement in the short run was interpreted as being complementary, not contradictory, to long-term desires. In this respect, Hamas escaped a binary perception regarding its relations with its ideological rivals and political opponents. It took care not to depict its social and political reality as a cluster of mutually exclusive, diametrically opposed categories, characterized by "either-or" relations. In short, Hamas recognized the limits beyond which it could not go on pursuing an "all or nothing" policy to advance ultimate political goals.

The multiplicity of policy devices that were adopted by Hamas enabled its leaders to manipulate normative rules in a pragmatic fashion. Indeed, Hamas leaders were able to move publicly from an "unrealistic" posture of conflict – of total moral commitment to a principle, at whatever cost – toward a more pragmatic bargaining posture, which entails some recognition that certain norms and interests are shared with the other side, and can be used as a basis to reach a workable compromise.[3]

Hamas's efforts to justify its position are best followed by analyzing its attitudes and policy toward the Oslo Accord and the establishment of the PA in Gaza and Jericho in June 1994, the issue of participation in the PA's institutions, and *jihad* against Israel or a temporary peaceful settlement. Its positions combined new political ideas with old beliefs, emphasizing long-range goals and short-term requirements. They demonstrated conformity with the formal Hamas doctrine while showing signs of political flexibility. Patterns of political adjustment in terms of controlled violence, negotiated coexistence, and calculated participation in the PA's emerging institutions became the main features of Hamas's political conduct.

Controlled Violence

Hamas, espousing a religious ideology, aspired to establish an Islamic state in all of Palestine. The liberation of Palestine was to be implemented by armed struggle against Israel, defined as *jihad*. The emphasis on this term was congruent with the set of Islamic symbols and beliefs constituting Hamas's political doctrine. Defined as an Islamic endowment (*waqf*) of the Muslim world as a whole, the duty of *jihad* was not only presented to be applied to any individual Muslim, but as a sole legitimate way to retrieve Palestine in its entirety. Still, Hamas was aware of the limits of its power, on both intra-Palestinian and regional levels. Hamas calculated its strategy on the basis of cost–benefit considerations. *Jihad*, a holy war against Israel, was subordinated to political calculations.

A policy of controlled violence became a key component in Hamas's political strategy and daily conduct. Hamas's concern about the population's day-to-day interests and immediate needs made it increasingly reluctant to translate its dogmatic vision into practice. Calculated policy and confrontational activities thus characterized its mode of operation. Recognizing the limits of its power, Hamas was careful not to step over the precipice and fall into an all-out confrontation with Israel. *Jihad* turned out not to be an ultimate goal but a political instrument amenable to restraints mandated by political considerations.

The Hamas policy of controlled violence against Israel persisted well after the Israeli–Palestinian Declaration of Principles (DoP), known as the Oslo Accord, which was signed on September 13, 1993. Again, it was a policy based on pragmatic profit/loss considerations rather than on bondage to a stated doctrine and rigid dogma. Succinctly expressing the pragmatic policy on terrorist attacks against Israel in the wake of the DoP, the head of Hamas's political bureau, Musa Abu Marzuk, stated that:

> military activity is a permanent strategy that will not change. The modus operandi, the tactics, means and timing are conditional on their benefit. They will change from time to time in order to inflict the heaviest damage on the occupation.[4]

That Hamas's armed struggle was perceived as a means, and not a goal in its own right, was made clear by the movement's leading figures in Gaza. Probably the most outspoken was Mahmud al-Zahar's:

We must calculate the benefit and cost of continued armed operations. If we can fulfill our goals without violence, we will do so. Violence is a means not a goal. Hamas's decision to adopt self-restraint does not contradict our aims, including the establishment of an Islamic state in place of Israel . . . We will never recognize Israel but it might be possible that a truce (*muhadana*) would prevail between us for days, months or years.[5]

Yet, Hamas in the West Bank and Gaza Strip was divided between two major trends regarding the use of violence: a politically-oriented current willing to adjust to the new political realities, which from the very establishment of the PA in June 1994 strove to reach an agreement which would allow it a legal and overt activity, and ways to share power through an envisioned Islamic party; and a military current, comprised mainly of 'Izz al-Din al-Qassam Brigades, who insisted on continued armed struggle and objected to any agreement with the PA which would mean the end of their status and organization.[6]

It is against this backdrop, and fears of confrontation with the PA – as a result of Israeli pressures on Arafat to eliminate Hamas and its social and religious infrastructure – that Hamas leaders repeatedly proposed, since 1995, a conditional cease-fire with Israel. Although many of Hamas's political leaders spoke out in favor of such a cease-fire, they were hardly in agreement regarding its terms. The following terms were mentioned by Hamas's leaders in the West Bank and Gaza: release of all the prisoners; removing the economic closure on the occupied territories; evicting all the settlers (sometime, the Jewish residents of East Jerusalem were also included in this category); and an end to the persecution of Palestinians. Such an agreement would have to be signed by the PA and Israel.

Aware of the Palestinians' initial popular relief at Israel's practical withdrawal from the occupied territories, Hamas forged a strategy that would secure its popularity among the Palestinian masses and arouse popular resistance to the Oslo process, but without being accused of causing its failure, which would perpetuate Israel's hegemony and usurpation of Palestinian land. Hamas pursued a policy of controlled violence against Israel and of dialogue and coexistence with the PA, despite the normative and political difficulties this entailed. The politics of adjustment was perceived by Hamas as preferable to the alternative of a head-on collision with Israel and the PA.

Negotiated Coexistence

The same pattern of controlled violence which Hamas had employed against Israel also characterized its efforts to seek a flexible strategy by which it could coexist with the PLO without being identified with the peace process or seem to have abandoned its original goal of establishing an Islamic state in historic Palestine. This approach found expression in various statements made by its most prominent leader, Shaikh Ahmad Yasin, already in 1988, as the following three examples show: First, Hamas did not rule out the possibility of a Palestinian state in the West Bank and Gaza Strip provided this was considered the first phase toward the establishment of a state in all of Palestine. Second, Hamas was ready to consider international supervision in the territories after the Israeli withdrawal if it were limited in time and did not require direct, clear-cut concessions to Israel. Third, Hamas would reject any attempt to enter into political negotiations with Israel over a peace agreement as long as the Israeli occupation continued; however, Hamas would not exclude such an initiative after a full Israeli withdrawal.[7]

Yasin's statements reflected a growing tendency within Hamas, already prior to the Oslo Accord, to bridge the gulf between the movement's agreed-on prose of reality while maintaining the poetry of its ideology. By adopting a strategy of neither full acceptance nor total rejection of the PLO's program of political settlement, Hamas was able to justify its position in normative terms, explicating such "concessions" as tactical moves. It is here one should look to understand a seemingly contradictory approach to the very idea of a political settlement with Israel. Hamas castigated the PLO's sanctioning of Palestinian participation in the Madrid conference of October 1991, defining it as "the conference for the sellout of Palestine and Jerusalem," while leading Hamas figures made statements about the admissibility, in principle, of a truce (*hudna* or *muhadana*) with the Jews. While a final peace settlement with Israel was forbidden – and, if signed, would be null and void *a priori* – Hamas left open the option of an agreement with Israel provided it assumed a temporary form denoting neither peace (*salam*) nor final conciliation (*sulh*). According to Hamas, these forms of relations with Israel coincide with the Muslims' interest (*maslaha*) and would not legitimize the enemy's presence on occupied Islamic land.[8]

Hamas demonstrated its flexibility by differentiating between the short-term goal of a Palestinian state in the West Bank and Gaza and the long-term goal of establishing a Palestinian Islamic state on the whole territory of Palestine that would replace Israel. Adopting this order of goals, Hamas effectively subordinated the former to the latter by emphasizing the transitional nature and temporary status of any political settlement with Israel.

Under Oslo, Hamas's political maneuverability and independent existence were threatened because Israeli occupation was to be replaced by a PLO-led Palestinian Authority. Hamas was aware that a new situation had emerged in which the Islamic movement would have to confront both Israel and the PLO if it were to adhere to its normative vision. Examining its uneasy options for political action, and seeking to preserve its political

position in the Palestinian society, Hamas was obliged to abide by its
perception of coexistence with the Palestinian Authority.

The rationale for this was clear. All-out confrontation would bolster the
movement's principles and militant image but risk its freedom of action and
possibly its very existence. More dangerous yet, it could erode Hamas's
ability to underwrite social and economic services for the community,
perceived as being crucial to maintain its popular influence. A "successful"
jihad against Israel – one that would end the peace process – would aggra-
vate the socioeconomic plight of the Palestinian society – for which Hamas
would be blamed – and alienate people from the movement. On the other
hand, cooperation with the PLO might place Hamas in a "divide and rule"
trap as a result of the co-optation of segments of the movement's leadership into the system, and undermine Hamas's bargaining position *vis-à-vis*
Israel and the PLO.

The main considerations in favor of a pragmatic approach had been
succinctly explained by Musa Abu Marzuq, head of the movement's
Political Bureau, shortly before the Cairo agreement on implementation of
Palestinian autonomy in Gaza and Jericho. In an article published in
Hamas's internal organ, *al-Risala,*[9] Abu Marzuq expressed concern at the
Israeli–PLO agreement, and described three major threats entailed in
Hamas's continued intransigence toward the current process:

1. A threat to Hamas's presence in Jordan, the "second arena of action
    after Palestine," due to joint Israeli and American pressure.
2. A growing negative perception of Hamas in the international arena as
    a murderous terrorist movement that targeted civilians.
3. Exposure of Hamas to domestic Palestinian criticism as it had no posi-
    tive alternative strategy to the peace process.

According to Abu Marzuq, Hamas's difficulty in coping effectively with
these threats derived from:

1. An identity of interests between the US, Israel, Jordan, and the PLO.
    Additionally, most Arab states and the international community
    supported the peace process and agreed that Hamas posed the main
    threat to its success.
2. Hamas's military inferiority *vis-à-vis* the PA's police and security
    agencies.
3. The Hamas infrastructure's dependence on external financial
    resources, which could be easily curtailed by PA legislation and admin-
    istrative restrictions.

The cumulative effect of the internal debate within Hamas was to
heighten its tendency to differentiate between an attitude toward the

"objective," namely Israel, and the perception of "actual situations." At the declarative level, expressed toward the objective, Hamas reiterated its intransigent rejection of Israel's legitimacy, maintaining that the solution to the conflict was a Palestinian Islamic state "from the river to the sea," i.e., Mandatory Palestine. Yet, blind pursuit of this attitude could paralyze Hamas's political maneuverability and force it to fight the PA or abandon its quest to provide an alternative political frame of reference to the existing order. That this extreme scenario did not occur was due to Hamas's attitude toward "actual situations," which revealed political realism and a recognition of concrete constraints that led Hamas consistently to express willingness to adopt the traditional Islamic concept of truce – *hudna* – with the infidels, in return for a Palestinian state in part of historic Palestine.

The legitimacy of *hudna* as a phase in the course of a defensive *jihad* against the enemies of Islam has been widely discussed – and accepted – by both radical and more moderate Islamic scholars since Sadat signed a peace treaty with Israel in 1979. The concept has been justified by historical precedents ranging from the Prophet's treaties with his adversaries in Mecca (the Treaty of Hudaybiyya, 628 CE) and the Jews of al-Madina, to the treaties signed between Salah al-Din al-Ayyubi and other Muslim rulers, and the Crusades. The common denominator underlying these precedents is that they were caused by Muslim military weakness and concern for the wellbeing (*maslaha*) of the Islamic community, and were later followed by the renewal of war and the defeat of Islam's enemies. In retrospect, these cases of *hudna* were legitimized in *realpolitik* terms and interpreted *a priori* as necessary and temporary pauses on the road of *jihad* against the infidels.

By interpreting any political agreement involving the West Bank and Gaza Strip as merely a pause on the historic road of *jihad*, Hamas achieved political flexibility without losing its ideological credibility. Having adopted the strategy of phases, Hamas was ready to acquiesce in the Oslo process without recognizing Israel; to support the establishment of a Palestinian state in the West Bank and Gaza Strip without ending the state of war or renouncing its ultimate goals; and to consider restraint, but not to give up the armed struggle, instead ascribing violent actions to uncontrollable groups and distinguishing between "political" and "military" wings within the movement, while claiming the right to launch operations from areas under Israeli rule. Political activity here and now was thus justified in terms of hereafter. Acceptance of a political settlement in the short run was interpreted as being complementary, not contradictory, to long-term desires.

Hamas's willingness to enter into a political settlement with Israel on a provisional basis, that is, without compromising its ultimate goals, enabled it to consolidate a working formula of coexistence with the PA. This involved the creation of joint *ad hoc* conciliation forums with Fatah and committees on national concerns such as the Palestinian prisoners held by

Israel. Hamas's willingness to maintain a negotiated coexistence with the
PA was reciprocated by the latter on grounds of cost/benefit calculations.
True, Arafat sought to weaken and divide Hamas and co-opt it into the PA,
but his cautious policy also reflected a preference for dialogue over head-
on collision. Since neither side could sustain the price of a full-fledged
attempt to eliminate the other, both preferred cautious acquiescence in the
other's existence, rather than risking their public legitimacy in a showdown.

Calculated Participation

Hamas's political strategy of neither official recognition nor total rejection
of the PA has been apparent in the movement's internal debate and concrete behavior concerning its participation in the PA's executive and
representative institutions. Hamas's need to ensure its survivability
and continued growth made necessary its access to power and resources.
On the other hand, Hamas had a vested interest in minimizing the damage
accruing to its political reputation by its participation in the PA, as this
might be construed as a deviation from its religious dogma.

Taking into account Hamas's refusal to recognize the PA, involvement
in its administrative apparatuses without either an official presence or
direct representation would furnish a useful means to gain some benefits
from the post-Oslo processes without paying the political cost of their
endorsement. Moreover, involvement would act as a safety valve for
Hamas, reducing the threats to its continued activity and public support.

Indeed, the strategy of participation through unofficial presence
dictated Hamas's behavior on the incorporation of its members to the PA's
executive bodies. Hamas encouraged its adherents to join the PA's administration on a personal basis. Hamas justified this by distinguishing
between two perceptions of the PA: as a sovereign political power, but also
as an administrative apparatus geared to provide services to the public.
While the former image represented political principles and national
symbols, the latter was perceived to be instrumental, linked to reality. As
a political center committed to enforce exclusive authority and articulate
collective ideas, common symbols, and collective beliefs, the PA was denied
Hamas's legitimacy. However, as an administrative apparatus designated
to enforce law and order and provide employment and services to the
community, the PA could be acknowledged.

Thus, although Hamas propaganda continued to discredit and de-
legitimize the PA's leadership, Hamas was careful not to alienate the rank
and file within the PA administration. This approach, and the PA's policy
of preferring coexistence over confrontation with Hamas, led the latter,
already in October 1993, to instruct its adherents to refrain from creating
a hostile atmosphere against the Palestinian police. On the contrary, police

officers were to be encouraged to collaborate in Hamas armed actions against Israel and even to "initiate suicide actions . . . exploiting their possibilities of [available] weapons and freedom of maneuver to support the resistance."[10]

Also, Hamas encouraged its members to fill official positions in the West Bank religious establishment, explaining that these were administrative positions, providing services to the community, without bearing representative significance. By reducing the significance of participation in the PA's administration to the individual level and underlining its executive aspects, Hamas could benignly portray such participation as unofficial, with no political or symbolic meaning.[11]

Flexible Thinking and Structural Features

Hamas was able to bridge the gap between its official dogma and "here and now" considerations as long as it justified pragmatic moves through normative terms and to engage in pragmatic initiatives that carried tolerable organizational risks. Islamic argumentation thus played an important role in legitimizing pragmatic conduct. Such argumentation probably helped facilitate the acceptance of pragmatic moves by the rank-and-file, and reduced the risk of division within the movement. The notion of *sabr* can serve as a typical example of Hamas's willingness and ability to invoke normative justification for public opposition and political moves that might have been perceived as deviations from religious dogma.

Sabr enabled the Hamas leadership to justify ongoing efforts to build the Islamic society from below, according legitimacy to the movement's preference of long-term religious and communal activities over a short-term avant-garde vision of revolution from above. It was in this context that Hamas drew a clear distinction between a permanent settlement of the Israeli–Palestinian dispute, which it unequivocally rejected, and a temporary settlement, which it deemed tolerable; between a short-term policy necessitating the temporary delay of ultimate goals in accordance with circumstances and constraints, and a long-term strategy based on firm adherence to Islamic radical vision; and between willingness to accept *ad hoc* arrangements of coexistence as the lesser evil, and denial of the PLO's and PA's legitimacy. *Sabr* thus served as a normative device of legal interpretation, providing Hamas with a measure of maneuverability to minimize the negative effects of deviation from the official dogma, which entailed pragmatic moves and responses.

Yet, the militancy of Hamas's grassroots activists, the vacuum within the senior and middle ranks due to arrests and the dependence on external funds meant growing influence by Hamas leaders outside the territories over the movement's mainstay in the Gaza Strip and the West Bank. The outside leaders, most of them deportees from the occupied territories, took the opportunity to try and deepen their control over the movement. In comparison to the inside members, the outside leadership consisted of relatively young, educated technocrats who belonged to the radical groups within Hamas. They associated themselves with the vision of political Islamism – that is, a revolution from above – rather than with religious revelation through ordinary processes of communal activity. This radical perception, which coincided with the militancy of the rank-and-file in the occupied territories, helped the "outside" Hamas to reorganize the movement's activity into a hierarchical order. This initiative was designed to accord the "outside" leadership control over the "inside" and secure the subordination of the latter's operational ranks.

Apparently, one might argue that the PA's growing political control, and the differences between Hamas's "inside" and "outside" leadership, would intensify the latter's effort to secure its influence within the movement through escalation of the military effort, driving a wedge between the military command and the "inside" political leadership. However, Israel's and the PA's massive pressure on Hamas, particularly on its military apparatus, weakened the "outside" control over the local leadership. Under these circumstances, the tension between the "outside" and "inside" leaders could have an adverse effect on Hamas's organizational unity, putting at risk the fragile coexistence between the two parties. In turn, such developments could undermine Hamas's ability to adopt a politics of adjustment and thus adjust itself to the new political reality.

That Hamas managed to avoid an organizational split and avert structural chaos was due to three main causes. First, the policy of the PA, which, as a matter of tactics, preferred dialogue and coexistence over a military confrontation with Hamas. Second, the fact that Israel withdrew the demand that the PA dismantle Hamas and was willing to be content with the PA's preventive steps against radical Islamic terrorism. Third, the provisional character of the Oslo Accords, which left unresolved, until the final status talks, key issues such as the future of Jewish settlements beyond the Israeli borders of 1967, Jerusalem, permanent political status of the PA, and the demarcation of Palestinian territory. In addition, Arafat's repeated commitment to the establishment of an independent Palestinian state, with East Jerusalem as its capital, helped bridge part of the gap between Hamas and the PA pertaining to the political goals of the peace process.

It was Hamas's internal weakness and the PA's and Israel's perception of the Oslo process, and the role of Hamas in this context, that rendered the politics of adjustment a preferable option to both Hamas's "inside" and "outside" leaderships. A strategy of all-out confrontation on the part of the "outside" leadership, in an attempt to undermine the Israeli–Palestinian Oslo process, would have exacted a high cost. In the short run, uncontrolled violence against Israel and the PA could disrupt the process. In the long run, however, the deterioration of the Oslo process would trigger violent retaliations by Israel – including further tightening of the closure of the autonomy areas – and the PA, producing growing public resentment against Hamas which could effectively alienate its local, non-military leadership. Thus, the effect of a policy of all-out confrontation by Hamas's "outside" faction could help consolidate the position of the PA and the "inside" Hamas leaders.

As for the latter, collaboration with the PA, or participation in its institutions to the point of *de facto* recognition of the PA, in disregard of the "outside" leadership, might have accorded the "inside" leaders personal political benefits. Yet, this would have generated extensive opposition among Hamas's rank-and-file, undermining the legitimacy of the "inside" leadership. Arguably, then, despite the "outside" leadership's control over material resources and the civil and military apparatus, as long as the nature of the permanent Israeli–Palestinian settlement remains vague and the PA's tolerant policy toward Hamas is sustained, the movement will probably continue to adhere to its politics of adjustment as a guiding political strategy.

Still, given the complex Palestinian political arena, one may argue that accelerated progress toward a permanent settlement would not lead Hamas automatically to reach the point of confrontation with the PA. Hamas is reform more than revolutionary; more populist than *avant-garde*; more political than military; more communal than universalist. Hamas is aware of cost–benefit considerations and has been markedly calculated in its decisions. Similarly, the PA has demonstrated pragmatism over extremism and has subscribed to the prose of reality rather than the poetry of ideology. Hamas has been cognizant of its limitations, though without admitting it; anxious to preserve Palestinian national unity – hence its extreme sensitivity to public opinion – particularly in view of the PA's volatile diplomatic process with Israel. Thus, one might assume that even under conditions of crisis in PA–Hamas relations, both sides would remain faithful to their basic inclination to avert a total showdown.

A Concluding Note

As demonstrated above, Hamas was far from being fixated on unrealistic "all or nothing" objectives and on modes of action based on a zero-sum political perception. Hamas, despite the perception that it only catered to fantasies, actually demonstrated a growing awareness of shifting political circumstances and a willingness to entertain cost–benefit policy calculations. Hamas, then, was definitely far different from its world image: a one-track organization possessing a monolithic, fanatic vision, unshakable fundamentalist interests, rigidly binary perceptions, and intransigent preferences. In fact, were Hamas to adopt such an unbending approach, it would be counterproductive, increasing the movement's isolation in the local Palestinian, inter-Arab, and international arenas.

Close examination of Hamas's declared principles pitted against its concrete actions shows that it was in Hamas's interest to become involved in political activity and not to exclude the possibility of a settlement – albeit of a temporary character – through non-violent means. Consequently, Hamas's political imagination and its organizational energies have for the most part been directed toward striking a balance between constantly growing conflicting considerations, competing demands, and contradictory needs.

Taking into account Hamas's fears that a strategy of clear-cut decisions would lead to the point of no return, as well as its need to search for a policy that balances national and local interests and maintains an equilibrium among multiple normative commitments, one cannot exclude the possibility that a continuity of the Israeli–Palestinian peace negotiations, and of patterns of coexistence between Hamas and the PA, may encourage the organization to search for political understandings with Israel. Probably Hamas's ability to justify such a move in the eyes of the radicals and gain rank-and-file support as well would depend, to a large extent, on its leadership's ability to adopt a strategy of political ambiguity. In such a strategy Hamas would rely on a third party – the PA and/or Jordan – to negotiate political understandings and modes of workable coexistence with Israel.

Looking at the dramatic shift in Israeli–Egyptian relations in the late 1970s, and at the developments in the Israeli-PLO conflict during the early 1990s, one cannot escape the conclusion that what had seemed improbable assumed an aura of inevitability. Often, people, movements, and nations terrorize the entire world just to become part of it.

Notes

1 See Mu'tamar 'Ulama' Filastin, "Fatwa al-Musharaka fi Mu'tamar Madrid wal-Sulh Ma'a Isra'il," Jerusalem, November 1, 1991.

2 Leaflet, "Bayan lil-Tarikh . . . La Limu'tamar Bay' Filastin wa-Bayt al-Maqdis," September 23, 1991; Leaflet, "Fatwa al-Musharaka fi Mu'tamar Madrid wal-Sulh Ma'a Isra'il," November 1, 1991.

3 F. G. Bailey, *Strategems and Spoils: A Social Anthropology of Politics* (New York: Shocken Books, 1969), pp. 174–81.

4 *Filastin al-Muslima,* June 1994.

5 *al-Quds,* October 12, 1995.

6 *al-Watan al-'Arabi,* November 4, 1994, p. 27; *al-Wasat,* September 28, 1995, pp. 23–4; *Kol Ha-'ir* (Jerusalem), March 8, 1996, pp. 68–71.

7 *Yedioth Aharonoth,* September 16, 1988.

8 Mu'tamar 'Ulama' Filastin, "Fatwa al-Musharaka fi Mu'tamar Madrid wal-Sulh Ma'a Isra'il," Jerusalem, November 1, 1991; Abdallah Azzam, *al-Difa'*

'An Aradi al-Muslimin Ahamm Furud al-A'yan (Jidda: Dar al-Mujtama, 1987), pp. 59–60.

9   *al-Risala* (Hamas's internal organ), April 21, 1994.

10 Hamas internal circular: "Siyasat wa-Madamin al-Khitab al-I'lami lil-Marhala al-Qadima (Ithra Ittifaq Ghazza-Ariha)," October 28, 1993.

11 *al-Quds*, October 2, 1994.

CHAPTER 11

The Palestinian Citizens of Israel and the Peace Process: The Case of an Unbuilt Bridge

REUVEN AHARONI AND JOSEPH GINAT

The Middle East peace process, beginning at the Madrid Conference in October 1991, aroused renewed interest in the situation and conditions of Israel's Palestinian Arab citizens. The peace process offered them many more opportunities to discuss their status and their fate in Israel freely. Israel and the PLO's mutual recognition eliminated many prohibitions. That which was once unimaginable and forbidden became a legitimate part of the new political reality. Visits made by Israeli Arab politicians and public figures to Tunis, Egypt,[1] and, after the Palestinian Authority was established, to Gaza as well, became routine. The intervention of Egyptian and Palestinian entities in Arab politics in Israel was no longer perceived as unacceptable, and Israeli Palestinian leaders asked their advice freely. Nor are they any longer afraid of the accusation that they are operating as a lobby for the national Palestinian movement, and the PLO now urges them to vote for the peace camp.[2] The Islamic movement has outspokenly intervened in Islamic matters in Jerusalem, and its leaders have embarked on missions of mediation between the PLO and Palestinian Authority and the Hamas.

In the occupied territories Palestinian Arab citizens of Israel were called "the inside Arabs," or "the 1948 Arabs," but ever since the PLO recognized the State of Israel the term "Israeli Palestinians" has begun to appear in a number of Palestinian publications. This is evidence of a new recognition that has gradually emerged in the newly evolving political reality. It recognizes that Israeli Palestinians are not part of the negotiations for the resolution of the Israeli–Palestinian conflict. A decade has passed since the Madrid Conference where the peace process began, and it is now possible to conduct a comparative examination of the issue before us regarding the peace process and its effects on the Arab community in Israel. This chapter is based on three main sources of information: interviews published by the Arab and Israeli press in Israel; an examination of the Arab parties' platforms; and the results of the Knesset and local Arab government elections since the peace process began. It also uses a survey conducted in January–February 2000 among a sample group of Arab citizens of Israel. We also examined various researchers' approaches as expressed in most of the academic conferences held during this period. From the Madrid Conference until several months after the signing of the Oslo Accords, Arab personages and media, as well as academic researchers and public figures in the Jewish sector, were intensely considering the role that the Arabs in Israel should play in the peace process. They looked at its effects on Arab society and politics as well as on the relations between Arabs and Jews in Israel. However, the worse the deadlock in the talks, the further this issue was pushed aside while the focus on the internal arena and its problems increased.

The Madrid Conference was widely covered in the partisan and the independent Arab press in Israel. Various approaches toward the peace process were already being formulated among the Arabs in Israel, approaches that are still manifested today. The writers and commentators emphasized the national pride and unity among all sections of the Palestinian nation, including its Israeli section. The Democratic Front for Peace, in its journal *al-Ittihad,* the Progressive Party for Peace in its journal *al-Watan,* and the Arab Democratic Party in its journal, *al-Diar,* all expressed support for the Madrid Conference and the positions presented by the Palestinians. The independent newspapers *al-Sunnara* and *Kul al-Arab* also expressed similar views. On one occasion two groups, *Abna' al-Balad* (Sons of the Country) and parts of the Islamic Movement, objected to the very existence of the conference and to Palestinian participation in its discussions. The first signs were also beginning to appear of a debate regarding the role of Israeli Palestinian citizens in the peace process and their fate after an agreement was reached, as well as the argument as to whether the PLO could represent them in the peace talks.

It seemed as though Palestinian Israeli citizens were well represented in the Madrid Conference, although there was no Arab representative in the Israeli delegation. Lutfi Mash'ur, editor of *al-Sunnara* newspaper, wrote, "they constituted a presence that would also continue during the negotiations." According to Mash'ur, a group of activists from Israel, along with Palestinians in the occupied territories and abroad, had prepared a special file including suggestions regarding the fate of the Palestinians in Israel, and they intended to raise the issue in the bilateral talks.[3] Some support for this was voiced by Radwan Abu Ayyash, later an official in the Palestinian Authority, at a meeting held in Umm Al-Fahem. He said that a special file pertaining to "Arabs of 1948" (the Palestinian Arabs who were in Israel since 1948) had been prepared for the discussions to be held in the future between Israel and the PLO after the arguments were over and the agreements signed. Abu Ayyash added that Knesset member Muhammad Mi'ari had participated in the Madrid Conference as a representative of the Palestinians in Israel.[4]

Later, Abu Ayyash explained that he had meant to say that "after an independent Palestinian state was founded, your matters [i.e., those of the Arabs in Israel] will be discussed with mutual understanding and in co-ordination with the independent Palestinian government, in accordance with what you see fit, and at your initiative."[5] Mi'ari himself explained the meaning of the mentioned "file," saying that if the Palestinian problem was to be referred to in principle, it should be kept in mind that the Israeli Palestinians constituted a fifth of the Palestinian nation. The Palestinian delegation included the issue of discrimination against the Palestinian Arabs in Israel under the general title of the "Human Rights" issues. They (the Palestinians) could certainly raise this issue for discussion, just as Israel could raise the issue of the Syrian Jews.[6]

It seemed that at this point there were those among the Arab public in Israel who considered it natural for the PLO or some form of Palestinian representation to speak on their behalf with representatives of the Israeli government, while believing that they could promote their affairs and rights in Israel. Mi'ari corrected himself by saying that after no Arab representative had been appointed on Israel's behalf, and after they had discovered that the matters of the Arabs in Israel would not be raised at all in the talks, an attempt was made to take an active and independent part and to achieve recognition.

Arab politicians in Israel considered the problems pertaining to the Arab community in Israel a legitimate issue clearly connected to the peace process, mainly to the matter of mutual recognition of Israel and the PLO. The Arab press in Israel showed clear signs that Arab citizens of Israel considered themselves part of the peace process, and demanded that the Palestinians as well as other Arab countries take them into account. On the other hand, Israel would have to consider them too.

Even now, more outspoken demands are beginning to be made regarding two topics that will receive an important place in the political agenda of the Palestinian minority in Israel. The first is the demand to link the problem of the Palestinians in Israel with Israeli withdrawal from the occupied territories, and the second, to establish independent organizations and institutions similar to those established by the Palestinians in the occupied territories.

The members of the Progressive Party for Peace were the most outspoken in these matters. Aziz Shehada linked his demand that Israel withdraw from the territories to the need to solve the problem of the Palestinians in Israel, whom the Israeli law called the "Arabs of Israel." He specified the issues at hand. "They suffer from various forms of discrimination, land appropriation, corruption of their national identity and division into religious communities, limitations concerning budgets, and development designed to pressure them to emigrate. But they will remain rooted in their land of origin – in the Galilee, in the 'Triangle' and in the Negev; peace will guarantee that they be given their national and political rights, their equality and the right to their lands, the right to budgets and to participation in the government relative to their proportion in the population."[7]

Shehada thus repeated his party's traditional stance, demanding a certain degree of autonomy for Palestinian Arab citizens in Israel and recognition as a national minority.[8] Muhammad Mi'ari, head of the party, said that "until these things are realized, we are closely following the process, supporting whatever the Palestinian leadership proposes in attempting to assess the situation, and the role we can fulfill according to the current rules of the game. We can do things that they (the Palestinians in the territories) cannot do. For example, they cannot make a non-confidence proposal in the Knesset.[9] In other words, Mi'ari and his party supported the idea that the Palestinian delegation could represent the Arab Israeli citizens.

Nazir Yunes, one of the founders of the Progressive Party, has stated, "The PLO did not represent us in Madrid. The Palestinians in Israel are the ones who should represent me in the negotiations concerning my fate as a Palestinian. We must act to establish independent organizations that will operate for the people, such as the political committees in the [West] Bank and the [Gaza] Strip."[10]

The Israeli Communist Party also took a stand regarding the Palestinian society within Israel, and particularly the party's role in the peace process. Emil Habibi wrote that the Communist Party contributed to the shift in the attitude toward the conflict among the Palestinians in general, Palestinian Israelis (Israeli Arabs), and Israelis. "It is no secret that we have reached a peace conference thanks to the position of the Palestinian Communists. They were the first to predict the future, and they emerged from darkness onto the path of democracy." He did not hesitate to accuse "certain Palestinian leaders" of preventing the peace conference between Israel and the Palestinians from occurring earlier. Israel, he claimed, missed the chance to utilize its Arab citizens as a bridge to peace, by discriminating against them and oppressing their aspirations for contact with their Palestinian brothers. However, he concludes, "I would like to calm the Arab public in Israel by saying that a central role awaits them in determining the future of this land – a role that must guide them in their everyday life."[11]

In another article written after the conference was adjourned, Habibi developed the idea he had presented earlier, answering both the objectors among the Arab minority in Israel and those who compared their fate with that of the Palestinians in the territories, stating, "We refused to accept the slogan *Al-Jalil qabel Al-Halil* (the Galilee before Hebron). We did not ask to send a delegation to Madrid and we did not ask to have our affairs discussed, because we will solve our problems along with the Israeli democratic powers." He believes that as a result of peace being achieved, most of the Israeli Arabs' problems will be solved.[12] In other words, Habibi disagrees with the opinion of those who claimed that the PLO represents the Palestinians in Israel as well.

This opinion was accepted by many leading figures and by the majority of the Arab public in Israel. Mi'ari also claimed that those who said the Palestinian delegation represented them meant representation only regarding matters of principle. This opened the debate within the Palestinian community in Israel as to how involved it should become in the peace process, what its role in the process should be, who should represent it, and whether there was room to plan various agreement possibilities regarding its status if and when a Palestinian state was established. Confusion, ambivalence, caution, and ambiguity marked the declarations made by Arab personages, as illustrated by Mi'ari's remark, "Our mission is to keep in touch with, but not become an integral part of the negotiations."

Approaches of Various Researchers and Personages

There is a tendency among researchers of Arab Palestinian society in Israel to link regional processes and events with events taking place in the local area. This is clearly manifested in the literature on the subject under consideration. Some researchers find a clear connection between the initial peace contacts that first began in September 1993 and the municipal elections held in November of that year. Researchers tried to find a similar connection regarding each one of the election campaigns for the Knesset and local municipalities held since the Madrid Conference and the Oslo Accords. This tendency led them to ask erroneous questions and to assume the existence of a connection between national politics and local events in the municipal arena.

For the Palestinian citizens of Israel, such a connection is groundless and basically artificial. They consider the large political processes distant arenas, controlled by forces that ignore them and their needs, relegate them to a marginal position and regard them as a forgotten playing card. In this sense, they see no difference between the Knesset and the various, constantly changing peace talk sites. Thus the local area remained by default the only arena for significant political activity. Moreover, the marginal role of the Palestinian Arab citizens in the peace process caused an intensification of activity in the local arena.

A good example of the disjunction between the two fields of activity is Umm Al-Fahem. In the 1992 Knesset elections, over 70 percent of its inhabitants voted for the anti-clerical Democratic Peace Front, while in November 1993, mayor Sheikh Ra'id Salah, leader of the Islamic Movement and objector to the peace process, won the municipal elections with more than 70 percent of the votes. This is no indication of the Islamic Movement's status throughout the entire sector. Salah was elected because of his personal reliability and a municipal activity that was considered successful and promising.

Seminars held at various universities and research institutions have dealt with the past and future effects of the peace process on the Arabs in Israel. Some of the questions researchers were asked included:

- How are the Oslo Accords affecting the Arabs of Israel?
- Will the discussion on the Palestinians in the occupied territories also encourage the Arabs in Israel to begin their own national struggle, or will the opposite perhaps occur, and the Palestinian Arab community try to integrate better into the state after the national tension is relieved?
- What about the Islamic Movement's position in Israel with regard to the peace accords?

The 1993 municipal elections served as a pretext for such a conversation. Sarah Ozacky-Lazar was the only one to directly discuss these questions. She stated that one of the most interesting phenomena observed was Arab society's total preoccupation with internal matters, while the national issue was not even considered in the elections – not even in the election propaganda of parties of a national character, such as the Democratic Front for Peace, the Arab Democratic Party, and the Islamic Movement. "It was as though the political issue, the Israeli–Palestinian conflict, had been resolved and was no longer discussed, while instead the talk was about the Palestinian Arab citizens' internal, civil struggle – that is, about their future status in Israeli society."[13]

At the same time, she found that the candidates' many visits to Tunis seemed to indicate an opposite tendency to the inward focus.[14] However, the visits made by local candidates to Tunis were not intended to affect the campaigns or to influence the direction of the peace talks. They were designed to show that the candidate recognized the PLO's supreme status and that the PLO recognizes the legitimacy of his candidacy – a preliminary condition without which it was impossible at the time to become a public figure among the Palestinian citizens of Israel. As time passed and the peace talks entered a cycle of crises and interruptions, the visits made by election candidates to the PLO leadership no longer served as a source of encouragement and inspiration. In the following election campaigns only marginal use was made of photo opportunities. This indicated that the peace process had almost completely ceased to exist as an issue in the election propaganda.

Alongside the seminars, many Jewish and Arab intellectuals, public figures, and researchers voiced their views and published their findings regarding the future of the Arab citizens of Israel following the anticipated peace between Israel and the Palestinians. Many surveys and studies were conducted, yielding an abundance of publications containing apocalyptic prophesies regarding an imminent *Intifada* among the Palestinians in Israel if their demands were not met in step with the progress being made in the peace process with the Palestinians. On the other hand, researchers such as Amiram Gonen and Rasem Hamaise made optimistic predictions regarding endless employment possibilities that would present themselves to the Arab citizens of Israel in the Palestinian Entity and Arab countries. The employment of Israeli Arabs in the Palestinian settlements and in the Arab countries would be so great as to do damage to the local economy of the Arab settlements in Israel.[15] These investigators also assumed that the government would redirect its attention to developing the Palestinian Entity and cut down its investment in the Arab towns, thus causing tension within the Arab population in Israel. This tension would become manifested in a social struggle of a national political nature, including strikes, demonstrations and protests.[16] Aluf Har-Even wrote, under the title "Will Civil Peace be Established?", that if the Arabs of Israel were not integrated into the government establishments, and the rate of economic development in their settlements continued to lag behind the economic development in the Palestinian Entity, they might demand autonomy within the borders of the Green Line.[17]

In one seminar, Eli Rekhess stated, "the Arab minority in Israel is at a turning point." He claimed that the implications of the accords for the Israeli Arabs were varied and sometimes contradictory. On one hand, Israel's recognition of the PLO and the Palestinian nation brought relief to Arab citizens of Israel, but on the other hand it also gave indirect legitimization to the recognition of their national status. In his view, the accords would, first, turn Palestinian Arab citizens of Israel into a "bridge" between Israel and the Arab world. At the same time, they would increase the socioeconomic differences between Arabs and Jews in Israel and perpetuate the marginality of the Arabs compared to the Palestinians in the territories, who would enjoy mobility by means of jobs and positions in all areas of Palestinian government.[18]

In fact, almost none of these results actually came to pass. Palestinian Arabs in Israel are self-focused and concentrate on their own matters, building an infrastructure of independent organizations and institutions. The Palestinians within the Palestinian Authority do not serve as a model to be imitated, by Israeli Palestinians, and they understand that as a people and a group they are not influential in the peace process. They are busy with the political development of the Palestinian minority that began to accelerate in the mid-1970s unrelated to the peace process. It was mainly influenced by changes and developments in the political mechanisms and economy in Israel and by routine contact with the Palestinian population in the occupied territories. Arab intellectuals and public figures in Israel affirm this.

The seminars served as a stage for Arab intellectuals and politicians. These groups presented their views on the peace process and its effects on Arab society in Israel, on which they are divided. In a seminar held at Tel Aviv University, Adel Mana' stated that after a Palestinian state was founded in the occupied territories, the Arabs in Israel would feel that they were the main victims of peace, since they would be left without a clear identity of their own. Therefore, Israel must become "the state of all its citizens" and maintain its Jewish character only symbolically.

Walid Sadeq said that following the signing of the accords between Israel and the PLO and the progress made toward a permanent status agreement, the government would, in practice, have to grant full equality to all its Arab and Jewish citizens. He expressed pessimism regarding the ability of the Palestinian community in Israel to serve as a bridge for economic cooperation between Israel and the Palestinians in the occupied territories, since they lacked the means to do so (such as capital, skilled manpower, etc.).

Salem Jubran, a writer and political journalist as well as the former editor of the *al-Ittihad* newspaper, put forth a different thesis. He claimed that the political climate had essentially changed following the Israel–PLO accords. "It was as though a heavy stone had been lifted off the Israeli Arabs following the accords. For the first time you feel that in practice what is good for the Jews is good for the Palestinians." Jubran assessed that greater cooperation would develop between Jews and Arabs in Israel, continuing, "While the Palestinians' right to self-definition is being realized in the form of a Palestinian state founded in the occupied territories, we are being excluded from this process with the PLO and Israel's agreement. My status in Israel is permanent. I am outside the political realization of the Palestinians."

Jalal Abu Tu'ma, former mayor of Baqa Al-Gharbiyya, emphasized the intentions of the Arabs in Israel to become more integrated in the fabric of Israeli life after the agreement was signed. However, their goal will be more focused than it has been in the past – that of achieving full equality with the Jewish population. If this goal is not attained, even in the age of peace, the potential for escalation will increase.[19]

Turning Outwards

The Arabs in Israel use the peace process mainly to attack the Israeli government and to point out their troubles. During the strike of the heads of the local Arab municipal councils, which took place in July and August of 1994, the strike leaders responded by saying that the Israeli government was making peace with its neighbors, but was making no effort whatsoever to resolve the problem of Israel's Arab citizens. True, they said, they are much better off than the Jordanians, but the comparison is not with them, but with the Jewish citizens of the state. In their distress, the heads of the Arab community threatened to go to the UN and present their concerns there, as other ethnic minorities had done in the past. This is undoubtedly a direct result of the effects of the peace process on the national agenda of the Palestinian citizens of Israel.

In recent years, the sacred principle of territorial sovereignty, forbidding any form of intervention in the internal affairs of countries – including cases of discriminations and persecution of ethnic minorities – is gradually being replaced by a new concept. According to this concept, human rights and ethnic minority rights are also within the responsibilities of the international community. Meanwhile, the position that the international community holds authority on matters of basic human rights through humanitarian intervention, contradictory to the principle of sovereignty, has been confined to extreme cases such as Kurdistan and Bosnia. It is possible, however, that claims regarding the deprivation of an Arab–Israeli national minority would not be rejected outright in international forums. Therefore, the Arabs in Israel are anxious to attain recognition as an ethnic national minority.

As early as July 1992, a document issued by the office of the Prime Minister's Advisor on Arab Affairs in Israel (before this function was abolished) indicated the increasing tendency of Arab citizens to turn to international bodies in protest of discrimination against them. This document was titled, "The Arabs of Israel and the International Community."[20] Indeed, the independently initiated contacts with Western organizations and groups by the heads of Arab municipalities began to bear fruit during 1991–2.[21] The continuous deprivation and discrimination with regard to routine budgets, development budgets, future planning and execution, the long-felt disappointment, and the internalization of the rules of the political game in Israel in recent years, have all pushed them outward.

The Madrid Conference constituted a first chance to voice these complaints, and Muhammad Mi'ari attended as an undisputed participant. He declared that he had come to talk with the world so that the Arab Israeli citizens would not remain outside the picture, and that picture included the sewers of Umm Al-Fahem. Before he departed on a tour of the United States shortly after the conference, he said: "We must not remain disconnected from processes that will affect us as well. We are part of the Palestinian nation, and every development is also our business. Our objective is to open channels to international organizations, to institutions that act on behalf of civil rights, to the UN and to the European community."[22]

In 1993, at least 160 volunteer organizations were active in the Arab sector. They were registered as non-political and non-ideological associations. This number does not include the Islamic Movement organizations. The European community's comprehensive program for the development of the Third World included a project designed to give aid to non-prosperous communities in the first world. The Arab sector in Israel is generally assigned to this category.

An important and exclusive source of financing for the associations of the Arab sector is a Palestinian fund operating from Europe, called the *al-Ta'aun*. In recent years this fund has made many contributions to the associations' activities, which mainly include community, education, social, cultural and health services. In July 1992, an organization called the Support and Counseling Service for Volunteer Organizations, founded in 1982, initiated a project "Equal Rights for Arab Citizens of Israel." In the first year following the Madrid Conference, one of the most important organizations, "The Galilee Association for Health and Research," headed by Dr. Hatem Cana'na, applied to sources abroad to ask for funds for establishing alternative health institutions. The sewage system of the town of Rameh was funded by this association.

The matter of the unrecognized Bedouin settlement of Ramiya, whose lands were designated for expanding the town of Carmiel, became the test case for Arab leadership and began to draw attention in many Arab countries. The Dutch embassy began to take interest in the sewage project of the town of Jaljuliya, and in May 1992 the State Department of the United States asked for information on the sewage of Kafr Qassem. The peak of this tendency to shift the struggle toward topics that would draw media attention in the West occurred in February 1992, when the Galilee Association applied to the International Water Tribunal in Hague, Holland, claiming that Israel was preventing unrecognized Arab settlements access to drinking water.[23]

How Palestinian Arabs in Israel Perceive the Peace Process

After the Basic Principles Accords between Israel and the PLO were signed in Oslo in September 1993, public debate on the Palestinian Israeli citizens' practical involvement in the peace process diminished. However, the accords were broadly supported. After they were signed, 63 percent of the Arabs in Israel expressed satisfaction with the agreement between Israel and the PLO – the "Gaza and Jericho First" agreement. Over 50 percent expressed the opinion that the PLO leadership and the delegation to the negotiations represented the expectations of the entire Palestinian nation.[24] Most of the newspapers supported the agreement. Samih Al-Qassem, editor of *Kul Al-Arab*, called it "the swallow heralding the Palestinian spring."[25] *Al-Ittihad* wrote, "From an agreement of the brave to the peace of the brave."[26] On the other hand, the *Islamic Movement Journal* expressed resolute objection.[27] However, the Palestinians in Israel quickly understood that they constituted a marginal factor in the process, and that their interests were considered an internal Israeli affair that should not be brought to discussion in international forums. Declarations and activity regarding this issue served primarily for internal political needs.

At the same time, there was a gradual intensification of the internal debate on the fate of the Israeli Palestinian citizens and their future status in Israel. The Palestinian minority succeeded for the first time in clearly defining its role in the general status of the Israeli–Palestinian conflict. Thus, alongside the mutual recognition achieved between Israel and the PLO, there was also the recognition that special and separate treatment must be given to the relations between Israel and its Jewish majority and the Palestinian citizens in the country. More spokesmen of the Palestinian public in Israel began to discuss issues at the center of this relationship, such as civil equality, the nature of the State of Israel, and the problems of lands and refugees.

The peace process did indeed arouse great expectations among the Palestinian citizens of Israel. The phrase, "My country is making peace with my people" became popular among the Arab public. However, from March 1996, when the right-wing government came into power, feelings of disappointment and frustration increased due to the deadlock in the political arena and the state's policies toward the Palestinians.

Two schools of thought were dominant among Arab intellectuals in Israel. One focused on the debate concerning all aspects of civil status, from equality to the image and nature of the state. As early as April 1992, Azmi Bishara, intellectual, political philosopher and activist, embarked on a new political path and founded "The Covenant of Equality." In its platform he suggested that Israel be the country of its Palestinian citizens just as it was the country of its Jewish citizens. Israel should acknowledge the Palestinian minority as a national minority with the right to cultural autonomy, which may also include economic and regional development.[28] The feeling that the peace process was riddled with obstacles led Arab intellectuals such as Professor Sa'id Zaydani to declare that they refused to be hostages of the results of the peace process.

Zaydani said, "There is no validity to the commonly-held belief that equal rights are dependent upon peace, just as there is no validity in the interdependency of war and discrimination."[29] Because it was felt that some devaluation had occurred in the concept of equality, intellectuals and educated political activists became increasingly active in order to promote the formula of "Israel as the state of all its citizens." In December 1996, "The Economic Committee of the Arab Masses in Israel" convened at the initiative of the Supreme Follow-up Committee for the Affairs of the Arab

Citizens and the Committee of the Heads of Local Arab Councils. Two of the organizers and initiators promoting this idea were Professor Zaydani, a resident of the village of Tamra and lecturer at Bir Zeit University, and Dr. Hanna Swed, mayor of Ilabun. The committee discussed six subjects:

- The national identity of the Palestinian citizens in Israel,
- The defense of lands and the future of unrecognized villages,
- The displaced residents of the villages destroyed in 1948 and the damage caused to the holy Muslim properties (the *Waqf*),
- The local Arab government's financial crisis,
- Problems of education and women's rights, and
- Health and welfare services.

The radical, ex-parliamentary movement *Abna' Al-Balad* expressed its support for this activity. Raja Ighbariya, one of the activists in the movement, attacked the tendency toward Israelization among some of the Arab intellectuals in Israel. He presented the new formula suggested by the committee. "A democratic state and a state of all its citizens" – as a victory for the concept that had been demanded for years to nullify the Jewish character of the state and grant its Arab citizens cultural autonomy.[30] The Israeli Communist Party maintained its objection to the definition "A state of all its citizens" and saw in it a retreat from the principle of "two states for two nations – Israel and Palestine." Salem Jubran, one of those who resigned from the party, claimed that proposing unrealistic slogans would only interfere with the struggle to end Israeli occupation of the territories and to found a Palestinian state, and that it would also interfere with a joint Arab–Jewish struggle for equality and for ending the occupation.

The second school of thought focused on looking outwards, at the implications of the political solution that was to be formulated when the peace talks were over. Its proponents reached the conclusion that a Palestinian state established at the end of the process would be a poor and wretched country, torn between separate territories (the West Bank and the Gaza Strip), with Israel controlling the passage between them, and large blocks of Jewish settlements at its heart. The peace accords would also force the Palestinian state to be non-democratic and authoritarian in order to retain power and to fight subversive terrorism. Therefore, a group of Israeli Palestinian intellectuals, including Azmi Bishara, Adel Mana', Nadim Rouhana and As'ad Ghanem, decided to direct their attention outwards and try to change the national Palestinian strategy.

The group members believe that instead of striving to establish an independent Palestinian state alongside Israel and making Israel the state of all its citizens, the Palestinians must aspire to establish a single dual national Palestinian–Jewish state. This state would be founded within the borders of Mandatory Palestine, and realize the aspirations and national needs of both the Jewish nation in Israel and the Palestinian people. This suggestion is a conceptual revolution in Israeli Palestinian political thought. It was stimulated by the first serious attempt to resolve the Jewish–Palestinian conflict – the Oslo Accords – and by the recognition of each party's right to exist as a legitimate political entity.

The Oslo peace process contemplated far-reaching territorial concessions by the Jews as well as the Palestinians in an attempt to establish "separation" between the two nations. According to this new concept, separation is not a practical goal because of the extremely small territory involved and the need to share limited resources. The existence of ideologically driven Jewish settlers within the Palestinian territories and the Arab–Palestinian minority within Israel that does not currently enjoy equal civil rights further complicate the separation ideal.

Azmi Bishara developed and expanded the concept from his experiences in "The Covenant of Equality." He tried to separate national territorial affiliation from citizenship in the State of Israel. The idea is that even without territorial separation, the two nations could each belong to their own exclusive state, and vote and be elected within it, subject to their rules and proud of their national emblems. Bishara considered two alternatives – integration of the Arabs into Israeli society or national separatism of the Arab minority, which would be granted cultural autonomy. Both are formulas for inequality. He offers a solution in his winding, acrobatic style: "To recognize the Arabs in Israel as a national minority within their own state. Not in the Jewish State, but within their own state as a national minority."[31]

The Peace Process in Arab Politics in Israel

In the Knesset elections as well, all the Arab parties emphasize their commitment to the struggle for equal civil rights, and all hint in their platforms at solutions such as "a state of all its citizens," cultural autonomy, and so on. They abandoned the Peace Talk arena, however, since the negotiations are conducted at political and government echelons where Arab Israeli citizens are not allowed to participate. The results of the 13th Knesset elections showed a decrease in the joint power of the three Arab parties: the Democratic Front for Peace, the Progressive Peace Party, and the Arab Democratic Party. While in the 1998 elections they obtained what added up to 60 percent of the Arab voters' votes, this time, half the Arab voters voted for Jewish Zionist parties. This indicated the Arabs' intense desire to remove the Likud party from government and their preference for a government that could promote the peace talks after the Likud had presented a rigid position at the Madrid Conference.

Another event that is exploited annually by Israeli Palestinians to make statements on the peace process is the "Land Day," which is celebrated on March 30.[32] After the 18th "Land Day" in 1994, Arab spokesmen pointed out the disappointment felt by the Palestinian Arabs in Israel regarding the difficulties of the peace process. They pointed out that ever since the Oslo Accords were signed in Washington, the "negotiation carriage" had remained stuck in the quagmire of endless talks and discussions. The Deputy Minister of Health at that time, Nawwaf Masalha, said that the Arab citizens in Israel were frustrated by the fact that they were being left outside the political process. They wished that their representatives, who supported the government (the Rabin administration) and its policies, would be allowed not only to express their support for the peace process passively but also to participate in the practical work and take an active part in the peace talks.[33]

The land issue continues to incite the Arabs in Israel and serves as a cohesive force. "Land Day" became more strongly emphasized after the peace talks with the Palestinians began. Arabs in Israel raised the 1950s land expropriation issue and the displaced person problem – people who were forced to leave their villages and move to other settlements within Israel's borders. About 31 percent of a representative sample of Arab citizens say that Arabs in Israel, had they participated in the peace talks, should have brought the land question up as first priority. About 27 percent say that the problem of the internal refugees of 1948 should become priority.[34] This means that over half believe that the problem of lands expropriated from existing settlements and lands belonging to the abandoned villages and their inhabitants now living in Israel are the most urgent problems in the era of the peace talks.

The PLO was actively involved in the politics of the Arab community in Israel, and, through them, in Israeli politics, particularly in the first two years following the Madrid Conference until the signing of the Oslo Accords. According to sources affiliated with Knesset Member Darawshe, his initiative to join his party to Rabin's coalition after the elections for the 13th Knesset was made with the PLO's encouragement. They noted in this respect that Yasser Arafat, the chairman of the PLO, even organized a warm reception for Darawshe and Knesset member Talab A-Sane' in Tunis at the end of 1992.[35] It appears that the whole affair resulted more from Darawshe and his party's desire to serve as a communication channel between the PLO and Israel, rather than Arafat's desire to become involved in Israel's political affairs. And indeed, Darawshe's initiative was attacked in the Arab press. An article in the weekly *Al-Sunnara* stated that "those among the Arabs of Israel who try to present themselves as mediators between the PLO and the Israeli government cause the organization great damage. The PLO does not need them, since it has formal channels within and without the occupied territories."[36]

At that time, Arab public figures and Knesset members were intensely active in the political process and the developments occurring in the occupied territories. They spent much time developing contacts with the Palestinian leadership in the territories, with high-ranking PLO officials, and with representatives of foreign governments after all the legal limitations on such meetings were removed. Personages such as Dr. Ahmad Tibi, Abd Al-Wahab Darawshe, Knesset Member Hashem Mahamid, and others, emphasized in their activities the interest of the Palestinian Arabs in Israel in resolving the "Palestinian problem," alongside their desire to stand out as politicians and to accrue credit among potential voters. Israeli Arab activity after the Madrid Conference was manifested in such issues as aiding the conciliation accords between Hamas activists and PLO activists in the Gaza Strip following the violent incidents between them in 1992. Another example was the mediation between the Israeli authorities and Palestinian entities in the 1992 incident at Al-Najah University in Nablus, when armed wanted terrorists took over the university during the elections for the student council.

The turning point of Arab politics in Israel took place when the Oslo Accords were signed in September 1993. The establishment of a firm basis for dialogue between the Israelis and the Palestinians drew a sigh of relief from the Palestinian Arab community and astonishment. On one hand, the accords and the ensuing process freed Arab Israeli citizens of many inhibitions. They no longer had to respond to accusations regarding their dual loyalty whenever they demanded full civil equality. The complication was solved – their Palestinian nation and their Israeli state were conducting a dialogue, and they were now free to look after their own interests. On the other hand, there was a sense of astonishment. Politicians in particular were feeling frustrated. In previous years they had tried to form a connection between Israel and Tunis, where the PLO leadership was seated after it was banished from Lebanon. But now, Rabin and Arafat had gone together to receive the Nobel Peace Prize, and Arab citizens in Israel were asking themselves where they belonged in the picture, not only for matters of honor, but also of affiliation. Nobody was asking for their help or mediation.

The mythological "bridge" concept of the Arab citizens in Israel thus was undermined. Since the Madrid Conference, Arabs in Israel had considered themselves a "bridge" to peace, and Arab politicians often used this metaphor in the media. And it appeared that Rabin and Arafat did not need such a bridge in order to shake hands. At the most, Palestinian citizens of Israel had served as a bridge upon which others trod, as Arab politicians often say cynically.

Talab Al-Sana' and the leaders of the Islamic Movement tried in November 1994 to mediate the kidnapping incident of Israeli soldier Nahshon Vaksman. The attempt failed, and Palestinians began to feel that the Israeli establishment did not want them as a mediator and that nobody needed them or desired their involvement. Nevertheless, Sheikh Abdallah

Nimmer Darwish, previously the leader of the central branch of the Islamic Movement, said, "for years we have waved two flags – peace and equality. Now things are proceeding toward peace, and we must rejoice. Now a window has opened to the Arab world, and our role is to be a bridge between Israel and the entire Arab world." Once again, the same mythological bridge, *al-sirat*. This is also the name of the Islamic Movement's monthly publication. It refers to a phrase from the Qur'an, which describes the bridge into hell that the faithful must cross on their way to heaven. The tension between the PLO and the Hamas following the abduction and murder of Nahshon Vaksman led Abdallah Nimmer Darwish to work toward building a bridge within Palestinian society. "Our role," he said, "is to make peace in the home. This is the Islamic Movement's unique role." He believed that peace between Hamas and the PLO was in the interests of both the Israelis and the Palestinians.[37]

And indeed, the Islamic Movement in Israel is the only political body that still defines its role, mission, and area of operation within the framework of the new political conditions that have developed as a result of the peace talks between Israel and the Palestinians. They see their role as the builders of a bridge that can serve as a communication channel. Its leaders walk on this bridge confidently on their way to missions of mediation and defense of the holy places in Jerusalem. They have exploited to the utmost the fact that the status of Palestinian Arabs in Israel and their leadership has improved since the peace talks began and their demands have become more legitimate.

When Dr. Sa'ib Arikat, a PLO loyalist in the West Bank, and Dr. Haidar Abd Al-Shafi', a member of the left-wing nationals in Gaza, developed an extreme and violent rivalry with two Hamas activist leaders in the Gaza Strip (Dr. Mahmud Al-Zahhar and Sheikh Abdallah Al-Rantisi), the two parties called on their Israeli colleague Sheikh Ra'id Salah, mayor of Umm Al-Fahem and head of the radical "northern" branch of the Islamic Movement, for help. He arrived accompanied by Ibrahim Nimmer Husein, chairman of the Committee of Heads of Local Arab Municipal Councils, and Tareq Abd Al-Hay, mayor of Tira. With their help, it was easier to conduct the negotiations between the rival parties in the occupied territories.

The Islamic Movement's involvement in matters concerning Jerusalem has increased continuously, parallel to progress in the peace process. The involvement of Palestinian citizens of Israel in Islamic affairs and in all aspects of the matter of the Al-Aqsa Mosque, is salient and important. Sheikh Ra'id Salah leads this activity as head of the Radical Northern Section of the movement. Since 1996, he has organized, in Umm-El-Fahem, an annual "Convention for Saving Al-Aqsa and the Islamic Holy Places in Jerusalem." He also initiated the digging, cleaning, and restoration of Solomon's Stables (the Marwani Mosque, in Palestinian dialect) and the opening of another gate in the wall surrounding Temple Mount.

Although the Israeli Palestinians' political agenda is different from that of the Palestinians in the territories and is centered on the struggle for equality within the State of Israel, there are still areas of mutual interest. The collective faith, the flourishing of religion in Israel and the territories, and the strengthening of social, political and religious ties alongside the peace talks have formed a firm bond between the two Islamic communities on both sides of the Green Line. The Muslim citizens of Israel believe that Arab Israelis are historically charged with the supreme mission of conserving the Muslim character of Jerusalem and its holy places, a mission that must be pursued in an age when talks are being conducted regarding the end of the Arab–Israeli conflict.

Sheikh Ra'id Salah and Sheikh Kamel Khatib, leaders of the activist branch of the Islamic Movement, have managed to harness Palestinian consensus regarding Jerusalem in the interest of their political needs. Whereas previously there was only endless quarreling between Jews and Muslims, these two leaders began to cooperate in an effort to contribute significantly to the only permanent resolution they believed in, the division of Jerusalem into two capitals – one Israeli and one Palestinian. The two men succeeded in making themselves and the Islamic Movement in Israel significant players in a playing field from which Israeli Palestinians had previously been excluded. Protection of the holy places was an honor that the Arab world had previously divided between King Hussein of Jordan, King Hassan of Morocco, and Yasser Arafat. For the first time, the Palestinian Arab citizens of Israel had carved themselves an independent niche and an influential position in the power structure of the conflict.

The fact that these two leaders of the Radical Branch had avoided participating in the Israeli political system has strengthened their spiritual authority and freed them to initiate ambitious moves in the regional arena. The religious function granted them due to their involvement in the opening of the mosque in Solomon's Stables and the building of the new gate in the walls of Temple Mount has opened to them and to the Arabs of Israel new and previously forbidden opportunities for political involvement in the peace process, with the blessing of the Palestinian leadership.

Analysis of the Issues

It is clear for the Arab Israelis that their struggle for equality within Israel has more importance to them than the Palestinian state issue, despite the fact that they have had protests and demonstrations regarding the Palestinian issue. For example, when the mayor of Nablus, Bassam Shaq'a, was fired, the students held one of the largest demonstrations. When the students were asked after the protest about the reason for such a big demonstration on that issue, each student referred to the equality issue. One student claimed that there were rumors that the Israeli government was going to expropriate land from the village. Another student claimed that her brother finished the Technion (the highly respected Israeli technical university) with higher grades than his Jewish fellow students, but has been unemployed for the two years since he finished his engineering studies.

Publicly the reason for the demonstration had been the Palestinian issue, but what really bothered them were issues of equality. It was easier to demonstrate on a national issue than on personal or communal issues. The Palestinian citizens of Israel only began in the late nineties to imitate the Jewish patterns of behavior and to demonstrate on matters relating to the struggle for equality. They took on such items as budgets for local councils, improving schools and buying new equipment for them.

During the time of the *Intifada*, there were two elections. The ballot box is a good place to protest, but there were no significant changes in the voting patterns by Arabs during the *Intifada*.

The Palestinian Arabs in Israel throughout the years thought that being Palestinian Arabs and Israeli citizens at the same time would enable them to serve as a bridge for peace. This did not happen in 1979 with the peace agreement between Egypt and Israel, and it did not happen in the period after the secret Oslo talks. Nor did it happen with the negotiations of an agreement with the Jordanians.

After the peace agreement was signed with Jordan in 1994, there were several joint committees between the Jordanians and Israelis on different subjects: agriculture, water, sewage, tourism, etc. Under the Oslo peace process a similar proliferation of committees took place between Israeli and the Palestinian Authority. However, none of the last three Israeli governments – Rabins', Netanyahu's and Barak's – have included representatives of the Palestinian Israeli Arabs on those committees.

This affects the Arabs' feelings. Had several of them been included in such committees, it would have given them a feeling of belonging and that they are part of the state.

Analysis of Findings from Investigations and Surveys

Palestinians in Israel are a national minority in a state in conflict with the national entity to which they belong. The Oslo process may resolve a very real identity problem that has plagued them. In other words, the state whose citizens they are will cease to battle with the nation to which they belong. Moreover, if peace is achieved between Israel and the Arab world, their ability to realize their civil rights and express their national identity may increase. Therefore, it is always interesting to examine the attitudes of Israeli Arab citizens toward the peace process. However, the measurement

of this public's attitudes using common research methods is extremely difficult, particularly regarding questions of high political sensitivity. Since the
peace process began, surveys and inquiries have been constantly conducted. The reliability of responses varies from one survey to another.

As early as 1993, the findings of a *New York Times* inquiry revealed that
the Declaration of Principles with the PLO was perceived by Arabs in Israel
as the first real and serious chance to eliminate discrimination against them.
The agreement was perceived as a means of achieving the status of citizens
with equal rights. Israeli Palestinian merchants and businessmen expressed
optimism, believing that foreign Arab markets would be opened for them,
since the agreement would put them in a position to serve as an important
bridge in trade contacts between Israel and the Arab world. The inquiry
notes that the agreement led the Arabs in Israel to demand to be made partners in the government system and to be included among the echelons of
high-ranking officials. Darawshe's struggle to join Rabin's coalition was
part of this trend. In the surveyors' opinion, the agreement also aroused
talk of "cultural autonomy," but not dissociation from Israel or unification with a Palestinian state.[38] In practice, hardly any business deals were
made between Israeli Arab factory owners and the Arab countries. Azmi
Bishara defined the relationships that would develop between the
Palestinian community in Israel and an independent Palestinian state as
resembling Israel's relationship with American Jews who support Israel but
retain their loyalty to the United States.[39]

A plurality (38%) of a group of Arab teenagers in 1998 considered the
achievement of peace to be the country's most important goal. However,
15 percent of them supported violent civil rebellion in response to offensive
government policies regarding the peace process.[40] The aspiration for peace
and the readiness to use violence result from the Arab population's
economic, social and political discrimination. Discrimination seeds the
potential for violence but also a desire for peace, in the hope that the Arabs'
position in Israeli society will improve in a state of peace, and that Israel
will become a state of all its citizens. It seems the Arab citizens of Israel are
presently exploiting the peace process in order to raise onto the public
agenda in Israel some existential and essential questions.

In August 1998, on the fifth anniversary of the beginning of the Oslo
process, a survey was conducted as part of the Tami Steinmetz Center's
"Peace Index Project." Its findings showed that the number of Israeli Arabs
who rated the peace process as having negative effects was three times
larger than the number of those who rated its effects as positive. The
surveyors explained this as being the result of the Israeli Arabs' high
expectations of the Oslo process in its early stages. Many of these expectations were never realized.[41] The surveyors concluded that some of the
interviewees hesitated to give answers that might anger the Jews or that
were politically sensitive.

The survey we conducted in a representative sample of Arab citizens in Israel in February 2000 was designed to examine two things:

*   Whether the peace process being conducted at the present time had any effect on the attitudes of Israeli Arab citizens regarding the State of Israel; and
*   To what extent it has affected matters of identity and civil status.

The survey focused on questions regarding Israeli Arab participation in the peace talks themselves, "Who could represent them – the Palestinian Authority or the Israeli government?" The purpose of the survey was to discover whether today's Arab citizens of Israel focused more on local issues that mattered to them or on national issues regarding the Israeli–Palestinian conflict. It tried to discover whether they were developing a tendency toward seclusion and isolation within the State of Israel as a result of the peace process.

Respondents' answers revealed the Palestinian aspect of their identity. There was no hesitation to reply candidly, even on politically sensitive questions.

The reliability of the survey results are lower, since it appears that the Israeli Arab sector is largely unanimous regarding these questions, beyond splintering factors such as occupation and education. Respondents were not asked about their support or objection to the peace talks with the Palestinians. That question was already answered in a survey of the peace index from August 1988, in which it was shown that 90 percent supported the regional peace process, and that a smaller majority supported the Oslo Accords. The results of our survey showed that about 65 percent favored the inclusion of Arab Israeli citizens in the peace talks, but only 24 percent thought that participation in the talks would significantly improve the status of Arabs in Israel, and only 29 percent believed that the peace talks would change their sense of inequality and discrimination.

The Palestinian Authority was perceived as an independent body that could not represent the Arabs of Israel. (Only about 18% believed it could represent them.) An interesting finding is that 58 percent are against being represented by the Israeli government in the peace talks; about 45 percent of those who said the Palestinian Authority could not represent them stated that the Israeli government could not represent them either.[42]

This indicates a tendency toward separatism, related perhaps to the tendency to try and achieve cultural and economic autonomy and to establish an independent organizational and institutional infrastructure. It also indicates a tendency to turn to international bodies and bring before them the problems of Arab society in Israel. Alongside the emerging Palestinian state, Israel's back yard is agitated. As stated by Muhammad Jabarin, one of the main activists among the nationalistic Arab intellectuals, "Arab

Israeli citizens are no longer indifferent. They want autonomy – at this stage, cultural and economic."[43]

Respondents were divided into three groups according to occupation:

- Self-employed, academics, managers, and students.
- Officials and employees in various service sectors.
- Non-professional laborers and the unemployed.

In the first group, nearly 44 percent preferred to place the lands issue at top priority. In the second group, a similar percentage preferred dealing with the issue of the 1948 refugees. The same percentage in the first group put the refugee issue in second place, and in the second group, 31 percent put the lands issue in second place.

Over 57 percent of the first group believed that the Permanent Status Agreement with the Palestinians would open up new demands regarding issues concerning the Palestinian minority in Israel. In the second group, only 37 percent thought so.

Only 28 percent of the respondents in the first group believed that the peace accords would change their sense of inequality and discrimination in Israel, compared with 44 percent in the second group. The lower the respondents' level of education and occupation, the stronger their feeling that the issue of inequality would not be solved by the peace talks.

Conclusion

The public debate among Arabs in Israel today focuses on the issue of civil equality and status in the State of Israel. In the past, Arabs in Israel struggled to be considered citizens with equal rights in Israel, believing that their national affiliation could be ignored. Now, after the *Intifada* years and deep into the peace process, they aspire to be defined as a national minority within the land of the Jewish people. Fifty years of disappointment have clarified to them the need for a separate, collective definition, which will enable them to fight for their human rights. Immediately after the peace process began, the Arabs in Israel began to take this struggle outside to the Western countries.

Two main approaches were popular among researchers of Arab society and politics in Israel. The first has claimed that the Arabs in Israel are increasing their interest in national Palestinian issues, parallel to the progress being made in the peace process. One of this approach's main proponents was Eli Rekhess. The second approach has claimed that the Arabs are now turning all their energy toward a discussion of internal issues related to equality and their status in Israel. Among the main spokesmen of this approach are Sami Smooha and As'ad Ghanem. The survey conducted for this chapter has proven the second approach to be correct.

The events of October 2000 shuffled the cards. Israel's Arab citizens took to the streets to express solidarity with their Palestinian brothers in the West Bank and Gaza Strip who launched the "al-Aqsa *Intifada*" following the failure of the peace talks in Camp David[44] and the disputed visit of Ariel Sharon, then a candidate for prime ministry, to the Temple Mount (al-Haram al-Sharif of al-Aqsa mosque) in Jerusalem.[45] They sought to utilize these events to voice sentiments that the Israeli establishment discriminates against the Israeli Arab community, neglects its needs, and ignores its distress.

The reaction of the Israeli police to the street disturbances was harsh. Three days of violence, stormy demonstrations and clashes with the police, ended with 13 Arab citizens killed. Arab citizens began to nurture hopes and expectations that their "awakening" (in Arabic "*hibba*," a term used by many of them) would make both the Israeli establishment and Israeli Jewish society realize how long the problems of country's Arab community have been neglected.

One year after the October disturbances, it was clear that all those hopes had been dashed on the rocks. The majority in Israel is of the opinion that the phase of the peace process that started in the Oslo Agreements has failed and come to an end. In February 2001 the majority voted for Ariel Sharon to make him the prime minister. The Arab community in Israel also has realized more than ever that they have a marginal role in the Palestinian national movement. From nearly every possible standpoint – political and economic – their distress is more intense than it was on the eve of the community's "awakening." During the same time the state has adopted a tougher stance *vis-à-vis* the Palestinians of the territories, there has been a serious deterioration in the relationship between the Israeli establishment and the Arab community within Israel.

While these lines are written, at the end of the year 2001, daily violence between Israel and the Palestinians continues. The growing connection between the Israeli Islamic Movement and its Palestinian counterparts has led to an increased involvement of Israeli Arabs in terrorist activities. For the first time an Arab citizen of Israel acted as a suicide bomber.[46] One week earlier, four Israeli Arab teenagers were arrested and charged with planting a bomb in one of the street junctions, and another group of Israeli Arab youngsters were arrested for having contacts with Hizballah.

The only positive development to emerge over the past year – from the standpoint of Israeli Arabs – is the growth of their collective sense of identity as a national minority that has legitimate rights as a group and has begun to harness its inner energies in a struggle to have these rights recognized. The past year's violence has embittered many Arab citizens and radicalized some of them. More and more voices are calling for a change in the nature of the State of Israel to a "state of its all citizens." The

involvement of the Israeli Palestinian minority in the peace process seems
farther away than ever.

Notes

1 Before the elections for the 13th Knesset in 1992, Abd al-Wahab Darawshe,
   head of the Arab Democratic Party, Muhammed Mi'ari, head of the progressive Peace Party and Ibrahim Nimmer Hussein, chairman of the Council
   of Heads of the Arab Local Municipalities, met in Egypt with government
   representatives in order to form a unity between the two parties along with
   independent bodies.
2 Professor Sami Smooha in an interview to the *Hadashot* newspaper, May 8,
   1992.
3 *al-Sunnara*, November 8, 1991.
4 Words spoken at the meeting on November 15, and published in *Al-Sunnara*
   on November 22, 1991. "The inside Arabs" is a common name in Arab press
   for the Israeli Arabs.
5 *al-Diar*, November 29, 1991.
6 From an interview held on November 29, 1991, quoted in Riad Kabha, and
   Sarah Ozacky-Lazar, *The Madrid Conference in the Eyes of the Arab Press in
   Israel* (Giv'at Haviva: The Insitute for Arab Studies, December 1991), pp. 8–9.
7 *al-Watan*, November 8, 1991.
8 See Y. Reiter and Reuven Aharoni, *The Political Life of Arabs of Israel* (Beit
   Berl: The Center for Research of Arab Society in Israel), 1993 (second edition),
   pp. 36–8; also see S. Ozacky-Lazar and As'ad Ghanern, *Autonomy for the
   Arabs in Israel – The Beginning of a Discussion* (Giv'at Haviva: The Institute
   for Arab Studies), 1990.
9 From an interview. See note 6.
10 *al-Sunnara*, November 22, 1991.
11 *Kul al-Arab*, November 1, 1991.
12 Ibid., November 8, 1991.
13 Kabha and Ozacky-Lazar, *The Madrid Conference*, p. 16.
14 Sarah Ozacky-Lazar in a lecturer at a seminar on the municipal elections in
   the Arab sector, December 1993.
15 Amiram Gonen and Rasem Khamaise, *The Arabs in Israel Following the
   Establishment of Peace* (Jerusalem: The Floersheimer Institute for Policy
   Research, November 1993), pp. 12–13.
16 *Ha'aretz*, December 19, 1993.
17 *Ha'aretz*, November 1992.
18 Eli Rekhess, in a lecture given at a seminar on The Palestinians and the Arab
   World following the Israel–PLO Accords. Tel Aviv University, December 22,
   1993.
19 These men said the above in a conference named "The Arab Citizens of Israel
   Toward the Twenty-First Century," Tel Aviv University, October 23, 1993.
20 Dr. Alex Bligh; "The Arabs of Israel and the International Community,"
   internal report by the office of the Advisor to the Prime Minister on Arab
   Affairs, Jerusalem, July 1992.
21 Examples are the comment made by US ambassador in Israel, William

Harrop, who expected the discrimination against the Arabs in Israel to occupy an important place in the Israeli–American agenda; and the Schifter Report by the American Justice Department which discussed civil rights in Israel in 1991 and first dealt with Israeli Arabs as well. See Reiter and Aharoni, *The Political Life of Arabs of Israel*, pp. 40–1.

22   Interview in *Ma'ariv*, September 1992.

23   *Kul al-Arab*, October 18, 1991. On the appeal to international organizations see Reiter and Aharoni, pp. 38–41.

24   *al-Sunnara* survey, September 5, 1993.

25   *Kul al-Arab*, September 1993.

26   *al-Ittihad*, September 1993.

27   *Saut Al-Haqq wal-Huriyya*, September 1993.

28   Interview in *Hadashot* newspaper, April 10, 1992.

29   Interview in *Ha'aretz* newspaper, December 5, 1996.

30   Interview for the *Fasl Al-Maqal* Journal, November 1996.

31   Azmi Bishara *Crisis in the Arab Leadership – Where is the Next Generation?* in A. Rekhess and Tamar Yagnes (eds.), *Arab Politics in Israel at a Crossroads* (Tel Aviv: Moshe Dayan Center, 1995), p. 52.

32   The first Land Day general strike protesting against planned land expropriations in the Galilee, as part of the plan to Judaise the region, took place on March 30, 1976. Six fatalities and 70 injured were the results of clashes with the police.

33   Interview, *Ha'aretz*, April 1, 1994.

34   Findings of survey conducted by Reuven Aharoni in February 2000.

35   *Ha'aretz*, January 11, 1993.

36   Munkidh al-Zu'abi, *al-Sunnara*, January 4, 1993.

37   Interview in *Ma'ariv*, November 1994.

38   New York Times, November 24, 1993.

39   Quoted in *Ha'aretz*, November 25, 1993.

40   Professor Efraim Ya'ar's research findings on Israeli youth, *Ha'aretz*, September 8, 1998.

41   Survey conducted as part of Professor Efraim Ya'ar and Dr. Tamar Herman's "Peace Index Project," the Tami Steinmetz Center, July–August 1998.

42   February survey, 2000.

43   Interview in *Ha'ir* newspaper, May 13, 1994.

44   The main issues under dispute in Camp David remained the question of sovereignty on the Temple Mount/al-Haram and the right of return of the Palestinian refugees.

45   The Palestinians in the territories and in Israel perceived Sharon's visit in al-Aqsa square as a provocation and an offense against the sanctities of the Islam.

46   On September 9, 2001 Muhammad Shaker Hubayshi from the village of Abu Snan in the western Galilee blew himself up in the town of Nahariya and caused four dead.

Part II

___

Countries with Peace Agreements with Israel:

Egypt and Jordan

CHAPTER 12

Lessons from Greek–Turkish Relations for the Arab–Israeli Conflict

DAVID KUSHNER

Aside from the peace process between Israel and its Arab neighbors, another "peace process" of sorts in this region has aimed to bring a solution to the dispute between the Greeks and Turks, particularly as it relates to the Cyprus question. In the latter case there has been no need to install formal peace between the contestants, nor has there been a need to achieve mutual recognition between them. Both Turkey and Greece – and this is true for their respective "client" communities on the island – have avoided slipping into all-out war and have been keeping the diplomatic channnels of communications open between them. Turkey and Greece have continued to share membership in the same NATO alliance. Yet, in the past decades,the relations between Turkey and Greece have been marked by some ups and downs, by episodes of considerable tension, little mutual trust, and occasional incidents reaching "near war" proportions at times. These were solved only with great difficulty and usually by outside mediation. Between one crisis and another – and by no means has Cyprus been the only trigger – there have been intermittent efforts to solve the outstanding problems and bring about a settlement to the conflict.

This "peace process" between Turkey and Greece over Cyprus may be divided into two main time periods.[1] The first began with the disruption of stability in Cyprus in 1963 in the wake of Greek attempts to bring about constitutional changes. The first Cypriot constitution of 1960, agreed upon by the Greek and Turkish communities as well as by Greece and Turkey, gave the Turks, though numerically only a fifth of the island's population, broad powers in an essentially Greek-dominated state. Headed by President Makarios, the Greeks, who had never been happy with the kind of system devised for their state, claimed that the constitution proved unworkable and that appropriate changes were necessary if the state was to be able to function at all. The ensuing stalemate soon led to the breakout of hostilities between the two communities.

Turkey, arguing that Turks on the island were facing annihilation, and basing its intervention on its status as one of the guarantors of the original Cyprus settlement, reacted by a degree of saber rattling, bringing about a real danger of confrontation with Greece. A measure of stability was restored with the expedition in March 1964 of a United Nations (UN) peacemaking force which differentiated between Turkish and Greek enclaves and resulted in an appointment of a UN mediator. However, all subsequent contacts between the communities and the mother states for the purpose of seeking a permanent settlement proved to be of no avail, failing largely over the basic disagreement over the constitution.

One low point in the Turkish–Greek relations came after the military coup d'état in Greece in April 1967 and the subsequent open support the new regime gave the defenders of *enosis*, or union, with Greece. Inter-communal strife began once again and Turkey threatened intervention should General George Grivas, the former guerilla leader, and Greek troops clandestinely sent to Cyprus not be removed. War between Turkey and Greece was averted only at the last minute thanks to diplomatic efforts (led by the United States) and Greece's agreement to withdraw its troops from the island.

The second phase began after the Turkish invasion of Cyprus in July 1974, which led to the occupation of almost 40 percent of the island and its total partition into two distinct zones – one Greek, the other Turkish. The invasion was triggered by a coup staged against President Makarios by Nicholas Sampson representing the *enosis* party among the Greeks in close cooperation with the military junta still ruling Greece. Turkey, which had been restraining itself from direct intervention until then, was adamantly opposed to such an outcome and finally decided to act in order to pre-empt the move at its inception. The resulting division of Cyprus into two parts has remained a reality ever since, and although contacts and negotiations between the parties continued intermittently, they have assumed a new direction. The Turks no longer accepted the previous concept of one unified state, but, claiming that the former system had collapsed, insisted on a settlement which would be based on a loose confederation between two separate zones and two separate governments for Turks and Greeks. The Greeks, while accepting in time the idea of a federal system with two separate zones, stood on the principle of a unified state and a strong central government.

Discussions of this as well as a host of other connected issues such as the withdrawal of Turkish forces, the size of the two zones, the question of refugees, and many others, have so far come to naught. A complicating factor has been the 1982 declaration of the Turkish Republic of Northern Cyprus. The Turks claimed that in the settlement this new state should be given equal status to the "Greek" state in the south, but the Greeks strongly refused, and the TRNC has not been able to win any recognition except that of Turkey. During the summer of 2000 relations between Turkey and Greece seemed to be an improved track, and there were new rounds of talks between the two Cypriot communities with UN mediation. In 2001 the leaders of the two communities met for the first time in years. [Editors note: On January 16, 2002 negotiations were launched under UN auspices to continue throughout the year.]

One difference between the Arab–Israeli peace process and the Turkish–Greek one becomes immediately clear. In contrast to the long dispute over Cyprus which has been dragging on for decades with no solution in sight, the Arab–Israeli conflict has witnessed some important breakthroughs in recent years. There seem to be several reasons for this. The Arab–Israeli conflict, for one, has been marked throughout its history by frequent eruptions of violence – and at times, outright war. For the parties concerned, these always entailed serious sacrifices and losses. Considering the fact that very often, at least in the past, the Arab–Israeli conflict also became embroiled in the Big Power contest for influence in the region, these eruptions also carried with them the danger of igniting a much broader conflageration. Hence a sense of urgency has been manifest in the attempts to bring an end to hostilities and solve the outstanding problems between the Arabs and Israelis. Although western powers, in particular, made several futile attempts in the past to solve the Arab–Israeli conflict, the real breakthroughs came when the parties themselves – beginning perhaps with Sadat's initiative – realized the futility and cost of pursuing the disputes between them and chose the path of peace.

In the conflict between the Turks and the Greeks over Cyprus, this element of urgency has been much less evident. It is true that the conflict did, at times, assume accute proportions with the danger of war erupting between Turkey and Greece – something greatly feared by NATO and the West. But both sides proved that they knew how to contain the crises between them – and once they were over, internal and external pressure to solve the basic problems at hand reduced considerably. There has been, furthermore, much less bloodshed between Turks and Greeks on the island than there has been between Arabs and Israelis; and on the whole, with the exception of some minor incidents, stability and peace have not been interrupted.

Both sides seem to have grown accustomed to the situation on the ground, happy that their respective interests were served, and hopeful that time was on their side. Their hard-line positions on this issue may have also served them well for the settlement of other problems they face. Thus the expression "window of opportunity" that has recently marked the efforts to achieve full peace between the Arabs and Israelis and which reflects the feeling of urgency felt on both sides has not been manifested in the case of

Cyprus. The Turkish–Greek conflict is one of those international conflicts that the world – and the contestants themselves – have been able to live with for many years.

If the "peace processes" in both cases seem to have gone in different directions, it is evident that the conflicts themselves – the Arab–Israeli and the Turkish–Greek – have shown some interesting common features. In both cases, not only have the specific issues themselves been difficult to solve, but they have been further complicated by the "burden" of history, by the deep-rooted ethnic, religious, and social divisions which have long separated the two national communities, and by the mere fact that both sides were basically fighting over the same piece of land. In this respect, it may be useful to take a broader view of Turkish–Greek relations over the years and see whether their fortunes could teach us something in regards to the prospects of the Arab–Israeli conflict.

The analogy must not, of course, be taken too far, and it is also impossible to equate exactly one side in the Turkish–Greek conflict with one particular side in the Arab–Israeli one. But the similarities are striking enough to warrant such a comparison and to attempt to draw some conclusions from the course of one conflict for the benefit of managing the other. While comparisons between two historical cases are always difficult and risky, it is still legitimate and possible to gain illumination and even make some reasonable predictions about one historical problem by drawing from the experience of another.

Historically, Turks and Greeks first came into contact with each other after the Seljuks defeated the Byzantines in the Battle of Manzikert in 1071 and opened Anatolia to Turkish settlement and rule. Later on, under the Ottomans, Turks moved on to the Balkans, and among their conquests were most of the areas identified today with Greece. In the Turkish Islamic state, Greeks were treated very much like other non-Muslim communities. According to Islamic tradition, they belonged legally to the *Ahl al-Dhimma*, and were tolerated and protected by the state in return for certain duties (as paying the poll tax) and limitations relegating them to a lower status in the population. But in practice, the Greeks fared well in the Ottoman Empire and, like the other non-Muslim communities, were permitted to lead their social and religious lives with little interference. Some became well integrated into the system. The Ottomans made good use of the Greeks' commercial and other skills, and members of the old and rich Greek families of Istanbul reached high positions in the sultan's service, especially in the eighteenth century.

This "idyllic" picture came to an end, however, when nationalism began affecting the Greek community, instilling in it a desire for freedom and self-rule. In the early 1820s, the Greeks launched the first real national uprising in the Ottoman Empire, which resulted in an independent Greece recognized in 1830. It is worthwhile noting that it was Europe, in a rare combination of forces between Russia and the West, reminiscent of the circumstances surrounding the rebirth of Israel in 1948, which was largely responsible for the Greek victory. European support for the Greeks was to leave a lasting impression on the Turks, and henceforth there was no question in the minds of Turks as to which side Christian and philhellenic Europe stood on.

Relations between Turks and Greeks were destined to further deteriorate in the coming years, as Greeks sought to unite under their flag all the areas inhabited by Greeks as well as those which belonged to them historically. The pattern was one of continuous Greek expansion – Thessaly in 1881, Crete in 1908, and the Aegean Islands and parts of Macedonia in 1912. In the eyes of the Turks, it looked as if Greece was on the road to continued aggrandizement, at Turkey's expense.

It was the First World War and its aftermath which led to the most bitter phase in Turkish–Greek relations. For the Greeks, the war represented a golden opportunity for accomplishing their "great idea," *Megali Idea* – the reunification of the Hellenic world under one flag. In 1917, Prime Minister Eleutherios Venizelos succeeded in his efforts to bring Greece into the war and, although the Greeks remained largely inactive, this afforded them the right to lay their own claims at the Peace Conference. In May 1919, with an eye on the future settlement and with the blessing of the Western powers, Greek forces occupied Izmir and its environs, and, by the abortive Treaty of Sèvres signed with the Ottoman government in August the following year, the area was to be recognized as a Greek-administered one, pending a possible union with Greece. From Izmir, the Greeks further advanced into Anatolia in a clear attempt to crush the Turkish nationalist movement. However, they were held back on the Sakarya River in 1921, and finally by the summer of 1922 were driven out of Anatolia, paving the way for the new peace conference in Lausanne.

This last chapter in the Turkish–Greek confrontation was no doubt the cruelest in the history of Turkish–Greek relations. It included massive destruction of villages, the massacring of civilians, and hosts of refugees on both sides. Arnold Toynbee, a first-hand observer, saw it as no less than a clash of civilizations. "Conflicts between civilizations," he wrote, "are terrible because civilizations are most real and fundamental forms of human society."[2] The war was basically between two peoples fighting over land each viewed as its own. It was also between two peoples divided by religious, cultural, and social differences as well as the long memories of past conflict.

There is no need to elaborate on the similarities between the course of the Turkish–Greek conflict up to that point and that of the Arab–Israeli one. With all the obvious differences between the cases, the Arabs, like the Turks, could and did see their enemies as being on a continued road of expansion at their expense, and as being, moreover, successful at their enterprise. Greeks, like the Zionist Jews, also seemed to enjoy the full support of the "imperialist" West. The Turkish War of Independence ended, it is true, in victory for the Turks, unlike the Arab fortunes in the Palestine war of 1948, but in both cases they were the low points in a long struggle for land between two ethnically and culturally divided communities whose interests were diametrically opposed. They were marked not only by terrible losses of life on both sides, but also by the creation of a massive refugee problem.

A point often emphasized by observers of the Greek–Turkish war is that the sight of the despised "second class" Greeks audacious enough to occupy Turkish lands and humiliate their former lords was one important factor in arousing the proud Turks to action in their fight for independence.[3] It is also the observation of many who have dealt with the Arab Israeli war of 1948 – as well as other encounters – that the experience of being defeated by "second-class" and "submissive" Jews was what for a long time made it so difficult for the Arab world to come to terms with the Jewish state.[4]

In the Turkish–Greek story, as it turned out, the most remarkable development after the signing of the Lausanne peace treaty in 1923 was the movement of both Turkey and Greece toward reconciliation and alignment. The Turkish–Greek exchange of population, agreed upon in Lausanne,[5] was virtually complete by the end of the 1920s. In the summer of 1930, a new agreement settling some outstanding issues was signed; in October of the same year, Venizelos, the architect of the Greek invasion himself, paid an official visit to Ankara, where he was warmly and enthusiastically received by President Mustafa Kemal Ataturk. A Treaty of Neutrality, Conciliation and Arbitration was then signed by the leaders, to be followed in 1934 by the Balkan Entente.

Several factors contributed to this new phase in the relationship: the physical "separation" between Turks and Greeks and the consequent removal of an important point of friction; the need for both states to stand together in the face of growing threats of war in Europe; and, not in the least, the farsightedness of both Ataturk and Venizelos. In any event, the foundations laid in the 1930s were to prove strong enough to sustain the good relations for another quarter of a century inducing the Turkish foreign minister at one point to describe them as *"une liaison pas d'amitie mais d'amour."*[6]

After the Second World War, both Turkey and Greece faced a new common challenge, that of Soviet expansionism. Both began to receive massive American aid, and they were both admitted into NATO in 1952 as full-fledged members. In 1954, a new Balkan alliance came into being, including Tito's Yugoslavia, along with Turkey and Greece. President Celal Bayar stated that Turkish–Greek cooperation was the supreme example of how two states which had been treated by each other with distrust for hundreds of years could agree on cooperation based on the realities of life.[7]

However, it was not long after this statement was made that a sudden change occurred once more. This came about as a result of the emergence of the Cyprus question. By the mid-1950s, Britain, under the pressure of the National Organization of Cypriot Fighters (EOKA) underground activities, expressed its readiness to leave Cyprus. The Greeks on the island were hoping to realize their long-cherished dream of *enosis* with Greece, but Turkey, motivated by a concern for the fate of the Turkish minority under Greek rule, as well as for the security of its southern border, voiced its all-out objection to any such settlement. The Turks argued that because of these concerns, and since Cyprus had belonged to them before it was handed over to Britain back in 1878, the least that it could accept was the division of the island.

This had the immediate effect of cooling Turkish–Greek relations, and soon led to serious incidents of violence between members of both communities. The friendship and confidence between the two peoples which had been built with such difficulty was destroyed in almost one stroke. The crisis was resolved for a short time by the agreements of Zurich and London in 1959, which prescribed full independence to Cyprus, ruling out any prospects of *enosis*, and with a constitution guaranteeing the Turkish minority a share in the political process. However, as we have seen, if there were any hopes for long-term peace and stability, they were soon shattered by Greek attempts to introduce constitutional changes, and the Cyprus story has cast its shadow upon Turkish–Greek relations ever since.

Inevitably the conflict has had the most adverse impact upon the relations between Turkey and Greece. Both states have seen it as their national duty to support their co-nationals on the island, and the whole question has assumed in their eyes the quality of a "national cause," with public opinion and party politics allowing governments little flexibility to change their positions. Relations between the two states have been further compounded by other issues, such as the questions of territorial waters, rights of exploration and exploitation of minerals in the Aegean seabed, and sovereignty over certain islands. More than once in the last decades, both states almost drifted into war, and no real solution has been found to any of the outstanding issues between them.

What then, in conclusion, can the Greek–Turkish experience teach us about the prospects and the nature of a settlement between Arabs and Israelis? Once again, a warning is due against drawing hasty conclusions from comparing seemingly parallel historical experiences. Still, we may be able to make at least the following general observations:

1 As the record of Turkish–Greek relations shows us, there evolved in the 1930s and 1940s a real reconciliation between the parties. It came when the futility and cost of previous struggle became all too evident, when few outstanding issues and opportunities of friction remained, and when, on the contrary, strong mutual interests drew both states closer to each other. A crucial factor was also the vision and farsightedness of the leaders involved who stood against historical myths, unrealizable aspirations, and emotional relics of the past which could block any compromise. Coming after a bitter and bloody struggle between the two nations, this phenomenon seems most significant for the future relations between Arabs and Israelis as well. It would lend support, perhaps even more than the commonly cited example of Germany and France, to optimistic views about the possibility of reconciliation between nations which had been bitter enemies in the past. It is possible to say that under conditions of peace, when a solution has been found to all outstanding issues between the parties, true cooperation and reconciliation between Arabs and Israelis can indeed be achieved and they will be able to cement and bolster whatever settlement is reached.

2 Little doubt exists that Turkish–Greek relations functioned best under conditions of maximum separation. It happened once when the exchange of populations between the two states in the 1920s removed much of the existing sources of friction and prepared the ground for the improvement in relations which followed. The same may be said for Cyprus after 1964, and more particularly after 1974, when the two communites on the island were totally separated from each other. The "functional" arrangement which was initially worked out for Cyprus and which left both sides at each other's throat had clearly not worked, while separation, though it has not brought about a solution to the problem, at least has brought a reduction of daily friction and bloody incidents. Although enmities did not end, at least talks between the parties could be held in a correct and constructive atmosphere. In the Arab–Israeli conflict, both sides seem to have come around to accepting this idea of separation, and from ideas of "a democratic secular state of Palestine" or "a greater Israel," the notion of "two states" has gained the upper hand among the parties concerned. It is also being accepted that in any future settlements between Israelis and Palestinians, the less presence and interference in each other's affairs, the greater the durability of the settlement.

3 In the 1930s, as we have seen, with the ostensible removal of all outstanding issues, Turkish–Greek relations considerably improved, but one potential emotional question, unnoticed at the time, did in fact remain between the two states – that of Cyprus. Once conflict erupted on this island, both the mother states of Turkey and Greece could not help but become involved, and the long historical feud between the two peoples was revived once more with all its great intensity. Identities and historical memories, as well as old national aspirations, proved difficult to erase completely; it turned out that just as it had been easy for past animosities

to be forgotten, so it was easy for them to resurge and embitter the conflict again. Here the role of public opinion cannot be overemphasized. The great emotional tones which were manifest in people's attitudes were quick to flare up and considerably force the hand of the governments concerned. The question of Palestine may be viewed as the Cyprus question of Arab–Israeli relations. It is, no doubt, as has been said so many times, the "crux" of the problem between the Israelis and the Arab world. Given the affinities between the Arab community in Palestine and other Arab communities, and the feelings of solidarity Palestinians enjoy in the Arab world, it is unreasonable to think that the latter would be able to forget or ignore their brothers in the future. Without a full settlement of the Palestinian issue, it is therefore likely to remain as a constant impediment to full reconciliation between Israel and the Arab world, and a true resolution of this long-standing conflict.

Notes

1   The basic facts connected with the Turkish–Greek conflict are too well known to warrant the extensive use of references. In general the literature on the Turkish–Greek conflict, including the Cyprus issue, is greatly infected by bias and one sidedness, depending on the particular background and views of the author. A good recent work which covers the entire story of the Cyprus problem is Clement H. Dodd, *The Cyprus Imbroglio* (Huntingdon: The Eothen Press, 1998).

2   Arnold J. Toynbee, *The Western Question in Greece and Turkey* (London: Houghton Mifflin, 1923), p. 136.

3   Halide Edib, *The Conflict of East and West in Turkey* (Delhi: S.M. Ashraf Lahore, 1935), p. 95; Lord Kinross, *Ataturk: A Biography of Mustafa Kemal: Father of Modern Turkey* (London: Quill Morrow, 1964), p. 181.

4   For example, Bernard Lewis, "The Consequences of Defeat," *Foreign Affairs*, January 1968; Walter Laquer, "Is Peace in the Middle East Possible?" *The New York Times Sunday Magazine,* August 27, 1967. Both articles are included in W. Laquer (ed.), *The Israeli-Arab Reader* (New York, Toronto and London: Bantam, 1969), pp. 342–68.

5   The agreement signed by Turkey and Greece, accompanying the peace treaty of Lausanne, prescribed the forced exchange of the Turkish and Greek populations between the two states, with the exception of the Greeks in Istanbul and the Turks of Western Thrace.

6   Ernest Jackh, *The Rising Crescent: Turkey Yesterday, Today and Tomorrow* (New York: Farrar and Rinehart, Inc., 1944), p. 201.

7   *The New York Times,* January 30, 1954, quoted by Ferenc A. Vali, *Bridge Across the Bosporus: The Foreign Policy of Turkey* (London: Johns Hopkins Press, 1971), p. 228.

CHAPTER 13

Peace with Israel in Egypt's Policy

YORAM MEITAL

The basic perceptions and attitudes of the Egyptian government with regard to the principles of peace with Israel were shaped more than twenty years ago. Since that time they have been re-interpreted in accordance with the changes of the situation in Egypt as well as in the Middle East in general. These images and policy guidelines were presented in public for the first time in President Sadat's historic speech on November 20, 1977 before a special session of the Israeli Parliament. Sadat emphasized:

> I did not come to you to conclude a separate agreement between Egypt and Israel, for this has no place in Egyptian policy.

He continued by amplifying that:

> any separate peace . . . is bound to fall short of establishing a durable and just peace in the entire area . . . did not come to you seeking partial peace in the sense that we put an end to the state of belligerency at this stage . . . This will not be the radical solution leading us to durable peace.[1]

But the next passage reveals the extent to which Egypt's attitudes had shifted in regard to the recognition of Israel and understanding for its security requirements. Sadat continued:

> I came here to you to build together a durable and just peace . . . You want to co-exist with us in this part of the world, and I tell you quite sincerely: we welcome you among us in all peace and security. This, in itself, constitutes a sharp turning point, a landmark in a historic and decisive change.[2]

As well as emphasizing the drastic shift in policy, Sadat also used the speech to reaffirm some of Egypt's long-standing positions on the conflict:

> Our land is not subject to bargaining nor is it a topic of debate. Our national and regional soil is to us the sacred valley in which God spoke to Moses . . .

There are certain facts that have to be faced with courage and clear vision. There are Arab territories which Israel occupied . . . We insist on complete withdrawal from these territories, including Arab Jerusalem . . . As for the Palestinian cause, no one can deny that this is the crux of the whole problem. No one in the whole world today can accept slogans raised here in Israel, ignoring the existence of the Palestinian people, and even questioning where is that people? . . . In all faith I tell you that peace cannot be achieved without the Palestinians . . . And direct confrontation with that Palestinian problem, the only language to deal with it for a just and lasting peace, is the establishment of their state.[3]

The Egyptian president summarized the elements of his speech by proposing a framework for Arab–Israeli peace based on five principles:

- Termination of the Israeli occupation of the Arab territories occupied in 1967.
- Achievement of the basic rights of the Palestinian people and their right to self-determination, including the right to establish their own state.
- The right of each state in the area to live in peace within secure borders guaranteed by agreed-upon procedures that would ensure the proper security of international borders, in addition to appropriate international guarantees.
- All the states of the area should be committed to conduct their relations with one another according to the aims and principles of the United Nations Charter, particularly not to resort to the use of force, and to resolve any differences among them through peaceful means.
- Termination of the present state of belligerency in the area.[4]

The revolutionary content of Sadat's Knesset speech reflected the complete transformation that had occurred in Egypt's position on the conflict with Israel. This shift ultimately led to the opening of negotiations between the two countries following Sadat's Jerusalem visit.

While Cairo's most basic aims remained unchanged and thus comprised an integral part of the speech, there had been much rethinking as to the means to achieve them, which was also made extremely clear in Sadat's speech. Before the November 1977 initiative, Sadat had frequently declared that Egypt could not enter into negotiations with Israel unless Israel first withdrew a further distance from the Egyptian territories it was still holding. Sadat's trip, and even more his words in the Knesset about Egyptian recognition of Israel and its right to exist in security, established a new pattern of relations between the two states. This in turn had provided the foundation on which the subsequent negotiations could be built. Preconditions had been dropped, and a negotiating process in which each side was free to bring up the arguments as it saw fit had been made possible. It may well be said that the Knesset speech was the first step on the road to normalization between the two states. By his initiative, Sadat had finally broken the status quo stalemate that had for so long overshadowed the political process.

Any examination of Egypt's policy during the momentous years of 1977–9 must without a doubt consider the effect of Sadat's extraordinary and influential personality. Yet, I would argue that it would be wrong to attribute all the changes that took place during these years to Sadat's personality alone. The fundamental change in Egyptian policy on the Arab–Israeli conflict must be viewed as part of a broader transformation encompassing the country's domestic, economic, and security policies. It was not so much the issue of Israel which Egyptian policy-makers had to measure up to, but – most of all – the need to act according to Egypt's most vital national interests in their entirety.

Sadat's peacemaking journey to Israel in November 1977 was a part of an overall re-orientation of Egypt's domestic, regional, and global policies. One of the main characteristics of this new orientation was the utilization of Egyptian foreign policy as a tool in the realization of domestic objectives. In addition, the need to deal with both the conflict with Israel and the social–economic challenges facing Egypt were the factors underlying a turn toward the United States. More than any other term, the "Open Door policy" (*siyasat al-infitah*) expresses the fundamental transformation that began in Egypt during the end of the 1970s.

According to this policy there is a direct linkage between the possibility of achieving stability on the borders along with accomplishing economic relief, and decreasing the domestic challenges the society and regime are facing. Domestically, the Open Door policy was expressed through the implementation of an economic policy that favored the free-market system, as well as liberalization of the fields of politics and the media. Gradually, the one-party system with its absolute control over the media was abandoned, and what developed in its place was a multi-party system that allowed freer possibilities of expression in the media. Although the Egyptian leadership viewed the Open Door policy as a general objective, they adopted a step-by-step approach that limited its implementation to a few defined aspects.[5]

The effort to carry out the Open Door policy was the background not only to Sadat's peace initiative of November 1977 and to the Egyptian–Israeli peace treaty (March 1979), but also to the complex relations that have since developed between Egypt, Israel, and the United States. During these years, Egypt consolidated its image in the eyes of the international community as the cornerstone for stability in the Middle East, and as a "key Arab partner in efforts to achieve an Arab–Israeli peace and strengthen moderate forces in the volatile Middle East."[6] As part of this process, a strategic alliance evolved between Egypt and the United States, which included intensive American economic, military and technological aid to Egypt. Despite differences of opinion on many issues Egyptian–US relations have been strengthened over the last two decades, and Egypt has received civil and military aid in the amount of $30 billion. This comprehensive support has enabled Egypt to renew its armed forces with sophisticated weapons, and as William Quandt in *The United States and Egypt* stated, "Besides selling arms to Egypt, the United States provides training for Egyptian officers, holds joint exercises with Egyptian forces . . . and carries out some cooperative security programs."[7]

The peace and the mutual interests between Egypt, the United States, and Israel have withstood the test of acute challenges. The sides remained faithful to their obligations, in spite of President Sadat's assassination and the outbreak of Israeli-Arab violence (particularly during the war in Lebanon), the *Intifada*, and acts of terror that targeted mainly innocent Jewish and Arab civilians. Although these challenges placed great stress on the fragile relations between Egypt and Israel, they did not change either side's fundamental approach or commitment to the agreements between them. Nevertheless, since the early stages of the peace with Israel, Egypt's public opinion in general considered their country's split with the Arab world as a heavy political, cultural, and national price.

This situation presented Cairo's decision makers with what appeared to be an underlying dilemma in their policy. In one scenario Egypt would be a central factor that could lead the Arabs to adopt moderate political stands and create essential conditions for stability in the volatile region of the Middle East. However, in times when relations with most of the Arab states and the Palestinians were cut off, Egypt's influence on regional developments decreased substantially.

In this situation, in the eyes of the Western states, Cairo's image as a regional power was reduced. Moreover, Egypt, under the leadership of Husni Mubarak, perceived the deteriorating relations between Cairo and most of the Arab states as harmful to the interests of Egypt. The efforts to reconcile with the Arab states, and more importantly with the Palestine Liberation Front (PLO), began to bear fruit in the second half of the 1980s. This process occurred while Egypt continued to honor most of the commitments of its peace treaty with Israel. Actually, Cairo presented its policy orientation as a model, i.e., a policy of settling the Arab–Israeli conflict by peaceful means based on the formula of "land for peace" and marked by full American partnership in all of its stages.

It seems that the most critical test of Egypt's Open Door policy and its relationship with the United States was the Gulf crisis and the war against Iraq. For many years the Egyptian government had tried to present its country as the image of moderation, and as a key instrument to achieving stability in the Middle East. During the Gulf crisis, Egypt's leadership understood that any attempt to evade their commitments would have severe repercussions for their country's standing in the eyes of the West, especially regarding the generous aid package granted by America. However, when the Gulf War was over, United States spokesmen announced that, "Egypt delivered the goods." In Egypt, the government declared that it had aligned itself with justice and international legitimacy. It believed that Egypt's firm stand in the war had led to important achievements: first and foremost the erasing of a substantial amount of the foreign debt as well as the initiation of successful economic reforms.

In addition, following the war with Iraq, the process of regional reconciliation was resumed, and the Camp David agreements became a point of reference for all sides. Egypt's senior decision makers invested tremendous efforts in maintaining the momentum of the peace process. They placed the signing of further agreements between Israel and its Arab adversaries – first and foremost with the Palestinians – as a top priority of Egypt's foreign policy. In this context, Egypt perceived the United States as a key player, and expected Washington to compel Israel to compromise on its positions, as well as to restrain its use of power against the Arabs.

Since the resumption of the peace process with the Madrid conference October 1991, the general attitudes in Egypt are as follows.

Egypt's decision makers and a substantial part of the public believe that following the Camp David agreements, the general trend of the *Arab–Israeli conflict has been changed fundamentally – from a "zero-sum game" over the right to exist to a dispute over territories and the terms of agreements*. Or, in the words of Osama al-Baz, Mubarak's senior political advisor, "*min sir 'a wujud ila sir 'a hudud,*" from a conflict over actual existence into a conflict over borders. In that sense, the Camp David agreements and concepts were indeed the "beginning of the end" for the Arab–Israeli long-term conflict – a historical compromise between the Arabs and Israel.

This framework prescribed that the Arabs ought to follow the Egyptian path and recognize Israel's sovereignty, territorial integrity, and its right to live in peace within secure and recognized boundaries as well as to terminate the state of war with Israel, to accept security arrangements and normalization of relations which satisfy Israel's demands. On the other hand, Israel should withdraw from Arab territories occupied in 1967, and fully implement its agreements with the Palestinians. This historical compromise, no doubt, is based on a concept in which the Arabs are compelled to neglect their old concepts and their struggle against the Jewish state. For Israel, the historical compromise with the Arabs, and especially the possibility of establishing an independent Palestinian state, was – and still is – a heavy blow to the ideology of *Eretz Yisrael* (The Land of Israel), which principally claimed the whole land of Palestine for the Jewish people.

Both *Egyptian decision makers* and other sectors of the public *believe* that any *serious standstill in the peace process may critically harm Egypt's most vital national interests*. These include primarily the current programs for economic reform as well as any initiative for developments, such as the

Tushka project, the goal of which is to move millions of Egyptians out from the narrow Nile valley and provide employment opportunities for them. Increasing the rate of development was described recently by President Mubarak "as a top priority" in Egypt's national agenda.[8] However this does not imply that Egyptian support for the Palestinians, Syrian and Lebanese people is in any way superficial, or that pan-Arab ideology is always sacrificed to the particularistic interests of the Egyptian state. My argument here is that Egyptian leadership believes that if the present stalemate in negotiations continues, the two pillars of peace, namely certainty and stability, will be rocked to their foundations. This in turn may have serious ramifications not only to the parties that are negotiating, but also for Egypt itself, which only during the last two or three years has begun to gain the benefits of the comprehensive economic reform programs that were implemented after the Gulf War.

As a result of this program, economic liberalization, and especially the privatization program gained momentum; inflation rates dropped to the level of 3.8 percent during 1998–9; hard currency reserves were estimated at $20 billion; foreign investment increased; the Egyptian pound and the country's balance of payments were stabilized; the stock market reached a record high; and the country's external debt dropped to $28.2 billion.[9] Undoubtedly the success of the economic reform is among the most important achievements of Egypt during the last decades. However there is still a long list of challenges yet to be addressed: the wide range of poverty and unemployment; the urgent need to increase exportation, attract foreign investments, and to decrease the deficit in trade balance (which was estimated at $12 billion last year). In addition to these economic considerations there is a demand in Egypt to accelerate the development of democratic practices in different fields.

Cairo holds Israel as mainly responsible for the deterioration in the peace process – primarily because of what the Egyptian public and leadership see as provocative policies by Israel's government. These include delays in fulfilling agreements with the Palestinians, unilateral acts such as its settlement activities, as well as Israel's ongoing military operations in Lebanon (and mainly its attacks against civilian infrastructures in Lebanon), in addition to extreme statements like "the soil of Lebanon will burn" (as Israel's Foreign Minister David Levy declared in February 2000, as part of his efforts to deter the Hizballah from carrying on their military operations against Israelis targets). All these acts and statements are perceived in Egypt as provocative steps that put obstacles in the path to peace, and are described as "illegitimate unilateral acts threatening the entire peace process."[10]

Over the past few years, *Egyptian society has become increasingly critical of the United States.* During the Gulf crisis there was incessant criticism in Egypt against what was perceived as American double standards in policymaking. The claim was that the American government did not hesitate to use political, general or military means against countries like Libya and Iraq, yet at the same time refrained from taking similar actions while Israel was breaching international agreements and harming Arabs in general, and Palestinians in particular. (Examples cited in Egypt were Israel's exaggerated use of force against the Palestinian population, its evasion of commitments according to the agreements signed with various Arab actors, and its refusal to sign the Non-Proliferation Treaty on Nuclear Weapons.) The demand of various individuals and institutions in America (especially the Congress) to re-examine the aid allocated to Egypt, and accusations hurled against Egypt for supposedly putting sticks into the spokes of the Israeli–Palestinian negotiations wheel, intensified the tension between the United States and Egypt.

However, despite the demands to cut back on the American assistance to Egypt, a few requests and assessments were published that recommended continuing American aid to Egypt.[11] It should be noted that many Egyptians believe that Zionist and Israeli individuals and institutions play a significant role in determining Egyptian–American relations. Nonetheless, despite some opposition to the strategic partnership between Egypt and America, the process of political talks has continued between the governments of Cairo and Washington, and the US aid to Egypt was reduced by only 5 percent.

A recurring cause of disagreement between Egypt and America concerned the issue of the balance of powers between Israel and her neighbors, especially pertaining to the completion of the peace process. The United States repeatedly stated her commitment to protecting Israel's independence, and refused to publicly denounce Israel's policy regarding nuclear arms. In Egypt, America's attitude was highly criticized, with emphasis placed on the fact that it gave rise to a situation in which only Israel had the military capability that was denied her neighbors – thus a cause for tension and instability in the Middle East. Egypt claimed that America's continual handling of Israel with "silk gloves" gave Israel a force-based advantage that affected its policy toward the Arabs in general and the Palestinians in particular. As such Egypt has come to regard itself as the leading Arab actor impelled to position itself in opposition to Israel, to balance the latter's unrelenting policy. The unanswered question was and still is whether the Egyptian and American leaders will be able to determine not only the political courses of action, but more importantly intervene in the oftentimes jingoistic public discourse to diminish the levels of hostility seething in both countries.

Since the mid-seventies, mutual interests and a similar general outlook on developments in the Middle East have formed the background for the foundation of the special relations between Egypt and the United States. From Egypt's point of view, relations with the United States and, as a part of them, the peace with Israel, were and still are basic factors in the orientation of the internal and external policies of Egypt. The end of the Cold War, the fall of the United Socialist Soviet Republics, and the trend toward reconciliation that developed in the Middle East since the Gulf crisis all reflect fundamental, local, and global changes. Despite this, even today, the conditions and needs that caused the United States and Egypt to develop such broadly-based relations still exist. At the same time, the relations between both countries will continually be re-examined.

About ten years ago, when there were such calls to re-examine US–Egyptian relations William Quandt published a research study that made numerous recommendations. Some of his findings became obsolete due to the Gulf War. However a substantial part of his argument remains valid today. In relation to the expectations and the mutual perceptions of both sides, Quandt emphasized:

> Both Washington and Cairo need to think about how to restructure their bilateral relationship to serve their mutual interests in the 1990s, particularly in light of the dramatic changes taking place in the international arena. For the United States, this requires that we see Egypt as it is, not as we imagine it should be. The cold war prism is particularly inadequate for assessing United States–Egyptian relations in the decade ahead. Nor should Egypt be viewed as another Israel . . . For the United States, the strategic value of Egypt resides in the fact that it is, on the whole, a force for stability in a volatile region, not that it is an ally in an anti-Soviet crusade. Egypt carries weight in inter-Arab circles . . . In effect, expectations should be lowered, both in Washington and Cairo. Although they do share many interests, their interests are not identical, and the two countries are not destined to become full-fledged allies. That does not mean, however, that they should not aim for a continuing special relationship built on mutual interests.[12]

Many in Egypt believe that there is a way out of the current standstill in the peace process – namely that Israel must fulfill all of the commitments that were agreed upon in the interim agreements with the Palestinians, as well as continue its negotiations with Syria and Lebanon. As such, negotiations between Israel and Arab parties should not be based "on a concept of supremacy" or attempts to impose the will of the strong.[13] Israel should put a halt to her intentions to impose her terms for agreements on the weak Palestinians or Lebanese leaderships. As for the Palestinian track, it is the responsibility of both Israel and the Palestinians to work hard toward the signing of a final status agreement, despite the potential explosiveness of the relevant issues as well as the domestic political pressures from opposing sectors in each society.

In the current stage of the peace process, the negotiations are focused on the most controversial issues of the Arab–Israeli conflict: withdrawal, borders, settlements, security, Jerusalem, refugees, normalization of relations, and the sharing of natural resources (especially water). However, from the Egyptian perspective, it is simply important that the Arabs and Israel keep advancing, no matter how slowly, toward the goal of achieving a comprehensive and just peace. From Cairo's standpoint, the most important result of the peace process was the creation of an atmosphere of stability in the Middle East. Stability, and only stability, could guarantee the successful continuation of the reforms in economics and politics that Egypt underwent. Nevertheless, one of the most acute issues preoccupying the Egyptian public opinion relates to the status quo in the post-peace Middle East, or "What Comes After," as was the front-page headline of the *al-Ahram Weekly* of February 3, 2000.

No doubt, Egyptian–Israeli attitudes on this issue are substantially different. There are many subjects on the agenda, most of which relate to Israel's position in the post-peace Middle East. These include Israel's military abilities – first and foremost her weapons of mass destruction – as well as its refusal to sign the Non-Proliferation Treaty on Nuclear Weapons. This concern relates to what seems from Cairo as a clear indication of Israel's efforts to minimize the leading role that Egypt has been playing traditionally in the Middle East.

Many in Egypt therefore claim that all Israel's efforts to build regional, economic, and technological cooperation are motivated by an "Israel in the center" approach. Consequently, since its inception, Egypt has opposed Shimon Peres's idea of "The New Middle East." Egyptian officials and non-officials alike describe this vision as a dangerous illusion "based on Egyptian labor, Gulf money and Israeli technological know-how."[14] Regarding this policy there appear to be two central positions in Egypt. The first negates the very basic perception of the Middle East and its peoples, as described in Peres's vision. The most common argument here is that:

> Without denying Israel's considerable achievements in the technological and economic fields . . . the Middle East is not an area of poverty and backwardness, as Peres stated. Nor is Israel the oasis of prosperity, somehow sanctioned by divine grace to lead the entire region out of the quagmire.[15]

The supporters of this approach suggest the adoption of an "Arab in the center" approach, which would lead to an all-Arab cooperation emphasis in a wide range of spheres.

Yet, according to the other approach, Egypt "cannot be more royal than the king." Or, as a high-ranking official declared in an interview with *al-Ahram Weekly,* "Once a settlement is reached, most countries of the region will be embarking on business with Israel. We [in Egypt] have no economic interest in isolating ourselves when the entire region would be going into a de facto integration."[16] So Egypt would have to do business with Israel.

An official attitude with regard to this issue can be found in the following words of Egypt's Minister for Information and Communication. In an interview, the minister was asked, "Is the government considering cooperation with Israel, the region's most active software provider?" His answer was: "The Israelis have exhibited interest in cooperating with us on hi-tech areas. They are very advanced in this area. We are definitely examining the potential for cooperation, but there is nothing concrete yet."[17]

The great interest of the Egyptian public in this issue can be found in various spheres. During the last years, the Cairo Book Fair has become one of the central avenues for public debate. It is no surprise that the program for the year 2000 includes the subject of the post-peace Middle East. As in previous years, Osama al-Baz addressed the public. His main arguments were as follows:[18]

- The peace process could be concluded within a one-year period.
- It would be a mistake to expect Egypt's role to become marginalized (*tahamish dur Misr*) in the post-peace order.
- There are signs that Israel has been trying to undercut Egypt's regional role.
- To guarantee its national interests and leading role in the region, Egypt must develop all its potentials and resources, including its military capabilities. Only a strong Egypt can protect both the country's own security, as well as the pan-Arab national security. If this is fulfilled, it will allow Egypt to play an instrumental role in the post-peace Middle East.

Yet a diverse opinion was put forth during this discussion at the Book Fair. Professor Hassan Nafaa, an economist from Cairo University, addressed the same issue but drew different conclusions. He predicted that Israel could dominate the region "not only because of its superiority, but because of Arab weakness and ineffectiveness." Professor Naffa also questioned the probability "of Arabs gathering around a single cause, once the Palestinian issue is settled."[19] What is clear is that both Egypt and Israel will continue to exercise power and influence in future Middle East politics and economics.

Notes

1 For the official text of Sadat's speech in the Knesset, see Arab Republic of Egypt, *White Paper on the Peace Initiatives Undertaken by President Anwar al-Sadat, 1971–1977* (Cairo: Government of Egypt, 1978), p. 172.
2 Ibid.
3 Ibid., pp. 176–9.
4 Ibid., p. 179.
5 For the interactions between the Open Door policy and Egypt's re-orientation during the mid-1970s, see Yoram Meital, *Egypt's Struggle for Peace:*

Continuity and Change, 1967–1977 (Gainesville: University Press of Florida, 1997), ch. 7.

6   Edward P. Djerejian, Assistant Secretary for Near East Affairs, "US Aid and Assistance to the Middle East," statement before the Subcommittee on Europe and the Middle East of the House Foreign Affairs Committee, Washington, D.C., April 28, 1993. US State Department *Dispatch*, Article 6, Vol. 4, No. 19, 93/05/10.

7   William Quandt, *The United States and Egypt* (Washington, D.C.: Brookings Institution, 1990), p. 33.

8   *al-Ahram*, November 14, 1999. For similar statement of the Egyptian president, see March 5, 2000.

9   Arab Republic of Egypt, Ministry of Economy, *Monthly Economic Digest*, February 2000.

10   *al-Ahram*, November 14, 1999.

11   Thus, for example, a report that was drawn up by two researchers, Robert Satloff and Patrick Clawson from the Washington Institute (July 1998) claimed, "In the end, an assessment of the costs and benefits of America's $1.3 billion in military aid suggests that maintaining the program at current levels – no increase, no decrease – is the approach that best advances United States interests," Satloff and Clawson, "United States Military Aid to Egypt: Assessment and Recommendations," *Policywatch*, 325, July 8, 1988. A similar conclusion was included in: William Quandt, *The United States and Egypt*, pp. 54–5.

12   Quandt, pp. 54–5. He also claimed, "Unless managed with skill and determination, and with continuing sensitivity to political realities, economic problems could undermine the foundations of a relationship that has served American interests well in recent years," p. 1.

13   See Mubarak's statement in *al-Ahram*, November 14, 1999.

14   See an article by Ibrahim Nafie, in *al-Ahram Weekly*, February 3, 2000. For Peres's vision and ideas see Shimon Peres, *The New Middle East* (New York: Henry Holt and Company, 1993).

15   Ibrahim Nafie, in *al-Ahram Weekly*, February 3, 2000.

16   *al-Ahram Weekly*, February 24, 2000.

17   Ibid.

18   See *al-Ahram Weekly*, February 3, 2000.

19   Ibid.

CHAPTER 14

Jordan's Perspective of Peace

MOHANNA HADDAD

Past Experience

The potential of the Hashemite Kingdom of Jordan is great due to the quality of its highly skilled citizens, but will remain limited, since it is a country small in size and poor in natural resources. On a very basic level,[1] Jordan will always be dependent on external resources. Its area is about 89,000 square kilometers, of which the productive and inhabitable area does not exceed one-tenth. Until the end of World War I, Jordan had formed a part of Syria called "Southern Syria."[2] The establishment of the state in the region in 1921 took place as a result of Britain's obligation toward the leaders of the Arab Revolution of 1916, led by the father of the founder of the State: Prince, and later on, King Abdullah.

As the Arabs joined the Allied Powers against Turkey and Germany during World War I (evidenced through the Hussein–McMahon correspondence), they demanded that an Arab state be established in the regions of Syria, Iraq, Palestine, and Transjordan.[3] This demand was rejected, but as compensation the Allied Powers, and Britain in particular, established the Kingdom of Iraq in 1919 to be headed by the abdicating King of Syria and the Emirate in Transjordan to be headed by Abdullah. The only chance for Jordan to survive was to accept the British Mandate, which continued for several decades. After its independence and promotion to Kingdom in 1946, a British officer was appointed as Chief-of-Staff of the Arab legion, or the Jordanian army.[4] The alliance with the Western powers, in effect, formed the backbone for the existence of the State of Jordan.[5]

After independence, Jordan became a member of the League of Arab States, taking responsibility for defending Palestine against the Zionist aggression. Very soon thereafter Britain decided to end its mandate over Palestine and to withdraw its troops. Despite attempts of King Abdullah to come to an understanding with the Zionist Organizations, the latter was preparing itself to be the independent alternative to the British Mandate's government in Palestine.[6]

The Jordanian Army was able to keep control of that part of Palestine, later to be called "the West Bank, despite the defeat of the Arab armies in the 1948 war." An understanding between the Palestinian notables and the Prince in a conference in Jericho in 1950 resulted in the Kingdom being restructured to include the regions held by the Jordanian Army in 1948.[7] As a consequence the population of the Kingdom tripled within two years and all the new inhabitants were granted citizenship. The expanded Jordanian state relied heavily on the Western powers for its existence and, in fact, had no other alternative to an alliance with the West. Britain continued assisting Jordan through grants of aid, which constituted the majority of resources for Jordan's economy, in addition to agriculture.[8]

The period between 1950 and 1958 was troublesome for Jordan. The enthroning of young King Hussein in 1952 coincided with the Egyptian revolution that paved the way for revolutionary movements seeking the independence of the Arab countries. Most of those movements were hostile to the Hashemite Monarchy. Alignment with the West was the Kingdom's only option if it wanted to maintain itself. The Hashemites in Baghdad were the only Arab supporters of the Hashemites in Jordan, and the former were terminated by a bloody coup d'état in 1958, leaving the Hashemite Kingdom in Jordan alone in a hostile region.[9] However, the support Jordan received from the West and the United States enabled the royal House to continue the struggle for survival, torn between a triangle of forces: two of which were Arab states and a third, which was the State of Israel.

Between 1960 and 1967, a new opponent appeared on the scene, the Palestine Liberation Organization (PLO) and other Palestinian organizations. These groups had the option of attacking the Kingdom not only from the outside, through collaboration with Egypt and Syria, but also from within, through Palestinians living in the Kingdom who formed the majority of the population.[10] Despite the addition of aid from the Gulf States to Jordan, the Western backing remained essential for the survival of the Kingdom.

The Six Day War and its aftermath brought the Hashemite Kingdom to the edge of disaster, but the leadership saved the country through skillful diplomacy that involved concessions to the Palestinian Liberation Organization. The Western powers, the United States in particular, played a prominent role during that period. The Palestinian organizations, which were boosted by financial help from the Arab oil countries, became a real danger to the survival of the Jordanian state.[11] The Jordanian army had to use force to restore order, which angered the neighboring Arab states who threatened military invasion. The Western world intervened and stabilized the situation by pressuring Syria to pull back its invading troops from Jordanian soil, especially through the intervention of Israeli fighter jets.[12]

This trend of Jordanian preference for the Western powers as allies, among them primarily the United States, continued through the following decades, resulting in the 1994 peace agreement. Even in the signing of a peace agreement with the State of Israel, Jordan asked the United States to be the witness, despite the fact that the negotiations between Jordan and Israel took place directly without direct US mediation.[13]

And this goes to show that the Jordanian leadership has exercised independence and individuality as a state among the Arab national entities, and has for decades charted its own course according to its own interests.[14] The Arab national dream and identity influence the decision-making of the current leadership, but not toward belligerency. The Jordanian Monarchy has sought to achieve the Arabic dream through education, consciousness, and popular choice.[15] Past efforts to impose the longed-for Arab Unity by force have proven fallacious. In 1994, Jordan signed a peace agreement with the State of Israel out of strategic considerations. This decision came about after international recognition of the need for a Palestinian state, leaving to the Palestinians primary responsibility for negotiating in their own way and with their own ability the recognition and characteristics of such a state.

Jordan and the Future: Proposed Scenarios

After an account of Jordan's history up until the signing of the Peace Agreement with the State of Israel, Ali Mahafza, a prominent historian of Jordan, provides several scenarios as to the future of Jordan.[16]

First, Continuation of the Status Quo

The first is the continuation of the present situation as is, without any significant change in the cultural, social, economic, or political fields; in other words it is the continued evolution of the struggling political system with all its internal contradictions and shortcomings. The current situation is characterized by the domination of the executive authority over the legislative and judicial ones, the weak performance of the legislative authority, the absence of popular control over the governments, the weakness of the political parties and the institutions of the civil societies, the widening gaps in national unity, and the continuation of Jordanian–Arab relations as they are at present with the continuation of the strong relations between Jordan, Israel, and the United States. This scenario includes the current economic crisis in its various manifestations, the external debts that put heavy pressure on the national economy, the widening gap between the rich and the poor, the continuous shrinking of the middle class, and the expansion of poverty, with all the accompanying features of social disorder and acts of violence. The eventual consequences are the corrosion of the legitimacy of the state or the regime, the possibility of reverting to the use of martial law, the halting of evolution toward democracy, and the augmentation of the tension between Jordanians of Palestinian and Transjordanian origin.[17]

Secondly, the Democratic Scenario

This scenario entails a deepening of the democratic system through the legislation of an adequate election law that would permit the actual representation of the various active powers and political orientations. This scenario also requires the election of representative councils that are able to exercise their constitutional power to control the executive authority by both questioning it and limiting its dominance. The councils should have the right of reconsidering laws and legislation that limit public and individual freedoms, and affect the basic rights of the citizen. A functioning democracy requires also the reconsideration of the judicial authority, establishing the rule of law, the practice of the alternation of rule, and reconsideration of the educational and informational policies that are used to fortify national unity. Underlying these institutional changes are the need for more freedom of the press, and the development of other news media; the opportunity of building the national economy on a more scientific basis; effective planning to reduce unemployment, limit poverty, and reduce the gap between rich and poor; and putting an end to profligacy of public expenditures. There should also be a more open attitude toward the Arab countries, improvement of the relations with them, and the establishment of an Arab common market to face international economic challenges that will confront the region in the coming decade.[18]

Thirdly, the Islamic Scenario

This scenario assumes that Islamicists come to power and the establishment of an Islamic state ruled by Islamic laws. Such a state would not allow non-Islamic forces to act or participate in the rule of the country, or to enjoy freedom of expression or worship. Women would be subordinate to husbands, would be obliged to wear the Hijab (veil), and a separation between the sexes would occur, similar to the situation in revolutionary Iran. Radio and television broadcasts would be censored, and the typical celebration of weddings as well as music would be prohibited. Such an environment would lead many to leave the country with little chance of their returning. The consolation is that the Islamicists have no alternative development plans and no economic or political programs to correct the deficiencies of the present situation, let alone to absorb and develop modern technology. Ali Mahafza believes this scenario is unlikely, because the people of Jordan have become accustomed to participation in the decision-making process, a social and economic class has been developed that rejects the Islamic ideology of rule, and the Islamicists have no comprehensive program to replace the existing one.[19]

Fourthly, the Palestinian–Jordanian Confederation

In case the Palestinians fail to reach an agreement with the State of Israel, or in case they unilaterally proclaim a state, Jordan will come under pressure to form a confederation with the new entity. In this case, Jordan and Israel would share sovereignty of the West Bank, as the new entity would not enjoy international recognition. Furthermore, Israel would maintain control over the Jordan valley, the Jewish settlements, the air space of the West Bank, the border crossings, and over water resources. This situation would neither answer the needs of the Palestinian people in their struggle for liberation from the Israeli occupation and quest for independence and liberty, nor would it meet the Jordanian people's expectations, who will not agree to a solution that conforms with its own ambitions but denies the Palestinians their rights. The situation in this case would be none other than one that oppresses both Jordanians and Palestinians. This confederacy might be highly dependent on the State of Israel and become an extension of it on both the economic and the cultural levels. It would secure for Israel its required cheap labor force, and serve as an intermediary for Israel's marketing of its industrial products to Arab countries.[20]

Fifth, the Crescent or Half Moon Scenario

This scenario proposes fundamental changes in the way that Middle East countries govern themselves – a change from authoritarian rule toward real democracy or the establishment of Islamic societies. It also implies changes in the international order that would weaken American hegemony in the Arab region and cause disequilibrium within the Israeli system. Although this scenario is not very likely, if implemented, it would result in a political and economic union among the Islamic countries of the region to face Israeli and the Western hostility, which constitute a threat to Islamic countries' interests in the region. The emergence of such a union, no doubt, would require a very high level of development among the peoples of the region and a high level of popular mobilization, as well as political wisdom by the regions leaders. Such a union should lead to progress in the economic situation in these countries, provided that there was an improvement in relations among the states of the Peninsula, the countries of the Nile Valley, and the Maghreb countries. This scenario would also be accompanied by progress in the relations with Islamic countries such as Turkey and Iran.[21]

Examination of these scenarios reveals the following attitudes, beliefs, and assumptions:

1. Discontent with the peace agreements between individual Arab countries and the State of Israel.
2. Treating Jordan from the point of view of a pan-Arabist, the scenarios imply that Jordan does nothing good and that changes are essential.
3. Either the notion of accepting the State of Israel in the region is refused categorically and Israel is eliminated, or implicit in these scenarios is the achievement of a comprehensive peace settlement between Israel and the Arab countries, so that Israel would feel safe despite any changes proposed in these scenarios.
4. The scenarios assume that the demographic make-up of Jordan is a divisive and not a complementary or symbiotic situation.
5. Though the Islamicists would play an essential role in the political arena these scenarios diminish their ability to present any program that could replace the present functioning one.
6. The second scenario – proposing the shift to democracy with representation of all the forces in the country – is based on the hypothesis that Jordanians of Palestinian origin will either one day give up their separate Palestinian national aspirations, or that they will come to rule Jordan. In this sense Jordan would have become the alternative Palestinian homeland and state. This could undermine the Hashemite Kingdom of Jordan for an alternative government instead.
7. These scenarios do not take into consideration the roles of the State of Israel and the international players, for they would not allow changes to occur in Jordan without trying to influence them. Nor do such scenarios consider the reactions of the State of Israel toward the status quo of the region.
8. The scenario of a confederation of Jordan with the Palestinian state has been a possibility that was first raised by the late King Hussein in the 1970s, but after the detachment in 1988 few have spoken of it. Fahd al-Fanik, a prominent Jordanian columnist, asserted in 2000 in an article that Jordan does not want confederation except as a means to get an independent state – because it views confederation as a solution for Israel's demographic problem. In a confederation there would be less rationale for Palestinians in the confederation to demand to return to their homes in Israel, since they would be living in their country. If anything, the movement of Palestinians resident in the West Bank would be into Jordan, and most likely Jordan would also be the place for the return of the Palestinian refugees from Lebanon. There probably would be financial compensation to the refugees and to Jordan to seal the deal. Israel would attempt to impose political, military, and economic hegemony over the con-

federation, and Jordanian independence under a trilateral confederation would be superficial, more like self-rule. Despite this, Israel does not want a confederation, since it could cause Israel to lose its Jewish and Zionist identity.[22]

A positive aspect of these imagined scenarios is the transition of Jordan to a modern state, under the model of the Western democracies, although the author in no way suggests a transition toward a secular state, and he does not suggest reconsidering the constitutional Islamic basis of the ruling system. That basis would put various limitations to the practices of the state both in its behavior in domestic affairs and in international relations.[23]

Notwithstanding the discussion of the above scenario, Jordan has already signed a peace agreement with the State of Israel, without intermediaries. Reading Moshe Zak's book on Hussein and peace, it becomes obvious that Jordan's continuity has been tightly connected to that of the State of Israel.[24] It was through this interconnection that the Palestinians reached the improved recognition as an autonomous entity they now enjoy. Jordan, however, does not feel entirely at ease with other Arab states about its relationships with Israel and the United States.

The Economic Situation

During the past ten years the Jordanian economy has made considerable progress.[25] Fundamental changes have taken place mainly due to the stability and security the Kingdom has enjoyed following the peace agreement of 1994. The main trend in this economic development is the focus on sustainable development. Jordan's efforts have centered on three main goals: Economic growth through attracting foreign investment, reducing unemployment to a minimum, and privatization. In his speech before the House of Notables, Prime Minister Ali Abul Raghib summarized the Jordanian policy as follows:

> Jordan realizes very well the size of challenges it faces to push the carriage of growth and development forward, and believes in the necessity of self-reliance and the use of the available economic resources to enhance the performance of our national economy and to raise the economic standard of living. We also believe that the world develops at a very rapid pace, and that it is necessary to manage and control this development with high quality professionalism in order to absorb modern technology rationally into the production process. We have to benefit from economic and commercial interaction with the developed countries in the various sectors and fields.[26]

In his speech he stressed the most important factors for development of the economy:

1. The economic adjustment program, as agreed upon with the World Bank, is a necessary national program until the internal and external disruptions are removed. It takes into account future additional burdens awaiting the nation. Key to the program's success are the reduction of debt and maintaining a minimal amount of foreign currency in Central Bank reserves.

2. The government has adopted a program of privatization in the water, electricity, transport, and communication sectors of the economy. Also included was privatization of the harbor of Aqaba and the trans- formation of that city into a free trade zone, in addition to the big projects in the potash and cement industries. Jordan has entered the international economy, and become open to the investment of international capital. The nation recognizes the inevitability of global- ization process, that the nation-state is limited in its ability to control this process, and that it is not desirable or possible to conduct a closed economic system of the past.

3. Important also is the relationship between the government treasury and the Central Bank, two entities that were interrelated and are now separated through a law giving independence to the Central Bank. This facilitates foreign investments, entry of international capital to the country, and the movement of capital to and from the country.

4. The adoption of sales taxes, from which the Jordanian citizen had previously been exempt, will enable the government to decrease the deficits in its budgets.

5. Very important is the steady transformation of the educational system. It is crucial to introduce computer education by the seventh grade, and efforts should focus on developing critical, scientific thinking and analytical skills through the teaching of mathematics in secondary and higher education. This implies a change from the traditional religious education, based on memorization and indoctrination, and is an unprecedented step in Arab educational systems. The goal is to follow the international orientation instead of promoting ethno-, religio-, or cultural-centrism.

6. The Free Industrial Zones (FIZ) in the country reduce bureaucratic red tape and give foreign investors an incentive to invest in the country. Presently Jordan has three(one in Sahab, near Amman, one in Irbid in northern Jordan, and one in al-Karak(providing work for some thirty thousand workers. In addition, there are free trade zones stemming from the proclamation of Aqaba as a free economic zone: one in Zerka, one in Jaber (near the Syrian border), and one in the south of the country. More free industrial zones in the Jordan Valley and the free trade zone with Iraq will expand the number of FIZs. In addition, there are the agreements with the Arab countries to connect Egypt,

Jordan, Syria, and Lebanon with a gas pipeline, in addition to the proposed Iraq–Aqaba Oil pipeline. In this way Jordan is opening its borders to internationalism and globalization. Stability and security are the backbone for economic development and prosperity.[27]

Foreign investment reached $650 million in 2000.[28] Tourism is also developing rapidly. Some 1,350,000 tourists visited Jordan the same year. The hotel industry expanded since 1995 at a growth rate of 500 percent, representing not only an increase in beds but, even more crucially, an increase in employment.[29] There has been a massive expansion in information technology. International commercial treaties with the European Union, the United States, the Arab States, and the signing of the GATT agreement, clearly reveal that Jordan has entered the international arena and the global market. Japanese, Chinese, and the Scandinavian interests in the country are expanding, not to speak of France England, Canadian, and other countries.

The Political Perspective

Relative to other Arab states, the political situation in Jordan is quite complicated. On one hand, it has to cope with its sister Arab states, and on the other it has to merge this relationship with its friendship with Western states and the State of Israel.[30] In the Arab world there are at least three ideological categories of states. One is based on the Ba'ath ideology and is generally hostile in its relations toward the West and particularly toward the State of Israel (Iraq and Syria).[31] A second is composed of states that are primarily based on Islamic rule (the Gulf states, Libya, and Sudan). A third is composed of more moderate states such as Egypt, Lebanon, and the Maghreb countries. Countries of the first two categories have had difficult relations with their neighboring states.

Internally, Jordan has to cope with a population that is more than half Palestinian in origin. These Palestinians possess Jordanian citizenship but are still committed to the restoration of a Palestinian state. They dominate the Jordanian economy and the private sector of the country. Additionally, they work in various public sectors, such as education, and are strong in the labor unions. Most of them are organized or affiliated with the Palestinian cause through ideological, social, or political organizations, or are still under the influence of the Palestinian Liberation Organization. These individuals are heavily influenced by the Palestinian struggle for self-determination and an independent state, and there are many East Jordanians of similar ideological orientation who support them and their aspirations.

Jordan must manage this situation at least until the Palestinians reach a settlement with the Israelis; but even after the achievement of a Palestinian state, Palestinians will still play a strong role in Jordanian society. The extent to which Palestinian groups affect the State of Jordan has been made explicit by various authors and columnists in the Jordanian daily newspapers and weekly magazines. Jameel al Nimri, a Christian political activist in the Communist party, expressed in an article how Jordan feels caught between a hammer and an anvil. "The political tension in Jordan becomes stronger both when it seems the Palestinians are close to an agreement with the Israelis in the peace negotiations, and when it seems they are very remote from an agreement."[32]

The reason, he suggests, is that Jordan feels left outside the negotiations. Even when the negotiating parties put Jordan into the negotiating arena, publicly Jordan can only back Palestinian demands. Jordan continues to be the outside party most sensitive to what happens to the Palestinian Authority. When the situation between Palestine and Israel becomes too heated, the heat is transferred to the interior of Jordan and the government is caught between two fires. On the one hand, the government must show solidarity with Palestinian demands for self-determination, and rhetorically support Palestinian rights and the *Intifada*. On the other hand, and at the same time, government support for the Palestinian cause must not overfuel the Jordanian Palestinians' ardor and protests to such a degree that the government cannot keep control and order.

Jordan is the outside country most affected by any deterioration in the Israeli–Palestinian negotiations. Although Jordan has considered the possibility of forced migration as a possible Israeli pre-intended goal, Israel's enduring occupation, confrontation, siege, and perpetration of violence on the Palestinians over such a long period of time has caused a gradual increase in Palestinians leaving the Palestinian Authority to escape the violence and drastic economic situation. It makes one wonder if this is not a premeditated goal of Israel's violence against those in the Palestinian Authority. Jordan is the recipient of most of the escaping Palestinians, and Jordan's socioeconomic and security costs have become too heavy. Jordan no longer enjoys the status of a "confrontation state" that would enable it to receive a large flow of economic aid from the Arab oil states. Jordan's status as such a country ended, despite the fact that the country still bears the major negative consequences of the Israeli–Palestinian conflict at the expense of Jordan's stability and development plan. This leads Jordan to support strongly the continuation of the peace negotiations. Yet, without real signs of an approaching comprehensive agreement on the horizon, fear and apprehension surface on Jordan's horizon because of the ambiguity of the future.

With Jordan largely left outside the peace negotiation process between Israel and the Palestinians, suspicions between the Jordanian and Palestinian leaderships increases. There are vital questions about several interests that Jordan has in the final settlement, as stated in the Jordanian–Israeli peace agreement. A final Israeli–Palestinian agreement will impact greatly on the internal affairs of Jordan; for example, the status of Palestinian refugees who are Jordanian citizens with respect to their right of return and/or compensation. There is also the question of Jordan's possible right to compensation for its hospitality to Palestinian refugees during more than a half century. The refugees, constituting 34 percent of the Jordanian population, are a potential source of internal instability, and the peace agreement with the State of Israel is no guarantee that the negotiating parties will not solve their problems in a final peace agreement at Jordan's expenses. If Israel intends to bring peace and stability to the region, particularly with its neighbors, a just settlement for all parties, including Jordan, is required as soon as possible.

Jordan's position on the Israeli–Palestinian negotiations is stipulated in its peace agreement with the State of Israel, namely that the final treaty should be a part of an overall and comprehensive peace in the region. Jordan cannot but insist on the right of the Palestinians to have their own state with East Jerusalem as its capital, as based the international conventions and United Nations (UN) resolutions. The problem of the refugees in Jordan must be solved, which Jordan believes should happen on the basis of UN Resolution 149 of 1949. These views were stated very clearly during a meeting of Parliament members, labor union and syndicate leaders and heads of the refugee camps in Jordan on January 13, 2001. Attendees expressed their refusal of the concept of an alternative home for the Palestinian refugees, since the right of return to their original homeland is sacred. At the same time, Jordan supports the Palestinian refugees as citizens of the Jordanian state. The attendees also insisted on Jordanian national unity, political and social stability, and security. These three elements form a red line and their violation would be considered intolerable, according to the Jordanian King in a speech to the National Council of January 2001.[33]

The most serious threat to domestic unity is from opposition ideological parties and the Islamicists. The majority in the Parliament and the courts support the government.[34] The professional unions and syndicates form the hard-core base of the opposition, and they confront the government. Members of the opposition were arrested after its anti-normalization committee published and distributed a so-called black list of all those who had any relations with the state and society of Israel. The debate on the right of the unions and anti-normalization committees continues, and has divided the nation into two camps. Many East Jordanians joined the first camp.

This domestic situation is parallel to that on the Arab front, where most relations between the member states in the League of Arab states are unclear, ambiguous, and are often plagued by fear and distrust. In this sense Shihada Abu Mur wrote an article in *al-Bilad* under the title, "the fear of Arabs from Arabs . . . is not a secret," stating:

> Political hypocrisy that dominates the official Arab interrelations requires that no one dare to state clearly the fears and skepticism he has about illegal ambitions of his Arab brother. Nor can one express clearly and openly that his existence, authority over his land, and his decisions are subject to threats exercised more by his Arab brother more than by the visible enemy and the foreigner!
>
> Arab rulers know this truth very well; politicians are very much aware of it; and national security officers in each Arab state are also. Mutual suspicion and the lack of trust in other Arab partners is the usual situation in formal inter-Arab relations. This does not date from recent times but is rooted in the long ago past. It is from this situation that each Arab state finds strong and sufficient justification to request protection from a strong foreign state when it feels threatened or exposed to a threat or to a conspiracy by an Arab sister state.[35]

The only other person to have previously said such things was Jordan's Prime Minister in 1967, Mr. Saad Jum'ah. In a book entitled *The Society of Hatred*, he began his first chapter by saying that every leader in the Arab world hates every other leader and everyone hates everyone.[36] It is exactly this lack of trust that constitutes a burden in the political relations among the Arab states. During various periods Jordan has suffered from conspiracies exercised by other Arab states. Fear from other Arab states has kept many political leaders from clearly stating where they stood, and many times the state chose to risk war rather than express its preference for a peaceful settlement. Recognizing this, Jordan has supported and taken part in successful peace negotiations. This was perhaps the result of King Hussein's long experience and the process of reconciliation within Jordan, in addition to the realization that security among nations is not one-dimensional. This has led the Western allies to view Jordan with far more credibility, as they realized that in many ways Jordan has been unique.

Jordan's new young leadership follows the political strategy of open relations, which are based on common interests with the other states, whether Arab or Western. The King has made it very clear through various statements that Jordan seeks good bilateral relations with all countries of the world and will not join any blocs. This has served the Kingdom well. The King's priorities are very clear: a stable internal situation, national unity, socioeconomic development, the battle against poverty and unemployment, peace, and national security. However in the absence of peace, none of the other goals can be achieved.

The Future of Jordan in the Middle East

Taking into consideration both the past and the present situation of the Hashemite Kingdom of Jordan, there remains a very important point to discuss in order to predict Jordan's prospects for the future. This point relates to the State of Israel.

It is true that Jordan signed a peace treaty with the State of Israel, and Jordan respects that treaty in word and deed. Yet, Jordan cannot be outside the developments of the Middle East in general, and particularly it cannot be outside the Arab camp in particular, especially when it concerns the Palestinian issue. This issue is vital for Jordan's survival. Jordan has opened its borders to Israelis and Israeli investment in Jordan and prepared the Jordanian public to accept Israelis as individuals and groups. Trade with the State of Israel continued to expand until the second *Intifada* in the territories of the Palestinian Authority, at which point most things came to a halt. Even during this difficult period, however, Israelis are found in the streets of Amman and in other Jordanian towns and cities, simply because Jordan believes in peace and decided to give enough time for the Palestinians and the Israelis to reach a satisfactory settlement agreement.

With hopes for peace after the 1994 agreement with Israel, Jordanians expected more progress in the economy than has been the case. As long as Israel and the Palestinians do not reach a solution, the situation will remain depressed and precarious. Fortunately, Jordan has begun to find new markets for its goods in various countries of Europe, and in the United States and Canada. Tourism declined after the *Intifada*, but now the stream of tourists to the country has returned to even higher levels than before. Had Israel and Palestinians made a political settlement, more investment would have streamed into the country and progress would have been far better.

The troubles in the West Bank affect Jordan dearly, for every time Palestinians are killed, Jordan also goes through the traditional condolence routine. The inhabitants of every single village in the West Bank or Gaza Strip have relatives with a diwan or village house in a city or town of Jordan. We live their sorrow every day and every night, and we share in their mourning. Many times our grief is even stronger, for we feel that we can do nothing for them except giving alms or aid.

At the very moment I write this, February 6, 2001, the results of the elections in Israel are being announced over the Lebanese Satellite Channel (LBC). Mr. Ariel Sharon has won. The Arabs from Lebanon, Palestine, the Arabs in Israel, Egypt and other countries, are all expressing their astonishment, not because of Sharon's victory but because of the choice of the Israeli people. Sixty percent of the Israeli public voted for Sharon, i.e., the vast majority of the Israeli Jews. The results of the elections are discouraging, but optimism is required. Israel and the Palestinians are in a kind of a catholic marriage whether they want it or not. They share a very small territory and they cannot remain at war forever. Jordan has far more in common with Israel and Palestine than it has in common with any other country of the Middle East. Cooperation among the three entities is needed for Jordan to prosper. Jordan looks forward impatiently to that time.

Jordan is pushing forward. The peace which Jordan made with Israel remains part of a comprehensive peace for the Middle East. Three peace treaties wait to be made: between Israel and the Palestinians, between Israel and Syria, and between Israel and Lebanon. Only then when this is accomplished will the region become truly attractive for more investment and prosperity. The Jordanian–Palestinian–Israeli triangle is still far from creation and current events discourage its optimistic proponents.[37]

To Conclude

The Middle East enters the twenty-first century with the rise of new leadership in several countries, and, hopefully, with new intentions and orientations. Jordan is a part of this region and welcomes the following century with a large smile, with courage and good intentions for its people, and for Arab and the other neighboring countries. Its leadership on the social, political, economic, and cultural levels realizes that the world is becoming a small village in which the state and the people have to make positive contributions. It has said farewell to the last century in which it had built two solid foundations, one of which was firmly laid by His late Majesty, King Hussein, through the peace treaty with Israel so that we will not have war anymore. The second is the new leadership of King Abdullah who sees the future with optimism and works tirelessly to achieve greater prosperity for Jordan's people and the region as a whole. Jordan is committed to working with all the benevolent people of this globe, Israel included, to serve humanity. Jordan is open to cooperation on the basis of equality, mutual respect, and mutual benefit. Israel has become a state like all the other states in the region through the peace agreement, and, as the King said in an interview: Jordan will not be affected by what happens in neighboring states.[38] The only hope we have in Jordan is that a comprehensive Middle East peace will soon be realized.

Notes

1   Asher Susser, *A Case Study of a Pivotal State*. Washington, D.C.: Washington Institute for Middle East Policy, 2000 (Policy Papers No. 53), pp. 64–73; Arnon Soffer, "Jordan Facing the 1990s: Location, Metropolis, Water," in Joseph Nevo and Ilan Pappe (eds.), *Jordan in the Middle East 1948–1988: the making of a pivotal state* (London: Frank Cass, 1994), pp. 26–44.

2   Mohanna Haddad, *Institutionalization of the State and the Formation of Society in Jordan* (Amman: Armed Forces Press, 1993), pp. 30–2 (Arabic); Ali Mahafzah, *The Contempoorary History of Jordan, the Period of the Emirate* (Amman: Armed Forces Press, 1973), (Arabic); Raphael Patai, *The Hashemite Kingdom of Jordan* (New York: Princeton University Press, 1958).

3   Hani Horani, *The Economic Structure in East Jordan 1921–1946* (Beirut: Research Center of the PLO, 1973), (Arabic); P. J. Vatikiotis, *Politics and the Military in Jordan* (London: Billing and Sons Ltd., 1969).

4   Ghali 'Odeh and Basheer al-Zu'bi, *Economic Cooperation between the Hashemite Kingdom of Jordan and the United Kingdom* (Amman: The Royal Scientific Society, 1994), (Arabic). See also the writings of John Bagot Glubb who was the Chief of Staff of the Arab Legion for a long period.

5   Moshe Zak, *Hussein and Peace: The Jordanian Israeli Relation* (Arabic translation by Dar al-Jalil), (Amman, 2000).

6   Suleiman Bashir, *The Roots of the Jordanian Tutelage: A study in Zionist archives* (Jerusalem, 1980).

7   Munib al-Madi and Suleiman Mussa, *The History of Jordan in the 20th Century* (Amman, 1959), n.p.

8   Ghaleb Abu Jabir, *Collection of the International Treaties and Agreements with Jordan 1923–1973* (Amman: The Ministry of Culture, n.d.), (Arabic).

9   Haidar H. Abidi, *Jordan : A Political Study 1947–1957* (London, 1965), pp. 12–13; Ann Sinai and Allan Pollack, *The Hashemite Kingdom of Jordan and the West Bank* (Washington, D.C., 1977).

10 Uriel Dan, "The Hashemite Monarchy 1948–1988: The Constant and the Changing – An Integration," in Joseph Nevo and Ilan Pappe (eds.), *Jordan in the Middle East*, pp. 15–25.

11 Robert B. Satloff, *Troubles on the East Bank* (New York: Praeger, 1986); Mohanna Haddad, "Palestinian Refugees and Identity in Jordan," a paper presented to the International Conference on Refugees, Oklahoma University, January 2000, published in Joseph Ginat and Edward J. Perkins (eds.), *The Palestinian Refugees: Old Problems – New Solutions* (Norman, OK: University of Oklahoma Press; Brighton and Portland: Sussex Academic Press, 2001), pp. 150–68.

12 Moshe Zak, *Hussein and Peace*, pp.84–5 (Arabic version).

13 Ibid., p. 56.

14 Gabriel Ben Dor, "Jordan and Inter-Arab Relations: An Overview," in Joseph Nevo and Ilan Pappe (eds.) *Jordan in the Middle East*, pp. 191–2.

15 Until now, we have nothing relating to re-evaluating the traditional Arab idea of Nationalism and Arab Unity despite the fact that it is becoming a truism that the country state, or *al-Dawla al-Qutriyya*, is going its own way regardless of the national ideology.

16 Ali Mahafzah, "Jordan . . . Where to?" in *The Arabs and their Neighbors* Al-Mustaqbal al-'Arabi Book Series no. 20 (Beirut: Center for Arab Unity Studies, July 2000), pp. 11–29 (Arabic).

17 Ibid., pp. 26–7.

18 Ibid., p. 27; see also Mustafa Hamarna and others, *The Jordanian Palestinian Relations . . . where to: Four Scenarios for the Future* (Amman: Center for Strategic Studies, Jordan University, 1997), (Arabic).

19 Mahafza, pp. 27–8; See also Dale F. Eickelman and James Piscalori, *Muslim Politics* (Princeton: Princeton University Press, 1996).
20 Mahafza, "Jordan . . . Where to?", 28–9.
21 Ibid., p. 29.
22 Fahd al-Farak, "The Confederation Which Nobody Wants," in *Al-Hadath*, January 4, 1999. (Original translation by Daniel Williams), *Jordan Digest* (http://landfiles.Williams.edu).
23 Kamal 'Abdullatif, "The Reconstruction of the Political Realm in the Arab Mind," in *'Allam al-Fikr*, Vol. 29, No. 3, 2001, pp. 95–109.
24 This is not only Zak's idea. Many authors have stressed this and many Arab nation political parties accused Jordan of this dependency. The accusation of treason addressed to the Jordanian regime, whether justified or not, stems from this very spirit, but all of them forgot that most of the Arab states owe their continuity to some support of one or more Western strong powers. Israel itself could not have survived was it not fully supported by the United States and other states.
25 *The Annual Budget Report of the Government of the Hashemite Kingdom of Jordan, Al-Ra'y*, January 29, 2001.
26 *al-Ra'y*, January 30, 2001, p. 35.
27 Ibid.
28 *al-Ra'y*, February 7, 2001, p. 5.
29 Ministry of Tourism, Annual Report 2000.
30 Yehuda Lukacs, *Israel, Jordan and the Peace Process* (Syracuse: Syracuse University Press, 1999).
31 Duriel Dann, *King Hussein and the Challenge of Arab Radicalism: Jordan 1955–1967* (New York: Oxford University Press, 1989); Gabriel Ben Dor, *State and Conflict in the Middle East* (New York: Praeger, 1983), pp. 355–73; Fuad Ajami, "The End of Pan Arabism," *Foreign Affairs*, Winter 1978/9.
32 *al-Hilal* weekly, January 9, 2001, p. 7.
33 *al-Ra'y*, January 14, 2001, p. 24.
34 These professional unions and the anti-normalization committee spread to the public lists of citizens described as traitors. Implicitly this accusation applies to the state as well for its action of signing peace with the State of Israel. Such practices belong to the past. The Unions and the Syndicates are social and economic organizations, not political ones. In the periods of the Martial Laws they acted as the political bodies of opposition. After the restoration of democracy, and despite the presence and functioning of the political parties, they still hold the view that they are the watchdogs of democracy.
35 *al-Bilad*, January 24, 2001, No. 391, p. 4. (Author's translation).
36 Sa'ad Jum'ah, *Mujtama' al-Karahiyyah* (The Society of Hatred) (Beirut: Dar al-Katib al-'Arabi, 1967).
37 Joseph Ginat and Onn Winckler, *The Jordanian–Palestinian–Israeli Triangle: Smoothing the Path to Peace* (Brighton and Portland: Sussex Academic Press, 1998).
38 *al-Ra'y*, January 7, 2001, front page.

CHAPTER 15

The Jordanian–Israeli Peace: The View from Amman

JOSEPH NEVO

Twenty odd years of a *de facto* peace between Israel and Jordan from the early 1970s, as well as King Hussein's persistent adherence to the notion of a political settlement to the Arab–Israeli conflict, gave rise to expectations that once a formal treaty was concluded, a genuine, "warm" peace (unlike the Israeli–Egyptian one) would prevail between the two states.[1] So far it has not transpired. It seems that the Jordanian public, even while ready to accept a formal accord between the two governments, has not yet become ready for reconciliation and normal relations between the two peoples.

This chapter juxtaposes King Hussein's and King Abdallah's perceptions of peace and normalization with Israel against the various constraints with which each of the two kings has had to cope. It also examines the activities of the anti-normalization forces, their motives, rationale, and impact on the Jordanian public. The intention here is not to take stock of what has or has not been achieved on the bilateral level during the first five years of the formal peace. It is an endeavor to study how the Jordanian public has perceived and evaluated the Jordan–Israel peace, its advantages and shortcomings both on personal and national levels.

From the early 1960s, and perhaps even earlier, King Hussein perceived *de facto* good relations with Israel as an essential component of Jordan's national security. Decision makers in Jordan estimated that the territorial integrity of their country, as well as the continuity and stability of its regime, were an Israeli interest too. The Israelis, so the Jordanians believed, would rather have on their eastern border a moderate and pro-Western conservative monarchy, strong enough to negotiate with the Palestinians and other domestic oppositions, yet not strong enough to threaten Israel. They would prefer that to an indigenous radical revolutionary regime, of the style that emerged in some Arab states following a military takeover, or to the possible disintegration of the state and its eventual annexation by

Iraq and/or Syria. That concept was somewhat shaken in the 1980s when a few Likud party leaders in Israel brandished the slogan "Jordan is Palestine," meaning that if a Palestinian state were to be founded in the future it should be established in Jordan, not in the West Bank, as the majority of Jordan's population were of Palestinian origin. Many among Jordan's political elite suspected that this was not merely the ideological caprice of a handful of political figures but a prescription for a concrete policy or an operational program to which the Israeli right was committed *in toto*. In the early 1990s, it proved obvious that that was not the case, but the apprehension of some Jordanians has not faded entirely.

Simultaneously, Jordan took pains, from June 1967 onward, to regain control over the West Bank, which had just been lost to Israel in the Six Day War. King Hussein was the first Arab leader to grasp – or at least to publicly acknowledge – that the Arabs could not retrieve their occupied territories simply by adhering to the Khartoum summit resolutions which referred to the consequences of that war (no recognition of Israel, no peace with Israel, and no negotiations with Israel). To oblige Israel to restore the territories, an appropriate *quid pro quo* was required, namely recognition by Israel and the attainment of a political settlement. This realization led, *inter alia,* to the adoption of UN Resolution 242 of November 1967 ("peace for territories"), of which King Hussein was a godfather.

Parallel to his adherence to Resolution 242 and to the public demand for an Israeli withdrawal, the king did not neglect any other available channel to promote the restoration of the West Bank, including direct meetings in secret with Israeli officials. Yet, even when negotiating such possibilities with the Israelis, Hussein remained committed to the all-Arab consensus: he could not and would not sign a separate peace treaty, even if Israel met his demands, as long as other Arab states did not join in and as long as the "Palestine problem" remained unsolved.[2]

The Egyptian–Israeli peace accord of 1979 and Hussein's decision in 1988 to abandon Jordan's claim to the West Bank paved the way to a formal Jordanian–Israeli peace. The former event was the precedent that guaranteed that Jordan would not be the first or the only Arab state to sign a peace treaty with Israel. The latter removed the major territorial bone of contention between the two countries. The question of whether or not Israel withdrew from the West Bank became less relevant to the Israeli-Jordanian bilateral agenda.[3] The Israeli–Palestinian mutual recognition, achieved in September 1993, provided a wide enough fig leaf for Jordan to maintain that the other constraint, the solution to the Palestine problem, was partially met. Jordan promptly entered into negotiations with Israel, which in October 1994 yielded a peace treaty between the two countries.

The full year that predated the peace accord constituted a sort of adaptation period for the Jordanian public to the idea of a formal peace with Israel. The fact that Israeli–Palestinian negotiations proceeded simultaneously with the Israeli-Jordanian ones made the latter appear more acceptable. When the peace accord was actually concluded the Jordanian public by and large adopted what may be defined as a fairly flexible wait-and-see attitude.[4] Many Jordanians wished to reap the economic rewards of peace through business relations with Israelis. In a public opinion poll taken in late July 1994 (three months before the peace treaty was concluded but at a rather advanced stage of the negotiations), 82 percent believed that their economy would benefit from peace with Israel.[5] On the other hand, many feared that such cooperation would result in Israeli regional economic hegemony. From the outset, some referred to it as "the king's peace." Indeed King Hussein took pains not only to achieve the peace treaty with Israel but also to fill it with substance.[6] A few Arab states, primarily Syria, criticized his approach. On the home front resistance to the whole project was centered around the general mainstream opposition to the regime, namely the Islamists and the pan-Arab left. They fought the peace treaty in any available venue: the parliament, the political parties, and the professional associations. The fact that the peace *did not* bring an instant remedy to the country's economic problems helped them turn it into a scapegoat and further fueled the resentment of a substantial section of the public.

Without doubt it was largely due to King Hussein's commitment and diligent efforts that the Jordanian–Israeli peace took a different course from that of its Egyptian–Israeli predecessor. More Jordanians than Egyptians have visited Israel (but still far less than the number of Israelis who have visited Jordan – even if the tens of thousands of Jordanians who work in Israeli illegally are taken into account). Israeli entrepreneurs have invested in job-creating projects in Jordan for which the local economy was in desperate need. A few Israeli-Jordanian joint ventures have been inaugurated and a number of bilateral agreements were signed between the two governments and have been duly implemented.[7] Some modest "fruits of peace" have truly ripened, and the general bilateral atmosphere is definitely less tense than that between Egypt and Israel.

On the eve of his death King Hussein was probably somewhat disappointed, not by the strategic decision to make peace but by Israel's response. He was not happy with the way Netanyahu's government conducted negotiations with the Palestinians, as it increased domestic and regional pressures upon him to take sides, which interrupted normalization and minimized ties with Israel. Obviously, the abortive attempt on the life of Khalid Mash'al (head of the Hamas political bureau in Amman) by Israeli agents also contributed to Hussein's anger with the Likud government.

Even so, Hussein's death and the removal of his brother Hassan from the decision-making circle – in other words the departure of the two greatest patrons of the peace with Israel – created a new situation.

Abdallah, the novice king, was well received in the Arab world and enjoyed ample support. As he was not guilty of his father's "crime" of making peace with Israel, the former "rejectionists" were ready to turn over a new leaf in their relations with Jordan. The renewed and improved ties with states such as Syria, Libya, Sudan, and Iran – which had deteriorated following the conclusion of the peace treaty – constituted an incentive to keep relations with Israel at a low profile. Anti-Israel forces inside Jordan followed suit and tried to persuade the new king, less diplomatically and more bluntly, to suspend ties with Israel and to freeze normalization.

Abdallah's view has been that peace with Israel should not be at the expense of the relations with the Arab world, and that cordial ties with the Arab states should not be at the expense of the peace treaty with Israel. Even though this was his official, public position he has more or less adhered to it on the practical level as well. On the face of it, this attitude matched that of the late King Hussein. But while Hussein always referred to the *peace* with Israel, Abdallah has reiterated his commitment to the *peace treaty*. That is, he feels bound more by the legal aspects of the treaty than by the conciliatory spirit and the general atmosphere of peace. Jordanian officials explained the differences between the two monarchs not in terms of a personal change, but simply that domestic and regional realities have shifted. They have speculated that had Hussein lived he would have had to follow the same course as Abdallah.[8] This change became more tangible following the formation of a new cabinet, the first one under King Abdallah, by Abd al-Ra'uf Rawabdah in March 1999. On the one hand, it contained no ministers involved in either the peace treaty or the peace process. It did, however, have among the newcomers two heads of professional associations, including the figurehead of the associations' anti-normalization committee (see below), the most vocal yet efficient instrument against normalizing ties with Israel. The impact of external and internal opposition to peace was clearly reflected by official statements, which included harsher and more frequent criticism of Israel. The Prime Minister and his ministers admitted that Jordan's peace with Israel was not without a price and explained that the relationship with Israel did not exist in a vacuum.[9]

The gap between the two kings' attitude to *normalization* was even wider. Hussein considered normalization to be the essence of the peace treaty and refused to regard it as hostage to Israel's good behavior or as a lever to pressure it to make more concessions to the Palestinians – as many advised him to do. Abdallah, on the other hand, maintains that normalization has nothing to do with government policy. It should be an independent decision, with discretion accorded to any individual or organization to decide whether or not to visit Israel or to cooperate with Israeli colleagues and counterparts.

The anti-normalization forces certainly welcomed this attitude. Under

King Hussein these forces (once again, the various Islamic groups, the pan-Arab left, and the professional associations) had led a continuous and intensive campaign against any form of normalization that led the government to consider curbing their activity. Under King Abdallah the professional associations continued to take the lead. Their supreme council, representing 13 professional associations (most of them dominated by Islamists or pan-Arab leftists) with almost 100,000 members, formed the anti-normalization committee, which was the vanguard, the initiator, and the major force behind the decisive actions against any hint of normalization. The committee, *inter alia*, boycotted the Arabic daily *al-Ray* for publishing an advertisement for the Israeli airline EL AL. They also published a "black list" of "normalizing" Jordanian individuals and organizations.[10]

The constitution of most associations strictly prohibits any ties with Israel or Israelis. Infringement of those rules carries severe economic sanctions. Jordanian law allows most professionals to practice only if they are members of the relevant association. The most telling instance is the case of the three Jordanian journalists who visited the University of Haifa as guests of the Jewish–Arab Center in September 1999. After the visit they found themselves nearly dismissed from their jobs. Only after they had publicly repented was the decision eventually revoked. It is also likely that some government pressure was applied as well, in order to prevent a serious predicament, even though most other anti-normalization activities have hardly elicited any official response either criticizing or supporting those measures. As one Jordanian journalist put it: "The government does not go out of its way any more to promote contacts with Israelis, but it has also dropped its threats to cut the professional association down to size and get them out of business of politics."[11]

Nevertheless, one has to bear in mind that normalization is a much more sensitive and loaded issue than the peace treaty. Many among those who may acquiesce in a formal peace, as a matter between the two governments, vehemently oppose normalization, which they regard as a direct threat to Arab tradition, culture, and even religion. In a public poll conducted in 1994 among professionals in Amman, 66 percent of the respondents supported peace talks with Israel. Less than half of them, however, were in favor of economic normalization, and a far lower percentage of them were willing to interact with Israelis.[12] The anti-normalization activists therefore, deliberately underline these arguments. The divergence between the official and popular view of the peace process is largely due to the intense campaign being waged by those activists.[13]

When King Abdallah succeeded King Hussein, Netanyahu's government was still in power. This gave the new monarch a pretext to pursue his father's reserved attitude toward Israel, adopted, as noted, in his last years. Moreover, the pressing domestic problems that King Abdallah faced provided him with a reason to avoid any reassessment or discussion regarding the future of the Jordanian–Israeli peace; the aforementioned challenges took obvious precedence to the ties with Israel and had to be met first.[14]

A few months after Abdallah's ascent to the throne, Ehud Barak became the Prime Minister of Israel and the excuse for keeping relations with Israel low key lost some of its validity. Even though the king made no secret of his satisfaction with the political change in Israel, bilateral relations remained low profile and ostensibly unchanged. This was, as noted, the price Jordan had to pay for the amelioration in its regional position and for its improved ties with the Arab states. Domestic constraints also played a part in deciding the future of the relations with Israel.

The fifth anniversary of the Israeli–Jordanian peace treaty in October 1999 (the first time when this event was marked under King Abdallah) offered a timely opportunity to evaluate the state of this peace after the trials and tribulations of the assassination of Prime Minister Yitzhak Rabin, the death of King Hussein, the era of Netanyahu's premiership, and the rise of Ehud Barak. The bottom line for most Jordanian commentators engaged in this stocktaking was that the five years-old peace was "a mixed bag of success and failure, disappointments and hopes, both political and economic." "The Jordanian peace with Israel," in the words of another observer, "is not a cold peace Egyptian style, nor is a warm peace as was originally intended by King Hussein and Prime Minister Rabin. It is something in between, maybe 'lukewarm' is the best word to describe [it]."[15] This state of affairs has enabled the many critics of the peace treaty to point to the empty half of the glass and the small number of its supporters to emphasize the full half.[16] In other words, as in any debate over a controversial issue the pros and cons being argued are not necessarily the most objective or relevant ones, but those supporting the debater's political views.

The main advantages of the Jordanian–Israeli peace, as perceived not only by its supporters but also by political analysts, are the following:

1. The major benefit of peace is peace itself: the end of conflict, tension, violence, and suffering.
2. Jordan enjoys, after almost five decades of a state of war, the demarcation of an internationally recognized border.
3. Jordan is no longer seen by Israel as substitute homeland for the Palestinians. As noted, such alleged Israeli intention was previously a major concern for many Jordanians.[17]
4. These first three "benefits" have relieved Jordan of severe economic, political, military and psychological burdens, and enable the kingdom to concentrate on pressing domestic issues.
5. Jordan has gained important new water resources.
6. There is considerable improvement in the economic situation: a tourist

boom, the writing-off of foreign debts, and increased foreign investments and financial aid.

7. Unique export opportunities have opened up, as the United States granted free trade access to Jordanian goods under the scheme of the Qualified Industrial Zones (QIZ). The first QIZ, near Irbid, has already created 5,000 jobs (some in Jordanian–Israeli joint ventures): in 1998 it exported nearly $500 million worth of goods to the American market. Discussion on the creation of another such zone, in the Aqaba–Eilat region, began in early 2000.

8. The peace treaty has extracted Jordan from the isolation and the economic plight it plunged into as a result of its stand during the Gulf War.

The disadvantages of the peace with Israel, as depicted by Jordanian observers, are more complex and can be divided into several categories. *The first* concerns the immediate impact of "the fruits of peace" on the economic welfare and the standard of living of the Jordanian population.

1. Only the state has benefited from the material and economic advantages of peace (if there have been any). They are not felt at the family level (except for workers in the tourist industry and in the QIZs).

2. The peace treaty created expectations that have not materialized. This has caused disappointment and bitterness.

3. Most Jordanians complain that their economic, water, and other conditions are probably worse than in 1994. The deterioration of the economic situation is attributed to the peace agreement.

4. Jordanians object to the obstacles and limits set by Israel on trade between Jordan and the Palestinian Authority. In 1998, trade between Jordan and the Palestinian territories stood at $30 million, compared to the $2.5 billion of Israel's trade with these territories.

The second category concerns the impact of the peace on Jordan's domestic life.

1. The peace treaty has had a negative impact on freedom and democracy in Jordan. It decelerated the democratization process that began in 1989; popular and political freedom has regressed since 1994. Claims have been made that the most controversial legislation, namely the press and publication law and the election law, were designed to nip in the bud any criticism and opposition to the peace with Israel, both in the media and in Parliament. Thus they constituted a retreat with respect to these aforementioned freedoms.[18]

2. The peace treaty may prevent Jordanians of Palestinian origin from adequately pressing their "legal and historical claims" against the State

of Israel. For Transjordanian nationalists, on the other hand, the treaty maintains the Palestinian majority in Jordan that which might challenge their dominant position. Moreover, Jordan may be reduced to a permanent dumping ground for Palestinian refugees.

The third category consists of issues exceeding the narrow bilateral aspects of the peace treaty. These refer to Israel's "bad behavior" and reflect solidarity with the Palestinians and pan-Arab sentiments.

1. Continued Israeli aggression against Palestinian, Lebanese, and Syrian lands.
2. Israel's arrogant, superior, apartheid-like attitude toward Palestinian and Arab rights.
3. No substantial progress has been achieved in the most significant issues of the Israeli–Palestinian negotiation, namely Jerusalem, settlements, water, land, refugees, and sovereignty.
4. The peace treaty has damaged Jordan's position in the Arab world.
5. Peace is perceived as an Israeli victory and as an Arab surrender. Hence Israeli-Arab relations are a zero-sum game.[19]

The claims contained in this last category are also the most repeated arguments of the anti-normalization forces. Despite being made by the most bitter foes of Israel and of the process, they ostensibly imply a conditional opposition: One is led to understand that *if* Israel reversed its attitude and became more responsive to Palestinian and Arab demands, opposition to the peace might be reconsidered.[20] There are, however, not a few diehard anti-Israelis who do not tolerate such speculation. They still adhere to the notion that the conflict with Israel is an eternal religious and cultural one. They deny the very right of the Jewish state to exist, and thus no compromise is admissible regardless of how Israel behaves. A Jordanian observer suggested, in mid-1995, that 60 percent of the Jordanian public held the former view while 20 percent belonged to the latter, "'rejectionist" group. The remaining 20 percent supported the regime's position, as they do on all issues.[21]

More than five and a half years have formalized a peaceful coexistence between the two states. The Jordanian-Israel peace is stable but not popular. It remains on solid ground but has yet to become the vibrant example of cooperation and prosperity that the late King Hussein and the late Premier Rabin hoped it would be. It can even be depicted as contradictory and complex arrangement consisting of close cooperation and deep hostility.

To judge from Amman newspapers and from conversations with Jordanians there is a tremendous curiosity regarding Israeli society and politics. Israel and Israeli-related issues are the subject of numerous daily headlines. Media reports are definitely *not* limited to the old style "know thy enemy" material. Certainly, not a few pieces and articles criticize Israel and emphasize negative aspects. On the other hand, detailed reports appear on issues such as the crisis over the transportation of turbines during the Sabbath, or analysis of the internal struggle within the Russian immigrants' party.

This approach, reflected from press coverage, is an indication of a state of mind that may be defined as a *passive normalization*. It characterizes the attitude of at least some segments of the Jordanian public to the peace treaty. Most Jordanians accept the peace with Israel as a given fact. Their genuine attitude to it may vary, according to the context of the discussion. On the declarative level and on the sphere of the collective public image, the Jordanians are differentiated "into two distinctive groups: a small minority that actively pursues mutually beneficial political, economic, and cultural relations with the Israelis, and a large majority that refuses to normalize relations with Israel *in the current political circumstances*" [my emphasis].[22] On the practical level, however, it seems that save for the "professional" anti-normalization activists, the peace treaty is not the prime concern of most Jordanians. It is reasonable to speculate that those activists constitute a relatively small group. Yet since they are well organized, vocal, and located in many key-points in the Jordanian society (parliament, media, professional associations, etc.), they manage to keep the issue of opposition to normalization in the limelight and to afford it maximal exposure. Admittedly, I am not familiar with any opinion poll in this respect that may corroborate or refute this impression.[23] I believe that the question of the peace with Israel (for better and for worse) occupies a lower place on the Jordanian public agenda than it did a few years ago. The economic situation, the poor standard of services provided by the government, Jordanian–Palestinian relations, women's legal and traditional status, and some other related issues seems to receive higher priority.

King Abdallah's attitude about the scope, nature, and contents of the future relations with Israel is being shaped by various contradicting constraints and he is in search of a golden mean between them. On the one hand, he has completed a successful first-year trial period and his position in Jordan and in the Arab world is stable and quite well established. He is reluctant to jeopardize this achievement by upgrading ties with Israel, an unpopular step in the eyes of both his internal opposition and some leading Arab states, particularly against the background of Israel's policy in Lebanon. Israel's bombardment of infrastructure facilities in Lebanon, in retaliation against Hizballah's activities, caused the king, in February 2000 to postpone a short visit to Eilat. (This scheduled visit was designated to "reward" Prime Minister Barak for the progress of the negotiations on the Israeli–Palestinian track and to provide an incentive for a more flexible Israeli attitude in its negotiations with Syria.)

On the other hand, King Abdallah believes that to cure the ailing Jordanian economy, privatization and globalization should be introduced, namely by selling public and government companies to private investors as well as integrating Jordan into the global economic system. The first move in this direction was made recently when Jordan was admitted to the World Trade Organization (WTO). The king is well aware that to create a sound and a suitable atmosphere to attract job-creating foreign investments, a mere formal peace is not enough. Jordanian economic experts reiterated, even before Abdallah's ascent to the throne, that economics cannot develop and thrive "until and unless an environment congenial to growth and prosperity is created first . . . , [U]nless the overall environment in the Middle East becomes conducive to investment and economic growth (and overall peace in the region appears to be a prerequisite) the economy will not be drastically changed."[24] This necessary regional stability can only be obtained through normalization.

To defuse the impact of these conflicting constraints King Abdallah has recently invested considerable efforts in endeavors to bring about a comprehensive peace in this region by promoting Israeli negotiations with Syria and the Palestinians. Obviously, a tranquil atmosphere of a political process might serve Abdallah's interests best. Nevertheless, regardless of the future of these negotiations, in the coming months he will have to take a crucial decision whether or not to make the peace with Israel more public and more visible.

Notes

1   See, for example, Adam Garfinkle, *Israel and Jordan in the Shadow of War* (New York: St. Martin's Press, 1992).
2   See Moshe Zak, *Hussein Makes Peace* (Ramat Gan: Bar Ilan University, 1996), [Hebrew].
3   It was still relevant however to Jordan's commitment to the Palestinians.
4   Rami Khouri, "The Paradox of Four Years of Jordan-Israel Peace," *Jordan Times*, November 24, 1998.
5   Results of opinion poll on the Washington Declaration. Center for Strategic Studies, University of Amman, August 1994.
6   The expectations about the economic rewards of peace were initially raised by the royal court in order to build public support for peace with Israel. Lori Plotkin, *Jordan-Israel Peace: Taking Stock 1994–1997*, The Washington Institute Policy Focus, Research Memorandum No. 32 (Washington, D.C., May 1997), p. 12.
7   On the economic results of the Israeli-Jordanian peace see Plotkin, *Jordan-Israel Peace*, pp. 3–25: Rami Khouri, "Jordan–Israel five years after the peace treaty: You shall not abhor the Edomite, for he is your brother," *Jordan Times*, October 23, 1999.
8   *Jordan Times* April 13, 1999.
9   Ibid.

10 *Arab al-Yawm*, June 1999; *al-Sabil*, February 9–15, 2000.

11 Rami Khouri, *Jordan Times*, October 23, 1999.

12 Hilal Khashan, *Partner or Pariah? Attitudes toward Israel in Syrian Lebanon and Jordan*. The Washington Institute Policy Papers, No. 41 (Washington, D.C., 1996), pp. 10, 23–7, 31.

13 Ibid., p. ix.

14 See, for example,: Amy Henderson "Analysts, Politicians see 'changing realities' in Jordan-Israeli-Ties," *Jordan Times*, April 13, 1999.

15 Amy Henderson, "Jordanian–Israeli peace treaty: Mixed bag of success, failure," *Jordan Times*, October 26, 1999; Fahed Fanek, "Five years of lukewarm peace," *Jordan Times*, October 24, 1999.

16 See, for example, Ahmad Y. Majdoubeh, "On the benefits of peace," *Jordan Times*, November 19, 1998.

17 One of the main reasons for Jordan to make peace with Israel, according to a Jordanian observer, was the willingness to "convert the cease-fire lines into internationally recognized borders and confirm that Jordan is Jordan." Fahed Fanek, October 24, 1999.

18 The one-person one-vote controversial election law that curbed the power of the Islamists in the parliament, was introduced in August 1993, before Israeli–Jordanian negotiations began. Anti-government factors claimed that the law was initiated in anticipation of the peace treaty. Suha Ma'ayeh, "5 years of peace between Jordan, Israel," *Jordan Times*, October 23, 1999.

19 *Jordan Times*, November 19, 24, 1998; April 13, October 23, 24, 26, 1999; *Al-Ray* October 23, 26, 1999; Abu-Odeh, Adnan, *Jordanians, Palestinians and the Hashemite Kingdom in the Middle East Peace Process* (Washington, D.C., 1999), pp. 234, 247; Plotkin, *Jordan-Israel Peace*, p. 14.

20 Fahed Fanek, "Five years of lukewarm peace," *Jordan Times*, October 24, 1999, wrote: "After five years the wounds [of the Arab humiliating defeats by Israel] have not healed yet . . . Israeli behaviour or misbehaviour can hasten or delay healing."

21 Plotkin, *Jordan-Israel Peace*, p. 27.

22 Rami Khouri, *Jordan Times*, October 23, 1999.

23 Indirect supporting evidence can be found in a public opinion poll conducted in mid-1996 which showed that the political role of the professional associations did not enjoy widespread public support: 43.3 percent supported limiting the role of professional association solely to work-related (as opposed to political) matters. Plotkin, *Jordan-Israel Peace,* p. 13, note 47.

24 Ahmad Y. Majdoubeh, *Jordan Times*, November 19, 1998.

CHAPTER 16

The Peace Process: A Jordanian Perspective

RATEB M. AMRO

Jordan is situated in what historically has been one of the most conflictive and contended-for areas in the world. It is a crossroads between three continents; and with the unstable current situation, the region has become even more vital to the interests of world groups and powers. Exogenous factors often affect the area. Wars and instability in the region have taken their toll on its resources as well as on the smooth continuity of its development efforts. The two peoples now inhabiting the area, the Arabs and the Jews, have – since the early part of the twentieth century and after more than eighty years of conflict and three major wars – endured bitter trials and tribulations.

Although they have labored for so long under conditions of hostility, these two peoples finally decided to see their hostile conditions for what they really are: emblems of an unnatural and sinister state of affairs, embodying both the fear of death and the silence of isolation. Together the Jordanians and Israelis have felt the fears that have mesmerized and prevented them from moving forward to create a bright future for their coming generations. They came to understand that this future could not be achieved, however, without establishing a direct dialogue at the highest level. The result of this was the Jordanian–Israeli peace treaty of October 1994. The treaty makes it possible for Jordan and Israel to become partners in shaping the future of all their peoples, and to seek for them a future of peace, stability, and security – the prospects for which are growing before our eyes.

On October 12, 1991, just before the convening of the Madrid conference, His Majesty the late King Hussein declared in an address to the nation:

> Peace demands no less courage than war. It is the courage to meet the adversary, his attitudes and arguments, the courage to face hardships, the courage

to bury senseless illusions, the courage to surmount impeding obstacles, the courage to engage in a dialogue to tear down the walls of fear and suspicion. It is the courage to face reality. From a purely bilateral angle, the Jordanian–Israeli perspective, so far, is bright and promising.

The Peace Process

The first tentative steps along the path to peace were taken at Madrid in October 1991. At that time, peace was a barely imaginable goal, lying far in the distance. There was no sense of trust or partnership between the parties, for the burden of history weighed heavily on them all.

There was no precedent in the Middle East for peacemaking on that scale, no effective channel of communication, and no established mechanisms for negotiation. The peace process has forever altered the political landscape of the Middle East. So thorough has this transformation been that, notwithstanding many problems, we are now within view of our ultimate goal. We stand poised on the verge of that accomplishment, long sought but always thought unattainable: a comprehensive, just, and lasting peace. And now we find ourselves for the first time contemplating together the shape of our common future.

These developments, astonishing as they would have seemed only a decade ago, have taken place against a background of deliberate, far-sighted and careful negotiation. I would now like to retrace some of the background in order to place these breakthroughs in context.

Jordan has been committed to a negotiated settlement of the Arab–Israeli conflict longer than any other regional party. It played an active role in formulating United Nation Security Council Resolution 242 and has consistently supported 242 and Resolution 338 as the basis for peace in the Middle East. The Jordanian commitment to the cause of peace has never been in question. Indeed, Jordan played a key role in the launching of the Madrid process far back in October 1991.

In the period immediately following the 1994 peace treaty between Jordan and Israel, many voices in the region were raised saying "Everything will be changed," "The Middle East will never be the same again," "This is new world, a new Middle East, and all the problems will be solved." And then, when we started our steps toward peace, the same voices were heard saying: "Nothing has changed," "Everything is back where it was before." Momentous events may happen quickly, as they surely did in some places, but time is needed to understand the changes that events have revealed, accelerated, or caused. By now it is becoming clear that there are indeed many changes occurring in this region.

These changes are related to two sequences: the first is short-term and regional – namely the settlement of the situation in the Palestinian National

Authority territories and future peace treaties between Israel and Syria and Lebanon; and the second is long-term and global – namely, the effort of the United States and the European Union to help the countries of the region to develop themselves economically. A new American policy has evolved for the Middle East, focused on different objectives. Its main aim is to prevent the emergence of a single hegemonic power that could dominate the region.

In the present situation, both the willingness of the other Arab countries to make peace with Israel and the American concern to push the process along, are vital. Many Arabs are beginning to realize that Israel is not their most pressing problem, nor is Israel the greatest threat that confronts them. At the same time there are so many bitter memories and such profound suspicion on both sides. Unfortunately, even now some of the parties do little to diminish and much to augment the lack of trust. The United States and the European Union can make a major contribution by convincing both sides of each other's steadfastness, fairness, and good faith.

The first sequence, if successful, will have its effect mainly on assuring regional security, at least over the long run. The important issue for the present and for the future of the region is the creation of a new and more equitable regional security arrangement and order, which conforms to the aspirations of the majority of the peoples in the region.

The Meaning of Regional Peace

The general public and politicians want a permanent peace for now and for all future generations. Wanted is a peace in which no party can make undue gains at the expense of the other. Any party that feels unduly wronged or greatly disadvantaged is bound to rise up against such peace at the earliest possible opportunity. A peace that collapses with power changes – whether in the region or in the world at large – is not a successful peace.

There is little doubt that world peace depends largely on achieving peace in the Middle East. If the present instability is allowed to continue it could endanger the entire human race, because of great power competition to control this vital region. If the human race is to maintain its claim of being civilized, it is imperative that humanitarian principles govern relations among peoples and nations. These principles should become the basis for the solution of problems of refugees and displaced persons, poverty, illiteracy, terrorism, and other issues that are detrimental to the advancement of Middle East peace and security; and, for this to be the case, respect for human rights must be part of the system.

We in Jordan have long been committed to peace in the Middle East, and we have had a clear view of the essential humanitarian elements for a lasting and durable peace. We believe in those elements, and the sooner they are encompassed, the sooner peace will succeed. Failing to incorporate humanitarian principles would be to perpetuate conditions for new conflicts and continuing instability.

Achieving peace brings to the force the following issues:

1 Palestinian–Israeli Peace: Commitments and Dividends

As Jordanians, we are absolutely committed to the peace process; and this commitment means the marshalling of all of our forces and capabilities toward fulfilling the requirements of the peace process with the hope of obtaining the long-term benefits and dividends that the peace process will bring. When we talk about our commitment, we are talking about an *irreversible* peace process. We are not talking about a trial period. We are not talking about a "let's see if it works" approach. We are planning on a peace process that must be made to work in an environment in which the objective conditions have been shaped by the end of the Cold War, the end of the Gulf War, changes within Israeli society, changes within Palestinian and Arab societies, changes in the balance of power, the requirements of ecology, the integration of new processes of development, economic changes in the world and the new globalization, as well as both objective factors and subjective factors. The goals and objectives of the leaders and peoples of Palestine, Israel, Jordan, Egypt, Syria, Lebanon, and, indeed, the entire Arab world around these countries, indicate that the process we are going through is not a process of tactical experimentation. If it is only a tactical ploy, or a sounding, or a strategy of gradualism in which the parties enter each stage with hopes of manipulatively creating advantages for themselves in negotiations in the next stage, then the process is of no value and futile. What we are talking about is a vision and a plan in which difficulties do not deter the policymakers from proceeding, but instead impel them to discover ways of improving the situation, ways of bypassing the problems, and ways of overcoming difficulties. They cannot retreat back to the starting line – to the old conflicts and old confrontations.

Focusing on how this peace process can work and what will make it work, we will find that this process can become irreversible. It can occur both by making use of the objective conditions and by translating into reality the objectives, targets, goals, values, and the commitment that the parties have made. And while I am specifying this for the Jordanian side, I believe that it is also relevant for the Israelis and for all the other Arab countries. In other words, if we were to assume that the Israelis were not serious, and that, subjectively and objectively, they are not looking to this process as irreversible, then our position would be completely different. Our assumption *is* that the Israeli side is as much committed to this peace process as we in Jordan are.

The Vision. Our vision is that of a long-lasting peace in the Middle East. It is of a comprehensive peace that includes Israel, Palestine, Jordan, Syria, Lebanon, and all Arab countries surrounding us. We envision a peace that creates regional institutions to uphold security requirements as well as political ones, and that allows the region to grow economically and prosper. In the realm of economics we envision a region in which there is mutuality and equality as well as a political regime that ensures these characteristics. By that, I mean an independent Palestinian state with Jerusalem as its capital, a state that is interdependent with Israel, Jordan, Egypt, Syria, Lebanon, and the countries around us, rather than continuously dependent on the Israeli economy, or enslaved by Israeli policies and military might. This is the vision. We must ask ourselves: "Is this feasible?" and "Is this attainable?" within the new regional approach to the peace process in our area.

We in Jordan are of the opinion that achievement of this vision of interdependence and regionalism would have various advantages for us, notwithstanding a number of potential impediments to its achievement. The quest for security leads to separation rather than to integration, and might propel us into areas that would result in the violation of human rights and democratic principles. Israel's focus on security provides a rationale for Israel's captivity of the Palestinian economy. I nonetheless recognize that concerns about security are understandable, and that without security for each country of the region it will be very difficult to achieve political, economic, and social interdependence, based on mutuality.

Settlements. Israeli settlements in the territories occupied since the 1967 Arab–Israeli war are areas that have been developed to house Jewish residents on Palestinian lands. They are designed and established in "blocks" to ensure control over Palestinian land and resources by confining the growth of Palestinian cities and villages. Furthermore, "roads and electricity nets, established to serve the [Jewish] settlements, bypass Palestinian villages, cut through Palestinian land, and further fragment Palestinian land and communities." The purpose of this fragmentation strategy is to transform "what were clearly Palestinian territories into an area 'under dispute.'"[1]

Various organizations, chief among them the World Zionist Organization (WZO), are involved in the settlement programs. With the "green light" from the Israeli government, the WZO enjoys a relatively free hand in planning and administering exclusively Jewish settlements. This scheme serves to release the government from the total responsibility in the settlement process.[2] As far back as 1977, the original "master plan" of the WZO regarding the occupied territories was "the creation of the scores of new settlements and the addition of tens of thousands of Jewish settlers."

Today, the Jewish population of the West Bank and Gaza strip is approximately 80,000.[3]

"The official plan for population dispersal in Israel," completed in 1985 by the interior ministry, "estimated that Israel's population (including the entire population of Israel and annexed Jerusalem, and the Jewish population of the occupied territories) would reach seven million by the year 2020." If Soviet Jewish immigration reaches the anticipated level of one million, Israel is expected to reach the seven million mark by 2010. Attractive incentives for settlers are a major ingredient of the Israeli settlement strategy. With billions of dollars in foreign aid and donations (and with a current $10 billion on hold from the United States earmarked for "housing development"), Israel offers generous tax exemptions, low or no interest mortgages, and commercial and industrial infrastructure.[4]

At the core of the Israeli–Palestinian conflict is the struggle over land. Arab states and the Palestinians stress that Israeli withdrawal from the territories is fundamental to achieving peace and a precondition to their recognition of Israel. As a result of Israel's massive program to erect Jewish settlements in the occupied Arab territories (the West Bank, Gaza Strip, Golan Heights, and East Jerusalem), a Jewish majority is being created over the indigenous Arab population, eliminating the possibility of any territorial compromise.[5]

Over the past 33 years, Israeli arguments justifying the government's aggressive settlement policy went from a need to "secure" its borders under the Labor Party to the Likud Party's more direct and open policy of expansion and annexation. The present settlement scheme in the West Bank was launched immediately following the 1967 war, based on a master plan by Labor Minister Yigal Allon to situate strategic military settlements along the Jordan Valley to defend Israel's eastern perimeter. Under the Likud party, which came to power in 1977, the military administration directed its efforts "at making Israel's control permanent." While "the façade of military administration has been maintained . . . the dominant purpose has become political and ideological – to settle in the whole region and to prevent the repartition of Eretz (Greater) Israel."[6] The policy of the WZO has been adopted by successive governments of Israel as a national priority, referring to Arabs in the occupied territories as minorities among Israelis.

Jerusalem. The most complicated issue in this conflict is Jerusalem. Without solving the Jerusalem issue, there will be no durable peace and stability in the region. Eastern Jerusalem is an occupied territory according to UN Security Council Resolution 242 (1967), and to all the subsequent Security Council resolutions concerning the Palestine question, Jerusalem, and other occupied Arab territories.

Refugees. The Palestinian community in Jordan, which is approximately half the population of the country, is at one and the same time a typically Jordanian community, and distinctly Palestinian. The Jordanian Palestinians aspire for a Palestinian state on the soil of Palestine. They share the dream of return, but being Jordanians, as well as Palestinians, they are also loyal to Jordan. If I may make an analogy, I would point to the Jewish communities of New York or California whose members are at one and the same time US and Israeli citizens. Members of the Jewish community of the United States (or of any other country) can always choose to live in Israel and enjoy their Israeli citizenship in application of the Israeli Law of Return of 1950. Jordanian Palestinians, similarly, could choose to live in the Palestinian state.

We in Jordan believe that the stability of each country in the region, particularly that of Israel and its bordering countries, is an integral component of the peace we hope to achieve. The Palestinian refugee community in Jordan has maintained its integrity and dignity due to the late King Hussein's skillful management of the Palestinians exodus to Jordan. His magnanimity and humanitarian treatment of the Palestinians gained worldwide appreciation, and included the granting of full citizen rights. His generosity enhanced rather than weakened the Jordanian–Palestinians' aspiration for return. It is my strong belief, however, that as long as almost half the population of Jordan is restless because of apprehension about a solution for their final identity and status, then real stability in Jordan – socially, economically, and politically – will always be compromised. These people are entitled, through the hard work of all the negotiating parties and within the context of a phased and final settlement, to choose the identity and citizenship they wish to maintain. As such they should be able to choose whether to reside either in Jordan, the Palestinian Entity (hopefully, the future state) in the West Bank and Gaza Strip or, whenever possible and mutually agreed-upon, in their original homes.

After 52 years it should be clear to both the Israelis and the international community that absorption of the Palestinians outside Palestine – in particular those who are registered refugees – is a "non-option." Just as the Israelis see themselves as a separate unique people who can live only in Israel, the Palestinians see themselves as distinct people whose identity is so inherently connected to Palestine that it is the only place they are willing to settle permanently.

2 The Syrian–Lebanese–Israeli Track

Although the situation between Israel and Syria and Lebanon is unstable, statements from both parties indicate an increasing acceptance of the necessity of peacemaking and the pragmatic considerations involved. It is Jordan's hope that they will find the common ground necessary to bridge the psychological barriers that exist on both sides. The Golan Heights is Syrian land occupied by Israel since 1967, as was the south of Lebanon.

3 Nuclear Weapons

There are dangers that threaten the Middle East region and the world as a result of the accumulation of the major arsenals of both conventional and nuclear weapons. Nuclear armament by a country such as Israel that has refused to sign the nuclear non-proliferation treaty (NPT) and has refused to allow the international organizations concerned to inspect its nuclear installation constitutes a danger to the Middle East. A report on Israeli nuclear armament by a group of experts appointed by the Secretary General of the United Nations, submitted to him in June 1981, stated that "Israel is capable of assembling a number of nuclear explosive devises within weeks, or perhaps days." Does that capability promote regional stability or peace?

Nuclear arms control is an issue that will remain on the front burner for the region. Meanwhile, the official Israeli point of view is that "Israel will not abandon its nuclear program before the attainment of peace in the entire region." This position spurs and makes inevitable the coming nuclearization of the region by one or more potentially hostile powers in the region acquiring nuclear weapons or perhaps building a nuclear weapons capacity. At best it can be postponed, limited, or perhaps controlled. But it cannot be prevented. A nuclear event in the Middle East, when it comes, will totally transform the situation in the region and the world.

4 Water

Water, agriculture, and food are basic issues that affect the daily lives of our peoples. The availability of food and the development of water resources as well sharing scarce water resources will play a crucial role in developing the Middle East region into a one of peace and stability.

5 Energy

Energy management is a high priority in practically every country in the world. While energy consumption in the industrialized world has reached high levels and seems to be tapering off, it is growing rapidly in the Middle East and will continue to do so into the foreseeable future. At the same time, it is well-known that Arab oil is threatened by depletion if alternative sources of energy are not developed, and if effective energy measures are not taken. Energy is one of the main factors with respect to achieving stability in the region.

6 Security and Human Rights

The quest for Palestinian independence, which will lead to Palestinian, Israeli, Jordanian, Egyptian, and Arab interdependence, is a quest for freedom, justice, equality, democracy, ecological sanity, and economic development. Achievement of this goal is dependent on taking steps that will achieve individual and collective security for both Israelis and Arabs.

Between the time President F. W. de Klerk and Nelson Mandela signed the agreement in South Africa and were readying for elections, some of the bloodiest events occurred in that country. But the two parties shared a vision and had the courage and patience to continue together; and through this they were able to create the miracle that we now see. The same miracle is possible in the Middle East, and that all our dreams are achievable if we work together. We must each pay part of the price that is required to make the long-term vision come about and we each must suffer through the difficulties that are inherent in the short term.

The Possible Economic Impact of Peace in the Jordanian Economy

This section has two central messages. *First*, most of the actions needed to position the Jordanian economy to benefit from the economic potential of peace in both the short and the long run are within the government's own span of control. They do not depend on the actions of others – not even Israel and the PLO. The *second* message is that the international community can and should assist Jordan in carrying out these actions since the success of the political agreements on peace will ultimately depend on the success of the region's economics.

In the short run, while peace may offer Jordan some immediate benefits arising primarily from an investment-led boom in the West Bank and Gaza (WBG), it also carries substantial risks to macroeconomic stability. The opening of branches of Jordanian banks in the WBG offers potentially large benefits in supplying financial services in a rapidly expanding economy. At the same time, however, it also exposes the Jordanian financial system to a new range of risks associated with operating in multiple currencies in a fragile environment. Jordan has the capacity to manage these increased risks through continued macroeconomic prudence and further efforts to strengthen the financial system.

In the longer term, peace offers Jordan, together with other countries in the region, the opportunity to benefit from a greater mobility of labor, capital, and expanding foreign investment. However, these long-run opportunities for the region at large carry with them significant challenges for Jordan. In a more open and competitive regional economy, expanded trade, and especially the growth of non-traditional exports, will offer an important opportunity for more rapid growth. The reforms introduced by the Jordanian government to improve efficiency and international competitiveness and to reduce the economy's dependence on external finance acquire even greater urgency in this environment. Although Jordan, compared with its regional neighbors, has somewhat of a head-start in building a more efficient, outward-oriented economy, it must maintain or accelerate that lead if it wishes to realize the long-term potential benefits of peace.

Jordan has traditionally been a society that has relied heavily on transfers from abroad, remittances of its citizens, and official aid to finance investments, and, even at times, consumption. The opening of new, attractive economic opportunities in the WBG may change traditional patterns of both foreign aid and direct foreign investment. Thus, Jordan needs a strategy to increase domestic savings, promote foreign investment, and remain an attractive location for capital transfers. A central element of that strategy will be a satisfactory resolution of outstanding debt; at the same time structural reforms designed to increase the attractiveness of private investments in Jordan are also essential.

The opportunities and risks for the international community are equally great. The durability of whatever political solutions result from the peace process will ultimately depend on economic success. The "peace dividend" for Jordan's population, as for those of other countries in the region, will be measured primarily in terms of the ability of the economy to return to a sustained growth of incomes and employment.

Conclusion

There are serious obstacles to overcome. The Arab–Israeli conflict has shattered the economies of the Middle East. Massive and constant expenditure on arms has wasted the region's resources, precluding much needed investment in more productive areas. This in turn has created an addiction to aid on the one hand, and to oil revenues on the other.

The conflict has created disparities, unserviceable debt burdens, and over-extended public sectors. It has stunted economic growth, prevented cooperation, and undermined international confidence. Given a climate of peace and a viable economic framework, the economies of the region will eventually recover. However this will take time, investment, and careful planning. The national investment and development projects that serve the region and its people will be absolutely essential. It is equally important that such projects be founded upon sound concepts and that they receive the support of the international financial institutions, governments, and multinational corporations alike.

Direct private investment will play a key role, as well as joint ventures and appropriate technology transfer. Those who seek to help the Middle East move toward a peaceful and prosperous future should consider how such channels could best be developed. However, peace requires an enduring structure to tackle the overarching problems of the economies of the region. Such a structure must allow for human cooperation, resource cooperation, and security. As a long-term goal, it is necessary to liberalize and dismantle all barriers in the region, whether in terms of trade, investment, labor, capital or services. A Middle East Free Trade Agreement (MEFTA) along the lines of NAFTA or EFTA is the objective. It is clear that different areas of the Middle East are endowed with different resources, labor, capital, and technology. So a free-trade regime would be in the interests of all the people of the region and would allow the Middle East to play a more dynamic and constructive role within the world economy. However, there is still a long way to go before conditions are sufficiently stabilized, equitable, and sustainable to realize that vision. International support will be absolutely vital in bringing about such conditions. Peacemaking inevitably creates uncertainty. Thus, the short-run fiscal aspect of peace is likely to be negative for Jordan.

Economic strategies alone, however, are not sufficient. They must be underpinned by an arrangement that can guarantee the security of all, and encourage cooperation among the parties. The bilateral tracks of the peace process involve only Jordan, Syria, Lebanon, the Palestinians, and Israel. The rest of the Middle East is represented only in multinational or multilateral talks. It is our hope that these multilateral talks will foreshadow the development of such arrangements; for if the Middle East is to enjoy a viable future it must above all find a neutral idiom and forum in which to discuss common challenges and the framework for collective action.

I believe that the Middle East has much to offer the world, but only if it is now set on a viable footing. For too long the region has been at odds with itself, squandering its potential and producing only instability. The atmosphere of uncertainty has prevented the evolution of representative institutions. It has encouraged the abuse of human rights and stifled creativity. With the resolution of the Arab–Israeli conflict a real possibility, we must consider how to devise a process of positive change. To be sure, there are difficult questions. We can take the easy way: avoiding them, and so give our assent to a future of chaos and darkness. Alternatively, we can set about the task of answering these difficult questions together. Jordan remains committed to peace, democratization, free trade, and human rights in the Middle East. The solutions proposed above are unusual and untested in the region, but the ways of the past have failed. I believe it is now time for a new way.

Notes

1   "Israeli Settlements: Are They Obstacles to Peace?" Settlement Watch, Washington, D.C., 1991.

2   John P. Richardson, "The West Bank: A Portrait," The Middle East Institute, 1984, pp. 116–17.

3   "Report on Israeli Settlements in the Occupied Territories," *Foundation for Middle East Peace*, Vol. 2, No. 4, Washington, D.C., July 1991.

4   Ibid.

5   Jackson Diehl, Washington Post Service, *International Herald Tribune,* October 17, 1991.

6   Meron Benvenisti, *The West Bank Data Project: A Survey of Israel's Policies* (Washington, D.C.: American Enterprise Institute, 1984), p. 38.

Part III

Countries without Peace Agreements with Israel

CHAPTER 17

Lebanon's Position in the Peace Process

KAIS FIRRO

Political statements from one Syrian and two Lebanese officials made on March 6 and 7, 2000 perhaps best reflect the position of Lebanon toward the current peace process. Salim al-Hus hastened to welcome the March 6 decision of the Israeli government to withdraw from south Lebanon with or without an agreement with Syria. To him the withdrawal meant that Israel had accepted the unconditional implementation off United Nations Security Council's Resolution 425 (March 19, 1978), which "calls upon Israel immediately to cease its military action against Lebanese territorial integrity and withdraw forthwith its forces from all Lebanese territory."[1] On March 6, 2000 an official Syrian statement judged the Israeli decision as a mere tactical move to separate the Syrian and Lebanese negotiating tracks, and warned that such a unilateral withdrawal would be no more than a new form of deployment of Israeli troops in Lebanese territory. The next day Lebanon President, Emile Lahud, declared that in the case of uni-lateral withdrawal without solving the problem of Palestinian Rrefugees in the country, Lebanon could not guarantee that Palestinian refugees would not in the future resume their attacks against Israel from Lebanese territories.

The last two statements seem to represent a coordinated response to the Israeli attempt to separate the Lebanese from the Syrian negotiating track. Even the Israeli withdrawal from south Lebanon could not elicit changes in the Lebanese position toward the peace process. Lebanese and Syrian officials continue to stress their united position, which calls for one single-track, *talazum al-masarayn*, in peace negotiations with Israel. The failure of Camp David negotiations along with the absence of the Syrian–Lebanese track put the entire peace process in jeopardy. In my view Israeli attempts to separate between the Palestinian, Lebanese, and Syrian tracks might lead to success in the short run, but will fail to achieve regional peace in the long run. I contend that the Lebanese case proves that the strategy of separation of the various peace tracks will not lead the region to peace but will probably lead to a new phase of conflict whose features no one can predict.

To assess the Lebanese position and its implications on the entire peace process, I will discuss three related topics: first, the historical experience of the Israeli–Lebanese relationship,; second, the Syrian presence in Lebanon and its impact on the defense and foreign policy of Lebanon, and the implication of this on the internal political game of the Lebanese elites and politicians; and finally, the future of the presence of Palestinian refugees on the territory of Lebanon.

Unlike the situation with Syria, there was no border dispute between Lebanon and Israel. The 1949 Armistice Agreement states, "the Armistice Demarcation Lines shall follow the international boundaries between Lebanon and Palestine." Article 8 of the agreement clearly states that under no circumstances can the Agreement be unilaterally abrogated. This article was again clearly reiterated in the terms of Resolution 425 and has been repeatedly endorsed by various other UN resolutions.[2] From 1949 until 1984, most of the Christian elites followed a policy of maintaining neutrality in the Israeli-Arab conflict while stressing that Lebanon would be the last country to sign a peace treaty with Israel. However most of these Christian elites saw Lebanon as an independent body *vis-à-vis* the Arab world, with special features in relation to the Arab environment. This independence was of course fictional and in foreign policy led to an overestimation of Lebanon's significance on the Western strategic chessboard. Israeli policy-makers came to the same conclusion as the Christian Lebanese elites, and until 1984 Lebanon was seen by the Israelis as a Christian country in which Maronite elites could determine – with Western and Israeli backing – its foreign policy. Three tests of this fictional independence prior to 1984 proved that Lebanon could not conduct a foreign policy based on Western or Israeli backing. The first test came during the Kamil Chamoun presidency, from 1952 to 1958, when his US-guided policy got him into trouble, leading to the breakdown of order and the eruption of the civil war. As he wrote in his *Crise au Moyen Orient*, Chamoun discovered that the United States abandoned him for the sake of its overall policy in the Middle East.[3]

The second test came in the years 1969–82, when Christian elites could not reconcile the conflicting interests of the Lebanese state and the revolutionary objectives of the Palestine Liberation Organization (PLO). The contradiction between these two sets of interests revealed the vulnerability of the Lebanese political system. This instability was the result of an internal balance of forces determined by clannish and sectarian considerations. The established Christian elites who maintained their neutrality in the Israeli–Arab conflict believed that "the strength of Lebanon lies in its weakness." But such neutrality was futile in the face of internal and external threats, and thus prevented Lebanon from steering an independent foreign policy. To rebuild the "Lebanese nationhood" and sovereignty, a new radicalized constituency under the leadership of Bashir Gmayel focused during the years of 1975 to 1982 on building military capabilities to protect the "nation." This radicalization became more pronounced in its anti-Arabism and in the cultivation of a semi-covert alliance with Israel.

This led to a third test. Israel attempted to exploit this new Lebanese radicalized constituency toward creating a peace formula that would guarantee the security of Israel's northern border and an independent foreign policy for Lebanon backed by the West. The 1982 Israeli invasion was seen as an opportunity to materialize this formula when it drove the bulk of the Palestinian military organizations out of southern Lebanon and Beirut, and destroyed the infrastructure of "the state within a state" which the PLO had established in Lebanon.

On September 1, 1982, one day after the last Palestinian guerrilla had left Beirut, President Reagan announced a new initiative to give substance to the Camp David Accord between Egypt and Israel. Later on, Secretary of State Shultz declared that the events in Lebanon had demonstrated that the United States had a special responsibility to bring peace to the region. Because it was a country militarily weakened – as US experts suggested – Syria was excluded from the new American initiative. While Israel rejected the Reagan Plan for the occupied territories, Israel gave Lebanon priority in the American initiative. On a visit to Washington in October 1982, Amin Gmayel received the impression that the United States was prepared to grant Lebanon a special place in its Middle Eastern policy. Then the semi-alliance between Israel and Amin Gmayel was translated into Israeli–Lebanese negotiations for an official agreement. On May 17, 1983 an agreement was signed. But both, the Israelis and Gmayel overestimated the place of Lebanon on the Western strategic chessboard and underestimated the role of Lebanese and Syrian opposition to the agreement, which soon became a dead letter.[4] Like Chamoun, Gmayel as well as other Christian leaders learned the hard way a basic element of realpolitik: "a *détente* with a regional superpower is more rewarding than an *entente* with an underdog."

From 1983 until 1991, Syrian and Lebanese leaders established norms of behavior for their two countries' unique relationship. General 'Aun was the last Lebanese leader incapable of reading the signs of the time. Apart from small groups from the opposition, most of the Lebanese politicians had learned that rebuilding Lebanon on anti-Syrian terms would remain an impossible task. A stable Lebanon is a Lebanon responsive to Syria's main regional and foreign policy concerns.

The rebuilding of Lebanon was the main goal of the Taif agreement of October 1989.[5] Implementing the agreement, the government, with Syrian support, began in 1991 to disarm the militias. Apart from the resistance forces (Hizballah) all militias have been disarmed. While the agreement stipulates that Lebanon and Syria will reach an agreement, "specifying the size and duration of the Syrian forces' presence" in Lebanon, it calls for the liberation of Lebanon from Israeli occupation under Resolution 425. Twenty days after disarming the militias, a Treaty of Brotherhood, Cooperation and Coordination was signed by Lebanon and Syria.[6] In addition to legitimizing the Syrian military presence in Lebanon, the treaty stresses that "the two countries' security requires that Lebanon not be made the source of a threat to Syria's security . . . and Syria . . . shall not allow any action that threatens Lebanon's security" (Article 3). In foreign policy the two "countries shall strive to coordinate their Arab and inter-national policies."[7] In September, the treaty was followed by "the Defence and Security Pact."[8] Thus, when the peace process was launched in the same year (1991), the Syrian and Lebanese tracks had already been merged. Furthermore, this outcome in defense and foreign policy reflected the change of the internal balance of forces among the Lebanese factions and political parties.

This change can be summed up by saying that the Lebanese civil wars since 1983 had resulted in a victory for the Arabist and Muslim orientation of Lebanon against the traditional Lebanist one, which had dominated Lebanon political life since its establishment in 1920. Clashes between Maronite factions accompanied by a large-scale migration of Christians from Lebanon put an end to the First Lebanese Republic. This led to the rise of the Second Lebanese Republic, in which an anti-Syrian policy in Lebanon was nearly impossible. General 'Aun was the last manifestation of Lebanism, which considers the Syrian presence in Lebanon as a threat to independence. Convinced that he could mobilize popular support, 'Aun decided in October 1989 to cross the Rubicon. However, he found himself waging his war alone without even the support of the many Christian factions. At the beginning of 1991, internal politics in Lebanon grew more and more dependent on Syria, regardless of the likes and dislikes of the Lebanese people. This dependency was not only the outcome of consistent policy of Syria toward Lebanon, but was and will continue to be related to the internal division among the Lebanese political elite. The elections of 1992, 1996 and 2000 testify to the state of dependency of this elite and its impotence to solve mutual distrusts.

During the years 1992 to 1996 the Syrians were able to use the Lebanese card for possible peace negotiations with Israel. Without going into detail on the ups and downs of the Syrian–Israeli negotiations, it is important to stress that the Lebanese card was played to seek a complete withdrawal of Israel from the Golan Heights. The Lebanese card enabled the Syrians to utilize two opposing options. On the one hand, they could engage in American, Saudi and Egyptian diplomacy, and meanwhile, on the other hand, they could maintain good relations with the Iranians, Palestinian Rejectionists, and Hizballah. Although the Americans as well the Israelis had demanded that Syria abandon the Iranian and Hizballah option, Syria was reluctant to respond. Yet in 1996, Asad seemed ready to meet the needs of Israel in the case of serious progress toward full withdrawal from Golan Heights.

The Israeli invasion of Lebanon and the new Israeli government that came to power that rejected full withdrawal from Golan Heights convinced Syria that abandoning the Iranian and Hizballah option before progress was made on substantial issues would jeopardize Syria's efforts to reach its goals and thus risk leaving Syria empty handed. The chain of events since the 1979 Camp David agreement for a separate Israeli peace with Egypt, and the setbacks in the Oslo's peace process framework, had implications that were not lost on President Asad.

In the absence of diplomacy during 1996 to 1999, military means were the only way for Israel to convince Syria to abandon its Iranian and Hizballah option.

Because the presence in south Lebanon cost Israel dearly, Netanyahu's government contemplated the idea of unilateral withdrawal from South Lebanon. To convince the Lebanese government, Netanyahu had to declare that he intended to implement Resolution 425, but he did so only through talks with the Lebanese government and international third-party guarantors. Lebanon rejected the Israeli proposal, considering it to be a deliberate attempt to separate the Syrian and the Lebanese tracks. In response the Lebanese government stressed its demand to see Resolution 425 implemented without any precondition. At the end of its mandate, Netanyahu's government "wanted to teach the Lebanese people and government a lesson," and bombarded the power plants near Beirut as reprisal for "acts of aggressions" by Hizballah. In fact, this was an attempt to change the rules of the game as formulated in the April 1996 accord. The Israeli hope that military operation would put pressure on Lebanon had the opposite effect. Hizballah gained wide popular support and Syria was able to employ the Lebanese card more than ever.

After Barak became the Israeli Prime Minister, the Syrian–Lebanese and Israeli track ran into difficulties. That Israel does not learn from the past is clear from the way it bombarded Lebanon's infrastructure, which again had a reverse effect. In June 2000 Barak fulfilled his promise to withdraw Israeli troops from south Lebanon in accordance with UN Resolution 425. It meant the return to the *staus quo ante,* which prevailed before the negotiations that culminated in the May 17 Agreement of 1983, and the return to the Armistice Agreement of 1949. The reason for a return to this latter agreement was to place obstacles to any separate treaty between Lebanon and Israel.

Today the peace process is in a crucial phase. It has two directions. One

would lead to a settlement with Syria and Lebanon, while continuing to
negotiate with the Palestinians for months and maybe years to reach a final
agreement. The other direction would be a peace process without Syria
and Lebanon, while accelerating the Palestinian track to marginalize
Syria's role in the international community. Maybe the latter would
deprive Syria of the use of its Lebanese card, and it certainly would press
the Syrian leadership to look for a new strategy. In my view, the statements
of the Lebanese officials concerning the Palestinian refugees in Lebanon,
and current Syrian statements, are clear indications that Syria is seeking a
new strategy. Without progress in the Syrian track, an agreement between
Israel and the Palestinian Authority will fail to satisfy Syria and its
Palestinian, Lebanese, and Iranian allies. Despite American criticism, Syria
has maintained close relationships with the rejectionist Palestinian
factions. Because the refugee problem in Lebanon has become a time
bomb, any serious setback in the peace process could cause it to go off.

Summing up, I think that a separation between Palestinian, Lebanese,
and Syrian tracks in this stage of the peace process cannot lead to a settlement but would instead usher in a new phase in the Israeli–Arab conflict.
Which course it will take no one can foresee. Excluding Syria and Lebanon
from the peace process also means inviting further difficulties for the
Palestinian track.

Notes

1 Text of UN. Security Council Resolution 425 (March 19, 1978) in Fida
   Nasrallah, *Prospects for Lebanon, The Question of South Lebanon* (Oxford:
   Center for Lebanese Studies, 1992), p. 33.
2 Ibid., pp. 33–42.
3 Camille Chamoun, *Crise au Moyen Orient* (Paris: Editions Gallimard, 1963),
   pp. 11, 424–31.
4 For further details see Theodor Hanf, *Coexistence in Wartime Lebanon,
   Decline of a State and Rise of a Nation,* (London: Centre for Lebanese Studies
   and I.B. Tauris, 1993), pp. 264–75.
5 On the Taif agreement see, Joseph Maila, *Prospects For Lebanon, The
   Document of National Understanding: A Commentary* (Oxford: Center for
   Lebanese Studies, 1992).
6 See Hanf, *Coexistence in Wartime Lebanon,* pp. 615–18; Albert Mansur, *Al-
   Inqlab 'Ala al-Taif* (Beirut: Dar al-Jadid, 1993), pp. 148–59.
7 Text of "The Treaty of Brotherhood, Cooperation and Coordination Between
   Lebanon and Syria, May 22, 1991," in the Appendices of the booklet, "The
   Questions of South Lebanon and Syria," part of a series "Prospects for
   Lebanon" (Oxford: Centre of Lebanese Studies, 1992), pp. 75–81.
8 Text of "The Defence and Security Pact Between the Lebanese Republic and
   the Syrian Republic, 1st September 1991," ibid., pp. 83–5.

CHAPTER 18

Lebanon and the Arab–Israeli Conflict

MARIUS DEEB

The Ironies of the Lebanese Situation

When one looks at how Lebanon has become embroiled in the Arab–Israeli conflict in the last thirty-four years, one is forced to think of all the ironies that surround this entanglement.

The first irony: Lebanon has avoided the Arab–Israeli wars, but ended up as a launching pad for guerilla operations. Lebanon has avoided participation in any of the Arab–Israeli wars except for that of 1948–9. The Lebanese–Israeli border was very peaceful and tranquil throughout the period from 1949 until 1967. After the June 1967 war the situation changed when the Palestinians and their leftist allies began attacking Israel from the Lebanese border, and these attacks in turn invited Israeli retaliation. The irony is that Lebanon, which was then a peaceful and democratic polity – that never constituted a threat to any of its neighbors – was compelled by the Palestine Liberation Organization (PLO) to become a battlefield of the Arab–Israeli conflict. Most of the Lebanese Christians were against the PLO's military operations from Lebanese soil. They believed that the PLO constituted a state within a state.[1] They were also sympathetic toward Israel because they shared with the Israeli Jews the feeling of being surrounded by an Arab Islamic world.

The very foundation of Lebanon as an independent country was based on the National Pact of 1943, which stipulated that Lebanon would neither remain under French protection nor would it be dominated by its Arab neighbors. The PLO's military activities violated the National Pact by subjecting Lebanon to the problems of its Arab neighbors. Although the National Pact created a genuine partnership of Christians and Muslims in ruling Lebanon, the very *raison d'être* of Lebanon was the presence of a large Christian community. The Lebanese Christians – who consciously averted from involvement in the Arab–Israeli conflict – found that their country was forcibly drawn by the PLO, into the conflict.

The second irony: although Lebanon has no territorial disputes with Israel, its border with Israel remains violent while the borders of other states are tranquil. There were never any territorial disputes between Lebanon and Israel, but the border between the two countries has been, since late 1967, plagued by violence. Meanwhile other Arab states bordering Israel have not permitted violent incidents across their borders with Israel. Jordan followed that policy long before its peace treaty with Israel in October 1994, in the aftermath of its expulsion of the PLO in July 1971. Egypt did the same as early as the first Egyptian–Israeli Disengagement Agreement of January 1974. Even Syria sealed off its border with Israel to guerilla operations since as of May 31, 1974.

The PLO exploited the existence of the Palestinian camps in Lebanon to use Lebanese territories to launch its attacks against Israel. When the mainstream PLO was obliged to evacuate, in the wake of Israel's Operation Peace for Galilee, from West Beirut in August–September 1982, Syria substituted the dissident PLO, and more significantly Hizballah, for Arafat's PLO. Consequently the Lebanese–Israeli conflict has not been solved because it has been part of Syria's strategy to keep it alive, whether under the late Hafiz Asad or his son, the present president of Syria, Bashar Asad. The reasons which underlie the Syrian strategy with respect to the Lebanese–Israeli border are complex. In my forthcoming book entitled, *Evil in the Levant: Syria's War on Lebanon and the Peace Process 1974–2001*, I expound fully, with supporting documentation, the basis and the goals of this Syrian strategy.

Hizballah, like its ideological masters in the Islamic Revolutionary Iran, regards its war against Israel and its allies in southern Lebanon as an imposed war (*harb mafrudah*). The truth is just the opposite. In fact Hizballah, which thrives on death and destruction, has fought and still is fighting in southern Lebanon because its very *raison d'être* is war. The very basis of Hizballah is what it calls war society (*Mujtama 'Harb*). The present Secretary-General of Hizballah, Hasan Nasrallah, stated as early as January 1987, that "when there will be in Lebanon two million hungry people, our mission will not be to provide bread for them, but to enable them to wage (*al-halat al-jihadiya*)."[2]

The proof that Israel and Lebanon never had any territorial dispute of significance was the demarcation by the United Nations (UN) of the blue line between Lebanon and Israel within two months of Israel's withdrawal and the dismantling of its security zone on May 24, 2000. This was done without any assistance from the Syrian-controlled Lebanese Government because Syria had prevented it from been helpful to the UN.[3]

Thus the war waged by Hizballah, prior to May 24, 2000, was a contrived and an artificial war with the objective of keeping Israel in the security zone rather than what it had claimed about "liberating" southern Lebanon. Syria was very upset about the Israeli withdrawal because it could have led to the pacification of the Lebanese–Israeli border. Before President Hafiz Asad died on June 10, 2000, he managed to find a pretext for the Lebanese government, which he controlled, and his proxy Hizballah to claim that the Israeli withdrawal has had not been completed. He argued that a piece of land called Mazari' Shib'a that is part of the Golan Heights belongs to Lebanon, and, unless Israel withdrew from it, Hizballah's military operations against Israel should continue. The senseless war waged by Hizballah against Israel is a contrivance of the Asad regime against Israel.

The third irony: all other border states of Israel, including Syria, have separate negotiations with Israel, while Lebanon is not permitted to do the same. Lebanon has been prevented by Syria to negotiate separately with Israel as Syria did during the Israeli governments of Itzhak Rabin and Shimon Peres from August 1992 until March 1996, and again during Ehud Barak's administration from December 1999 until January 2000. The reasons are glaringly obvious. First, Lebanon could easily sign a peace treaty with Israel, following in the footsteps of Egypt and Jordan. If Lebanon is left alone to make peace with Israel, then it will neither be a cold peace like that between Egypt and Israel, nor a lukewarm peace like that of Jordan and Israel, but it will be a real genuine peace. Second, contrary to all appearances there is no hostility felt by the various Lebanese communities toward Israel.

The Attitude of the Lebanese toward Hizballah's War Against Israel

The vast majority of the Christians want peace with Israel, and feel no hostility whatsoever toward the Israelis. The Patriarch of the Maronite Catholic community, Cardinal Sfair, has publicly declared his position on southern Lebanon, a stand that represents not only the Maronite community but also all the Christian communities of Lebanon. He demanded "the spread of the Lebanese State's authority in the South."[4] This could only mean that southern Lebanon should not be left to for Hizballah to dominate and to launch operations from it against Israel. Sfair called for the withdrawal of Syrian troops from Lebanon in accordance with UN Resolution 520 of 1982. Because of Syrian domination, Lebanon is neither independent nor sovereign. Syria not only nominates the politicians of Lebanon but also its civil servants and even members of the judiciary.[5]

The Greek Orthodox journalist Jubran Tueni, who is the present publisher of the most prestigious and influential newspaper in Lebanon, *Al-Nahar*, concurred with the declaration issued by Sfair and stated that the issues which Sfair has raised have been frequently raised by the vast

majority of the Lebanese themselves. Tueni strongly objected to allowing
Hizballah to hold armed rallies, and called for the return of the legitimate
authorities to southern Lebanon. He said this would make the villagers feel
protected by the Lebanese government and thus encourage them to return
to their families and properties.[6] Tueni has a profound understanding of
the history of the conflict in southern Lebanon. In an article written on
August 10, 2000, he praised the officers and the rank and file of the contin-
gents of the Lebanese Army in Marji'yun who refused to join the renegade
officer Ahmad al-Khatib who established in 1976 the breakaway
Lebanon's Arab Army, which was "under the control of the Palestinians
and was financed by the Iraqi Ba'ath." "We all remember [in 1979] when
the Lebanese state asked permission from Arafat and his allies to let the
Lebanese Army to be sent to southern Lebanon, and how they refused.
They wanted to keep southern Lebanon aflame to serve the Palestinian
cause !"

After the Israeli withdrawal from the security zone in May 2000, Tueni
argues that there should be no authority in southern Lebanon except that
of the Lebanese state with and all its institutions. Hizballah should neither
be allowed to have checkpoints to stop travelers on the roads nor to raid
villages and arrest people in their homes. Otherwise southern Lebanon
would revert to the days of the armed Palestinian presence, which "constituted a state within a state." The Lebanese authorities should close down
the "Fatima Gate" which is used by "whoever wants to harm Lebanon by
means of undertaking actions against Israel." Tueni invites "the heroes of
throwing stones and Molotov cocktails to proceed to another Arab–Israeli
border. Let them go to the Golan Heights, but I doubt whether the Syrian
state would allow the rekindling of the conflict at its borders."[7]

Jubran Tueni defends those who served in the South Lebanon Army, and
condemns the fact that they have been singled out and imprisoned for no
reason whatsoever. He quotes a letter sent by a former member of the South
Lebanon Army who is incarcerated in the Roumieh prison, and who was
going to spend Christmas alone without his wife and children, in which the
prisoner states that he was indicted because he loved his homeland and was
attached to his land. Tueni points out that all those who carried arms from
other regions of Lebanon were given a general amnesty except those of
southern Lebanon.[8]

The Sunni community has been dispelled of its illusions after its support
of the PLO in the late 1960s to the early 1980s, which had brought disaster
to Lebanon. Prime Minister Rafiq Hariri was displeased with Hizballah's
operations against Mazari' Shib'a. Hizballah mounted an operation that
killed an Israeli soldier and wounded two others, on February 16, 2001, the
ninth anniversary of the assassination by Israel of Hizballah leader 'Abbas
al-Musawi.[9] Prime Minister Hariri issued a statement that was critical of
Hizballah's action, but he had to recant on February 18, 2001, after meet-

ing Hizballah officials and endorsing their operation. The reason: because Hizballah operates in accordance with Syrian instructions.[10]

Even the majority of the Shi'i community who have not been enticed or entranced by the Khomeini ideology know very well that the operations by Hizballah have brought nothing but death and destruction to southern Lebanon. The proof is in the continuous demand by people in southern Lebanon for the return of the legitimate authorities represented by the Lebanese Army to keep law and order and for its deployment at the Lebanese–Israeli border.

A news article that details the social and economic situation in the security region of southern Lebanon, eight months after the Israeli withdrawal, shows that the people there complain about the absence of legitimate government authority that could provide security and law and order in the region.[11] Syria vetoed the deployment of the Lebanese Army because it wanted to keep the region in turmoil and under its proxy, Hizballah. Five hundred soldiers and another five hundred members of the Gendarmerie were sent to southern Lebanon, on August 9, 2000, but they were confined to the army barracks in Marji'yun and Bintjubail.[12] The whole former security zone, irrespective of whether the villages are Shi'i or Christian, became the exclusive domain of Hizballah, which is "energetically creating new realities on the ground which would make it be difficult to alter them in the future."[13] The villagers of southern Lebanon are not convinced by Hizballah's propaganda that claims that sending the Lebanese army to southern Lebanon is an "American-Israeli demand," and is "for the security of Israel and not for the security of Lebanon."[14]

The Attitude of the Lebanese toward Syrian Domination: The Primacy of Freedom

The very basis of Lebanon as envisaged in National Pact of 1943 is that the Lebanese polity will enjoy all the basic freedoms of the press, speech, and religion, as well as free elections. The Christians of Lebanon are, sui generis, unlike the Christians in other countries of Middle East, because they revere their freedom, and absolutely refuse to live as *Dhimmiyyun*, that is, subservient to their Muslim compatriots.[15] When Jubran Tueni, in an open letter addressed to Bashar Asad in March 2000, called for the withdrawal of Syrian troops from Lebanon, he was attacked and belittled by the Syrian Foreign Minister, Faruq al-Shar'. The latter claimed that Syria will withdraw its troops only if the request comes "from the Lebanese government [which Syria controls] or from the representatives of the Lebanese people [who have been chosen by Syria] . . . and not from a person [Jubran Tueni] who writes in a Lebanese newspaper [*al-Nahar*]."[16]

Jubran Tueni challenged al-Shar' by pointing out that it is not surprising

that al-Shar' has no understanding how a journalist could represent the
Lebanese public opinion, because

> the press in Syria, as it is in all political systems of the same ilk, does not repre-
> sent public opinion but the opinion of the regime in power . . . perhaps with
> the passage of time, and through al-Shar''s travels abroad . . . he would
> discover the importance of free press, and the importance of public opinion
> which are bases of democratic systems. While waiting for Minister al-Shar'
> to comprehend this aspect of the problem . . . we shall continue writing our
> opinions and transmit the points of view of the Lebanese, because we are
> convinced that Lebanon is the model to emulate. To adjust to the new
> civilized world, others [Syria] have to follow in the footsteps of Lebanon and
> not vice-versa !.[17]

The primacy of freedom is not confined to the Christians, but other
religious communities cherish it as well. 'Alaya' al-Sulh, the eldest daughter
of the founding father of the National Pact of 1943, Riyad al-Sulh, wrote
an article in al-Nahar, on November 21, 2000, in which she reminded the
readers that Lebanon became independent in 1943, before Syria. The prime
ministers of the two countries, in the case of Lebanon it was her father, and
in the case of Syria it was her maternal uncle, congratulated each other
officially and in a civilized manner. Mutatis mutandis, Lebanon does not
need to wait for Syria to get its Golan Heights to have peace in southern
Lebanon.

The two tracks, the Lebanese and the Syrian, are different, and their
political systems are different. The very bases of the Lebanese polity are
freedom and pluralism. Lebanon was the bulwark of the freedom of
thought and a refuge for those in the Arab world who suffered from sub-
jugation and oppression. Now there is an attempt to impose on Lebanon a
monolithic ideology. Syria should deal with Lebanon on an equal footing
and should stop interfering in its domestic affairs. Al-Sulh maintained that
it would be easier for Syrian troops to leave Lebanon now than it was for
them to enter Lebanon in 1976.[18]

The Shi'i leader of Jabal'Amil, Kamil al-As'ad, the former president of
the Chamber of Deputies for almost decades prior to 1982, openly attacked
in a TV interview on January 14, 2001 the present dominant leaders of the
Shi'is and other communities as instruments of the Syrian Intelligence
Services.[19] The last three parliamentary elections in 1992, 1996, and 2000
were rigged while, in contrast, the elections held in 1972 were free. Prior to
the elections of 2000, al-As'ad predicted that the process of elections would
be controlled. On July 30, 2000, al-As'ad returned to his hometown
al-Taybay in the Marji'yun district and gave an eloquent defense of
democracy, calling the rule of the people through their representatives who
are fully accountable to their electorate. He, bemoaned the present condition of the people of the South who are oppressed and downtrodden,

suffering from deprivation and poverty because they are robbed of their allocations by the corrupt and hegemonic militias of Hizballah and Amalthe. Al-As'ad's public call for the return of democracy and free elections was shared by thousands who attended the rally, and who welcomed him at the ruins of his family residence.[20]

The Druze leader Walid Junblat, who has been a major ally of the Syrians, called publicly in October 2000 for the redeployment of Syrian troops in Lebanon in accordance with the Ta'if Agreement of 1989 that Syria itself had imposed on Lebanon. Syrian proxies immediately attacked his position. 'Asim Qansu, the vice president of the pro-Syrian Ba'ath party in Lebanon, accused Junblat of ingratitude because the late Syrian president "Hafiz Asad gave Junblat whatever he wanted."[21] This was a reference to the arms, logistics, and manpower (dissident Palestinians and other leftist militias) support given by Syria to Junblat's Druze militia in its battles against the Christian Lebanese Forces and the national Lebanese Army from 1983 until 1990. The President of the Chamber of Deputies, Amal's leader Birri, who is also a Syrian proxy, declared publicly that Junblat had become a persona non grata in Syria and would not be permitted to visit Damascus, where he kept an office for the last two decades. On November 6, 2000, 'Asim Qansu raised the ante and accused Walid Junblat of being "an agent of Israel."[22] This was an allusion to the special relationship that the Druze have always enjoyed with Israel, as their co-religionists have regularly served in the Israeli Defense Forces. Under the pressure of threats from Syrian proxies, Junblat was forced to recant his demand for the redeployment of Syrian troops in Lebanon, and was forgiven by the Syrians.

Hizballah as Syria's Ideal Weapon in its War against Lebanon and the Peace Process

The role of Hizballah, as envisaged by the Asad regime in Syria, is to create a senseless and contrived conflict toward Israel. Hizballah has been the major instrument of the late Syrian president Hafiz Asad in confronting Israel in southern Lebanon. The prevalent view that Hizballah represents only Iran only is erroneous. Hizballah is the embodiment of the strategic alliance between Iran and Syria. But it is the latter that controls it and sets its agenda. The evidence comes directly from the horse's mouth, that is, from the leader of Hizballah himself, Hasan Nasrallah. On the fortieth day following the death of Hafiz Asad, Hasan Nasrallah gave a speech eulogizing Hafiz Asad and called him "the great leader (*al-Qa'id al-'Azim*)."[23] Nasrallah added that the leaders of Hizballah felt joyful when they were informed that Hafiz Asad was elated and very proud of Hizballah's victory over Israel (the Israeli withdrawal on May 24, 2000). Nasrallah addressed the late Asad by stating: "Victory was the work of your hands; the fruits of your thought, and [a product] of your school of struggle and waging war."[24]

Nasrallah showered praise on the new Syrian president, Bashar Asad, whose support is much needed for the continuation of Hizballah's role in Lebanon and the region.[25] Conversely, for Bashar Asad, Hizballah is absolutely indispensable for Syria's continued war on the Lebanese polity and the peace process. Hasan Nasrallah was invited to speak to a Syrian Youth congress, held in Damascus, celebrating the take-over of power by the Ba'ath Party. He told his audience that the liberation of southern Lebanon was done with Syrian help: "Syria has changed the equation and proved that Israel is not invincible."[26]

When the Israeli withdrawal from the security zone took place on May 24, 2000, Syria contrived a pretext for its proxy, Hizballah, to continue to be heavily armed and to wage war against Israel by claiming that Mazari' Shib'a, which is part of the Golan Heights, is occupied Lebanese territory. On October 11, 2000, the Syrian president Bashar Asad himself stated that "Mazari' Shib'a is a Lebanese territory occupied by Israel, and it is the right of the resistance (al-Muqawamah) to struggle against the occupier."[27] On October 7, 2000, Hizballah matched its threats with deeds by launching its first guerilla operation since the withdrawal of the Israeli forces from Lebanese territories on May 24, 2000 against Mazari' Shib'a. The operation resulted in the capture of three Israeli soldiers. Earlier on the same day, and most probably coordinated with Hizballah as a diversion, around one thousand Palestinians, who traveled from their camps in Beirut, demonstrated in support of their Palestinian compatriots at the Marwahin Gate, throwing stones and Molotov cocktails at an Israeli post on the other side of the border. The Israelis retaliated by firing at the Palestinians, killing two persons and wounding twenty others.[28]

The popular Lebanese Deputy Albert Mukhayber, who no one dared to challenge in the August 2000 Parliamentary elections for the Greek Orthodox seat in Northern Matn, criticized the Lebanese government for allowing Hizballah to launch an operation against the Israelis on October 7, 2000. Mukhayber, expressing the views of the vast majority of the Lebanese, pointed out that he "has been repeatedly warning the Lebanese authorities of militias [Hizballah] which have been making numerous attempts to open a new military front on Lebanese territory to serve the interests of others [Syria]."[29] Mukhayber added that "if the Arabs fear these wars on their lands, we are telling them loud and clear: Lebanon has paid the head tax (Jizya) of the Arab–Israeli struggle for too long, so enough is enough!"[30]

The leader of Hizballah, Hasan Nasrallah, tried to justify the operation of October 7, but he sounded somewhat on the defensive. Nasrallah gave three reasons for the operation against the Israelis. First, that the three Israeli soldiers were abducted to exchange them for the Hizballah prisoners held by Israel. Second, that the operation's objective was the liberation of Mazari' Shib'a. Finally, although the operation was planned before September 28, it was in support of the Palestinian *Intifada*.[31] On October 15, 2000, Nasrallah publicly announced that an Israeli businessman, Elhanan Tennenbaum, was in captivity in Lebanon after he was lured to Lebanon by Hizballah operatives in Europe.[32] This shows that Hizballah operates independently from the Lebanese authorities, as an abducted Israeli was brought to Lebanon without the Lebanese government's knowledge.

The role of the Palestinians in Lebanon has become greater since the *Intifada*. On October 21, 2000, two armed guerilla fighters were killed trying to attack the Mazari' Shib'a region. On January 26, 2001, two Palestinian members of Ahmad Jabril's Popular Front for Liberation of Palestine-General Command (PFLP-GC) were killed and their guerilla operation was foiled by the Israelis. Ahmad Jabril, in a public speech delivered in Lebanon, on November 23, 2000, criticized those who are demanding the withdrawal of Syrian troops, and described the military presence of the Syrians and the Palestinians in Lebanon as a "Pan-Arab right (*Haq Qawmi*)."[33] Nasrallah has urged the Palestinians to continue their *Intifada* by what he called "low-technology" operations like that of the Palestinian bus driver who killed eight Israelis on February 14, 2001.

Commemorating the assassination of the Hizballah leader 'Abbas al-Musawi by Israeli helicopters in 1992, Hizballah attacked an Israeli army convoy on February 16, 2001, killing one soldier and wounding two others. Nasrallah boasted in a rally held in memory of 'Abbas al-Musawi that Hizballah's operation scored "a direct hit."[34] There is no doubt whatsoever that Syria utilizes Hizballah to continue its war against Lebanon and the peace process. Hizballah's plays a destructive role to keep the situation in Lebanon in turmoil. As the noted Lebanese sociologist and writer Waddah Shararah has pointed it out, Hizballah has contributed to the continued Lebanese economic crisis as it has prevented the Lebanese state from extending its authority and regaining its power to collect revenues without which no economic recovery is possible.[35]

In a meeting of the Lebanese Cabinet in early February 2001, the cabinet minister Pierre Helou asked whether Lebanon will be "a Hanoi or a Hong Kong." Will Lebanon be "open to military confrontation or open to large foreign investments?"[36] It seems that Syria under Asad (whether the late father or the present son) has decided that the answer is Hanoi. Hizballah is fulfilling this mission. It is not surprising that Hizballah supports strongly the Syrian military occupation of Lebanon because without it Hizballah will not survive. Nasrallah maintains that Syria is needed in Lebanon to prevent sectarianism from re-emerging, while in fact the quintessence of Hizballah is the embodiment of sectarianism. It is the ultimate irony that Syria imposed Hizballah on the Lebanese as the so-called liberator of

southern Lebanon when Israel wanted to leave Lebanon as early as June
1983, and Hizballah's attacks on the Israelis were meant to create artifi-
cially a hostility which that had not existed between Israel and Lebanon
since 1949. The Shi'i clergymen who are close to Syria, like al-'Allamah
Muhammad Husain Fadlallah, and the Mufti al-Ja'fari 'Abd al-Amir
Qabalan, had to reaffirm in their Friday *Khutbahs* that the Lebanese should
fear Israel and not Syria,[37] knowing very well that the Lebanese public
opinion holds the opposite view.

If Lebanon were left alone to make peace with Israel, it would be a real
peace for two basic reasons. First, the topographies of southern Lebanon
and northern Israel are similar with villages and towns close to each other.
Lebanon's borders with Israel are different from Egypt's where the Sinai
desert separates Egypt from Israel, and even different from Jordan's where
the Jordan River valley as well as uninhabited arid regions separate Jordan
from Israel. No geographical barrier exists between Lebanon and Israel
and many of the tributaries and springs of the Jordan River, like the
Hasbani, the Wazzani, and the Derdarah, originate in southern Lebanon.

Second, the Lebanese, descendants of the Phoenicians, are by nature
traders, entrepreneurs and adventurers, who have traversed the globe for
economic opportunities, and therefore would be elated by open borders
with Israel for the exchange of goods and services.

It flies in the face of the vast majority of the Lebanese to have Hizballah
imposed on them by Syria as the so-called heroes of the liberation of
southern Lebanon, when Hizballah's ideology and practice constitute the
antithesis of what the Lebanese polity is all about. Lebanon since its independence has been based on tolerance, pluralism, freedom, and democracy.
In contrast Hizballah is an obscurantist, intolerant, fundamentalist,
monolithic, and violent organization. Hizballah has been responsible for
numerous terrorist operations, including: the blowing up of the American
Embassy in Beirut in April 1983 and again in September 1984; the bombing
of the US Marines and the French Foreign Legion headquarters of the
Multi-National Forces in October 1983; the assassination of the President
of the American University of Beirut, Malcolm Kerr, in January 1984; the
hijacking of the TWA airliner in June 1985; the kidnapping and killing of
several American and French nationals in Lebanon from March 1984 until
December 1991; the blowing up of the Israeli Embassy in Buenos Aires in
March 1992, and the building of the Argentine-Israeli Mutual
Cooperation, in Buenos Aires, in July 1994.

There is a very strong feeling among the Lebanese that they have been
forced to pay a heavy price for the "war of others (*harb al-akharin*)" on their
territory. They have realized the hollowness of the so-called "war of liberation (*harb al-tahrir*)" fought, by Hizballah, against Israel in southern
Lebanon. The mind-set of Hizballah is best exemplified by how Hasan
Nasrallah, their leader, depicted the stoning at Fatimah Gate: it has "a

moral and cultural value [sic]."[38] This mind-set is totally alien to the vast majority of the Lebanese population.

In conclusion Lebanon will remain a battlefield for those like Hizballah, and its patrons Syria and Iran who have no interest in ending the conflict with Israel. The key to ending this vicious circle of conflict perpetrated by Syria and its proxies is to end the Syrian military occupation of Lebanon. Hizballah will not survive if its Syrian master is ousted from Lebanon because, contrary to all appearances, Hizballah is detested by the vast majority of the Lebanese people. Then, and only then, would permanent peace be realized between Lebanon and Israel.

Notes

1 When 'Arafat was asked in September 1993 whether he had any experience in governing a territory, he answered in the affirmative citing his experience in ruling Lebanon.
2 *al-Nahar*, January 27, 1987, p. 5.
3 See John Kifner, "UN Criticizes Lack of Help by Lebanon," *The New York Times*, August 13, 2000, p. 7.
4 *al-Nahar*, September 21, 2000, p. 1.
5 See the interview with Patriarch Sfair by Chantal Rayes in the *Liberation*, November 30, 2000.
6 *al-Nahar*, September 21, 2000, p. 1.
7 Ibid., August 10, 2000, p. 1.
8 Ibid., December 30, 2000, p. 1.
9 *The Washington Post*, February 17, 2001, p. A24.
10 *al-Nahar*, February 19, 2001, p.1.
11 Ibid., January 19, 2001, p. 4.
12 *The New York Times*, August 10, 2000, p. A6.
13 *al-Nahar*, January 19, 2001, p. 4.
14 *al-Nahar*, August 14, 2000, p. 5.
15 This characteristic of the Lebanese Christians have been missed by the latter-day post-orientalist Western scholars on the Middle East as well as pundits and policy-makers, because they lack an understanding of Middle Eastern realities in a profound manner.
16 Ibid., June 7, 2000, p. 1.
17 Ibid., June 8, 2000, p. 1.
18 Ibid., November 21, 2000, p. 1.
19 Ibid., January 15, 2001, p. 3.
20 Ibid., July 31, 2000, p. 4. Kamil al-As'ad did not name Hizballah and Amal as such but referred to them as "the roller or the bulldozer(bulldozer (*al-mihdalah aw al-jarrafah*)."
21 Ibid., October 13, 2000, p. 1.
22 Ibid., November 7, 2000, p. 1.
23 *al-Ba'ath*, July 21, 2000, p. 1.
24 Ibid.
25 Ibid.

26 *L'Orient-Le Jour*, March 1, 2001, p. 3.
27 *al-Safir*, October 12, 2000, p. 1.
28 *al-Nahar*, October 8, 2000, p. 1.
29 Ibid., October 10, 2000, p. 3.
30 Ibid. Albert Mukhayber uses the word *Jizya* (the head tax on Muslims under Muslim rule) instead of the word *Daribah* which simply means tax, to imply that Lebanon has been singled out because of its large number of Christians.
31 Ibid., October 8, 2000, p. 4.
32 Ibid., October 16, 2000, p. 1.
33 Ibid., November 24, 2000, p. 5.
34 *The Washington Post*, February 17, 2001, p. A24.
35 Waddah Shararah, *Dawlat Hizballah* (Beirut: Dar al-Nahar li-Nashr, 1996), p. 362.
36 *al-Nahar*, February 19, 2001, p. 2.
37 Ibid., November 11, 2000, p. 4.
38 Ibid., September 19, 2000, p. 5.

CHAPTER 19

Syrian–Israeli Relations on the Eve of the Peace Process

MOSHE MA'OZ

Syrian–Israeli relations play a pivotal role in o the current Middle East peace process; no comprehensive, stable, and durable peace can be achieved without a Syrian–Israeli political settlement. In many respects, the course of events since 1978 has transformed the Arab–Israeli conflict – which started largely as a result of the Arab-Jewish dispute in Palestine going back to the 1880s – into a Syrian–Israeli confrontation. Egypt, the veteran leader of the all-Arab campaign against Israel, first signed the 1978 Camp David Accords, then the 1979 peace treaty with Israel. Since then it has maintained peaceful relations with the Jewish state. With Jordan, there has been *de facto* peaceful coexistence since 1970, and an official peace treaty since 1994. Israel and the PLO have been engaged in a peacemaking process since the Oslo Accord, signed in 1993. Iraq has officially been in a state of war with Israel since 1948, but in fact has played no more than a marginal role in the military struggle against it: in 1973 by dispatching two armored divisions to the Golan front; and in 1991 by launching some 40 Scud missiles against Israel. Otherwise, since 1980 it has made use of its military power in the Gulf region, first against Iran and later against Kuwait. Following the destruction of its military machine in 1991, Iraq is not expected, in the near future, to play a major role in any new Arab–Israeli military confrontation.

Thus, during the last two decades Syria and Israel have become the two major protagonists in the Middle East conflict, the two main rivals not only with regard to the Golan Heights but to some degree also over influence in Lebanon as well as the fate of the Palestinians. Indeed, Israel and Syria each control large sections of the Palestinian people (Syria also has certain Palestinian guerrilla organizations under its control) and both are thus able to affect the settlement of the Palestinian problem – the core of the Arab–Israeli conflict as well as of the current peace process.

What, then, were the positions of Damascus and Jerusalem concerning the Golan, Lebanon, and the Palestinians prior to the Madrid peace conference (1991), and to what extent did they signify the policies of both parties at that conference?

Positions since 1967

Broadly speaking, the positions of both parties were far apart at the Madrid conference (1991), even though they had undergone important changes since 1967: Israel had hardened its stand on both the Golan and the Palestinian issues since the early 1980s, whereas since the late 1980s Syria adopted more flexible attitudes toward Israel and the Palestinian problem. Israel has accepted in 1968 United Nations (UN) Resolution 242 of November 22, 1967 which *inter alia* called for "withdrawal of Israel's armed forces from territories occupied in the recent conflict" and the "termination of all claims or states of belligerency and respect for and acknowledgment of the sovereignty, territorial integrity, and political independence of every state in the area and their right to live in peace within secure and recognized boundaries, free from threats or acts of force."[1]

Significantly, the Israeli cabinet had earlier unanimously adopted (on June 19, 1967) a resolution to the effect that "Israel offers to conclude a peace treaty with Syria on the basis of the international boundary and Israel's security needs . . . " namely, "demilitarization of the Syrian Heights . . . and an absolute guarantee of the free flow of the River Jordan's sources into Israel."[2] Syria rejected this offer and Israel subsequently withdrew it. But after the Likud party's rise to power in 1977, Menachem Begin, the new prime minister, stated that "Israel will remain in the Golan Heights, but in the framework of a peace treaty we will be ready to withdraw our forces from their present line to a [new] line that will be . . . a permanent boundary."[3] The guidelines of Begin's new government also indicated Israel's readiness to participate, without preconditions, in the Geneva peace conference on the basis of UN Resolutions 242 and 338 (of 1973).[4]

Yet in view of the belligerent position of Syria and Israel's security needs, Israeli Labor and Likud leaders, both before and after 1977, periodically called for the retention of the Golan Heights under Israeli control. As a result, in December 1981 the Israeli Knesset passed, by a majority vote, the Golan Heights Law, applying Israeli law, jurisdiction, and administration to the area. Half a year later, in June 1982, the Israeli army invaded Lebanon with the declared aim of destroying the Palestinian Liberation Organization's (PLO's) military infrastructure; in fact, however, the Israeli Defense Forces (IDF) also attacked Syrian troops – without provocation on their part – and temporarily established positions some 25 miles west of Damascus.

Subsequently, Israel's hostile attitude toward Syria intensified in reaction to the Damascus-sponsored war of attrition against Israeli troops in Lebanon during 1983–5 and the alleged Syrian attempt to blow up an El-Al plane at a London airport in 1986.

Both Likud and Labor leaders (not to mention factions further to the right) continued during the late 1980s and early 1990s to assert that Israel should not return the Golan to Syria, even in exchange for peace. Yitzhak Rabin, for example, while Israel's defense minister, declared in June 1988 that he did not regard Syria under Asad as a partner for peace. The formula of land for peace was therefore irrelevant as far as Syria was concerned.[5] Following Syrian and Egyptian reconciliation in 1989, which could have been interpreted as signaling a new flexible Syrian attitude toward Israel, Rabin stated: "We don't see a change in the Syrian position."[6]

Syrian Positions

In fact, however, the Syrian position regarding Israel has significantly changed since 1967. Following the Six Day War, Syria did not even participate in the Arab summit at Khartoum (August 29–September 1,1967) which *inter alia* approved the following principles: "No peace with Israel, no recognition of Israel, no negotiations with it."[7] The Syrian regime's official organ, *al-Ba'ath*, stated on August 31, 1967: "The Israeli enemy will be liquidated only by means of force,"[8] and, unlike Israel, Syria rejected UN Resolution 242.

However, following his ascent to power in 1970, the new Syrian president Hafiz Asad was ready to accept the resolution in March 1972. His only condition was that Israel withdraw completely from all occupied Arab territories and that the rights of the Palestinians be guaranteed.[9]

To be sure, Asad has never relinquished the military option as the major component of his struggle against Israel; but unlike his predecessor, Salah Jadid, Asad also regarded diplomacy and political maneuvering as important ingredients of his overall strategy *vis-à-vis* Israel; such maneuvering was necessary, to use his own words, to "facilitate the military campaign . . . to gain time or to acquire the sympathy of international public opinion."[10] Accordingly, Asad has developed Syria's military power with massive Soviet help, while simultaneously – notably at periods of military weakness – adopting diplomatic action, mostly directed toward the United States, in his confrontation with Israel. Thus, for example, he joined Anwar Sadat in launching the October 1973 war against Israel but, having been defeated, he accepted UN Resolution 338 of October 22, 1973 calling for a cease-fire and the implementation of UN Resolution 242. Subsequently, he initiated a war of attrition against the IDF, yet simultaneously conducted a diplomatic campaign against Israel

– trying to utilize Henry Kissinger's mediation efforts to secure a satisfactory disengagement agreement in the Golan (May 1974).[11] Significantly, following this agreement, Asad entertained for the first time the idea of signing a peace agreement with Israel within a comprehensive political settlement of the Arab–Israeli dispute based on UN Resolutions 242 and 338. This remained predicated, however, on Israel's full withdrawal from all occupied territories and on the rights of the Palestinian people being safeguarded through the establishment of a Palestinian state in the West Bank and Gaza.[12]

To be sure, Asad's peace overture was primarily intended to win over American public opinion and gain the Nixon administration's support for an Israeli withdrawal from the Golan, Sinai, the West Bank, and Gaza and – if possible – to push a wedge between the United States and Israel. To do so, Asad renewed diplomatic relations with the United States (June 1974) and even indicated his willingness to integrate, possibly alongside Sadat, into an American-sponsored Middle East peace process.

However, Asad's bold diplomatic efforts failed in the face of the combined Israeli–Egyptian–United States positions: Israel was not willing to make further withdrawals from the Golan (beyond that of 1974) or to recognize the "national rights" of the Palestinians. Golda Meir, then Israel's prime minister, declared early in March 1974 that the Golan was an inseparable part of Israel. Earlier, she had stated that there was no such thing as a Palestinian people. The Israeli government was prepared for further partial withdrawals from Sinai (following those of 1974) as part of another Egyptian–Israeli agreement, but would keep the Golan and thus further widen the split between Sadat and Asad. As it turned out, Asad's pleas and pressures notwithstanding, Sadat was prepared to accept separate partial deals with Israel. His policy was supported by Kissinger's step-by-step diplomacy, much to the dismay of Syria and the Union of Socialist Soviet Republics (USSR), who advocated an overall Arab–Israeli settlement.[13]

Having failed to recover the Golan by, in his own words, "political action," Asad harshly criticized Sadat for his "total submission to Israel's demands [and for causing] a breach in Arab solidarity."[14] He severely denounced Israel as a "racist fascist state" and threatened it with "another October war."[15] Simultaneously, the 12th National Congress of the Ba'ath party (convened in July 1975) stated that, following the recovery of the territories lost in 1967, Syria would continue the struggle against Israel "toward liberating all the Palestinian lands."[16] Alongside these statements, Asad embarked on an ambitious strategy aimed at establishing a north-eastern front against Israel, which was to consist of Syria, Iraq, Jordan, Lebanon, and the Palestinian Liberation Organization (PLO). However, in reality only Jordan was inclined to work toward military, political, and economic integration with Syria (and that, too, only for a limited span of time). Iraq, meanwhile, rejected Asad's approach, arguing that Syria continued to adhere to UN Resolutions 242 and 338, to a diplomatic rather than a military solution.

Indeed, in 1976–7 Asad renewed his diplomatic initiative toward Israel on lines similar to his 1974–5 attempt. Syria was again exposed to a potential Israeli threat following Damascus' intervention in the Lebanese civil war and the deployment of its troops near the Lebanese–Israeli borders. To neutralize this threat, Syria, under American auspices, reached the tacit "red line" agreement with Israel in South Lebanon (Spring 1976),[17] which acknowledged the interests of both sides there. Subsequently (late 1976 and early 1977), Asad suggested a resumption of the Geneva negotiations to the Carter administration, aimed at reaching a peaceful solution to the Arab–Israeli conflict. He stated that he was willing to sign a "peace agreement" (though, in fact, a closer look shows that he meant no more than a non-belligerency agreement) provided Israel withdrew from all territories occupied in 1967 and agreed to the creation of a Palestinian state in the West Bank and Gaza. Asad also implied that the United States should have the major role in mediating such a settlement.[18]

However, once again Asad's overture was foiled by the combined policies of Israel, Egypt, and the United States. Like the Labor coalition government before it, the Likud government in Israel (since 1977) continued to insist on a separate settlement with Egypt, with no linkage whatsoever to either the Syrian or Palestinian issue. For various reasons, Egyptian president Sadat also continued to believe that a comprehensive Arab–Israeli settlement was not feasible and thus opted for the more limited objective of recovering Sinai from Israel. Finally, in November 1977, he made his historical trip to Jerusalem, which led to the 1978 Camp David Accords and the 1979 Egyptian–Israeli peace treaty. Both agreements were facilitated by US President Jimmy Carter. This symbolized a retreat from his previous support for a comprehensive settlement, a move that deeply frustrated Asad.[19]

Asad's Doctrine of Strategic Parity and its Failure

Under these circumstances, Asad almost entirely abandoned his diplomatic efforts. For the next decade, he concentrated his energies and skills on building, with the massive help of the Soviet Union, a military option *vis-à-vis* Israel. The underlying concept was Asad's doctrine of strategic balance, or military parity, with Israel. His goals were the following: to build a strong and credible military machine capable both of deterring Israel from attacking Syria and of effectively defending Damascus should such a simultaneous attack occur; to use his armed strength at the appropriate time to launch a limited or all-out war against Israel, primarily in order to recover the Golan Heights; but also to negotiate a comprehensive political settlement with Israel from a position of military strength.[20]

Asad's need to strengthen his military power *vis-à-vis* Israel became a great deal more urgent during the early 1980s: Since the Likud government had come to power, Israel had increasingly supported the Christian Maronites' opposition to Syrian control of Lebanon; then, in June 1982, it invaded South Lebanon, attacked Syrian troops and advanced along the Beirut–Damascus route in the direction of Damascus. Iraq, Syria's rival as well as potential military ally, had been engaged in a bloody war against Iran since 1980, thus indirectly strengthening Israel's hand *vis-à-vis* Damascus. Egypt did not exercise any tangible pressure on Israel to withdraw from Lebanon, while in the United States, the Reagan administration "opted to back the Israeli action, at least insofar as it was aimed at effecting a pro-Western order in Lebanon."[21] In reaction to the growing Israeli menace, Asad not only engineered a war of attrition by proxy against Israeli troops in Lebanon, but also substantially enlarged and modernized his armed forces and his weapons system in a further attempt to attain a strategic parity with Israel.

Nonetheless, despite his vast efforts, Asad was unable to achieve a strategic balance with Israel, although he presumably succeeded in reaching a quantitative military parity with it. Following their build-up, the Syrian armed forces could possibly deter Israel from attacking Syria, or else effectively defend Damascus against an Israeli Defense Forces (IDF) offensive. They were presumably also capable of grabbing parts of the Golan in a surprise assault, although they were likely to be defeated in the ensuing all-out war with Israel, due to the IDF's qualitative superiority in both conventional and non-conventional weapons. Consequently, Syria was unable to counterbalance Israel's strategic superiority at least for many years. This prompted Asad, since 1988, to revert once again to diplomacy and to seek to integrate Syria into the Middle East peace process.

Among the reasons for Syria's failure to attain parity were the severe economic difficulties it ran into in the 1980s, caused largely by the huge military build-up (which absorbed some 65% of the yearly budget), by the costly military involvement in Lebanon, by mismanagement and corruption in various public sectors, as well as by the decrease in Arab aid and international credits. The prolonged economic crisis, which led to high inflation and created great poverty as well as starvation, forced the government to make major cuts in defense spending, including a reduction in the size of the army.[22] In addition, Syria's military capability was significantly reduced as a result of the crucial change in Moscow's policy toward Damascus and toward the Arab–Israeli conflict. True, following the conclusion of the 1980 Soviet–Syrian Treaty of Friendship and Cooperation and particularly during 1982–4, the Soviet Union supplied Syria with huge quantities of weapons, including sophisticated long-range missiles. But other than Yuri Andropov (1982–4), Soviet leaders, notably Michail Gorbachev, made a point of supplying weapons calculated to strengthen Syria's defensive rather than its offensive capabilities. For example, the Soviets did not equip the Syrian army with the accurate long-range SS 23 ground-to-ground missiles, despite repeated requests from Damascus to do so. In later years, Moscow apparently reduced the shipment of arms to Syria and requested payment in hard currency for its arms.[23]

In addition, Syria did not, during the early 1980s, consistently enjoy Soviet military and political backing when confronted with an Israeli threat, notably during the 1982 invasion of South Lebanon. Most crucially, following the rise of Gorbachev in 1985, Soviet policy toward the Syrian–Israeli (as well as toward the Palestinian–Israeli) conflict changed dramatically. During a visit by Asad to Moscow in April 1987, Gorbachev told him bluntly that "the reliance on military force in settling the Arab–Israeli conflict has completely lost its credibility." The Soviet leader also pointed out that Moscow would no longer support Syria's doctrine of strategic parity with Israel, and urged Asad to seek a political settlement to the conflict. Gorbachev offered Soviet help in doing so.[24] Subsequently, Gorbachev continued to send messages to Damascus through the new Soviet Ambassador, Aleksandr Zotov (appointed in early 1989), again urging Asad to relinquish "illusions about a military option against Israel."[25]

Indeed, by mid-1988, Asad realized that Syria did not possess a military option for an all-out war against Israel. The change in Soviet policy was not the only reason. Another was that the end of the Iraq–Iran war (more or less in Baghdad's favor) exposed Syria – which had supported Iran – to a new Iraqi threat, whether on its eastern borders or by means of Iraqi-sponsored subversive activities in Lebanon. It also led to Syria's growing isolation in the Arab world. Consequently, Damascus could not rely on military backing from Iraq (let alone from Egypt) in case of war with Israel; the need to adopt a diplomatic course of action thus became more urgent. Yet, in order to revert to diplomacy, Damascus first needed to mend fences with Egypt – the major Arab power and the champion of a diplomatic breakthrough with Israel – as well as with the United States and Western Europe. The latter was seen in Damascus as potentially helpful in working for a favorable political settlement with Israel. (It must be indicated that previously, in October and November 1986, the United States had recalled its ambassador from Damascus, Britain had severed diplomatic relations, and both the European community and the United States had adopted sanctions against Syria because of its involvement in the bombing attempt of an El-Al plane in London on April 17, 1986.)[26]

Damascus' New Diplomatic Venture

At the end of 1988, after a decade of Syrian hostility to Egypt over the Egyptian–Israeli peace treaty, Damascus started to transmit conciliatory signals in the direction of Cairo. In December 1988, Asad publicly stated that he "acknowledged the importance of Egypt in the Arab arena" and that Syrian–Egyptian cooperation had always been compatible with the interests of the Arab world.[27]

In May 1989 Egypt was readmitted to the Arab League, after a ten-year absence. Syria no longer objected, and in late December 1989, full diplomatic relations between Syria and Egypt were restored. In mid-July 1990, Asad paid his first official visit to Egypt in thirteen years, thus acknowledging that Sadat's peaceful-diplomatic approach had the advantage over his own belligerent–rejectionist policy toward Israel. Upon his departure from Cairo, Asad stated: "We are ready to join the peace process . . . we accept UN Resolutions 242 and 338 and we still call for a just and comprehensive peace."[28] Asad made similar statements earlier that year in his meetings with American senators and particularly in his talks with former American President Carter, in Damascus in March 1990.[29]

Indeed, alongside its conciliatory approach to Egypt, Syria was seeking a rapprochement with the United States. Under the Reagan administration, Washington developed a hostile attitude to Damascus on account of its alleged involvement in anti-American "state terrorism," notably in the 1983 attack on the US Marines compound in Lebanon and the bombing of Pan-American flight 103 in 1988. But toward the end of the Reagan administration (i.e., at the same time as the change in Asad's approach), the United States itself became interested in improving relations with Syria, partly because of its major role in releasing American hostages and partly because of Damascus' potential capability of restoring order and stability in Lebanon. Indeed, the United States and Syria began to cooperate on these two issues, thereby noticeably enhancing their relationship, particularly during the Bush administration. Yet, for the time being they remained in disagreement regarding the settlement of the Arab–Israeli dispute: whereas the United States advocated a step-by-step process under its sponsorship, starting with Israeli–Palestinian negotiations, Syria insisted on convening a conference of Israel and all Arab states under UN auspices, notably with the participation of the USSR, then still Syria's major ally. However, by 1990 and particularly following the Iraqi invasion of Kuwait, Damascus significantly changed its stance, moving closer to the American position.

Syrian Attitudes toward the Madrid Peace Conference

To be sure, Asad and other Syrian leaders continued for several years to publicly depict Israel as an aggressive and racist state, a neo-crusader entity alien to the region that should be fought.[30] But this harsh ideological position notwithstanding, Asad made major attempts – much bolder than in 1974–5 and 1976–7 – to use diplomacy in the confrontation with Israel, notably through combining American support and coordination with other Arab states. He was prompted to do so because, beginning in 1988–9, Syria's chances for diplomatic gains greatly improved, while simultaneously, as we have seen, its military option significantly diminished. We have already referred to the deleterious effects of the change in Soviet policy, exacerbated (from the point of view of Damascus) by the demise of the Soviet Union.

The Iraqi menace was neutralized by the destruction of Baghdad's military machine in the 1990–1 Gulf War, but this also eliminated for quite some time Syria's potential strategic depth or backing in case of war with Israel. On the other hand, the US victories in the Cold War and in the Gulf demonstrated its global military superiority and its readiness to use military power in order to assist its allies in the Middle East – whether Kuwait or Israel – against external aggression. America's new predominance, no longer challenged by Moscow, increased Syria's political and economic dependence on the United States while somewhat diminishing Israel's status as a strategic asset for the United States. Washington thus assumed a role as the major broker for a Syrian–Israeli settlement.

Unlike the Israeli government, Asad adjusted his policies to these new global and regional realities even before the Iraqi invasion of Kuwait in August 1990. Yet this invasion offered him a unique opportunity to emerge from his predicaments and to solidify his new orientations. By joining the American-led campaign against Iraq, Syria was able to neutralize or even remove the Iraqi menace, consolidate its indirect control over Lebanon, end its regional isolation, erase its image as a "terrorist state" in the West, and turn itself into a respectable member of the American–Arab coalition. Subsequently, Syria expected to be rewarded by the United States, mainly through support for its attitudes in the newly launched Arab–Israeli peace process.

Washington, for its part, valued Damascus at that juncture not only for its contribution to Lebanon's stability and for adding to the Arab legitimization of the American campaign against Iraq, but also for its potentially crucial role in the peace process. This new American–Syrian bond of mutual interests was demonstrated by Secretary of State James Baker's visit to Damascus in September 1990 and by Asad's meeting with President George Bush in Geneva in November 1990 – his first with an American president in thirteen years. And following the Gulf War, Asad responded in July 1991 to the American-engineered Arab–Israeli peace process by adopting new, flexible positions more or less consistent with the American terms. These represented a major departure from Syria's formerly inflexible conditions. For example, Syria had previously demanded a fully-fledged international conference under United Nations (UN) sponsorship, to meet only after an advance commitment by Israel to withdraw from all occupied territories, including East Jerusalem. Furthermore, at such a conference, whose resolutions would be binding, the Arabs would negotiate with Israel jointly, rather than separately, and indirectly rather than directly; the Palestinian people should be represented by the PLO and be entitled to establish an independent state in the occupied territories, including East Jerusalem. Under the new American terms, Syria now agreed to convene a regional conference under United States and Soviet sponsorship, with only a passive UN observer, and, following the opening of the conference, it would conduct direct negotiations with Israel. Syria also dropped the demand that Israel should commit itself in advance to withdraw from the occupied territories or that the PLO should represent the Palestinians. Nor did Damascus insist on the establishment of an independent Palestinian state, demanding only that the "Palestinian problem" must be "resolved."[31]

While these new positions, which various US government officials and other observers depicted as a diplomatic breakthrough, primarily represented Syrian concessions on procedural issues, they also touched on certain matters of substance. Yet, on the most essential points, Syria did not change its position: it continued to demand the withdrawal of Israel from the entire Golan Heights, as well as from South Lebanon, the Gaza Strip and the West Bank, including East Jerusalem. Syrian Vice-President Abd al-Halim Khaddam stated, for example, on October 5, 1991, that, "Not a single Arab participating in the peace process can sell out one inch of the occupied territories or a single right of the national Palestinian rights." Syrian Foreign Minister Faruk al-Shar'a, in his militant anti-Israeli speech at the opening of the Madrid peace conference (October 31, 1991), made certain statements which were reminiscent of passages broadcast in a Radio Damascus commentary on October 8, 1991: "Syria and all the Arabs adhere to the Golan Heights, Jerusalem, the West Bank and Gaza. We will not bargain over our territories or relinquish our rights."[32]

In return for these territories Syrian leaders offered a "peace agreement" with Israel, which in fact was devoid of full recognition of Israel and was certainly open to be interpreted as no more than a non-belligerency agreement. Indeed, around the same time, in an interview with an American journalist, Asad evaded the question whether or not he accepted "the existence of a Jewish state in the Middle East."[33] Other Syrian officials repeatedly insisted that peace with Israel should not include full diplomatic relations nor economic cooperation or cultural ties, etc. Accordingly, Syria refused to attend the "third round" of the peace negotiations designed to discuss these latter issues. And when the Syrian Vice-President was asked about Damascus' position on Israeli attempts to attend a meeting in Turkey on regional water problems, he said, "Israel has no right to a single drop of water in the region. It is absolutely unacceptable for Israel to be a party to any arrangements on water or any other issues in the region."[34]

Possibly Syria's stiff refusal to recognize Israel's legitimacy and to sign a full peace treaty with it represented a bargaining position in the negotiation process; and once Israel would commit itself to withdraw from all occupied territories and implement the national rights of the Palestinians, Asad would have agreed to sign a full peace treaty with Israel, as Sadat did in 1979. Yet it would appear that Asad, while determined to recover the entire Golan – just like Sadat did regarding Sinai – would, unlike Sadat, also somehow also insist on a clear-cut settlement of the Palestinian issue. This attitude stemmed from Syria's deep historical commitment to the ideas of Arab nationalism and because of the crucial need of the minority Alawi regime in Damascus to gain legitimacy in the eyes of the Syrian Sunni-Muslim majority population.

Israeli Positions

Unlike Sadat, the visionary and brave leader of a more cohesive society, Asad was not likely to make a historical trip to Jerusalem and appeal directly to the Israeli public in order to win its trust. Such a move was improbable, not only because of Asad's different personality traits and style or his ideological and domestic constraints. It was also because Asad was aware that he had a very slim chance to convince the Israelis to give up the Golan. For one thing, Israel's Prime Minister Yitzhak Shamir, unlike Begin who made peace with Sadat, was a rigid and suspicious leader (much like Asad himself) lacking historical vision, and inclined to maintain the status quo with Syria as long as possible. Even more significant was that a majority of Israelis were reluctant to give up the Golan, whether from strategic considerations, psychological motives, or both. For, unlike Sinai, a big desert distant from Israel's population centers, the Golan is a small plateau of some 500 square miles. Topographically and strategically, it controls the northern Galilee and Lake Tiberias, and had been used, prior to the 1967 war, to shell Israeli villages. Given Syria's aggressive record and its image of brutality, it is no wonder that public opinion polls since 1967 have consistently shown that some 90 percent of Israeli Jews wish to keep the Golan.[35]

Yet, since the end of the Gulf War and the beginning of the peace process, more Israelis were willing to give up part of the Golan in return for real peace with Syria – 28 percent or 33 percent (respectively, in two polls) – as against a majority of 57 percent or 65 percent who opposed any territorial concessions to Syria.[36] Significantly, according to yet another poll (of October 1991), 55 percent of Likud members were prepared to give up part of the Golan – provided it was demilitarized – for peace with Syria, compared to 42 percent who were against.[37]

It would indeed appear that whereas more Likud members were then prepared to make some territorial concessions in a demilitarized Golan (but not in the West Bank which they regard as part of the Land of Israel), more Laborites refused for security reasons to give up even part of the Golan (but were prepared to withdraw from the bulk of the West Bank and Gaza). Indeed, former Defense Minister and Labor co-leader Rabin declared in June 1990 that he would rather retain the Golan even if this prevented peace with Syria than make peace with Syria and relinquish the Golan.[38]

Nevertheless, once the peace process started, the Labor party late in 1991 adopted a new platform on the Golan which stated somewhat ambiguously: "The peace treaty with Syria will be based on Security Council Resolutions 242 and 338, whose meaning is the principle of territorial compromise within a framework of a full and viable peace, in which the security needs of Israel will be provided for . . . in any peace agreement with Syria and in the [accompanying] security arrangements Israel's presence and control, both [through] settlement and militarily, in the Golan Heights . . . will continue."[39]

As far as the Likud government was concerned, its official position regarding the Golan had not changed since Israel launched its peace initiative in May 1989. This initiative which was "based on Resolutions 242 and 338," and calls for "the establishment of peaceful relations [with] . . . . those Arab states which still maintain a state of war with [Israel]," but it neither mentioned Syria specifically nor did it suggest the application of UN Resolutions 242 and 338 to the Golan Heights.[40] Indeed, Shamir and other government ministers had repeatedly stated their opposition to returning the Golan Heights to Syria in return for peace.

In March 1991, for example, Shamir declared: "The Syrians will tell us that they want the Golan Heights and we shall tell them – No! . . . Undoubtedly the Golan Heights is part of Israel . . . this is the government's position . . . [UN] Resolution 242 has nothing to do with the Golan."[41] At the end of July 1991, following Syria's positive reply to President Bush's peace initiative, Israel defense minister Arens asserted that there would be no negotiation with Syria over the Golan.[42]

Even assuming that this uncompromising official Israeli position represents a bargaining posture and that ultimately Israel would be prepared to give up part of the Golan for full peace with Syria – even then, Syria would almost certainly reject such a deal, insisting on the return of the entire Golan. Consequently, having no expectation that Israel would return the

Golan of its own free will, Asad had directed his diplomatic efforts mainly toward the United States, trusting that Washington would deliver the Golan. In Asad's words: "The U.S. . . . reaffirmed its commitment to the UN resolutions, which it had agreed to in 1967, 1973 and in the '80s . . . We only ask the United States, the Soviet Union and other permanent members of the UN Security Council to abide by what they voted for . . . The United States has not recognized the Israeli annexation of the Golan. It rejected this annexation and the other countries of the world have taken similar attitudes."[43] Asad was certainly correct in his description of the American official position regarding the Golan and in fact the US interpretation of UN Resolution 242 is close to – even though not identical with – his own. It is in any case closer than Shamir's (who held that Israel had already fulfilled the resolution by giving back Sinai to Egypt). Asad was thus predicating his new diplomatic strategy on US pressure against Israel to give up the Golan for full peace – and security arrangements such as demilitarization etc. – which Asad might be willing to accept. Alternatively, if Israel refused, Asad was counting on forming a better relationship with the United States, obtaining American economic assistance, and possibly pushing a wedge between the United States and Israel. For example, he would expect the United States to cool its relations with Israel, withhold loan guarantees, and reduce economic aid as well as political and military support,[44] thus weakening the fabric of Israel's society and propelling the Jewish state into a growing global isolation. Furthermore, assessing that it may by then have broad international backing, Syria might be tempted to resume a military posture *vis-à-vis* Israel. In keeping with this approach, Asad reportedly warned American officials that if peace with Israel were not attained within one year, Syria would revert to the military option.[45]

Whether or not Asad intended to employ his military power against a rejectionist Israel, he had substantially stepped up his military build-up since early 1991. Syria used the $2 billion pledged by Saudi Arabia and Kuwait for its participation in the Gulf War to purchase new and modern arms including strategic-offensive systems. In addition to hundreds of modern Soviet-made tanks and aircraft from the Soviet Union and Czechoslovakia, Syria also ordered Scud-C and M-9 long-range (600 km) missiles from North Korea and China, respectively.[46] Although it was not known at the time (early 1992) how much of the arms on order were actually delivered, it could be assumed that Syria had purchased the new weapons in order to deter Israel from attacking Damascus, to negotiate with Israel from a position of military strength, and to signal to Israel and the United States that Syria is prepared to resort to a military option if the peace process failed.

Still, Asad was unlikely to initiate a war against Israel as long as the peace process continued, and particularly not before the presidential elections in the United States and the parliamentary elections in Israel (November 1992).

To sum up, notwithstanding the fact that the military component of this scenario – and other scenarios may, of course, materialize as well – it can be concluded that owing to various constraints and considerations, Syria has since 1988 adopted a new diplomatic approach to the problem of regaining the Golan Heights and settling the Palestinian problem. The overtures made toward the United States represent a major departure from Syria's previous refusal to accept various American diplomatic schemes involving direct negotiations with Israel. "Mr. Asad seems to have finally bought an argument that the Egyptians and others have been trying to sell him for a long time: if he wants to get the Golan Heights back, in the long term he will create more pressure on Israel and on the United States by saying yes instead of saying no."[47]

By contrast, the Israeli government, which for many years prior to 1977 had been prepared to give up territories occupied in 1967 in return for full peace with its Arab neighbors, changed its positions. After handing back Sinai to Egypt, the Likud government refused to make further territorial concessions – whether to Syria or to the Palestinians. This stand was regarded as "rejectionist" not only by all Arab nations, but also by most of the world community – and by a significant number of Israelis, too. It was only following the election of Labor leader Yitzhak Rabin, prime minister in 1992, that Israel significantly changed its positions regarding the peace negotiations with Syria (and the Palestinians).

Epilogue: An Outline of the Syrian–Israeli Peace Negotiations[48]

Peace negotiations between Israel and Syria started following the Madrid peace conference (October 1991) and were conducted mostly in Washington, D.C. with American participation. During the first phase – up until the June 1992 Israeli elections – there was hardly any progress in the talks between the representatives of Syria and of the Israeli government headed by Shamir. The major bone of contention between the two parties was interpretation or applicability of UN Resolutions 242 (1967) and 338 (1973) regarding the Golan Heights, namely, the formula "land for peace." Syria insisted on full Israeli withdrawal from the Golan and was prepared to offer in return a peace agreement with Israel, which, in effect, represented a non-belligerency pact devoid of diplomatic relations and normalization. Israel, by contrast, demanded full peace with Syria but refused to commit itself to full withdrawal from the Golan, adhering to its own interpretation of UN resolutions. Only after the election of Rabin as Israel's prime minister did the new Israeli delegation announce that UN

Resolution 242 was applicable to the Golan. Rabin's new formula regarding this issue was as follows: the extent of withdrawal in the Golan would depend on the extent of peace with Syria.

In a long series of intricate negotiations between Israel and Syria from August 1992 to March 1996, significant progress was made and mutual understanding (not formal agreement) achieved on several important issues.

- Israel agreed to totally withdraw from the Golan on condition that full peace normalization and proper security arrangements would be implemented.
- Syria agreed to conclude a peace agreement with Israel which would include diplomatic relations, certain security arrangements, and cooperation in several issues: tourism, communications, and trade as well as the flow of water from the Banias river to the Jordan River.
- Lebanon would also sign a peace agreement with Israel, while other Arab states would be encouraged to follow suit.

By contrast, Syria still refused to conduct full economic relations with Israel, to reduce its military forces (some five divisions) along the Golan line and to the establishment of ground early warning stations – notably on the Hermon Mount – to be manned by Israeli personnel. Syria did agree, though, to the demilitarization of the Golan and adjacent regions on a mutual basis and at a ratio of 6 to 10 (in Israel's favor) to be supervised by American aerial systems.

The parties did not agree on the exact demarcation of the new Syrian–Israeli boundary. Syria insisted on the June 4, 1967 line, which, in certain areas, ran west of the international boundary (the 1923 British–French line), namely, including Israeli territories. Israel apparently adhered to the international border but was inclined to suggest a new "peace boundary" which would take into consideration Syria's demands, provided the Israeli security concerns were satisfied.

By early February 1996 it appeared that Israel and Syria were unable to overcome their differences and reach a peace agreement. Asad declined to accept a suggestion by Shimon Peres, Israel's new prime minister (since November 1995), to conduct several summit meetings aiming at finalizing an Israeli–Syrian peace accord. And as opposition to his peace policy grew in Israel, Peres decided to call for early elections (in May 1996), calculating that after his election he would accelerate the negotiations with Syria and reach a peace agreement. Meanwhile, both parties would continue to discuss various bilateral issues. Reportedly Asad agreed to Peres' suggestion.

But in early March 1996 Peres ordered a stop to the negotiations with Syria, ostensibly because Damascus refrained from denouncing the series of bloody Hamas attacks on Israeli citizens in Jerusalem, Tel Aviv, and Ashkelon in February and early March. The new Israeli government, headed by Binyamin Netanyahu (since June 1996) expressed the desire to resume peace negotiations with Syria. But the new administration refused to acknowledge the achievements and accept the informal understandings reached with Syria under the previous Israeli government. In its new guidelines, Netanyahu's government also articulated its refusal to withdraw from the Golan. Subsequently, however, Netanyahu conducted indirect secret talks with Syrian leaders, but these ultimately led nowhere.

The Syrian government continued to call for the resumption of the negotiations but insisted that they should continue on the basis of the "agreement" reached by the parties by March 1996. In other words, Syria demanded that Israel should commit itself to a total withdrawal from the Golan as a condition to resuming the bilateral talks. Simultaneously, Syria continued to exert military pressure on Israel by means of Hizballah's guerrilla warfare in southern Lebanon.

Following the election of Ehud Barak as prime minister (May 1999), peace negotiations were resumed between Israel and Syria, with active American participation. But in March 2000, they ended in a new stalemate.

Notes

This chapter is a revised version of my article, "Syria, Israel and the Peace Process," in *From War to Peace: Arab–Israeli Relations 1973–1993*, ed. Barry Rubin, Joseph Ginat and Moshe Ma'oz (Brighton and Portland: Sussex Academic Press, 1994), pp. 157–81. Cf. my book, *Syria and Israel: From War to Peacemaking* (Oxford: Oxford University Press, 1995).

1 C. H. Dodd and M. Sales (eds.), *Israel and the Arab World* (London: Routledge and Kegan Paul, 1970), p. 183.
2 R. Pedhazur, *Ha'aretz* (Tel Aviv), May 3 and August 11, 1991. Cf. G. Rafael, *Destination Peace* (New York: Madison, Inc., 1981), p. 177.
3 Cited in I. Rabinovich, "Israel, Syria and Jordan," paper presented at the Council of Foreign Relations, New York, October 1989; cf. A. Drysdale and R. A. Hinnebusch, *Syria and the Middle East Peace Process* (New York: Council of Foreign Relations, 1991), p. 114.
4 Y. Nedava (ed.), *The Arab–Israeli Conflict* (Ramat Gan, 1983), p. 273, (in Hebrew).
5 *Ha'aretz*, June 8, 1988.
6 *New York Times*, December 29, 1989.
7 Dodd and Sales, *Israel and the Arab World*, p. 174.
8 Ibid., pp. 175–6.
9 Damascus Radio, March 8, 1972.
10 Interview with *al-Nahar* (Lebanon), March 17, 1971.
11 For details, see M. Ma'oz, *Asad – The Sphinx of Damascus:. A Political Biography* (New York: Grove/Atlantic, Inc., 1988), pp. 94–7.
12 *Ibid.*, pp. 97ff.

13 *Ibid.*, pp. 102–3; William B. Quandt, *Decade of Decisions* (Berkeley: University of California Press, 1977), pp. 261ff.
14 Damascus Radio, October 6, 1975; *Newsweek*, September 22, 1975.
15 Ma'oz, *Asad*, p. 104.
16 Drysdale and Hinnebusch, *Syria and the Middle East*, p. 112; Ma'oz, pp. 105–6.
17 Rabinovich, *The War for Lebanon* (Cornell: Cornell University Press, 1984), pp. 49, 106.
18 Asad's interviews with the *Washington Post*, December 1976 and with *Time*, January 17, 1977. Further details in Ma'oz, *Asad*, pp. 138ff.; Drysdale and Hinnebusch, *Syria and the Middle East*, pp. 114–15.
19 For an excellent study on this issue, see W. B. Quandt, *Camp David, Peace Making and Politics* (Washington, D.C.: The Brookings Institute, 1986).
20 For a more detailed discussion, see Ma'oz, *Asad*, pp. 146–8, 177ff.
21 Helena Cobban, *The Superpowers and the Syrian–Israeli Conflict* (Washington, D.C.: Center for Strategic and International Studies, 1991), p. 38.
22 For details, see Drysdale and Hinnebusch, *Syria and the Middle East*, pp. 44ff.; *International Herald Tribune*, August 7, 1984; D. Hopwood, *Syria 1945–1986* (London: Routledge, 1988), pp. 112–14; *Washington Post*, November 15, 1986; *Al-Dustur*, March 31, 1986; *Jerusalem Post*, January 29, 1987; A. Cowell, "Trouble in Damascus," *New York Times Magazine*, April 1, 1990.
23 Cobban, *The Superpowers and the Syrian–Israeli . . .* , pp. 52ff.; Drysdale and Hinnebusch, *Syria and the Middle East*, pp. 166–7; see also E. Karsh, *The Soviet Union and Syria* (London, 1988), pp. 81ff.
24 Karsh, *The Soviet Union and Syria*, p. 92; Cobban, *The Superpowers and the Syrian–Israeli . . .* , pp. 57–8.
25 *Al-Qabas* (Kuwait) January 27, 1989, quoted in *The Middle East Journal*, Summer (1989), p. 502; see also Drysdale and Hinnebusch, *Syria and the Middle East*, pp. 166–7.
26 *Middle East Journal*, Spring 1987, p. 277.
27 *Ha'aretz*, December 23, 1988; *Middle East Journal*, Spring 1989, p. 286.
28 *New York Times*, July 17, 1990 and July 15, 1990.
29 *Ha'aretz*, March 19, 1990.
30 Asad's speech, Damascus Radio, March 8, 1988; Asad's interview with *Newsweek*, April 3, 1989; Asad's speech, Damascus Radio, March 8, 1990.
31 Cf. *New York Times*, July 17, 1991; interview with Syria's foreign minister, Faruk Shar'a, *Newsweek*, July 1, 1991; *New York Times*, April 19, 1991; *Pravda* (Moscow), July 17, 1991, quoted in *The Soviet Union and the Middle East*, Vol. XVI, No. 7 (Jerusalem: Hebrew University, 1991), pp. 1–2; *Al-Ba'ath*, December 25, 1991.
32 Quoted in *FBIS*, October 10, 1991, p. 27.
33 In an interview with Lally Weymouth, *L.A. Times*, July 29, 1991. Syrian Foreign Minister al-Shar'a, in his Madrid speech, also rejected the notion of Jewish nationhood, speaking of Jews as merely belonging to a religion rather than forming a nation.
34 *FBIS*,; *op. cit.*; *al-Hayat*, August 28, 1991.
35 Poll-taker Hanoch Smith, *The New York Times*, March 24, 1991.

36   *FBIS*, July 25, 1991, pp. 29–30, quoting *Jerusalem Post*, July 22 and *Hadashot*, July 24, 1991.

37   Israel Radio, October 5, 1991.

38   *Yediot Ahronot*, June 17, 1990.

39   *Spectrum* (Labor Party monthly), December 1991, p. 11.

40   For its full text, see the *Jerusalem Post*, May 15, 1989.

41   *Yediot Ahronot*, March 19, 1991; Drysdale and Hinnebusch, *Syria and the Middle East*, p. 205; cf. Shamir's conversation with the Golan settlers, Israel Radio, 7 August 1990.

42   Israel Radio, 28 July 1991, quoted in *FBIS*, 29 July 1991; cf. Drysdale and Hinnebusch, *Syria and the Middle East*, pp. 205–6; *New York Times*, July 17, 1991.

43   Interview with Lally Weymouth, *L.A. Times*, July 29, 1991; cf. Thomas Friedman, *New York Times*, July 15, 1991; Damascus Radio, July 30, 1991; *Al-Ba'ath*, December 25, 1991 and January 17, 1992.

44   Cf. Asad's interview with Lally Weymouth, *op. cit.*; cf. *Al-Ba'ath*, January 17, 1992; Damascus Radio, January 15, 1992.

45   *Ha'aretz*, July 22, 1991.

46   *Defense News*, August 20, 1991; *Ha'aretz*, March 17, 1991.

47   Thomas Friedman, *New York Times*, July 17, 1991.

48   For full accounts, see Ma'oz, *Syria and Israel*; Itamar Rabinovich, *The Brink of Peace: Israel and Syria 1992–1996* (Princeton: Princeton University Press, 1998), (Hebrew, Tel Aviv, 1998).

CHAPTER 20

Israeli–Syrian Peace Negotiations (December 1999–March 2000): A Missed Opportunity?

EYAL ZISSER

Ehud Barak's victory in the Israeli general elections of May 1999 brought about a renewed wave of expectations of a quick resumption of the Israeli–Syrian negotiations and even of a conclusion of a peace agreement between the two countries. It should be noted that Barak's victory over Netanyahu was decisive. For the first time the political draw that had existed for years between the two main blocs in Israel – right and left – was broken. Barak won the election by a 56 percent majority with Netanyahu receiving only 44 percent of the votes. Barak received a similar percentage of the support even among the Jewish settlers in the Golan Heights. These results were interpreted as granting Barak a broad mandate to put his political views into action and to complete the peace negotiations on the Syrian track, even at the expense of painful territorial concessions on the Golan Heights.[1]

However, no such breakthrough in the Israeli–Syrian peace negotiations occurred. The negotiations renewed in Washington in December 1999, and the talks subsequently held in the town of Shepherdstown, Virginia in January 2000, did not produce any results. The talks ended shortly after they had begun, leaving the Israel–Syrian negotiations at an impasse. It would even appear that the psychological barriers that had existed between the two countries – suspicion, distrust, and animosity – had grown in the wake of the failure of the talks. The burial of the peace process on the Syrian and Lebanese tracks, at least for the foreseeable future, was announced in Israel and the United States in the wake of the failure of the Geneva summit between President Clinton and the late President Hafiz al-Asad in March 26, 2000.[2] Furthermore, the optimistic assessments on a peace agreement in the near future between Israel and Syria were quickly replaced by pessimistic evaluations of a possible confrontation between the two countries following Israel's unilateral withdrawal from south Lebanon toward the end of May 2000.[3]

What indeed had happened between Syria and Israel and, of course, the United States? Why, against all expectations, had the Israeli–Syrian negotiations in early 2000 not yielded the expected fruit of a peace accord between the two countries? It should be mentioned that conventional wisdom in Syria, the Arab world, Israel, and the West, held that both Israel and Syria were interested in reaching a rapid conclusion to the negotiations and the signing of a peace agreement, and that the conditions present in each of the countries had created a golden opportunity for reaching such an agreement.

Syria and Israel Along the Road to Peace – Historical Background[4]

Syrian–Israeli peace negotiations began in October 1991 with the convening of the Madrid Conference. President Asad's readiness to join the peace process initiated by the United States represented a substantial change from his traditional policy toward Israel. Asad was now prepared to seriously consider the possibility of negotiating peace with Israel, the nation that he had considered until then to be an eternal enemy. This *volte face* in Asad's attitude to the conflict with Israel must be understood against the background of Syria's weakened international standing following the collapse of the Soviet Union and Iraq's defeat in the Gulf War.

In practice, however, the Syrian–Israeli peace talks began only following the elections in Israel in June 1992, which brought Yitzhak Rabin to the post of Prime Minister. The Rabin government expressed its readiness – at first only hinted at, but later unequivocally in messages passed on to the Syrians by the then American Secretary of State, Warren Christopher – for Israeli withdrawal from the entire Golan Heights to the June 4, 1967 border line. However, this readiness was conditional on an acceptable Syrian response to Israel's demands in the areas of security arrangements and normalization of relations between the two states.[5]

The reaction of the Syrians to the flexibility shown by Israel was to make a number of gestures designed to promote the peace negotiations and especially the Syrian–American relations. These included allowing members of the Jewish community in Syria to emigrate, hosting a delegation of Israeli Arabs who had come to Damascus in March 1994 to express their condolences to President Hafiz al-Asad on the death of his son Basil who was killed in a car accident, and, finally granting Syrian Foreign Minister, Faruq al-Shar' the first interview of its kind on Israeli television in October 1994. Also noteworthy was Asad's declaration, following the summit meeting with President Clinton in Geneva in January 1994, that Syria was ready to establish a "peace of the brave" with Israel and to maintain "regular relations" with it.[6]

However, despite the progress that had been made in the Syrian–Israeli negotiations in the years 1992–6, the two countries failed in their attempts to achieve a breakthrough. They did not succeed in tearing down the psychological barriers of hate, animosity, and especially the suspicion and distrust that had grown up between them over the years. In addition, they also failed to close the remaining gaps in their respective positions on everything that had to do with the exact details of the expected peace agreement.

The assassination of Yitzhak Rabin, and later on the defeat of Shimon Peres in the Israeli general elections in May 1996, put an end, at least temporarily, to the Syrian–Israeli negotiations. The new Israeli Prime Minister, Benjamin Netanyahu, did not share Rabin's readiness that Israel withdraw to the June 4, 1967 border line. Netanyahu even managed to extract a letter from Secretary of State Warren Christopher, stating that Rabin's message to the Syrians regarding his readiness to withdraw to the 4 June border line, according to international law, was not an agreement or commitment binding on the Netanyahu government.[7] Thus, for most of Netanyahu's term of office, 1996–9, the Syrian-Israel negotiations were at an impasse, although both Syria and Israel were careful not to break them off entirely and continued to declare their commitment to the peace process.

Following Netanyahu's defeat in the Israeli May 1999 general elections, it became known in Israel that Netanyahu was engaged in secret negotiations with the Syrians during the course of 1998. These contacts were maintained by Ron Lauder, an American businessman and close friend of Netanyahu. According to media reports, the negotiations were halted when the Syrians requested that Netanyahu provide them with a map on which the border line to which he was prepared to withdraw was clearly marked. Netanyahu refused to comply with this request, apparently because of political difficulties that he encountered within his government and his coalition.[8] However, the Lauder episode does teach us that even during the Netanyahu era Asad was prepared to examine closely and carefully the possibility of achieving peace, of course on the condition that all his demands were met. This lent support to the impression held by many in Israel – that Asad had made a strategic choice to make peace with Israel, and that the Syrian president had even begun to show increasing interest in reaching such an agreement.

The Barak Era – Turning Over a New Leaf

When Barak entered the office of prime minister, he was faced with the same dilemma that the late Prime Minister Yitzhak Rabin had faced seven years earlier after he had achieved victory in the 1992 elections. This dilemma related to which of the two tracks in the peace process should be pursued more energetically: the Israeli–Palestinian track or the Israeli–Syrian (and the Lebanese) track. Barak, like Rabin, was inclined at first to invest his efforts in the Syrian one. This track was viewed as more attractive and more promising than the Palestinian track, since the problems involved in it and the obstacles to progress in its path appeared to the innocent observer to be much easier to solve than those on the Palestinian track. After all, differences with Syria focused on the question of the June 4, 1967 border line, and related to a relatively small land area. Thus, it appeared that once both sides had reached agreement on that, a breakthrough in the negotiations toward peace could be achieved. It also appeared that Barak lent an ear to those in Israel, mainly in the security establishment, who assessed that Asad's deteriorating state of health and his desire to make his son his heir as ruler of Syria, made him a more effective and congenial partner than he had been in the past, and even prompted him to establish considerable urgency to achieving peace with Israel.[9]

The first harbinger of matters gaining impetus on the Syrian–Israeli track in the peace process appeared in a series of interviews with Asad and Barak at the end of June 1999 by the British journalist Patrick Seale. This journalist was known in the West as Asad's personal biographer and close friend. The interviews, which appeared in *al-Hayat*, included mutual compliments each of the men paid the other. Barak called Asad "the builder of modern Syria," and Asad declared that "Barak is a strong and honest leader interested in peace."[10]

However, despite the optimism and good will voiced in both capitals, Israel and Syria needed one-half year longer to renew the negotiations. This was because the Syrians made renewal of the talks conditional on Israel's commitment to withdrawing to the June 4, 1967 border, claiming that when the talks between the two sides ended in March 1996, they already possessed Rabin's commitment to such a withdrawal. The Syrian position was expressed in a series of articles by Patrick Seale published in *Al-Hayat* arguing that this commitment had been left with the Americans as a deposit. Seale also reported that the Syrians had a letter in their possession that President Clinton had sent President Asad in June 1995 in which Clinton wrote:

> "As I told you in Damascus, and emphasized to your Foreign Minister, I have in my possession the commitment by Prime Minister Itzhak Rabin to withdraw to the 4 June 1967 border."[11]

While Israel did express its readiness to renew the talks from the point at which they had ceased in early 1996, it claimed that it had its own definition, different from that of the Syrian's, concerning just what that point was. Spokespersons for Israel repeatedly claimed that Rabin's readiness to complete withdrawal to the June 4, 1967 border was hypothetical, and in any case, was conditional on Syria's complying with Israel's security and other demands.[12]

The Americans finally succeeded in overcoming the differences in the positions of the two sides, bringing the Syrians and the Israelis back to the negotiating table. Following the visit of Secretary of State Madeleine Allbright to Damascus and Jerusalem in early December 1999, President Clinton announced the resumption of the Syrian–Israeli negotiations. It seems that the Americans had purposely created the necessary ambiguity that would allow both sides to negotiate with each other – with each side believing it was getting what it wanted. Syria agreed to renew the talks on the assumption that they would be resumed at the point at which they had been broken off, i.e., that it had an Israeli commitment to withdrawing to the June 4, 1967 border already in its pocket. Israel, on the other hand, renewed the talks on the assumption that it had *not* made such a commitment. The price for this ambiguity would be paid by both partners as well as the United States later on in the negotiations.[13]

The Israeli–Syrian Peace Negotiation – Washington and Shepherdstown (December 1999–January 2000)

The negotiations between Israel and Syria were renewed on December 15, 1999 in Washington, at the senior political level of Israeli Prime Minister Ehud Barak and Syrian Foreign Minister Faruq al-Shar'. The negotiations were renewed, but beclouded by a stern speech made by al-Shar' at the opening ceremony in which he accused Israel of prolonged aggression against the Syrians. Al-Shar' also refrained from shaking hands with Prime Minister Barak in front of the cameras. He expressed the Syrian concept of peace with Israel in this way:

> It goes without saying that peace for Syria means the return of all its occupied land, while for Israel, peace will mean the end of the psychological fear, which the Israelis have been living in as a result of the existence of occupation, which is undoubtedly the source of all adversities and wars. Hence, ending occupation will be balanced for the first time by eliminating the barrier of fear and anxieties and exchanging it with a true and a mutual feeling of peace and security. Thus, the peace, which the parties are going to achieve will be established on justice and international legitimacy, and, thus, peace will be the only triumph after 50 years of struggle . . . We are approaching the moment of truth, and there is no doubt that everyone realizes that a peace

agreement between Syria and Israel and between Lebanon and Israel would indeed mean for our region the end of a history of wars and conflicts and may well usher in a dialogue of civilization and an honorable competition in various domains – the political, cultural, scientific and economy.[14]

However, despite the Syrians' demonstratively chilly attitude toward their negotiation partners, there were feelings of optimism in Israel and even in Damascus as to the chances of achieving a breakthrough on the Syrian track within a short time. This optimism had its roots in the observation that for the first time the political wills and even the interests of all the leaders of the region had come together in a unique situation that would, as was hoped, facilitate reaching a Syrian–Israeli peace agreement.

With regard to Asad, the assessment both in Israel and in the United States was that the Syrian president had begun to show, for the first time since the Syrian–Israeli peace negotiations started, some interest in reaching a peace agreement, and realized that it was to Syria's clear advantage to do so. And the time for reaching this agreement was running out. Asad's deteriorating state of health was also mentioned as one of the factors that might motivate him to be more flexible on this point of reaching an agreement with Israel. This flexibility would allow him to see in his lifetime the return of the Golan Heights to Syria. In view of the fact that in the last few years of his life Asad had been focused mainly on ensuring that his son Bashar would be his heir, one may also assume that he would have been interested in a peace agreement that could facilitate his son's establishing his rule. American and Israeli sources also mentioned Asad's desire to use President Clinton's last year in office to promote relations between Damascus and Washington, mainly to obtain financial aid, in view of the serious rapidly deteriorating condition of the Syrian economy. Finally, Israeli sources pointed out the increasing realization in Syria that Ehud Barak was determined to withdraw Israeli troops from South Lebanon by July 2000, a move that might take away from Asad an important bargaining chip vis-à-vis Israel, and in fact the important chip which prompted many Israelis to support withdrawal from this area.[15]

As for Prime Minister Barak, he continued to declare that reaching an agreement with Syria was a central goal in his policy which he believed would change realities in the Middle East, and would lead to an improvement in Israel's strategic standing. The fact that Barak was clearly losing ground in Israel because of socioeconomic and other domestic problems was also considered to serve as possible motivation for him to invest efforts in promoting the peace process with Syria. In the first months of the year 2000, Ehud Barak indeed made substantial strides toward the Syrians, at least in Israeli terms. Barak took a number of steps designed to prepare the groundwork in Israeli public opinion for far-reaching concessions on the Golan Heights – in fact, withdrawal from all of the Golan Heights – simultaneously sending a message to the Syrians that he was prepared to make such concessions. Thus Barak declared that four of his predecessors – Shamir, Rabin, Peres and Netanyahu – had agreed to withdraw to the June 4, 1967 line.[16]

However, despite the ideal starting place of the peace talks between Israel and Syria, first in Washington and later in Shepherdstown, the two sides failed to achieve a breakthrough. Although Israel was ready to express its readiness to withdraw to the June 4, 1967 line, it remained unclear to the Syrians just what was behind this emerging Israeli flexibility, and what this line *was* in Israel's view. Thus, while during the Washington talks held on December 15–16, 2000, the Syrians agreed to Israel's demand that these talks focus on setting an agenda for future negotiations, in Shepherdstown they rejected the Israeli demand that the discussion on the demarcation of the June 4 line be preceded by a discussion on the other components of the peace talks. Following the first round of talks in Shepherdstown, held January 3–10, 2000, the Syrians announced that they had no intention of arriving for a second round as long as Israel refused to first discuss the demarcation of the June 4 line.[17]

The Geneva Summit (March 2000) – The Sea of Galilee Shore

A final effort to propel the Israel-Syrian talks into action was introduced by the Americans in a meeting between Presidents Clinton and Asad in Geneva on March 26, 2000. During the meeting, Clinton presented Asad with a proposal on behalf of the Israeli Prime Minister Ehud Barak, designed to rescue the Israeli–Syrian negotiations from the impasse they had reached. This proposal was based on Barak's readiness in principle to accept the June 4 line as the future border between Israel and Syria, but in return Barak demanded that changes be made in this line so that Israel would retain sovereignty over the entire northeastern shore of the Sea of Galilee.[18]

For Barak, it seems that ensuring Israeli presence on the shore of the Sea of Galilee was a red line, since Syria's return to the shore would grant Syria the status of a littoral country and, in keeping with international law, sovereignty over at least part of its waters. It also appeared that Barak was concerned about the reaction among the Israeli public. According to public opinion polls, they would find it difficult to come to terms with the sweeping and complete concession on the Golan Heights and the return of the Syrians to the Sea of Galilee. Barak may also have wanted to retain some maneuvering space on the subject of the border line as long as Israel still did not know what peace agreement with Israel the Syrians were prepared to sign. However, it is also quite possible that Barak may have believed that for Asad the June 4 line was a symbol and that his adherence to it was a matter of prestige – and not necessarily rooted in any real Syrian interest in the territory itself. Thus, Barak believed that as soon as Israel expressed its readiness in principle to accept this line, Asad would be prepared to take a more flexible stand on the actual demarcation of it, and in effect, leave Israel the northeastern strip of the shore which the Syrian army had held prior to the Six Day War – on the condition, of course, that the new border line is to be called the June 4 line.[19]

Following the failure of the Geneva summit, Barak declared that he had good reason to assume that the Syrians would accept the compromise proposal regarding the demarcation of the June 4 line. He stated:

> We had gained the impression we did not because we had conducted any seances in the evenings there (in Shepherdstown), but rather because that was what the Americans believed according to what they had been told. We had reason to think that the Syrians understood that Israeli sovereignty over the waters included a strip of ten or thirty or seventy meters from the water, while we believed that we needed several hundred meters. However, at the meeting in Geneva it became clear that Asad was not prepared to accept even that. Clinton told me that already at the beginning of the meeting he had told Asad that Israel expected to control the shore, and Asad immediately reacted sharply. In other words, that the Syrians were not prepared (for this). Clinton then said to Shar', "Listen, we understood differently"; and Shar' squirmed and stammered.[20]

Indeed, in the first five minutes of the Asad–Clinton summit, it became clear that negotiations had run into difficulty. Asad refused to listen to the compromise proposal presented on behalf of Ehud Barak, and declared that Syria demanded the northeastern shore of the Sea of Galilee, and thus water rights in the Sea. Asad also told Clinton that the northeastern shore of the Sea of Galilee had been in Syrian hands prior to the Six Day War, and that he himself had swum in the waters of it, had fished there and eaten its fish.[21]

Following the failure of the Geneva summit, spokespersons in both Israel and the United States were quick to lay the Syrian track to rest. Ehud Barak stated that peace with Syria would have to wait for the next generation, that the window of opportunity for achieving peace with Syria had closed – or at best, only a crack was left open."[22] The Israeli government also made a binding and official decision regarding the withdrawal of the IDF from South Lebanon, a move that Barak had postponed as long as the negotiations with Syria were progressing. On May 24, 2000, the IDF did withdraw from South Lebanon. Syrian and Lebanese leaders were quick to announce that they had no intention of serving as police to defend Israel's northern border. They also stated that Israel needed to take into account that resistance to it would continue even after the withdrawal and that there would be quiet on Israel's northern border only if it reached an agreement with Syria.[23] Israeli sources brought up the possibility that Syria or the Hizballah might turn Palestinians living in Lebanon against Israel, thus taking action of some kind against it.[24] Israeli leaders, including Chief of General Staff Shaul Mofaz and even Prime Minister Barak himself, each threatened on their sides that a stiff response would also be directed against Syrian targets in Lebanon. Thus, the optimistic assessments regarding an imminent Israeli-Syria peace agreement had been replaced by those of an imminent deterioration in the situation that could possibly lead to an all-out confrontation between Israel and Syria.[25]

What Went Wrong?

On the assumption that Asad indeed wanted peace with Israel and that in his desire for peace he found Barak and Clinton to be eager and enthusiastic partners, the question must be asked: "Why did the sides fail in their efforts to achieve such a peace at the beginning of the year 2000? Have the psychological barriers between the two countries remained as insurmountable as they were? And was the difficulty in resolving possession of several hundred meters along the shore of the Sea of Galilee truly the reason a peace agreement was not achieved between Syria and Israel"?

It would outwardly appear that what separated Syria and Israel were basically disputes over a narrow strip of land several hundred meters long along the northeastern shore of the Sea of Galilee. In Syria's view, however, these few hundred meters had become an issue in principle concerning national pride; and it was these meters that had made the difference between peace with honor, which Asad wished to achieve, and peace with surrender, which the Syrians refused out of hand. Also from Israel's point of view, the issue became a matter of principle touching not only on the question of water, but on the question of Israeli national pride as well. Syria's insistence on regaining the entire Golan Heights and in addition, land that had originally been part of British Mandatory Palestine (which had been captured by Syria in 1948), accompanied by Syria's grim and hostile attitude toward Israel, was considered by many Israelis to be an insult to national pride and a witness to Syria's unwillingness to negotiate peace. Indeed, public opinion polls held in Israel showed that Syria's[26] insistence on the June 4 line prevented many Israelis from supporting the peace agreement forming between the two countries.

Public Opinion and Decision Making in Israel and in Asad's Syria

The fact that the majority of the Israeli public opposed the return to the June 4 line, which apparently motivated Barak to adopt a tougher position on this question, is significant. It would indeed appear that as a result of pressure from public opinion in Israel and as well in Syria, that at the last moment, both Asad and Barak recoiled from making difficult decisions. This put a halt to the considerable progress that had been made in the Israeli–Syrian negotiations.

In the Israeli context, it should be noted that after Barak was elected prime minister and especially after signs appeared of his readiness for substantial concessions on the Syrian front, there was also growing opposition in Israel to the emerging peace settlement with the Syrians. Public opinion polls did indeed indicate that the Israeli public was divided on the question of the Golan Heights. Within this public a considerable percentage were in favor of making substantial concession on the Golan Heights. On the other side there was a solid majority which was opposed to giving up the entire area, and especially to concede to the Syrian demands for Israel's withdrawal to the June 4, 1967 line.[27]

It seems that Damascus had failed, and apparently had not even attempted, to encourage in Israel a "peace camp" – to put pressure on the government of Israel to decide in favor of concessions on the Golan Heights, or that would assist the Israeli government in convincing its Israeli public to support such concessions. There were those in Israel who compared Asad's behavior to that of Sadat in this situation. While the Egyptian president's historic visit to Israel in 1977 resulted in the establishment of the peace camp ("Peace Now"), that put pressure on the Begin government to soften its position in the peace negotiations with Egypt, Asad used Hizballah as a means of putting pressure on Israel to accept Damascus's demands. The use that Asad made of Hizballah did have results, since many in the Israeli public tended to support a peace agreement with Syria because they wanted to put an end to the prolonged bloodletting in Lebanon. Nevertheless, at the same time it also aroused doubts concerning Syria's sincerity, and in any case left a bitter taste in the mouths of many Israelis.[28]

In Syria as well, for the first time since the beginning of the Israeli–Syrian peace negotiations in 1991 – and apparently against the background of the feeling that a peace agreement was imminent – voices were heard criticizing the regime for what appeared as its readiness to reach a peace settlement with Israel. For instance, 'Uqla 'Ursan, the Chairman of the Arab Writers' Association in Damascus and a member of the Ba'ath party, published an article criticizing what he called the flexibility that Syria had shown in its negotiations with Israel.

We reject and will continue to reject in the future, any possibility of recognizing the Zionist enemy. We will also continue to fight against any evidence
of normalization with it, since we view this as a "struggle for survival" and
not "a struggle for borders" [a hint at what Foreign Minister Faruq al-Shar'
had said on the White House lawn in Washington in December, 1999 –
E.Z.].[29]

The embarrassment in which the Syrian regime found itself in the wake
of these words was manifested by Foreign Minister Faruq al-Shar''s readiness to explain and justify before the members of the Arab
Writers'Association that the Syrian regime was now prepared to negotiate
with Israel, and perhaps even to reach a peace agreement with it. Shar''s
address was filled with apologetic attempts to justify himself – thus, full of
contradictions. On the one hand, Shar' once more reminded his audience
that the Arab world had suffered a defeat at the hands of Israel, a defeat
which had left no option but to mount the road to peace. He also admitted
that the conflict with Israel had turned from a battle for existence to a battle
over borders. On the other hand, Shar' declared that he was still committed,
as a veteran member of the Ba'ath party, to its vision and long-range goals,
and thus to the destruction of the State of Israel. Shar' stated:

Israel is stronger than all the Arab states together, and in addition to that,
the United States is its strategic ally and supplies it with every form of
weaponry from the rifle to the missile and up to planes and supercomputers
which are not even to be found in Europe . . . I should like to stress the
extent of this aid – both direct and indirect, the official and the unofficial –
that arrives in Israel from the United States. The Israeli budget is twenty
times larger than the Syrian budget, and the military budget of Syria does
not reach seven percent of the Israeli military budget. It should be borne in
mind that world weapons prices are the same for everyone, and there is no
inexpensive weaponry which Syria receives, or expensive weaponry which
Israel procures for itself. All weapons are expensive, and all the spare parts
are sold at the same price everywhere in the world – in Moscow,
Washington and London.

The real question facing all of us with regard to peace, and I mean genuine
peace as Asad's Syria understands it, is: Will a peace of this kind allow Israel
to expand and establish "Greater Israel?" I believe that a war could better
assist it to achieve this goal, since there is no military balance between the
Arabs and Israel. However, if we turn military confrontation into political,
economic, trade and cultural competition, we will neutralize the power of the
military weapons that Israel has at its disposal, and thus the result of competition of this sort could be better for us . . . since a situation of peace
transforms this conflict into political, ideological, trade and economic
conflict, in which we could be in the preferred position . . . if the Israelis are
not prepared to return the occupied lands to their legitimate owners, they
are sending a message to the Arabs that the conflict between us and them is
a conflict of existence and not a conflict of borders. In any event, the Israelis

possess the concept of a conflict of existence and they treat the Arabs like Indians who have to be annihilated.

After his address, Shar' was asked:

In your address, do not the use of terms such as "a confrontation between cultures and civilizations" that is in the future to replace the military confrontation [between Israel and the Arabs] create a kind of recognition of the rights of the Zionist movement over Palestine, and does it not clash with the principles of the Ba'ath party?

Shar''s answer was edifying;

The Ba'ath party contends that the return of all of Palestine is a long-term strategic aim that will not be able to be realized in one stage . . . Even in the thinking of the Ba'ath Party, there is a differentiation between the various stages of the struggle for the liberation of Palestine . . . According to this differentiation, the first stage is the return of the occupied Arab lands and the ensuring of the permanent national rights of the Palestinian Arab people.[30]

The internal debate going on in Syria over the issue of peace with Israel revealed the difficulty that this country has had in maintaining a policy of peace with its neighbor. Indeed, the difficulties in overcoming the differences of the northeastern shore of the Sea of Galilee are only the tip of the iceberg. A high wall of suspicion and hostility still exists between Syria and Israel. This wall has remained in place because of the inability, to say nothing of the lack of desire, on the part of Damascus to adopt a policy of peace toward Israel and to maintain a dialogue not only with the Israeli government, but also with the Israeli public. With no policy of this kind, every government in Israel, including that of Ehud Barak, might find it difficult to recruit public support for the painful concessions (complete withdrawal from the Golan Heights) necessary in reaching a peace agreement with Syria.

Syria's obduracy on this issue clearly demonstrates the deep chasm between the Israeli and Arab concepts of peace. The Israeli public wanted peace with Syria to be a "warm peace," based on broad and deep normalization of relations – including commercial, tourism, and cultural ties. The hope of maintaining a warm peace with its Arab neighbors was considered a critical objective among the Israelis, since a peace agreement meant painful territorial concessions on Israel's part (withdrawal from the Golan Heights), thus the people in Israel wanted to be convinced that Syria was indeed desirous of peace. While Syria did want a settlement with Israel, it wanted it to be more of a formal and even a technical nature. It envisioned a settlement which was not more than a state of non-belligerency in diplomatic relations. So in Syria there was an aversion and overall opposition to the idea of establishing warm peaceful relations with Israel, as well as deep fears about genuine and meaningful normalization of relations with its neighbor. If this were the case, it would, in the view of many Syrians, allow the latter to establish a "New Middle East," to use Shimon Peres' terminology, e.g., to gain economic and political control of the Middle East exploiting its economic superiority.[31]

A clear expression of this approach by Damascus was seen not only in Shar''s refusal to shake Ehud Barak's hand, as if the latter leader had the plague, but also in the hostile tone that the Syrian media has adopted toward Israel. A prominent example of this tone is evident in an editorial by Muhammad Khayr al-Wadi, editor of *Tishrin*, the official Ba'ath party organ, in which he denied the Holocaust, and claimed that Israel's acts are worse and more serious than those of which it accuses the Nazis. This editorial, which aroused considerable reaction in Israel, was published at the height of the Syrian–Israeli negotiations. It said in part:

> Zionism hides its dark pages in its black history, while inventing stories about the incinerator [the Holocaust] which the Jewish people endured. It even exaggerates the number of people [who ostensibly died in that Holocaust] to astronomical numbers . . . . Zionism is not satisfied with that alone. It also tries to choke off the voices trying to tell the truth, and tries to disprove these claims. In this it has two aims. One is in order to extort more money from Germany and European institutions and governments . . .The second, in order to use it as a whip and means of pressure on anyone who is an enemy of Zionism so as to be able to accuse him of anti-Semitism. Israel, which presents itself as the heir to the victims of the Holocaust, has carried out crimes against the Arabs of a far greater scope, crimes that are even worse than those ostensibly committed by the Nazis. After all, the Nazis did not expel entire peoples from their homelands and did not bury people and captives alive, as did the Zionists.[32]

Asad: Failing Health and the Question of the Succession – An Obstacle on the Road to Peace

Syria's failure throughout the decade of peace negotiations with Israel to adopt a policy of peace had its roots to a considerable extent in the character and personality of President Hafiz al-Asad of Syria. Asad was a slow-moving leader, as well as very closed and suspicious. Moreover, in many respects Asad was a product of Arab world of the 1950s and the 1960s – a world characterized by nationalist fervor, anti-West, and thus anti-Israel. Unlike other leaders, Asad remained firmly planted in the past and clearly found it difficult to adapt himself to the changing realities all over the world as well as in the region.[33]

However, over and above that, it must also be borne in mind that at the beginning of the year 2000, Asad was a different leader from the one who the Israelis – or more precisely the American mediators – had met during the initial stages of the negotiations in the first half of the 1950s. There is indeed another possible explanation of the failure of the effort to establish peace at the beginning of that year: that is, Asad's state of health. He showed an inability to function, to make definite decisions, and even to show the flexibility necessary to his position – mainly because of a depressed feeling that his "days were numbered." He also expressed a desire to grant priority and even exclusivity to the task of ensuring his son Bashar's succession. Thus in early 2000, Asad was an ailing leader in the final phases of both a physical and mental decline – a leader who was isolated from others, sunk within himself. He was a leader who had in essence ceased to function. It would appear that Asad himself was aware of his deteriorating condition, and the failure of the meeting with Clinton in Geneva may have had something to do with his decision not to take any chances in signing an agreement with Israel, and to focus most of his efforts on ensuring Bashar's succession.[34]

The United States – What More Could Be Done?

In light of all the aforementioned, the role played by the United States in the negotiations is worthy of attention. This role was a significant one, especially because, in Syria's view, the peace process was designed to establish peaceful relations between Washington and Damascus. However, to the disappointment of the Syrians, and later of the Israelis, the Americans refrained from playing an active role in the negotiations, and retreated to the position of a "postman" passing messages back and forth between the two sides. The Syrians claimed that the Americans, who had been entrusted with Rabin's deposit, should have taken more active measures to realize it, while the Israeli side complained that the Americans should have exerted more pressure on the Syrians to take more confidence-building measures toward Israel. The Americans' response to this was that they had no real bargaining chips allowing them to pressure either Syria or Israel. The administration's situation regarding the Syrians was even more serious. It lacked the means of luring Syria into moving the negotiations forward in view of the anti-Syrian lobby in Congress that might have foiled any move that the administration could make toward improving relations with Syria, and mainly granting it economic aid.[35]

Epilogue – The Death of Hafiz al-Asad and Bashar al-Asad's Rise to Power

On June 10, 2000, Hafiz al-Asad passed away, exactly 33 years after he had lost the Golan Heights to Israel. With his death, all eyes turned to his son Bashar who was quickly declared Asad's successor.

Conventional wisdom held that Bashar would need some time to stabilize his rule at home before he turned his attention to renewing the peace process. However, at the same time it was clear that promoting the peace process is a necessary and vital step if Bashar is to extricate Syria from its political isolation and especially from its economic difficulties.

It should be mentioned that Bashar, born in September 1965, was two years old when Israel captured the Golan Heights. Thus there were many in Israel and in the West who assessed that he did not have the bitter resentment of the past, or the hostility that characterized his father's attitude toward Israel. Bashar also spent a number of years practicing medicine in Great Britain, and even took the trouble to present himself as a ruler versed in Western ways and as wanting to bring Syria into the twenty-first century, integrating it into the world at large. It is difficult to assume that Bashar will be able to divorce himself from his father's explicit legacy on the territorial issue. Nevertheless, Bashar may be shown to be a more convenient partner in negotiations with Israel, as he may conduct public diplomacy with Israel, and should know how to make intelligent use of the Western and Israeli media. These steps that were so lacking in his father's administration may very well move the peace process forward and bring about the awaited breakthrough. Support for these assessments can indeed be seen in reports from Damascus, according to which Bashar will be prepared to renew negotiations with Israel, although he does demand Israeli withdrawal to the June 4, 1967 border.[36]

As a result, it is still too early to know whether Bashar's rise to power will lead to the breakthrough on the road to peace. Will Bashar succeed in stabilizing his rule? Will he be prudent and flexible on the territorial question on which the two sides still disagree? Will he demonstrate openness and conduct public diplomacy with Israel, including holding a dialogue with it? One must also remember that Bashar will need an Israeli partner to negotiate peace with; and the question is whether such a partner will be found, when taking into consideration the current political turmoil in Israel. All that remains is to wait and see what the new era in Syria under Bashar will bring to the Israeli–Syrian negotiations.

Notes

1   *Yedi'ot Aharonot*, May 20, 28, 1999; *Ha'aretz*, May 20, 1999.
2   See *Ma'ariv*, March 31, 2000, *al-Hayat*, April 8, 2000.

3 See *Ma'ariv*, March 31, 2000; see also *Ha'aretz*, May 25, 2000; for the Syrian position see *al-Ba'ath*, April 12, 2000.

4 For historical background on the Israeli–Syrian peace negotiations see Itamar Rabinovich, *The Brink of Peace: The Israeli–Syrian Negotiations* (Princeton, NJ: Princeton University Press, 1998); Moshe-Ma'oz, *Syria and Israel: From War to Peace Making* (New York: Oxford University Press, 1995); Helena Cobban, *The Israeli–Syrian Peace Talks, 1991–1996 and Beyond* (Washington, D.C.: United States Institute of Peace Press, 1999); Eyal Zisser, *Asad's Legacy: Syria in Transition* (New York: New York University Press, 2000); see also Interview with Syrian ambassador to Washington Walid al-Mu'allim, *Journal of Palestinian Studies*, Vol. XXVI, No. 2 (Winter 1997), pp. 401–12.

5 See *Ha'aretz*, August 29, 1996; *al-Hayat*, November 21, 22, 23, 1999; See also, Itamar Rabinovich, *The Brink of Peace*, pp. 138–57.

6 See Eyal Zisser, "Syria," in *MECS* (Middle East Contemporary Survey) (Boulder: Westview Press), Vol. XVIII (1994), pp. 639–48; Vol. XIX (1995), pp. 612–17.

8 See *Ha'aretz*, May 29; July 15; November 25, 1999; see also *Ma'ariv*, November 31, 1999.

9 See an interview with Gen. 'Amos Malka, head of the Israeli Military Intelligence, *Bamachane*, July 9, 1999; see also *New York Times*, July 18, 1999.

10 *al-Hayat*, June 23, 1999.

11 *al-Hayat*, November 21, 22, 23, 1999.

12 See *Ha'aretz*, September 10, 1999.

13 *See al-Thawra*, December 22, 1999; *Ma'ariv*, December 9, 10, 1999.

14 Reuters, December 15, 1999; *Tishrin*, December 17, 1999.

15 See *Ha'aretz*, December 10, 17, 1999; *Yedi'ot Aharonot*, December 10, 31, 1999.

16 Israeli TV, Channel 1, January 27, 2000; *Ha'aretz*, January 28, 2000.

17 *New York Times*, January 10, 11, 2000.

18 See *Washington Post*, March 29, 2000; see also *Ma'ariv*, March 31, 2000.

19 *Ma'ariv*, December 24, 1999; *Yedi'ot Aharonot*, March 31, 2000.

20 See Barak's interview to *Ha'aretz*, May 19, 2000.

21 *al-Nahar*, March 28, 2000; see also Mustafa Talas' interview to R. al-Sharq, July 10, 2000.

22 *Ma'ariv*, March 31, 2000.

23 See *al-Ba'ath*, April 20, 2000; *al-Hayat*, April 27, 2000.

24 See interview with Gen. 'Amos Malka, head of the Israeli Military Intelligence published in *Ha'aretz*, May 31, 2000.

25 See *Ha'aretz*, January 24, 25, 2000.

26 See *Ha'aretz*, January 6, 2000, January 24, 2000.

27 Ibid.

28 See *Ha'aretz*, March 17, June 25, 2000.

29 *al-Usbu' al-Adabi* (Damascus), December 12, 1999; see also 'Uqla 'Ursan, "Bidun Musafaha" (without shaking hands), *al-Usbu' al-'Adabi*, December 18, 1999.

30 *al-Safir*, February 13, 2000.

31 See Uri Savir, *The Process: 1,000 Days that Changed the Middle East* (New York: Random House, 1998), pp. 297–328; for the Syrian position, see an

interview with 'Aziz Shukri of the Damascus University, *al-Wasat,* February 3, 1997.
32 *Tishrin,* December 31, 1999.
33 For more on Asad see Eyal Zisser, *Decision Making in Asad's Syria,* The Washington Institute, Policy Paper, February 1998; see also Eyal Zisser, "Asad of Syria – the leader and the Image," *Orient,* vol. 35 (2/94), pp. 247–60.
34 See *Ha'aretz,* March 6, 2000; *al-Nahar,* March 30, 2000; *Sunday Times* (London), April 7, 2000.
35 See (*Middle East Institute*), Symposium on "America and the Middle East Peace: Interests, Responsibilities, Limitation," March–April 1998, pp. 19–44; see also an interview with American diplomat by the author, Tel Aviv, June 4, 2000.
36 See *al-Hayat,* July 14, 2000, Reuters, July 19, 2000.

CHAPTER 21

Iraq and the Middle East Peace Process, 1968–2000

AMATZIA BARAM

Political Arabism surfaced in Iraq (or "Mesopotamia" as it used to be called at the time) in a more or less organized fashion following the Young Turks' coup d'etat in Istanbul in 1908. In response to the new Turkish rulers' inclination to emphasize the secular Turkish rather than Islamic Ottoman identity of the empire, Arab army officers, paramount among whom were people who hailed from Baghdad and Mosul, formed a secret society, al-'Ahd (the Covenant). This was one of three main such Arab groups that demanded political rights on the basis of Arab culture and identity. Their practical demands ranged all the way from political autonomy to political independence for the Arabs, which would entail complete separation from the Ottoman Empire. However, the public exposure of these early Arab nationalists was extremely limited due to there being no more than a few scores of activists and the limitations on their movements and public discourse.

Mass education and propagation of Arab nationalism arrived in Iraq only with the accession of King Faysal I to Baghdad's throne in August 1921. Immediately upon arrival to power, in the wings of the British occupation of Iraq, the new king established a state educational system. This he put under the supervision of Sati' al-Husri, a pan-Arab ideologue who had served under him in Damascus between 1919 and 1920. Husri's educational system emphasized pan-Arab nationalism above any other value. The teaching of history and geography was carefully tailored to suit this goal. These subjects were taught almost exclusively in order to foster the pan-Arab identity among the children. This was done through specially written textbooks and the employment of pan-Arab teachers, many of whom were asked to come from Palestine, Lebanon, and Syria. One of the most central issues within the curricula was the Palestinian problem. Anti-British and anti-Zionist sentiments were encouraged among the children.

Palestine was described as the neck, linking the two parts of the Arab homeland: the Arab East (Arabia, Iraq, Syria, Lebanon, and Jordan) with Egypt and the Arab West (North Africa).[1] As such, in addition to it being an integral part of the Arab homeland, it gained very special emphasis, and preventing the Zionist movement from developing there became of paramount importance. Another pan-Arab educator, Dr. Sami Shawkat, who showed even greater zeal, adding to Husri's pan-Arabism some fascist hues, succeeded Husri. The liberal Shi'i educator Fadil al-Jamali, whose commitment to pan-Arabism was no less impressive than Husri's, replaced him, in his own turn. During the first 20 years of the existence of this monarchy, all children who graduated from primary, intermediate, and high schools received massive doses of pan-Arab sentiment.

The success of Husri's educational system was near total. The educated and half-educated strata in Iraqi society grew to be deeply attached to Arab issues, including those far away from the national borders of Iraq. It is hardly surprising that despite the fact that Iraq had no borders with Palestine, of all the Arab capitals it was Baghdad which experienced the first large-scale anti-Zionist demonstration. In February 1928, no less than 40,000 demonstrators, led by students and teachers of the Teacher's Training College of Baghdad, stormed the city demonstrating against a visiting British dignitary, Sir Alfred Mond, a confidante of Lord Balfour – who was identified, as a result, with the 1917 Balfour Declaration.[2] Pan-Arab sentiment, with the Palestine issues at its core, became a powerful tool in the hands of politicians in Baghdad who were attempting to undermine their competitors in the government of the day and return to power. By accusing their opponents of neglecting Palestine and succumbing to British pressures, Iraqi politicians had a reasonable chance of toppling the government. Appearing as the staunchest defenders of Palestine against Zionism also served the Hashimite monarchy in its quest for Iraqi hegemony in Syria and more generally in the Fertile Crescent and the Arab world. Thus the Palestinian issue became both a major domestic and foreign policy concern in monarchical Iraq – so much so that when the government of Muhammad al-Sadr decided in May 1948 to send Iraqi troops to fight against the newly born State of Israel, this bought the government and the Regent 'Abd al-Ilah a few months of relative tranquility after a long period of social-economic unrest.[3]

After he had destroyed the monarchy and assumed power, General 'Abd al-Karim Qasim steered Iraq clear of pan-Arab policies; but even he needed to cover his flank in his struggle against Egypt's Gamal 'Abd al-Nasir, and was the first Arab leader to establish a regular battalion of the Palestinian Liberation Army, consisting of Palestinian ex-patriots who lived in Iraq. The first regime of the Ba'ath party (February–November 1963) paid little attention to the Palestinian issue, but the successor, General 'Abd al-Salam 'Arif, docilely towed the militant anti-Israeli line of 'Abd al-Nasir. His elder brother, General 'Abd al-Rahman 'Arif, who took over in 1966 following his brother's death in a helicopter crash, was caught unprepared by the May–June 1967 crisis. Even though he sent a brigade-size tank force to the Jordanian front, most of it was lost in the desert on the way, decimated by the Israeli air force.

The fact that he sent such a small force and that this force was largely lost presented a golden opportunity for the clandestine Ba'ath party. Even though Iraq was far from being a democracy at the time, the regime could not or would not stop a Ba'athi mass demonstration, denouncing General 'Arif for "corruption and inefficiency."[4] As we are told by Saddam Hussein himself, it was 'Arif's failure in the Six Day War of June 1967 that enabled the young Ba'athi activist to convince a key person, Colonel Hammad Shihab, Commander of the Tenth Armored Brigade, the most powerful unit in the Iraqi army, to break his vow of allegiance to 'Arif and help the Ba'ath party to topple him. Saddam's argument was that by his failure to act properly in the war, 'Arif broke his own "commitment to the lofty values and honorable ideals" of the Arab nation. "For the honor of this (Arab) people, its history and future," Saddam argued, 'Arif had to be removed; and Shihab agreed, on the condition that 'Arif's life would be spared (a promise he kept).[5]

Phase One: Radical Ideology, Radical Practice, 1968–1970

When the Ba'ath regime came to power in a bloodless coup d'etat which overthrew the 'Arif regime, they were at a serious disadvantage. They had only a few hundred activists on whom they could rely as many members had left the party during its underground years. They were also extremely unpopular as a result of their failure to hold on to power in 1963 and as a result of the mass killings of Communists, both real and perceived. Finally, the Iraqi army was flooded with supporters of Egypt's 'Abd al-Nasir, who had no sympathy at all for the Ba'ath party. In addition, it will be remembered that they managed to come to power largely as a result of the poor performance of their predecessors in the Six Day War.

For all these reasons, turning the Palestinian issue into their main propaganda focus seemed to be a good way to re-capture the imagination and support of the Iraqi public. Thus, both on the ideological and practical level, their policies vis-à-vis Israel were the most extreme in the Arab world, and indeed, in the history of Iraq. On the practical level, they kept an army of at least 18,000 soldiers mainly in Jordan with a small force in southern Syria as well, with two divisional commands.[6] This expeditionary force represented around one-fifth of the Iraqi army; and having to supply this force through one thousand kilometers of bad desert roads was a huge economic burden which cost Iraq more than one-third of its oil revenues in the years 1968–70.[7] No less important, Iraq had a low-intensity military confrontation on its eastern border with the Shah's Iran, and by sending so many troops to Jordan it weakened its own hand. Last but not least, recurring confrontations with Israel cost the Iraqi dispatch force casualties on a continuous basis.[8]

On the ideological level the Ba'ath regime coined the slogan "*Kull shay' min ajli al-Ma'raka*" ("Everything for the [Palestine] battle").[9] Indeed Palestine became by far the single most important component in the regime's propaganda warfare against its opponents at home and rivals in the Arab world. All the Arab regimes, including the Egyptian and Syrian ones, were accused of betraying the Palestine issue. Iraq called for an immediate resumption of a full-fledged war against Israel – something Egypt, Syria, and Jordan could have hardly afforded to do. Furthermore, the Ba'ath regime tried to bring the PLO under its influence, and promised that through the battle to liberate Palestine, new revolutionary forces would be born. These forces, apparently guided by the Ba'ath party, would eventually spread from Palestine to the whole Arab world to topple all its regimes without exception and install new revolutionary governments.

In other words, the Ba'ath regime of Baghdad believed, or claimed to believe in those days, that through the battle to liberate Palestine they would eventually be able to take over the Arab world as a whole. This process was alternately called "the Arab Revolution" or "the Permanent Arab Revolution," no doubt inspired by Leo Trotsky's theory of action. Consequently, in response to the Egyptian acceptance of the Roger's Plan (put forth by US Secretary of State William D. Rogers) in July 1970, which put an end to the War of Attrition against Israel, the Baghdad-based pan-Arab leadership called upon the Arab masses to "join the Permanent Revolution – whatever the price – until the liberation of Palestine and the liberation of *all the Arab countries* . . . (and their inclusion) in democratic, socialist (Ba'ath style) Arab unity."[10]

Phase Two: Pragmatic Practice, Radical Ideology, 1970–1982

When in the summer of 1970 the tension between the Hashamite regime of Jordan and the Palestinian armed organizations approached a boiling point, the Ba'ath regime of Iraq announced that in the case of confrontation, it would place all its forces in Jordan "under the command" (*tahta tasarruf*) of the Palestinian organizations. In fact, even as early as January 1970, a senior Iraqi declared that Iraq's forces had already been placed "under the command" (*tahta amr*) of the "(Palestinian) leadership of the armed struggle."[11] In one case they even announced that the Iraqi forces had already been placed under the Palestinian command. At the same time, however, the Minister of Defense, Hardan 'Abd al-Ghafar al-Tikriti, visited Amman and promised King Hussein Iraqi neutrality. When the battles in Amman started, the Iraqi forces withdrew a few miles east of the main road leading from the Syrian border to Amman, thus keeping away from the military confrontation, but also clearing the way for Syrian forces to advance on the Jordanian capital.

The Iraqi inaction earned the Ba'ath regime severe criticism from the Palestine Liberation Organization (PLO) and radical Arab circles. As it was defined by the regime itself, the Ba'ath regime found itself "powerless . . . to act in a way commensurate with the measures of the conspiracy and the magnitude of the [party's] slogans . . . and commitments . . . the September (1970) events . . . were used by the regimes and circles hostile to the party . . . which severely damaged its reputation . . . in the Arab masses."[12] The result was that, following an internal struggle in the party's leadership, a pragmatic political line emerged. According to this new line, Iraq had to change its priorities. Ideologically, or as it was often defined, on the level of long-term strategy, Iraq should remain staunchly dedicated to the total liberation of Palestine. However, in practice, or on the short-term tactical level, it should dedicate all its energies to its own interests. This meant that the Iraqi forces should be withdrawn from Jordan and Syria and placed along the Iraqi–Iranian border. It also meant that Iraq should concentrate on military aggrandizement and on economic development, and should stay away from Arab–Israeli confrontations, even if this meant a postponement of the liberation of Palestine for ten or twenty years.[13] Only when it was fully ready for war with Israel, and after it had achieved a major leap forward on the socioeconomic level, should Iraq engage Israel again – and this time for the decisive battle. This would also be the moment when Iraq would become "a center of revolutionary pan-Arab radiation to the whole (Arab) area."[14] Namely, the first phase of self-development and of building its armed forces would serve as the basis not only for the liberation of Palestine, but also for Iraqi leadership of the Arab world.

Because the regime had to convince its domestic audience as well as its Arab supporters outside of Iraq that detaching itself from the Arab–Israeli conflict did not mean an abandonment of the Palestinian issue as a whole, its anti-Israeli and anti-Western rhetoric remained as extreme as it had been when it had come to power in July 1968. It made great efforts to convince its audiences that on the strategic level it had remained totally loyal to its pan-Arab commitment. Any Arab country that hinted readiness to talk to Israel was met with the most severe Iraqi condemnations. One instance of this was when Hafiz al-Asad's Syria developed the theory of phases: e.g., eliminating Israel through a number of phases, including diplomatic negotiations. When this occurred, Syria was accused by Baghdad of treason. Iraq's demand of the Arab states was, rather than actually going to war (for which the Arabs were not yet prepared), to retain a war-like attitude.

As Deputy Chairman of the Iraqi Revolution Command Council (RCC), Saddam Hussein explained to an Egyptian journalist:

> We do not imagine that the Arabs are capable of smashing the Zionist enemy and we do not believe that the world will allow us [now] to smash it . . . I do not say that the war will continue in the same way as the October [1973] War happened . . . but it will continue in [retaining] the atmosphere of war.[15]

Additionally, the Iraqi leadership under Saddam's influence adopted a "phases" strategy over Palestine, but it was different from the Syrian one. While Damascus envisaged a switch from war to diplomatic negotiations and back on the way to destroy Israel,[16] Baghdad would allow no negotiations. All phases must be hostile and unilateral. For example, war may be followed by a cease-fire and economic and diplomatic pressure, to be followed again by war; but any positive bilateral or multilateral contacts with the enemy were seen as the beginning of a compromise over the whole land of Palestine.[17]

Indeed, there is little doubt that it was Saddam Hussein who initiated or at least was the most energetic initiator of the new and pragmatic Iraqi-centered line. An important component of that line was an emphasis on the Iraqi entity, partly at the expense of the pan-Arab identification of the Iraqis. The most important component in this new identity was Iraq's historical greatness. As Saddam Hussein described it, even if it postponed its re-entry, there was absolutely no fear that Iraq would defect from the decisive battle against Israel because Iraq has always led the Arab battle against the Jews, even in remote antiquity – and continuing this battle was its destiny. When, following the Camp David Accords, he agreed to start cooperating with Syria despite the hissing animosity between the two Ba'ath regimes, the RCC under his control reminded the Iraqi and Arab audiences:

> Iraq has always had a well-known part in the struggle against Zionism and in the liberation of Palestine, since the era of the Assyrians and Babylonians and in the era of Salah al-din al-Ayyubi, then in the 1948 war and the war of October 1973 and to this very day.[18]

In a speech in the Shi'i south a few months later, he explained again:

> The agents of imperialism do not wish to see a greater and greater Iraq (for fear) that the Arabs would become powerful, because the power and glory of the Arabs (grow) from the power and glory of al-'Arab Iraq ('izz min 'izz al-'iraq) . . . The Zionists who are crouching on your land, who are they and where did their conceit come from? They are three million usurpers assembled from all parts of the world and they are supported by a qualitative gap in action and understanding . . . [However], if we want to return to history we shall find out that . . . from here Nebuchadnezzar emerged and arrested those elements which had tried to debase the land of the Arabs, the land of

Cana'an in Palestine [sic!] and he brought them, chained, to Babylon. From
here emerged (also the Assyrian kings) Shalmanesser and Sargon II . . . to
liberate the Arab land from the filth of those who had wanted to usurp it.
These people, who inherited the usurpation from those [whom
Nebuchadnezzar exiled to Babylon], . . . are today assembled on the land of
Palestine, creating the Zionist Entity.[19]

I personally provided this quotation to the Israeli prime minister's office
in late 1980. My own analysis at the time was that the Iraqi leadership was
trying to mobilize public Shi'i support in view of Ayat Allah Khomeini's
ascendancy to power in Tehran (it will be remembered that the speech was
made in the Shi'i south) but, at the same time, refrain from any concrete
timetable for the liberation of Palestine. After all, the immediate danger
was Khomeini, not Menachem Begin. But according to one source close to
him, Prime Minister Begin, whose sense of history was proverbial, received
the report and went ballistic. Saddam Hussein's European-style reconstruction of "Iraqi" national history and glory struck at Begin's
innermost European-style sense of identity. Apparently, the memory of
Nebuchadnezzar gave him an extra push when he decided to launch the
aerial attack against Iraq's nuclear reactor in June 1981. Saddam's
invocation of Nebuchadnezzar did not go unnoticed by Begin's court
journalist, who used it a few years later as one of his arguments designed
to justify the operation.[20] The total success of the operation represented a
major embarrassment for Saddam, and throughout much of the Iraq–Iran
War, he repeatedly promised his army officers to avenge the destruction of
the reactor.

Many years later, Saddam was still unable to forget Begin's response to
his interpretation of Iraq's history. In 1999, in a meeting with middle-level
Ba'ath party officials in the Shi'i south, not far from the ruins of Babylon,
the Iraqi president returned to the same theme. This time, however, he
conveniently forgot that it was he who started this battle of clashing
national historical memories almost exactly twenty years earlier, stating:

The enemies are retaliating [by embargoing Iraq's women and children]
because Nebuchadnezzar took them as captives. They are fearful about the
future; they fear that Iraq may achieve prosperity and thwart the expansionist, racist and aggressive Zionist ideology which is targeted against the
Arab nation.[21]

In fact, Saddam even explained US motivation when they bombed
Baghdad in December 1998 in terms of the United States being "mindful
of the history of Babylon": since time immortal, he contended, only by
conquering Babylon could any power hope to become "master of the four
directions," as the Americans wish to become.[22]

Phase Three: Pragmatic Practice, Dual-Track Rhetoric in the Iraq–Iran War, 1983–1989

Following his invasion of Khomeini's Iran on September 22, 1980, Saddam must have felt that attacking a staunch anti-American, anti-Israeli, and pro-Palestinian regime required some explanations. Six days after he launched his offensive, he declared victory – although the war continued eight more years – and he made a solemn promise:

> Brothers: this [fighting Khomeini] is a great honor for the Iraqi army, the army we have prepared, and still are preparing . . . to liberate Palestine. Those who fought in Zayn al-Qaws, Sayf Sa'd al-Muhammara and Ahwaz were asphalting the road to Jerusalem, Ramallah Hebron and Jaffa.[23]

This speech, too, added to Prime Minister Begin's resolve to bomb the Tammuz nuclear reactor in the face of strong opposition in his own government and military and intelligence community.[24] By mentioning Jaffa, Saddam made it very clear that, at least ideologically speaking, he was committed to the early and full-fledged elimination of the State of Israel. Throughout the war, almost every time the enemy was mentioned, it was not just Iran, but rather "the Persian–Zionist enemy." This way, the fear and revulsion so long associated with Israel were expected to stick to Khomeini's Iran too. This was particularly important in relation to the Shi'a. In April 1983, however, following the hurried and humiliating withdrawal of Iraq's troops from almost all the Iranian territories conquered since September 1980, the Iraqi leader sounded much more subdued. While the barrage of anti-Israeli rhetoric continued unabated, including the identification between Zionism and Khomeini's "Zoroastrianism," the actual commitment to the early elimination of Israel disappeared. Consequently, in an interview with a Palestinian intellectual who wanted to know whether Iraq would at long last free itself to deal with Israel and when this would take place, the Iraqi president was very evasive:

> Tell them [the Palestinians] that no Arab, close or distant, in Palestine or outside of it, should imagine that we are distant from him or ignoring his sufferings . . . However, the expression of our feelings will only come when the hour which we expect . . . arrives . . . Tell your brothers in the [West] Bank and the [Gaza] Strip that each battle has its circumstances.[25]

Namely, Saddam postponed Iraq's involvement on the battlefield and implied that even when Iraq joined the Palestinian fray, it would only seek to liberate the West Bank and the Gaza Strip, i.e., the territories conquered by Israel in June 1967. In the same interview, Saddam also departed from his regime's previous policy of isolating Egypt because of its separate peace with Israel. In his new view, the correct approach now was to draw Egypt closer to the Arab world, to "return (Egypt) to the lap" (*ihtidanuha*) and thus encourage and help it to forsake its peace with Israel gradually, "thread by thread," rather than "in a dramatic and immediate fashion." Even though Saddam went out of his way to emphasize that this new approach has nothing to do with Egypt's support for Iraq in its war with Iran, since then Iraq has exerted vigorous efforts to return Egypt into the Arab League.

Three months earlier as Iraq was still reeling from the defeats in Abadan and Khorramshahr, Tariq 'Aziz, then foreign minister, divulged to *Le Mond* that Iraq was actually pushing the Palestinians and Jordanians into each other's arms so that they could jointly start peace negotiations with Israel.[26] Iraqi spokesmen made it clear to Western audiences that Iraq would never join such negotiations but neither would it sabotage such a process. Likewise, Iraqi diplomats explained to Israeli and American interlocutors that after the war Iraq would dedicate all its energies to reconstruction, completely forsaking the path of war. This is what Ambassador Nizar Hamdun told Generals Ori Or and Avi Ya'ri at the home of Professor Nadav Safran in Boston in 1986. This is also what Prime Minister Sa'dun Hammadi, Foreign Minister Tariq 'Aziz, and Ambassador Barazan Ibrahim Hasan al-Tikriti, Saddam's half brother, told General Avraham Tamir in two meetings in 1988 and 1989.

They never promised to sign a peace agreement, but they did make it clear that after the war Iraq would not return to the Rejectionist Front: it would approve of a Palestinian–Israeli peace, and concentrate on its reconstruction. Meetings between Iraqi diplomats and Israelis and Zionist American Jews were no longer a taboo, as Iraq needed American support against Iran. Furthermore, in 1984–6 Iraq engaged in extensive negotiations with Israel's Prime Minister Shimon Peres through American intermediaries (mainly Bechtel Company) over the construction of a large oil pipeline from Haditha through Jordan to Aqaba. Iraq wanted Israeli and US guarantees that the pipeline would not be harmed by Israel, and for that was ready to pay a handsome annual protection fee.[27] Strictly in the foreign media, Iraqi officials were quite open over the project, but demanded clear-cut guarantees against "Israeli sabotage."[28] The project never materialized, apparently because the Iraqis were never too serious about it: the domestic price they would have to pay for tacit cooperation with Israel could be too high, especially after the destruction of Tammuz. It would seem that the whole project was embarked upon in order to exert pressure on the Saudis to allow Iraq to build a pipeline through its territory, which eventually they did. Still, the very fact that Iraq was ready to appear for a while as "kissing Israel," even if through a Jordanian–American glass, was a major change in Iraq's approach.

For the domestic record, Saddam announced in a published interview with a Zionist American Jew, Congressman Steven Solarz, that "the Israelis" (apparently as individuals, as different from "Israel" as a political entity) deserve "a secure situation" (*halah aminah*).[29] Also, every Iraqi knew by then that the hard line toward Egypt because of its peace agreement with Israel was over. Even more illuminating was the attitude toward Lebanese President Amin Jumayyil, who signed on May 17, 1983 a peace agreement with Israel. Following a conversation between the two presidents, it was announced that an agreement had been reached that Saddam would receive Jumayyil's envoy for discussion of the agreement with "the Zionist Entity." Na'im Haddad, President of the Iraqi Parliament, announced that Iraq's objection to the agreement notwithstanding, Iraq would continue to support Jumayyil against Israel (sic!). The Pan Arab leadership argued that the crimes of Damascus (of occupying parts of Lebanon, supporting Iran, and negotiating peace with Israel) overwhelmingly outweighed those of Beirut; thus, one should not be too hard on Jumayyil, who played a weak hand and had to survive under harsh political circumstances. Furthermore, it agreed that Lebanon should stick to the letter of the agreement. Its only demand was that it go no further in normalizing relations with the "Zionists."[30]

At the same time, however, albeit far less frequently than ever before, one could still come across in the Iraqi media a continued long-term commitment to the ideal of the total "liberation of Palestine" and the elimination of "Israel" (in inverted commas), or the "Zionist Entity."[31] Much more common were claims that since the days of Chaldean Babylonia, the Jews and the Persians had been bent on the destruction of Iraq.[32] The conclusion, albeit mostly by implication, was that whatever Iraq does, Israel would always seek to destroy it; hence Iraq had no choice but to destroy Israel. The duality of, on the one hand, an implied acceptance of Israel within its pre-1967 borders, and on the other a commitment to destroy it, was never discussed explicitly. Thus, party members could have interpreted it as a continuation of the party's now-traditional differentiation between short-term tactics and long-term strategy. Equally, however, it could also be understood as a gradual departure from traditional party doctrine of the total "liberation" of Palestine.

Phase Four (1989 to the Mid-1990s) – Radical Action, Radical Rhetoric

The first months after the Iraq–Iran war seemed to be a direct continuation of the war period: Iraq's main enemy was now Syria. Its military support for Syria's arch-enemy in Lebanon, General Michel 'Awn, was stepped up as the Israeli Navy turned a blind eye to this support. Only when Saddam sent Soviet-made Frog 70–km missiles to Lebanon did Israel force the ships that carried them to turn back (according to another source the missiles were stopped in Jordan). But toward mid-1989, Iraq reversed its policy. In July and August, Iraqi aircraft flew reconnaissance sorties near the Israeli border and a joint Iraqi–Jordanian fighter wing was established.[33] In December 1989 Iraq launched its three-stage ballistic missile, Tammuz. Even though it was only partly successful, the launch thrilled the Iraqi media to such an extent that it brushed aside all its controls and presented it as the first step on the road of eliminating Israel.

In April 1990, Saddam, fearing an Israeli raid on Iraq's newly-built nuclear installations, threatened that if Israel did attack, he would "burn half of Israel" in return, apparently with the chemically-tipped missiles of which he boasted. From then on, and particularly after the invasion of Kuwait, the Iraqi leadership and media adopted a very extreme political line, promising to punish Israel if the international alliance attacked Iraq. Twenty-four hours after the Gulf War began, the first missiles landed in Tel Aviv.[34]

On the ideological level too, this period, extending throughout the 1990s, was typified by the most extreme slogans promising Israel's destruction. In the same way that in the 1980s Zionism was identified with the Iranian enemy, it was now identified with the Anglo-American anti-Iraqi policies – beginning with the Gulf War – through the international embargo and the No Fly Zones, and all the way to theories of American–Zionist conspiracies to weaken the Arabs by keeping Iraq weak and eventually, to turn all Arabs into slaves. Thus, in a wide-ranging article, Salah al-Mukhtar, the editor of the daily owned by 'Udayy Saddam Hussein, discussed an American–Israeli plan which he called "Plan 2000" formulated in the 1970s, which aimed at turning Israel into the only important industrial and economic center in the Middle East. This center, he believed, was to be surrounded by a vast rural and underdeveloped Arab hinterland, which would be kept away from any scientific and technological advancement.[35]

The implied conclusion was that Israel's very existence could not be tolerated. Dr. Bahnam Abu Suf, Iraq's most prominent Mesopotamian archeologist, discussed at length the ancient enmity between the Jews and the peoples of Mesopotamia. Since the beginning of time, Jews have been aligning themselves with the West against the East, and receiving support in return.[36] The Jews also worked together with the Persians from the East in order to destroy Babylon in the sixth century BC, and before that they made a crucial contribution to the destruction of Assyria.[37] It has to be made clear that even though the Jews exiled in Babylon benefited from the Persian victory, there is no evidence whatsoever that there was any Jewish–Persian collusion. Likewise, there is no historical evidence of any cooperation between the Jews and other forces against the Kingdom of Assyria. Iraqi ideologues who presented the modern Iraqi people as the offspring and cultural heirs of Babylon and Assyria found it very useful, however, to create a historical connection between the Jews and the ancient Persians; this reinforced their claim that the Iraq–Iran War, initiated by Saddam Hussein, was nothing but a continuation of a Jewish–Persian conspiracy from a long way back. In this way the responsibility of the Iraqi leadership for this disastrous war could be played down. Not surprisingly then, another Iraqi journalist concluded an article dealing with Israel's right to exist by stating:

> The existence of the Zionist Entity on the land of Palestine is null and void. It is impossible to turn this non-existence into solid reality . . . thus it is impossible to reach peace [with Israel] because something which does not exist cannot lead to peace.[38]

In an interview one year after the Gulf War, Saddam Hussein gave a typical answer to the question of why he was not afraid of the Israeli military response to the Iraqi missiles launched against Tel Aviv and other cities:

> All the forces that attacked Baghdad were Israeli [forces]. Zionism [however] preferred not to use some of its weapons, because it preferred to control the situation at the end of the war.[39]

Gone were the days when Iraqi spokesmen implied that Israel within its pre-1967 borders could be acceptable to them. Hasan al-Kashif commended the killing of Israelis by Palestinian guerillas and explained that killing those people inside pre-1967 Israel proves that "the whole of Palestine, and not just the West Bank and the Gaza Strip, is the (exclusive) homeland of the Palestinian people."[40] In his annual Army Day speech in January 1996, Saddam reminded his listeners of the exploits of the Iraqi army on the Palestinian front:

> The valiant Iraqi army is one of the few Arab armies . . . that fought outside of the borders of the country . . . against the army of the Zionist enemy. This army's stands are still recalled . . . on the battlefields in Sinai, the Golan, and occupied Palestine, in Jennie [West Bank], Far Quasi [Israel], Nobles [West Bank] . . . Raman Hakovesh [Israel] . . . Kfar Yona [Israel] . . . Kakun [Israel] . . . It is a great honor for this army of Arabism that its aircraft were the only aircraft of all armies that defied the Zionist Entity's air defences roaring over the skies of Palestine to pound their targets inside the Zionist Entity. It is a great honor for this army that its al-Hussein and al-'Abbas were the only missiles among those of all Arab armies that pounded their targets inside that usurping, aggressor entity.[41]

Among those most outspoken about Iraq's commitment to eliminate Israel has been the Iraqi president's elder son 'Udayy, the owner of *Babil*. We see this, for example, in mid-1995, when in his rivalry with both his cousin, Hussein Kamil, General of the Army and Director of the Military Industry Organization, and with his uncle, Minister of Interior Watban Ibrahim Hasan, he wrote in a front-page editorial:

> Our role and ultimate conviction is that an end must be put to Israel and its men, one by one . . . Throwing the Israelis into the sea as demanded by the late Egyptian leader, Gamal 'Abd al-Nasir, was not good enough, as those Jews who could swim might survive.

To buttress his anti-Jewish rhetoric, 'Udayy quoted one of the Prophet's sayings: "There will come a day, the stone shall speak and say: 'there is a Jew behind me, come and kill him!'" As 'Udayy saw it, destroying the Jews, then, was simply "an application of a prophetic saying."[42] Still, 'Udayy was careful not to mention a timetable.

From the start, Baghdad objected to the post-Gulf War Madrid process. Thus, for example, a senior journalist, Hasan al-Kashif, wrote expressing his thoughts against the January 1992 Moscow peace conference, arguing that it was meant to encourage economic and other cooperation between Arab States and "the Zionist Entity."[43] The most common nickname for those Arab countries that were negotiating peace with Israel (Egypt, Syria and Jordan in the first place) was *'Arab al-Taswiya* ("The Arabs of the Settlement").[44]

Occasionally it is possible to come across hidden admiration for Israel and the Zionists: for example, Salih 'Abbas Muhammad al-Ta'I's Ph.D. dissertation on the role of propaganda in Israel's foreign policy is full of admiration for the potency of this propaganda machine and suggests establishing an Arab body that would operate in a similar fashion.[45] Still, this was counterbalanced by occasional fairly vicious anti-Jewish expressions. So, in the first of a series of such articles in the daily of the ministry of defense, a journalist who only used the initials "T.S.," explained that Jews are using human blood in their religious rites.[46] Another, Munir 'Abd al-Karim, when responding to a resolution by the US Congress recommending the relocation of the American embassy to Jerusalem, called upon all Arabs to "resist turning Jerusalem into the capital city of the murderers of Jesus."[47]

Phase Five (1994–2000): Pragmatic Practice, Dual Track Rhetoric

Since 1994 this uniform picture of hatred and fear acquired a surreal nature when, alongside it, information of renewed Israeli–Iraqi contacts began to leak. In the summer of 1994, there were persistent rumors that at least two of Yitzhak Rabin's cabinet ministers, Baghdad-born Moshe Shachal and Basrah-born Binyamin (Fuad) Ben Eliezer, were conducting negotiations with Saddam Hussein's regime over some kind of an Israeli-Iraqi rapprochement. Likewise there were rumors that Israeli official responsible for South Lebanese affairs, Uri Lubrani, had met with some Iraqi businessmen and intelligence officers, apparently for a similar purpose.[48] According to Jordanian TV, which based itself on other Israeli sources, Iraq, in its negotiations, agreed to consider entering the peace process. Anonymous Iraqi officials told the Jordanian media:

> "Iraq is interested in getting sanctions lifted or at least relaxed." Israel and the US, they disclosed, expect Iraq, in exchange for lifting the embargo, to absorb some 300,000 Palestinian refugees, mainly from refugee camps in Lebanon.[49]

Officially speaking, however, Iraq denied the whole story, arguing that there were absolutely no contacts with Israel.[50] The US official response was not long in coming. As reported by a well-informed Lebanese journalist from Washington, according to anonymous American officials the Clinton administration rebuked Prime Minister Rabin who, for his own part, promised to stop these Israeli-Iraqi contacts.[51]

Indeed, I myself, in an interview which I conducted with the then White House chief Middle East officer in late July 1994, was asked to deliver personally to Prime Minister Rabin the United States sense of being offended and outraged at these Israeli-Iraqi contacts. As the senior official saw it then, the United States was making every effort to keep the embargo on Iraq in place in the face of growing international pressures to lift it. Israeli-Iraqi negotiations greatly weakened the American position because they enabled Saddam Hussein to present the United States as being abandoned even by its closest ally in the Middle East. There was no doubt that some Israeli-Iraqi contacts were indeed underway. In my conversations back in Israel, these contacts were not denied, but it seems that the American warning did have a limited effect, since in late 1994 they were put on hold. Still, since mid-1995 there were renewed rumors that Cabinet Minister Ben Eliezer resumed indirect talks with Iraqi officials. The murder of Prime Minister Yitzhak Rabin and the later electoral defeat of Prime Minister Shimon Peres, his Labor successor, effectively put an end to these contacts. The important conclusion, however, is that, as long as the Israelis were willing, the Iraqi side too was ready for covert indirect discussions. Having secured for itself sufficient deniability the Iraqi regime even made certain that these discussions would be publicized.

Occasionally since 1994, one could even come across very pragmatic, and moderate rhetoric. For example, in an interview in Rome in June 1994, Tariq 'Aziz declared:

> Iraq has no bilateral dispute with Israel. Our sole concern is the protections of the rights of Arab peoples who are in contact with Israel, [their] violated

rights . . . as long as the embargo remained, we will be excluded from the region and rendered unable to make any contribution [to the peace process].[52]

It is important to point out, though, that until 1999 such moderation was demonstrated almost exclusively in interviews with the non-Arab, and, certainly, non-Iraqi media. In the latter, much more common were expressions of total rejection of any peace process with Israel, let alone normalization. Thus, for example, Salah al-Mukhtar, Editor-in-Chief of *Babil*, responded to the Cairo agreement of May 1994 with a ferocious attack on Arafat:

Upon signing the documents of the Cairo agreement, Yasir Arafat said . . . "our two peoples (Palestinians and Israelis) share a joint fate" . . . previously his message was that the fate of the Palestinians was intertwined with that of the Arabs! He is now championing a strategic alliance with Zionism, which necessarily must be anti-Arab . . . Arafat has obviously abandoned the Palestinian people's goals . . . are we talking about a grand old scenario that called for certain people [the Jews] to make it to the top and to facilitate for others [the Palestinians] to be swept out of their way?[53]

Still, in 1999, new voices were heard. In December 1999 an Iraqi diplomat confirmed a report in Israel's *Ma'ariv* according to which Iraq was asked to join the peace process in exchange for the embargo being lifted. The diplomat provided an Iraqi response by quoting Foreign Minister Muhammad Said al-Sahhaf and Deputy Prime Minister 'Aziz. According to the two most senior officials engaged in the formulation of Iraq's foreign policy immediately under Saddam (as Iraq had no border with Israel),

there is no need for it . . . to get involved in the peace process . . . besides, it will not obstruct any agreements signed by Arab states with Israel. Iraq is eager to maintain at their best its relations with Arab countries that had already signed such peace agreements [Egypt and Jordan] and those who intend to sign such agreements [Syria, the Palestinians].[54]

Indeed, a few days later Tariq 'Aziz elaborated on this theme, and in the process formulated clearly and explicitly the Iraqi dual track approach to Israel and those Arabs who now wish to make peace with it. In an interview with LBC Satellite TV, which most Arabs but no Iraqis can view, he cautioned, "there can be no change in our (negative) position on Israel." Yet, he continued:

When Arab countries reach agreements with Israel, that is their business. When Jordan signed a treaty with Israel we did not interfere . . . we have . . . a [negative] political and ideological analysis [of peace with Israel] that does not have immediate impact on a country's behavior. Iraq as a state is not a party to the Arab–Israeli conflict . . . it has no dispute with Israel over territory, water resources or other issues as the case with Lebanon, Syria, Jordan or Egypt. Hence we will not enter into this game. This is an old Iraqi strategy: in 1948 the Iraqi army took part in the war against the Zionist gangs . . . [Afterward] the neighboring countries went to Rhodes and signed an agreement. Iraq did not take part. It withdrew its forces from Jordan and Palestine . . . there is a difference . . . between [anti-Israeli] ideological–political analysis and sentiments on the one hand, and the responsibilities of a state on the other. The Iraqi state does not have anything over which to negotiate with Israel.[55]

'Aziz explained in detail what Iraq's long-term strategy and ideological conviction were in a conference on "The Future of Zionism" in Baghdad in September 1999. He complained that certain Arab states are mistaking a fleeting moment for a permanent sea change in world politics. The disintegration of the USSR and the rise of the United States to world supremacy created a new reality that pushed these Arabs into making peace with Israel – and this is understandable. However, this does not change the fact that the "Zionist Entity" is "a racist, aggressive and expansionist movement." It is the enemy of "the Arab cultural plan, which means full independence, Arab unity at a minimum, Arab solidarity . . . economic, social, technological and scientific progress." "The trouble is that now those Arabs who had believed in these principles are trying to "brainwash" the rest of the Arabs into believing that this is no longer the case and that long-term peace with Israel is possible. They also promise that peace will improve the lot of the Arabs, and argue that the advocates of pan Arabism, like the Iraqi regime, are holding the Arabs back. Thus they are mixing tactical political concessions, which may be a necessary evil, with long-term strategy that should not be changed:

> The Zionist movement and its entity in occupied Palestine . . . cannot come to terms with the Arab cultural project. It is seeking hegemony, expansionism, . . . [It is] aggressive and inhuman, . . . [using] murder, lies, forging historical facts, occupying the land of others, launching wars . . . How can two projects that contradict each other in term of nature and outcome meet?[56]

Even more explicit was Saddam statement in his 1999 Revolution Day speech, the most important speech each year:

> Brothers, Palestine is an Arab land and the home of the Palestinians. It is a part of the greater Arab homeland . . . It houses the first *qiblah* and the third holiest site. . . . Palestine is Arab and Zionism [as a political entity] must leave it. If any [individual] Jew wants to coexist with its people [the Palestinians, but fails to accept] his rights and duties . . . then each [Jew] should return to his [previous] country.[57]

Saddam does not explain what the "rights and duties" of those Jews who are willing to stay in Palestine are, but at least there may be no doubt that, as he describes it, the "Zionist entity" must disappear altogether from the map of the Middle East.

Conclusion

Since 1994, and more clearly since 1999, Iraqi spokesmen returned to their 1983–9 duality. Its essence is a pragmatic political approach to the peace process and those Arabs who engaged in it, combined with continued adherence to radical long-term goals. As in the 1980s, Iraq now too needed Western and Arab support – this time no longer against Iran, but rather against the UN-imposed embargo. Vitriolic attacks in the dominant style of the years 1968–80 against Egypt, Jordan, and Syria for their relations or negotiations with Israel would have denied Iraq this crucial support, meager as it is. The difference is that in 1999, 'Aziz, the regime's foremost foreign policy spokesman, provided a detailed map of the Iraqi red lines: Iraq itself will never engage in peace negotiations with Israel.

Agreements between other Arab countries and Israel are acceptable, but only if they are publicly recognized as a necessary evil, namely, only as long as those countries are fully aware that such agreements are purely tactical maneuvers to be followed by renewed struggle. In his last Revolution Day speech of the millennium, President Saddam Hussein sealed 31 years of party rule by confirming that as a political entity, Israel is unacceptable to the Iraqi Ba'ath.

What are the chances of an eventual Iraqi–Israeli rapprochement? At least judging by past experience, all the covert mutual overtures lead to nothing, and not by coincidence. In the 1980s, and again in the mid and late 1990s, the Iraqi leadership had a deep interest in creating the impression that secret talks were taking place, but as equally deep interest in denying it for fear of losing support at home – mainly in the party and armed forces. Sixty or seventy years of extreme anti-Zionist, anti-Israeli and, occasionally, anti-Jewish rhetoric have created their own momentum that has been difficult to reverse. Furthermore: to date, for Baghdad extreme anti-Israeli rhetoric has its own benefits. By presenting Israel and "world Zionism" as the main forces behind the embargo and the Anglo-American alliance, it has been hoped to persuade the Iraqi public and the Arabs that the international isolation and economic disaster are unavoidable – the results of unending Zionist machinations. As such, they are not the fault of the president and his advisors.

At the same time, however, Iraq has to consider the option of abandoning all that, showing true moderation toward Israel, and somehow even joining the peace process in exchange for the lifting of the embargo. Iraq could "test the water" by conducting a deniable covert dialogue with Israel and the United States. While covert, it admittedly still involves a dual risk of exposure and rejection – but then, there are no free meals in politics. As far as this author can tell, Iraq has never attempted such an option.

What are the considerations of the Israeli side of the equation? Since the 1984–6 oil pipeline negotiations and the 1986 discussions between Ambassador Nizar Hamdun and the Israeli army generals in Boston, all contacts, direct and indirect, have ended with no results. This happened when the Arab world was already having a fruitful dialogue with Israel. No doubt, the 1981 Israeli bombing of the nuclear reactor and the weapons shipments to Iran between 1981 and 1986 did little to dispel Iraqi fears and suspicions, but Saddam Hussein could only blame himself; both his personal and his regime's promises since 1968 to exterminate Israel left him with no friends in Jerusalem. All the same, however, Israel did nothing to stop the gushing torrent of weapons streaming into Iraq through Jordan's port of Aqaba, though stopping it would have been relatively easy.

The Israeli position began to change in 1983 following Tariq 'Aziz's interview in *Le Monde*. In 1986, the US–Israeli weapons' deals with Iran were exposed and the Iranian option became a laughing stock in the Israeli media and an embarrassment in Washington, D.C.. This was the moment when now-Foreign Minister Peres turned his undivided attention to Iraq, but with no results. On the part of the Iraqi regime, a combination of persistent fears of Israeli support for Iran and raids, an unfinished account over the destruction of the reactor, and the need to have a reliable hate object prevented a meaningful change. Following the invasion of Kuwait, having failed to deter the Allied forces by his threat to bomb Israel, attacking it became necessary. An Israeli response had the potential of unhinging the international coalition – and this was Saddam's hope. For Israel, this was the fourth sign of Saddam's recklessness, following the threat to burn it, the invasion of Kuwait and the decision to stay and fight.

The complete failure of all previous attempts to reach a rapprochement left Israel with a sense that the Iraqi regime is not truly interested in it but, rather, in deniable contacts, in weakening the American resolve to keep the embargo in place. Revelations of Iraq's astounding achievements in its military nuclear and biological programs, combined with conviction that it is still bent on the development of such weapons, increase Israeli concern. This could be an incentive for a dialogue, but what poses a formidable obstacle on the way of a fruitful dialogue is an Israeli assessment that Saddam's finger on the non-conventional trigger is too light for comfort (recalling his 1990–1 non-conventional threats, as well as the use of chemical weapons in the Iraq–Iran War and against the Kurds in 1988).

It is far from clear that he has learned his lesson and that his strategic decision-making has become more responsible. Under such circumstances, allowing him to develop these weapons again with the huge funds he will have at his disposal once the embargo is over is a very risky policy, even if Saddam joins the peace process – which he is not very likely to do.

American objection is yet another obstacle. Finally, Saddam's mass murder of Kurds in the Anfal Operation of 1988, of Shi'is in 1991, and of many others throughout his rule became a moral obstacle but, admittedly, in international relations, morality still plays a marginal role.

Notes

1 See, for example, Reeva Simon, "The Teaching of History in Iraq Before the Rashid Ali Coup of 1941," *Middle Eastern Studies* (January 1986), pp. 39–51. Phebe Marr, "The Development of a Nationalist Ideology in Iraq, 1920–1941," *The Muslim World*, Vol. LXXV (1985): pp. 85–101.

2 See Peter Sluglett, *Britain in Iraq 1914–1932* (Oxford and London: St. Antony's College and Ithaca Press, 1976), pp. 159–60, 243.

3 See Michael Eppel, *The Palestine Conflict in the History of Modern Ira: The Dynamics of Involvement, 1928–1948* (Ilford, Essex: Frank Cass, 1994), especially pp. 177–94.

4 Majid Khaduri, *Socialist Iraq* (Washington, D.C.: the Middle East Institute, 1978), p. 19.

5 Amir Iskandar, *Saddam Hussein, Munadilan wa Mufakkiran wa Insanan* (Paris: Hachette, 1980), p. 108.

6 According to *Reuter*, 18,000, June 26, 1970; *al-Ahram*, March 26, 1969; according to President Bakr the number of Iraqi troops on the Palestine front was more than 50,000, *al-Jumhuriyya*, July 18, 1971.

7 President Ahmad Hasan al-Bakr, *Masirat al-Thawra Fi Khutab wa Tasrihat al-Rais* (Baghdad, 1971), pp. 231–2.

8 For more details see A. Baram, "Qawmiyya and Wataniyya in Ba'athi Iraq: the search for a new Balance," *Middle Eastern Studies*, Vol. 19, No. 2 (April 1983), pp. 188–200; A. Baram, "Saddam Hussein: a political profile," *The Jerusalem Quarterly*, No. 17 (fall, 1980), pp. 131–4.

9 See for example, Ahmad Hasan al-Bakr, *Masirat al-Thawra*, pp. 49–51, 57–9, 90–4, 242; Defense Minister Hardan al-Tikriti, *al-Jumhuriyya*, December 26, 1969.

10 For "The Permanent Revolution" see for example, the Pan-Arab Leadership's communiqué against 'Abd al-Nasir's acceptance of the Roger's Plan, *al-Jumhuriyya*, July 28, 1970. For the Arab Revolution and its meaning see, for example, Michel 'Aflaq, *Nuqtat al-Bidaya* (Beirut, 1973), pp. 86–9; *al-Thawra al-'Arabiyya*, the internal magazine limited to party members only, No. 7–12, 2nd year, Baghdad, 1969, p. 236, a communiqué for May 15; 'Abd Allah 'Abd al-Da'im (Deputy Secretary General of the Pan-Arab Leadership), *Mawaqif* (Beirut), No. 8, 2nd year, March–April 1970, pp. 32–3; The National Bureau of Culture, *Political Report, The Tenth National Congress* (Baghdad, March 1970), p. 73, 82; Ahmad Hasan al-Bakr, *Masirat al-Thawra Fi Khutab wa Tasrihat al-Rais* (Baghdad, 1971), pp. 57–8, the President's speech for Fath day.

11 For example, RCC Member and Minister of Interior, General Salih Mahdi 'Ammash, *al-Jumhuriyya*, January 3, 1970; see also President Bakr on July 19, 1970, *Masirat al-Thawra*, pp. 238–9; also pages 254–5; and the Iraqi commander in Jordan, *al-Jumhuriyya*, September 2, 1970.

12 Hizb al-Ba'ath al-'Arabi al-Ishtiraki, *Thawrat 17 Tammuz al-Tajriba wal Afaq* (The Resolutions of the 8th Regional Party Conference), (Baghdad, January 1974), pp. 171.
13 Saddam Hussein as quoted in the Communist magazine, *Tariq al-Sha'b*, May 1, 1978.
14 A. Baram, "Qawmiyya and Wataniyya in Ba'athi Iraq . . . ," p. 194.
15 *al-Mus.awwar*, January 28, 1977; see also *al-Siyasa* (Kuwait), January 17, 1981.
16 See *Syrian Arab News Agency*, August 4, 1975, the Damascus-based Pan Arab Leadership's communiqué at the end of the 12th Congress of July 1975.
17 For example, Saddam Hussein, *al-Thawra* , *al-Jumhuriyya* , October 29, 1974; interview to Kuwait's *al-Siyasa*, January17, 1981.
18 RCC Communiqué following the Camp David Accords, *al-Thawra* October 2, 1978.
19 *Wa'i al-'Ummal* (special supplement), February 17, 1979.
20 See Shlomo Nakdimon, *Tammuz Be Lehavot* (Tammuz in Flames), 2nd edn. (Tel Aviv: Ha Makor Press, 1993), p. 207.
21 *Baghdad Republic of Iraq Radio Network*, July 13, 1999, in *FBIS-NES-DR JN1307221599*, July 13, 1999.
22 *al-Thawra*, September 6, 1999, a speech to army officers.
23 *Baghdad Voice of the Masses in Arabic*, September 28, 1980, in *FBIS-NES-DR* September 29, 1980, p. e7.
24 Nakdimon quoting Begin, *Tammuz Be Lehavot*, p. 272.
25 Saddam Hussein's interview with the Palestinian intellectual Nasir al-Din al-Nashashibi, *al-Anba*, April 28, 1983.
26 *Le Monde*, January 6, 1983.
27 See, for example, good reports in *The Washington Post*, February 25, 1988; *The New York Times*, February 25, 1988; *Ma'ariv*, April 7, 1988.
28 See *Middle East Economic Survey*, July 30, 1984; *Jerusalem Post*, August 15, 1984.
29 *al-Jumhuriyya*, January 3, 1983.
30 For the discussion between the presidents *Iraqi News Agency*, May 19, 1083; for Haddad, *al-Anba'* (Kuwait), May 21, 1983; for the Leadership's communiqué *al-'Iraq*, May 23, 1983.
31 See, for example, " The Last Days of 'Israel'," in *al-'Iraq*, November 18, 1985.
32 See many examples in A. Baram, *Culture, History and Ideology*, pp. 109–11.
33 Michael Eisenstadt, *The Sword of the Arabs: Iraq's Strategic Weapons*, the Washington Institute For Near East Policy, Washington, D.C., Policy Paper 21, 1990, pp. 41–3.
34 For details on this period see Amatzia Baram, "The Iraqi Invasion of Kuwait: Decision Making in Baghdad," in A. Baram and B. Rubin, *Iraq's Road to War*, 2nd edn. (New York: St. Martin's Press, 1996), pp. 5–36.
35 *Babil*, March 15, 1992.
36 *Babil*, March 18, 1992. See also, *Afaq 'Arabiyya*, November 11, 1985.
37 *Babil*, March 19, 1992.
38 *al-Thawra*, January 20, 1992.
39 *Babil*, January 29, 1992.
40 *'al-Iraq*, February 20, 1992.

41 *Baghdad Iraq TV Network in Arabic*, January 6,1996, in *FBIS-NES-DR*, January 11, 1996, p. 29.
42 *Reuter*, from Baghdad, June 3, 1995.
43 *al-Thawra*, January 28, 1992.
44 See, for example, Hasan al-Kashif, *al-Thawra*, January 23, 1992.
45 *Babil*, February 2, 1992.
46 *al-Qadisiyya*, February 15, 1992.
47 *al-'Iraq*, October 28, 1995.
48 *Israel Radio Channel 2 in Hebrew*, Jerusalem, 1700 GMT, August 7, 1994; *Mid-East Mirror*, August 5, 1994.
49 *Jordan Times*, August 10, 1994.
50 Two senior Iraqi diplomats, *Al-Hayat*, August 17, 1994; *al-'Arabi*, (Cairo), August 15, 1994; Tariq 'Aziz: "There have not been any secret or official contacts (with Israel) nor are there any now," *L'Independente*, June 29, 1994, p. 10 (in Italian).
51 Hisham Milhem in *Radio Monte Carlo*, August 12, 1994, in *FBIS-NES-DR JN 1208173694*, August 12, 1994.
52 *L'Independente*, (Rome), June 29, 1994, p. 10.
53 *Babil*, May 8, 1994.
54 *al-Sharq al-Awsat* (London), December 17, 1999, p. 5.
55 *LBC Sat TV in Arabic* (Beirut), January 2, 2000, in *FBIS-NES-DR* January 4, 2000.
56 *Baghdad Republic of Iraq Radio Network*, September 12, 1999, in *FBIS-NES-DR*, September 12, 1999.
57 *Iraq TV Network*, July 17, 1999, in *FBIS-NES-DR*, July 17, 1999.

Part IV

Jerusalem and the Peace Process

Creative Approaches for the Coexistence of National and Religious Identities in Jerusalem

ENRICO MOLINARO

In antiquity and in the Mediterranean until the Millet system of the Ottoman Empire, the model of the collective identity was based on ethnic–cultural features, without sharp distinctions – within the community – between the "secular" and the "religious" groups. Secular and religious models of identity were introduced to the Middle East by western European conquerors, particularly Napoleon and the British, respectively.

Jerusalem and its holy places are the symbolic frontier of the Middle East conflict involving the very definitions of the collective identities of the groups raising claims in that conflict: Jews–Arabs on one hand and Christians–Muslims–Jews on the other. This distinction follows an apparent dichotomy between prevailing territorial/national-oriented or universal/religious-oriented models of collective identity. The overlapping of these two models adds complexity to resolving this conflict that requires innovative solutions.[1] This chapter suggests policy options that can be directly applied to the current permanent status negotiations, and alternative terms to use in place of controversial words (such as "sovereignty') that, in the negotiations on the Holy Places of Jerusalem, have the potential to be a source of political manipulation.

The Different Meanings of "Status Quo" in Jerusalem

Negotiators may try to take into account as much as possible temporary "status quo" arrangements in order to avoid the obstruction of peace compromises by national or religious controversies.

The Latin expression "status quo" is frequently used in diplomatic and political language as well as in legal literature. It literally means the situation as it is, and it denotes the preservation of the existing state of affairs.

The entire original phrasing of this short Latin expression was *in statu quo ante*, in the state (things were) before. The expression, initially common only in British diplomatic language, came into general usage after Victor Hugo employed it in the introduction of his *Les Orientales* (1829): *Le statu quo européen, déjà vermoulu et lézardé, croque du côte de Costantinople.*[2]

The original expression was *statu quo*, in the Latin ablative form. It is now, however, commonly referred to as *status quo*, adopting the nominative form. In particular, in state practice, as well as in the theory of international law, the expression started to be used mainly in connection with the legal effects of war.[3]

After the termination of a state of war, two different options were generally taken into consideration. One option was that the situation preceding the war (*status quo ante bellum*) would be restored. In the second case the situation of the belligerents at the end of the hostilities became the legal basis of a new *status quo post bellum* (or *status quo nunc*).[4] A similar distinction has been applied also to the Holy Places of Jerusalem.[5]

The Final Act of the Helsinki Conference on Security and Cooperation in Europe may be considered as another example of recognition of an existing situation. According to this document, "frontiers can be changed, in accordance with international law, by peaceful means and by agreement."[6]

One can conclude that in any instance of a frozen situation by a status quo agreement peaceful changes are possible provided the consent of the other interested parties is given. The Status Quo regime in the Holy Places of Jerusalem, as well, requires the consent of all interested parties in case of change in its implementation.[7]

Any stable relationship may be labeled as status quo. In international law, however, the *status quo de facto*, "in order to justify the word *status*, must be more than an occasional conglomerate of changing facts"[8] showing a minimally stable structure.

When the expression refers to a certain legal situation – the *status quo de jure* – on the other hand, "even if the facts do not correspond to the law, is always linked to a factual situation."[9] In the case of the Holy Places in Jerusalem the Status Quo *de facto* has been distinguished from the Status Quo *de jure* mainly because of its temporary, as opposed to permanent, nature.[10]

More generally, the expression status quo may refer to different aspects of the Jerusalem question: the "cultural/religious status quo" in the city or the "Status Quo" of the Holy Places in the narrow sense. I intend to stress the importance and the peculiarity of the latter meaning of the term by writing it with capital letters in order to distinguish it from the other uses of status quo as applied to the Jerusalem question. This is also the solution adopted during a long period of time in several documents, including the

Cust's Memorandum and the Basic Agreement between the Holy See and the Palestine Liberation Organization (PLO), mentioned below.[11]

Similarly, the expression "Holy Places" in this chapter has been capitalized when used in this context, assuming a rather narrow meaning related exclusively to those places regulated by the Status Quo.[12]

An additional meaning refers to the political situation on the ground as "frozen" since 1967, due to the outcome of the Arab–Israeli conflict, pending a final solution to be negotiated by the relevant parties. This situation is commonly defined, also by journalists and diplomats, as the "political status quo."

The Relationship between the National Communities ("the Political Status Quo")

Paragraph 4 of Article V of the Oslo peace process Declaration of Principles (hereinafter DoP) states, "The two parties agree that the outcome of the permanent status negotiations should not be prejudiced or pre-empted by agreements reached for the interim period."[13] The "agreements" stipulated by the parties during the "interim period," therefore, should not be interpreted as aimed at modifying the political–territorial situation on the ground. The apparent goal of the provision, in other words, is to avoid a situation in which the outcome of the permanent status negotiations would be "prejudiced or pre-empted" before they actually take place.

One may wonder whether this provision implies also an international obligation on the parties to refrain from any act involving a change of the situation on the ground ("the political status quo"). Certainly, as in any other agreement of this kind, the parties must behave according to the principle of good faith.

In the opinion of Professor Yehuda Blum, former Israeli Ambassador to the United Nations, a pattern of "constant Palestinian attempts to change the existing *status quo*, by creating *faits accomplis* on the ground to enhance the PLO's bargaining posture in the projected permanent status negotiations concerning the future of Jerusalem," has marked the period since the signing of the Declaration of Principles.[14]

One example mentioned by Professor Blum is the "New Orient House," located "in the eastern part of the city, which had served as the office locale of the Palestinian contingent in the Jordanian–Palestinian delegation to the Madrid conference and to the subsequent Washington talks prior to the signing of the DoP."[15] The building, according to Professor Blum, has been transformed into a *de facto* PLO Mission in Jerusalem. The PLO flag has been flying over the building, and official visitors to Israel have been hosted there as if they were entering exterritorial "Palestinian" soil.

More recently, on August 10, 2001, in the aftermath of a terrorist attack in Jerusalem in which a suicide bomber killed 15 people, the Israeli police moved into the Orient House. An Israeli flag has replaced the Palestinian flag hoisted atop the building; however, it was later removed.[16]

According to "an intelligence document obtained by *Ha'aretz*," used as "the legal basis for the decision to seize control of Orient House . . . the actions of the Palestinian security service in East Jerusalem have tilted the balance of power in favor of the Palestinians and eroded Israeli control in the eastern half of the city."[17]

The report adds that the Israeli police "have difficulties preventing Palestinian security services from operating in the area as they work under-cover in civilian clothes."[18] In particular, the report lists the following categories of activities carried out by the Palestinian security services in Jerusalem:

- Collecting intelligence information
- Enforcing directives from the Palestinian leadership
- Preventing activities harmful to Palestinian interests
- Guarding Palestinian VIPs and offices
- Presenting a presence of intelligence officials at central sites and carrying out patrols
- Policing the Palestinian population with regard to criminal matters.[19]

According to Israeli Foreign Minister Shimon Peres, "after the six-month seizure injunction against the Orient House expires, Israeli control of the building will be reconsidered."[20] Among other declarations of protests against the Israeli move, Nabil Sha'ath, Palestinian Minister for International Cooperation, was quoted as saying that the Palestinian Authority wants the United Nations to restore the "Jerusalem status quo"[21] to the situation before the Orient House's seizure.

Another example given by Professor Blum of PLO attempts to change the status quo in Jerusalem relates to the appointment of the Grand Mufti of Jerusalem, an issue that apparently could be related more directly to the religious dimension of the controversy on the city.

In the wake of the death of Suleiman Ja'abari, the incumbent Mufti appointed by Jordan one year earlier, on October 15, 1994 the Government of Jordan appointed his successor (as it had since 1948, including the period since 1967), Sheikh Abdul Kader Abdeen, chief justice of the Islamic courts. According to Dr. Sami Musallam, Jordan had appointed Ja'abari "without due consultation with the PLO."[22]

The following day, Hassan Tahboub, a member of the Palestinian Authority in charge of *Waqf* (Moslem Religious Trusts) Affairs, im-mediately made, on behalf of Chairman Arafat, a counter-appointment, calling the Imam of al-Aqsa Mosque, Sheikh 'Ikrima Sabri, to the post.[23]

Dr. Musallam, adds that Sheikh Sabri, "a man known for his strong personality, . . . was the Imam who led the prayers at al-Aqsa when President Sadat of Egypt visited Jerusalem and prayed at the Mosque in 1979."[24]

According to Blum, agents of the Jericho-based Palestinian preventive security service, headed by Jibril Rajoub, had been posted on the Temple Mount/Haram al-Sharif Compound in order "to isolate the Jordanian-appointed mufti and to prevent him from functioning."[25] Moreover, in the wake of his appointment "as Mufti, Sheikh Sabri accompanied the Turkish Prime Minister on her tour and prayer in al-Aqsa Mosque as well as attended meetings with her at the Orient House."[26]

In this context, on December 26, 1994, the Israeli Knesset adopted the "Gaza/Jericho Agreement Implementation (Limiting of Activities) Law" by a vote of 56 to 6, with 32 abstentions.[27]

The law establishes two different limitations for the Palestinian Authority and the PLO, respectively. Only the former needs a written permit from the Government of Israel if it wants to open or operate any representation (including any institution, office, or agency) in Israel, or to hold any meeting (including marches, convocations, and conferences) on its behalf or under its auspices.

The Government, however, may order that any of the PLO representations be closed or that a meeting convened by it be cancelled. These provisions were introduced together with parallel legislation intended to incorporate the May 1994 Cairo Agreement between Israel and the PLO on the Gaza Strip and the Jericho Area into Israel's legal system.[28]

The 1994 law thus bars any activity in Israel of the PLO or the Palestinian Authority, "of a political or governmental nature or other similar activity within the area of the State of Israel which does not accord with respect for the sovereignty of the State of Israel without the agreement of the State of Israel."[29]

On the other hand, several decisions taken by the Government of Israel have been considered attempts to change the political status quo in the city. A recent example is seen in the reaction of several United Nations members in the Security Council debate on the recommendations concerning Jerusalem adopted during the Israeli Cabinet meeting on June 21, 1998, chaired by the then Prime Minister Benyamin Netanyahu.

The Israeli Cabinet decided to adopt a plan for the expansion of Jerusalem's jurisdiction westwards and the creation of an umbrella Jerusalem municipality, officially with the intention to streamline services in the Jerusalem region.

On June 30, 1998, however, the Russian Federation representative defined such decisions in the 3900th Security Council meeting as "unilateral actions aimed at changing the demographic composition and borders of Jerusalem in violations of the status quo."[30] Similarly, the representatives of China and France claimed during the same meeting that the Israeli decisions "change" or "would clearly alter the existing status quo" in Jerusalem.[31]

The Relationship between the Territorial/National Authority and the Different Communities Present in the City ("the Cultural/Religious Status Quo")

As stated above, the expression status quo, when related to the international dimension of the Jerusalem question may refer also to other meanings. One of them includes all the norms applying to the relationship between the territorial authority on one side and the different communities present in the city on the other.

A detailed and comprehensive analysis of this category of norms goes far beyond the purpose and the scope of this chapter. I have listed the main principles related to this broader status quo in Jerusalem, in the document quoted below titled "Statement of policy for the protection of the cultural–religious status quo."[32]

I have further suggested the idea that international law may have incorporated this wider group of principles, either by virtue of a sort of international local custom (or objective regime) or by virtue of the legally binding effect of several unilateral declarations issued on the subject of the Holy Places by the various territorial authorities which have been ruling the city over the centuries.[33]

The status quo, in this respect, relates to all aspects and established principles embodied in the regulations enacted by the Ottoman Empire *vis-à-vis* the different communities of Jerusalem. These principles include the protection of the ways of worship, and access and pilgrimage to the main places of worship – within Jerusalem or in its immediate proximity – of significant importance for the followers of the three monotheistic religions.[34] Moreover, these traditional principles also guarantee the cultural interests of the different communities present in the city.

A close examination reveals that, *vis-à-vis* the special privileges, immunities, or exemptions granted to the various communities present in Jerusalem, the practice of the different territorial powers that administered the territory under examination was broadly coherent. Some specific aspects of this long established practice even went beyond the minimum standard of similar rights granted by the majority of the other countries in the world in the context of freedom of religion and worship.

This cultural–religious status quo in Jerusalem, internationally recognized as a world cultural heritage, refers to a spiritual and eschatological face to the Jerusalem question, which stems from the universal religious interest in the fate of the city. According to Berkovitz, "Eight principles are acceptable to all parties concerned and have never been disputed by anyone:

1. Protection of the Holy Places.
2. Respect for their dignity and sanctity.
3. Freedom of worship.
4. Freedom of access and exit.
5. Proper maintenance.
6. Exemption from taxation.
7. Observance of the "status quo" in its broad sense.
8. Precedence of the public interest in matters such as safety, health, and proper conduct, over the above principles."[35]

The last part of paragraph 2 of the Declaration by the European Council on the Middle East Peace Process held in Florence on June 21–22, 1996 (known also as "the Florence Declaration"), for example, referred to this broad meaning of the cultural–religious status quo in Jerusalem. The reference to "the need to respect the established rights of religious institutions" does not contradict, however, the Status Quo in the narrow sense:[36]

> The European Union encourages all parties likewise to re-engage themselves in the peace process, to respect and implement fully all the agreements already reached and to resume negotiations as soon as possible on the basis of the principles already accepted by all parties under the Madrid and Oslo frameworks. These cover all the issues on which the parties have agreed to negotiate, including Jerusalem, noting its importance for the parties and the international community, not least the need to respect the established rights of religious institutions.[37]

Additionally, the expression status quo is used in Israel "in the context of relations between secular and religious Jews in Israel – compromise arrangements on matters concerning the Jewish faith, such as respect for the precepts of Judaism in public places and in the army, safeguarding the rights of the religious establishment, and the application of religious law in marriage and divorce proceedings."[38]

The Relationship between the Recognized Communities in the Holy Places ("the Status Quo in the Narrow Sense")

Origins of the Status Quo in the Christian Holy Places of Jerusalem

The delicate compromise in the Holy Places of Jerusalem eventually known as the Status Quo has crystallized since Ottoman rule (1517–1917) of the city. Following the conflicting claims of the different Christian communities, the Ottoman government promulgated a set of Firmans (Imperial decrees), which attempted to impose a temporary truce to settle disputes on respective rights and interests with regard to several important Christian sacred sites. According to L. G. A. Cust in his *The Status Quo in the Holy Places* (1929), the Christian Holy Places affected by the Status Quo are the following:

> The Holy Sepulchre with all its dependencies, the Deir al Sultan, the Sanctuary of the Ascension, the Tomb of the Virgin (near Gethsemane), the Church of the Nativity.
> The Grotto of the Milk and the Shepherds' Field near Bethlehem are also in general subject of the Status quo, but in this connection there is nothing on record concerning these two sites.[39]

The front page of Cust's important confidential work (or *"vade mecu,"* as H. C. Luke, the Chief Secretary to the Mandatory Government of Palestine called it, in his Introductory note to the book), clarified that "The accounts of practice given in this Print are not to be taken as necessarily having official authority."[40] Nevertheless, the author defines his book in the Introduction as

> the first attempt to discover and codify as far as is possible what is the practice at the present time, and, irrespective of what is claimed, what are the existing rights that thus the Palestine Government is bound to preserve.[41]

Given the inability of the interested Christian communities to find a proper and equitable solution based on mutual consent, and taking into account the apparent difficulty of an ordinary judicial settlement, this kind of arrangement has since been known as the Status Quo in the Holy Places.

The Sultan Habdul Mejid substantially reaffirmed the pre-existing situation since 1757, after making reference to a careful examination that had been conducted by a committee of lawyers appointed by the Porte in an important Firman. This Firman, or Sultan's decree, enacted in 1852, constitutes a sort of official declaration of the Status Quo in the Holy Places, "to serve constantly and for ever as a permanent rule."[42] According to the aforementioned Cust:

> The present position therefore is that the arrangements existing in 1852 which corresponded to the Status Quo of 1757 as to the rights and privileges of the Christian communities officiating in the Holy Places have to be meticulously observed, and what each rite practiced at that time in the way of public worship, decorations of altars and shrines, use of lamps, candelabra, tapestry and pictures, and in the exercise of the most minute acts of ownership and usage has to remain unaltered. Moreover, the Status Quo applies also to the nature of the officiants.[43]

In other words, the Status Quo became a sort of truce imposed by the territorial government upon the different conflicting Christian communities. This truce is comprised of a legal regime dividing space and time for the use (for religious purposes) and possession of the Holy Places among the aforementioned communities.

The Status Quo's Extension to the Jewish–Muslim Holy Places from the British Mandate until the Basic Agreement between the Holy See and the PLO

The Status Quo principles originally applied exclusively to the Christian Holy Places. Since the end of the Ottoman rule in Jerusalem, the British Mandatory power started to apply by analogy this arrangement to the Jewish and Muslim shrines as well as to the relationship between the respective communities. According to the above quoted Memorandum, *The Status quo in the Holy Places,*

> The Wailing Wall and Rachel's Tomb, of which the ownership is in dispute between the Moslems and the Jews, are similarly subject to the Status quo.[44]

It is beyond the scope of this chapter to ascertain the specific contents of the Status Quo arrangements between the different communities. Nor will the extent to which the traditional principles applied to the new Status Quo established by Israel after 1967 among the Christian, Muslim, and Jewish communities in their respective Holy Places be examined here. This chapter's focus is limited to a clarification of the meaning of the Latin expression as applied to the Holy Places of Jerusalem. According to Professor Itzhak Englard, presently Judge on the Supreme Court of Israel:

> The Mandatory Power strove hard to retain the existing system of rights of the various religious communities in the Holy Places, as it was bound to do under international law.[45]

Moreover, Herbert Samuel, High Commissioner and Commander-in-Chief at the time of the Mandate in Palestine, wrote that:

> The Mandate, in its thirteenth article, gave a clear direction. By it the Mandatory assumed full responsibility, and undertook to preserve existing rights and the free exercise of worship, subject, of course, to the requirements of public order and decorum. The duty of the Administration, therefore, was to secure the observance of the status quo . . .
>
> Fortunately, during the last five years no serious difficulties have in fact arisen. The Government has been strictly impartial in maintaining whatever arrangements existed under the former régime, even to the extent of continuing in their functions the Moslem family who are the hereditary

doorkeepers of the Church of the Holy Sepulchre. Its impartiality has been recognized by the several creeds and churches and sects . . . [46]

Several international agreements contributed to give international legal relevance to this special arrangement between the different communities in the Holy Places. The most significant recent example is offered by article IX of the peace treaty between Israel and Jordan signed on October 25, 1994. The full text of the article, titled "Places of Historical and Religious Significance and Interfaith Relations," reads as follows:

1. Each Party will provide freedom of access to places of religious and historical significance.
2. In this regard, in accordance with the Washington Declaration, Israel respects the present special role of the Hashemite Kingdom of Jordan in Muslim holy shrines in Jerusalem. When negotiations on the permanent status will take place, Israel will give high priority to the Jordanian historic role in these shrines.
3. The Parties will act together to promote interfaith relations among the three monotheistic religions, with the aim of working toward religious understanding, moral commitment, freedom of religious worship, and tolerance and peace.[47]

The above quoted provisions seem to confirm, at least indirectly, the Status Quo in the Holy Places. However, the only provisions included in international documents signed by Israel mentioning explicitly the expression "Status Quo" have so far been article 4, § 1, of the Fundamental Agreement between Israel and the Holy See (13 December 1993) on one hand and Paragraph 8 (e) of the preamble as well as article 4 of the Basic Agreement between the Holy See and the Palestine Liberation Organization, signed on 15 February 2000, on the other.

These agreements, though formally concluded outside the Middle East peace negotiations' context, were signed during the same period of time of the current peace negotiations. Article 4, § 1 of the Fundamental Agreement, reads as follows:

§ 1. The State of Israel affirms its continuing commitment to maintain and respect the "Status quo" in the Christian Holy Places to which it applies and the respective rights of the Christian communities thereunder. The Holy See affirms the Catholic Church's continuing commitment to respect the aforementioned "Status quo" and the said rights.[48]

Article 4 of the Basic Agreement between the Holy See and the PLO is very similar to the parallel article of the Fundamental Agreement quoted above:

Article 4.
The regime of the "Status Quo" will be maintained and observed in those Christian Holy Places where it applies.[49]

Paragraph 8 of the Preamble of the Basic Agreement includes a similar provision (section e), but in this provision the adjective "Christian" has been dropped from the reference to the Status Quo "in those Holy Places where it applies":

> Preamble, Paragraph 8 (e).
> Calling, therefore, for a special statute for Jerusalem, internationally guaranteed, which should safeguard the following: a. Freedom of religion and conscience for all b. The equality before the law of the three monotheistic religions and their institutions and followers in the City; c. The proper identity and sacred character of the City and its universally significant, religious and cultural heritage; d. The Holy Places, the freedom of access to them and of worship in them. e. The Regime of "Status Quo" in those Holy Places where it applies.[50]

One possible explanation for this difference may be the implied confirmation of the progressive extension of the Status Quo principles also to the Jewish–Muslim Holy Places. This interpretation seems to be confirmed also by the general context of the Preamble's provisions, which refer both to the broader cultural/religious status quo[51] and to the Status Quo in the narrow sense.

Some Remarks about the Status Quo System

One should take into consideration, in order to understand the complexity of the Status Quo arrangement, that it relates to the relationship among communities responding to and bound by rules belonging to separate, original respective systems of law (for instance, the Canon Law for the Latin Catholic community). Special courts, moreover, generally have the specific task to apply these rules for each of the different recognized communities.

The object of the Status Quo arrangement relates to events and behaviors that have a proper meaning only in a transcendental, or ritual, context. Should one try to apply some sort of municipal law analogies, such terms as rights of property, possession or use might be adopted. That terminology, however, cannot aptly explain the type of relationship at stake, because of the different context where the Status Quo rules have to be construed and applied. According to Professor Englard:

> By its very nature, the dispute over the Holy Places lies outside the usual framework of settlement by means of law.[52]
> It is difficult, however, to define precisely what legal rights derive from the status quo. These "rights" do not fit easily into the traditional categories of law, such as proprietary rights. The Supreme Court of Israel has touched upon the question where Justice Landau has said "we may perhaps regard

the right of access to a Holy Place as a kind of easement (or servitudes) in the sense of the (Israeli) Land Law (of 1969)."[53] Dr. Berkovitz, who dealt with the question in his doctoral thesis on the Holy Places, has suggested that the rights should be treated as sui generis.[54]

One might draw the conclusion, from the point of view of the theory of law that a kind of *sui generis, ad hoc*, system of law has come into existence. This rather coherent, sufficiently organized, set of norms has showed its effectiveness over the years and, in its basic legal structure, over the centuries. If this is true, then the only hermeneutic legal context where the norms of the Status Quo may be correctly construed seems to be its own context, namely the Status Quo system of law.

Other systems of law, such as international law, the law of the recognized religious communities or the law of the territorial rulers generally take into account the Status Quo system of law, even though they may not mention it explicitly, as an autonomous source of law (*lex specialis*) that may prevail over general rules.

In this context, one may say that if there is any international obligation on the part of the territorial authority, this may stem from a special application of the principle of non-interference, which thus has become a corollary of the Status Quo in the Holy Places. In this sense, according to Ferrari:

> While . . . the status quo which governs the relations of the various Christian communities attending the Church of the Holy Sepulchre . . . is far from perfect, it nevertheless . . . provides proof that the sharing of the same Holy Place among a number of different religious communities is possible. Particular attention should be paid to the provisions excluding modifications of the status quo that are not agreed upon by the religious communities, and preventing any interference from external powers.[55]

More recently, on November 14, 1994, the Patriarchs and the Heads of Christian Communities in Jerusalem signed an important Memorandum on the Significance of Jerusalem for Christians, confirming the *Status quo* in the Christian Holy Places. The Memorandum, signed by the Greek Orthodox, Latin and Armenian Patriarchs, the Custodians of the Holy Land, the Coptic, Syriac, Ethiopian Archbishops, the Anglican and Lutheran Bishops and the Greek Catholic, Maronite and Catholic Syriac Patriarchal Vicars, under the headline "Legitimate Demands of Christians for Jerusalem," reads as follows:

> *11. . . . Those rights of property ownership, custody and worship which the different Churches have acquired throughout history* should continue to be retained by the same communities. These rights which are already protected in the same Status quo of the Holy Places according to historical "firmans" and other documents, should continue to be recognized and respected.[56]

The various confirmations of the Status Quo, however, are not to be interpreted as a decision on the part of the various interested communities to consider it as a perfect arrangement, to be maintained permanently, without any possibility of change or improvement in order to meet new and unpredictable needs. On the contrary, the Status Quo, by definition, allows such improvements, provided they receive the consent of all interested parties.

In this context, one may consider the difficulty in preserving a certain situation when other circumstances change. For example, in modern times, one should take into account any improvement or change imposed by new or unforeseen needs in the use of the Holy Places, such as the introduction of electrical lights, or the need to provide toilets to the pilgrims, particularly for special events.

Practical Proposals for the Permanent Status Negotiations on Jerusalem

Alternative definitions of sovereignty for the negotiations on the political status quo

Given the potentially misleading effects of the term *sovereignty*,[57] a distinction between its different meanings may help to describe the new agreements to be negotiated by the parties on the political–territorial status quo.[58] This includes the possibility of drawing special arrangements between the parties, each of whom may exercise governmental powers in areas under territorial jurisdiction of the other.

Saint Peter's Square in Rome – where the Holy See owns the area under international law, with Italy exercising various governmental powers – is an example from contemporary practice. Each of the two parties to the negotiations on Jerusalem may establish part of their capital *abroad*, namely in an area under the territorial jurisdiction of the other party.

Recognizing the distinctions between the three main meanings of *sovereignty* as *independence, authority,* or *title* suggested below may help clarify the real issues at stake in the ongoing negotiations on the political–territorial status quo of Jerusalem.

These different nuances correspond to three different aspects of the Jerusalem question. The discussion of *independence* does not exclude any of the solutions discussed in the negotiations on Jerusalem. This aspect of *sovereignty* refers to the manner in which states exercise their powers in international law and may be distinguished from *title* and *authority*.

The parties are free to separate the discussion on the actual exercise of *authority* in the city from the *title* to it. Until now, Israel and the PLO, in negotiating their rights in Jerusalem, have not needed to ascertain in advance to whom the city presently belongs.

International law does not prohibit the parties from freely distributing, limiting, or even sharing their respective governmental powers in Jerusalem according to the described criteria of *functional, territorial, and personal jurisdiction.*[59]

Statement of policy for the protection of the cultural/religious status quo

The following Statement of Policy is based on an analysis of the documents that the parties involved in the Middle East Peace negotiations and the UN issued on the religious and cultural dimension of Jerusalem.

The selected principles apply today, as a sort of broad cultural and religious status quo, to the relationship between the territorial authority, on one hand, and the communities living in Jerusalem on the other.

This author assumes that the parties that have a recognized interest in the Holy Places consider most of the cardinal points quoted below as internationally binding, whose full respect may help preserve the peaceful and dynamic coexistence between the different collective identities represented in the city. The author has discussed a draft copy of this Statement of Policy at several conferences on Jerusalem (some held behind closed doors) with Palestinian and Israeli participants on an individual basis.

Among them, the conference held in El Escorial (Madrid), Spain, on August 5–9, 1996 at the Complutense University, the International Colloquium held in Toledo, Spain, on March 17–18, 1998, organized jointly by the Arab Study Society and the Jerusalem Institute for Israel Studies and the International Conference held in Bellagio, Italy, on July 13–17, 1998, organized by the Rockefeller Foundation, with academicians and diplomats from Israel, Egypt, Morocco, Saudi Arabia, the Palestinian Authority, and the Kingdom of Jordan.

Different versions of the Statement of Policy have been published by and reprinted in various journals, among them, the Palestinian weekly, *The Jerusalem Times* (November 8, 1996), the *Bulletin of the Christian Information Center* (No. 393, November–December 1966), a newsletter reporting about the major Christian recognized communities present in Jerusalem, *La Nuova Frontiera. International Human Rights and Security Review* (Year IV, n. 12, Spring 1998) *Hiwarat* (n. 5, February 1999), monthly newsletter of *Arabroma. Website of the Rome Group for Arab Culture* [www.arabroma.com], and *Nonviolence*, an Internet site linked to the Latin Patriarchate of Jerusalam [www.lpj.org/Nonviolence]. A draft of this Statement of Policy follows.

Preamble: special objectives of the authorities administering the city

The government/s or administering authority/ies (hereinafter, "the Government") in discharging administrative obligations in Jerusalem shall pursue the following special objectives:

(a) To protect and to preserve the unique religious and cultural interests of Christians, Jews and Moslems related to the city; to this end, to ensure that order and peace, and especially religious peace, reign in Jerusalem;

(b) To foster co-operation among all the inhabitants of the city in their own interests, as well as to encourage and support the peaceful development of the relations between the Arab and Jewish peoples throughout the area under British Palestinian Mandate until May 14, 1948; to promote the security, well-being and any constructive measures of development of the residents, having regard to the special circumstances and customs of the various peoples and communities.

Principles applying to the Holy Places, religious buildings and sites

1. Existing rights in respect of the Holy Places and of religious buildings or sites shall not be denied or impaired.

2. Insofar as the Holy Places are concerned, the liberty of access and visits to the city and the Holy Places therein shall be guaranteed, in conformity with existing rights, to the residents of Jerusalem as well as to all other persons, without distinction of nationality, subject to requirements of national security, public order and decorum.

    Similarly, freedom of worship shall be guaranteed in conformity with existing rights, subject to the maintenance of public order and decorum.

3. Holy Places and religious buildings or sites shall be preserved. No act shall be permitted which may in any way impair their recognized sacred character. If at any time, it appears to the Government that any particular Holy Place, religious building or site is in need of urgent repair, the Government may call upon the community or communities concerned to carry out such repair. The Government may carry it out itself at the expense of the community or communities concerned if no action is taken within a reasonable time.

4. No taxation shall be levied in respect of any Holy Place, religious building or site that was exempt from taxation on May 14, 1948, date of the termination of the League of Nations Mandate in Palestine.

No change in the incidence of such taxation shall be made which would either discriminate between the owners or occupiers of Holy Places, religious buildings or sites, or would place such owners or occupiers in a position less favorable in relation to general incidence of taxation than existed on May 14, 1948.

Religious and cultural rights of the local communities

1. The personal status and family law of the various communities and their religious interests, including endowments, shall be respected.
2. The Government shall ensure adequate primary and secondary education for the Arab and Jewish community, respectively, in its own language and its cultural traditions.

The right of each community to maintain its own schools for the education of its own members in its own language, while conforming to such educational requirements of a general nature as the Government may impose, shall not be denied or impaired. Foreign educational establishments shall continue their activity on the basis of their existing rights.

Religious and cultural rights applying to all visitors and residents

1. Freedom of conscience and the free exercise of all forms of worship subject only to the maintenance of public order and decorum shall be ensured to all.
2. No discrimination of any kind shall be made between the inhabitants on the ground of race, religion, language or sex.
3. All persons shall be entitled to an equal protection of the law.
4. Except as may be required for the maintenance of public order and good government, no measure shall be taken to obstruct or interfere with the activities of religious or charitable bodies of all faiths or to discriminate against any representative or member of these bodies on the ground of his religion or nationality.
5. No restriction shall be imposed on the free use of any language in private intercourse, in commerce, in religion, in the Press or in publications of any kind, or at public meetings.

Practical proposals for the Status Quo in the narrow sense

As a practical proposal, it may be useful to hold a series of meetings between specialists, focused on the following two issues:

(a) A definition of the "Status Quo" regime in the Holy Places of Jerusalem in view of the Israeli–Palestinian negotiations.
(b) Suggested policy options to settle potential disputes between the

religious communities on the interpretation and the implementation of the "Status Quo" principles: 1. Ordinary judicial jurisdiction, 2. Political settlement, 3. A special body in charge of such disputes, namely a body that is recognized by the concerned parties as being able to take decisions independently from the interests of the parties, while at the same time taking them into due account.

The possibility should be considered of inviting religious experts or authorities to the suggested meetings, which could produce better results if they were informal, confidential, and based on a legal/practical-oriented approach, rather than purely political or religious.

Such meetings could be held under the auspices of a third party considered relatively neutral. The European Union or individual European countries may play a significant role, given their traditional interest in the Holy Places.

General features of the Status Quo legal regime

As mentioned above, it may be useful for a group of experts from different fields (law, history, comparative religions, etc.), specializing in the subject of the Status Quo, to meet. The purpose of such meetings would be to determine the general features of a legal regime that, though ancient and crystallized, has never been formally clarified in a complete and generally recognized framework. If one should summarize the main general principles characterizing the Status Quo system of law, one may try to list the following guidelines:

- Requirement of the consent of the representative bodies of the communities with a recognized vested interest in the Holy Places for any change in the Status Quo, the legal regime dividing space and time for the use (for religious purposes), and possession of those places. Different interpretations may arise regarding the nature of the body entitled to represent the various communities. A broad consensus, however, seems to exist on this sensitive issue.
- Territorial power's authority over public order, safety, and decorum in the Holy Places and its obligation of non-interference in the internal matters of the aforementioned communities. These communities (with a recognized vested interest in the sites) are the only bodies authorized to manage the Holy Places. Different interpretations may arise about who is entitled to represent the territorial power's authority. The above principle, however, applies regardless of the answer that the negotiations on Jerusalem may give to this question.
- Need for continuous, uninterrupted exercise of existing rights in the Holy Places for their maintenance.

- Possibility to separate the different aspects of access, possession and worship, which may belong to different representative bodies of the communities.
- Immunity from ordinary judicial jurisdiction over the settlement of disputes between the representative bodies of the communities on the Status Quo in the Holy Places in the narrow sense described above. This includes the possibility of setting up a special body competent in dealing with this category of disputes.

Policy Options for the Settlement of Disputes on the Status Quo of the Holy Places

The topic of the settlement of disputes in the Holy Places has rarely been dealt with in scholarly literature,[60] in part due to the extreme complexity of the issues. Research in this field requires in-depth knowledge and familiarity with several subjects, each with a distinct methodology, scholarly fields such as law, history, and political science. In fact, even if we limit our focus to the legal aspects of the issue at stake, an exhaustive study of the topic would require mastery of the details of municipal law (procedural, criminal, civil, and constitutional), comparative law, international law, and the laws of recognized religious communities (such as canon law for the Catholic Church).

The issue of the jurisdiction over the settlement of disputes on this sensitive subject is not limited only to the Christian Holy Places, but also includes the Muslim and Jewish Holy Places,[61] as various decisions by the Israeli Supreme Court demonstrate.

Among the several questions to be answered are: How should the current practice of judicial jurisdiction over the settlement of disputes concerning the Holy Places be interpreted? Is jurisdiction on the substance of the disputes suspended or in abeyance?

The main question refers to whether and to what extent the ordinary courts have competence to decide in these matters. A possible alternative is that either the territorial government or a neutral third body should decide disputes on substantive rights and claims in the Holy Places.

Moreover, if existing principles require the appointment of such a special body, its nature and composition have to be determined, along with who should have the power to appoint its members. Similarly, it has to be decided how this neutral body should be organized, whether it should consult with representatives of the recognized religious communities, and what should be the procedure of this consultation.

An additional question is whether this special body should be permanent or temporary, and in which kinds of disputes would it be called in.

Separate considerations may determine the answer to the procedural question of who should decide when such disputes require this third-party intervention. One of the most sensitive, from the political point of view, is the question of who should have the duty and power to implement the decisions of such a body.

The questions listed above help in the understanding of the aforementioned complexity of the issue, as well as the extreme sensitivity of the topic. For this reason it is necessary to focus on the following two issues.

First, what would be the respective roles of ordinary courts, the territorial government, and a third-party ad hoc body in the settlement of Holy Places disputes? And secondly, how a body could be appointed whose authority would be recognized by the relevant parties in any dispute, and that can decide independently while taking the interests of these parties into account?

Because of the said complex nature of the issues involved, the approach to the topic should be, by necessity, multidisciplinary. An additional example of the described complexity emerges from considering terminological issues related to the very definition of such controversial concepts described above as "Holy Site," "Status Quo," "Religious Community."

Clear answers emerging from the described analysis may have practical implications. A solution may be found which is acceptable to all of the parties involved in the issue of the Holy Places of Jerusalem.

Concluding Remarks

The expression status quo is used in many different senses but rarely defined in its specific context. One cannot but hope that the scholar as well as the diplomat, when dealing with the Jerusalem question, will try to clarify the meaning given to the expression.

Indeed, especially if the aim is to find a possible solution for the longstanding conflict over the city, one should avoid using a terminology that sometimes has proven to be misleading, too often generating confusion and useless controversies.

In this chapter three different meanings of the Latin expression have been examined. Each of them refers to the relationship between different group identities. The first, the political–territorial status quo, regulates the relationship between the national group claiming control over the city: Palestinians and Israelis.

The second, the religious–cultural broad status quo, applies to the relationship between the territorial authority exercising pro-tempore control over the city on one hand and the traditional religious–ethnic communities on the other.

The third meaning refers to the Status Quo *par exellence*, which applies to a selected number of Holy Places where long-standing controversies have developed over the time since, at least as the Christian Holy Places are concerned, the Ottoman rule on the city.

Each of the described meanings refers therefore to different aspects of the conflict over the city and its Holy Places, which acquire symbolic meanings far beyond the border of the area in question.

For each of the aforementioned aspects of the Jerusalem controversy, practical proposals have been suggested. This author hopes that the proposed approach may help not only to resume negotiations on the necessary mutual concessions, but also to win the consent of both the Israeli and Palestinian publics on the path to a permanent settlement of the conflict.

Notes

1 On the idea of Jerusalem as a frontier city see also Menachem Klein, *Jerusalem. The Contested City* (Jerusalem: The Jerusalem Institute for Israel Studies, 2001), pp. 1, 9–18, and the bibliography quoted there.

2 See "*Statu quo*," in Aldo Gabrielli, *Si dice o non si dice?* (Milano: Mondadori, 1969), p. 511.

3 See Wilhelm G. Grewe, entry "Status quo," in Rudolf Bernhardt, ed., *Encyclopedia of Public International Law* (Amsterdam: Elzevire Science, 2000), p. 687.

4 See ibid.

5 See Sélim Sayegh, *Le Statu Quo des Lieux-Saints. Nature juridique et portée internationale* (Roma: Libreria Editrice della Pontificia Università Lateranense, 1971), pp. 56–7.

6 *Declaration of Principles Guiding Relations between Participating States,* Section I, paragraph 2, quoted in Grewe, p. 689.

7 See *infra*, section 2.3.a, n. 1.

8 Grewe (see note 3), p. 689.

9 Ibid.

10 Sayegh, *Le Statu Quo*, pp. 103–10.

11 See *infra*, section 1.3.a. and 1.3.c., respectively.

12 I wish to thank Professor Shabtai Rosenne for having kindly reminded me of the limits of this graphic solution since in Arabic and Hebrew documents, for instance, neither the expression "Status Quo" nor "Holy Places" may be capitalized.

13 UN Doc. A/48/486–S/26560 (Annex), October 11, 1993; reproduced in *International Legal Material* 32 (1993), pp. 1525–44.

14 Yehuda Blum, "From Camp David to Oslo," *Israel Law Review*, 28, nos. 2–3 (Spring–Summer 1994), p. 218, n. 20.

15 Ibid.

16 See Peter Hirschberg, "Officials say Orient House conquest a signal to Arafat; Palestinians vow 'war for Jerusalem'," *Ha'aretz*, August 11, 2001.

17 Ibid.

18 Nadav Shragai, "Report: PA activities threaten Israeli control in Jerusalem," *Ha'aretz*, August 11, 2001.

19 Ibid.

20 Nina Gilbert and Etgar Lefkovits, "Peres: We'll rethink Orient House in 6 months," *Jerusalem Post,* August 15, 2001.

21 "News Flashes," *Ha'aretz,* August 15, 2001.

22 Sami F. Musallam, *The Struggle for Jerusalem: A Program of Action for Peace* (Jerusalem: PASSIA, 1996), p. 109.

23 Yehuda Blum, "From Camp David to Oslo," *Israel Law Review,* p. 28, nos. 2–3 (1994), p. 218, n. 20.

24 Musallam, *The Struggle for Jerusalem,* p. 110.

25 Blum, "From Camp David to Oslo," p. 218, n. 20.

26 Musallam, *The Struggle for Jerusalem,* p. 110.

27 See Ruth Lapidoth, "Jerusalem in the Peace Process," *Israel Law Review,* p. 28, nos. 2–3 (1994), 428; Blum, "From Camp David to Oslo," p. 218, n. 20.

28 See Lapidoth, "Jerusalem in the Peace Process," p. 428.

29 www.israel.org/mfa.

30 Security Council, 3900th Meeting (AM & PM), SC/6541, on June 30, 1998.

31 Ibid.

32 See *infra,* section 2.2.

33 Enrico Molinaro, "Religious Freedom in the Holy Places of Jerusalem," (in Italian), *I diritti dell'uomo. Cronache e battaglie* (1995), p. 59 ff.; *id.,* "Israel's Position on Jerusalem and international Norms for the Holy Places," *Jerusalem Letter* No. 342 (Jerusalem: Jerusalem Center for Public Affairs, September 16, 1996), p. 3 ff.

34 Shmuel Berkovitz, "The Legal Status of the Holy Places in Israel," Ph.D. diss., (in Hebrew), The Hebrew University of Jerusalem, 1978, p. xi.

35 Shmuel Berkovitz, "Proposals For the Political Status of the Holy Places Within the Context of a Peace Treaty," in Ora Ahimeir, ed., *Jerusalem – Aspects of Law,* Discussion Paper No. 3, 2nd revised version (Jerusalem: The Jerusalem Institute for Israel Studies, 1983), p. xi.

36 See *infra,* the following section.

37 Declaration by the European Council on the Middle East Peace Process held in Florence on June 21–22 , 1996.

38 Ruth Lapidoth,"Freedom of Religion and of Conscience in Israel," in *Freedom of Religion in Jerusalem* (Jerusalem: The Jerusalem Institute for Israel Studies, 1999), p. 36, n. 36.

39 L. G. A. Cust, *The Status Quo in the Holy Places,* with an Annex on The Status Quo in the Church of the Nativity, Bethlehem, by Abdullah Effendi Kardus, MBE, formerly District Officer, Bethlehem Sub-District (Jerusalem: Printed for the Government of Palestine by His Majesty's Stationery Office, 1929), p. 12.

40 Cust, *The Status Quo in the Holy Places,* front page.

41 Ibid., p. 1; emphasis in the original text.

42 Walter Zander, *Israel and the Holy Places of Christendom* (Worcester: The Trinity Press, 1971), p. 180 (translation of the 1852 firman in English).

43 Cust, *The Status Quo in the Holy Places,* front page.

44 Ibid., p. 12.

45 Itzhak England, "The Legal Status of the Holy Places," in O. Ahimeir (ed.), *Jerusalem – Aspects of Law* (Jerusalem: The Jerusalem Institute for Israel Studies, 1983), p. v; see also Enrico Molinaro, "Religious Freedom in the Holy

Places of Jerusalem" (in Italian), *I diritti dell'uomo. Cronache e battaglie* (1995), p. 58.

46 Herbert Samuel (High Commissioner and Commander-in-Chief), *Report of the High Commissioner on the Administration of Palestine, 1920–1925* (London: Printed and published by his Majesty's Stationery Office, 1925), pp. 48–50.

47 *Peace Treaty between the State of Israel and the Hashemite Kingdom of Jordan* (Jerusalem: Israel Information Center, 1994), p. 15.

48 For the full text of the Fundamental Agreement, see, among other sources, *International Legal Material* 33 (1994), p. 153; Eugene J. Fisher and Leon Klenicki, eds., *A Challenge Long Delayed. The Diplomatic Exchange Between, the Holy See and the* State *of Israel* (New York: Anti-Defamation League, 1996), pp. 49–53.

49 For the text of the Basic Agreement see the Internet site of the PLO'S Negotiations Affairs Department: www.nad.plo.org.

50 Ibid.

51 See *supra*, section 1.2.

52 Englard, "The Legal Status of the Holy Places," p. iv.

53 *The Orthodox Coptic Metropolitan Patriarchate v. The Government of Israel*, (1979), 33 *P.D.* (I), p. 238.

54 Englard, "The Legal Status of the Holy Places," p. v.

55 Silvio Ferrari, "The Religious Significance of Jerusalem in the Middle East Peace Process: Some Legal Implications," *The Catholic University Law Review*, vol. 45, no. 3 (1996), p. 738.

56 Emphasis in the original text. For the text of the Memorandum see the Internet site of the Holy See: http://www.greatjubilee2000.org/Documents/documents.html.

57 Ian Brownlie, *Principles of Public International Law* (Oxford: Clarendon Press; New York: Oxford University Press, 1998, 5th edn.), p. 106; Louis Henkin, *International Law: Politics, Values and Functions. General Course on Public International Law, Recueil des Cours*, p. iv (Dordrecht/Boston/London, 1989), pp. 24–5; Jean Maritain, "The Concept of Sovereignty," in W. J. Stankiewicz (ed.), *In Defence of Sovereignty* (New York/London/Toronto, 1969), pp. 61–4. On the distinction see also this author's forthcoming paper, "Alternative Definitions of Sovereignty Drawing on the European and Mediterranean Legal Heritage: an Analysis of Coexisting National and Religious Identities in Religious Indentities in Jerusalem," in a volume by *Institut des Etudes Poltiques Méditerranéennes* (Monte Carlo, 2001.

58 See *supra*, 1.1.

59 For a broader analysis see this author's "Alternative Definitions of Sovereignty."

60 Walter Zander, *Israel and the Holy Places of Christendom* (Worcester: The Trinity Press, 1971); *Idem.*, "On the Settlement of Disputes About the Christian Holy Places," *Israel Law Review* 8 (1973), pp. 331–66; *Idem.*, "Jurisdiction and Holiness: Reflections on the Coptic-Ethiopian Case." *Israel Law Review* 17 (1982), pp. 245–73; Shmuel Berkovitz, "The Legal Status of the Holy Places in Israel," Ph.D. diss. (in Hebrew), The Hebrew University of Jerusalem, 1978; *Idem.*, *The Legal Status of the Holy Places in Jerusalem* (in

Hebrew). (Jerusalem: Jerusalem Institute for Israel Studies, 1997), *Idem.*, *Conflicts on the Holy Places* (in Hebrew), (Or Yehuda: Hed Arzi Publishing House, 2000); Claude Klein, "The Temple Mount Case," *Israel Law Review* 6, (1971), pp. 257–65.

61 See *supra*, section 1.3.c.

CHAPTER 23

Jerusalem in the Peace Process

MANUEL HASSASSIAN

It has become self-evident that lasting peace in the Middle East can be attained only with the establishment of an Independent Palestine with East Jerusalem as its Capital. This is in fact the core issue, while matters such as personal security for Israelis, regional cooperation, and the proliferation of weapons of mass destruction are only symptoms and not the root cause of the conflict.

Given that the Oslo process failed to fulfill the national aspirations of the Palestinians, we must learn the lessons for the inevitable future phase of negotiations. Ultimately, there is no alternative other than to negotiate a peace agreement between the Palestinians and the Israelis. Even if a regional war breaks out, the parties will eventually succumb to the political realities and return to negotiations.

Accordingly, both sides must learn the lessons from the previous period of talks, draw conclusions from mistakes made, and focus the energy of their think tanks, strategic thinkers, and security establishments on being prepared for the appropriate time when the negotiations will be restarted. Furthermore, both sides need to keep the channels of diplomatic communication open with each other, even if at a bare minimum, so as not to start from zero once again.

It is certainly provocative to talk about peace at this time, but more provocative is the deafening silence among the Israeli Left and the Palestinian mainstream. As a whole, both sides are hardly talking to each other, and it seems they have forgotten that it is they who will jointly resurrect the peace process in the future, despite the fact that at this time they both feel betrayed by the other side.

Rather than engage in the political warfare and finger pointing of who is responsible for derailing the peace process, it is more constructive to attempt to examine the faults in the process itself. Thus it will be possible to rebuild its foundation by finding common ground where Palestinians and Israelis can join to meet as equal partners in negotiations, with true intentions of arriving at peaceful agreements to our national disputes.

It would, however, be naïve and self-deceiving of us to approach each other without first recognizing the differences and asymmetries which compose both our actual power and perceived imagery of the other. It is therefore of the utmost importance to convey to the Israeli side the Palestinian position and explain the reasons why such a position exists. Through this effort, we also hope to understand Israel's position and see where we can meet on common ground, with the full intention of making peace, and not based on coercive muscle flexing or checkmate tactics.

The Palestinian position is a culmination of current and historical facts that have affected the public sentiment and negotiation status of the Oslo peace process. Unfortunately, a great deal of public goodwill, hope, and support for the peace process has been squandered at the hands of Israel, which has consistently engaged in unilateral acts intended to prejudice the outcome of negotiations. All this has occurred despite the fact that both the Israeli and Palestinian side openly agreed in the Oslo Accords not to take any steps that might prejudice the status and position of the final stage of negotiations.

Despite such agreements, the Palestinians witnessed the continued expropriation of their land for new settlements and bypass roads, the closure of Jerusalem to "non-residents," and Palestinian Jerusalemites have faced an increasing array of hardships just by remaining in their city. Such unilateral actions have substantially eroded the confidence of Palestinians in the good will of their Israeli counterparts. Furthermore, when Palestinians realize that such acts are part of an official and systematic state policy that is both organized and well-funded, it becomes obvious to them that Palestinian concerns and the overall desire for peace is secondary on the Israeli agenda. Israel simply cannot expect to have the land, the security and peace while giving nothing but limited control over the crumbs of the Occupied Territory, crumbs that have the highest concentration of "rowdy" and "unlawful" Palestinians.

All the future possibilities and past and present tribulations of the Palestinian/Israeli and the Arab/Israeli conflict, in all its dimensions, are realized, symbolized, and crystallized in the question of Jerusalem. Jerusalem is blessed (or perhaps cursed) with a religious, political and military history caused by divergent, discordant and conflicting claims that impact on the city's future. Indeed such an outlook demonstrates to the unbiased observer the impossibility of a "neat" solution. While the multicultural, rich history and conflicting claims of Jerusalem are definitely obstacles toward arriving at a solution, they do not necessarily constitute a death knell. However any solution in Jerusalem must involve a process that gradually integrates the communities, thus creating a system whereby interactions between the sides are conducted on a basis of equality. The goal should be to have freedom for all who hold Jerusalem as sacred.

Three decades ago, Israeli forces occupied the West Bank and Gaza Strip. Part of this conquest naturally included the occupation of Arab East Jerusalem. Despite the fact that international law and UN resolutions explicitly forbid the acquisition of land by force and the alteration of the status of Jerusalem, Israel wasted no time in declaring Jerusalem its "unified" capital city and has worked methodically and systematically toward realizing this myth. The Judaization of Jerusalem – the imposing of a Jewish landscape both physically and demographically – has continued without interruption throughout the peace process, as though Jerusalem were a non-negotiable issue off limits in final status negotiations. Israel has moved swiftly without a hint of shyness to implement a series of Israeli laws and practices that prejudice the outcome of negotiations by changing the landscape to suit its interest.

Fundamental to this strategy is Israel's policy of settlement construction for "Jewish only" neighborhoods, while at the same time severely limiting the construction and land use for the Palestinians. Such policies have intentionally retarded the prospects for Palestinian sovereignty in the city by confining Palestinians to scattered, under-developed neighborhoods fenced in by two belts of ever expanding settlements. Furthermore, Israeli policies have restricted Palestinian economic development and habitation. The central business district in Arab East Jerusalem has been unable to expand since the occupation and no other industrial or commercial areas have developed. Israel also has used its power over residency laws to bar non-Jerusalem Palestinians from living and even entering the city. Today, from a population of zero in 1948, there are now no less that 180,000 Jewish settlers living in 34 percent of occupied East Jerusalem – a number that almost equals the number of Palestinian residents who live cramped into 13 percent of the eastern half of the city. This is a testament to the success of the Israeli settlement strategy, which is considered colonialism by the Palestinians.

Through the confiscation of lands in East Jerusalem, Israel has been able to take control of strategic and ideologically significant sites. It built large settlement blocks to strengthen its demographic (and also its military) control of the newly occupied territory. The Israeli strategy has unmistakably been to consolidate its control over the entire city and erase the Green Line. Yet its strategy is fundamentally flawed. The hope that with the passing of time, the question of Jerusalem will be decided by ongoing de facto demographic and physical changes is simply not plausible. Neither is it a possibility that the world will magically forget that East Jerusalem is a part of the West Bank and that Jerusalem must be a multicultural city and not for Jews and Jews only.

Moreover, it is clear that without Palestinian sovereignty in Arab East Jerusalem, without the room for habitation development or the expansion of our central business district, Jerusalem will always be a source of instability rather than progress. Israel understands that by giving back these vital areas, Palestinians will be able to live, develop, and nurture East Jerusalem Arab identity. If Israel is allowed to continue in this manner and does not allow Palestinian East Jerusalem to be a viable city and the political and economic heart of the emerging state, it will remain a marginal, backwater city that is characterized for its slums more than the beauty of its landmarks and holy sites.

Unfortunately, history has always tended to favor the acquisition of territory by military force and the same holds true with the Israeli occupation of lands beyond the border of June 4, 1967. Also, Jerusalem as a city embodies the aspirations of a diverse group of communities and faiths. This is perhaps the steepest challenge of all: the challenge to stretch itself thin enough to satisfy the quarreling powers that claim sovereignty and jurisdiction over their respective "holy soil."

It is no secret that the question of Jerusalem, with or without the fateful "Peace Process," remains one of the largest impediments to achieving peace between the Palestinians and Israelis. Finding a solution that will satisfy the needs of the two communities will indeed be a formidable challenge and requires an effective and flexible negotiating process. Part of the problem is that many involved in the negotiations and even those sponsoring the negotiations believe that the question of Jerusalem is a zero-sum conflict.

To demonstrate the previous point, let us review recent events to see how Jerusalem was dealt with in the context of the peace negotiations.

Jerusalem between Camp David II and Taba Negotiations

In Camp David II, Israel proposed that it maintain long fingers deep into the West Bank and also insisted on a large security zone along the Jordan Valley. This would functionally divide the West Bank into three separate units. Also it is important to note that through the Modiin settlement area near Latrun, the Shamron block in the north would be territorially joined with the Greater Jerusalem blocks to form one solid unit.

In Taba, Israel refined the rough edges. Israel gave up the Shilo settlement east of Ariel and gave up some of the smaller finger extensions like Kedumim and Beit El but insisted on keeping the large blocks of settlements. Furthermore, in Taba, the major settlement blocks including Givon, Adumim, and Etzion would have the capacity to expand from 250 percent to 300 percent over the next 15 years, while the Palestinian areas would be able to grow only marginally.

Also in Taba, the negotiation tools that were developed in second-track negotiations came into play. Issues like the "Holy Basin" and the "open city" as serious options for land swaps were discussed.

Evidently, Camp David II and Taba negotiations did not fully integrate the Palestinian position with regard to Jerusalem. A national Palestinian consensus on Jerusalem appears to form around the following components: Jerusalem as the capital for both Palestinian and Israeli sovereign states within the pre-1967 internationally recognized borders and to be administered by two municipal bodies, one Palestinian and the other Israeli. The two municipalities will co-operate with regard to decision-making, provision of municipal services, and infrastructure projects. In addition, there will be an equitable allocation of land use and respect for ownership rights, freedom of worship and access to Jewish, Islamic and Christian holy sites and geographic contiguity of Palestinian-held areas of Jerusalem with north and south West Bank. Finally, Jerusalem will be one city, open to all to circulate, live, and work. Obtaining Israeli acceptance for this position will be difficult but not impossible in the light of the following formulation.

According to Michael Dumper, a specialist on Jerusalem, a Palestinian negotiating agenda designed to achieve these goals needs to be framed by two overarching strategies: compatibility and reciprocity. Compatibility is straightforward and will not meet too many Israeli obligations. It refers to the importance of ensuring that whatever is agreed on Jerusalem should be both consistent and compatible with positions adopted in the other Permanent Status negotiations. Border permeability, employment and residency rights, economic and fiscal arrangement, security and policing co-operation should all be compatible with other arrangements negotiated between Israel and the rest of Palestine. It would be both pointless and unworkable, for example, to agree to *hard* or impermeable borders between most of the West Bank and Israel, but have *soft* or permeable borders for the areas between East Jerusalem and Israel. Irredentists on both sides could simply enter each other's territory via Jerusalem. This requirement for compatibility, however, need not exclude some special arrangements for Jerusalem as a result of its unique status of the site of Holy Places for three religions and the site of two national capitals. Thus questions over access to holy places, taxation on religious property and the operations of embassies will need to reflect this status.

Furthermore, according to Michael Dumper:

> The issue of reciprocity is more contentious but will be crucial in the attempt to maintain a national consensus. The ceding of land, of restitution claims, of access, of jurisdiction etc., must all be in exchange for other "goods" on the part of the Israelis, although not necessarily the same goods. Thus, each meter of the border, each house, and garden with a settlement, each municipal service and legal jurisdiction obtained by the Israeli needs to be accompanied by a *quid pro quo* for Palestinians. It also needs to be established from the outset that the Palestinian position outlined above is not simply a starting point. It needs to be met by a reciprocal concession by Israel on de jure recognition of Arab East Jerusalem as the Palestinian capital and the

return of refugees. From the detailed surveys carried out by Professor Segal and his team and from recent Israeli opinion polls, such a prospect cannot be ruled out completely.

The solution to the question of Jerusalem must and can only depend upon an incremental divesting of psychological impediments. As such the goal should be to accept the other not as enemy, but as a potential ally that contributes to the essential, magnificent, and all too often tragic character of Jerusalem. With that, let me share several points.

Any solution that is to be imposed upon the city must include a plan that focuses upon the economic and social commonwealth of the Israelis, but more so, of the Palestinians. We have already seen how concerted efforts on behalf of the Israeli government have had devastating effects on Palestinian Jerusalemites in all realms of life. Such a commonwealth would promote development and growth, hence eradicating the main problem of socioeconomic inequality between Israeli and Palestinian neighborhoods. It is precisely the socioeconomic dimension of the peace process that has recently taken on such a vital role, for it has the capacity to solve the most detrimental problems which Palestinians suffer from daily as the result of closure.

I find it important to note that a future settlement must address and promote the process of democratization. Essential in the path to this goal is the development and sustenance of a civil society, and therefore, any solution must recognize this. Self-governed bodies and institutions cannot survive and flourish if there is no absolute freedom in election, no accountability, or no transparency in the handling of public affairs. Here non-governmental organizations (NGOs) not affiliated with either side can play a pivotal role in preserving the physical and functional unity of the city. They can be used to promote trust and facilitate the creation of a forum where people from both sides can have positive mutual interaction. NGO involvement has already proven itself to be a productive avenue for members of each community to gather, interact, and share with the other side.

Furthermore, I believe any solution must try hard to promote the following two ideals: justice and inclusion. Justice is an element essential to any solution, for when left in abeyance the result is often the continuation of protracted conflict and bloodshed. Furthermore, the desire for justice does not easily disappear: when a Palestinian family loses its home due to house demolition, all residents of that house will bitterly remember their treatment of injustice by the power which authorized it. Such activities scar – perhaps permanently – the psyche of those who suffer such injustices. Unfortunately, there is a high percentage of Palestinians from Jerusalem who have such grievances. As Teddy Kolleck so accurately said, "Never have we given the Arabs a feeling of being equal before the law." It is for

this reason that the second element of inclusion must be a necessary ingredient in any solution. Palestinians have felt so left out of consideration with
the political decisions that have directly (many times gravely) affected their
lives.

In addition, the practices of the Israeli government have also had grave
consequences on all non-Jewish interests in the city. Such a policy has even
led to a law forbidding archeological research that would predate Jewish
existence in Palestine. Israeli policy has been strictly exclusionary, and has
therefore been harmful for all the communities both in Palestine, the Arab
World, Europe, Asia, the Americas and anywhere else where Jerusalem is
held sacred. Jerusalem is instrumental to so many religions and to so many
lives. Therefore, its future role must include this universality. The whims of
an Israeli or Jew simply must not be allowed to dictate the fate of Jerusalem.
Jerusalem is too precious to too many other people. In this, justice and
inclusion become the facets of the same essential idea that must be
preserved if bloodshed is to be spared. In order for this to happen, there is
a need to strip ourselves from old modes of thought that restrict us to
believe in the zero-sum, "fixed-pie" nature of Jerusalem. New thinking and
new approaches need to be put forward by participants in the Middle East
and abroad. Ultimately, the fate of Jerusalem, while a sensitive subject to
the immediate parties involved, is also an issue of wider international
concerns because it relates to the peace of the region, and the world.

Concluding Remarks

The implementation mechanism is one of the most important issues in
negotiations and perhaps has been given the least focus. The experience of
the Oslo Process has shown that the Israelis have difficulty implementing
past agreements. Again, it is not so important that each side trust the other
completely, more important is that there are safeguards in place that will
ensure that agreements are implemented in full by both sides and gives
guarantees that each side will not prejudice the outcome of an agreement.
A mechanism must therefore be established wherein a third party, possibly
a multinational force, be created to both monitor and enforce the implementation of agreements on both sides and be given the mandate to enforce
these agreements through various means. Various Palestinian and international circles have discussed such a force as a way of de-escalating the
current *Intifada*. However, an international force at this time would more
than likely have a weak and unclear mandate (unless the international
community would suddenly decide to implement UN Resolution 242 and
338) and would do more harm than good.

However, once there is an agreement between the two sides an international force is vital to giving guarantees that the agreement will be

implemented and in keeping the peace. If an adequate implementation mechanism is not created, the process of interim agreements will inevitably continue and we will be fated to repeat history.

To sum up:

1. Palestinians and Israelis alike must accept that political sovereignty cannot be regulated over questions of faith. This is dominantly a political issue and must not become a battle between religions.
2. The religious centrality of Jerusalem cannot be used to obfuscate the national context.
3. As there is no conclusive historical or archeological evidence proving that Jerusalem was ever the political capital of any distinct nation, especially a modern nation, the Palestinians reject any attempt to de-legitimize their national connection to Jerusalem on the basis of this argument.
4. Neither side desires a return of Jerusalem to the status quo ante of 1949–67. However, the Palestinians will not accept a unified city on any basis other than full national equality and will accept nothing less than a viable and prosperous capital.
5. Full integration requires equal and unlimited access to all areas of the city in terms of unrestricted movement and freedom to invest as well as accessibility and protection of all religious sites.
6. The sensitivity of the Jerusalem question requires a solution to be built on three premises:
    (a) Jerusalem cannot be divided physically as such a division would be mutually detrimental.
    (b) Without both Israeli and Palestinian sovereignty in Jerusalem, there will be no permanent peace involving the sharing of both the territorial aspects and those pertaining to its future socioeconomic and political development.
    (c) Religious, ethnic, and cultural identities cannot be negotiated and therefore Jerusalem must become an open city that maintains its pluralistic and universal character.

One could infer that through a strategy based on UN Resolution 242 and 338, and with the principle of equitable reciprocity along with tactics of disengagement and phasing, it is possible for the Palestinians to engage in realistic and productive negotiations with the Israelis.

CHAPTER 24

The Palestinians: From the Sidelines to Major Player in Jerusalem

MOSHE AMIRAV

The "Jerusalem Problem" as a Changing Policy Paradigm

In July 2000, at Camp David in the United States, the international community turned its gaze toward the political breakthrough between the Israelis and the Palestinians when they convened, under the auspices of the President of the United States, for a decisive discussion on the permanent peace settlement between them. One of the key issues that, in particular, aroused the interest of the international community, and which rapidly emerged as one of the obstacles to a permanent settlement between Israel and the Palestinians, was the "Jerusalem problem," as it has been defined since the beginning of the twentieth century.

What is the "Jerusalem problem"?

The definition of the "Jerusalem problem" has changed three times in the course of the twentieth century. To a large extent, how the problem is defined depends on the political "players." Based on a short historical review, the definition has changed each time that the political players have.

Until the 11th of December 1917, the date Jerusalem was taken over by the British General Allenby, the Jerusalem problem was defined as a problem of the "holy places." The European powers, especially Britain and France, used this definition in order to weaken the main player in Jerusalem – the Ottoman Empire – in their demand for a foothold in the holy city. The "policy paradigm" attempts to explain changes in the international political arena by formulating political ideas and definitions on the one hand, and power changes among the political players on the other. Thus in

1917 the *colonial policy* paradigm, which had adopted the definition of the importance of the "holy places," was replaced by a new definition – "the Jerusalem problem" – which from this point on became an *"international problem."* The international community has replaced the Ottoman Empire in the role of key player in Jerusalem's political arena.

In 1922 the League of Nations granted Britain the mandate over the Land of Israel and authorized it to keep Jerusalem in trust for the international community. When Britain left the Land of Israel in 1947, the international community resumed debate on the "Jerusalem problem." Evidence that the problem was not part of the "Jewish–Arab Conflict" can be seen in the 1947 Partition Resolution, in which the United Nations determined the unique and different status of Jerusalem as *"corpus separatum,"* a separate body to be governed by an international authority. This resolution – No. 181 of the UN General Assembly – was rescinded as soon as the outcome of the war in the region determined the physical and political division between the two new players: Jordan and Israel.

In the new paradigm, the "Jerusalem problem" was transformed in 1949 from an international problem into a *political–territorial problem between Israel and Jordan.* This political–territorial paradigm, like the former one, also endured for about 30 years. The Six Day War did not change it, and in the years between 1967 and the *Intifada* that erupted in the late 1980s, the problem was still perceived, as was its solution, in terms of finding a compromise between the two main players – Israel and Jordan – over the city. The reservations of the Arab states about Jordan's ruling the Old City until 1967 and the reservations of the international community about its annexation by Israel after 1967 did not alter the policy paradigm. The international demand to restore "Arabness" to the Old City was interpreted in international, Arab and Israeli public opinion as a "re-division" between Israel and Jordan. There was a lack of symmetry in the demands of the two key players. While Israel sought to achieve recognition of the city as its historical and political capital, Jordan strove to achieve religious and political status in the city, but did not seek to turn the city into its capital.

The Palestinian *Intifada* that erupted in December 1987 marked the beginning of a shift in the policy paradigm and of the composition of the players in the arena. Among the main factors triggering the change were King Hussein's withdrawal of responsibility for the West Bank and the strengthening of the Palestinians' status in the Arab-Muslim sphere. This process was coupled by the national consolidation of the Arab minority in the city in a "Palestinization" process that pushed aside the "Jordanization" and contained the "Israelization" that Israel had hoped for. From this point a new policy paradigm began taking shape, a new player entered the scene – the Palestinians – and the "Jerusalem problem" began to be redefined. The new definition of the problem was as a national one – for which player will Jerusalem be the capital: for the Israelis or the Palestinians?

Israel had hoped that Jordan's military collapse in 1967 and the policy of "determining facts on the ground" which it has adopted since then, would leave it the only player on the scene. However, it was gradually forced, while its status was being eroded, to agree to accept the new paradigm. The willingness of every Israeli prime minister, from Menachem Begin to Ehud Barak, to discuss Jerusalem as part of the solution to the Israeli–Palestinian conflict, helped to reinforce the new paradigm. The Oslo Agreements in the early 1990s and Israel's proposals at Camp David in 2000 finally crystallized it. Henceforth, the "Jerusalem problem" would no longer be defined as a religious, international or purely territorial problem, but rather as one that lies at the very core of the conflict between two national movements, with each wishing to stake a claim to the city as its own historic capital. The veteran players – the European powers, the UN, the Vatican, the Arab League, the Muslim world, and Jordan – who had laid claims on Jerusalem in the past, cleared the arena and left it to only two players: the Israelis and the Palestinians. Any compromise settlement agreeable to the two would be acceptable to them.

Despite Israel's political control over East Jerusalem since 1967, its "policy of creating facts on the ground" has not succeeded in achieving the strategic goal of resolving the fate of the city. The Palestinians, on the other hand, have succeeded in achieving their strategic goal of changing the policy paradigm in the city and of presenting themselves as a player with equal rights *vis-à-vis* Israel. From the sidelines of the political stage, the last player to lay a claim to the city at the beginning and in the course of the twentieth century, the Palestinians have managed to push the veteran actors, and primarily Jordan, off the stage. They have also forced Israel to accept them as its sole partner in negotiating a permanent arrangement for Jerusalem. To understand the process that led to the consolidation of the new paradigm for Jerusalem, it is necessary to analyze the policy objectives of Israel and the Palestinians since 1967, examine the strategies adopted, and evaluate the results of each side's policy in the struggle over the city.

In this chapter I will examine the goals, methods of implementation, and the results of the Palestinian policy from 1967 to the present. Israeli policy calls for another parallel analysis.

The Theoretical Framework: How the Changes in the Policy Paradigm Can Be Explained

How did events, circumstances, and policy tools lead to a shift in the Jerusalem paradigm and in the elevation of the Palestinians from the sidelines of the political arena to be a major player?

In recent years the literature dealing with processes of change in policy paradigms has attributed the process to the varying weight of the players and shifting definitions of policy problems. Two approaches provide us with these explanations:

- *The policy networks and policy communities approach* attributes the processes of change to the players' changing weights.[1]
- *The policy problems definition approach*[2] claims that events and circumstances become policy problems only when they are defined as relevant to policy.

Within this theoretical framework, which is based on the social structuring approach, the definition of policy problems is characterized as *a process in which the circumstances become problems by players who succeed in redefining them.* Many researchers have used this approach of explaining policy processes from the initial stage of determining the agenda, up to the choice of policy tools.[3]

Research in these areas presents the researcher with a number of methodological problems, including:

1. Determining criteria for identifying the processes of change;
2. Identifying the relevant policy areas in which the players operate; and
3. Creating criteria for evaluating the players' success or failure in achieving their objectives.

In the present research, I have relied, to a large extent, on the policy problems definition approach and especially on the work of Scharpf.[4] He proposes examining a policy community or players by the scope of interests that they represent, the degree of stability and perseverance with which they succeed in realizing their objectives, and the results of the change in terms of the acceptance or non-acceptance of the new policy paradigm. The criteria for identifying the processes of change in the policy paradigm of the following study will be the extent of the PLO's success, as a marginal player in the 1960s, in rallying around it the interests of the international community, the Arab states, and especially the Palestinians, and in the 1980s, in their attempt to prevent the other side (Israel and Jordan) from formulating the policy problem according to their needs. Two areas of policy are relevant: the international sphere and the Israeli sphere, of which the objectives and strategies will be identified for each.

The Palestinians defined a change in the policy paradigm as a strategic goal. This change was essential, in their view, in order to achieve their national goal: *East Jerusalem as the capital of the Palestinian state.* The processes of change can be examined in two policy spheres. Within the *international sphere*, the objectives were obtaining international recognition, mobilizing the United States on their side, and pushing Jordan out of the arena. Within the *Israeli sphere*, the objectives were containment of the policy of "determining facts on the ground" to prevent an irreversible situation in the city. The measure of success would be the willingness of all the other players – Israel, the UN, the United States, Jordan, the Arab League, the Vatican, and the Muslim states – to adopt the new policy paradigm.

The Policy Spheres: Objectives and Strategies

The centrality of Jerusalem in the national-Palestinian ideology – as in the national ideology of the Jewish People – was reflected from the turn of the twentieth century in the policies of the Palestinians and the Jews. Their goals were identical: the establishment of an independent state throughout the territory of the historical Land of Israel whose capital is Jerusalem.

In the hundred years of conflict between the two national movements, political constraints deflected Jerusalem from the top of the Zionist list of priorities, and it sometimes seemed as if more important national objectives had pushed Jerusalem to the margins of the Zionist endeavor. In Zionism's early years, and even after the establishment of the State of Israel, Jerusalem was not at the top of the list of priorities of the Zionist enterprise. The willingness of the Zionist leaders, headed by David Ben-Gurion, to relinquish the city in the thirties and the forties, was a result of a pragmatic list of priorities, which recognized that more than constituting an asset, the city constituted an obstacle to the objective of establishing an independent state.[5]

The Palestinian national movement faced similar political constraints in the early 1960s, when East Jerusalem was under Jordanian rule. At that time the Palestinians adopted a pragmatic approach, preferring to place the emphasis on establishing an independent Palestinian state rather than "liberating" the Old City from Jordanian "occupation." An expression of this position can be found in the PLO's agreement to downplay its claim on Jerusalem in order to obtain Jordanian legitimacy, which enabled it to convene its inaugural assembly at the Intercontinental Hotel in Jerusalem, on May 28, 1964. In spite of the fact that the Organization's charter determined that Jerusalem would be the seat of the Palestinian National Council,[6] the drafters of the charter, as well as that of the Palestinian Covenant, avoided mentioning the city as their future capital, although they did indicate that it would serve as the domicile of the Palestinian National Council.

The unwritten understanding between Jordan and the PLO was that the Palestinian claim was over the western part of city under Israeli rule, as part of the liberation of Palestine's occupied lands.[7] Israel's occupation of the Old City and the annexation of East Jerusalem in 1967 allowed the PLO to express outright for the first time its demand for Jerusalem as a whole, and to challenge the Jordanian demand for the return of East Jerusalem. From that time until the mid-1970s the Palestinian consensus expressed the demand for Jerusalem as the capital of the Palestinian state. There is no difference between the western and the eastern parts – neighborhoods in West Jerusalem such as Baka, Musrara, Katamon, Malcha, and Ein Kerem would be treated the same way as those in the eastern part of the city and in the Old City. Only in the late 1980s, as part of the PLO's willingness to reach a settlement with the State of Israel, did a historical compromise take shape, allowing the relinquishing of West Jerusalem while being content with the eastern part based on the ceasefire lines of 1949. It is noteworthy that this compromise is unacceptable to the rejectionist organizations and the fundamentalist religious organizations, all of whom see Jerusalem as holy *Waqf* land, not one centimeter of which can be relinquished.[8]

The PLO's willingness in the Declaration of Independence in 1989 to abandon the program in stages, whereby the State of Israel would be abolished and replaced with a secular democratic state, led naturally to what Haled El Hasan, one of the founders of the organization, called: *"Vakiya,"* or coming to terms with reality in Jerusalem. The political solution, according to the pragmatic approach, is not only to have two countries existing side by side, but also two capitals existing side by side.[9]

However, in the 1960s the Palestinians were very far from fulfilling any of their dreams in Jerusalem. For years they had no significant position compared to the central "players" in the Jerusalem arena. During the Mandate it was Britain, subsequently Jordan and Israel; the international community, the Arab League, the Vatican, and even the UN did not view the Palestinians as a legitimate "player" in this arena. In the argument "to whom does Jerusalem belong," only three players were reckoned with until the 1970s – the international community (as reflected in UN Resolution 181 of 1947), Jordan (who ruled the Old City until 1967), and Israel (which annexed East Jerusalem and unified the entire city in 1967).[10]

The Palestinians' strategic goal, as formulated in the late 1980s, was to become a legitimate "player" with no less a valid claim on the city than Israel. In order to attain this strategic goal, the Palestinians formulated two spheres of reference toward which the policy was directed. It was necessary to adopt a different strategic policy in each of these spheres in order to achieve their national objectives.

The first sphere was the international community, which first had to recognize the Palestinians as a nation entitled to a country and not simply as refugees seeking a solution. The international community was asked to recognize Palestinian national rights over the city. In this sphere emphasis was placed on two bodies: The United States, whose patronage Israel

enjoyed, and the Arab League, which was required to remove Jordan's
claim of ownership over the city and the Islamic holy places.

Israel was in the second sphere. In view of the facts created on the
ground, there was a need to establish counter-facts that would consolidate Palestinian's claim to being the legitimate partner over the city. The
Palestinians adopted a different strategy for each of the two policy spheres
marked by features that can be defined as strategies of *recognition,
expelling, and containment.*[11]

The international community's position on Jerusalem was expressed in
two historical decisions: Resolution 181 of 1947 to internationalize the city,
and Resolution 242 of 1967, which mandated Israel's withdrawal from the
occupied territories. The two resolutions did not express any recognition
of the Palestinian's status in Jerusalem. The position of the Arab and the
Muslim world bore considerable importance, and in this respect the PLO
strove to push aside Jordan from its status of claiming sovereignty over the
city and as guardian of the Islamic holy places. In the Israeli sphere,
the PLO worked toward containing the Israeli policy that sought to create
"an irreversible reality" in East Jerusalem. In order to create "a reversible
reality" in Jerusalem, the Palestinians would have to maintain an ongoing
popular resistance to the occupation, to determine counter-facts to the
Israeli ones already on the ground. It would also have to formulate an institutional infrastructure for *"the capital in the making,"* adopting a similar
pattern as that adopted by the *yishuv* [pre-statehood Israel] in its struggle
for "the country in the making."

An examination and evaluation of the results of the Palestinian policy
shows that the Palestinians have achieved all their national objectives in the
above two policy spheres. They adopted strategies and advanced them step-
by-step toward these national objectives, and by the late nineties they had
achieved their goal. The international community, the United States, the
Arab League, the Islamic states, and even Israel recognized them in practice *as a major player in the talks on the future of Jerusalem.*

The position supported by the international community for many years,
in which an international regime would be set up in the city, was no longer
valid. The Palestinians achieved recognition and support, including that of
the United States, for their demand to divide the city between them and the
Israelis. The Arab and Muslim policy – which in the past had been
accepted, albeit with no small reservations – and Hussein's senior status in
the city and over the holy places was replaced in the 1970s and 1980s with
unequivocal support for the Palestinian position. The political struggle in
the Arab arena and the *Intifada* in the occupied territories in 1987 brought
about Jordan's withdrawal from its role as a political player on the
Jerusalem stage. Guardianship over the holy places, which the Arab and
the Islamic states had claimed in the eighties, had, by the end of the nineties,
been handed over to the Palestinians.

The Israeli attempt to transform the annexation of East Jerusalem into a fait accompli also failed. To oppose the Israeli's policy of "determining facts on the ground," the Palestinians established counter-facts, expressed mainly by preventing international recognition of Israel's actions in Jerusalem on the one hand, and by transforming integration and unification processes into processes of segregation and confrontation in the city on the other.[12]

It is doubtful whether Israel's enterprise of building new neighborhoods in the eastern part of the city after 1967 strengthened territorial control in this part of the city, which, from an urban point of view, was connected to the surrounding Arab metropolitan area. Furthermore, the demographic objective of increasing the Jewish majority in the city was not achieved. The percentage of Jews, which Israel wished to increase to 80 percent-90 percent, and thus to determine the uni-national character of the city, continued to decrease, with a corresponding increase in the proportion of Arab residents. By 1999 the percentage of Arabs had reached almost 33 percent. The Arab annual growth rate of 3.5 percent in the city, as opposed to the Jewish growth rate of 1.5 percent, has strengthened the transformation of Jerusalem into a *bi-national city*.

Israel's inability to achieve unequivocal conquest during its thirty years of rule in the city, its compromise with Palestinization processes, and Prime Minister Ehud Barak's agreement to divide the city in the July 2000 Camp David talks for a permanent arrangement in the city, reflect the achievements made by Palestinian policy in the Israeli sphere. To a large extent their success in the two spheres – the international and the Israeli – brought them closer to their goal: transforming East Jerusalem into the capital of the Palestinian state.

The International Sphere – Strategy of Recognition: The United States' Shift to the Palestinian Side

In the struggle for international recognition for legitimization of their demands over Jerusalem, the Palestinians wished to change fundamentally the positions of the UN and the United States on this issue. From the beginning of the twentieth century, the international community supported the position that Jerusalem "belongs" to the international community. This was expressed by the League of Nations in the Mandate Articles of July 22, 1922, which entrusted the city as part of the British mandate, and wherein Britain's status was defined as "keeper of the holy places," and as responsible for the city on behalf of the League of Nations.

Also the recommendations of the Peel Commission in 1937, which for the first time mentioned the possibility of partitioning the Land of Israel between the Jews and the Arabs, indicated in Section 10 that the division of Palestine (*Eretz Israel*) was subject to the decisive need to safeguard that the holiness of Jerusalem and Bethlehem would not be desecrated and that the whole world would be ensured free and safe access to them. This is "a holy trust of the civilization in the full sense of the wording of the Mandate – not just on behalf of the people of Palestine (*Eretz* Israel), but rather on behalf of the masses of people of other countries for whom these places, either or both, are holy."[13]

The recommendations of the 1947 report of the United Nations Special Committee on Palestine (UNSCOP) and the General Assembly Resolution of November 1947, also express the position of the international community, which considers Jerusalem a "*corpus separatum*" – a separate body, to be placed under special UN rule. The 1967 resolutions of the UN General Assembly and of the Security Council also did not contradict the position that a special international authority would be preferable for the city. Even prior to 1967, the international community refused to recognize the results of the 1948 war, whereby Israel held the western city and Jordan the Old City.

Since 1967, the Palestinians' struggle for the recognition of their claims over the city has paralleled their international struggle for recognition of their right to self-determination in the territories of the West Bank. The more established their status in the institutions of the UN became, the closer the Palestinians came to attaining this objective. The dissolution of the 1947 resolution to make Jerusalem an international city, Jordan's exit from the Jerusalem game, and the peace process in the Middle East between Israel and the Palestinians placed the Palestinians on center stage in Jerusalem.

According to the Palestinians, the United States is at the center of the international sphere. Its dual status as a superpower and as Israel's patron has conferred on it, in the Palestinians' view, a key position in determining the city's future. The position of the United States has fluctuated between the internationalization solution and the solution of a Jordanian–Israeli agreement on its future. On June 19, 1967, President Johnson first expressed the United States' position on the question of Jerusalem by skirting the territorial–political aspect and opting to emphasize the problem of the holy places within the city. This hinted at the possibility of a solution that combines the historical UN position, as expressed in General Assembly Resolution 181 of 1947 and Security Council Resolution 242 of 1967. An arrangement of functional internationalization of the holy places and territorial compromise between Israel and Jordan in Jerusalem appeared to the American president as an appropriate solution to the Jerusalem issue. This problem, according to the Americans, cannot be solved without a comprehensive Middle East peace settlement. United States ambassador to the UN Arthur Goldberg also expressed this view in his speech to the UN in July 1967, in which he stated, among other things:

I wish to clarify that the United States does not accept or recognize these measures [that were adopted in Jerusalem] as altering the status of Jerusalem ... We do not believe that the problem of Jerusalem can be realistically solved in separating it from other aspects relating to Jerusalem and the Middle East situation. The most fruitful approach for a discussion on Jerusalem's future calls for addressing the overall problem as one aspect of the broader arrangements that must be made to restore a just and durable peace in the region.[14]

This approach to a solution for Jerusalem as a settlement between Israel and the Arab States, and especially Jordan, found support in those years in the first American peace proposal for the Middle East, presented by American Foreign Secretary William Rogers in 1969. In his plan of December 9, 1969, Rogers determined: "Both Israel and Jordan should have a role in administering the political, economic, and religious life in the city."[15] President Ronald Reagan's plan of September 1, 1982, which speaks of autonomy for the Palestinians, also mentions Jordan and Israel as the parties connected to the issue of Jerusalem.

Not only did the Israeli government, headed by Menachem Begin, reject in 1982 the American president's plan. It was also rejected by PLO Chairman Yasser Arafat, since the Jordanians and not the Palestinians were designated as Israel's negotiating partner on the future of the occupied territories and Jerusalem. Only in the wake of the *Intifada* and the process leading up to the Madrid Conference were the Americans persuaded to replace the Jordanian option with the Palestinian option. From this point on, American foreign secretaries – George Shultz and James Baker – would attempt to involve the PLO and the inhabitants of East Jerusalem in the political process, recognizing that United States historical policy, in which Jordan was the natural partner for the agreement on Jerusalem, would have no chance of succeeding.

In the late 1980s, Foreign Secretary Baker formulated the Five Point Plan in which for the first time America indicated its willingness to grant the PLO its greatest international political achievement to date – the participation of representatives from East Jerusalem in the peace talks. The American Foreign Secretary's meetings with PLO representatives (internal) at the Orient House in East Jerusalem, symbolized, more than any other, the turning point in the US position. The pressure exerted by the PLO on the United States bore fruit when in the letter of guarantees that the Americans delivered to the Palestinians on October 18, 1991 in exchange for their willingness to enter the peace talks, it became unequivocally clear that the United States saw the Palestinians, and not Jordan, as a partner in the talks on the city's future.

The American letter of guarantees (that was concealed from the Israelis) marked three achievements for the Palestinians. The letter confirms that the United States does not recognize the annexation of East Jerusalem to Israel.

Furthermore, the Arab residents of the city are entitled to choose their representatives to the Palestinian Authority and to be represented in the delegation to the negotiations, and that the permanent settlement would include a discussion on Jerusalem. The argument between President George Bush and Prime Minister Shamir regarding the status of East Jerusalem – in the context of the use of budgets allocated for the absorption of immigration from the former Soviet Union – further sharpened the American administration's position. The United States defined the areas of East Jerusalem as occupied territory and viewed them in the same way as the West Bank territories that would be destined to come under Palestinian rule in the future.

The return of the Labor party to power in 1992 and the Oslo Agreements of 1993 further advanced the talks regarding Jerusalem and led the Americans to take a position very similar to that of the Palestinians on the issue of Jerusalem. In 1993 President Clinton's administration became actively involved in the negotiations between Israel and the Palestinians. In spite of the President's support for Israel, his position on Jerusalem was similar to that of his predecessors. In a meeting between Clinton and Rabin in Washington on November 12, 1993 on the subject of advancing the Oslo Agreements, Clinton made the relocation of the United States embassy to Jerusalem conditional upon its implementation as part of the permanent agreement with the Palestinians.

Initiatives undertaken by US Republican Senator Robert Dole and Congressman Newt Gingrich in 1995 to immediately transfer the embassy to Jerusalem, were regarded by Foreign Secretary Warren Christopher as "an unwise proposal which jeopardizes the success of the peace process . . ."[16] On October 24, 1995 the House of Representatives and the Senate passed an order directing that the embassy be transferred to Jerusalem no later than May 31, 1999. However, President Clinton used his authority to postpone the implementation of the order by six months and refused to sign it on the grounds that it would damage the peace process and thereby threaten the essential security interests of the United States. Other joint resolutions by Congress and by the House of Representatives recognizing Jerusalem as the undivided capital of Israel did not change the President's position that transferring the embassy and the recognition of Jerusalem during the negotiations could harm the process.

In July 2000, Israeli and Palestinian delegations convened in Camp David for talks on the permanent settlement. The subject of Jerusalem was postponed to the end of the talks. On the fifth day of the summit, in which President Clinton, Prime Minister Barak and Chairman Arafat participated, Israel first proposed, informally, the division of Jerusalem. The solution would be based on determining new municipal boundaries for the two cities: Al-Quds in the east and Jerusalem in the west. The Israeli proposal spoke about extending Jerusalem and annexing Ma'aleh

Adumim and Givat Ze'ev on the one hand, and transferring the "fringe" neighborhoods such as Shuafat, Beit Hanina, and Zur Bacher, with about 130,000 Arab residents, to full Palestinian sovereignty on the other. The internal Arab neighborhoods and the Old City, with about 70,000 Arab inhabitants, would enjoy considerable municipal autonomy (the Arab neighborhoods would enjoy the status of self-administered urban neighborhoods and the Old City would be under special administration), but would remain under Israeli sovereignty. Israeli sovereignty would be retained over the Temple Mount, but the Palestinians would be given administrative control and the Authority's Chairman Arafat would be defined as protector of the holy places. The Palestinians would be permitted to reach the Haram al-Sharif by means of a road and bridge under Palestinian sovereignty, which would save the Palestinians from having to pass Israeli roadblocks on their way to the Temple Mount.

The negative Palestinian reaction led President Clinton to propose his own ideas, which amended the Israeli proposal with regard to the status of the internal neighborhoods and the Old City.

The American proposal, as formulated toward the end of the summit, included three options:

1   To postpone by consent a permanent settlement for Jerusalem or, alternatively for the Old City, and in the meantime to sign a permanent settlement relating to all other issues.
2   To amend the Israeli proposal with regard to the internal neighborhoods by granting full Palestinian sovereignty over them, and agree on Palestinian control of the Old City without sovereignty.
3   To alter proposal No. 2 – allowing Palestinian control without sovereignty over the internal neighborhoods and Palestinian sovereignty over the Christian and Muslim quarters of the Old City.[17]

The reservations of the two delegations, the Israeli and the Palestinian, about the American proposals concerning Jerusalem and the lack of clarity regarding the status of the Temple Mount were among the major reasons for the failure of the Camp David talks.

Several months later, President Clinton formulated his own detailed proposal for a permanent settlement between Israel and the Palestinians and presented it as a presidential proposal to the two sides. In his proposal, which he presented on December 23, 2000, the principle with regard to Jerusalem was determined as "whatever is Arab will be Palestinian and whatever is Jewish will be Israeli." With regard to the Old City, the President proposed establishing a "special authority" whereby the Christian and Muslim quarters would be under Palestinian sovereignty and the Jewish quarter and part of the Armenian quarter would be under Israeli sovereignty. Two alternatives were proposed for the Temple Mount. In the

first, the Palestinians would receive sovereignty over the Mount and the
Israelis would receive sovereignty over the Wall and a special, unclear,
linkage to the underground area beneath the Temple Mount. The second
alternative proposed that the Israelis would receive sovereignty instead of
linkage to the underground space. The city would be divided according to
the spatial distribution of the neighborhoods, and the continuity between
the Jewish and the Arab neighborhoods would be maintained by means of
overhead roads, bridges, or tunnels.

The two sides chose not to respond negatively to the presidential
mediation document. The Palestinians had reservations about the Israeli
linkage to the underground space and about the possibility that territorial
continuity would not be maintained between the Arab neighborhoods. The
Israelis had reservations about the Palestinian sovereignty over the Temple
Mount and about the possibility that the holy area outside the city,
especially the Mount of Olives, would be under Palestinian sovereignty. In
spite of the Israeli reservations concerning Jerusalem and other issues, the
Israeli government decided on December 29, 2000 to respond positively in
principle to the US proposal.[18] The negative Palestinian position, even
though phrased in the form of reservations and requests for further clarification, actually put an end to the presidential proposal.

While the new administrations in Israel and in the United States are not
committed to Clinton's presidential proposal with regard to Jerusalem,
nevertheless, from the Palestinians' point of view it can be said that they
achieved their strategic goals. For the first time, the international community recognized them as a partner with the same rights as Israel to
discuss the city, and for the first time an American administration had
recognized their claims on the eastern part of the city; And for the first time,
an Israeli government had agreed to divide Jerusalem.

The Arab-Muslim Sphere: The Strategy of Dispossessing Jordan of Jerusalem

Two stages can be discerned in the struggle to abolish Jordan's senior status
in Jerusalem and to obtain the support of the Arab League and the Muslim
world for the Palestinians' claims on Jerusalem. The first stage is the
struggle that the Palestinians waged to obtain Arab recognition of their
political claims on the city, claims that were not obvious in the 1960s. This
stage ended with an impressive achievement for the Palestinians in which
they succeeded in pushing aside Jordan's claims on the city. The second
stage is the struggle waged by the Palestinians in the 1990s to obtain
Muslim recognition of their claim for sole status as guardians of the Islamic
holy places. In reality, it was the peace process with Israel that enabled the
Palestinians to penetrate Jerusalem and take control of the al-Haram al-

Sharif mosques, the Muslim *Waqf*, and the Supreme Muslim Council. And it was this penetration that assisted Arafat in establishing his status as sole guardian of the holy places.

The Israeli conquest of the Old City in 1967 shocked the Arab and the Muslim countries, which at that time had about 50 members in the UN. Led by Jordan, these countries initiated a large number of UN resolutions condemning the Israeli occupation and preventing Israel from obtaining recognition of the unilateral annexation. The collective Arab demand at the time spoke about restoring "the Arab character of Jerusalem" without explicitly mentioning its future political status or which country would be responsible for the Islamic holy places.

Until 1974, resolutions of the Arab summit conferences did not mention the rights of the Palestinians over the city. Long-standing reservations on the part of the Arab states, from the period of the annexation of the West Bank to Jerusalem by King Abdallah[19] and the internal power struggles in the Arab League, somewhat clouded the position of the Arab League regarding the city's future. The process of transferring the political "birthright" to the city to the Palestinians began at the Rabat Conference in 1974, when the conference participants decided, for the first time, that all future liberated Palestinian land would be transferred to "an independent Palestinian national authority." The recognition of the PLO, and not Jordan, as "the sole legal representative of the Palestinian people," marked the beginnings of a process of eliminating Jordan's responsibility for the fate of Palestine, afterwards for the fate of Jerusalem, and finally for the fate of the Islamic holy places on the Temple Mount.

In the Camp David talks in 1978 between Israel and Egypt, Sadat emphasized the "Arab character" of Jerusalem. Egypt, like the rest of the Arab states and Muslim countries, leaned toward a settlement that would ensure Palestinian sovereignty over East Jerusalem, but would leave the guardianship of the Islamic holy places in the hands of the Arab nations.[20] This approach also found expression in the first peace initiative put forward by the Arab nations at the Fez Summit Conference in Morocco, in September 1982. For the first time the conference resolutions mention that East Jerusalem would become the capital of the Palestinian state.[21] The question of the status of the holy places was left open in the Fez resolutions. Saudi Arabia, Morocco, and Egypt thought it would be possible to separate political sovereignty in the city from the question of sovereignty over the holy places. Yet, they still entertained the possibility of the religious administration of these places remaining in their hands under a political Palestinian umbrella.

The notion of a separation between political sovereignty in the city and religious sovereignty was originally a Jordanian idea.[22] Jordan felt that what was holy to Islam should be liberated and placed under Jordanian safekeeping irrespective of the liberation of Jerusalem. In Hussein's opinion, Israel would not relinquish its sovereignty in East Jerusalem, but would be prepared, under certain conditions, to relinquish the Temple Mount, and he saw himself adopting the role of guardian of the Islamic holy places. Arafat, who was aware of and disturbed by Jordan's position on this issue, vigorously strove to prevent the acceptance of the principle of separating political from religious sovereignty. For this reason he pushed to have himself elected at the beginning of the 1980s to the position of vice-chairman of the Conference of Islamic States. His election at the League's conference in Fez in 1982 enabled him, henceforth, to present the liberation of the Haram al-Sharif from the Israelis as both a political and a religious objective.

In the late 1980s the Palestinians succeeded in shaping the policies of the Arab states and the Muslim countries within the context of the possibility of peace with Israel. Thus, for example, the Arab Summit Conference in Casablanca in 1989 adopted all the resolutions of the 19th session of the Palestinian National Council of November 1988. The resolutions of the Palestinian National Council defined the Arab and the Muslim consensus as recognition of and peace with Israel, and presented the proposed compromise in Jerusalem: its division into two capitals, Jerusalem in the west and Al-Quds in the east. The recognition of West Jerusalem as the capital of Israel by the Arab and the Muslim world is, from this time on, the compensation promised to Israel by the Palestinians in exchange for its willingness to allow the Palestinian capital in the eastern city.[23]

King Hussein's announcement, during the *Intifada*, renouncing his responsibility and any political claim over the West Bank and Jerusalem did not put an end to Jordan's claim for status over the holy places in Jerusalem. From then on, Arafat would also struggle for the Palestinians' exclusivity in claiming political sovereignty over the Islamic holy places.

The talks between Israel and Jordan yielded a peace agreement between the two countries on July 25, 1994. In the section later inserted in the peace agreement, which was signed in Washington in September 1994, Jordan and Israel tried to determine a *fait accompli* regarding the status of the holy places in Jerusalem. The lack of clarity shown by the Arab states toward the status of the Islamic holy places in their conferences since the Fez Conference in 1982 and the possibility that the Palestinian claim to the holy places would be overridden by one of the Arab states led Hussein to determine a *fait accompli*, whereby he would be guardian of the holy places. In the Washington Declaration it was determined that "Israel respects the current special role of the Hashemite Kingdom of Jordan with regard to the Muslim holy places in Jerusalem. When the negotiations for a permanent settlement are conducted, Israel will give high priority to Jordan's historical role in these holy places."[24] Rabin and Hussein personally formulated this section with the intention of separating the discussion over the political sovereignty of the city from the religious status of the holy places

(Moshe Kochanovsky, Ministry of Defense's legal advisor, and one of the Declaration's writers, *Ha'aretz*, November 27, 1995). Prince Hassan, Hussein's brother, expressed his country's position lucidly by stating that Jordan had never relinquished, nor would it ever relinquish its responsibility over the Islamic holy places in East Jerusalem.[25]

This Israeli–Jordanian accord supplied the pretext for the Palestinians to raise the question of the responsibility for the holy places in a number of international Arab forums, a question which the Arab states had preferred to leave open up to that time. Arafat announced, "no Arab or Israeli leader rules the holy places in East Jerusalem. This right is given solely to the Palestinians." Attempts to mediate between the Palestinians and Jordan on this issue failed. Prince Hassan, the Crown prince, initially tried in November 1994 to persuade the Palestinians that Jordan was acting in this matter as an emissary of the Arab and Muslim world in order to extricate the holy places from Israel, and that this is in fact in the Palestinians' interest. Arafat was not convinced and decided to transfer the decision to the Conference of Islamic States. In December 1994, the Conference of Islamic States convened in Casablanca. Jordan was supported by Qatar, Yemen, and Oman, and the Palestinians by Saudi Arabia, Egypt, and Morocco.

The Palestinians' supporters at the conference tried to convince Arafat to agree, as a compromise, to the establishment of a committee on behalf of the Islamic Conference. This would hand guardianship over the holy places to Jordan until the Palestinians gained control in East Jerusalem. Their efforts failed due to pressure from Saudi Arabia, claiming that the separation between religion and politics, as put forward by Hussein regarding Jerusalem, was foreign to Islam. The phrasing of the summary announcement of the conference clearly constituted a significant victory for the Palestinians. It stated that the Islamic states were to assist them in the future negotiations so that all the authority and the areas of responsibility in the conquered lands, including the exalted Jerusalem, would be transferred to the National Palestinian Authority. Furthermore, the announcement stated that the authority in Jerusalem, during the period of transition, should be transferred to the Palestinian Authority and not remain under Jordanian trusteeship.[26] These decisions were a resounding slap in the face for King Hussein who stormed out of the conference before it had ended.

Concurrent with the diplomatic activity in the Arab states, the Palestinians sought to determine facts on the ground with regard to the holy places. In October 1994, following the death of the Mufti of Jerusalem – Sulieman el Jaber – one of King Hussein's most loyal followers, a virulent argument erupted over who had the authority to appoint his successor. By virtue of the authority that was held by the King of Jordan since 1967, Hussein appointed his follower Sheikh A'abdin to the position. At the same time, Arafat appointed his follower, Sheikh Akrama Sabri, to the same position. For some time both filled the position until, gradually, Sabri's followers pushed A'abdin's followers from their posts. In 1998, upon Sheikh A'abdin's retirement, Sabri took control over the Mufti's institutions and determined *fait accompli* that he was the sole Mufti on the Temple Mount.

The followers of the Palestinian Authority also concurrently began to take control over the asset-rich *Waqf* and the Supreme Moslem Council. In 1994 a PLO supporter, Hassan Ta'abuv, was chosen as chairman of the department, and Feisal Husseini as his deputy. In January 1977, Arafat decided to appoint 18 representatives to the Supreme Moslem Council, a body with a majority of Jordanian supporters, in order to strengthen the West Bank's representation at the expense of the East Bank. All of them were, of course, his followers, thereby creating a majority for his supporters on the Council.

Once the issue of the holy places was decided in the Palestinians favor, the Palestinians completed the circle of achievements among the Arab states and the Islamic countries. The road was now open for demanding not only political sovereignty, but also sole religious status in the city; for not only had all Jordan's claims been dismissed, but also those of Egypt, Morocco, and Saudi Arabia.

The Israeli Sphere: Policy of Containment – Popular Resistance Strategy

The Palestinians' inferiority in their struggle against Israel in the city itself called for a consolidation of strategies that would contain Israel's policy of "creating facts" on the ground. Israel's policy was based on the assumption that changing the geopolitical reality in East Jerusalem would lead to a historical conclusion and an irreversible situation in the "united" city. The overall Israeli goal was to create an irreversible geopolitical reality in the area and in the city, in order to prevent any possibility of dividing the city in the future.

Israeli policy was conducted in two spheres, the first, international – in which it strived to achieve international recognition for its sovereignty over the city and its status as the capital of Israel. The second, an internal sphere, in which Israel determined four objectives as part of the conception of "determining a *fait accompli*." First, in terms of demographics, the Israeli objective was to increase the Jewish majority in the city. Second, in the territorial area it was to shift the distribution of Jewish settlement in the eastern city to prevent any possibility of linking the Arab neighborhoods to the West Bank. Third, in the economic sphere, the goal was to create an economic infrastructure that would attract Jewish immigration to the city and ensure financial resources to bridge gaps and improve the residents' standard of living. And, finally, in the political arena the objective was to bring about normalization and prevent political unrest. With regard to the Arab minority, a policy was adopted that sought, on the one hand, to bring about their "Israelization" and on the other, to reduce their demographic and economic influence.[27]

An analysis of Palestinian actions from 1967 to the present time reveals three strategies of containment: The first strategy was *popular resistance* by the Arab residents of Jerusalem to Israeli rule. This resistance, which was expressed both in a popular uprising and acts of violence throughout the years, reached its climax in the *Intifada* in the late 1980s.

The second strategy was based on *creating counter-facts to the facts created by Israel on the ground*. *Vis-à-vis* the Israeli attempt to reduce the influence and power of the Palestinian minority, the Palestinians adopted a policy of *"Tzumud"* (national survival) by developing a complex system of "give-and-take" relationships with the Israeli government. "A dialogue of acts," as it was called by Meron Benvenisti. Feisal Husseini stated: "We do not create facts on the ground, we are the facts on the ground," his intention being the demographic, economic, and economical empowerment of the minority, which Israel tried to diminish by all possible means.

The third strategy was that of *political consolidation and the creation of an infrastructure for the capital in the making*. Facing the Israeli attempt to preserve the traditional elite within the municipal areas of Jerusalem, the *mukhtars* of the villages annexed to Jerusalem and the Jordanian supporters, the PLO strove to create an alternative leadership supported by and representing the popular social classes. Palestinianization and development of the national and local institutions formed the organizational backbone of the capital in the making.

Already in June 1967, a few days after the occupation, Israelis discovered that in contrast to Arab populated areas conquered in 1948, in which the Arabs came to terms with the new reality, here, in Jerusalem, their work was far more difficult. Jordan and the PLO called on the residents of Jerusalem to resist the occupation and to express this politically. The National Direction Committee, set up that month under the leadership of Sheikh Abdel Hamid el Tsaich, one of Hussein's followers,[28] initiated acts of political protest against the occupation. Members of the Jordanian municipal executive, headed by Ruchi el Hatib, refused to cooperate with the Israeli municipality and demanded their reinstatement as the independent Jordanian Jerusalem municipality.

The Bar Association sent a petition to the UN requesting that the international community intervene in Israel's actions, and the teachers announced that they would not open the school year if they were forced to teach the Israeli Arab curriculum. On August 6, 1967, the first announcement of popular resistance appeared, with a call for a general strike. The announcement called for maintaining Jordanian Arab identity (and not necessarily Palestinian): "We have called a general strike so that the world will hear your outcry, and to prove that you are steadfast in your refusal to accept the plans and the laws of the Zionists and that you belong to the Arab nation on both banks of the Jordan. Long live Jordan on both banks, long live Arab Jerusalem."[29]

The first political strike in the city broke out the following day, completely paralyzing life in East Jerusalem, and surprising the Israeli government by its magnitude. Among Israeli policy-makers there were those who considered restoring the military government to the eastern part of the city. Along with the popular uprising and protest orchestrated by Jordan, independent political activity also commenced on the ground. Leftist organizations – students' and pupils' associations, trade unions and the Arab Women's Association – began to take strong protest actions and to struggle against the occupation. The National Direction Committee, which called for a moderate struggle, was accused by these organizations of cooperating with Israel. The boycott of Israeli rule and non-cooperation with it quickly turned into a pattern of political action on the part of East Jerusalemites. The two most prominent features of the boycott were refusal to accept Israeli citizenship and the boycott of municipal elections.[30]

The boycott of Israeli rule caused the Palestinian population considerable damage over the years. Non-acceptance of Israeli citizenship, as well as the refusal to accept compensation for the expropriation of their lands or to be partners in the city council in the distribution of municipal resources, were expressions of the popular resistance, which was soon joined by violence and terrorism. The choice of violence and terrorism along with political resistance enjoyed little public support in the initial years; most residents preferring the popular rebellion and the passive resistance led by the National Direction Committee. Over the years, the longer the occupation continued and as the PLO's political power in the world gained momentum, more and more Palestinians in Jerusalem joined the armed struggle.

On September 17, 1967 the first explosive device was planted in the newly united Jerusalem. The device, placed amateurishly, did not explode and was found and dismantled by the security forces. Two days later, however, another bomb exploded next to the neglected Hotel Fast located on the old border. Seven passersby were injured, thereby initiating terrorist activity in Jerusalem, which continued intermittently until the *Intifada*. In 1968 a booby-trapped car exploded in the Machaneh Yehuda market, killing 12 people and injuring 54. A year later bombs were detonated in the Supersol on Agron Street and in the cafeteria of the Hebrew University. In the three years from 1967 to 1970, there were 79 acts of sabotage in Jerusalem, but in the ensuing years the security forces almost totally succeeded in preventing any acts of this kind in the city.

At the end of 1987 the popular resistance to the occupation of Jerusalem had grown into a raging storm that combined with the waves of violence of the *Intifada* in other parts of the West Bank and the Gaza Strip. If Israel hoped that the actions it took in the 1970s and 1980s toward consolidating its rule and enforcing order and security in the eastern city would prevent what had happened on the West Bank, it was greatly disappointed. An expression of the surprise and the disappointment was provided by the legendary mayor, Teddy Kollek, who defined the new reality in Jerusalem in terms of "shattering the vision of the unity of the city" or "the death of coexistence."

Both Jews and Arabs perceive the period of the *Intifada* as one of the turning points in the history of the relationship between the majority and the minority in the city. By its extreme nature, the *Intifada* polarized and completed the process of separating the Arab minority in Jerusalem from the ruling Jewish majority. It succeeded in leaving a mark of national separation in Jerusalem, and thus thwarted the twenty-year Israeli national effort to unify the city, since 1967.

Teddy Kollek was not the only person to express what he saw as the collapse of the dream of the united city. In his book, published at the start of the *Intifada*, Meron Benvenisti, who had followed Israeli policy since he served in 1967 as Kollek's assistant for Jerusalem affairs, wrote: "We have to start from the beginning, to compile a new dictionary of concepts that will match reality, and the dictionary cannot be compiled without eliminating obsolete vocabulary."[31]

The Israeli population's shock at the intensity of the Palestinian civil uprising in their capital can be compared to the shock experienced by the city's Arabs after the conquest of 1967. *Ha'aretz* newspaper, in reviewing the 1,000 days of the *Intifada* in Jerusalem, wrote:

> In both sides of this city each person lives in his own tent. The Arab side has already exhausted the severance processes as part of the steps decided by the leadership of the uprising. The Jewish side, in the circumstances, also finds itself disconnecting itself . . . [32]

The *Intifada* recorded the longest Arab strike in the history of Jerusalem; previous strikes during the 1936 Arab Revolt lasted for a few months. During the Jordanian and Israeli period they continued for a few days. During the *Intifada* the general strike lasted for three consecutive years.

Between 1988 and 1992 there were 18 murders in the city, scores of injured, 45 attempted murders, 67 bombs, 703 Molotov cocktails thrown, 2,008 cases of Israeli vehicles set on fire and destroyed, 14,540 cases of stone throwing, and 3,404 violent protests (as reported to the municipality's executive by the commander of the Jerusalem District Police Force, on November 2, 1992). From the Israeli point of view, the 1967 "city line" had returned. Since the *Intifada*, the ethnic division line between the communities has become the border that marks the division of the city.[33]

Many places mentioned in the literature and the songs of the *Intifada* are connected to the Palestinians' collective experience, such as Jaffa, Haifa, Nablus, Jenin, Bethlehem, and Gaza; but chief among them is Jerusalem.[34] The *Intifada* built Jerusalem as the renewed national and religious center of the Palestinians, and the call for national liberation repeatedly mentioned Saladin, the liberator of Jerusalem from the Crusaders.

The Policy of Containment: Strategy of "Determining Counter-Facts"

With or without an agreement we have to do everything to create facts on the ground every day, and quickly, in order to ensure the future of the holy places in Jerusalem and its Arab character.[35]

The strategy of creating counter-facts, like that of the "popular resistance," is proactive. Its aim is to curb the two objectives of Israeli policy – reducing the Jerusalem Arab population's power and their percentage of the city's overall population; and creating processes of integration and cooperation in the "united" city.[36]

The Israeli policy of reducing the power of the Palestinians was expressed in three areas: demographic – by planning and building limitations that would lead to reducing their proportion of the population; territorial – by expropriating their lands in order to build new [Jewish] neighborhoods; and economic – by preventing economic development in the eastern city and increasing the Palestinians' dependence on the Israeli economy.

The integration processes that Israel promoted in Jerusalem were designed to prove that the city was united and developing normally for the benefit of all its residents. A policy of "Israelization" was adopted toward the Arabs in the city, on the assumption that the Arabs of Jerusalem would undergo the same socio-political processes, as did Israeli Arabs after 1948. The internal contradictions in Israeli policy since 1967 paradoxically secured the success of the Palestinian strategy. The building of the new Jewish neighborhoods in the 1970s created an economic boom that improved the standard of living of the city's Arab population. After many years of a scarcity of jobs and a slump in economic development, which marked the period of Jordanian rule in the city, the Israeli authorities opened up economic opportunities that put an end to the negative migration trends that had characterized the city's Arab population until 1967. The provision of advanced health and medical services reduced Arab infant mortality and increased the life expectancy of the elderly population. The granting of financial benefits promised by the Israeli welfare system, such as National Insurance payments, raised the standard of living and personal income of the Arab residents of Jerusalem far above that of their brothers on the West Bank. On the other hand, Israel failed in its attempts to develop an economic infrastructure that would widen employment opportunities for the Jewish residents. The building of satellite settlements around Jerusalem led to the migration of tens of thousands of Jews from Jerusalem to these settlements.

The Israeli policy led to steady growth in the percentage of the Arab minority in the city. From about a quarter in 1967, the percentage of Arabs in the city grew to about a third in 2000,[37] the annual rate of growth in the 1980s and 1990s being about 3.5 percent per annum. Parallel to this, starting in the 1980s, the Jewish population in the city was characterized by a negative migration trend. The rate of Jewish population growth in the 1980s and 1990s fell to only 1.5 percent.[38]

The Israeli attempt to shape the image of Jerusalem as a uni-national city with an insignificant Arab minority of 10–15 percent failed. The continuation of current demographic trends guarantees the bi-national character of the city. The proportion of Arabs in the city, according to the Central Bureau of Statistics as well as research conducted for the Jerusalem municipality by Professor De La Pergola, will, within 20 years, reach 40 percent or even 45 percent of Jerusalem's overall population. While in the demographic area the Palestinians had the upper hand, in the competition for the Arab geographical space their position was inferior. About a third of the area of East Jerusalem was expropriated for the building of the new neighborhoods. Nevertheless, the Palestinians adopted a strategy of counter-facts, primarily involving attempts to purchase land and assets offered for sale by Palestinians, mainly in the Old City and its environs, and imposing the death penalty on anyone attempting to sell or trade Palestinian land to Israelis or engaging in illegal building.

In July 1995 the establishment of the Palestinian Investment Company was announced, and a year later the Organization for the Development of the Old City was established. These two organizations, with the help of overseas Palestinian financial magnates, founded "The Jerusalem Development and Investments Foundation" with initial capital of $100 million, and began acquiring assets and land in East Jerusalem.[39] Concurrently, the Palestinian Authority set up a loans fund for encouraging building in the city.[40] The money was transferred through the Orient House to Palestinians who obtained municipal building permits. According to Feisal Husseini, about nine million dollars was distributed in 1997 for these loans.[41]

At the same time, Feisal Husseini began fund-raising through the "Jerusalem Foundation" set up by the King of Morocco in January 1995. Morocco's pledge of $500 million was not realized and Husseini only managed to raise some tens of million dollars. The Palestinians' weakness in raising funds and in acquiring assets and land led them to raise the penalty against land dealers. The prohibition against the sale of land to Israelis has been in force almost since 1967, and the Jordanian government was strict about bringing land dealers in Jerusalem and the West Bank to trial in Amman. In 1997, the Palestinian Legislative Council passed an explicit law on this subject, and religious leaders decreed a religious prohibition on these acts. The Palestinian cabinet determined that this transgression would lead to the imposition of the death penalty and instructed the General Intelligence Services to prevent these transactions. The General Intelligence Services located 16 land dealers, three of whom were murdered in 1997, and about a dozen others were arrested.

The Israeli policy of reducing the proportion of Arabs in the population was expressed in the planning and building laws, which prohibited or limited Arab building in most of the Arab neighborhoods. The demographic growth of the Arab population and housing shortage led to illegal construction, mainly in the north and the northeast parts of the city. Construction was carried out in Arab areas within and on the outskirts of the neighborhoods, as well as on reserves of vacant land between the Palestinian neighborhoods.[42] The Palestinian leadership welcomed the phenomenon and promised assistance to anyone whose home was destroyed by the authorities. In parallel, a legal department was opened in the Orient House, which dealt in filing court petitions against any intention to demolish homes.

In the 1980s and the 1990s the number of illegal buildings in East Jerusalem grew considerably. The figures are not exact, but the municipality estimates that this involved thousands of homes; the municipality has obtained demolition orders for about 1,000 of these, but their implementation has been impeded by repeated court hearings. Illegal construction by Jerusalem's Arabs causes planning and urban damage to the city. In the past decade, building has spread in northeastern Jerusalem and is liable to undermine Plan E1, which is designated by the municipality to link Ma'aleh Adumim to Jerusalem. In the north of the city, the illegal construction prevents territorial continuity from Neve Ya'akov to the northern Jewish neighborhoods and to the center of the city. Palestinian construction on the municipal borders of the city blurs the annexation lines and links East Jerusalem to the West Bank.[43] There is good reason why Ehud Olmhert, the Mayor of Jerusalem, has made the battle against illegal Arab construction his major rallying cry against the government's helplessness to control the phenomenon. "This is a cancer that now threatens Israel's sovereignty over Jerusalem," Olmhert claims, "and I intend to prepare for massive enforcement . . . the Palestinian Authority has infiltrated and spread into every area of life and the government tends to ignore it."[44]

According to data from "Ir Shalem"[45] and the Jerusalem municipality, between 1992 and 1997, 70 to 84 homes were demolished.[46] The demolition of homes ceased during the Barak administration, but in the Sharon government, the new Internal Security Minister, Uzi Landau, and the Mayor, Ehud Olmhert, have again declared their intention to destroy homes built illegally.

The Palestinians defined their policy in Jerusalem as one of "*Tzumud*" – steadfastly holding onto the city at any price. For this to succeed, they created a complex system of interdependence intended to benefit them in their dealings with the Israeli authorities. Their limited willingness for what Meron Benvenisti has called "a dialogue of actions" was characterized by their willingness to accept practical benefits from the authorities, without relinquishing the flavor of the resistance or the political boycott. For example, all the Arab residents of the city agreed to accept the status of resident and to hold an Israeli identity card, but only very few (6,000 out of 200,000) applied for Israeli citizenship. The Palestinians agreed, under protest, to pay municipal and government taxes, in order to avoid breaking the law, which could result in sanctions and the closing of their businesses. They worked in Israeli institutions in the western city in order to raise the level of their income and build new neighborhoods (which they call "settlements") in the eastern city, although they refused compensation for the expropriation of their lands on which these neighborhoods were built.

Concurrently, they created autonomous systems of health, transportation, education, economics, culture, and religion in order to strengthen their community and prevent its disintegration. They firmly refused to adopt patterns of Israelization similar to those of Israeli Arabs. Thus, for example, for almost two years they shut down the educational system in East Jerusalem, when Israel tried to force the Israeli Arab curriculum upon them. They refused to be subordinate to the Muslim-religious system of jurisdiction of the Kadi Kifo – the Ministry of Religion's official authority on Muslim matrimonial law in Israel. Their refusal led to Israel relinquishing the struggle on these and other issues, leaving them with considerable autonomy – far more than that enjoyed by Israeli Arabs.

Research examining the dimensions of separation and integration in politically mixed or polarized cities, points to Israel's failure to reinforce integration trends between Arabs and Jews in the city.[47] In the three aspects usually used to examine these trends – the socioeconomic, the spatial-geographic, and the political – Jerusalem compares badly with other polarized cities in the world. Social and economic interdependence is almost always the result of constraints and not of free choice. Partnerships and joint businesses do not exist beyond the ethnic boundary. There is almost a complete overlap between ethnic origin and social status, and there are virtually no social contacts or mixed marriages. Spatially, there is a notable separation in residences, businesses and services, as well as visually: extreme differences can be seen in the development level of the neighborhoods. As far as the institutional–political aspect is concerned, there is a noticeable institutional separation in almost every area of public life.

Israel's willingness to enable the institutional–political separation of Jerusalem Arabs began in the 1970s, the underlying assumption being that "Jordanization" was preferable to "Palestinization." Jordan's gradual withdrawal from the economic, social, cultural, and political nodes of influence in Jerusalem in the 1980s and the 1990s allowed the Palestinian Authority to penetrate these areas. The Shamir government's interest in developing independent Palestinian leadership in 1991, in light of the possibility of a political settlement on the West Bank, paradoxically strengthened the institutional–political attachment to the PLO and accelerated Palestinization processes. These processes came to a head in January 1996 when, for the first time in its history, elections were held in East Jerusalem for the Palestinian National Council. The Arab residents of the city were not only permitted to vote, but also to be elected to the legislative institutions and to the Palestinian government (the cabinet).

Vis-à-vis the Israeli strategy designed to abolish the previous border, the Palestinians adopted a counter-strategy to maintain it. The researchers Michael Romann and Alex Weingrod claim in their book that: "Since 1967 the national ethnic gap between the residents of both parts of the city has deepened to the point where a line has been created in their consciousness ... the crossing of which is perceived as dangerous ... The border created deep differentiation as well as different living arrangements and behavioral patterns on each side."[48]

The Policy of Containment: Strategy of Building the National Institutions – "The Capital in the Making"

The Palestinian struggle to build national institutions is to a large degree reminiscent of the institutional organizational patterns that were the legacy of the pre-state Jewish settlement in its struggle against British rule. These patterns have been especially prominent in Jerusalem and were expressed in the Palestinians' attempt during the 1990s to widen the autonomous institutional infrastructure that had been set up in the city in the 1970s and 1980s.

Even before the Oslo Agreements, in which Israel agreed not to interfere with and even to encourage the activities of the existing Palestinian organizations in East Jerusalem[49] – dozens of Palestinian institutions operated in East Jerusalem – such as the Labor Bureau, trade unions, workers' associations, charity organizations, and councils that assisted the population in various areas, such as housing, tourism, health, research institutes, colleges, newspapers, and cultural institutions. Furthermore, the

Palestinians had autonomy in the spheres of education, transportation, and religious institutions such as the Supreme Muslim Council, the Muslim *Waqf*, and the Sha'ari Court.[50]

All these constituted an organizational base and a legal precedent for the next stage, in which the Palestinians sought to institutionalize the national institutions in Jerusalem, which were meant to be the foundations for "the capital in the making." The first institution that developed from an academic research institute into a type of miniature "foreign ministry" was the "Orient House." In the heart of East Jerusalem, not far from the "American Colony" hotel, which served as the main meeting place for overseas journalists, Feisal Husseini founded the Society for Arabic Studies in 1979 as a center documenting the Palestinians' activities. In the 1980s, under this guise, Husseini worked toward coordinating support for the PLO in Jerusalem and, among others, to activate his supporters in the city and distribute money for various national goals. From March 1991 until the Declaration of Principles in 1993, the Israeli government agreed that the work of the "technical committees" – expert committees that prepared the position and the working papers of the Palestinian delegation to the bilateral and multilateral negotiations with Israel – would be coordinated there. Prime Minister Yitzhak Shamir permitted – in spite of criticism directed against him in the government on this issue by a number of ministers, Ariel Sharon among them – the Orient House to operate freely as the Palestinians' diplomatic center, in the hope that it would in time constitute a counterweight to the PLO in Tunis.[51]

From 1991 to the time that the PLO located itself in Gaza in June 1994, the Orient House operated as the PLO's unofficial political extension in Jerusalem. In the period between the Madrid Peace Conference and the Declaration of Principles between Israel and the Palestinians, about 47 political meetings took place at the Orient House from September 1993 to March 1995 with representatives of the United States, France, Britain, and Russia. Subjects relating to the negotiations were discussed and assistance agreements signed.[52] From the signing of the Oslo Agreements until the summer of 1995, the representatives of 29 additional countries visited the Orient House, including one prime minister, two deputy prime ministers, five foreign ministers, two deputy foreign ministers, nine ministers, and many ambassadors.[53] The Palestinian flag flies over the building.

The threats made by Palestinian extremists toward Husseini and his people because of their willingness to attend the Madrid Conference led Shamir's government to approve quasi security autonomy for the site. Palestinian security guards, who started protecting the Orient House against Palestinian extremists in the first stage, and against Jewish extremists at a later stage, constituted a precedent that led in 1994 to the entry of Jibril Rajub's Palestinian security forces to undertake policing activities in all parts of East Jerusalem. The Palestinian security personnel are perceived by the Palestinians as a symbol of Palestinian sovereignty over the site and do not permit the Israeli security and police forces to enter the area of the Orient House offices. An incident took place in 1996 when the Palestinian security personnel refused to allow the Israeli bodyguards of the Egyptian Foreign Minister and the Turkish Prime Minister to accompany them on their visit to the Orient House.

Gradually, national departments developed at the Orient House that took care of municipal issues, the obtaining permits to visit relatives in Arab countries, building and renovating schools, the economic development of the eastern city, as well as legal areas such as ruling in civil disputes and approving land transactions, while circumventing the Israeli legal system. The Orient House also coordinated national activity such as the elections to Palestinian Authority Council, the Palestinian Center of Statistics, and the Palestinian Authority's working papers on the subject of Jerusalem leading up to the talks on the permanent settlement in the city, in 2000.[54]

The Palestinian Authority's entry into Gaza reduced the need for the Orient House's diplomatic activity. Arafat's attempts to reduce the power of Husseini, who, in his opinion, had become too independent, led, at the end of the 1990s to the creation of Palestinian power centers in competition with the Orient House, such as the office of the Palestinian Governor of the Jerusalem District in Abu Dis and the national offices in Ramallah and Gaza. Following the Declaration of Principles between Israel and the Palestinians, which prevented East Jerusalemites from acting as part of the Palestinian Authority, Feisal Husseini was appointed as holder of the Jerusalem portfolio in the PLO Working Committee and not to the cabinet of the Palestinian Authority. This, of course, did not prevent him from enjoying ministerial status as a permanent participant in the cabinet meetings. He himself admitted that the Palestinians were seeking in this way to prevent Israel from legally ceasing activities at the Orient House.[55]

The activity of the Palestinian Security Forces in Jerusalem began in the middle of 1994 as part of the security accords following the Oslo Agreements. Similar to the Orient House affair – in which Prime Minister Shamir assumed that Israeli interests necessitated limited political activity – in the affair of the introduction of Palestinian security forces into East Jerusalem Prime Minister Yitzhak Rabin assumed that Israeli interests necessitated limited preventive security activity. In both cases, the Palestinians used Israeli consent for the loophole precedent and rapidly expanded the activity, so much so that the two prime ministers changed their minds and tried, unsuccessfully, to turn back the tide.

It should be mentioned that the main factor enabling the entry of Palestinian security personnel into the eastern city had to do with the results of the *Intifada* and not with the Oslo Agreements. As a result of the *Intifada*, Israel's control in East Jerusalem weakened, governmental and municipal bodies reduced their activities there, as did the Israeli police and the security forces. The *Intifada* resulted in the resignation of Palestinian policemen who had served on the Jerusalem police force, as well as made it difficult to recruit Palestinian agents and collaborators in the eastern city. For a long time the Jerusalem police force had avoided imposing law and order in East Jerusalem, which had led to an increase in crime and virtual anarchy in that part of the city.

In May and June 1994, the Palestinian security forces began operating in East Jerusalem. At first, they acted against local crime and arrested drug, sex, and prostitution offenders. They uncovered and returned stolen property to the Jerusalem police and operated an intelligence service throughout the eastern city. In the second stage, the security forces introduced a tourist police force whose task was mainly to prevent tourists from being robbed. An incentive was provided for the Palestinian tourism policemen by the churches, which paid part of their salaries and raised the average level of their pay above that of the Palestinian policemen in the territories of the Palestinian Authority. In the third stage, the Palestinian security forces began undertaking political activities, which included supervising the sermons in the Al-Aqsa mosque, registering residents of the eastern city going on the Haj to Mecca, and arresting and investigating elements opposed to Arafat. Thus, for example, they arrested the human rights activist Basam Id, and the journalist Daud Kutav, who expressed criticism and exposed incidents of corruption in the Palestinian Authority.[56]

During 1995, Rajoub's preventive security mechanisms operating in East Jerusalem were joined by personnel of the general intelligence commanded by Amin El Hindi, by the presidential security personnel, formerly Force 17, and by security personnel attached to the Governor of the Jerusalem region – Jamil Atman Nasser. In the first half of 1997, the general intelligence forces commenced operating against land dealers selling Palestinian land to Jews. In that same year, the Palestinian security forces had already become a visible and familiar part of East Jerusalem's scenery, and its residents saw in them a legitimate national mechanism that should be listened to and with whom they should cooperate.[57]

Attempts were made by the Rabin and Netanyahu governments to reduce the activities of the Palestinian national institutions and security forces in the eastern city following the signing of the Oslo B Agreements, which set clear restrictions on the activities of the Palestinian Authority in Jerusalem, and also in the wake of the Law for Implementing the Agreement with regard to the Gaza Strip and the Jericho Region (Limitation of Activity) that was passed by the Knesset on December 26, 1994. However, it was difficult to change the facts that had already been determined on the ground. The Likud government, which took office in 1996, continued its attempt to close the national institutions and stop the activity of the

Palestinian security forces. But it was no longer possible to turn the clock back and to stop the national activity in Jerusalem.

It was in both sides' interest – the Israelis and the Palestinians – not to turn the issue into a problem that would impede the peace progress or cause a flare-up that would exacerbate the situation in Jerusalem. The Palestinians thus responded by reducing the scale of the security activity by reducing the international profile of the Orient House's activities, and by closing some of the national offices. On the other hand, both the Rabin and the Netanyahu governments avoided such drastic measures as closing all the institutions and of completely discontinuing the activities of the security forces. The tacit arrangements between the Israeli government and the Palestinians were approved by the High Court of Justice, when at the end of January 1996 it dismissed a petition filed by the left-wing "Be'Tzedek" organization against the Israeli government for not striving to implement the Oslo Agreements and for allowing the Palestinians to operate in Jerusalem. The High Court preferred the state's claim of the need to exercise caution and sensitivity, which resulted in arrangements and compromises in this matter.[58]

By 1997 about twenty institutions of the Authority had been set up in East Jerusalem with the direct or indirect assistance of the Palestinian Authority. A security document leaked to the media named the institutions and their activity. The document stated:

> From the list of institutions, it appears that the Palestinian Authority is active in Jerusalem and exercises its authority there in a number of areas, from religious issues to energy and education.[59] This reflects the concerted efforts of the Authority to set up the infrastructure for an alternative government in the city and to undermine Israel's authority in Jerusalem.

Among the institutions listed in the document, in addition to the Orient House, the religious institutions and the security forces, are the offices of education, youth and sport; the office of mapping and geography administered by Halil Tofaqji that is preparing, among others, a list of Arab assets in the western city, which are currently worth billions of dollars;[60] the offices of the Palestinian Housing Council, among whose directors are the Authority's Minister of Justice and its Housing Minister; the Islamic National Committee for the Struggle Against the Settlements, located in the offices of the Mufti on the Temple Mount; the Institute for Palestinian Wounded, which provides for the needs of the disabled on the West Bank who were injured since 1936 (through 1948, 1967 and two *Intifadas*) in belligerent acts. The Palestinian Energy Center aspires to be, and took care to publish that it is "part of President Arafat's office."

In addition to the official offices, the Authority assisted in setting up non-governmental organizations (NGOs). In 1994 the cabinet of the Palestinian Authority passed a resolution to support these organizations as they contribute to the cohesion of civil society on the one hand, and, according to Allam Jarrar,[61] Vice-President of the Palestinian Council for Justice and Peace, to the struggle against the occupation, on the other. NGO bodies are also active in assisting the population in the areas of health, education, and culture. Of the 36 organizations in the West Bank, 18 operate in Jerusalem and they encompass hundreds of active members.[62]

Summary and Conclusions

In summary, it is appropriate to mention a number of theoretical, historical, and political lessons that emerge from the change that occurred in the political paradigm and in the renewed definition of the "Jerusalem problem." A new player does not change the policy paradigm. The networks and policy communities approach, in isolating the processes of change, emphasizes the *totality* of the changes in the status of *all* the players as a condition for change in the policy paradigm. From this we see that not only did the Palestinians' success in achieving their objectives lead to a change in the definition of the Jerusalem problem, but also that the totality of the changes in the positions and the situation of *all the players*, and perhaps Israel especially, is what led to the changes we have described.

The events and the circumstances connected to the approach adopted by the international community – and especially the Arab states and the United States – led to the problem being defined anew. As such the search for a solution was approached from different directions than had been the case in the past. From the moment that the problem was defined anew – as a national problem between Israel and the Palestinians – it is easier to explain the determination of the parties' national agenda and the policy tools chosen to achieve their objectives. Henceforth, the researcher only has to examine the extent to which the implementation strategy of the players matched their respective policy goals. The greater the match between the implementation strategies and the objectives, the better the anticipated results. The unwillingness or inability of the international community to force upon the two sides, Jordan and Israel, the international status of the city in 1948 brought about a change in the policy paradigm and a renewed definition of the "Jerusalem problem." It was transformed from an international problem to a political–territorial problem, and the international community's main interest lies in the desirable border demarcation between the two players who divided the city between themselves according to their military capability in the 1948 war.

Until 1967 the Zionist–Israeli approach was pragmatic, expressed by a willingness to relinquish Jerusalem in the 1930s and 1940s,[63] and to be content with the western part in the 1950s and 1960s. However in 1967 this approach was replaced by an uncompromising ideological approach expressed in the conception of the unity of the city.

An examination of the Israeli implementation strategy reveals gaps and contradictions between it and the specific objectives such as the demographic, the territorial, the economic, and the political. Thus, for example, a contradiction was created between the strategy of the territorial expansion of the city and the demographic objective, which sought to turn the city into a uni-national city with a large Jewish majority. The strategy of creating identity between the Arab population of the city and the West Bank Arabs, and granting autonomy in areas such as education, economics, transportation, and religious status contradicted the political objective of "Israelization" and led to the inevitable result of "Palestinization."

The Israeli ideological approach prevented the achievement of compromises that were possible with Jordan or with the Palestinians in the initial years. Two examples among many: The rejection by Prime Minister Golda Meir of the plan presented by the American Foreign Secretary Rogers in 1970. According to this plan, Jordan was to obtain limited political status in the eastern city and full control over the Islamic holy places on the Temple Mount. A second example: rejection of the proposal made by Sadat, Egypt's president, at the autonomy talks at the end of the 1970s for a separate Palestinian municipality (under Israeli sovereignty) in the eastern city, and Arab control (the Arab and the Muslim states) over the Temple Mount. The Arab Palestinian approach, which was ideological until the 1970s and demanded the whole of united Jerusalem under Arab–Jordanian sovereignty, had already been replaced by 1974 with a pragmatic approach. The expression of the pragmatic approach lies in the willingness to divide the city between Israel and the Palestinians according to the 1967 borders.

An examination of the Palestinian implementation strategy, as described in our work above, reveals congruence and continuity with their objectives. While the Israelis strive toward a resolution in terms of which "it is all mine" and seek the status of single player on the Jerusalem stage, the Palestinians' demands were more realistic, replacing the Jordanians' partner status with their own in the division of the city.

The strategies they chose matched their national claims for historical compromise in united Palestine and were expressed in the idea of two countries for two nations within the 1967 borders. The willingness of the international community, and especially the United States, to redefine the "Jerusalem problem" and to see Palestinians as partners with the Israelis in its division into two capitals constituted a strategic achievement whose importance is difficult to exaggerate. If to this we add the Palestinians' willingness on this issue at the beginning of the 1990s and at the Camp David conference in 2000, then the Palestinians' achievement has even greater significance.

From this it follows that not only the Palestinians' "success" or the Israelis' "failure" constitutes an explanation of the policy paradigm change. This change is an integrated result of circumstances and events in which many players took part. From Israel's point of view, the paradigm change was an informal admission of a new reality that was created in their capital: a reality of a bi-national city, divided between two nations, that seek it as their historical, religious, and political capital.

Notes

1 Frank Baumgartner, "Independent and Politicized Communities: Education and Nuclear Energy in France and in the United States," *Governance*, Vol. 2, No. 1 (1989), pp. 42–66. See also William D. Coleman and Grace Skogstad, "Policy Communities and Policy Networks: A Structural Approach," in William D. Coleman and Grace Skogstad (eds.), *Policy Communities and Public Policy in Canada* (Toronto: Copp. Clark, Pitman, 1990). ch. 1, pp. 15–31.

2 Deborah A. Stone, "Causal Stories and the Formation of Policy Agendas," *Political Science Quarterly*, 104 (2) (1989), pp. 281–301. See also David Dery, *Problem Definition in Policy Analysis* (Lawrence, KS: University Press of Kansas, 1984); Janet A. Weiss, "The Power of Problem Definition: The case of government paperwork," *Policy Sciences*, 22, (1989), pp. 97–121; and Ann Schneider and Helen Ingram, "Social construction of target populations: Implications for politics and policy," *American Political Science Review*, 87, (1993), pp. 334–47.

3 Michael Howlett, "Policy Instruments, Policy Styles and Policy Implementation: National Approaches to Theories of Instrument Choice," *Policy Studies Journal*, Vol. 19, No. 2, (1991), pp. 1–21. See also S. Linder and Guy Peters, "Instruments of Government: Perceptions and Contexts," *Journal of Public Policy*, Vol. 9(1), (1989), pp. 35–8; and David Rochefort and Roger W. Cobb, "Problem Definition: An Emerging Perspective," in Rochefort, David and Roger W. Cobb (eds.), *The Politics of Problem Definition: Shaping the Policy Agenda* (Lawrence: University of Kansas, 1994), pp. 1–31.

4 Fritz W. Scharpf, "Decision Rules, Decision Styles and Policy Choices," *Journal of Theoretical Politics,* Vol. 1, No. 2, (1989), pp. 149–76.

5 On the attitude of the Zionist movement, which from its beginnings was conflicted about the city's place in the national list of priorities, see Moti Golani, "Zionism Without Zion? Position of the Yishuv's Leaderships and the State of Israel on the Jerusalem Question – 1947–1949," in Avi Bareli, ed., "Divided Jerusalem," *Idan 18* (Jerusalem: Yad Ben-Zvi, 1994).

6 Yehoshafat Harkabi, ed., *Arabia and Israel, 3–4: Resolutions of the Palestinian National Councils* (Tel Aviv: Am Oved, 1975), [in Hebrew].

7 Menachem Klein, *Doves in Israeli Skies – the Peace Process and the City* (Jerusalem: Jerusalem Institute for Israeli Studies, 1999), p. 37; and Arnon Yuval and Ohana Arie, *PLO – Portrait of an Organization* (Tel Aviv: Ma'ariv Publishers, 1985), p. 30.

8 The Islamic rejection movement – the *Hamas* – expresses most noticeably the fundamentalist approach with regard to Jerusalem, and views the whole

of Palestine, and in any event the whole of Jerusalem, as a religious unit. Palestinian lands are Islamic *Waqf* (religious trust) of every generation of Muslims to the end of days; they cannot be relinquished in whole or in part. See Paz Reuven, *The Islamic Covenant and Its Significance: Data and Analysis*, (Tel Aviv: Dayan Center, Tel Aviv University, 1988). Furthermore, the *Hamas* views Palestine as "Greater Jerusalem" and the land of Palestine is known as "Al Asra'ah" (the night journey) land and as "Al Ma'araj" (the ascent to heaven), traditional concepts according to which Mohammad rose to heaven from Jerusalem. This perception parallels the religious Jewish perception, which believes that Jerusalem is destined to expand and envelop the whole Land of Israel as "Eretz Zion Ve'Yerushalayim" [Land of Zion and Jerusalem].

9   In a meeting I held with Haled El Hasan in February 1990, in Stockholm, he expressed his regret that the Israelis' rejectionist approach to the idea of the secular democratic state had forced the Palestinians to compromise and agree to two states existing side by side. He especially criticized the approach of dividing Jerusalem into two cities, which he sees as a political necessity but also an expression of the two nations' lack of wisdom. "It is similar," he said to me "to a person who has a special, large, and precious stone made from all the precious stones in the world, and he has to share it with his friend. If they divide it, both will lose its quality and uniqueness; if they keep it jointly, they will be able to show it proudly to the whole world. The same applies to Jerusalem, which could have been a symbol of reconciliation between nations, a model for imitation by polarized cities and national conflicts, if the sides would be prepared to say: It is ours, instead of saying: It is mine."

10   On July 24, 1967, twenty-two Palestinian leaders on the West Bank signed a petition which stated that Arab Jerusalem is "an integral part of Jordan . . . annexation of Arab Jerusalem is an invalid act that the occupation authorities unilaterally enforced against the will of the residents of the city who oppose this annexation and believe in the unity of the Jordanian homeland. See Meron Benvenisti, *A Place of Fire* (Tel Aviv: Dvir Publishers, 1996), p. 216.

11   The strategies with regard to Jerusalem are somewhat parallel to the national strategies adopted by the Palestinians in their national struggle. These strategies are expressed in the Proclamation of Independence that the Chairman of the PLO Arafat read at the 19th session of the Palestinian National Council in Algiers on November 15, 1988. It contains two spheres of reference. The Israeli sphere involves strategies of linkage and struggle, whereas the international sphere calls for strategies of attaining recognition of the Palestinians' national rights, and putting pressure on Israel to accept the principle of the division of the land into two countries under Resolution 181 of November 1947. See Anne Lantadris, *Palestinian Resistance and Urban Change in Jerusalem – 1967–1994*, (Pessia: The Palestinian Academic Association for International Affairs, 1995), (Arabic). Lantadris also mentions two policy spheres: the international sphere – with the recognition of the countries of the world, and especially the Arab world, of the Palestinian people's rights to Jerusalem; and the policy sphere toward Israel – which mentions the resistance strategies, containment of the Israelis, and building an infrastructure of autonomous national institutions.

12 On segregation processes, escalation of political confrontation in the city, and Palestinization of the Arab minority that led, contrary to Israeli policy, to linking East Jerusalem to the West Bank. See Meron Benvenisti, *Facing a Sealed Wall* (Tel Aviv: Wiedenfeld and Nickelson, 1973); Meron Benvenisti, *A Place of Fire* (Tel Aviv: Dvir Publishers, 1996); Michael Romann, *Reciprocity Between the Jewish and Arab Sectors in Jerusalem* (Jerusalem: Jerusalem Institute for Israeli Studies, 1989); Shmuel Berkovitz, *Problem of the Holy Places* (Jerusalem: Jerusalem Institute for Israeli Studies, 2000); Moshe Amirav, *Israel's Policy in Jerusalem Since 1967* (Jerusalem: Municipality Publishers, 1992).

13 White paper 5479, Peel Commission, 1937, Section 10, official translation as presented by Benvenisti, 1996.

14 American Foreign Policy (1967), *Near and Middle East*, Doc. VII-52.

15 Shlomo Slonim, "The United States and the Status of Jerusalem," in *Israel Law Review*, Vol. 19, No. 2 (1984), p. 216.

16 Geoffrey W. Watson, "The Jerusalem Embassy Act of 1995," *The Catholic University of American Law Review*, Vol. 45, No. 3 (1996), pp. 841–3.

17 The Israeli and the American proposals are from publications in the press and from personal discussions the author held with members of the Israeli delegation and with government policy-makers.

18 On the Israeli and Palestinian strategy regarding Jerusalem in Camp David, see Menachem Klein, *Breaking the Taboo – Negotiations for a Permanent Settlement on Jerusalem* (Jerusalem: Jerusalem Institute for Israeli Studies, 2001).

19 On April 12, 1950 the Arab League decided to prohibit the annexation of parts of Palestine by any of the states in the region; the possibility was even considered at that time of expelling Jordan from the League. See Moshe Hirsh, Dvorah Hausen-Kuriel, and Ruth Lapidot, *Where To Jerusalem? Proposal Regarding the City's Future* (Jerusalem: Jerusalem Institute for Israel Studies, 1994).

20 Menahem Klein, *Jerusalem in Negotiations for Peace – Arab Positions* (Jerusalem: Jerusalem Institute for Israeli Studies, 1995).

21 Sela Avraham, *Unity Within a Divide, Arab Summit Conferences* (Jerusalem: Magnes Publications, 1983), p. 259.

22 Sassar Asher, "Hussein's Position Regarding the Future of the West Bank," *The New East* (1979), p. 28; and Klein, (1999), p. 27.

23 *Palestine El Taura,* June 4, 1989.

24 *Ha'aretz,* June 10, 1990; September 28, 1990; June 1, 1994; July 13, 1994; July 20, 1994; July 26, 1994; July 27, 1994; November 16, 1994; December 16, 1994; December 20, 1994; December 22, 1994; July 11, 1995; August 15, 1995; October 27, 1995; July 28, 1995; January 30, 1996; February 9, 1996; February 27, 1997; May 25, 1997; May 26, 1997; June 2, 1997; July 3, 1997; July 4, 1997; February 10, 1998; June 4, 1998; June 17, 1998.

25 *Davar*, November 2, 1994.

26 See *al-Quds,* December 16, 1994 and March 2, 1998; *Ha'aretz,* July 27, 1994 and December 22, 1994.

27 On Israel's policy in Jerusalem see: Amirav, *"Ha'aretz,"* August 1, 1991; Amirav, *"Ha'aretz,"* June 23, 1994; as well as Moshe Amirav, *Israel and*

Palestine Political Report (Paris, No. 201, 1992); Amir Chechin, Bill Hutman, and Avi Melamed, *Separate and Unequal* (Cambridge, MA: Harvard University Press, 1999); and Michael Romann, *The Israeli Establishment in East Jerusalem – Arrangements and Lessons Learned* (Jerusalem: Jerusalem Institute for Israeli Studies, 1995).

28 Subsequently expelled because of his activities on behalf of Jordan, he joined the Palestinian organizations and was later elected as Chairman of the Palestinian National Council.

29 Benvenisti (1973), p. 262.

30 According to Ministry of the Interior data, by the late 1990s only 6,000 out of 200,000 Arabs in East Jerusalem have applied for and received Israeli citizenship. Participation in the municipal elections was as follows: 1978 – 14.4 percent; 1983 – 18.4 percent; during the period of the *Intifada* in 1989, the percentage fell to 2.7 percent; and in 1993 stood at 7 percent (Benvenisti, 1996).

31 Meron Benvenisti, *The Bullet and the Club* (Tel Aviv: Kav Adom Publications, 1998).

32 *Ha'aretz*, September 28, 1990.

33 For a detailed discussion see I. Zilberman, *The Palestinian Uprising (Intifida) in Jerusalem, Initial Research Report*, Jerusalem (1998); Michael Romann, "The Effect of the *Intifada* on Jewish–Arab Relations in Jerusalem," *The New East*, 34 (1992), p. 162.

34 Ami Elad, "The Sacredness of the City of Jerusalem in *Intifada* Literature," in Aharon Leish, ed., *The Arabs in Jerusalem* (Jerusalem Institute for Israeli Studies, 1992), pp. 151–61.

35 Dr. Erikat, member of the Palestinian delegation to the talks with Israel, in an interview to the El-Arab staff, Cairo Radio, November 8, 1993, as quoted in Klein (1999), p. 113.

36 Cecilia Albin, *The Conflict Over Jerusalem: Some Palestinian Responses to Concepts of Dispute Resolution* (Jerusalem: PASSIA, 1990).

37 The number of Arabs in Jerusalem in 1967 was 64,000 – 25.8 percent of the population. In 1999, the number of Arabs in the city was 209,500 – 32.4 percent of the overall population.

38 Data from the *Jerusalem Statistical Yearbooks* for those years.

39 Klein (1999), p. 202.

40 *"Kol Ha'ir" [City Voice]*, February 9, 1996; March 7, 1997; April 11, 1997.

41 *Ha'aretz*, June 17, 1998.

42 *Ha'aretz*, June 10, 1990; July 3, 1997; July 4, 1997.

43 Klein (1999), p. 207.

44 *Ha'aretz*, June 2, 1997.

45 Ir Shalem, *"Easter Jerusalem: Planning Situation,"* Jerusalem (1998).

46 *Ha'aretz*, June 4, 1998.

47 On comparative separation trends in Jerusalem, see: Meron Benvenisti, *Jerusalem – City with a Wall in its Center* (Hakibbutz Hameuchad: Kav Adom Publishers, 1981); Michael Romann, "Integration and Separation in the Relations Between the Jewish and Arab Sectors in Jerusalem – Methodological Test," in *City and Region*, No. 19 (Jerusalem: Jerusalem Institute of Israeli Studies, 1989); and Scott A. Bollens, "On Narrow Ground – Urban Policy and

Ethnic Conflict," in *Jerusalem and Belfast* (New York: State University of New York, 2000).

48 Michael Romann and Alex Weingrod, *Living Together Separately, Arabs and Jews in Contemporary Jerusalem* (Princeton: Princeton University Press, 1991).

49 *Ha'aretz*, June 4, 1998.

50 One of Arafat's conditions for signing the Oslo Agreement was Israel's promise not to close any of the Palestinian institutions in Jerusalem. The promise is contained in Foreign Minister Peres's letter to the Norwegian Foreign Minister Holst. See Klein (1999), p. 109.

51 Sami F. Musalam, *The Struggle for Jerusalem: A Programme of Action for Peace* (Jerusalem: PASSIA, 1996), p. 60; and Klein (1999).

52 Mabat L'Shalom, "A View to Peace," *Ha'aretz*, July 13, 1994.

53 *Ha'aretz*, August 15, 1995.

54 Klein (1999), p. 132; *Ha'aretz*, December 16, 1994; December 20, 1994; Mabat L'Shalom (1995).

55 *Ha'aretz*, February 9, 1996; Kol Ha'ir, February 9, 1996.

56 *Ha'aretz*, November 16, 1994; November 20, 1994; May 25, 1997; May 26, 1997; Kol Ha'ir, March 7, 1997.

57 *Ha'aretz*, February 27, 1997; February 10, 1998; Klein (1999), p. 140.

58 *HCJ rulings 2142/95*, Volume 49, Fifth Part (5755–5756, 1995); and *Ha'aretz*, January 20, 1996. On the struggle between the Palestinians and the Rabin and Netanyahu governments concerning the activities of the Palestinian institutions and security forces in East Jerusalem, see the detailed and exhaustive review of Klein (1999), pp. 185–91.

59 *Ha'aretz*, February 12, 1997; September 9, 1998.

60 *Yediot Aharonot* (Tel Aviv weekly magazine) March 15, 1996.

61 Jarrar Allam, *Israel and Palestine Political Report*, Paris, No. 201 (1998).

62 See: Jarrar Allam, "Palestinian NGO's Directory" (1998) – http://www.people.org./ngos./plngo/htm.

63 See Golani (1994), pp. 32–3.

CHAPTER 25

Demarcating Jerusalem's Borders

MENACHEM KLEIN

Many Israelis tend to support the conclusion that peace has to be carried out by the peoples and between the peoples of the formerly hostile nations – that the mission of peace building should be undertaken by various extra-establishment elite groups, i.e., professionals, academics, NGOs etc. They prefer adopting the bottom-up approach rather than the top-down strategy, whereby governments build peace negotiating directly, or through back-channel diplomacy when public negotiations have broken down. Then, the mission of peace building is taken by various extra-establishment elite groups, i.e., professionals, academics, NGOs etc. My argument is that peace should be found first and foremost by elite groups, mainly political leaders. This is demonstrated by the lessons of what Israelis call "co-existence" in Jerusalem and what the Palestinians deem the Israeli occupation.

It is the responsibility of political leaders to tell their people what the options are, as well as their consequences. Political leaders must be ready to tell their people the truth. The Israeli government, however, is acting on the assumption that public opinion will not tolerate any compromise on Jerusalem. And if the Israeli leadership is unwilling to make any compromises on Jerusalem, this will lead to a breakdown of the entire peace process.

The need to formulate a comprehensive approach to the question of Jerusalem has become starkly evident. Jerusalem can no longer be left "until the end" if there is to be progress in the peace negotiations as a whole. Past experience of Israel–PLO negotiations shows that it is important to be able to maneuver among questions of differing degrees of importance. The greater the number of such issues, the greater the leeway for bargaining in the negotiations. Most important is that without addressing the question of Jerusalem it will be impossible to reach agreement on other issues on the agenda.[1]

The Limits of Israeli Unilateral Deeds

Israel has ruled Jerusalem for a longer period than Britain did (1918–48), and for almost twice as long as the Jordanians (1949–67). In historical perspective, Israel has chalked up quite a few achievements in the city. The most prominent of these is the fact that it is now impossible to return to the reality that prevailed there before the 1967 war.

In 1967, in the wake of the Six Day War, Israel annexed East Jerusalem and extended the municipal borders of the city as a whole. The annexed territory included not only the Jordanian city, which covered 6.5 square kilometers, but also an additional 64.4 square kilometers of West Bank villages and some lands belonging to Bethlehem and Beit Jala. In doing so, the Israeli government turned two peripheral cities – the Jordanian city and the Israeli city, which itself covered 38.1 square kilometers – into the country's largest city, with an area of 108.5 square kilometers. In 1993 the city's territory was enlarged even further, to 126.4 square kilometers. Up until then both cities had lain at the end of narrow corridors. The Jordanian city had been a peripheral city, far from the capital in Amman and under its sway. The Israeli capital was located at the end of the Jerusalem corridor, a narrow strip of land that linked it to the coastal plain and to the rest of the country.[2]

Demographic considerations have shaped Israeli policy in East Jerusalem since 1967. The Israeli establishment has invested vast resources in an effort to maintain a demographic balance that would ensure stability over time of the situation existing at the time of annexation: 74.2 percent Jews vs. 25.8 percent Arabs. Paradoxically, however, the annexation momentum has had the effect of increasing the Palestinian presence in East Jerusalem. At the end of 1998 the demographic balance stood at 68.4 percent Jews and 30.9 percent Arabs. Israel's effort over the past 33 years to tilt the demographic balance in the city increasingly in its favor has failed, despite building housing for Jews on a massive scale and limiting Arab building rights.

Over the years, 34 percent of East Jerusalem's territory has been expropriated while 56 percent of the remaining areas have been designated green open spaces. All that remains for the Palestinian sector is 14 percent. Between 1967 and 1994 a total of 24.8 square kilometers of land was expropriated, out of a total of 70.5 square kilometers that was annexed by Israel in 1967.[3] From 1967 to 1997 there was public construction of 38,350 housing units for Jews on more than 25 percent of the area of East Jerusalem that was expropriated from Arabs, while not a single apartment for Arabs was built on this land. Only 8,890 housing units were built for Arabs during this period, constituting only 12 percent of total construction in the city, of which only 600 were public housing units for Arabs, which had been built at the beginning of the 1970s.[4] At the beginning of the 1990s the Arab public in Jerusalem suffered from a shortage of some 20,000 housing units.[5]

Moreover, zoning plans have been completed for only 39 percent of the 45.5 square kilometers that were left under Arab ownership in East Jerusalem after the expropriations. Since 1967 there has been no general master plan for the Arab city, and this makes it difficult for Palestinians to obtain building permits. Up until the 1980s ad hoc building permits were granted, and since then neighborhood zoning plans have been prepared. Yet there is no master plan integrating the East Jerusalem neighborhoods into the municipal system that answers the needs of the population on the super-neighborhood level. Only 7.3 percent of the area of East Jerusalem is in practice available for construction for Palestinians. The available land lies largely in built-up areas and is concentrated in a region defined geographically as "northeast." In terms of available housing units, it is generally permitted to build only one or two floors, so according to the approved plans it is possible to add less than 5,000 housing units.[6] A low construction density has been set in the building plans for East Jerusalem, out of design considerations and out of a desire to preserve its village character, and out of political and demographic considerations in order to limit the population of the eastern city.[7]

The average housing density in East Jerusalem is 2.21 housing units per dunam (1/4 acre), as opposed to 6.1 units in Jewish areas. In 1995 the average housing density in East Jerusalem was twice as high as in West Jerusalem – 2.1 people per room in the Arab sector as opposed to 1.1 in the Jewish sector. In East Jerusalem, 27.8 percent of the Arabs live in homes where there are three or more people per room, as opposed to only 2.4 percent in Jewish Jerusalem.[8] The conclusion is that the residents of East Jerusalem are relatively rich in land, but poor in floor space.[9]

Israel's attempts to reverse this trend of demographic development by confiscating Palestinians' ID cards, depriving Palestinians of residency rights in the city, and demolishing illegally built houses within the city and in the metropolitan region have only demonstrated the non-viability of this approach. Israel estimated that between 50,000 and 80,000 of East Jerusalem's 180,000 inhabitants had moved to the suburbs outside the Jerusalem city limits, although their lives continued to be centered on Jerusalem.[10] By law, as upheld by the Supreme Court, permanent residence status terminates automatically if the holder of the document remains outside Israel for seven years, even if he makes brief visits.[11] According to the Palestinians, Israel used these measures to confiscate some 4,000 identity cards.[12] Israel reported that between 1967 and 1996 the residence status of 3,874 people had expired, including those who had moved from Jerusalem to other countries.[13] In the period from the beginning of 1996 to the summer of 1999 the residence status of another 2,711 people was revoked,[14] of which only about 200 were Jerusalem residents who had moved into the suburbs; most of them lived outside the West Bank.[15]

In the final analysis, Israel's policy accomplished little, since it brought about no change in Jerusalem's demographic balance. On the contrary, under the new policy between 20,000 and 30,000 residents of the suburbs returned to live in Jerusalem in harsh housing conditions so as not to lose their Israeli identity cards and their residence rights. The demand for housing rose and prices spiraled upwards, housing density increased, and housing and living conditions worsened.[16] Demographic growth and the shortage of housing and land for the residents of East Jerusalem led to large-scale illegal construction in the Jerusalem area,[17] especially in the city's north and northeast, on vacant land separating the Palestinian neighborhoods. Arab construction is spontaneous private construction, not planned from above by the local or national leaderships,[18] although both welcomed the phenomena.

Since 1997, the Palestinian Authority has attempted to encourage housing construction by issuing its own building permits in the Zone B areas of the Jerusalem district. A total of 1,777 such permits have been issued thus far, in response to 2,977 official requests. It is reasonable to assume that the actual number of Palestinians seeking permits is even larger.[19] Such construction created contiguity between the Arab neighborhoods in the city's north, preventing them from remaining isolated islands surrounded by Jewish neighborhoods and connecting them with Ramallah. Palestinian construction tightens East Jerusalem's links to Palestinian Authority, blurs Israel's annexation lines, and even threatens to surround and isolate some of the Jewish neighborhoods in the city's east.

To battle illegal construction, the Ministry of the Interior and the Jerusalem municipality adopted a policy of demolishing illegal buildings at various stages of construction, such as skeleton, foundations, and the expansion of existing buildings. The relation between the implemented demolition orders and the number of building violations identified by the municipality is as much as about 8 percent according to Ir Shalem's data, and about 4 percent according to municipal figures.[20] In addition, Israel's civil administration has carried out demolitions in the West Bank suburbs of Jerusalem. Between July 1997 and July 1998 the Civil Administration demolished 29 structures in the Jerusalem area, about half of the total number of demolitions in the West Bank as a whole.[21]

Undivided Area

The principle of non-partition of the city by means of border barriers has become part of the international consensus, and is also accepted by Arafat. In a statement made in Stockholm at an event marking the tenth anniversary of the PLO's recognition of Israel and condemnation of terror,

Arafat set out the guiding principles for a permanent settlement. With regard to Jerusalem he stated that the city should remain open

> to all its inhabitants without prejudice. The city must remain physically undivided by roadblocks and fortifications. There is no solution to the Jerusalem question unless the interests of all sides are taken into account, together with standing firm on halting the Judaization of Jerusalem and the preservation of the rights of all communities and of adherents of all the monotheistic faiths equally.[22]

The Palestinian dependence on the income generated in the western part of the city is another reason for preserving an open city. The incomes of Jerusalem's Arabs are affected by its being an open city. The openness enables the movement of tourists through both sides of the city and also creates a mutual economic dependence between unequal elements. The strong Israeli side needs Arab manual laborers, and the Arabs are dependent on their incomes from their work places in West Jerusalem. The daily income in the Palestinian district of Jerusalem is also higher than in the rest of the West Bank and Gaza Strip; in 1997 this was NIS (New Israeli Shekels) 82.6 in Jerusalem as opposed to NIS 61 elsewhere.[23] Moreover, the health and welfare services that the residents of East Jerusalem receive from Israel leave them with more available income than the Palestinians who live under the Palestinian Authority. Even though the inhabitants of East Jerusalem constitute only 8.6 percent of the Palestinian population in the West Bank and Gaza Strip, the national income per person in East Jerusalem is 55 percent higher than in the West Bank and 70 percent higher than in the Gaza Strip; it is, however, some 20 percent lower than that in Israel.[24]

Indices of local product also underline the economic dependence of Arab Jerusalem on Jewish Jerusalem. The gross local product in the Palestinian district of Jerusalem is more than 13 percent higher than the gross local product in the rest of the Palestinian districts.

Furthermore, the fact that about 50 percent of the city's residents live in what was the Jordanian ruled area renders any idea of evacuating the new Jewish neighborhoods blatantly infeasible. However, the possibility of leaving them under Palestinian sovereignty is equally problematic. What character would the capital of Palestine have if half of its inhabitants were Israelis? The unavoidable solution is to bring about Palestinian agreement to annex these new neighborhoods to West Jerusalem. This should be part and parcel of a process of "give and take," not a coercive act by the stronger party.

Obligations will be mutual and adopted freely, and mandate the imposition of limitations on sovereignty in Jerusalem. Just as no return is possible to the situation of June 4, 1967, it is equally impossible to turn the annexation lines of June 27, 1967 into a permanent border. Though the common wisdom in Israel is that the permanent borders of the city will be those fixed in the 1967 annexation, whoever examines the situation on the ground will see that this is simply impossible. The criteria by which Israel determined the annexation boundary are no longer valid or relevant. From its status in 1967 as a city at the dead end of a land corridor, a "cul de sac" city or two "cul de sac" cities, Jerusalem has become a metropolitan area. Small Arab villages that were not included in the annexation for demographic reasons such as Abu Dis or al-Azariyeh have become integrated into the urban/suburban grid. East Jerusalem functions as an urban and political center and provides income and services for a larger population that resides outside the municipal boundaries. In short, both boundary lines of June 1967 belong to history, not the present. The current municipal boundaries not only make no sense functionally, but will also have to bend to political realities that have emerged following the implementation of Oslo Agreements. The need now is to redraw the city's boundaries, not least because the present boundaries arbitrarily divide most of neighborhoods in the eastern part of the city.

Initially, Israeli–Palestinian agreement is required regarding the criteria for the new demarcation. I personally believe that the boundaries should be expanded and adapted to the scale of the developments over the past 33 years. This promising direction should be undertaken cautiously, not unilaterally by the dominant Israeli side but in cooperation with the Palestinian partner, while demonstrating consideration for the various lines that currently crisscross the city. The Jerusalem area is fragmented along ethnic–national, demographic, functional, political and metropolitan lines.

Despite the tremendous efforts and massive investments of funds and resources, Jerusalem remains a divided city shared by two peoples with different cultures, different heritages intertwined but disparate economies, conflicting collective agendas, and contrasting national aspirations. Israel has not succeeded in breaking down the religious, national, and ethnic dividing lines between the principal populations in the eastern city. The new Jewish neighborhoods are functionally part of West Jerusalem, while East Jerusalem is an Arab city. The residents of the Arab neighborhoods enjoy the benefit of a road system that links them to West Jerusalem while circumventing the Arab-populated areas. The Arab inhabitants naturally need a separate road system to link them with their compatriots, fellow Arabic speakers, and co-religionists. Geographically and topographically, the Jewish presence beyond the June 4, 1967 borders is massive and dominant and expresses ownership. For Israel, Jerusalem has been acquired through construction, but Israel's success is only partial. The two populations on the eastern side of the city do not mix, nor is the minority assimilating into the majority.

While viewing Jerusalem not only from visionary heights but also from sidewalk-level, one might identify the following five soft lines dividing Jerusalem:

1. The ethnic–national boundary between Israeli-Jews and Palestinian-Arabs. This boundary penetrates the Eastern city, with the Israeli-Jews living there either in separate neighborhoods or in isolated enclaves inside massively Arab populated areas. The ethnic-national boundaries also run along West Jerusalem where many blue collar Palestinians work under Israeli employers.

2. The municipal boundary. This is also a political boundary, since it is the boundary of the Israeli unilateral annexation. It divides the State of Israel and the PA and the occupied territories.

3. The functional border or the boundaries of the metropolitan area within which east and west parts of the city function separately as urban centers. The centers provide services, sources of income, working places etc. to both the city residents and to those living in Jerusalem's suburbs outside the municipal boundaries. The Israeli building boom in Jerusalem and the rights that the annexation granted to its residents have turned the city for the Palestinians living on its periphery into a focal point of employment, commerce, services, communications, and political activity. Even though Israel's annexation is very much questionable under international law,[25] daily life has functionally expanded the city's borders, and they are so perceived as borders by Israelis, as well as by most Palestinians, especially those who live in Jerusalem.[26]

4. In the annexed eastern city there are certain unofficial functional arrangements dividing actual authority and local services between Jews and Arabs. Culturally, linguistically and religiously, the identity of East Jerusalem's inhabitants is Muslim or Christian Arab. Their spatial identity is unique and manifestly distinct from that of Jerusalem's Jewish inhabitants. Culturally and religiously, it is not only the Muslim religious institutions that create the different character of East Jerusalem. Businesses and commercial establishments are open and public transportation functions on the Jewish Sabbath and holidays, in glaring contrast to the situation in Jewish Jerusalem. On the symbolic level, sovereignty is expressed by the simple fact that the inhabitants of East Jerusalem bear Israeli identity cards. The practical side is the benefits, payments, and services that the holders of Israeli ID cards receive, alongside the obligations and payments imposed on them. An Israeli ID card brings with it a variety of benefits inasmuch as it implies official affiliation with Israel. These benefits include the right to vote in municipal elections, social benefits, health and welfare payments (at an average of $354 per person per year in 1999 prices) from Israel's social security system,

residential rights in Jerusalem, freedom of movement into and out of the city in times of closure, freedom of employment and movement inside and outside the city Jewish Jerusalem. However, it is important to distinguish between the "strong," full symbolic identity of citizens of Israel and the "weak" symbolic identity of the residents who are not citizens. Holding a resident ID card creates only a "weak" symbolic link with Israel. The Israeli resident status of East Jerusalem Palestinians establishes nothing about their political ties or their national identity.[27]

5. The Oslo II agreement also introduced the categories and definitions of Zones B and C into the Jerusalem area. The Oslo Agreements prohibit, at Israel's insistence, the Palestinian Authority from operating in Jerusalem, but from the Palestinians' point of view, Zones B and C, and even more so the Palestinian cities in Zone A, are a subject to which East Jerusalem can be attached in discussions about the permanent settlement. However, the Oslo II lines were intended to be temporary, make it difficult for the inhabitants of the Arab space, which from an urban point of view had previously functioned as a single unit, to live as they used to live. In Al-Sawahra, for example, the border between Israeli Jerusalem and the Palestinian district of Jerusalem runs straight through the neighborhood. Ever since May 1994 when Israel and the Palestinian Authority began implementing the Oslo Agreements, the political map within Jerusalem and its environs has changed. Until 1994 there was a single border as far as Israel was concerned, the annexation boundary, which was also, the Jerusalem municipal limits. The establishment of the Palestinian Authority and its penetration into Jerusalem has made the Jerusalem political border complex. The entrance of the Palestinian Authority into the cities bordering on Jerusalem to the south – Bethlehem – and to the north – Ramallah – have restricted the metropolitan functions of East Jerusalem and the space it occupies.

The closure line is not simply a municipal boundary but also a political one, marking the area of Israeli sovereignty in Jerusalem. The damage the closure has caused to the Palestinian status of East Jerusalem serves the purposes of the Israeli government. While it was not imposed for this purpose, the longer it has lasted the more the Palestinians have come to perceive this as the major reason for its persistence. True, East Jerusalem has not reversed its linkage to nor its desire to become part of the Palestinian Authority and has not accepted the Israeli annexation, but its connections with the Palestinian hinterland have been attenuated and have become more difficult than they have been in the past, because of the closure. The pressure on the Arab inhabitants of Jerusalem has increased and they have found themselves caught between, on the one side, the annexation line and the closure that has cut them off from the West Bank, and on the other side the national–ethnic line that divides the city.

In conclusion, there are several boundaries in Jerusalem, as opposed to one deep rift line. Theoretically, many boundaries might exacerbate a conflict and encourage deterioration, even bloodshed. Since Jerusalem's different boundaries overlap only partly, the variety helps to moderate the conflict and to create flexible, soft, and permeable boundaries in Jerusalem. Thus the key questions are first, how and secondly who may make use of this type of boundaries in order to promote peace and build confidence? Institutionalizing this situation will create the possibility of maneuvering among the different types of boundaries, and will contribute to the resolution of the issue of sovereignty.

Irreversible Realities

The Arabs of East Jerusalem are not Israeli citizens but only permanent residents. In other words, about a third of the inhabitants of Israel's capital city do not recognize it as such and reject Israeli citizenship. In comparisons with Jerusalem's non-Zionist ultra-orthodox Jews, the latter legitimize the State of Israel, enjoy its citizenship, and contribute to its self-determination as a Jewish state. The Arabs in East Jerusalem, on the other hand, are neither Israeli citizens nor Jews. The hope that the Arabs of East Jerusalem will become Israeli Arabs is a pipe dream. A whole series of differences distinguishes the Arab population in the Galilee and the Negev in 1948 from the population in East Jerusalem in 1967. Furthermore, the developments that have taken place in each of the two population groups since 1967 are radically different: Israelization vs. Palestinization.

When, in 1948, Israel conquered areas in which there were large numbers of resident Arabs, the population was largely a rural one scattered over a large area. Beyond this geographic aspect, and the low level of urbanization and modernization that characterized this population, the Palestinian population of 1948 lacked a political leadership and autonomous institutions that functioned more or less properly. This was apparently because the leadership dissolved with the flight of many of its members and the arrest, by the British, of others, and because it had been deeply divided after the rebellion of 1936–9.[28] None of this was the case in East Jerusalem in 1967, and less and less so thereafter. In 1967, Jerusalem was home to a Palestinian community with a solid consciousness of itself, a local leadership, and a tradition of political leadership, deriving from the Palestinian institutions of the British Mandate period and in the Jordanian kingdom. In the period that preceded the Israeli occupation, Jerusalem was not a remote rural area but rather a city of great religious importance, and Jordanian oversight of religious sites had granted legitimacy to the

Hashemite dynasty, even if from an administrative and political point of view Jordan's rule over the city had been marginal.

Beyond this, the lack of contact between the Arabs of Israel and their Palestinian and Arab brethren over the space of 19 years had led to far-reaching changes among them. Unlike the Arabs of East Jerusalem, only a minority of Palestinians in the State of Israel has social and family links to the inhabitants of the West Bank and Gaza Strip. The East Jerusalem Arabs are politically linked to the institutions of the territories, and the vast majority of them boycott Israel's municipal and political institutions. The Arabs of Israel, in stark contrast, are active participants in Israeli politics, and one of them, Knesset Member Azmi Bishara, was in 1999 a candidate for Prime Minister. The ethnic–geographic boundaries between them and the dominant and ruling Jewish majority have been open since the dissolution of the military government over Israel's Arab population in 1966. In many cases, the Arabs in Israel even cross over the ethnic–cultural border and assimilate the norms of the majority as part of the process of Israelification they are undergoing.[29] Many of them have adopted Israeli identity, and the major stream among the Arabs of Israel demands that his country's government treat them as citizens with equal rights.

In practice this is movement in two opposite directions. While the Palestinians in Israel are intensifying their demands for equal division of resources and access to the collective institutions, the process of separation has intensified among the Palestinians of East Jerusalem. The Palestinians in Jerusalem do not want to penetrate the heart of the political structure and change the division of power and resources, but rather to detach themselves from Israeli rule. Until the Oslo Accords, the official demand of the Palestinians was to separate Jerusalem into two sovereign municipal entities while keeping the city undivided physically. Since then, the peace process has produced other forms of dividing positions of control, administration, and resources in Jerusalem between Jews and Arabs.

The demographic considerations will ultimately oblige Israel to locate a Palestinian framework within which the Arabs in Jerusalem will be able to realize their political rights at both the municipal and the national level. The elections for the institutions of the Palestinian Authority that were held in January 1996 could serve as a point of departure for future arrangements that will confer citizenship and the right to vote in elections for Palestinian national institutions. Concurrently, the Arab residents of Jerusalem will establish their own municipal institutions and they will become partners in the municipal and regional administration of the city.

In the absence of a permanent, comprehensive political settlement, the residents of East Jerusalem are perceived as a threat to Israeli sovereignty and at best as an exotic backdrop. This state of affairs has enabled successive Israeli governments to practice an ongoing structural discrimination toward the residents of East Jerusalem in distribution of resources, installation of infrastructure, and supply of services. It should be remembered that the East Jerusalem Arabs make up 30 percent of the city's population, but received, in 1995, only about 7 percent of the city's budget.[30] At a special cabinet meeting in 1999, the municipality presented further data on the East–West gap in the city, gaps running from 300 to 1,000 percent, depending on the area. In Jewish Jerusalem there were 743 inhabitants per kilometer of sewage pipe; in Arab Jerusalem 7,362 inhabitants. In Jewish Jerusalem there were 690 inhabitants per kilometer of sidewalk, as opposed to 2,917 in the East.[31] According to municipality data from 1999, the sum required closing the gap between Arab and Jewish Jerusalem was more than NIS 1 billion.[32] Under current budgetary conditions and the social needs of Israeli society, it is difficult to expect the government to come up with NIS 1 billion for a population that rejects Israeli citizenship.

In addition, the underlying conception of the investment policies, as laid down by Likkud governments, is fatally flawed. Will the equalization of services and infrastructure in the Eastern City to the standard in the Western City induce 200,000 Palestinians to rush to the Interior Ministry in order to acquire Israeli citizenship and thank Israel for its beneficent annexation? Will Israel as a Jewish state wish or be capable of absorbing about 10 percent of the residents of the West Bank and the Gaza Strip?

A permanent settlement in Jerusalem without the more equitable allocation of resources for the benefit of the Arab residents of metropolitan Jerusalem is inconceivable, but those resources have to be found outside Israel. Israel has to let Palestinians, Arabs and whoever is interested participate in the economic regeneration of Arab Jerusalem. In short, a new package deal should be offered to the Palestinians in Jerusalem. Instead of per capita payment and public discrimination, Israel and the state-to-be Palestine have to agree on providing these people national identity, ensuring their right to realize the principle of self-determination and self-rule based on equitable democratic principles. Arab and international investments, Palestinian state and municipality services, the openness of Jerusalem's job market for the city's Arab residents, and developing its attraction to tourists are the main components of the economy of peace in Jerusalem.

In the absence of a settlement, a "land grab" and "power grab" has developed in East Jerusalem. Both sides took unilateral steps, such as unauthorized building by Palestinians inside the municipal boundaries and close to it; the confiscation of ID cards and demolition of unauthorized buildings by Israel, as well as the building of new Jewish neighborhoods inside the municipal area and expanding Israeli settlements in the metropolitan area of Jerusalem. But Israel, as the stronger party, has enjoyed a striking advantage. However the Palestinian presence can be neither erased nor ignored any longer. As Faisal al-Huseini has quipped, the Palestinians are not creating facts on the ground, but rather they *are* the facts.

In order to meet the symbolic importance and needs, a permanent settlement in Jerusalem must launch a process in which the mutual historic, religious, and national aspirations of each side throughout the entire area of metropolitan Jerusalem will be recognized. In the future, competition over space and the reciprocal threat must be replaced by a model of partnership and a quest for unifying frameworks while keeping the two population groups separate.

Controlling the Religious Extremists

There is a widespread assumption that at the heart of the conflict is an unbridgeable religious dispute symbolized by the Temple Mount. But the question of the holy places is not congruent with the Jerusalem question, and the question of Jerusalem is not an exclusively religious matter. It has been shown to be politically possible to manage the religious conflict in the city. The question of the holy sites is one component among others in the Jerusalem file. In order to regulate religious tension and prevent it from sliding into and exacerbating the already existing national tension in the city, the Israeli authorities have, since 1967, given the Muslim and Christian authorities autonomy in the management of their holy sites.

In the law for the preservation of holy sites, legislated in 1967, Israel promised these sites full protection from desecration and harm, free access to visitors and tourists, and freedom of religious practice in all the holy sites. Entry to the Temple Mount is permitted to all in the framework of the visiting hours set by the managers of the site, in keeping with Muslim ritual requirements. In fact, Jewish freedom of worship on the Temple Mount was seriously restricted after the occupation in 1967 out of fear of strong Muslim protests. In summary, Israel, which bears the responsibility for Jerusalem and the Temple Mount, has succeeded, since occupying East Jerusalem in 1967, in keeping the issue of Jerusalem a political rather than a religious problem. The Jerusalem syndrome, as a pathological religious phenomenon, has not destroyed the political frameworks. In other words, politics has thus far succeeded in overcoming the religious element in Jerusalem. It has enlisted religion in its service while simultaneously controlling it. The problem of Jerusalem is not congruent with or identical to the problem of the Temple Mount, and the question of the Temple Mount will not prevent political negotiations on Jerusalem. The Temple Mount has remained one of the components of the question of Jerusalem, and the politicians hope to neutralize it, if not resolve the disputes over it. So far Israeli and Palestinian politicians have succeeded in managing the city's religious affairs and in restraining pressures of various kinds, mainly by extreme Jewish elements, to dramatically change the status quo in the holy Muslim shrines. As such, it has abided by the concept of a holy place. A holy site is not any place, but a defined site that imposes restrictions and reservations. A settlement at the holy places must demonstrate consideration for the essential character of the sites in question, while deflecting government and the politicians to the sidelines. Freedom of worship, security, public order, and free access to all holy places should be preserved, and at times further developed. Furthermore, pluralistic and multicultural features of Jerusalem's identity must be encouraged. Administration of the holy places by the religious authorities has become an accepted prospect that is difficult to challenge.

It is worth noting that according to the Beilin–Abu Ma'azen plan, the Temple Mount will be declared under extra-territorial, de facto Palestinian sovereignty, and the Palestinians would be permitted to fly their flag above it. Also, the Beilin–Abu-Ma'azen understanding extends the limits of the Old City beyond its walls and includes the Valley of Jehoshafat and the Mount of Olives, with their plethora of holy sites sacred to the monotheistic religions. Consequently, such an approach might lead both sides to guarantee a unique status not only for the holy sites but also over the extended "sacred zone" which will be administrated jointly.

Both sides must ensure freedom of worship at the holy places and guarantee freedom of access to them. Although security concerns of both sides must be recognized, there should not be exclusive access to the city for one people at the expense of the other. In addition, Palestinians residing outside the Jerusalem area shall enjoy the right to have an access to their holy places inside the area, and vice versa. However, the status quo on the Temple Mount must be left intact. Palestinian recognition of the historic, religious, and national rights of Israel and of the Jews need not be translated immediately into granting Jews the right to pray in the Temple Mount compound.

Conclusion:
Foundations of a Palestinian–Israeli Agreement

1 *Collective Rights and Equality*. Both Israelis and Palestinians in Jerusalem and outside the city alike have morally equal right to self-determination, and to engage in state building as an expression of their national aspirations. Also, the two peoples have collective rights and national aspirations in Jerusalem. Both peoples should be allowed to express these rights and aspirations in Jerusalem and achieve mutual and international recognition. The Palestinians must recognize Israeli rights in the city, including those in the eastern part of the city. Palestinians will be related to as equal partners with national aspirations and rights, not as a demographic threat.

It should be noted that equality as a principle does not rule out the option of using a "give and take" strategy. Concessions in one area should be compensated for in other one and thus an overall equality will exist.

2 *Power Sharing*. Sharing authority in city management and democratic principles of self-governance should be applied on all levels. The two national communities, on equal footing will share the authority applied in the Jerusalem area. Two sub-municipalities, one Jewish and one Arab, would together form an umbrella municipality. The Arab sub-municipality would include territory presently outside the city's boundaries as well as most of the current Arab areas of East Jerusalem. The Jewish sub-municipality will include West Jerusalem and the Jewish neighborhoods in East Jerusalem. Israel would recognize the area of the Arab sub-municipality as the Palestinian capital, and the Palestinians and the world would recognize West Jerusalem as Israel's capital. Territorial contiguity between Arab neighborhoods on the one hand, and between the Jewish ones should be a guideline in Jerusalem's city planning and development programs. The Old City would have a special status. By creating Greater Jerusalem, its current access corridors would expand and the city reconstituted as the hub of a circle instead of being a frontier city.

3 *Human and Communal Realities*. Any solution or plan for the future of Jerusalem should take into consideration the human and communal realities on the ground. It means that Israeli "settlements" in Eastern Jerusalem will not be dismantled and Palestinians who owned property in West Jerusalem will neither be automatically able to return nor receive adequate financial compensation. Palestinian real estate lost in 1948 and 1967 wars and by Israeli confiscations shall be compensated on the national level either by an Israeli recognition of the Palestinian historical relationships and rights or by giving back unbundled confiscated land.

4 *Differentiating between Jerusalem and the West Bank*. The solution in Jerusalem will be different to that in the West Bank in spite of the fact that the two areas will not be disconnected from one another. Furthermore, the uniqueness of Jerusalem might be expressed by empowering Israeli and Palestinian local authorities *vis-à-vis* their respective national governments. Greater Jerusalem administration will be different in its structure and authorities than any other local administration in either state.

Opinion polls shows that there are areas that are high in priority for Israelis and low for Palestinians, such as the Jewish Quarter of the Old City, West Jerusalem, and the new Jewish neighborhoods in East Jerusalem. On the other hand, there are areas that are high in Palestinian priorities, and low for Israelis: the Arab quarters of the Old City, the Arab suburbs, and the Arab downtown area. Reflecting not only subjective viewpoints but also political and urban realities, these results show that the Jerusalem question is negotiable and there is enough room in which decision-makers may maneuver. It also seems that a majority of Israeli Jews and Arab

Palestinians would not object to redefine the boundaries of Jerusalem, especially if it will be explained as a need to keep the city "Jewish" or "Palestinian," respectively. The Israeli-made city boundaries are neither sacred lines nor immutable, and may be made smaller or larger in order to redefine the cake, and share it. Creative ideas such as entrusting the Jerusalem area administration with its different municipal authorities will hopefully pave the way to implementable solutions that leaves much to the eye of the beholder.

5 *The Concept of Sovereignty.* There has been a dramatic change in the concept of sovereignty in international law. It has rid itself of the idea that there is only absolute sovereignty. Professor Ruth Lapidot, among others, has shown in her research that sovereignty is no longer perceived as a zero-sum game but as a multidimensional variety of options. Some of these could definitely be suited to the complex reality of Jerusalem. Today the concept of sovereignty under international law does not imply one meaning and is not identical with the "either/or" model, either "mine or yours." International law provides us other models of sovereignty such as the joint sovereignty model which might be applied in a city-state; or the suspension of sovereignty, or its dilution, that may be appropriate at the Holy Sites; functional sovereignty (division of powers and responsibilities according functions); and shared sovereignty (including effective control and de facto sovereignty to one side and de jure sovereignty subjected to certain limitations to the other side). Two concepts worthy of consideration in Jerusalem would be Palestinian sovereignty in some areas, shared sovereignty in other areas where there could be a symbolic Palestinian sovereignty and de facto Israeli rule, or vice versa. Moreover, there is an option that one side will have limited powers in territory that is under the sovereignty being vested in the other side.

The principle of an open city should be applied to the entire metropolitan area. Freedom of movement, employment, and certain agreed residency rights should be preserved for all Jerusalem area residents, visitors and employees, and Jews and Arabs alike. Along the implementation of the open area principle, special security arrangements must be concluded in order to guarantee security and order in the metropolitan area. An agreement on special border arrangements must be part and parcel with keeping the metropolitan area undivided and open. The international border at the west boundary will function as such only for Palestinians wishing to enter Israel. The same should apply to the Greater Jerusalem borders on the north, east and south edges of Greater Jerusalem for Israelis willing to enter Palestine. One should not rule out the option to build checkpoints for Israelis only at roads leading to the state of Palestine and vice versa for Palestinians at roads going to Israel. The construction of these checkpoints may be similar to that of payment station at the entrance/exit of payment roads, including a free route to Israelis or Palestinians driving to their own state.

While it may be difficult to check every passenger, this model provides a compromise between two different principles that both should be preserved in any final status agreement: the principle of an open metropolitan area on the one hand, and that of two cities or capitals connected to their respective sovereign and secured hinterland on the other hand. Therefore the Jerusalem area will contain permeable administrative boundaries between two city halls while the international border will be situated outside them.

6 *A Preference for Arab Jerusalemites in Israeli Job Market.* Special arrangements shall insure the priority of Arab Jerusalemites to enjoy access to the Israeli job market, in order to promote the economy of Jerusalem's Arab city and maintain its residents' higher income *vis-à-vis* the rest of the Palestinian area. Such arrangements will limit the economic attractiveness of Jerusalem and minimize blue-collar immigration to the city from the non-Jerusalem territory of the Palestinian state.

The good news is that the question of Jerusalem is not the most difficult issue to be resolved in the Israeli–Palestinian track. The bad news is that not too many people have heard the good news.

Notes

1 The following discussion is based on my books *Doves Over Jerusalem's Sky: The Peace Process and the City 1977–1999* (Jerusalem: The Jerusalem Institute for Israel Studies, 1999), [in Hebrew]; and *Jerusalem – The Future of a Contested City* (New York and London: C. Hurst, 2001).

2 Meron Benvenisti, *A Place of Fire* (Tel Aviv: Dvir, 1996), p. 57; Maia Choshen, *On Your Data Jerusalem 1997: Existing Situation and Trends of Change* (Jerusalem: Jerusalem Institute of Israel Studies, 1998).

3 "*East Jerusalem: Planning Status*," published by Ir Shalem (an Israeli NGO), Jerusalem, 1998.

4 Daniel Seidman, "Before Beginning to Destroy" in *Ha'aretz*, August 17, 1997.

5 "A Policy of Discrimination: Land Confiscation, Planning and Construction in East Jerusalem," published in Hebrew by B'tselem (an Israeli NGO), Jerusalem, 1995, pp. 32–6.

6 *Ha'aretz*, January 4, 1996; Seidman, 17 August 17, 1997.

7 Ir Shalem, "*East Jerusalem: Planning Status.*"

8 Benvenisti, *A Place of Fire,* p. 133; *Ha'aretz*, August 17, 1997; Choshen Maia and Shahar N'ama, eds., *Jerusalem Statistical Yearbook*, 1998, p. 130.

9 *Ha'Aretz*, August 15, 1995, September 3, 1995, August 17, 1997; Ir Shalem, "*East Jerusalem: Planning Status.*"

10 *Ha'aretz*, January 26, 1997, March 17, 1997.

11 "The Silent Transfer: The Revocation of Residence Status from Palestinians in East Jerusalem," published in Hebrew by B'tselem and Center for the Defense of the Individual, Jerusalem, April 1997.

12 *www.pna.net,* November 25, 1997.

13 *Ha'aretz*, September 9, 1998.
14 *Ha'aretz*, July 21, 1999, June 16, 1999.
15 *Kol Ha-Ir*, August 22, 1997.
16 *Ha'aretz*, June 2, 1997, June 10, 1997, June 17, 1998; *Kol Ha-Ir*, August 22, 1998.
17 *Ha'aretz*, June 10, 1996, July 3, 1997, July 4, 1997, July 16, 1997.
18 *Ha'aretz*, July 9, 1997, July 10, 1997.
19 Data provided by Orient House and the Palestinian Ministry of Local Government.
20 *Ha'aretz*, August 21, 1996, August 22, 1996, August 25, 1996, August 26, 1996, September 18, 1996, September 20, 1996, May 29,1997, July 13, 1997, July 16, 1997.
21 *al-Quds*, August 1, 1997; B'tselem, 1997; *Ha'aretz*, August 4, 1997, March 2, 1999.
22 *al-Ayam*, December 6, 1998.
23 Awartani Faisal, "Labor Force Indicators in Jerusalem," unpublished report in English, 1998.
24 Data of the Jerusalem Institute of Israel Studies for 1996.
25 Yehuda Blum, "Zion by International Law was Redeemed," *Ha Praklit* 27 (1971), pp. 315–24; Blum, "East Jerusalem is not Occupied Territory," *Ha Praklit* 28 (1972–3), pp. 183–90 (both in Hebrew); "Demolishing Peace: The Policy of Mass Demolition of Palestinian Homes in the West Bank," published by B'tselem, 1997, pp. 20–3; Yoram Dinstein, "Zion by International Law will be Redeemed," pp. 5–11; and "It really wasn't Redeemed, or: Not by Demonstrations but by Action," *Ha Praklit* 27 (1971), pp. 5–11 and pp. 519–22; Ruth Lapidoth, *Jerusalem Legal Aspects – Background Papers for Policy Makers*, Jerusalem Institute for Israel Studies, 1997; Ian Lustick, "Has Israel Annexed East Jerusalem," *Middle East Policy* 5 (1997), pp. 34–5.
26 Jerome M. Segal, "Is Jerusalem Negotiable?" Jerusalem: Israeli/Palestinian Center for Research and Information (IPCRI), 1997, p. 37; Jerome M. Segal and Izzat Sa'id Nader, "The Status of Jerusalem in the Eyes of Palestinians," Center for International Security Studies, University of Maryland, 1997, pp. 39–42.
27 On currency, media, health, religious courts and the Holy Islamic Sites, the autonomy of the local Palestinian establishment, political ties, and political participation of East Jerusalem Arabs as well as on planning and construction see Klein, 1999 and Klein, 2000.
28 Arnon-Ohana Yuval, *The Sword at Home: The International Struggle in the Palestinian National Movement* (Tel Aviv: Tel Aviv University, Hadar and Dayan Center, 1989); Yosef Nevo, *The Political Development at the Arab-Palestinian Movement*, Ph.D. dissertation, Tel Aviv University, 1977; Yahoshua Porat, *From Riots to Rebellion: The Arab Palestinian Movement, 1929–1939* (Tel Aviv: Am Oved, 1978).
29 Adel Mana and Kusai Haj Yehiye, *Mabruk: The Arab Wedding Culture in Israel*, Ra'anana: Center for the Study of Arab Society in Israel, 1995; Elis Rekhes, "The Arabs of Israel and the *Intifada*" in Gad Gilbar and Asher Sasser, eds., *In the Eye of the Conflict: The Intifada* (Tel Aviv: Dayan Center

of Tel Aviv University and Kibbutz Ha-Me'uchad, 1992), pp. 99–127 (in Hebrew).

30 *Ha'aretz*, July 10, 1995; Danny Rubinstein, "Thirty Percent of the Residents, Only Seven Percent of the Money," *Ha'aretz*, November 20, 1996.

31 *Ha'aretz*, March 25, 1999; *Kol Ha-Ir*, April 16, 1999.

32 *Kol Ha-Ir*, April 16, 1999.

CHAPTER 26

The Future Status of Jerusalem: Views of the Israeli and Palestinian Publics

EPHRAIM YUCHTMAN-YA'AR

The purpose of this chapter is to describe and analyze the attitudes of the Israeli and Palestinian populations toward some critical aspects of the future status of Jerusalem. The issue of Jerusalem is, of course, one of the most difficult obstacles to reaching the ultimate goal of a permanent peace accord between the Israelis and the Palestinians on the basis of mutual concessions. Judged from the initial positions of the political leadership of both sides, the difficulty in attaining an acceptable compromise over Jerusalem stems from two main factors that are related to each other. On the one hand, the city is of utmost importance to the Israeli and Palestinian peoples alike. On the other hand, there is a wide gap between their aspirations concerning the city's proper status and its place in the respective Palestinian and Israeli states.

Thus, the Palestinian Authority insists that the only acceptable solution is to divide the city, so that East Jerusalem would become the capital of Palestine and West Jerusalem the capital of Israel. In contrast, the new Israeli government[1] asserts that it will accept nothing less than the status quo, namely, that Jerusalem should remain an undivided city and the capital of Israel.[2] It is precisely because of the wide gap concerning the future status of the city, together with its unequivocal importance to both sides, that this issue was deferred along with a few other outstanding issues, such as the Palestinian refugees, to the final phase of negotiations.

Notwithstanding that both the Israeli government and the Palestinian Authority are the legitimate representatives of their peoples, any proposed solution to the problem of Jerusalem would require the support of their constituencies. Without a reasonable degree of such support, any agreement about the city may prove impractical and detrimental to the overall peace effort as well as to these authorities' legitimacy. In order to avoid such developments, the leaders of both sides need to know as precisely as possible what their peoples feel and think about possible solutions for Jerusalem.

This does not necessarily mean that they should formulate their policies only according to their peoples' desires, since these may prove to be unrealistic. Political leaders are expected to lead their nations rather than be led by them, particularly when courageous and imaginative policies are needed to put an end to painful situations such as the century-old strife between Israel and the Palestinians. Nevertheless, knowing the "voice of the people" is important for national leaders at least for two main reasons. First, it enables them to assess how far they can go in terms of compromise without risking the emergence of a powerful opposition to their policy. Second, by knowing where the public stands, they can use various means of education and persuasion so as to narrow the gap between ideal and real solutions. The responsibility of political leaders is to influence their people as much as to be influenced by them.[3] We believe that this principle is highly relevant to the discourse between the leaders and their publics in both the Israeli and Palestinian cases. We also expect that the results of national public opinion surveys, such as reported in this paper, will be understood in the spirit of this principle.

Methodology

This chapter presents the main results of coordinated attitude surveys conducted in December 1999 by the JMCC (the Jerusalem Media and Communication Center of East Jerusalem) and the Tami Steinmetz Center for Peace Research, Tel Aviv University. The surveys were based on interviews with randomly selected males and females who represent, respectively, the adult Palestinian (West Bank and Gaza Strip) and Israeli-Jewish populations, including the residents of the occupied territories. The Palestinian survey was based on face-to-face interviews with about 1,200 people. The Israeli poll involved some 1,000 respondents[4] who were interviewed by telephone. In addition to the results of the coordinated surveys, we will present some findings pertaining to the Israeli public only, based on surveys conducted at different points during 2000.

The Subjective Importance of Jerusalem

The first group of findings pertains to several questions that probe the importance of Jerusalem for Israelis and Palestinians relative to other major issues. The first question was formulated as follows: "In your

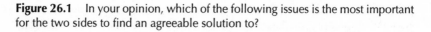

Figure 26.1   In your opinion, which of the following issues is the most important for the two sides to find an agreeable solution to?

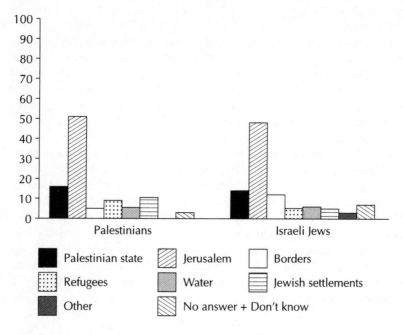

opinion, which of the following issues are the three most important for the two sides to find an agreeable solution?" The respondents were presented with a list of six issues and asked to indicate which they considered the most important, the second most important, and the third. The list of issues, along with the order and frequencies by which they were chosen, are provided in figure 26.1.

Figure 26.1 reveals that both the Israeli and Palestinian respondents regarded the future status of Jerusalem as the most important issue. In fact, compared with all the other issues, Jerusalem is in a league of its own, surpassing the rest by a wide margin. Moreover, the percentage that put this issue at the top of the list was nearly identical in the two groups. Thus, as seen in the first column of figure 26.1, Jerusalem was chosen as most important by 48.4 percent and 51.0 percent of the Israelis and the Palestinians, respectively. In comparison, only 14 percent of the Israelis and 16 percent of the Palestinians selected the next issue in order of importance, the establishment of a Palestinian state.

Another way to assess the relative importance of the six issues is to calculate an average percentage score for each of them on the basis of the weighted frequencies of the first, second, and third choices (see figure 26.2). Accordingly, the percentages of the first and the second choices were

Figure 26.2   Which of the following are the most important issues for the two sides to find an agreeable solution to?

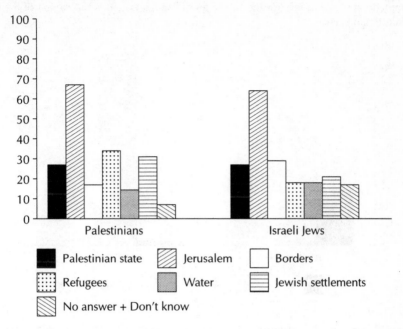

weighted three times and two times as much, respectively, as those of the third choice. The result is that Jerusalem receives a score of 64.0 among the Israelis and 67.0 among the Palestinians, whereas its nearest rivals obtain much lower scores of 29.0 (the borders issue) among the Israelis and 34.0 (the refugee problem) among the Palestinians.

Taken together, these results show clearly and consistently that the future status of Jerusalem is by far the most prominent issue both for the Israelis and Palestinians. In order to probe more specifically how important Jerusalem is for ordinary Israelis and Palestinians, respondents were presented with functionally equivalent questions. The Israelis were asked: "If the issue of Jerusalem was the last obstacle to signing a comprehensive peace agreement with the Palestinians, would you agree that East Jerusalem become the capital of a Palestinian state?"[5] Complementarily, the Palestinians were asked if they accepted the Israeli demand that even after the establishment of an independent Palestinian state, Jerusalem remains united and the capital of Israel (with the same specification regarding the peace agreement as given to the Israeli respondents). The results for both questions are presented in figure 26.3.

As can be seen from figure 26.3, both the Israelis and the Palestinians are unwilling to compromise on the future status of Jerusalem even if this

Figure 26.3   If the issue of Jerusalem is the last obstacle to the signing of the peace agreement, would you agree that (for the Palestinians) the city of Jerusalem is the unified capital of Israel; (for the Israeli Jews) East Jerusalem is the capital of the Palestinian State

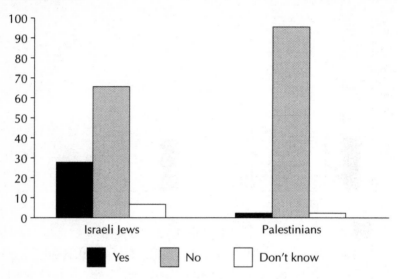

would ensure the signing of a peace agreement. Interestingly, the Palestinians tend to be more adamant on this issue than the Israelis, with 95 percent of them rejecting the idea that Jerusalem as a whole would be the capital of Israel compared to 66 percent of the Israelis who do not agree that East Jerusalem would become the capital of Palestine.[6] Still, these figures indicate that at the level of ordinary citizens, neither the Israelis nor the Palestinians are ready to sacrifice their national aspirations concerning the status of Jerusalem for the sake of a peace agreement.

Granted that the Israelis and Palestinians reject each other's desired solutions for Jerusalem, the final series of findings on both Israelis and Palestinians involves attitudes toward various alternative solutions for the problem of Jerusalem. Respondents were presented with a list of seven such options and asked which of them they regarded as the best permanent solution for the city's status. The seven options and the frequencies with which they were chosen are shown in figure 26.4.

It emerges that none of the seven solutions gains the joint support of even an appreciable minority in either group. For the Israelis, the dominant choice (81.0%) is, again, keeping Jerusalem united and the capital of Israel, with all other solutions receiving 1–7 percent. As expected, the Palestinians are virtually united in their rejection of the preferred Israeli solution, with only 1 percent agreeing to it. However, none of the other alternatives, including the division of the city into East Jerusalem as capital of Palestine

Figure 26.4   What is the best permanent solution to the problem of Jerusalem?

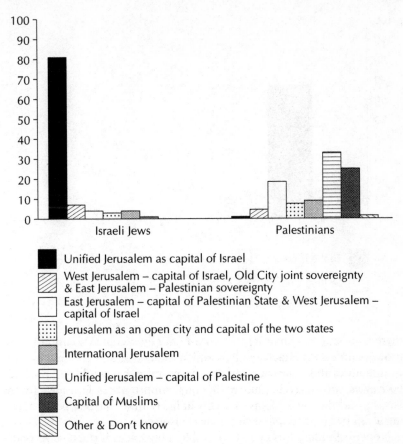

and West Jerusalem as capital of Israel, gains consensual support among the Palestinians. The most popular choice among the Palestinians was keeping Jerusalem unified as the capital of Palestine, but it was embraced by only one-third of them (32.9%). Note that this choice accords with the Israeli desire to keep Jerusalem a united city. The next most popular choice (25%) was for Jerusalem to be the capital of Muslims; the third was for East Jerusalem to be the capital of the Palestinians and West Jerusalem to be the capital of Israel (18.5%). Note that this is the option preferred by the Palestinian Authority. Each of the remaining options was favored by 1–9 percent of the Palestinian respondents. It is worth emphasizing that both the Israelis and the Palestinians reject the ideas of making Jerusalem the joint capital of the two states or of turning it into an international city.

Taken together, the findings indicate that the two peoples' sentiments on Jerusalem are similar in intensity but diametrically opposed. Consequently,

Figure 26.5   To whom is the issue of Jerusalem more important?

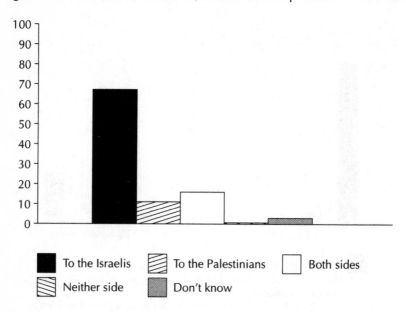

there is little if any chance to reach a mutually accepted solution to this problem unless the Israeli and Palestinian leaders are able to convince their communities about the necessity of a compromise that would be painful for both sides. Moreover, because of the equal importance of Jerusalem for the Israelis and the Palestinians, it seems unlikely that a lasting peace agreement can be attained unless this issue is resolved.

Notwithstanding this climate of public opinion, is it possible to find a way of bridging the gap? One possible way is, perhaps, to sensitize each of the two communities to the importance of Jerusalem for the other. Mutual awareness of this kind may reduce the sense of deprivation and injustice that each side is likely to experience if one side gets something that the other strongly desires. Whether such an effort would be helpful or not, it is clear that at least so far as the Israeli public is concerned, there is today little awareness of the importance of Jerusalem for the Palestinians. This assessment is based on the Israeli respondents' answers to the following question:[7] "Within the framework of negotiations between the Israelis and the Palestinians toward the achievement of a permanent agreement, to whom is the issue of Jerusalem more important – the Israelis or the Palestinians?" The results are shown in figure 26.5.

Thus, 67.2 percent believe that the city is more important to the Israelis, 11.1 percent that it is more important to the Palestinians, and only 18.0 percent believe that Jerusalem is of equal importance to both sides.

Figure 26.6   Reasons for the importance of Jerusalem

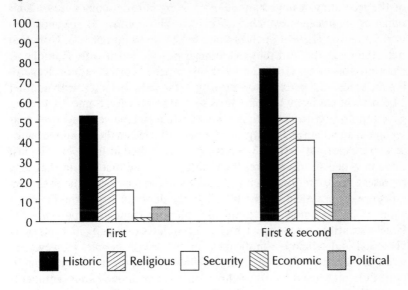

However, when the same question was presented to the Israelis at the end of July 2000, shortly after the Camp David summit, the results were somewhat different. The percentage of those who believe the city is more important to the Israelis declined to 50.8 percent, while the percentage who believe the city is equally important to the Israelis and the Palestinians went up to 33.3 percent. This highly significant change may be attributed to the influence of media reports according to which the Israeli government was willing, during the negotiations, to turn over the Arab neighborhoods of East Jerusalem to the Palestinians. It is therefore possible that the increase in the Israelis' cognizance of the city's importance to the Palestinians stemmed from the government's apparent recognition of the Palestinians' claim to East Jerusalem. We believe that such a change is indicative of the vital role that political elites can play in influencing their peoples to understand the other side and accept the need for costly compromises. It goes without saying that to be effective, such an effort must be made by both the Israeli and Palestinian elites.

Granted the significance of Jerusalem for the Israeli public almost as a whole, we tried to discern what are the main components of this attitude. Thus, the respondents were presented with a list of five possible reasons for keeping Jerusalem united and the capital of Israel, and asked which of those reasons were the most important and second most important for them. The results are shown in figure 26.6.

The findings indicate that the most salient reason for keeping Jerusalem a united city and the capital of Israel is its historical significance. For 76.4

percent of the respondents, this is either the most important reason (53.0%) or the second most important (22.4%). Next in order comes Jerusalem's religious significance, which 51.5 percent chose either as the most important reason (22.4%) or the second most important (29.1%). Note that both the historical and religious dimensions are laden with symbolic or emotional meanings rather than with instrumental considerations. Regarding the latter, 15.8 percent gave priority to the security factor, with another 24.6 percent choosing this factor as second in priority. Some 7.1 percent gave top priority to the political factor, while 16.6 percent regarded it as second in importance. Finally, just 1.8 percent selected the economic factor as most important, with 6.3 percent putting it second in order. The last three in order of importance, then, differ from the first two in that they represent more "rational" considerations. In other words, the main significance of Jerusalem for the Israeli public does not stem from the city's value as an economic and political center, or from its importance for Israel's security. Instead, the Israeli public relates to the city in terms of its historical and religious significance for the Jewish people. However, in terms of the potential for changing public attitudes, the task may in fact be more difficult when these are anchored in national and religious sentiments rather than in the domain of rationality. It is difficult to bargain or negotiate over objects that are of symbolic and affective value. Of course, this point pertains to the Israelis and Palestinians alike.

Attitudes toward Jerusalem's Neighborhoods

Any discussion of the future status of Jerusalem must consider critical questions pertaining to its geographic, ethnic, and national composition. Jerusalem is a hilly city, composed of various quarters and neighborhoods scattered over relatively large areas.[8] Yet the municipal boundaries of Jerusalem have undergone various changes over time, depending on who was in power in the city. For example, as noted by Klein (1999),[9] the city's boundaries were expanded during the Jordanian rule in April 1952, by the annexation of the neighborhoods of Silwan and Ras al-Amud. Similarly, Jewish neighborhoods built after the war of 1967, such as Pisgat Ze'ev and Ramot, were incorporated into the city's jurisdiction by the Israeli authorities. In light of these historical transformations, it is important to find out what are the perceptions and attitudes of ordinary people in regard to the city's boundaries.

To explore this question, we gave our respondents a list consisting of ten widely dispersed neighborhoods of the city. Half of them are inhabited mostly by Jews (Neve Ya'akov, Pisgat Ze'ev, Ramot, Gilo, and Har Homa) and half by Palestinians (Shu'afat, Sheikh Jarah, Ras al-Amud, Wadi Joz, and Abu Dis). For example, Neve Ya'akov and Pisgat Ze'ev are two Jewish

Figure 26.7a   Which of the folowing neighborhoods are part of Jerusalem?

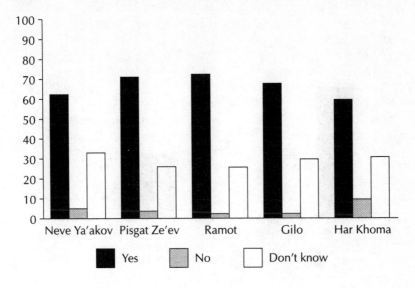

Figure 26.7b   Which of the folowing neighborhoods are part of Jerusalem?

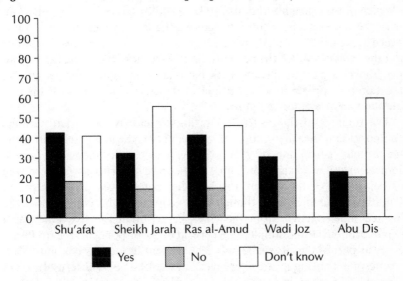

neighborhoods located close to the northern edge of the city, just north of the Palestinian neighborhood of Shu'afat, whereas Wadi Joz and Sheikh Jarah are much closer to the Old City. We then asked the following two questions: "When you think about Jerusalem, which of the following

Figure 26.7c   Which neighborhoods are part of Jerusalem?

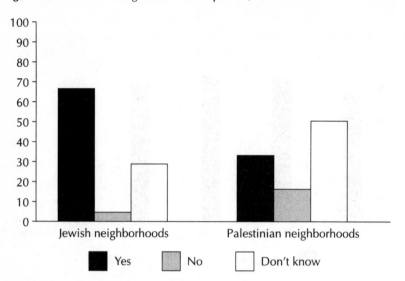

neighborhoods are in your opinion part of the city and which are not?" and, "Which of these neighborhoods can be ceded by Israel in the negotiations with the Palestinians, if this will remove the last obstacle to achieving a peace agreement?" Underlying these questions was our interest in finding out the extent to which the perceptions and attitudes regarding the various neighborhoods are affected by their national composition and geographic location (i.e., proximity to the center of the city). The results for the first question are presented in figures 26.7a, 7b, and 7c.[10]

The findings of figures 26.7a, 7b, and 7c clearly show that national composition rather than geographic proximity is the main factor affecting the Israelis' perception of which of the ten neighborhoods are part of Jerusalem and which are not. Thus, all the Jewish localities were perceived as being part of the city by much higher percentages than any of the Palestinian localities, even though all five of the Jewish communities are located much farther from the city's center than the five Palestinian neighborhoods. For example, 70.8 percent of the respondents regard Pisgat Ze'ev as part of the city while only 29.6 percent feel that way about Wadi Joz despite its being located very close to the heart of Old Jerusalem. On average, 66.6 percent regard the five Jewish neighborhoods as part of Jerusalem, whereas for the Palestinian neighborhoods the figure is half as small – 33.2 percent. However, note that the respondents tended to avoid the answer "doesn't belong to the city" even with respect to the Palestinian communities. The common answer for those places was "don't know" on average, it was given by 50.5 percent of the respondents in regard to the

Table 26.1 Perceived belonging of Jewish and Palestinian neighborhoods to Jerusalem by residency? (in percentages)

	Jewish Neighborhoods			Palestinian Neighborhoods		
	Yes	No	Don't know	Yes	No	Don't know
Residents of Jerusalem	90	5	5	51	21	28
All others	60	4	36	30	16	54

Palestinian neighborhoods. This answer can apparently be interpreted in more than one way.

An interesting question raised by these results is whether the Jewish residents of Jerusalem differ from the rest of the Jewish respondents on this issue. Are Jerusalem's residents more inclined to perceive the various neighborhoods as part of their city, regardless of their ethnic composition, since they "know better," or do they make the same distinction between Jewish and Palestinian localities as the rest of the Jewish public? To probe these matters, we divided the original sample between the two groups of respondents and compared their answers, with the results shown in table 26.1. For the sake of parsimony, the ten localities were grouped according to the distinction between Jewish and Palestinian neighborhoods. Note that a "yes" answer means that the neighborhood is regarded as part of Jerusalem, and "no" that it is not.

The figures shown in table 26.1 are revealing in several respects. First, the residents of Jerusalem are much more inclined than the rest of the Jewish citizens to see both the Jewish and the Palestinian neighborhoods as part of Jerusalem. Second, both groups are much more inclined to regard the Jewish neighborhoods as parts of the city by comparison with the Palestinian ones. The combined effect of these two factors – residency of the respondents and national composition of the neighborhoods – yields large gaps in the perceptions of which localities belong to the city. Thus, 90 percent of the residents of Jerusalem regard the Jewish neighborhoods as part of the city while only 51 percent of this group view the Palestinian neighborhoods the same way. Correspondingly, 60 percent of the respondents who do not live in Jerusalem perceive the five Jewish communities as part of the city compared to only 30 percent of this group who have the same perception about the five Palestinian communities. Also noteworthy is the finding that within both groups, respondents who do not consider the Jewish or the Palestinian localities as part of Jerusalem are much more likely to say that they do not know where these places belong than to say that they definitely are not parts of the city. This finding applies to the Jewish as well as the Palestinian neighborhoods, though not to the same degree.

Figure 26.8a If Jerusalem is the last obstacle to the signing of the peace agreement, which of the following neighborhoods of Jerusalem can Israel cede?

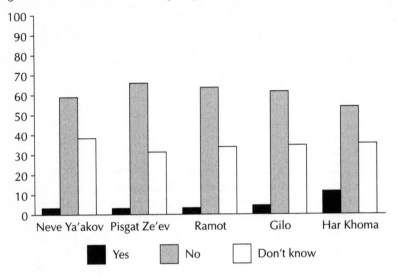

Figure 26.8b If Jerusalem is the last obstacle to the signing of the peace agreement, which of the following neighborhoods of Jerusalem can Israel cede?

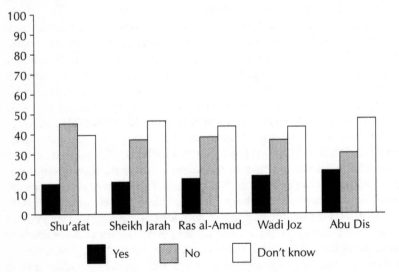

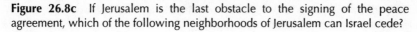

Figure 26.8c If Jerusalem is the last obstacle to the signing of the peace agreement, which of the following neighborhoods of Jerusalem can Israel cede?

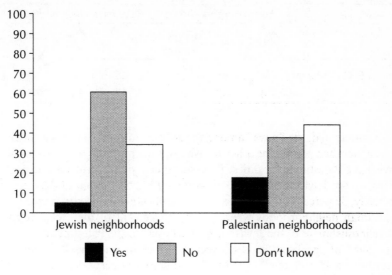

Apart from their perceptions about which of the ten neighborhoods belong to Jerusalem, we now turn to the more critical question of which of these neighborhoods the respondents believe Israel could cede to the Palestinians if this would remove the last obstacle to a peace agreement. The answers are presented in figures 26.8a, 8b, and 8c.

As can be clearly seen, almost all of the respondents are not prepared to cede any of the Jewish neighborhoods, including those that were constructed well beyond the 1967 borders. Moreover, only a small minority, ranging from 15.0 percent (Shu'afat) to 21.6 percent (Abu Dis), is willing to relinquish the Palestinian neighborhoods. However, the percentages of those who explicitly oppose relinquishing either the Jewish or the Palestinian neighborhoods are not as high as might be expected, given the figures that have just been mentioned. Thus, with respect to the Arab neighborhoods, only 38 percent say they should not be ceded to the Palestinians, with the rest (44%) having no clear position on this matter, saying they do not know. In other words, those who oppose relinquishing the Palestinian neighborhoods are not a majority. The comparable figures for the Jewish localities are 61 percent who oppose giving them up and 34 percent who do not know. In other words, a clear majority opposes ceding these neighborhoods. Note, however, that it is not an overwhelming majority.

To what extent do the Jewish residents of Jerusalem differ from the rest of the Jewish public on this issue? The findings are shown in table 26.2.

Table 26.2 Readiness to cede Jewish and Palestinian neighborhoods of Jerusalem by residency? (in percentages)

	Jewish Neighborhoods			Palestinian Neighborhoods		
	Yes	No	Don't know	Yes	No	Don't know
Residents of Jerusalem	7	86	7	25	57	18
All others	4	57	39	17	35	48

As anticipated, the "nays" among the Jerusalem residents are considerably higher than among the other Jewish respondents, both in regard to the Jewish and Palestinian localities. Thus, 86 percent of the former are against giving up the Jewish neighborhoods compared to 57 percent of the latter. Similarly, 57 percent of the Jerusalem residents are unprepared to cede the Palestinian neighborhoods whereas only 35 percent of the others reject the relinquishment of the Jewish neighborhoods to the Palestinians.

In light of the large gaps between the Israelis and the Palestinians regarding their preferences for the future status of Jerusalem, it is very likely that the two sides will have to resort to outsiders to help overcome this problem. Furthermore, there are several entities claiming that they have certain rights in Jerusalem and should therefore take part in negotiating its future. In light of these considerations, our final question was: "Who should be a side in the agreement over the future status of Jerusalem?" The respondents' order of preferences was as follows (note that the answers were not restricted to one choice):

Israel	95%
The Palestinian Authority	59%
The United States	44%
The United Nations	36%
Jordan	25%
The Muslim *Waqf*	19%
The Vatican	16%
Do not know/did not answer	5%

Only Israel is almost unanimously (95%) accepted as a legitimate side to the negotiations over Jerusalem. A majority, too, perceives the Palestinian Authority, as a legitimate side, albeit much smaller – about 60 percent. The minority that does not approve of the Palestinian role is divided between those who believe that Israel is the only legitimate party and those who are willing to accept some other players, particularly the United States and the United Nations. However, neither of those two, nor any of the other entities, is approved by a majority. As for Jordan, the *Waqf*, and the Vatican, those few who accept them as legitimate sides apparently had in mind their historical rights to the holy places. Overall, it appears that the majority of the Israeli public believes that the Israelis and the Palestinians themselves should resolve the problem of Jerusalem.

Conclusions

The findings that we have presented generally reaffirm the prevailing assumption that Jerusalem is the most difficult issue on the negotiating table between the Palestinians and the Israelis because of the city's unrivaled importance for both peoples and the wide gap between their aspirations for its future. Thus, while for the large majority of the Israeli public there is only one acceptable future for Jerusalem, namely, it's being the undivided capital of Israel, the Palestinian public unanimously rejects this idea. However, the Palestinians are divided among themselves about the solution for the city, with none of the listed options favored by a majority. In fact, less than 20 percent of the Palestinians regard the "official" Palestinian position of dividing the city into two capitals as the best permanent solution. One-third of the Palestinian respondents want the city as a whole to become the capital of Palestine, and one-quarter want it to be the capital of all Muslims. Clearly, none of these three solutions is likely to be accepted by the Israeli public. In fact, from an Israeli perspective the latter two, which when combined are preferred by a majority of the Palestinian respondents, represent much more radical solutions than the "two capitals" solution.

Notwithstanding these pessimistic observations, one must take into account that ordinary citizens, too, are capable of understanding the distinction between desired and acceptable solutions, particularly if their legitimate leadership makes such a distinction. Under this assumption, we believe that both the Israeli and Palestinian publics can be persuaded to accept the idea of keeping the city functionally undivided while dividing it politically into two capitals. Note in this regard the relatively high proportion of Israelis who do not perceive the Palestinian neighborhoods, some of which are located at its heart (e.g., Sheikh Jarah and Wadi Joz), as part of the city. Moreover, in an earlier survey done within the framework of the "peace Index,"[11] we found that nearly half of the Jewish public believes that the city is already divided in practice between East and West Jerusalem. It appears, therefore, that the Israeli public could be persuaded to accept the "two capitals" formula, provided that it would satisfy the historical and religious sentiments that the Jews have for the city, particularly its religious sites, such as Temple Mount and the Wailing Wall. On the same grounds, it seems reasonable to believe that the Palestinian public can be convinced that this formula constitutes the best realistic solution for their own claims and sentiments about Jerusalem. Ultimately, the realization of this solution depends on the willingness and ability of both nations' political leadership to persuade their peoples that the problem of Jerusalem can be solved only if each side understands the city's importance to the other.

Notes

1　Following the elections of February 6, 2001, the Labor government under Ehud Barak was replaced by one headed by the Likud leader Ariel Sharon. The previous government apparently was willing to satisfy the Palestinian demand that East Jerusalem become the capital of Palestine.

2　For various Israeli and Palestinian views on possible solutions to the problem of Jerusalem, see: *Dialogue on Jerusalem*, Passia meetings 1990–1998, ed. M. S. Hadi (Jerusalem: PASSIA, 1998); J. M. Segal, *Is Jerusalem Negotiable?* (Jerusalem: Israel/Palestine Center for Research and Information [IPCRI], No. 1, July 1997).

3　In addition to these two reasons, rulers can use public opinion as a means to improve their bargaining position in negotiations.

4　Actually, the original Israeli sample size of about 1,000 was divided between 500 Jews and 500 Israeli Arabs. In this paper we will be concerned with the Jewish sample only.

5　Before presenting this question, the Israeli respondents were asked if they believed that the Palestinians would eventually have an independent state. Seventy-nine percent answered affirmatively, 13 percent negatively, and 8 percent did not know.

6　In two surveys of the Israeli public conducted in July and December 2000, the results were practically identical to those obtained in December 1999.

7　This question was presented to the Israeli respondents only.

8　For basic demographic and geographic facts about Jerusalem since 1967, see M. Goshen, *Jerusalem on the Map* (Jerusalem: Jerusalem Institute for Israel Studies, 1998).

9　M. Klein, *Doves over Jerusalem's Sky: The Peace Process and the City 1977–1999* (Jerusalem: Jerusalem Institute for Israel Studies, 1999), p. 35.

10　For an earlier study using a similar approach regarding the importance of different neighborhoods to the Israelis and the Palestinians, see Segal.

11　The Peace Index is a monthly Poll concerned with various aspects of the peace process between Israel and the Arab world. It has been conducted since June 1994 by the Tami Steinmetz Center for Peace Research at Tel Aviv University headed by Professor Ephraim Ya'ar and Dr. Tamar Hermann.

CHAPTER 27

Temple Mount – al Haram al-Sharif: A Proposal for Solution

JOSEPH GINAT

The issue of Jerusalem, and to a certain extent its holy sites, has been examined by many scholars. For the past seven years, Professor Ephraim Ya'ar and I have been conducting research to create a solution for the Temple Mount issue. We wrote a draft of a concrete proposal and submitted it to a number of the region's leaders, including the late Prime Minister Yizhak Rabin and Foreign Minister Shimon Peres. It was also submitted to Danny Naveh, who served as Benjamin Netanyahu's Cabinet Secretary. When Ehud Barak was elected Prime Minister we sent him the proposal as well. We received no negative comments on our proposal; however, Danny Naveh did not comment at all. While Rabin, Peres, and Barak reacted positively to the content of the proposal, due to the charged political nature of the issue they were unable to embrace it publicly.

We considered discussing the subject in an academic framework, and we therefore applied to the Rockefeller Foundation for funds to convene a conference on the issue of Jerusalem. The representative of the Rockefeller Foundation, Mr. Clifford Chanin, was at first reluctant, but once we convinced him that representatives of the Palestinians and other Arab countries would agree to participate in such a conference, he agreed to support it.

The first meeting of the conference took place in July 1998 in Bellagio, Italy. It is important to stress that at the initial meeting all of the Arab participants were hesitant to deal with the Temple Mount. They preferred instead to focus on the purely political aspects, such as the sovereignty of the city. Arabs from Jordan, Egypt, Morocco, and Saudi Arabia, as well as Palestinian Arabs, participated in the conference, and there were nine Israelis and three American participants. The outcome of the Bellagio meeting was a draft thinking-points paper. The second meeting of the conference took place in December 1999 in Amman, Jordan. Progress was made, but there was not yet a consensus on a solution among all the participants.

The third and final meeting of the conference was convened under the auspices of the University of Oklahoma's International Programs Center in January 2000 in Amman, Jordan, and was concluded in Jerusalem. The third conference was led by Ambassador Edward Perkins, the director of the International Programs Center at the University of Oklahoma and former US ambassador to several countries and to the United Nations. Saudi Arabian and Moroccan scholars did not participate in the third meeting, as they had in the first two conferences on this subject. We held a press conference in Jerusalem on January 23, 2000, two days after the conclusion of the conference, but did not distribute copies of the agreed upon conference paper.

Following are the "Negotiating Jerusalem: Guiding Principles" that resulted from the conference. Except for one Israeli scholar who abstained, all of the participants voted in favor of the proposal. We presented the proposal to the Israeli prime minister through the minister in charge of Jerusalem, Haim Ramon, only two hours prior to the press conference. It was also forwarded to Palestinian Chairman Arafat through Abu Ala, President of the Palestinian Parliament. The guiding principles of negotiating Jerusalem were presented to King Abdullah of Jordan and President Mubarak of Egypt at the same time by the Jordanian and the Egyptian participants of the conference. At the January 23 press conference there were many Arab journalists representing not only the Palestinian Authority but the regional Arab media as well.

We were subsequently notified that Chairman Arafat accepted the proposal. This proposal, which is comprehensive of the entire negotiating process, has relevance to the Temple Mount problem, and is therefore presented here.

Negotiating Jerusalem:
Guiding Principles:
January 23, 2000

First released to the office of the Prime Minister of the State of Israel at 0900 hours, January 23, 2000 in Jerusalem.

Released to the Office of the Chairman of the Palestinian national Authority at 1000 hours, January 23, 2000 in Abu Dis.

Subsequently presented to: His Majesty King Abdullah bin Al Hussein of the Hashemite Kingdom of Jordan and to President Muhammad Husny Mubarak of the Arab Republic of Egypt.

Recognizing the historic opportunity that Arabs and Israelis have at the beginning of the new millenium to secure comprehensive peace between them, *being cognizant* of the looming deadline for a final settlement of the Palestinian–Israeli conflict,

believing that neither party can resolve the conflict unilaterally,

understanding the central importance of Jerusalem to Palestinians and Israelis, religiously, culturally, and politically,

considering the significance of Jerusalem to Muslims, Jews, Christians, and other communities and to many states, including Jordan, which has played a significant role in East Jerusalem for several decades,

accepting the principles of equity, fairness, and reciprocity among the parties in searching for a lasting settlement,

having examined and debated the issue of Jerusalem in several sessions over the last two years, and having overcome serious disagreements in the process,

we, a group of international academics and practitioners, including Israelis, Palestinians, Jordanians, Egyptians, Americans, and others, acting as individuals,

resolved to put forth the following **Guiding Principles** for the final settlement of the Jerusalem issue:

Neither the imposition of annexation nor the partition of Jerusalem could serve as a basis for the final status of the city. Jerusalem is to be the capital of both Israel and Palestine in Jewish West and Arab East of the city, respectively and on equal footing.

Palestinians and Israelis shall be sovereign over their respective capitals as stipulated in the first principle above.

The unique religious, cultural, and historical importance of the walled part of Jerusalem to both sides requires special arrangements for this part to be negotiated by the parties.

The wholeness of Jerusalem should be upheld, with open access to Israelis and Palestinians alike.

Governance of the city must be respectful of Jerusalem's important pluralistic and multicultural character. The protection and preservation of the unique religious interests of Christians, Jews, and Muslims must be guaranteed, and freedom of worship and access to holy–places must be granted.

The status quo in the administration of holy places should be maintained, and a coordination mechanism among the various religious authorities should be introduced.

Principles of self-governance of all communities and at all levels must be equitable and democratic.

It is necessary to resolve the issue of Jewish neighborhoods/settlements in and around Jerusalem beyond the 1967 "green line," and to reconcile existing realities with the existing agreements between the parties and with relevant international resolutions.

Residents of Jerusalem, including non-citizens, shall be subject to equitable rules and regulations to be agreed upon by Israel and the Palestine Liberation Organization.

Municipal arrangements in Jerusalem must be consistent with above principles. Among the possible arrangements consistent with these principles is the establishment of two municipal councils in the two respective capitals and a coordination commission for the entire city with equal representation.

No unilateral step that would affect the final status and boundaries of Jerusalem, beyond the 1967 green line, should be taken prior to final agreement.

Participants

Dr. Mohammed Ali, *Jordanian*	Professor Manuel Hassassian, *Palestinian*
Mr. Rateb M. Amro, *Jordanian*	Professor Saad Eddin Ibrahim, *Egyptian*
Dr. Taisir Amre, *Palestinian*	Mr. Abdullah T. Kanaan, *Jordanian*
(Amb.) Tahseen Basheer, *Egyptian*	Dr. Menachem Klein, *Israeli*
Professor Dale Eickelman, *American*	Professor Moshe Ma'oz, *Israeli*
Dr. Khalil Elian, *Jordanian*	Mr. Rami Nasrallah, *Palestinian*
Dr. Bahieldin Elibarchy, *Egyptian*	(Amb.) Edward Perkins, *American*
Professor Abraham Friedman, *Israeli*	Dr. Hussein Ramzoun, *Jordanian*
(Gen.) Shlomo Gazit, *Israeli*	Dr. Itzhak Reiter, *Israeli*
Professor Joseph Ginat, *Israeli*	Professor Shimon Shamir, *Israeli*
Dr. Motti Golani, *Israeli*	Professor Shibley Telhami, *American*
Dr. Mohammad Jadallah, *Palestinian*	Mr. Khalil Tufakji, *Palestinian*
Professor Mohanna Haddad, *Jordanian*	Professor Ephraim Ya'ar, *Israeli*

This project was funded by the Rockefeller Foundation and sponsored by the Center for Peace Studies of the International Programs Center at the University of Oklahoma.

*   *   *

With respect to resolving differences over the Temple Mount, in informal meetings among the members of the delegations at these three conferences

I was told that in peace negotiations it was important to resolve the political issues first and only then to tackle the religious problems. We must remember that the last conference held in January 2000 was half a year prior to the failed Camp David Summit. The Oslo peace process still held promise, and participants emphasized that on Jerusalem it was extremely important to preserve the status quo, allowing Jews and Arabs to co-exist in two adjacent capitals. There was hope for a political settlement, after which the sides would examine the issue of the Old City and religious sites. Some of the conference attendees voiced the view that it would be impossible to solve quickly a conflict of over 100 years, such as the Temple Mount, and that a period of co-existence and cooperation was desirable before dealing with such a sensitive issue.

The explanation for their position is, however, more complex. Most of the Muslim World sees the Temple Mount as a religious matter, and only secondarily as a political issue. There is a Muslim committee for oversight of Jerusalem, and the entire Muslim World elected the King of Morocco as the committee chairman. Yasser Arafat was appointed only as deputy chairman. Thus, it is apparent that Haram al-Sharif is to the Muslim World an even broader issue than the political issue of Jerusalem, and must be dealt with separately. Undoubtedly, the Arab countries fully support East Jerusalem as the capital of Palestine, but that does not imply that they want the Temple Mount to be under Palestinian sovereignty as well. They consider it a separate subject.

At the meetings of this third conference on Jerusalem, Professor Ya'ar and I became all the more convinced that the ideal solution for the Temple Mount issue was embodied in our proposal. And, as will be seen at the end of this chapter, with the unfortunate disrupture of talks on political issues for almost two years, I now believe that talks on the Temple Mount using the Ginat–Ya'ar proposal should proceed. The proposal should not be too controversial, and if adopted could improve the atmosphere for political negotiations.

In the proposal we emphasize that the management of the site itself would be under a Muslim committee.[1] It would include the Palestinians, but they would not be the sole managers. We eliminate the term "sovereignty" completely, because we believe that the late King Hussein's conception of the holy places was and remains the most realistic:

> My religious faith demands that sovereignty over the holy places in Jerusalem resides with God and God alone. Dialogue between the faiths should be strengthened; religious sovereignty should be accorded to all believers of the three Abrahamic faiths, in accordance with their religions.[2]

In December 2000, Ephraim Ya'ar and I met with Egyptian dignitaries, among them academics and retired politicians. Our general impression was that they accepted our proposal, although some of them indicated that it might still need additional modifications. The mere fact that after reviewing the proposal they recommended only minor changes demonstrated a *de facto* acceptance on their behalf. Stemming from their reactions, we presented the proposal to dignitaries and academics in Jordan. We received a similar response.

Following is the proposal as it was presented to the Egyptians and the Jordanians:

Temple Mount – al-Haram al-Sharif: A Suggested Solution

Temple Mount is the third holiest place to Islam, after Mecca and Medina, and yet is the only one not under full Muslim rule. Jewish people regard Temple Mount as the holiest of places, where the Jewish temple had once stood, and according to Jewish faith will only be rebuilt once the Messiah appears. As long as this has not happened, the mountain itself is forbidden and many observant Jews avoid approaching the Mount itself.

Muslims the world over perceive Temple Mount as a place of religious, rather than of political significance. Islamic countries wish fervently for the establishment of a Palestinian state with Jerusalem as its capital; these same countries are of the opinion that Temple Mount should be under a joint Islamic management, with the Palestinians as partners, rather than have the Mount managed exclusively by Palestinians.

The Islamic world elected the king of Morocco to chair the Jerusalem committee, with Yasser Arafat merely his second in command. When king Hasan II of Morocco died the Muslim world did not even wait for the 40 days of official mourning to end before electing his son, king Muhammad VI, to succeed him as chairman of the Jerusalem committee.

We think the entire management of the Temple Mount should be turned over to the Islamic committee. Egypt, the largest Islamic state in the region, which also has peaceful relations with Israel and Jordan, should preferably play a central role in this committee. Discussions would be held at two levels: coordination at the inter-Islamic level and with the Israelis. The Temple Mount should be transferred to the full control of an Islamic body.

The management of Temple Mount itself should also be carried out at two levels:

Everyday management, should be by Jordan, the Palestinians, and Egypt; and overall policy management by Egypt, Jordan, Palestine, Morocco, and Saudi Arabia.

Since Jews perceive Temple Mount as the most sacred place to their religion, the Temple Mount managing committee should take this into account. The Islamic managing committee should designate a place near the entrance gate to Temple Mount where Jews would be permitted to pray.

Obviously, on Fridays or on any Muslim religious holiday Jews would not be permitted to enter the Haram al-Sharif compound to pray near the Western Wall. The Islamic committee would also determine the maximum number of Jewish worshippers at any one time.

We are not suggesting here the construction of any structure whatsoever, but rather an area for short prayers east of the Wailing Wall within the Haram al-Sharif. The final decision on this issue would be placed in the hands of the members of the Islamic committee, and their designation of such a prayer area would not be a prerequisite for the transfer of absolute management of the Temple Mount to the Islamic committee.

The Ginat–Ya'ar proposal is practical, and, more importantly, would be a permanent solution. In our proposal there is no reference to the concept of sovereignty. We refer only to the management of the Temple Mount. Moshe Hirsch, in his study on the functional approach and the future arrangements of Jerusalem and the Temple Mount, says that he does not present a specific solution to the future of the Temple Mount or Jerusalem in general. He only indicates the possibility of using different functional arrangements as a basis to a future agreement between the sides.[3] In contrast to Hirsch, the Ginat–Ya'ar proposal is presented as a tenable solution. Whereas Hirsch suggests that the Palestinians should consult other Muslim countries on the issue of management, we propose, instead, that the management should be by a group of Muslim countries, including the Palestinians, but not by the Palestinians alone.

In February and March of 2001 I met twice with the Sephardic Chief Rabbi, Rabbi Baqshi Doron, together with a high official from one of the Arab countries who read the Ginat–Ya'ar proposal. The Arab official indicated that he liked it. He wanted to know the reaction of the Chief Rabbi toward the proposal. Chief Rabbi Doron did not have any objection to the proposal, although he said he could not comment on Jewish prayer on the Temple Mount.[4] As to the issue of sovereignty, he was very firm that no one in the world can relinquish it.[5]

Professor Ya'ar and I sent a copy of our above proposal to Prime Minister Barak and asked for a meeting during Camp David. We thought that the question of the Temple Mount should not be discussed in that summit, since we consider it a religious, not a political, issue. On the basis of information "leaked" about the Camp David summit deliberations, the media reported that President Clinton had suggested that the Temple Mount could have "schizophrenic sovereignty"; that is, the Palestinians could be granted sovereignty above ground and the Israelis could have sovereignty underground. Prime Minister Barak agreed to this proposal.[6] President Clinton opined that the Israeli public would not oppose this creative solution.

Professor Ya'ar and I believe that Jordan should be involved in any talks

regarding the future of Temple Mount because of Jordan's historical role
in protecting the religious sites:

> The peace talks between Israel and Jordan produced the Washington
> Declaration signed by Rabin and Hussein on July 25, 1994. One of the
> Declaration's sections relates to Jerusalem's holy places. This section, later
> copied in substantially similar language into the Israeli-Jordanian peace
> treaty of September 1994, confirmed Palestinian apprehensions about Israeli
> activities in Jerusalem, and rekindled discord between the PLO and Jordan.[7]

The Washington Declaration states that:

> Israel respects the present special role of the Hashemite Kingdom of Jordan
> in Muslim holy shrines in Jerusalem. When negotiations on the permanent
> status takes place, Israel will give high priority to the Jordanian historic role
> in these shrines. In addition the two sides have agreed to act together to
> promote interfaith relations among the monotheistic religious.[8]

Menachem Klein refers to His Royal Highness Prince Hassan of Jordan
saying that:

> Jordan had never, and would never, relinquish its responsibility over the
> Islamic holy places in East Jerusalem. In his view, it was necessary to do
> everything to separate the religious and political issues in East Jerusalem, not
> only in an interim period, but also in a permanent settlement.[9]

On January 17, 2001, less than a month before the Israeli special election
for prime minister (February 6, 2001), Professor Ya'ar and I were invited
to the prime minister Barak's home. For over two hours we tried to
convince him that our proposal would be more feasible than the
Clinton–Barak approach. We suggested that he contact President
Mubarak and King Abdullah as well as King Muhammed VI of Morocco
to find out if they would support our proposal. If the proposal were to be
presented to Arafat from other Muslim leaders, it would elicit a different
reaction from it being presented in the context of Israeli–Palestinian discussions. We also emphasized that when we showed our proposal in Egypt and
Jordan, the reference to the possibility for Jews to pray on the Temple
Mount had not traumatized them. Although Prime Minister Barak did not
have any negative comments throughout the discussion, we both felt that
he was committed to the idea of shared sovereignty instead of our proposal.

Most Orthodox Jews refrain from entering the Temple Mount. The main
reason is that no one knows the exact location where the Jewish Temple
once stood. If Jewish people walk on the Temple Mount, they might be
walking on the site of the holy of holies, where only the high priest was
allowed to enter once a year on the Day of Atonement (Yom Hakippurim).
There are several theories as to where the Temple used to stand. It is not in
the scope of this chapter to discuss this issue, but I will just mention that

the most traditional and common theory is that the Temple stood where the Dome of the Rock is located today. A second theory was put forth by the late Rabbi Goren, who was the chief rabbi of Israel. According to him, only the western part of the Temple was under the Dome, and the central part with the altar was on the plateau west of the Dome. The holy of holies, according to his theory, was on the steps leading to the Western Wall.[10] Rabbi Goren felt that Jews were allowed to walk anywhere on the Temple Mount except for the aforementioned steps. A third theory by Dr. Asher F. Kaufman claims that the Temple was located north of the Dome of the Rock and that the holy of holies was located directly in front of the Golden Gate (gate of mercy).[11]

It is implausible that the Temple could have been adjacent to the east side of the Western Wall. Herod the Great leveled the area of the Temple around 20 BCE. Thus if we propose that Jews be permitted to pray on Temple Mount but adjacent to the east side of the Western Wall, there is no way that Jews standing there would violate religious prohibitions. According to our proposal, there would not be any additional building (such as a synagogue) on the Temple Mount, and the members of the Temple Mount committee can decide the exact site, days, and number of people who can pray.[12] I should emphasize again that the entire issue of the possibility of Jews praying on the Temple Mount would not be a pre-requisite for negotiating the site with the Muslim world; in the end the decision will be up to them.

Some people, among them politicians and academics, who saw and agreed with our proposal claimed that it was too late to implement it, because at Camp David Yasser Arafat had received a proposal from President Clinton to obtain sovereignty over the Temple Mount. I think that with the failure of Camp David, all the proposals and ideas up for discussion remain open to rereading and reinterpretation. Moreover, if after consultations with Israel, other Muslim leaders accept and present the proposal to Yasser Arafat, it would have a better chance of succeeding.

Some critics assert that the Camp David talks failed because of the Temple Mount sovereignty issue. If they are correct, there is little room for further progress or compromise. However, I believe that the refugee issue was actually what prevented Arafat from signing a deal at Camp David. Neither Arafat nor any other Palestinian leader will be able to remain in his position if the issue of the right of return is relinquished.[13] I personally believe in the advice of the participants in the Jerusalem conference, embodied in the above "Guiding Principles for Negotiating Jerusalem," namely that the peace process with the Palestinians must advance in stages. It is simply not possible to solve a conflict of 120 years in the course of a one-week summit, such as was attempted at Camp David. The "Guiding Principles" can serve as an excellent guideline for future political dis-cussions in the context of two capitals for two states.

The Temple Mount issue, among other religious issues, has to be dealt with in a completely different framework of discussions, one that is not political. An example of a different forum for such matters is the case of the Deir es-Sultan Monastery. The keys to the Deir es-Sultan corridor leading into the church of the Holy Sepulchre were formerly held by representatives of the Coptic (Egyptian) church. The State of Israel turned the keys over to the Ethiopian church. Both the Copts and the Egyptian government sought a decision by the Israeli Supreme Court on this matter. (In Professor Ya'ar's and my opinion an acceptable solution should be found which would give the Copts an equal status to the Ethiopians.)

Another example has to do with the Holy Sepulchre. Since the Ottoman Empire, the Easter celebrations and some of the ceremonies in the week prior to Easter have not taken place without an official representative of the ruling government (the Ottomans [Turks], British, Jordanians, and now the Israelis). During the first Easter after the 1967 war, the Prime Minister of Israel assigned the advisor on Arab affairs to represent the government. I was the deputy advisor at the time, and because the advisor, Shmuel Toledano, was unable to attend, I participated in his place. Even then I thought that Israel should change this practice. Why should a representative of the government oversee a religious ceremony, especially of another religion? The events included the "washing of the feet" on Thursday, the ceremony of Good Friday, the Friday night ritual, the Saturday fire ceremony, and the Easter ceremonies on Sunday. As these are purely religious issues, they should be purely religious ceremonies, run by religious leaders without the intervention of the government.

Returning now to the questions of procedures and timing of issues in the peace process, at the time of the three conferences on Jerusalem described earlier in this chapter, it was not foreseen that after the Camp David Summit that talks would breakdown and the second *Intifada* would produce a prolonged violent uprising. The Mitchell Mission (led by former US Senator George Mitchell) and US efforts led by CIA Director George Tenet to end the violence have at the date of writing this chapter in April, 2002 not achieved a cease-fire nor resumption of negotiations. There is still the expectation that a cessation of violence will be achieved and the parties will return to political negotiations. I suggest that when political discussions resume, the negotiators should separate the political issues – the refugees, settlements, the Jordan Valley, the water issue, and the political status of Jerusalem – from the religious issue of the Temple Mount. Contrary to the advice of many of the participants in the three conferences on Jerusalem, I no longer believe political issues should be solved prior to addressing the Temple Mount question. Because of the breakdown of talks and the poisoned atmosphere due to almost two years of violence, I now think resolving the Temple Mount problem first could greatly enhance the possibilities for successful negotiation of political issues.

I believe that the Palestinian refugee issue is the most complicated problem in the peace process, and I do not agree with Yizhak Reiter's assertion that the solution of the Temple Mount is the key to reaching a permanent agreement between Israel and the Palestinians,[14] but I repeat that reaching agreement first on the Temple Mount could make reaching a final peace accord easier. For one thing, once the religious issue of the Temple Mount is solved, the Muslim countries that will participate in its management could be in a position to have a positive influence on the entire process.

The Ginat–Ya'ar proposal is a viable solution to the Temple Mount issue. The proposal has been examined by Egyptians, Jordanians and Moroccans, and by scholars and retired politicians. The emphasis of the proposal is the separation of the political issue of Jerusalem from the religious issue of the Temple Mount, and to thereby allow the negotiating parties to move toward a solution for a permanent peace in the political sphere. Resolution of the Temple Mount issue should not be delayed.

Notes

1   In the talks between the Egyptians and the Israelis following the late President Sadat's visit to Israel (November 24, 1977) the Israeli Prime Minister Menachem Begin was willing to agree to self-rule for each denomination regarding the holy places in Jerusalem. He also suggested that countries which do not border Israel – such as Saudi Arabia, Morocco, and Iran – could participate in the management of the holy places. See Menachem Klein, "Temple Mount: A Challenge, Threatening, and Promising on the Path to an Agreement," in Yizhak Reiter, ed., *Sovereignty of God and Men: Sanctity and Political Centrality on the Temple Mount* (Jerusalem: The Jerusalem Institute for Israel Studies, 2001), p. 273 [in Hebrew].

2   Quoted from Menachem Klein, *Jerusalem; The Contested City* (London: Hurst & Company, 2001), p. 163. Adnan Abu-Odeh – who was a minister in the Jordanian government and was very close to the late King Hussein – introduced in 1992 the idea of separating political sovereignty and religious sovereignty. See Adnan Abu-Odeh, "Two Capitals in an Undivided Jerusalem," *Foreign Affairs*, 17 (1992), pp. 183–8.

3   Moshe Hirsch, "The Functional Approach and the Future Arrangements of Jerusalem and the Temple Mount," in Yizhak Reiter, *Sovereignty of God and Men*, pp. 338 and 350.

4   For more reference regarding the Jews and the Temple Mount see Amnon Ramon, "Beyond the Western Wall: The Attitude of the Israeli Government and the Jewish Public of all its Aspects on the Temple Mount (1967–1999)," in Yitzhak Reiter, ed., *Sovereignty of God and Men*, pp. 113 and 142. See also Shmuel Berkowitz, "Status of Temple Mount and the Western Wall in Israeli Law," in Yizhak Reiter, ed., *Sovereignty of God and Men*, pp. 183 and 240.

5   Ifrah Zilberman, "Confrontation of the Mosque – The Temple in Jerusalem and in Ayodhya," in Yizhak Reiter, ed., *Sovereignty of God and Men*. Zilberman refers to I. England's paper, "The Legal Status of the Holy Places

in Jerusalem," *Israel Law Review,* No. 4, Vol. 28 (1994), p. 1, which states that in confrontations between religious groups on "holy places," the parties in the conflict feel it is difficult to give up what they feel is their "right." From their perspective the rights come from a divine source, and, therefore, a human being does not have a mandate to relinquish those rights.

6   The idea behind this proposal is that the Muslims would not be allowed to dig on the Temple Mount to try to reach the possible remains of the Jewish Temple.

7   See Klein, *Jerusalem: The Contested City*, p. 162

8   Walter Laqueur and Barry Rubin, eds., *The Arab–Israeli Reader: A Documentary History of the Middle East Conflict* (New York: Penguin, 1995), p. 655.

9   See Klein, *Jerusalem: The Contested City*, p. 163

10 Rabbi Shlomo Goren showed me diagrams of his hypothesis in 1972.

11 For the entire theory see Asher S. Kaufman, "Where the Ancient Temple Stood?," *Biblical Archaeologist Review*, Vol. 9, No. 2 (1983), pp. 42–59. There is no indication that the contemporary Ottoman walls of the Old City, including the Golden Gate, are exactly above the walls and gates at the time of the Second Temple. The entire area of the contemporary Golden Gate east of the eastern wall of the Temple Mount is a Muslim cemetery. As such it is unlikely that any excavations can take place there.

12 Obviously it cannot be less than 10 people because in Judaism a quorum (minyan) is no less than 10 men.

13 For more details, see Joseph Ginat and Edward J. Perkins, "Concluding Remarks," in Joseph Ginat and Edward J. Perkins, eds., *The Palestinian Refugees: Old Problems – New Solutions* (Norman, OK: University of Oklahoma Press; Brighton and Portland: Sussex Academic Press, 2001).

14 Yitzhak Reiter, "The Status Quo of Temple Mount – al-Haram al-Sharif – Under Israeli Control 1967–2000. Appendix: The Status Quo as a Point of Departure for a Future Arrangement," in Yitzhak Reiter, ed. *Sovereignty of God and Men*, p. 318.

CHAPTER 28

Postscript, May 2002

JOSEPH GINAT, EDWARD J. PERKINS, AND EDWIN G. CORR

The experience, knowledge, detail, analyses, options explored, and recommendations that are encompassed in this book by experts on Middle East are of great worth for all those interested in the negotiation of a lasting peace for that region. The book draws upon and brings together research and observations on the Middle East from such disciplines as political science, law, sociology, and anthropology. The content is particularly important for those who are or will be involved in the negotiating process, both for officials and diplomats directly negotiating and for the numerous, strong and influential persons of the Middle East, the United States and Europe who are actively and meaningfully engaged in citizen diplomacy that has proved to have a growing impact on official negotiations and talks. The book may become imminently more valuable as there now are increasing prospects and hopes for a return to the negotiating table after almost two years of strife. The period has been marked by growing numbers of innocent victims of despairing violence and by diminishing mutual trust between Israelis and Arabs.

These remarks are being written in May 2002 after twenty months of conflict that began as the second *Intifada* after now Prime Minister Ariel Sharon's provocative visit to the Temple Mount on September 28, 2000. The violence began with rock-throwing youths and steadily escalated to guerrilla warfare, Palestinian suicide bombers and a full-scale mobilization of the Israeli Defence Forces (IDF) who invaded and occupied Palestinian Authority controlled territory on March 30, 2002. Palestinian suicide bombers had attacked, killed, and maimed Israeli civilians within the state of Israel and in response the IDF used well trained, powerfully armed soldiers with tanks and aircraft in the Palestinian Authority area, killing and wounding not only armed men but also unarmed civilians, and bull-dozing about 100 buildings in the middle of the Jenin refugee camp that has been the origin of many Palestinian suicide bombers.[1] The reason that many of the buildings were demolished was that Palestinians had planted mines and explosive traps throughout the buildings. Aside from the horrendous death and destruction on both sides, the physical infrastructure of the Palestinian Authority was largely destroyed, and the economies of Israel and especially of the Palestinian Authority were greatly damaged.

The political landscape is uncertain. Some think a goal of the Sharon government was to destroy the Palestinian Authority and Arafat by demolishing their power to govern, and that the IDF came close to doing that. Israel, from October 2000 until the summer of 2002, has been unified by what most Israelis have regarded as a renewed strong threat to national survival, namely suicide-bomber killings within the Israeli state, and by perceptions of growing signs of anti-Semitism – especially in Europe, not to speak of the Islamic world. The same instinct for national survival against 35 years of Israeli occupation of what Palestinians consider to be their rightful lands, and the March 30, 2002 full invasion of the Palestinian Authority by the IDF, has further reinforced the resolve of the Palestinians and increased solidarity among Arabs. There are, however, those in Israel who question the Sharon government's destructive policies and comportment, and ask if they were necessary and ethical. Others question whether the military campaign indeed accomplished the goals for which it was implemented. There are also persons from the Arab world questioning their own past actions, the efficacy and accountability of their governments, and what are the next steps needed to gain greater legitimacy, better governance, and formal recognition of a territorially viable Palestinian state.

These same questions are being asked in other parts of the world, including the United States, which has for decades stood strongly with Israel. The situation and how to address it is complicated for the United States and other nations by an as yet unclear response to the "world war on terrorism" launched by the US after the September 11, 2001 terrorist attack on New York City and Washington, D.C., and by conflicting US political and economic interests in the Middle East. There are doubts about how US policies, actions, and non-actions square with promoting the ideals of self-determination, democracy, and respect for human rights (both by governments and non-governmental groups) that Americans cherish.

This Postscript discusses first the current situation and prospects for Israeli–Palestinian negotiations. The highlights of the content of negotiations during the Barak government are then briefly described, followed by comments on specific issues that must be resolved in order to reach a final peace agreement.

Developments that Augur for Return to Negotiations

The twenty months of violence was preceded by seven years of intermittent negotiations that culminated in meetings at Camp David under the auspices of President William J. Clinton, July 11–25, 2000; at Sharm el-Sheikh, Egypt, October 16, 2000; and at Taba, Egypt, January 21, 2001, in which Israel and the Palestinian Authority moved close to an agreement. Though unsuccessful, "the negotiations that took place between July 2000 and February 2001 make up an indelible chapter in the history of the Israeli–Palestinian conflict . . . taboos were shattered, the unspoken got spoken, and, during that period, Israelis and Palestinians reached an unprecedented level of understanding of what it will take to end their struggle."[2]

After steadily increasing levels of violence during the second *Intifada* that culminated in a series of Palestinian suicide bomber attacks against civilians within Israel, Sharon invaded the Palestinian Authority on March 30, 2002 in what was the largest Israeli ground offensive in twenty years. The invasion followed a suicide-bombing massacre of civilians observing the Passover in a hotel in Netanya. The question now is whether the two sides remain sincerely interested in seeking a negotiated solution, and, if so, can they overcome increased distrust and hatred and return to the negotiating table. In the opinion of the co-editors, this is the only feasible, lasting solution. Sooner or later the Israelis and Palestinians must learn to live together peacefully in two fully established sovereign states, and the Israelis and all Arab states must establish normal relations. Developments that began in February 2002 and new events that continue to occur could lead to serious talks toward these ends.

Yasser Arafat wrote an article, published in the *New York Times* on February 3, 2002, in which he condemned terrorist attacks by Palestinian groups, and stated, "These groups do not represent the Palestinian people nor their legitimate aspirations for freedom." Arafat made clear that he believes a final settlement will include an independent and viable Palestinian state alongside Israel in the territories occupied by Israel in 1967. Significantly, when calling for a "fair and just" solution to the plight of Palestinian refugees, he also wrote that "Palestinians must be realistic with respect to Israel's demographic desires." Regarding the siege of his headquarters in Ramallah, Arafat responded, "The personal attacks on me currently in vogue may be highly effective in giving Israelis an excuse to ignore their own role in creating the current situation. But these attacks do little to move the peace process forward, and, in fact are not designed to." Arafat concluded, "Palestinians are ready to end the conflict . . . But we will only sit down as equals, not as supplicants; as partners, not as subjects; as seekers of a just and peaceful solution, not as a defeated nation grateful for whatever scraps are thrown our way. For despite Israel's overwhelming military advantage, we possess something even greater: the power of justice."[3]

On February 11, 2002, the Peres–Abu Ala peace proposal was published in the Israeli press. It called for the immediate establishment of a

Palestinian state, immediate resumption of final status talks, and immediate implementation of the Mitchell and Tenet proposals without waiting for Sharon's stipulated seven days of quiet. Israeli recognition of the State of Palestine would have occurred even though major issues remained unresolved. Comprehensive negotiations would have begun eight weeks after the cease-fire and lasted a year, followed by a year for implementation of the agreement. Final borders would be based on UN Resolutions 242 and 338. Prime Minister Sharon, who was kept informed of the negotiations, characterized the plan as illusionary and dangerous. Some members of the Likud, one of them a member of the cabinet, stated that a Palestinian state will never be established and therefore the plan was not viable. The plan was finally doomed when on February 12, 2002, Yasser Abed Rabbo, the Palestinian minister of information, said that the boundaries would have to be the boundaries of 1967, including Jerusalem.

On February 21, 2002, *The New York Times* ran an editorial and a story by Henry Siegman about an interview of newsman Thomas Friedman with Saudi Arabia's Crown Prince Abdullah who said that his country was ready to sign a peace treaty with Israel if Israel were to sign a peace accord with the Palestinians. The Saudi Government then released the same information. The editorial stated that the Saudis were now willing to accept Israeli control over the Wailing Wall and Jewish neighborhoods in East Jerusalem. One of the reasons the Camp David talks failed was Saudi Arabia's refusal to endorse such compromises on Jerusalem.[4] A summit meeting of the twenty-two nation Arab League, including such unflinching foes of Israel as Iraq and Syria, was held in Beirut, Lebanon on March 28, 2002. The member-states unanimously approved the Saudi proposal, based not on land for peace, but on full normalization of cultural, economic, and political relations between the Arab states and Israel in return for Israel withdrawing to pre-1967 borders. Of course a number of difficult details and issues, including some adjustments of borders and territory, will still have to be worked out to make such a settlement possible. The Arab initiative could offer Palestinian leaders critical political and cultural support to crack down on violent opposition groups, such as Hamas and Islamic Jihad, and to compromise on issues of refugees, Jerusalem, and borders.[5]

Although Israeli forces continued to occupy militarily much of the Palestinian Authority, international pressures and creative international diplomacy led the Israelis on May 2, 2002 to free Chairman Yasser Arafat from his headquarters in Ramallah, where the IDF with tanks and soldiers had him penned in for more than three weeks. From the Israeli point of view the siege was not of Arafat but of the four assassins of an Israeli cabinet member who were in the headquarters with Arafat. With the intervention of the American and British governments, the four assassins were put in prison in Jericho (West Bank) under British and American supervision. The Israeli government's allegations that Arafat was responsible for and must stop completely all suicide bombings, and Israeli threats/sound-ings about exiling Arafat, left the impression with much of the outside world that Arafat, too, was a prisoner of the IDF, not just the four assassins.

Following the IDF invasion, 39 armed Palestinians fled from the Israeli soldiers seeking them into the 1,700 year old Church of the Nativity, constructed as a shrine over the site where many believe Christ was born. Clergy and a number of other Palestinians were also in the Church, and these were joined by a group of international "peace activists." The IDF surrounded the Church with tanks, soldiers, and snipers. After inter-national pressure and much bargaining throughout 39 days, 13 of the most wanted terrorists were exiled to Europe, and 26 lesser wanted armed Palestinians were sent to Gaza on May 9, 2002. Others in the Church had been freed during the last days of the siege or were released on the last day.

After the Israeli invasion of the Palestinian Authority, President Bush on April 4, 2002, with Secretary of State Colin Powell at his side in the White House Rose Garden, called upon Chairman Arafat to condemn terrorism and suicide bombing, and on the Israelis to halt incursions and begin troop withdrawals. On April 6, President Bush clarified that he meant withdrawal "without delay." Secretary Powell also departed on April 6 for a visit to Europe and the Middle East, and on that same day, Condoleezza Rice, the US National Security Adviser, told the press that "without delay" means "right now." President Bush on April 9 said the Israelis must continue withdrawing from the Palestine Authority area, but they did not. Ari Fleischer, the White House spokesman, told reporters that "the President believes that Ariel Sharon is a 'man of peace'" on April 11, and then on April 17 (13 days after the Rose Garden speech) said the President understood the need for the Israelis to continue the siege of Arafat's Headquarters in Ramallah. He repeated his description of Sharon as a "man of peace."[6]

The general impression in the United States was that Secretary Powell had only limited success during his trip to the Palestinian Authority and to Israel. Evidently, the President did not give him sufficient leverage to persuade Prime Minister Sharon to withdraw Israeli troops and to enter into talks with the Palestinians. Some felt that the Secretary had been some-what humiliated by Sharon.

Prime Minister Sharon, in a briefing on April 23, 2002, announced that the Israelis had completed Operation Defensive Shield, although all troops had not yet been withdrawn, and that he had proposed a regional peace conference at which Israel would present a peace plan containing three phases:

1. A complete cessation of violence, hostilities, and especially incitement which leads to violent terrorist acts.

2.   A long-term intermediate agreement, similar to an armistice.
3.   A permanent agreement, in which Israel's final borders and the
     Palestinian's final borders would be established, ending the conflict
     between Israel and the Palestinians, and between Israel and the Arab
     countries. This agreement must be based on Israel's right to exist in
     secure borders and provide for normalized relations with all countries
     in the region."[7]

During Prime Minister Sharon's visit to Washington, May 6–7, 2002,
however, his public statements seemed aimed at further discrediting Arafat,
getting approval for Arafat's ouster, and delaying any serious talks directed
toward a final peace agreement. By emphasizing the building of barriers
and a buffer zone between Palestinians and Israelis, he left any possibility
of Israel's recognition of a Palestinian state to the future, and was vague
about when a regional peace conference might be held. Sharon continued
to insist that Israel must win completely its "war against terrorists" in
Palestine, and that the governing authority there would have to be
thoroughly reformed into an honest, transparent entity that demonstrates
that it takes firm measures to suppress all terrorist activities before Israel
would discuss a permanent political arrangement.

    While in Washington, Sharon accused the Saudis of supporting
terrorism and suicide bombers' families. He and his delegation presented
documentation purporting to show both Arafat's and the Saudis' direct
involvement in terrorism against Israel. Prime Minster Sharon had openly
declared support for a regional summit after the Saudi and Arab League
peace proposal, and in Washington he again referred to the possibility of
a regional conference, perhaps to be held in Turkey, for discussions on how
to achieve security for Israel and peace and order in the Palestinian territories. He did not publicly endorse the Saudi and Arab League initiative
that many think could be a significant development after decades of
searching for a means toward Middle East peace.

    On May 2, 2002, the Bush Administration announced that it was joining
with Europe, Russia, and the United Nations in a conference on the Middle
East early in the summer. Powell has referred to this group as the "quartet."
The meeting will be at the ministerial level, not chief of state, thus avoiding
a meeting between Sharon and Arafat, with whom Sharon has said he will
not meet. Secretary of State Colin Powell said the conference would address
issues of security, economic reform, humanitarian needs and the "political
way forward," but US officials have emphasized that the meeting, though
important, is not intended to be a major event, such as the Madrid conference. President Bush repeated his earlier commitment to a Palestinian state
while warning that such a state could not be built "on a foundation of terror
and corruption," and he reiterated his call for an end to Israeli occupation
of the Palestinian Authority.[8]

The same day the Bush administration announced the conference for summer 2002 on the Middle East, both houses of the US Congress adopted resolutions expressing strong solidarity with Israel in a "common struggle against terrorism as it takes necessary steps to provide security to its people by dismantling the terrorist infrastructure in the Palestinian areas." The vote was 94 to 2 in the Senate and 352 to 21 in the House. The White House unsuccessfully tried to have the cited language removed. The White House was able to have added to the House resolution a provision calling for "action to alleviate the humanitarian needs of the Palestinian people."[9]

The more active role begun by the United States government in 2002 seemingly derives from the alarming situation of the Middle East during the previous months, and from the US accord with the Saudi Government at a meeting of Saudi Crown Prince Abdullah with President Bush at the Crawford Ranch in Texas during the last week of April 2002. News reports and comments by official sources revealed that the United States had agreed with the Saudis to employ more strongly US influence with Israel to move that government toward an acceptable negotiated solution, and that the Saudis, along with other friendly Arab states (i.e., Egypt and Jordan) would exert pressures on the Palestinian leadership to quell terrorist type attacks and provide more accountable governance. In short, the idea is that moderate Arab states friendly with the United States will manage the Palestinians and Arafat, while the United States will manage the Israelis and Sharon. The sensitivity of Israel and Palestinians to outside opinion and pressure will be discussed below. Of course, neither the Israelis nor the Palestinians are "manageable" if they think vital interests of their nations are at stake.

Lack of US attention toward the Middle East during the first year of the George W. Bush administration is in stark contrast with the intensive involvement of President Clinton, especially during the last year of his government. President Bush campaigned primarily on domestic policy issues and that is where he devoted most of his time during his first year in office. His national security concerns focused on missile defense and his foreign policy priority was Latin America. This all changed with the September 11, 2001 terrorist attack that put the "war on terrorism" and foreign affairs to the top of his agenda. During the initial response to the September 11 attack, the Israeli–Palestinian conflict remained on the margin. The US government seemed to give Sharon free rein. Within the Middle East it was Iraq and Iran that were focused upon, along with North Korea in Asia, as an "evil axis" threatening the United States and the rest of the world with terrorism and the development of weapons of mass destructions.

The Israelis strove, fairly successfully, to define their conflict with Palestine as part of the US war on terrorism. Palestinian suicide bombers helped the Israelis in this regard, and few would dispute Israel's right to go into the Palestinian Authority after terrorists. A *Washington Post* editorial, however, pointed out that the problem of equating Israel's campaign against terrorism with the US-led world war on terrorism, as Prime Minister Sharon and some of his American supporters do, is that it disregards the decades-long Israeli–Palestinian struggle over territory and sovereignty. Palestinian national aspirations are recognized as legitimate by the United Nations and were tacitly accepted by Israel when it signed the Oslo Accords of 1993, although the Likud Party and parts of Prime Minister Sharon's coalition government are devoted to Israel's control and settlement of the territories occupied in the 1967 Six Day War as necessary to defend against the Palestinian threat to Israel.[10] The Israeli campaign is in this way distinct from the US-led campaign in Afghanistan. One must distinguish between legitimate defense against terrorism and using counterterrorism to justify unacceptable gains. Some think the Israelis may have been trying to do both.

It is important to note that Prime Minister Sharon himself has said that a Palestinian state is in the end inevitable, and a poll published in the Tel Aviv newspaper *Maariv* on May 10, 2002 "showed 57 percent of Israelis favoring a regional peace conference on the notion of two states for two peoples." Moreover, on May 14, 2002 the newspaper Y*ediot Ahoronot* reported that an overwhelming majority of Likud Party members disagreed with the Party's Central Committee – controlled by Sharon's rival Benjamin Netanyahu – resolution adopted on May 12, 2002 never to allow the creation of a Palestinian state.[11]

Perhaps the shift in US attention to the Middle East in 2002 began when Vice President Richard Cheney toured the Middle East in March to sound out governments about US policy on and about Arab support for bringing down Iraq's Sadaam Hussein. Instead of dealing with Iraq, Cheney was forced to respond to enjoinders for the US government to use its influence with the Israelis to force their withdrawal from Palestine and to return to negotiations with the Palestinians. Subsequent meetings between the US President and chiefs of state of friendly Arab countries further reinforced this, and culminated with Saudi Crown Prince Abdullah's meetings with President Bush in Texas.

The same day that the United States announced the forthcoming summer conference of the "quartet" powers on the Middle East, Jordan's Prince El Hassan bin Talal, the Chairman of the Board of Visitors of the Center for Peace Studies that has its headquarters at the University of Oklahoma, in his capacity as the Moderator of the World Conference on Religion and Peace (WCRP), called for a peaceful end to the Israeli siege around the Church of the Nativity where both Christian clergy and armed Palestinians were entrapped. His Royal Highness Prince Hassan, as a believing Muslim and on behalf of and united with his religious colleagues, asked that the Church be accorded the protection that holy sites of the Middle East have been accorded historically. Moreover, he called for:

"First, upon Israeli and Palestinian leaders to work together to immediately (a) withdraw the Israeli military forces from all the areas earmarked under the jurisdiction of the Palestinian Authority; (b) reject, condemn and take legally permissible action against all terrorism; (c) effect a formal cease-fire; (d) respect human rights and the commitments under the mutual agreements concluded between them; and, (e) begin political negotiations aimed at the establishment of a just and durable peace;

"Second, upon the member states of the Arab League to continue their laudable efforts to have a comprehensive peace established;

"Third, upon the United Nations to take immediate steps necessary to create peace through mandates and instruments available to it;

"Fourth, on all the states around the world to use their good offices in building peace and desisting from action that could further exacerbate the conflict;

"Fifth, upon the United States to actively exercise its peacemaking role, with the vigour commensurate with its capacity;

"Sixth, upon the world community to unite in extending financial and technical assistance for the rehabilitation for war damages and the development of the Palestinian territories; and finally;

"Seventh, upon believers around the world, especially the Jews, Christians and Muslims of the Holy Land, to unite in solidarity for Peace in the Land of Peace."

Prince El Hassan bin Talal
Majlis El Hassan
Jordan[12]

Prospects for Successful Negotiation of a Final Treaty

To begin this section, we will describe two events that occurred as this Postscript is being written: a May 14 speech by Prime Minister Ariel Sharon to the Israeli Parliament that casts a shadow over prospects for beginning negotiations and reaching a final peace agreement; and the encouraging Arab summit held at Sharm el-Sheik, Egypt on May 10–12, 2002, followed by a speech by Chairman Yasser Arafat to the Palestinian Authority Parliament on May 15, 2002 about reforming the Authority.

Prime Minister Sharon opened his speech by invoking Biblical links between the Jews and the Holy Land. He told the Parliamentarians that Israel will not enter into any peace negotiations until thoroughgoing reforms in the Palestinian Authority's social, economic, legal, and security systems have created a new Authority, and there has been a complete halt to Palestinian violence and incitement against Israel. He spoke of eventual negotiations toward permanent peace after a lengthy intermediate stage of calm. Sharon did not rule out a Palestinian state, but made clear that this was a far-off possibility.

At the initiative of President Mubarak of Egypt, a summit meeting between President Mubarak, Crown Prince Abdullah of Saudi Arabia, and President Bashar Al-Assad of Syria took place in Sharm el-Sheikh, May 10–12, 2002. Also attending were two representatives of the Palestinian Authority: Mr. Nabil Sha'ath, a member of the Palestinian Authority cabinet, and Mr. Mohammed Dahalan, who is in charge of the PA Security Services in the Gaza Strip. The Palestinians were not official participants to the conference, but their presence was significant, as was especially the participation of President Assad of Syria.

This summit was a follow-on meeting to the Saudi Arabian Proposal for Peace in the Middle East and the Beirut Arab League Summit. The Sharm el-Sheikh summit was a good beginning for progress toward a comprehensive peace arrangement for the region. The attendees denounced all kinds of violence, and their statement did not distinguish between a legitimate struggle and terror. The condemnation was against all kinds of violence. Professor Ginat believes that if the Palestinian people oppose the use of suicide bombings, Hamas will have to follow suit. The Summit participants were very supportive of the Palestinian people, but the name of Chairman Arafat was not mentioned in the Summit communiqué.

Chairman Arafat addressed the Palestinian Legislative Council in Ramallah on May 15, 2002. He acknowledged that he had made mistakes in his governance, and called for reforms to make for a more democratic, honest, and responsible government.[13] The next day, Arafat proposed that elections should be held in the Palestinian Authority, and called upon the Legislative Council in Ramallah to formulate drastic reforms.[14] President Bush announced his intent to send CIA Director George Tenet to the Palestinian Authority to assist the Palestinians in re-building and re-structuring the Palestinian security forces. The security forces have as their first mission the security of the Palestinian people, and not just the security of the Israelis. The co-editors of this book believe that the Sharm el-Sheikh summit was timely. Arafat seems already to be responding to moderate Arab friends of the United States to take measures that could move forward the chances for negotiations. The constructive involvement of Arab countries and leaders in searching for a solution to the Middle East crisis is an essential ingredient to restart progress toward a comprehensive peace process.

The developments mentioned above, notwithstanding the Fabian tactics being employed by Prime Minister Sharon, would seem to auger well for a return to the negotiating table – not just the Israelis and the Palestinians but also the Arab states and Israelis for regional negotiations. These possibilities have provoked increased study and creative thinking about the ingredients for such accords. The talk of new negotiations has also raised again questions as to what degree the Israelis and the Palestinians, and other Arabs, are truly committed to reaching an agreement for the establishment and permanent acceptance of the states of Israel and of Palestine and normalized relations among all states of the region.

At this point, the co-editors think it useful to remind readers of the second principle of Senator George Mitchell for negotiating on long-standing, seemingly intractable conflicts, such as Ireland or the Middle East, which President David L Boren cited in his Preface to this book:

> "It is important to establish early, and to repeat consistently, a determination not to yield to men of violence. In every circumstance . . . men of violence on both sides will be determined to wreck the peace process . . . to bomb, murder, assassinate, and destroy to get their way, in the hope that the other side would eventually capitulate."

On the matter of willingness to negotiate sincerely, in the past one usually questioned the extent to which Palestinians and Arabs in general really are willing to accept Israel. Chapters of this book point to contrary statements and positions of the Iraqis and Syrians and to the support of Iran, Iraq, Syria, and Lebanon of terrorist groups such as Hamas, Hizballah, and Islamic Jihad that are openly committed to the destruction of Israel. In this case, however, because of the occupation of Palestine and reported statements of Prime Sharon, the questioning begins with whether Israel still is willing to permit the creation of a sovereign, integrated, and independent Palestinian state – not merely allow a puppet state configured to look like Swiss-cheese in terms of its territorial contiguity.

As previously stated, there are some who believe that an objective of the Sharon government in its occupation of Palestine, and its destruction of not only the security infrastructure but even of school and financial records, was to put an end to the Palestinian Authority. At the Ministry of Education, the IDF stripped computers of their hard drives and blew them up. Soldiers also destroyed Palestinian television studios and ransacked banks. Even if flattening the Authority was not a Sharon government objective, there are those who consider that the aggressive occupation of the Palestinian Authority did not contribute to the goal of indefinitely removing the threat of Palestinian terrorism against Israel.

General (Res.) Shlomo Gazit, former head of Israeli Intelligence, gives

Operation Defense Shield a negative balance sheet. In a piece in *The Jerusalem Post* on April 16, 2002, he praised the IDF and said the Operation had impressively resulted in the killing and arrest of a large number of terrorists and the seizure of their killing material, that IDF regular and reserve fighters had demonstrated their competence in fighting in a difficult urban environment without heavy losses to IDF personnel, and that the Operation had reduced the number of deadly attacks by suicide bombers against Israeli targets. He argued, however, that the Operation had failed in terms of the central goal: eliminating the motivation that causes young Palestinian men and women to carry our attacks against Israel. This, he said, can only be achieved by the "permanent presence of a security authority that rules over the entire Palestinian territory and acts effectively against any attempt at terrorist organization." He added that Israel surely does not want that responsibility, and that the Operation had so crushed the Palestinian apparatus that it cannot presently fulfill that role. Despite a contrary intent, the Operation only strengthened Arafat's personal status while leaving him with zero capacity to enforce a real cease-fire, even if he wants to do so.[15]

General Gazit's analysis has been validated by further suicide bombings, such as the one that forced Sharon to cut short his trip to Washington and return to Israel on May 8, 2002. Despite repeated public condemnation of terrorist attacks on civilians by Arafat since then, there was another major attack on Israeli civilians on May 19, 2002. These attacks also validate the claims by Arafat that he is not capable of stopping all Palestinian terrorist activities by groups such as Hamas. The very fact that the Israeli government postponed, or called off, sending the powerful IDF into Gaza after Hamas terrorists following the May 8 attack seems to show the absurdity of Sharon's constant position that Arafat could stop all such attacks if he only wanted to do so. The Bush Administration, after statements joining with Sharon to blame Arafat and call for him to prevent all terrorist attacks, finally acknowledged, through public statements of both Vice President Richard Cheney and National Security Advisor Condoleezza Rice, that Arafat does not have the capacity to stop all bombings.

Casting doubts also on Israeli sincerity to negotiate for a final peace agreement is the irritating issue of Israeli settlements in the West Bank and Gaza, and the unwillingness of the Israelis to date to halt the expansion of settlements, much less to abandon more than a few insignificant settlements to reach an accord with the Palestinians. *The New York Times* of April 26, 2002 reported that during the previous week, when Israeli army officers had proposed uprooting several dozen isolated Jewish settlements in the West Bank and the Gaza Strip, "Prime Minister Ariel Sharon had angrily dismissed the idea at a cabinet meeting, saying that as long as he was in power there would be no discussion of removing a single settlement." Settlements have long been a bone of contention for the United States with Israel. President George Bush (father) in 1993 threatened to withhold $10 billion in loan guarantees from Israel if it did not freeze its settlement building. The number of Israelis living in settlements in Gaza and the West Bank grew from 100,000 to 200,000 during the 1990s, and 200,000 Israelis now reside in neighborhoods of East Jerusalem that were captured from the Palestinians by Israel in 1967.[16]

Doubts about the sincerity of Palestinian and Arab commitment to the existence of Israel also loom large – very large to the Israelis. Few would think that Iraq and Iran have changed fundamentally their opposition to an Israeli state. Libya and Syria both initially voiced opposition to Saudi Arabia's regional peace proposal, and then acceded to it at the Arab League Summit. No one doubts that significant numbers of Arabs in every state retain the view that Israel has usurped Arab lands with international backing, and that such land should immediately or eventually be recovered, if by no other means than by greater Arab population growth over Israeli population growth. However, the bold and welcome Saudi initiative and its unanimous backing by the Arab League should be sufficient for all parties to put doubts aside and to urge all parties to move forward deliberately toward a comprehensive peace settlement.

In their struggle to establish sovereign, independent, well-functioning states, Israelis and Palestinians have been acutely sensitive to, even if they have not always heeded, the perceptions and positions on the Middle East of the outside world. Israel was created through external support of the international community and through actions of the League of Nations and the United Nations. In later years, however, Israel has regarded the United Nations as unbalanced, namely favorable toward the Arabs *vis-à-vis* Israel; it resists United Nations participation in anything related to Israel. Israelis have been able consistently to rely on the United States to exercise its veto in the UN Security Council to protect Israel's interests as defined by Israel. The most recent example was US government help to prevent an assembled UN inspection team from visiting Jenin, where the IDF had been accused of human rights violations during its attack on and siege of the town and the refugee camp there. Arabs have asked why the US government prevents UN examination of Jenin while insisting on UN inspections of Iraq for weapons of mass destruction. It will be interesting to see how much influence the US presidency actually has and is willing to exercise with Israel. Sharon certainly took his time in responding to President Bush's pleas for Israeli withdrawal of the IDF from the Palestine Authority. There are strong domestic political constraints and incentives not to pressure the Israelis.

Palestinians became sensitive to world opinion in the 1970s. They realized that as the weaker party in the negotiations and struggle they needed outside backing to offset US support for Israel. The PLO leadership dropped its demand for regaining "historic Palestine" and instead began to base demands on international law, especially on United Nations resolutions as they (and others) interpret them. The apex of Israelis' and Palestinians' adherence and sensitivity to world opinion was at the beginning of the Oslo Peace Process. Neither side was happy with the conditions on their participation, but both felt it in their interests to come to the table.[17] The recent Israeli invasion of the Palestinian Authority and Prime Minister Sharon's calls for reform of the Palestinian Authority are likely to bring more international organization and participation in Palestinian–Israeli matters. However, as in the case of Israel, it remains to be seen how much influence can and will be exercised over the Palestinians and Yasser Arafat by the United States, the quartet partnership, the United Nations, and by the Arab League states, especially the Saudis, Egyptians, and Jordanians.

The Yatom, Amirav and Ginat Proposed Initiative for Israel

Maj. Gen. (Res.) Danny Yatom, former top aide to prime minister Ehud Barak and a former head of Mossad; Dr. Moshe Amirav, lecturer in public policy at Haifa University, an expert on the Jerusalem conflict, a former member of the Likud Central Committee, and a contributor to this book; and Professor Joseph Ginat, a Middle East expert, former advisor to prime ministers on Arab affairs and director of the Israel Academic Center in Cairo, Egypt, and co-editor of this book, published in the April 19, 2002 edition of *The Jerusalem Post* a piece entitled "An Initiative for Israel." The article is repeated here as part of the co-editors' concluding remarks, and should serve as a basis for further comments on the content of negotiations.

Although the situation has never looked so gloomy, our assessment, based on accumulated personal experience in security and Middle East affairs, is optimistic. Two recent developments have opened a window of opportunity for resolving the Middle East conflict: the proposals presented by the Arab League at its Beirut summit a few weeks ago, and Prime Minister Ariel Sharon's announcement of Israel's readiness to participate in regional peace talks.

It is not enough, however, that both the Arab countries and Israel want talks. Israel would be expected to come to such a summit with concrete plans for negotiating peace with Syria and the Palestinians. In this article we present some ideas for an Israeli initiative. In our opinion, the proposals of the Arab League provide a rare opportunity to change the historical Israeli–Palestinian equation. This equation is based on the assumption that peace with the Arab world will only come after a solution to the Palestinian problem. In the Israeli–Palestinian equation, the return is low and the price is high. In the new Arab-Israeli equation, the return for Israel is high and the price is worthwhile.

To illustrate the advantage of this new equation, let us look at the two issues that were the stumbling blocks toward reaching a permanent settlement at Camp David: the Temple Mount and the Palestinian refugees. It would be easier for Israel to reach a Pan-Arabic solution to the question of the Temple Mount than to agree on solely Palestinian sovereignty. The same goes for the question of refugees where Israel cannot breach the historical Palestinian claim for the "right of return." The resolutions of the Arab League facilitate a new formula of a "just solution" based on UN Resolution 194, instead of the "right of return."

The formula also provides an opportunity to solve the conflict Israel has with Syria. The main obstacle to an agreement between Israel and Syria was the latter's demands for Israel's withdrawal to the June 1967 border as a precondition to negotiations. The Syrians also refused to specify how they would have fulfilled all of Israel's needs. With Syria, Israel's main interests are security and normalization, not territory.

We want to state that actually Israel and the Palestinians were not so far from reaching an agreement. On the issue of territory, for example, the Palestinians consented to 80 percent of the settlers remaining in blocks of settlements to be annexed to Israel. They suggested that those blocks will consist of 2.6 percent of the West Bank while Israel insisted on at least 8 percent. Is 5.4 percent an unbridgeable gap?

The lessons from the Oslo process demand that the parties relate in the interim agreement to each of the permanent status components and that a mechanism to resolve disputes be established. Here is our proposal for a practical interim agreement. It should include the establishment of a Palestinian state on 65 percent of the territories leaving 35 percent for the permanent settlement.

This 35 percent includes the blocks of settlements, the Jordan Valley, and Jerusalem under Israeli control. Israel will evacuate all settlements in the Gaza Strip and all the isolated settlements in the West Bank. A Palestinian municipality will be established in east Jerusalem. It will operate during the interim period under Israeli law, as do other Arab municipalities in Israel. The parties will begin negotiations to define the final status of the Old City, which would consist of one square kilometer. The Old City will be under an agreed "Special Regime" which will embody elements of cooperation.

The Arab League formula on the question of refugees will be accepted in principle. Israel, Palestine, and the international community will accept Resolution 194 and the formula of a "just solution" to the Palestinian refugee problem. According to this formula, only a symbolic number of refugees will return to Israel. The rest will be given a choice between returning to their new Palestinian homeland, rehabilitation in the countries where they reside, or emigration to a third country.

There will be an international framework to mediate disputes comprised of the presidents of Russia and the United States (Vladimir Putin and George W. Bush) and two representatives from the Arab League, President Hosni Mubarak from Egypt and King Abdullah from Jordan.

Such an interim agreement would cause Israel to make painful concessions, but would also serve its interests. Here are three examples.

Evacuation of isolated settlements in the West Bank and all settlements in Gaza serves purely security interests. Separation from the Arab residents of Jerusalem serves Israeli demographic interests. The Palestinian population in Israel is growing at the rate of 3.5 percent per year compared with a 1.6 percent growth of the Jewish population. Without dividing the city, the Arab minority will reach a majority of 55 percent over the next 25 years.

The third and perhaps most important advantage in the interim agreement is a "separation plan" in which Israel will erect a fence for effective control of the border with the Palestinian state. Terrorists easily enter Israel today because there is no such barrier. In case the Palestinians refuse to negotiate peace on the basis of no violence, Israel will have to immediately implement a unilateral separation based on the components of the interim agreement suggested above.

There is an assumption that a permanent agreement between Israel and the Palestinians will end the historic conflict in the Middle East. We want to turn this equation around: peace with the Arab world, and especially with Syria, will allow Israel to achieve peace with the Palestinians. Today, Palestinian Authority Chairman Yasser Arafat's extremist positions block the possibility of having a practical dialogue with the Palestinians. The Arab League initiative bypasses this obstacle by adding a strong and more important partner to the negotiations. Not only will the return be higher, but also the price Israel will pay will be lower.

The ongoing conflict puts a heavy burden on Israel, Syria, and the Palestinians. It also has not served Zionism in reaching its main goal. It was not territory that Zionism was seeking through history, rather, as Theodore Herzl phrased it in his book *Alteneuland*, "a secure home for the Jewish people."[18]

Corr/Perkins' Critique of Yatom, Amirav, and Ginat Proposal

Ambassadors Corr and Perkins admire the creative and pragmatic thinking of General Yatam. Dr. Amirav, and Professor Ginat. Their proposal offers advantages to all parties involved that are undeniably attractive. They articulate and promote concepts that are very much in mode in Israel at this time – the need for an interim agreement and a separation by barriers of Israel and Palestine. These two elements were included in the Sharon "proposal" of April 23, 2002, and were highlighted by Sharon during his May 6–7, 2002 visit to Washington. However, Professor Ginat's two co-editors of this book are concerned that a plan involving an interim agreement without more specificity on the details of the final agreement is not likely to win approval of the Palestinians, and probably not that of their Arab backers. The two co-editors think the United States should maximize the opportunities of the Saudi and Arab League proposal.

Talks that do not enunciate the goals of a final settlement and the general outline of territories of Israel and Palestine will likely stall, although the final borders need not be completely delineated. Ambassadors Perkins and Corr believe that Sharon's idea that Palestinians will have limited autonomy on about half of the West Bank for 10 to 15 years while the world reforms Palestinian governance to meet Israeli standards is a sure formula for continued violence from desperate people. Negotiations need to start soon, and they need to deal more certainly with what will constitute a final comprehensive peace treaty.

A review of Arafat's position in the Camp David talks may provide some indication of how he and other legitimate Palestinian leaders might react in future negotiations if the final outcome is not fairly clear. Mr. Robert Malley, as Special Assistant to President Clinton for Arab–Israeli Affairs, was a member of the US delegation at the Camp David talks. Mr. Hussein Agha has been involved in Palestinian affairs for many years, including in Israeli–Palestinian relations. Agha and Malley argue persuasively in their book, *Camp David: The Tragedy of Errors* (*The New York Review of Books*, August 9, 2001), that a major reason for the inability of Arafat to accept the "generous" proposals supposedly put forth by Prime Minister Barak and President Clinton was that Arafat inextricably links interim and permanent issues as "part and parcel of each other."

At Camp David, Arafat knew that Prime Minister Barak had not complied with a number of interim actions to which he was formally committed, "including a third partial redeployment of troops from the West Bank, the transfer to Palestinian control of three villages abutting Jerusalem, and the release of Palestinians imprisoned for acts committed before the Oslo agreement." Moreover, Agha and Malley argue that the ambiguity in the approach of Prime Minister Barak, and President Clinton's multiple presentations on the variations of Israel's initially "unmovable red lines," left the Palestinians with the perception that the Israelis never really put forth a full and definitive proposal. This was in part because Barak did not want the Palestinians to consider Israeli proposals on the table as concessions. Barak and Clinton wanted Arafat to accept general proposals as "bases for negotiations."

"According to those 'bases,' Palestine would have sovereignty over 91 percent of the West Bank; Israel would annex 9 percent of the West Bank and, in exchange, Palestine would have sovereignty over parts of pre-1967 Israel equivalent to one percent of the West Bank, but with no indication of where either would be. On the highly sensitive issue of refugees, the proposal spoke only of a 'satisfactory' solution. Even on Jerusalem, where the most detail was provided, many blanks remained to be filled in. Arafat was told that Palestine would have sovereignty over the Muslim and Christian quarters of the Old City, but only loosely defined 'permanent custodianship' over the Haram al-Sharif, the third holiest site in Islam. The status of the rest of the city would fluctuate between Palestinian sovereignty and functional autonomy. Finally, Barak was careful not to accept anything. His statements about positions he could support were conditional, couched as a willingness to negotiate on the basis of the US proposals so long as Arafat did the same."[19]

In the eyes of the Palestinians, they had seen Oslo as a surrender, of their having given up on the war for the whole of historic Palestine (as they viewed it). They saw Oslo as an agreement to concede 78 percent of mandatory Palestine to Israel. Acknowledgment of repeated allegations by commentators on Camp David that Israel was generously offering land to the Palestinians or was making concessions was interpreted by the Palestinians as confirming Israel's Biblical right to the land, something the Palestinians reject. The Palestinians felt that they were the ones being asked to make concessions, not the Israelis. And even so, if they were to grant such concessions they wanted certainty about what they were agreeing to. Arafat seems to fear that in negotiations the Israelis set traps and seek to prevail through piecemeal or salami negotiating tactics.

Given the Israeli track record, Corr and Perkins doubt that the Palestinians will in future negotiations be any more disposed to buy into an interim agreement than they were at Camp David, unless they have better knowledge of what the final agreement will be. Additionally, it is certain that Palestinians' trust in the Israelis has not grown since Camp David. The guarantee of credible outside powers (i.e., the United States or the quartet powers, and the Arab League) that the promised final agreement will be implemented on an agreed upon schedule will likely be required. Palestinians are probably going to want to know the specifics of the end game before buying into interim arrangements like that proposed in the Yatom, Amirav, and Ginat proposal, which is completely independent of and has nothing to do with Prime Minister Sharon.

They are even less likely to respond positively to Prime Minister Sharon's demands, which, in contrast to the Yatom, Amirav, and Ginat proposal, do not offer the immediate establishment of a Palestinian state in more than half the territories. Furthermore, in contrast to the Yatom, Amirav, and Ginat proposal, which proposes the immediate abandonment of settlements in Gaza and of some in the West Bank, Prime Minister Sharon has not pledged to dismantle even one settlement – always a sensitive matter with the Palestinians.

In response to Corr and Perkins' critique of the Yatom, Amirav, and Ginat proposal, Professor Ginat points out that Prime Minister Barak wanted and tried to reach a final agreement with the Palestinians without any interim period. It did not work. Instead, the outcome was the *Intifada* and twenty months of escalating violence.

Professor Ginat personally would have liked a comprehensive peace and final agreement, but after the events since the start of the *Intifada* in

September 2000, he does not believe it possible to reach a final agreement in one stage. Therefore, the Yatom, Amirav, and Ginat proposal is to establish immediately the Palestinian state, and immediately dismantle the settlements in the Gaza Strip and all the scattered settlements in the West Bank prior to a final agreement. These immediate acts, Ginat argues, would help to rebuild trust and enable the successful negotiation of the final accord within a period of two years. The process would be facilitated merely by the fact that negotiations would be between two states – Israel and Palestine.

The crux of the difference between Ambassadors Perkins and Corr with Professor Ginat is how much specificity the Palestinians and Arabs will need to entirely abandon violence as one of the tools for pressuring for a final agreement. The greater are Palestinian doubts about being able to achieve the end of occupation and reach what they consider to be a reasonable final solution (generally but not strictly in accord with UN resolutions), the less likely are Palestinians to abandon or control violence against Israelis, especially those settled in the occupied territories. And normalization of relations with Arab countries in the region is related to reaching an acceptable arrangement with the Palestinian Authority. The Saudis and the Arab League at long last seem to offer an opportunity for a comprehensive peace.

Professor Ginat stresses the importance of Israel negotiating on two fronts – with the Palestinians and Syrians – simultaneously. He and his colleagues argue that by working at the same time on two fronts it is sometimes possible to speed a negotiated settlement more quickly. The Syrians participated in the Beirut Summit and approved the "normalization" proposal, so the possibility of simultaneous negotiations is real.

Ambassadors Corr and Perkins also see possible advantages in "dual negotiations" of the Israelis with the Arab states and Palestinians, but caution that such negotiations could have pitfalls. The PLO had given up Palestinians' claim to "historic Palestine," recognized Israel's right to exist, and made concessions to Israel that other Arabs had not conceded by the beginning of the Barak government. When the Barak government initially gave lower priority to negotiations with the Palestinian Authority and unsuccessfully attempted to play the "Syrian card," there was much resentment. Dual negotiations will require sensitivity and balance. There will be many players and competing interests among them that can be exploited but can also derail negotiations.

Comments on Specific Issues for Negotiation

The remainder of this Postscript focuses on specific issues that must be resolved in negotiations to reach a final agreement. These subjects have been treated thoroughly in the chapters of this book. They will be reviewed first in terms of their discussion within previous talks, and then some issues individually.

Negotiations during the Barak Government

Ehud Barak was elected Prime Minister of Israel on July 5,1999. From the very beginning of his term, he was determined to reach a comprehensive agreement and sign a peace treaty with the Palestinians. The first negotiations took place on July 29, 1999 in the Laromme Hotel in Jerusalem. Gilad Sher, the chief of staff of the prime minister's office, headed the Israeli delegation. The Palestinian delegation was headed by Saib Erakat, a member of the PA cabinet and the PA spokesman, and Mohammed Dahlan, chief of PA Preventive Security Service in the Gaza Strip. On the agenda were several key issues. The Israeli interest was to keep Jerusalem under Israeli sovereignty and preserve the Jewish connection to the holy places in the capital. As such, most of the settlers were to be concentrated into several areas (blocks) under the sovereignty of Israel, the Palestinian state that would be established would be demilitarized, there would not be an Israeli acknowledgement of having caused the Palestinian refugee situation, and there would be no implementation of the right of return. However, the Israeli side was willing to acknowledge the need to compensate the refugees, and to participate in an international effort to rehabilitate them.[20]

The second stage of discussions resulted in the Sharm el-Sheikh memorandum of September 4, 1999. In the Sharm el-Sheikh meeting, held at the Jolie Ville hotel, there was a big ceremony in which the entire Palestinian and Israeli leaderships participated. Also present at the meeting were American Secretary of State Madeleine Albright and the entire US delegation, President Hosni Mubarak of Egypt and his senior minister, and King Abdullah of Jordan and his staff. President Mubarak, Albright, and King Abdullah signed as witnesses to the agreement. The main achievement of the Sharm el-Sheikh memorandum was that the two sides agreed there would be only a short period from the interim agreement to negotiations over a comprehensive agreement on permanent status. The Palestinian side was obligated to security cooperation, as well as to all the stipulations of the Wye River Accord, including the collecting of weapons from civilians and the detention of suspected terrorists. Both sides agreed not to change unilaterally the status of the West Bank and the Gaza Strip. There was an agreement that Israel would release 350 prisoners in two stages, and a joint committee would be established to recommend the release of additional prisoners. On the following day, September 5, 1999, the Israeli cabinet approved the memorandum with two ministers opposing. This precipitated the first in a series of coalition crises.[21]

Between April and June 2000 the Swedish government made special efforts to conduct secret talks in Sweden in an effort to speed the entire Middle East peace process along. This was called the Stockholm agreement, although no agreement was reached. Many maps were prepared in the course of the talks, but in reality little resulted from the meetings.

Another look at Camp David, July 11–25, 2000

Camp David was briefly examined earlier from the Palestinian viewpoint. This section will include insights to both Israeli and Palestinians positions. When Prime Minister Barak left for Camp David there had already been a vote of no confidence against him in the Knesset by a vote of 54–52. The Prime Minster was selected by direct elections at that time, however, and there was no operative significance to the vote. Barak still had a direct mandate from the people, and before he left, he declared, "I don't go alone, together with me there are two million voters."[22]

As has been widely reported, the discussions at Camp David were very intense and complex. On Saturday, July 15, Madeleine Albright went to Yasser Arafat and told him, "You'll have a state." Arafat responded, "I do have a state, and if Barak doesn't want to recognize it now I don't care that it will not be recognized for another twenty years. Our situation is like South Africa, the entire world supports me."[23]

The most difficult questions that were posed in the Camp David discussions were the issues of Jerusalem and the Palestinian refugees. Barak and the members of his delegation decided that they had to delineate their policy on exactly how many refugees they were willing to absorb into Israel. Dan Meridor, a member of the Israeli cabinet, indicated that it would be a delusion to believe that the number would be less than 100,000. Regarding Jerusalem there were very significant gaps related to the Old City and the sovereignty on Temple Mount. Also there was the issue of the need for a passage (corridor) east of Jerusalem between Bethlehem and Ramallah. Yossi Ginossaur, who was previously in the Shin Bet (similar to the American Federal Bureau of Investigation) and since the time of the late Prime Minister Rabin had served as a liaison between Rabin, and later Peres and Barak, to Yasser Arafat, claimed that Jerusalem would be the issue that would make or break the agreement. He emphasized that among the Palestinians there is a misunderstanding of the importance of Temple Mount to the Jewish people. He felt that the Temple Mount should be dealt with first, and only then the issue of the Palestinian and Israeli neighborhoods of Jerusalem.[24]

Amnon Shahak, previously chief of staff and a member of Barak's cabinet, emphasized that there were large parts of Jerusalem that he did not consider part of "his" Jerusalem. He believed it was in the interest of Israelis to give (or transfer) the Arab neighborhoods of East Jerusalem to the Palestinian Authority, so as to have as few Arab residents as possible remain under Israeli sovereignty. But, he asserted, "we can not give up sovereignty to Arafat on Temple Mount, which is the basis of Jewish culture." At same time Shahak understood that Israel should not manage the Muslim holy sites. Israel's Attorney General, Elyakim Rubinstein, referring to the Temple Mount, said that the responsibility for managing the Temple Mount should be given to the representatives of the *Waqf* (Islamic trust or endowment). Furthermore, the archaeological sites would be under Israeli control, and the sides should agree on an area where Jews could pray.[25]

In a meeting on July 17, Madeleine Albright asked Abu Mazen, a member of the Palestinian delegation, how Arafat would react if it turned out that there was a division between Abu Mazen and Arafat regarding the issue of Jerusalem. Abu Mazen replied, "I cannot oppose him, I'll resign, and you have to remember that any concession over Jerusalem is a threat of death to Arafat."[26] At Camp David, Arafat did not make any concessions over Jerusalem. Arafat said to President Clinton that a billion Muslims would never have forgiven him. He continued, "If I will not get full sovereignty in East Jerusalem I don't have a mandate to make any concessions." Clinton was enraged, and said to Arafat, "You are leading your nation and the entire region to a disaster." Arafat rejected all the American proposals and suggested that the talks be postponed for two weeks. He reiterated that he would not sign any agreement without al-Quds [Jerusalem], and that he was ready to wait twenty years to sign an agreement, since first he had to consult with the entire Muslim world. Barak's reaction was to declare that there was no partner for peace, in the deepest meaning of those words. President Clinton invited Arafat to his cabin, and told him that he had suggested to President Mubarak and King Abdullah to delay negotiations over the issue of Jerusalem for two years, and that he wanted Arafat to agree to those terms. Arafat replied, "I invite you to my funeral if you insist on your demands regarding Jerusalem."[27]

On the issue of the Palestinian refugees Prime Minister Barak said that Israel would not agree to the right of return, but that Israel was willing to consider absorbing a limited number of refugees on a humanitarian basis or for family reunification. The Israelis remained firm about four principles: (1) that all the people who are considered Palestinian refugees would receive full rights without any discrimination in the places where they currently dwell; (2) that the status of a Palestinian refugee would be designated meaningless from both legal and practical points of view; (3) that the Palestinian refugees would be rehabilitated in the places where they lived, a third country, or in Palestine; and (4) that the refugee camps would be dismantled and then rebuilt and developed, to become part of the social, cultural, and legal system of their environment. In addition, UNRWA would be declared obsolete, and all its duties and responsibilities would consequently be transferred to the hosting countries.

The Palestinian position was that a just solution must be based on UN Resolution 194. The Palestinians insisted on the right of return under which each refugee who had resided within Israel's boundaries until 1948 and would like to return to Israel would be able to do so. The Palestinians promised that they would persuade the refugees to select other places rather than Israel to settle. An exception would be for the Palestinian refugees in Lebanon, who would be permitted to return to Israel. The Palestinians demanded that Israel pay reparations to the refugees for their suffering, for their being uprooted, and for their loss of their property.[28]

In order to avoid a collapse of the talks in Camp David, President Clinton suggested three possible alternatives. One, a delay on solving the issue of Jerusalem to a further date, for perhaps five years, or a partial solution that would leave unresolved only the issue of the holy places. Second, custodial sovereignty to the Palestinians on Temple Mount in addition to Israeli sovereignty (in other words an arrangement of dual sovereignty), and a special regime on the Old City in addition to Palestinian sovereignty over the Arab neighborhoods of Jerusalem. Third, Clinton suggested functional Palestinian autonomy over the Arab neighborhoods in Jerusalem, and full Palestinian sovereignty over the outside neighborhoods. The Old City would be divided: the Muslim and Christian quarters to the Palestinians, the Jewish and Armenian quarters to the Israelis. The Palestinians did not agree, and on July 25, 2000 the Camp David chapter ended.

The Sharm el-Sheikh and Taba meetings

Gilad Sher indicates that there were 38 meetings for negotiations between the Israelis and the Palestinians from the end of Camp David in July until the beginning of the violence at the end of September 2000. Most of the meetings took place in Jerusalem.[29] The first meeting was planned originally to take place between Barak and Arafat on September 25, 2000 in the home of Abu Mazen, but the meeting took place instead in Barak's home in Kochav Yair. The outcome of this meeting was a meeting of Israeli and Palestinian negotiators in Washington. The two issues to be discussed were refugees and the Temple Mount. At this time, according to Sher, the Palestinian refugee issue was identified as the main obstacle. The Israelis emphasized to the Americans that it should be made clear to the Palestinians that Israelis will not commit national and political suicide, while they were willing to show flexibility over Jerusalem and the Jordan valley. The Americans suggested using the language "right of return to their 'homeland'," without using the specific term Palestine or Israel. The Israelis demanded that it be specified that their "homeland" is the State of Palestine. The delegations went back to their countries on September 28, thinking that after the Day of Atonement, October 9, 2000, there would be continued meetings and that Arafat and Barak would meet once again.

On September 28, 2000 Ariel Sharon, who was a member of parliament at the time, along with several members of his Likud party, visited Temple Mount. About 1000 Muslim demonstrators were on Temple Mount, but there were not any serious encounters between police and the demonstrators. Even the Shin Bet and the Israeli Military Intelligence did not anticipate any severe consequences, but, needless to say, they failed in their assessment. Twenty-two Arab countries condemned the visit, calling it an insult to the sacredness of Islam. The following day there were demonstrations. Five Palestinians were killed, 50 were wounded, and 60 Israeli police officers were wounded, and the situation in the West Bank and Gaza began to seethe. As the events unfolded a decision was taken, with the intervention of President Clinton and Mubarak, to hold another summit, which took place on October 16, 2000 in Sharm el-Sheikh, Egypt. Participating were President Clinton, UN General Secretary Kofi Annan, Prime Minister Barak, Chairman Arafat, King Abdullah, and President Mubarak. It is important to note that King Abdullah said that the current violent conflict engendered by Sharon's visit to the Temple Mount finished the Israeli–Palestinian dialogue and turned it into a broader Arab–Israeli one.[30]

George Tenet, the Director of Central Intelligence of the United States, who has played an important role in trying to mediate the conflict, specified the immediate steps to be taken by both sides, but not before 48 hours of complete quiet and the resumption of the security cooperation. Everybody was hoping that after Sharm el-Sheikh the violence would stop, but it did not. It only escalated, and at that stage Tunisia and Morocco announced the severing of ties with Israel. Meetings were held to try to find ideas to stop the violence, such as one between Amnon Shakak and Arafat on October 31, 2000. Right after that meeting Peres proposed creating a "Peace Corps" to work in the territories. Barak rejected that idea.

The next meeting between Israeli and Palestinians representatives was at Bowling Air Force Base near Washington. There was a lot of tension between the sides. Again the issues of Jerusalem, Palestinian refugees, security, and borders were raised. The Israeli delegation flew to Egypt and met with Mubarak in Sharm el-Sheikh on December 28, 2000. Gilad Sher emphasized to Mubarak that on the Haram al-Sharif (Temple Mount), "there is a need for a creative but logical solution that expresses the faith of both sides." Sher added that Israel would not sign any contract that gives the sovereignty on the Holy of Holies of the Jews to the Palestinians. As to the right of return, Sher asserted that there was no way to apply it within the boundaries of Israel.[31]

All negotiations were stopped due to the New Year holiday. The following and last negotiation attempt was made starting January 21, 2001, in Taba, Egypt. Yossi Beilin, who was the minister of justice in Barak's cabinet, said that everyone emphasized their commitment to try to complete what was not solved at Camp David, and that everyone stressed the need to put an end to the violence that had become a nightmare. According to Beilin, Abu Ala said that the Palestinians were not committed to Clinton's plan. Saib Erakat corrected him, and said that they agreed to Clinton's plan as a basis, but that they had their conditions.[32] In Taba the Palestinian refugee issue was dealt with in more depth than in all other previous meetings. The Palestinians asked the Israelis, in an informal meeting, "Why do you fear the right of return?" And Beilin's answer to him was, if most of the refugees were to ask to move to Israel, it would cease to be a Jewish state. Yossi Beilin, in an effort to show that Jew's desire for their own state was not a dislike of Palestinians, showed the Palestinians documents, one of which was from April 28, 1948, written in Hebrew and Arabic. In it, Jews told the Arabs of Haifa, "We don't harbor any hatreds towards you, don't destroy your own homes by your own hands. Do not cut yourselves off from your sources of work. Do not bring a catastrophe upon yourself. Our city in Haifa is your city, it is a joint city."[33]

The remaining issue was the right of return, and the implementation of UN Resolution 194. Beilin felt that the solution could be along the lines of President Clinton's idea, which has been previously mentioned.[34] The talks in Taba ended Saturday night, January 27, 2000, without any signed document. Both sides felt that they came closer to an agreement than ever, but on a practical basis there were only pronouncements that there was a basis to rebuild trust.[35]

Yasser Arafat: Relevant or Irrelevant?

The personal enmity between Ariel Sharon and Yasser Arafat is historic. A major objective of Sharon is not only to marginalize Arafat but to exile him from Palestine. This is obvious to all observers, especially since the March 30, 2002 IDF invasion of the West Bank and imprisonment of Arafat in his headquarters in Ramallah. Repeated demands that the confined Arafat stop the suicide bombers while the IDF destroys the communications, police, and societal infrastructure that might enable him to do so, and Israeli attempts to demonstrate that Arafat has been behind and financed suicide bombings, exacerbate the situation.

Early in the Sharon administration, the Israeli cabinet made a decision that Yasser Arafat was no longer relevant, and that there would not be any more negotiations with him. It seems that the Israeli leaders fail to understand that by declaring Arafat irrelevant, they have actually made him more relevant than ever. The Bush administration, being persuaded that the Sharon government's actions can justifiably be considered part of the war on terrorism, has demonstrated full support and understanding for Sharon's position, claiming that it was imperative that Arafat make a serious effort to clamp down on militants.[36] After the IDF besieged Arafat in Ramallah – not allowing him to leave, with Israeli tanks waiting several hundred yards from his headquarters – there was initially, while permitted, a pilgrimage to see him, not only by Palestinians but also by delegations from the European Union (EU), members of European parties, and even by Israelis.

According to Danny Rubinstein, "if one is to judge by the behavior of the members of the Palestinian leadership, none of them think that Arafat's days are coming to an end." They recognize that the Palestinian opposition is increasing, and exactly because of that fact they know that there is no alternative but to support the Palestinian Authority headed by Arafat. The Palestinian population at large know that the Israeli government wants to get rid of Arafat, and therefore more than ever they support him.[37] An Arab member of the Israeli Knesset, Hasham Mahamid, returning from a meeting with Arafat said, "Don't even dream of successors to Arafat." And Tawfiq Tirawi, who is head of the Palestinian Intelligence in the West Bank, stated, "Any Palestinian leader that will come to power on an Israeli tank, I will personally hang in Ramallah's city square."[38] The Palestinians have rallied behind Arafat, with hundreds of journalists, academics, and regular citizens marching under the slogan, "Defend the Palestinian territories and defend our President Arafat."[39]

Abu Ala, on a visit to Canada, proclaimed that all the talks about the possibility of replacing Arafat are foolish. "If you don't talk with Arafat, you won't find any other Palestinian to talk with." The Palestinian media announced that Sharon had failed in his attempt to persuade anyone but himself that there is a need to replace Arafat. And a member of the Palestinian cabinet, Hassan Asfour, sitting near Arafat during the announcement, added, "We have one president, we don't have fights like those in Israel between Ariel Sharon and Shimon Peres." Danny Rubinstein states that it is guaranteed that the popular support for Arafat is extremely high and will remain that way. The more he is hated or boycotted, the more his prestige rises within the Palestinian territories.[40]

The European Union adopted the French resolution to call for elections in the West Bank and Gaza, which would give an accurate picture of who the Palestinians support as their leader. Representatives of the EU declared that Israel and the General Assembly of the UN should recognize the Palestinian state as a first step after the end of violence. The intent is to legally establish the Palestinian state before any further negotiations, after a cessation of the violence.[41]

The co-editors of this book believe that the very fact that up to the time of the March 30, 2002 invasion that Shimon Peres was meeting with Abu Ala, and that Sharon himself met with the three most important Palestinian deputies, would seem to indicate that Arafat *is* relevant. As long as PLO leaders support Yasser Arafat he remains relevant. It is not the role of national governments to make decisions or even suggestions for other "states," or to interfere in their decisions, even if they are adversaries. Even when at war, a state cannot decide for the other side who their leaders and representatives will be. Ariel Sharon had personal experience with that during the 1982 Lebanon War when he inaugurated a Lebanese president, Bashir Jumayyil. A few days later President Jumayyil was assassinated. Sharon apparently has not learned the lesson.

Unilateral Separation

The Yatom–Amirav–Ginat proposal called for unilateral separation of Israel from Palestine, and the same concept is embodied in Prime Minister Sharon's announced plans to establish security for Israeli citizens. As the escalation of violence grew between Palestinians and Israelis, more and more politicians, organizations, and individuals advocated unilateral separation. The Association for Peace and Security in Israel, whose members are mainly retired generals and colonels, as well as former personnel from other security organizations, published a leaflet entitled "We say peace to the Palestinians," and called for unilateral separation. The pamphlet recognized the "dead end" that the political leadership has brought the country to, and the possibility that the violent confrontation might deteriorate to a very bloody war.

The writers of the proposal for a unilateral separation emphasize that it would not provide a permanent solution to the Israeli–Palestinian conflict. In their words it is, "a temporary arrangement initiated by Israel." The main goals of the program are: (1) to ease the burden of the security arrangements on the budget; (2) to improve and reinforce the ability of the security forces, and to narrow the dangers and the threats to the Israeli public; (3) to minimize friction points with the Palestinian people; (4) to reduce the danger of escalation, and the likelihood of a general war; and (5) to slow down the negative demographic process through which, from the Israeli point of view, the Jews are becoming a minority in the historical boundaries of the Land of Israel.

The crux of the plan is a shortening of the lines to be defended, which would necessitate the evacuation of settlements and other military positions. The separation program does not entail any steps within Jerusalem. The future boundaries between the two states is to be determined in comprehensive negotiations. Israeli settlements which are adjacent to the Green Line and east of it would remain under Israeli control until a final border is established. The international border crossings on the Jordan River and Rafiah would remain under Israeli control, at least for now, until there was joint supervision coordination between Israel, the Palestinians, Jordanians and Egyptians. The plan would be coordinated as much as possible with the United States, the Palestinian Authority, and Arab countries in the region. Members of the Association particularly emphasized that unilateral separation would not bring about a comprehensive solution; they simply want to establish conditions that will be better and more effective than the current situation while avoiding the possibility of further escalation and deterioration.[42]

We the co-editors would like to indicate that Joseph Ginat and General Shlomo Gazit, who have contributed to this volume, are members of this Association, and General (retired) Gazit is a member of the Board of the Association. A. B. Yehoshua, the famous Israeli author, who received the Israel Prize for Hebrew Literature, published an article in which he also endorsed and justified the notion of unilateral separation. According to Yehoshua:

> Today, after the Palestinians' violent outburst, there is no alternative but to adopt the model that succeeded in Lebanon along our border with the Palestinians. True, there are a great many differences between the security zone in Lebanon and the West Bank and Gaza Strip, and consequently, the withdrawal cannot be whole and absolute, nor will it bring about the total quiet that has descended on the border with Lebanon (sic). Nevertheless, the principle can be applied here, too, with a reasonable degree of effectiveness, which will lighten the suffering and reduce the high price in blood that both sides are paying for a borderless existence.
>
> If the Palestinians consider the withdrawal their victory, as Hezbollah viewed the unilateral withdrawal as its victory – all the better. If these feelings of "victory" ultimately bring about agreements and the quiet we had in the past, which is psychologically very understandable, they are very worthwhile. For 120 years of conflict, we have inflicted defeats and humiliations that only generated a passion for revenge and induced more fighting.[43]

Yehoshua's plan for unilateral separation includes 11 major points, the crux of which are summarized here. First of all, separation will depend on and be carried out by Israel alone; Yehoshua also asserts that, although desirable, international support is not vital. His plan is for Israel to withdraw from 85 percent of the territory conquered in 1967, with the aim to leave Palestinians contiguous blocks of territory after the evacuation of roughly 50,000 settlers. Yehoshua's plan is for Greater Jerusalem to remain in Israel's hands; a border fence would be built around the city, and the three main settlement blocs, with official border crossings where appropriate. In addition, the Jordan Rift Valley would remain in Israel's hands, with the possibility that it could be given to the Palestinians after an extended period of time. Finally, a tax to implement the border separation would be imposed on all Israelis, and civil guard units would be set up to guard the fence.

Yehoshua recognized – contrary to the situation now, after continuing

Palestinian suicide bombings in Israel and the violent Israeli invasion of Palestine – that at the time of the proposal's publication there was little support for it on either the Israeli right or left. The resistance from the right, he claimed, was that from Sharon's perspective, "the 42 percent of the area under discussion that has already been conceded to the Palestinians is more than enough." Yehoshua identified criticism of separation by leftists as concern that Jerusalem and the rest of the territory will remain in Israel's hands indefinitely, thus precluding the eventual signing of a permanent peace treaty. Yehoshua responded by asserting that,

> a "hard" border is essential in peacetime, too, and it will make it possible for the post-Arafat Palestinian leadership to do battle against terrorism more effectively. No longer will they be able to say that they have no control over the despairing members of Hamas and Islamic Jihad . . . Even now, the temporary and unsophisticated fence in the Gaza Strip is preventing hundreds of terrorist attacks in Israel.[44]

Shlomo Baum, from the Jaffa Center for Strategic Studies at Tel Aviv University, also deals with the unilateral separation, noting that the deadlock of the Oslo process and the failure of Barak's efforts that caused the second *Intifada* raised a debate within the Israeli public. Unilateral separation has several different aspects such as security separation, comprehensive separation, and separation with retreat to a border line that, according to Baum, Israel will decide upon. He expressed concern that with the current strength of the right in Israel that separation would further impede the evacuation of the few settlements that was agreed upon. At the same time, according to Baum, those who are against the separation assert that if it results in giving territories to the Palestinians, it will reinforce the view of some Palestinians that violence is the best way to achieve their goals, in place of political negotiations. In addition, unilateral separation could make the Palestinians feel they are imprisoned in cages, thus creating greater feelings of despair that could lead to even more violence.[45]

The head of the Israeli Shin Bet, Avi Dichter, also made a recommendation on this issue before the committee of security and foreign affairs in the Knesset on February 12, 2002. He claimed that a physical separation in the West Bank is a critical need. Dichter emphasized, however, that his recommendation as head of the Shin Bet only applied on a security level.[46]

A former director of the Shin Bet, Ami Ayalon, came out in support of the idea of unilateral separation, but not for security reasons. He claimed that it was essential to evacuate the settlements; his perspective is that because Israel and the Palestinians are still far removed from having the European model of borders between countries, unilateral separation was necessary. According to Ayalon, "Only when we evacuate the settlements and the Palestinian state is created will the Palestinians have a real cause to fight terrorism."[47]

The co-editors of this book do not oppose unilateral separation as a necessary, though hopefully not long-lasting, measure. However, as pointed out, it cannot be a substitute for intense and sincere efforts to negotiate a final agreement, even if the final agreement consists of phased but mutually agreed upon stages that culminate in the fulfillment of a final arrangement and peace. It is necessary to look at the total situation. Gaza is currently surrounded by a fence, and almost every day there have been repeated Palestinian mortar attacks (though not suicide bombings) staged from there by Hamas. Physical barriers will not provide the answer to terrorism; a solution can only be arrived at through negotiations.

Suicide Bombings and Assassinations

Suicide bombings are morally reprehensible and unacceptable. Judaism, Christianity, and Islam condemn them. Carried out against civilian targets, they are to be twice condemned. Acts of violence by armed forces against civilians are also wrong, though sometimes impossible to avoid. Palestinian and Arab leaders and Islamic clergy need to leave no doubts in the minds of their audience and electorate about the wrongness of suicide bombings. Glorifying suicide bombings and bombers, as did the Palestinian Ambassador in London by calling them "heroes worthy of flowery tributes," is unacceptable behavior. In a sense, broad popular Palestinian, Arab, and Islamic support for suicide bombers is more to be feared than the suicide bombers themselves, for such a situation promises continuing and growing terrorism.[48]

During the second *Infitada* Israel adopted a policy of retaliation by assassinating militants from Hamas and Islamic Jihad. There is no doubt that those people initiated and sent bombers to commit suicide. And there is no doubt that all these militants are responsible for causing injury to scores of innocent people, and are morally culpable for their actions. But the question that arises, is, whether it is strategically effective to adopt this policy, and whether it has any value in terms of prevention or deterrence of future attacks. Whenever Israel assassinates, the response unfailingly has been several more suicide attacks that cause civilian casualties.

According to Danny Rubinstein:

> Israel's assassinations today generate far more damage than the benefits they are supposed to bring . . . There are perhaps other military intelligence techniques of fighting terrorism and there is no need for ethical and legal debates on this issue – simply because the practical aspect is so obvious. The policy of assassination is a boomerang that hurts Israel badly.[49]

The situation in the territories, according to Rubinstein, is such that the number of militants far outweighs Israel's capability to control them through "liquidations"; thus, although such actions are highly supported by Israeli public opinion, the policy does little to improve Israel's security situation.[50]

Jerusalem

This volume devotes several chapters to the issue of Jerusalem – the city itself, the various surrounding neighborhoods, as well as the Temple Mount. As previously indicated, although most religious Jews are opposed to entering the Temple Mount, in recent years more and more rabbis support a change to previous strictures. Such a practice would have severe security implications. Nadav Shragai, a journalist who wrote a book on the Temple Mount, claims that many people from the Shin Bet think that the very fact that it is closed to non-Muslims by the Muslims themselves creates a potential Jewish underground or the possibility of random individual saboteurs. According to Shragai, Sharon said to one of his close advisors, "We will wait for the right occasion. The mountain will not remain closed for a long period for non-Muslims."[51]

The Temple Mount should be open for everyone, just like any other religious site. Freedom of religion and freedom to visit holy places should be universal. It would not be wise, however, to try to force Muslims to open the Temple Mount for non-Muslim visitors. Israel has to convince other Arab countries, the EU, and the US to put pressure on the PA to reopen the Temple Mount as it was before September 2000.

The co-editors of this book support the ideas of Ya'ar and Ginat (see Ginat's chapter 27) as a solution for the Temple Mount. The religious issues pertaining to the Mount should be dealt with separately from the political issues of Jerusalem. Yossi Ginossaur, in the Camp David discussions, as recorded above, suggested that it would be useful to solve the issue of the Temple Mount before tackling political issues, which supports Ginat's argument.

Palestinian Refugees

In the earlier volume to the *Studies in Peace Politics in the Middle East* series, *Palestinian Refugees: Old Problem – New Solutions*, there were 25 chapters, ten of which were written by Palestinians and Arabs from Jordan and Egypt. The issue addressed throughout was the "right of return." Different solutions were proposed. Some authors proposed that Israel should formally agree to the right of return, knowing that in reality not many refugees will return to the Palestinian state.[52] Throughout the discussions at Camp David, other negotiations, and mainly at the Taba talks, much attention was directed to the problem of the Palestinian refugees. When the violence ends, or if negotiations start even before it ends, and both sides reach an agreement about evacuating part of the settlements, on set boundaries, on the Jordan Rift Valley, on Jerusalem – the Old City, Temple Mount, etc. – there will still be the refugee issue to resolve. Many of the Israelis and Palestinians who participated in Camp David and other meetings, as well as all those who prepared the background material for the negotiators, state that the most difficult issue to resolve is that of the Palestinian refugees.

Yasser Arafat was quoted earlier as having said to President Clinton during the Camp David negotiations that he would be inviting Clinton to his funeral if he were to sign an agreement without Jerusalem. Several prominent Palestinians have told us that were Yasser Arafat to sign an agreement without a solution to the right of return, he would not survive even one day. Moreover, no other Palestinian leader who might succeed him in the future will be able to reach a final agreement without resolving the issue of the right of return.

Throughout the Camp David, Taba, and other talks even a moderate person like Yossi Beilin has been adamant against full implementation of the right of return. There were many suggestions and ideas, like President Clinton's "homeland" proposal, to which Israelis insisted on an agreement specifying the Palestinian state as the Palestinians' homeland. In a conference held by the Tami Steinmetz Center for Peace Research, Ginat suggested that it is crucial to find a solution that makes constructively ambiguous the term "right of return."[53] We must search for such a constructive ambiguity. Israeli negotiators' acceptance even partially of the right of return would cause an earthquake among the Israeli public. The main issue is not the number of refugees but the concept of the right to return itself.

According to the UNRWA there are today 3.7 million Palestinian refugees, out of which 1.5 million are in Jordan, 1.4 million in the West Bank and Gaza, 380,000 in Syria, and 380,000 in Lebanon. The real numbers are much less than that – many refugees who are registered at UNRWA left the camps and emigrated to North and South America or Europe. Those who are in Jordan have Jordanian citizenship, while those in the West Bank and Gaza will be rehabilitated within the Palestinian state. The real number of refugees in Syria is between 180,000 and 220,000. Refugees in Syria have a permit and the possibility to earn money.

The main issue is in Lebanon, where the refugees have no legal status. However, Beilin states that countries like Canada, the United States, and other European and Scandinavian countries are willing to absorb more than the number of refugees in that country, which does not exceed 200,000. And, it would be possible to absorb those refugees who would like to return to Palestine into the Palestinian state. If it would be acceptable to the major parties in negotiation of a regional settlement, the richer nations of the world might proceed to establish a large fund to finance and offer visas to Palestinian refugees in Lebanon who meet reasonable requirements to migrate to countries outside the Middle East.

Among the many solutions that have been suggested, one is to rehabilitate the camps in Jordan, Syria, the West Bank, and Gaza by turning them into attractive municipalities. No one has yet studied seriously the possibility of compensating the state of Lebanon by building plants, factories, and other working opportunities for the Palestinian refugees, and also for Lebanese who dwell in those areas. As the international community will probably have to participate financially in solving the Palestinian refugee issue, it has been suggested that the European Union should tackle the Lebanese component.

Throughout the negotiations at Camp David, Israelis spoke about 40,000–50,000 refugees that Israel was willing to absorb. Yossi Katz, chairman of the Knesset Committee, suggested that Israel would absorb 100,000 refugees. Donna Arzt wrote a comprehensive study on the refugee issue and also contributed a chapter in the first volume (*The Palestinian Refugees: Old Problems – New Solutions*) of the current series. In both her studies she analyzed the issue, and her conclusion is that Israel has to absorb about 70,000 refugees.[54] Thus in our proposal, the maximum that Israel would have to absorb would not exceed 70,000–80,000 refugees. In actuality, we believe that the numbers would be much less. It is important to remember that a third generation has already been born in the camps. Many have married spouses from the surrounding area, and their social and cultural interactions are in the place where they currently live. To leave the areas where they are living would be to uproot, and turn them into refugees for a second time. Thus the rehabilitation and rebuilding of the camps should be a major focus.

The key to solving the concept of the right of return is "constructive ambiguity" – to find a formula that would help both sides feel satisfied that they had not made excessive concessions on the issue. The Palestinians must be able to claim that Israel recognized the right of return; and the Israelis must be convinced that they are not agreeing to commit demographic suicide. Israel would not be able to absorb more than the aforementioned reasonable number of about 70,000 to 80,000 refugees.

Settlements

In the co-editors' opinion the Israeli settlements in Gaza are only creating needless casualties and friction between the two sides, as well as causing the diversion of necessary resources and soldiers from other places. We believe that Israel should unilaterally dismantle all its settlements in Gaza. In the

West Bank, the isolated settlements, which comprise about 20 percent of all the settlements, should also be evacuated to allow for contiguity of Palestinian territory. Israel can maintain three important blocks of settlements. This evacuation of settlements should be taken unilaterally by Israel, as it is in Israel's security interest. It would, as well, greatly facilitate negotiations over the other remaining and complicated issues.

Final Comments

Palestinians and Israelis now face the most difficult period since the signing of the Oslo Accords. Prime Minister Ariel Sharon long insisted on having seven consecutive days of complete quiet. There were almost seven days of quiet, and then the Israelis assassinated Raed Karmi in Tulkarem in January 2002. Karmi was no angel; he initiated several suicide attacks. But the perennial question is whether it is more important to be right or to be smart. Assassinating Raed brought a chain of suicide attacks and escalated the violence.

The co-editors of this book feel that negotiations should start as soon as possible. Until Palestinians can reasonably expect the establishment of a viable Palestinian state in the foreseeable future, the dream of Israel to live in a true peace will remain a fantasy, because it is also fantasy that Israel can control Palestinians while there are ever growing settlements and Palestinian aspirations for a viable state alongside a legitimate and Arab recognized Israel are not progressing. We believe that if there are negotiations – even if they take place under fire – it will be easier for Arafat to control the violence. Just as Israel does not believe in what Arafat is saying, the Palestinians do not believe that the Israelis really intend to resume substantive negotiations. The main question is: Does Prime Minister Sharon really want to resume negotiations?

Sharon turned down the idea of a *hudna*, the Arabic cultural cease-fire (see the Introduction). Even the Shin Bet said that a cease-fire achieved on a religious and cultural basis would have a higher chance for success than any other type of cease-fire. What could Sharon have lost by letting President Katsav appear before the Palestinian parliament to request a *hudna*? There was so much to gain that it is difficult to understand why Prime Minister Sharon turned down the idea.[55]

As pointed out earlier, in a similar manner Sharon turned down Shimon Peres' proposal with Abu-Ala. It would seem that Prime Minister Sharon is mostly interested in continuing the status quo. Just as his visit to Temple Mount was motivated partially by internal Likud politics, currently Sharon is using external events to fend off criticism and a possible bid to unseat him by former Prime Minister Benjamin Netanyahu.

From an abstract point of view, not a humanitarian or moral point of view, it almost does not matter how long the violence will continue. At the end of the day the parties will have to sit and come to an agreement. They are fairly close now to agreement on all terms. The pity is all the blood that is being needlessly spilled in the meantime. In response to another round of bloodletting and subsequent criticism from both the Israeli right and left, Sharon remarked that, "Israel has never lost a war, and Israel will win this war."[56] The co-editors feel that it is not important who "wins" the war, but who "wins" the peace, for in peace both sides will gain.

Notes

1   Personal communications of Joseph Ginat with Danny Rubenstein of *Ha'aretz,* who said that several journalists from *Ha'aretz* had established this number of destroyed buildings.
2   Hussein Agha and Robert Malley, "Camp David: Tragedy of Errors," *The New York Review of Books,* Midsummer Issue, Vol. XLVIII, Number 13, August 9, 2001, pp. 59–65.
3   *The New York Times,* February 3, 2002, Op-Ed page.
4   Editorial, "A Peace Impulse Worth Pursuing," *The New York Times,* February 21, 2002, p. A26; Henry Siegman, "Will Israel Take a Chance?" *The New York Times,* February 21, 2002, p. A27.
5   Fawaz A. Gerges, "What's Behind the New Arab Momentum," *The New York Times,* March 15, 2002, p. A23.
6   Fareed Zakaria, "Colin Powell's Humiliation," *Newsweek,* Vol. CXXXIX, No. 17, April 29, 2002, p. 28.
7   "PM Sharom: Free from the Threat of Terror, We Can Move Towards Peace Negotiations" in "The Week in Review," April 22–26, 2002, prepared by the Israeli Consulate in San Francisco, available at mailto:culture@houston. mfa.gov.il
8   "U.S., In Surprise, Announces an International Meeting to Tackle the Middle East," *The New York Times,* May 3, 2002, p. A1.
9   Alison Mitchell, "House and Senate Support Israel in Strong Resolutions," *The New York Times,* May 3, 2002, p. A10.
10 Editorial, "Terrorism and Nationalism," The *Washington Post National Weekly Edition,* May 6–12, 2002, p. 24.
11 Editorial, "Mideast Bombast and Diplomacy," *The New York Times,* May 14, 2002, p. A22; and James Bennet, "Sharon Makes Palestinian Reforms a Condition for Talks," *The New York Times,* May 15, 2002, p. A3.
12 Prince El Hassan bin Talal, "Peace in the Middle East" issued in HRH's capacity as the Moderator of the World Conference on Religion and Peace, May 2, 2002.
13 "Leaders back Saudi plan" *The Norman Transcript,* May 12, 2002, p. D8: Steven Erlanger, "Rebuffing Sharon, Party Repudiates Palestinian State," *The New York Times,* May 13, 2002, p. 1.
14 Edward Cody, "For Arafat, Pressure From All Sides, The Palestinian leader takes the blame and calls for reforms, but specifics are skimpy," *The Washington Post National Weekly Edition,,* May 20–26, 2002, p. 16.

15 Shlomo Gazit, "Negative balance sheet," *The Jerusalem Post, Internet Edition*, April 16, 2002.
16 Editorial, "Israel's Historic Miscalculation," *The New York Times*, April 26, 2002, p. A26.
17 Ghassan Khatib, "Getting past the misunderstandings" in "World opinion & the conflict" of *Bitterlemons.org* [bitterlemons@bitterlemons.org], an internet newsletter that presents Palestinian and Israeli viewpoints on prominent issues of concern, April 22, 2002, Edition 14.
18 Danny Yatom, Moshe Amirav, Joseph Ginat, "An initiative for Israel" in *The Jerusalem Post, Internet Edition*, April 19, 2002.
19 Agha and Malley, "Camp David: Tragedy of Errors," p. 7.
20 See Gilad Sher, *Just Beyond Reach, The Israeli–Palestinian Peace Negotiations, 1999–2001* (Tel Aviv: Miskal – Yediot Aharonot Books and Chemed Books, 2001), p. 41.
21 Ibid., pp. 56–7.
22 Ibid., p. 151.
23 Ibid., p. 163.
24 In Joseph Ginat's meetings with Arab high officials and academics, he discovered that they were unaware of the Jewish relationship to the Temple Mount. They were skeptical that a Temple ever existed there. Some of them think the Temple existed on another mountain. A few of them referred to Mount Gerizim. The mistake is that there was a temple on Mt. Gerizim, but this is the sacred center of the Samaritans.
25 Sher, *Just Beyond Reach*, pp. 179–80. See in chapter 27, Ginat and Ya'ar's proposal regarding the possibility of Jewish people praying on the Temple Mount. It is important to point out that the Attorney General, Mr. Rubinstein, is an Orthodox Jew. Many religious Jews refrain from entering the Temple Mount, as was explained in the paper.
26 Ibid., p. 183.
27 Ibid., pp. 189, 193, 194.
28 Ibid., pp. 213–15. The refugees in Lebanon have not received citizenship, in contrast to the situation in Jordan and the West Bank, where all of them received Jordanian passports. The refugees of Gaza received papers that allow them freedom of movement, but without any citizenship. Thus the Lebanese Palestinian refugees have been in the most difficult situation.
29 Sher, *Just Beyond Reach*, p. 244.
30 Ibid., pp. 304–6.
31 Ibid., p. 370. See an example for a creative solution regarding the Temple Mount in Ginat's chapter in this volume.
32 Yossi Beilin, *Manual for a Wounded Dove* (Tel Aviv: Miskal – Yediot Aharonot books and Chemed Books, 2001), pp. 199–200.
33 Ibid., p. 206.
34 Ibid., pp. 207–8.
35 On February 14, 2002, *Ha'aretz* newspaper published a document termed an EU non-paper describing the final position of the negotiations at Taba on all the permanent status issues. The document was prepared by EU Special Representative to the Middle East, Ambassador Moratinos, through consultations with both the Israeli and Palestinian sides. Ambassador Moratinos was

present at the talks but was not a participant; and, as previously mentioned, the Taba talks produced no official document. The document discusses issues including territory (West Bank and Gaza), the issue of Jerusalem (including the holy sites), the refugees, and security. Yossi Beilin, who was one of the main Israeli representatives in the Taba talks, was interviewed on Israeli radio and television on the same day the document was published, February 14, 2002, and said that basically the document represents the essence of the talks; although he indicated that the document in and of itself didn't adequately reflect the positive atmosphere which prevailed at the talks.

36 *Herald Tribune,* January 29, 2002, p. 6
37 *Ha'aretz,* January 20, 2002, p. 3.
38 *Yediot Aharonot 24 Hours,* p. 10. February 13, 2002.
39 *Herald Tribune,* January 21, p. 4.
40 *Ha'aretz,* February 11, p. 8.
41 *Ha'aretz,* February 10, p. 3.
42 "We say peace to the Palestinians," a leaflet published by The Association for Peace and Security in Israel, November 2001.
43 *Ha'aretz Week's End,* February 13, 2002 p. b1.
44 Ibid.
45 Shlomo Baum, "Unilateral Separation, Strategic Update," Jaffa Center for Strategic Studies (JCSS) Tel Aviv University, Volume 4, Number 3, November 2001, p. 15.
46 *Yediot Aharonot,* February 13, 2002, p. 3.
47 Ami Ayalon, Channel 2 interview, February 1, 2002.
48 Editorial, "A Muddled Strategy," *The Washington Post National Weekly Edition,* May 6–12, 2002, p. 4; Steven Erlanger, "Sharon Party's Hard Line Unlikely to Convince Him," *The New York Times,* May 14, 2002, p. 11.
49 *Ha'aretz,* January 21, 2002, p. 5.
50 Ibid.
51 *Ha'aretz,* January 17, 2002, p. B3.
52 Joseph Ginat and Edward J. Perkins (eds.), *The Palestinian Refugees: Old Problems – New Solutions* (Sussex Academic Press and University of Oklahoma Press, Brighton and Norman, 2001).
53 Joseph Ginat "Israeli–Palestinian Negotiations: Academic discussion points, with practical consequences," in *Is the Israeli–Palestinian conflict solvable?,* edited by Tamar Hermann and Ephraim Ya'ar (Tel Aviv: Tami Steinmetz Center for Peace Research, 2002), pp. 139–48.
54 Donna Arzt. *Refugees into Citizens: Palestinians and the End of the Arab–Israeli Conflict* (New York: Council on Foreign Relations, 1997); and Donna Arzt in Joseph Ginat and Edward Perkins (eds.), *The Palestinian Refugees: Old Problems – New Solutions,* pp. 122–38.
55 "Pros and cons of killing Karmi," *Maariv,* January 22, 2002, p. 7. For more details about the possible visit of Katsav to Ramallah, see *Ha'aretz Week's End,* January 4, 2002, p. B1.
56 *New York Times,* February 18, 2002, p. A7.

Contributors

Reuven Aharoni teaches in the department of Eretz-Israel studies of the University of Haifa. His research fields are Bedouin societies and the Arab Palestinian society in Israel. He is the author of, with Shaul Mishal, *Speaking Stones: Communiques from the Intifada Underground* (Syracuse NY: Syracuse University Press, 1994); *Twofold Pass – Illegal Immigration and "Rekhesh" of 544 Company of Electricity and Machinery in the British Army during World War II* (Ramat El al: Yad Tabenkin, 1957) (in Hebrew); and, with Ytzhak Reiter, *The Political Life of Arabs in Israel* (Bect Berl: The Institute for Israeli Arab Studies, 1993) (in Hebrew).

Moshe Amirav earned his masters degree at New York University and his doctorate at the London School of Economics. He is currently an associate professor of political science and public safety at Haifa University and Bect Berl College. He has been a research scholar at Stanford University and Stockholm University, and was the director of Engineering, Roads and Transport for the Municipality of Jerusalem and director general of the Israeli Highway Safety Administration. He served as an advisor on Jerusalem to Prime Minister Barak and is the author of published articles and papers and of two books: *Ein Karem-Journey to the Village of God* (Jerusalem: Ariel, 1988) (in Hebrew); and *The Jerusalem Problem: Positions and Solutions, 1917–1992* (Stockholm: University of Stockholm, 1992.

Rateb M. Amro is director general and founder of Horizon Center for Studies and Research in Amman, Jordan. He was director of the Occupied Territories of the Ministry of Foreign Affairs. He is a retired colonel of the Jordanian Army Forces, and is the author of articles and of chapters of books, including "A Jordanian Perspective" in Joseph Ginat and Edward J. Perkins (eds.), *The Palestinian Refugees: Old Problems – New Solutions* (Norman, OK: University of Oklahoma Press, 2001; Brighton: Sussex Academic Press, 2001).

Amatzia Baram is chair of the department of Middle East history at the University of Haifa where his research focuses on the Ba'ath regimes of

Iraq and Syria. He serves as an advisor to various branches of the Israeli government and was an advisor to Prime Minister Shimon Peres, 1984–88. He is a trustee of the International Policy Institute for Counter-Terrorism in Israel. His doctorate is from the Hebrew University in Jerusalem, and he has held fellowships at the Woodrow Wilson International Center for Scholars, St Antony's College, Oxford, the Rockefeller Foundation, and the US Institute of Peace. The author of over 40 articles and chapters in edited books, he is the author of *Culture, History and Ideology in the Formation of Ba'athist Iraq*, and editor of *Iraq's Road to War*.

Fredrik Barth is currently professor of anthropology at Boston University. A Norwegian citizen, he earned his undergraduate degree at Artium Oslo, his master's degree at the University of Chicago, and his doctorate at Cambridge University. He has taught in Bergen and in Oslo as well as Boston, and has done extensive fieldwork in the Middle East, Sudan, Papua New Guinea, Bali and Bhutan. Professor Barth has published more than 100 professional articles and 18 books, including *Political Leadership Among Swat Pathans* (London, 1959); *Models of Social Organization* (London, 1966); *Ethnic Groups and Boundaries* (Oslo, 1969); *The Last Wali in Swat* (Oslo, 1985); *Cosmologies in the Making* (Cambridge, 1987); and *Balinese Worlds* (Chicago, 1993).

Gabriel Ben-Dor is a professor of political science at the University of Haifa. He was former rector, chairman of the department of political science, director of the Institute of Middle Eastern Studies, and chairman of the Jewish–Arab Center at Haifa University. He was senior research associate at the Dayan Center for Middle Eastern and African Studies at Tel Aviv University. He has served on the boards of numerous educational, public and corporate organizations, and is on the editorial board of the *International Journal of Middle East Studies*. He earned his doctorate at Princeton University and is the author of over 100 scholarly articles and seven books, including *The Druze in Israel: A Political Study*; with David B. Dewitt, *Confidence Building in the Middle East*; and, with Ofra Bengio, *Minorities and the Arab State*.

David L. Boren is the president of the University of Oklahoma. He is a former US senator, a former governor of the state of Oklahoma, and a former state legislator. As a United States senator, he was the longest-serving chairman of the Senate Select Committee on Intelligence. He is widely respected for his longtime support of education, his distinguished career as a reformer of the American political system, and his innovations as a university president. A graduate of Yale University in 1963, he majored in American history, graduated in the top one percent of his class, and was elected to Phi Beta Kappa. He was selected as a Rhodes scholar and earned a master's degree in politics, philosophy, and economics from Oxford University in 1965. In 1968, he received a law degree from the University of Oklahoma College of Law. He served as a member of the Yale University board of trustees. He was chairman of the department of political science and chairman of the division of social sciences at Oklahoma Baptist University. He is the co-editor, with Edward J. Perkins, of *Preparing America's Foreign Policy for the 21st Century* (Norman, OK: University of Oklahoma Press, 1999); with Edward J. Perkins, of *Democracy, Morality and the Search for Peace in America's Foreign Policy* (Norman, OK: University of Oklahoma Press, 2002); and is the author of numerous articles and chapter contributions in edited works.

Edwin G. Corr is associate director of the International Programs Center of the University of Oklahoma. He was the Henry Bellmon Professor of Public Service, a professor of political science, and the director of the Energy Institute of the Americas at the University of Oklahoma. He published *The Political Process in Colombia* (Denver: University of Denver, 1972), co-edited, with Stephen Sloan, *Low-Intensity Conflict: Old Threats in a New World* (Denver: Westview Press, 1992); co-edited, with Max G. Manwaring and Robin Dorff, *The Search for United States Security: A Forward Strategy for the 21st Century* (Praeger, 2002); and has contributed chapters to a number of edited works, and published articles, both in English and Spanish. A career Foreign Service Officer, he served as the United States ambassador to Peru, to Bolivia, to El Salvador, chargé d'affaires in Ecuador and as deputy assistant secretary of state for international narcotics matters. He was a Peace Corps director and a US Marine Corps infantry officer.

Marius Deeb is a lecturer at the School of Area and International Studies of the Johns Hopkins University. He has taught at George Washington University, Georgetown University, the American University in Beirut, Princeton University, Kent State University and Indiana University; and has lectured at a number of other institutions. He received his doctorate from Oxford University and specializes in comparative politics, Islamic politics and modern history of the Middle East.

Khalil Elian is an associate professor of economics and finance at Amman University for Graduate Studies. He has served as the senior economist for USAID financed economic projects, the head of the finance and administrative department of the Education Department of UNRWA in Amman, and as a project officer and researcher for the Amman Chamber of Commerce and the Industrial Development Bank in Amman. He served as a Jordanian delegate to UN Specialized Organizations in Geneva. He is the author of many research papers, reports and journal articles.

Kais M. Firro earned his doctorate at the University of Nice, France and is professor of Middle Eastern history at the University of Haifa. He has written extensively on the economic history of Syria and Lebanon in the nineteenth century. He is the author of *A History of the Druzes* (Leiden, 1992); *The Druzes in the Jewish State* (Leiden, 1999); and *Inventing Lebanon: Nationalism and State* (Tauris, 2002).

Shlomo Gazit completed 33 years of service in the Israeli Defense Forces. Following the 1967 Six Day War he served as coordinator of Israeli Government Operations in the Occupied Territories (1967–74), and following the 1973 Yom Kippur War, he served as director of Israeli Defense Force of Military Intelligence. Among his many writings on Israeli and Middle East strategic affairs are *The Carrot and Stick* (1985), and *Trapped* (1999) on Israel's policy in the occupied territories. He was the editor of *The Middle East Military Balance* during the years 1990–95.

Joseph Ginat is a professor of anthropology at the University of Haifa and is the co-director of the Center for Peace Studies at the International Programs Center at the University of Oklahoma. He is former chairman of the Israeli Academic Center in Cairo, Egypt and a former chairman of the Jewish–Arab Center at the University of Haifa. He was a Fulbright professor at the University of Oklahoma and a visiting professor at the University of Utah, Brigham Young University, Tel Aviv University, and Concordia University (Montreal, Canada). He is the author of many articles and books on the Middle East, including, with I. Altman, *Polygamous Families in Contemporary Society, Coping with Challenging Life Style* (Cambridge: Cambridge University Press, 1996); with M. Ma'oz and O. Winkler (eds.), *Modern Syria: A Pivotal Role in the Middle East* (Brighton and Portland: Sussex Academic Press, 1999); and, with Edward J. Perkins (eds.), *The Palestinian Refugees: Old Problems – New Solutions* (Norman: University of Oklahoma Press, 2001).

Mohanna Haddad received his doctorate from the State University of Utrecht. His dissertation was titled "Arab Perspectives of Judaism: A Study of Image Formation in the Writings of Moslem Arab Authors 1948–1978." He holds the rank of professor at Yarmouk University, Irbid, Jordan. Professor Haddad has six books published in Arabic and some 60 articles published in Arabic and English. He became the first professor from an Arab country to spend his sabbatical year at Israeli universities in 1999/2000.

bin Talal, His Royal Highness Prince Hassan is a pluralist, believing in consensus and respect for the other. His Royal Highness Prince El Hassan bin Talal believes in societies in which all peoples can live, work, and function in freedom and with dignity. This goal has been the moving force behind his interest and involvement in humanitarian and interfaith issues, with particular stress on the human dimension of conflicts. His Royal Highness has initiated, founded, and is actively involved in a number of Jordanian and international institutes and committees. He co-chaired the Independent Commission on International Humanitarian Issues (ICIHI), 1983, and he is currently chairman of the Arab Thought Forum, president of the Club of Rome, moderator of the World Conference on Religion and Peace, chairman of the Policy Advisory Commission for the World Intellectual Property Organization, and founding member and vice chairman of the foundation for Interreligious and Intercultural Research and Dialogue (Geneva). His Royal Highness is the author of five books: *A Study on Jerusalem* (1979); *Palestinian Self-Determination* (1981); *Search for Peace* (1984); *Christianity in the Arab World* (1994); *Continuity, Innovation and Change: Selected Essays* (2001); and is the joint author, with Alain Elkann, of "*Essere Musulmano*" (To be a Muslim) (2001). His Royal Highness is the chairman of the Board of Advisors of the Center for Peace Studies of the International Programs Center at the University of Oklahoma.

Manuel Hassassian is a professor of international politics and relations, and is currently the executive vice president of Bethlehem University. His latest books are *Palestine: Factionalism In the National Movement 1919–1939* (in English) and *The Historical Evolution of the Armenian Question and the Conflict over Nagorno Karabagh* (in English). He has published extensively in academic journals on the Palestine Liberation Organization (PLO), the peace process, democracy and elections. He is the president of the Rectors' Conference at the Palestinian Ministry of Higher Education.

Menachem Klein is a senior lecturer in the department of political science of Bar-Ilan University, Israel, and a senior research fellow at the Jerusalem Institute for Israel Studies. His latest books are *Jerusalem: The Future of the Contested City* and a forthcoming *Breaking a Taboo: Negotiating Final Status Agreement on Jerusalem, 1994–2001*, as well as a number of articles on the PLO's policy and ideology, Jerusalem as a frontier city, and the ambivalent relationship between intellectuals and politicians.

David Kushner is a professor of Middle East history at the University of Haifa. He is currently the director of the Israeli Academic Center in Cairo, Egypt. He earned his bachelor's and master's degree from the Hebrew University, and his doctorate in Islamic Studies from the University of California at Los Angeles (UCLA). His specialization is Ottoman and modern Turkish history. His publications include *The Rise of Turkish*

Nationalism, 1876–1908 (London: Frank Cass, 1977); *Palestine in the Late Ottoman Period: Political, Social and Economic Transformation* (Jerusalem–Leiden: Yad Izhak Ben-Zvi, 1986); and *A Governor in Jerusalem: The City and Province in the Eyes of Ali Ekrem Bey, 1906–1908* (Jerusalem, 1995) (in Hebrew).

Moshe Ma'oz is professor of history of the Middle East at Jerusalem's Hebrew University. He is a leading expert on Syria and was assistant advisor on Arab issues to Prime Minister Ben-Gurion, advisor to the Knesset Committee for Foreign Affairs and Defense, advisor on Arab affairs to Defense Minister Ezer Weizman and a member of the Advisory Committees on Arab–Israel Relations to prime ministers Shimon Peres and Yitzhak Rabin. He is an author of five books, including *Assad, The Sphinx of Damascus: A Political Biography* and *Syria and Israel: From War to Peacemaking*, as well as numerous articles in scholarly journals and chapters of edited books.

Yoram Meital earned his doctorate in history from the University of Haifa. His research is on modern Egypt and the history of the Jewish community in Egypt. Among his recent publications are *Jewish Sites in Egypt*, the Ben-Zvi Institute for the Study of Jewish Communities in the East (Jerusalem: The Hebrew University, 1995) (in Hebrew); *The Economic Dimension of Peace Treaties: The case of the Egyptian–Israeli peace treaty* (Tel Aviv: Tel Aviv University, 1995) (in Hebrew); and "Reactions in Egypt toward the Islamic dimension of the Gulf crisis" in *Hamizreh Hehadash,* Vol. 36 (1994/5), pp. 160–71.

Shaul Mishal is an associate professor in the department of political science at Tel Aviv University. He was the head of the Institute for Israeli Arab Studies, and has been a visiting professor at Yale University and Harvard University. Among his publications are *West Bank/East Bank: The Palestinians in Jordan, 1949–1967* (New Haven, CT: Yale University Press, 1978); *The PLO Under Arafat: Between Gun and Olive Branch* (New Haven, CT: Yale University Press, 1986); and, with Reuven Aharoni, *Speaking Stones: Communiques from the Intifada Underground* (Syracuse: Syracuse University Press, 1994).

Enrico Molinaro is a research fellow of the Harry S. Truman Research Institute for the Advancement of Peace. He is currently completing his doctorate at the Hebrew University of Jerusalem. He focuses on the freedom of religion and worship in the communities in the areas administered or to be negotiated by Israel and the Palestinian Authority. His publications include "Alternative Definitions of Sovereignty – Drawing on European and Mediterranean Legal Heritage: An Analysis of Co-existing

National and Religious Identities in Jerusalem" in *Politics and Economics in Search for Stability in the Mediterranean Region* (Monte Carlo: Institut de Etudes Politiques Méditerranéenes, 2002).

Joseph Nevo is a professor in the department of history of the Middle East at the University of Haifa. He has been a visiting professor at Carleton University, Ottawa; York University, Toronto; Princeton University; and St Antony's College, Oxford, England. His recent publications include, with Alan Pappe, *Jordan in the Middle East 1948–1988: The Making of a Pivotal State* (London: Frank Cass, 1994); *King Abdullah and Palestine – A Territorial Ambition* (Oxford: St Antony's College in association with Macmillan, 1996).

Edward J. Perkins is the William J. Crowe Jr. Chair Professor of Geopolitics and the executive director of the International Programs Center at the University of Oklahoma. He was appointed as US permanent representative to the United Nations, with the rank and status of ambassador extraordinary and plenipotentiary; US representative in the UN Security Council; director general of the Foreign Service; US ambassador to the Commonwealth of Australia; US ambassador to South Africa; and US ambassador to Liberia. He received his bachelor degree from the University of Maryland and his masters in public administration and doctorate of public administration from the University of Southern California. He has received numerous awards. As ambassador to South Africa he worked to end apartheid. He has published numerous articles in his areas of expertise. He is editor of, with David L. Boren, *Preparing America's Foreign Policy for the 21st Century* (Norman, OK: University of Oklahoma Press, 1999); with Joseph Ginat, *The Palestinian Refugees: Old Problems – New Solutions* (Norman, OK: University of Oklahoma Press, and Brighton: Sussex Academic Press, 2001); and with David L. Boren, *Democracy, Morality and the Search for Peace in American Foreign Policy*, (Norman, OK: University of Oklahoma Press, 2002).

Robert L. Rothstein is the Harvey Picker Distinguished Professor of International Relations at Colgate University. He has written and edited nine books and 70 articles. The most recent book is an edited collection entitled *The Israeli–Palestinian Peace Process – Oslo and the Lessons of Failure* (Brighton and Portland: Sussex Academic Press, 2002).

Onn Winckler is a lecturer in the department of Middle Eastern history at the University of Haifa and deputy director of the Jewish–Arab Center at the University of Haifa. His major fields of academic research are demographic and economic history of the modern Arab world. His recent publications include *Population Growth and Migration in Jordan,*

1950–1994 (Brighton and Portland: Sussex Academic Press, 1997); *Demographic Developments* and *Population Policies in Ba'thist Syria* (Brighton and Portland: Sussex Academic Press, 1999); co-editor, with Moshe Ma'oz and Joseph Ginat. *Modern Syria: From Ottoman Rule to Pivotal Role in the Middle East* (Brighton and Portland: Sussex Academic Press, 1999); "Population Growth, Migration, and Socio-Demographic Policies in Qatar" in *Data and Analysis*, Tel Aviv University, the Moshe Dayan Center for Middle Eastern and African Studies, July 2000; and "The Challenge of Foreign Workers in the Persian/Arabian Gulf: The Case of Oman," in *Immigrants & Minorities*, Vol. 18, No. 2 (July 2000), pp. 23–52.

Ephraim Yuchtman Ya'ar is a professor of sociology and former dean of the faculty of social sciences at Tel Aviv University. He is the current head of the Tami Steinmetz Center for Peace Research and the incumbent of the Rapoport Chair in Sociology of Labor. In 1997 he was named the first recipient of the Special Fulbright Itzhak Rabin Award for his academic achievements in the study of peace and democracy. He has had several books published as well as numerous articles in academic and intellectual journals. Since 1994, he has written a monthly column entitled "The Peace Index" for the Israeli daily, *Ha'aretz.*

Eyal Zisser is a professor of Middle Eastern and African history and a research fellow at the Moshe Dayan Center for Middle East and African studies at Tel Aviv University. He was a visiting research fellow at the Washington Institute for Near East Policy. He has published *Syria under Asad – At a Crossroads* (Tel Aviv: HaKibbutz Hameuhad, 1999) (in Hebrew); and *Lebanon – Challenge of Independence* (London: I.B. Tauris, 2000); and numerous articles.

Index

United States *(continued)*
  increased peace process role (2002), 388–90
  Iranian weapons' deals, 263
  Israeli invasion of Lebanon (1982), 216
  Israeli–Iraqi contacts, 259
  Israeli–Syrian peace negotiations, 232–3, 242
  Jerusalem issue, 305–6, 307, 308–12, 330
  Jordan, 79, 152, 153, 159, 173
  key role in Middle East, viii, xvi
  Lebanon, 194, 195
  mediator role, 5–7
  new Middle East policy, 180
  pressure on Israel, 30
  protection of Israeli interests at UN, 395
  Saddam on, 252
  Saudi Arabia, 389
  solidarity resolutions with Israel, 388–9
  Syria, 213–14, 215, 217, 218, 219–20, 223, 224, 234
  UN examination of Jenin, 395
  unilateral separation plan, 409
  United Nations Resolution 242, 223
  world war on terrorism, 384, 389
The United States and Egypt (Quandt), 143
University of Oklahoma, xiii
UNRWA, 404, 414
'Ursan, 'Uqla, 238–9
US Agency for International Development, 33

Vaksman, Nahshon, 9
Venizelos, Eleutherios, 135, 136
virtual communities, 55–7

Wadi Araba Agreement (1994), 69, 70
Wadi Joz, 362, 363, 364, 366, 369
al-Wadi, Muhammad Khayr, 241
Wailing Wall, 277, 369
Waqf, 305, 313, 316, 325, 404
Washington Declaration (1994), 378
Washington Post, 389–90
al-Watan, 105
water resources
  Arab settlements access to, 113
  as component of peace package, 185
  Israeli–Syrian relations, 221
  as issue to be dealt with in final status talks, 3
  public opinion polls, 356–7
Weingrod, Alex, 324
West Bank

Camp David Summit (2000), 86, 295
economic feasibility, 32
establishment of Palestinian independent state, 71–2
included in Jordan (1950), 152
Israeli cession rumors, 37*n*
Israeli settlements, 4, 30, 183, 397, 415–16
Jordan abandons claim to, 168, 301, 314
Jordan's attempts to regain control, 168
occupation by Israel (1967), 69, 77
opening of Jordanian banks, 186
Sharm el-Sheikh memorandum (1999), 402
Yatom, Amirav and Ginat proposal, 397
Winckler, Onn, 13, 77–82
World Bank, 33, 158
World Tourism Organization, 82
World Trade Organization (WTO), 176
World Travel and Tourism Council, 81–2
World Zionist Organization (WZO), 182, 183
WTO, 176
Wye River Accord, 402
WZO, 182, 183

xenophobia, xii

Ya'ar, Ephraim Yuchtman
  Israeli public opinion on Oslo process, 13, 83–90
  Jerusalem issue, 17, 354–70
  Temple Mount, 17, 371, 374, 375, 377–8
Ya'ri, Avi, 254
Yassin, Ahmde, 8, 95
Yatom, Danny, 396–401
Yediot Ahoronot, 390
Yehoshua, A. B., 410–11
Yemen
  Jerusalem issue, 315
  remittances from emigrant labor, 79
Young Turks, 246
Yugoslavia, 136
Yunes, Nazir, 107

al-Zahar, Mahmud, 93–4, 119
Zak, Moshe, 157
Zaydani, Sa'id, 114, 115
Zerka, 158
Zinni, Anthony C., 7
Zionism, 83, 304
Zisser, Eyal, 15, 229–45
Zoroastrianism, 253
Zotov, Aleksandr, 217
Zur Bacher, 311